THE LINE OF BATTLE

THE LINE OF BATTLE

The Sailing Warship 1650-1840

Editor: Robert Gardiner

Consultant Editor
Brian Lavery

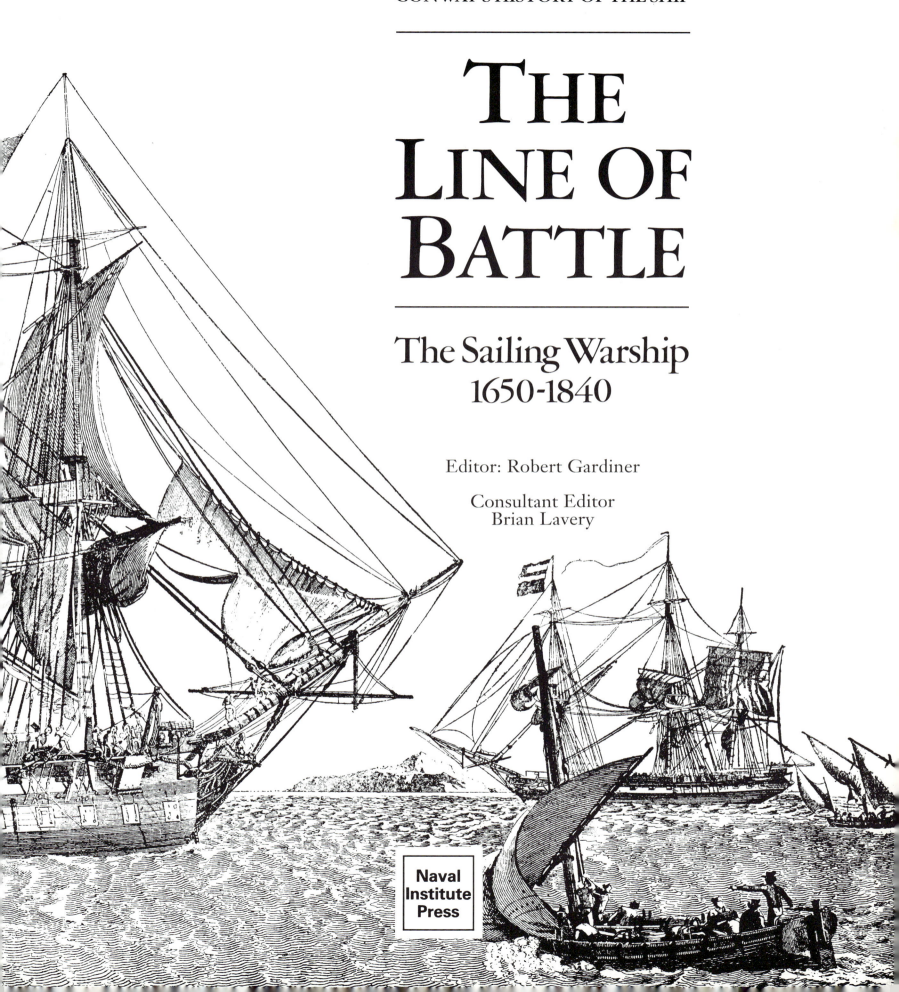

Naval
Institute
Press

Series Consultant	Dr Basil Greenhill CB, CMG, FSA, FRHistS
Series Editor	Robert Gardiner
Consultant Editor	Brian Lavery
Contributors	John Franklin Robert Gardiner Jan Glete John Harland Karl Heinz Marquardt Nicholas Tracy Chris Ware

Frontispiece: The archetypal warship of the age was the two-decked line of battle ship, of which the 74-gun rate was the dominant class from the mid-eighteenth century onwards. This Beaujean engraving from the end of the Napoleonic War depicts a British 74 signalling to a frigate, the cross-section of naval craft being completed by a storeship and a schooner in the background and ships' boats in the foreground.

© Conway Maritime Press Ltd 1992

First published in Great Britain 1992 by
Conway Maritime Press Ltd
101 Fleet Street
London EC4Y 1DE

Published and distributed in the United States
of America and Canada by the Naval Institute
Press, Annapolis, Maryland 21402

Library of Congress Catalog Card No. 92–60196

ISBN 1–55750–501–2

Manufactured in Great Britain

Contents

Preface

THIS is the second title in an ambitious programme of twelve volumes intended to provide the first detailed and comprehensive account of a technology that has shaped human history. It has been conceived as a basic reference work, the essential first stop for anyone seeking information on any aspect of the subject, so it is more concerned to be complete than to be original. However, the series takes full account of all the latest research and in certain areas will be publishing entirely new material. In the matter of interpretation care has been taken to avoid the old myths and to present only the most widely accepted modern viewpoints.

To tell a coherent story, in a more readable form than is usual with encyclopaedias, each volume takes the form of independent chapters, all by recognised authorities in the field. Most chapters are devoted to a ship type, but some broader topics are necessary to give added depth to the reader's understanding of developments. A degree of generalisation is inevitable when tackling a subject of this breadth, but wherever possible the specific details of ships and their characteristics have been included (a table of typical ships for each relevant chapter includes a convenient summary of data from which the reader can chart the evolution of the ship type concerned). Except for the earliest craft, the series is confined to seagoing vessels; to have included boats would have increased the scope of an already massive task.

The history of the ship is not a romanticised story of epic battles and heroic voyages but equally it is not simply a matter of technological advances. Ships were built to carry out particular tasks and their design was as much influenced by the experiences of that employment – the lessons of war, or the conditions of trade, for example – as purely technical innovation. Throughout this series an attempt has been made to keep this clearly in view, to describe the *what* and *when* of developments without losing sight of the *why*.

The series is aimed at those with some knowledge of, and interest in, ships and the sea.

It would have been impossible to make a contribution of any value to the subject if it had been pitched at the level of the complete novice, so while there is an extensive glossary, for example, it assumes an understanding of the most basic nautical terms. Similarly, the bibliography avoids very general works and concentrates on those which will broaden or deepen the reader's understanding beyond the level of the *History of the Ship*. The intention is not to inform genuine experts in their particular area of expertise, but to provide them with the best available single-volume summaries of less familiar fields.

This volume describes the warship from the evolution of the specialist line of battle ship in the 1650s to the end of sail as the principal mode of propulsion. Neither of these events can be pinpointed to a precise year so in order to give a complete picture there is some reference outside the 1650–1840 dates of the subtitle. This is a period in which the design of merchant ships and warships diverged steadily; it is true that merchantmen continued to be taken up as makeshift warships, and that many naval small craft derived from mercantile prototypes, but it was quickly established that only purpose-built vessels were fit to stand in the line of battle and perform the many duties of a naval cruiser.

Merchantmen were banished from the frontline by a tactical and technological revolution that placed emphasis on large numbers of guns carried on the broadside, increasing weight of firepower, and the rigid discipline of line ahead tactics to take advantage of these developments. Manoeuvre-and-board battles were replaced by gunnery duels where superior firepower became the decisive factor. In the line of battle individual ships were not free to choose suitable opponents but had to take on their opposite number, whatever their size; this tended to drive out the smallest rates, and with them went the hired or purchased merchant ships (a seventeenth-century East Indiaman might be the size of a Third Rate, but she was more lightly built, carried guns of smaller

calibres and, certainly in merchant service, was never manned at a level that allowed sustained broadside firing).

The battlefleet became the arbiter of sea power, but navies that could not compete successfully at this level turned to the age-old strategy of the *guerre de course* or attack on trade. For this a faster, more seaworthy but less heavily armed vessel was ideal; the fleet also needed an 'all-weather' scout that could outsail a battleship but outgun anything smaller, and these requirements came together to produce the first genuine cruiser designs. In fact, the process of specialisation within the fleet accelerated at this time: many of the familiar types of small craft were first tried between 1650 and 1700, while an entirely new method of land-attack, the bomb vessel, was introduced.

Compared with the late-medieval emergence of the three-masted ship or the nineteenth-century revolution of steam and steel, the period in between may seem one of little progress. It was certainly described as such by earlier historians, but while the advances were incremental and individually unspectacular, the overall effect was highly significant. It will be clear from the chapters that follow that between 1650 and 1840 the wooden warship became not only larger, better constructed and more powerfully armed, but the very nature of its capabilities was changed dramatically: from being little better than a coastal, summer-only force, the battlefleet and its consorts developed into a powerful and flexible weapon that could be employed in virtually any seas, in all but the heaviest weather, all the year round. The world-wide campaigns of the late eighteenth century, or the ceaseless drudgery of blockade duty, were only made possible by enhanced seaworthiness and more rugged construction, so with this instrument, sea power became a far more powerful and influential factor in world history.

Robert Gardiner
Series Editor

Introduction

GUNS were first fitted to fighting ships as early as 1340, but purely as supplementary weapons. With the invention of the gunport, which allowed the gun to fire through the side of a ship rather than over the gunwale, it became possible to mount much heavier guns lower in the hull, thus maintaining the stability of the ship. Nevertheless, even major ships of the sixteenth century did not rely on the broadside as their main force; they considered their chase guns, firing directly forward, as their main armament, and turned the ship to bring each gun to bear one after another. During the first half of the sixteenth century, loading techniques began to improve, so that guns could be fired much more often during a battle; ships had to be faster, and therefore longer in proportion to their breadth, and this caused them to carry a much smaller proportion of their armament firing forward. Very large ships were built to reflect the prestige of the state, and these were even less suitable for turning round in action. As a result, the broadside, rather than the forward firing guns, began to predominate.

A ship is naturally long and narrow, and from this it might be concluded that the broadside is the obvious way to mount a heavy armament; but history does not bear this out. The rowing galley carried all its heavy guns firing forward, and twentieth-century vessels, such as the submarine and the torpedo boat, also had forward firing weapons. But in the seventeenth, eighteenth and nineteenth centuries, technology could not produce a single large weapon which could be mounted forward. There was an effective limit on the size of naval guns, as a man could not handle a projectile larger than about 42 pounds. For a substantial armament, a major warship had to carry a large number of guns, and the great majority of these had to be mounted on the sides.

The use of the broadside had many implications. A ship could not normally advance on an enemy at the same time as firing on him, and this had a profound effect on naval tactics; it gave a certain advantage to the defence, and it was difficult to obtain a decisive result without taking a certain amount of risk. The broadside also inspired the line of battle, the main tactical formation over several centuries – clearly the fleet had to form a single line if it was to deploy its gun power to best effect. There remained many ships, such as frigates and sloops, which did not form part of the line of battle, but these still used the broadside in action. Only the very smallest vessels of war, such as the rowing gunboats, could concentrate all their power on a single gun firing forward.

Navies and warfare

The age of the sailing line of battle, roughly from 1650 to 1840, was a period of intense competition between the European powers, punctuated by many wars. It saw the later years of the revolutionary English republic, up to 1660, and the English 'Glorious Revolution' of 1688; the American Revolution of 1776, the French Revolution of 1789, and the Industrial Revolution of the late eighteenth century. Each of these events, except the last, inspired or helped inspire a war in itself, and contributed to the general insecurity in the European sphere of influence. Other wars were caused by the rivalry over trade (such as the Second Anglo-Dutch War), by dynastic disputes within Europe (The War of Spanish Succession), or by colonial disputes, especially in the Americas (The War of Jenkins' Ear and the Seven Years War). In the more crowded waters of the Baltic, the expansion of Russia and the ambitions of Sweden caused yet more conflict.

The epoch began with the rapid decline of Spanish power in Europe (though her great overseas empire was to survive intact almost to the end of the age of sail). The Dutch had played a major part in the Spanish decline, and their epic eighty-year struggle for independence had established the United Netherlands as a major naval power. With France and England weakened by internal struggle the Dutch seemed particularly strong. However, with the end of the English Civil War in 1649 and the execution of Charles I a kind of unity was found, and a great fleet was built. The Dutch were defeated in the First Anglo-Dutch War (1652–4), but reformed their fleet over the next ten years. Many fierce battles were fought in the Second Anglo-Dutch War (1664–7), but ultimately the English ran out of money, and the Dutch raid on the Medway in 1667 caused them great humiliation. In 1672 the English and French combined to attack the Netherlands by land and sea. By this time the English people had no wish for this kind of war, and the naval part of the campaign was not particularly successful. England made a separate peace in 1674, though the land war between France and the Netherlands continued until 1678. The Dutch succeeded in retaining their independence, but at great cost. After the power of France revived under Louis XIV, they had to look continually at the possibility of an invasion by land, and their days as a great sea-power were over. Furthermore, warships were increasing in size, and Dutch harbours and coastal waters were too shallow to allow them to build bigger ships.

For a time, France became the leading sea-power. Louis XIV had succeeded to the throne in 1643, but it was 1661 before he began to take real power. The centralised monarchy, very different from the federal republic of the Netherlands or the limited monarchy of England, allowed him to impose high taxes, while the substantial population and resources of France provided the manpower and material to build a large navy as well as a standing army. Louis' great minister, Colbert, rebuilt the navy after its collapse during the previous decade. Initially, he bought ships from the Dutch, and then copied from them, but soon he was developing native talent. By 1675, it was reported to the English Parliament that the French fleet had 96 ships, while the Dutch had 136, and the English 92. By 1677 the French were ahead, and were said to have 209 ships of all types, including galleys. Despite the great 'Thirty Ships' programme of 1677, political divisions in England prevented them from keeping up, while the resources of the Dutch were already overstrained.

In 1688–9, war broke out between France and a coalition which included Britain, the Netherlands and Spain. Louis' navy had its greatest triumph in 1690, when it defeated the Anglo-Dutch fleet at the Battle of Beachy Head; but the French high command showed, not for the last time, that it did not know what to do when it had maritime superiority. The planned invasion of England was delayed for too long, and in 1692 the tables were turned when the French were defeated at Barfleur, and a large part of the surviving battlefleet was annihilated at La Hogue. The French navy continued to increase in strength for some years as new ships came off the stocks, but France's days as the leading seapower were over. Instead, the French turned to the *guerre de course*, fitting out small, fast privateers to raid enemy commerce. This caused considerable concern among the trading classes in England, and the navy was pressurised into devoting more effort to commerce protection.

By the 1690s the British ruling classes recognised that, whatever other differences might exist within the country, a strong navy had to be maintained. Parliament voted several large sums for building more ships (though the actual vessels produced were not always well

The dominating influence on the development of warships between 1650 and 1840 was the line of battle, graphically represented by this print of the St James Day battle between the English and Dutch in 1666. Devised to exploit the advantages of broadside firepower, it made the approach difficult and was not readily adapted to forcing decisive results until breaking the line became a common tactic in the late eighteenth century. (NMM)

conceived). It came to be accepted that these ships should be maintained on the Navy List, even after the lifetime of a particular vessel had ended. By the finish of the war in 1697, the English navy had 323 ships, including 118 of the line, and France had been been overtaken as the greatest naval power in the world. Britain was in the position she was to retain for more than 200 years, until long after the end of the age of sail.

The next major European conflict, the War of Spanish Succession (1702–14), produced no new ideas, and few major naval battles, largely because the French did not seriously contest the dominion of the seas. The French navy reached its nadir around 1720, with only forty ships. It began to revive around 1730, not only in strength but also in creative ideas. In the years that followed it developed both the 74-gun ship and the frigate, helping to create the widely held belief that French design was immeasurably superior to British. The Spanish too had something of a revival, and performed quite well when war broke out with Britain in 1739. The British had fallen into complacency and stagnation during their years of effortless supremacy, and were surprised by the quality of the new French and Spanish ships. Eventually they learned to adapt these designs to their own purposes, and by the end of this round of wars, in 1763, the British had again established total superiority by means of several great victories. They had also gained control of North America and India.

The greatest challenge to British seapower came after the revolt of the American colonists, beginning in 1775. France, Spain and eventually the Netherlands declared war on Britain, leaving a balance of forces of ninety effective

British ships of the line against sixty-three French and fifty-eight Spanish. There was no decisive battle in European waters, but the combined fleet failed to exploit its superiority. After 1780 the focus of the war shifted to North America and the Caribbean, where numerous battles were fought. In 1782 the British were decisively victorious at the Saintes, in the West Indies. Although the lost control of America, they were able to retain most of their other possessions, and their seapower.

The wars between Britain and the forces unleashed by the French Revolution lasted from 1793 to 1815. Alliances varied during these years, but there were times when Britain was faced with the same combination of forces as in 1780. This time the different naval powers could be defeated one by one, and the Dutch (beaten at Camperdown in 1797) and Spanish (defeated at St Vincent in 1797 and Trafalgar in 1805) were almost totally destroyed; neither country ever recovered as an independent naval power, even of the second rank, during the age of sail. The French, however, soon recovered from such disasters as the Nile and Trafalgar; near the end of the wars in 1815, they still had a fleet of sixty-three ships of the line.

The central naval struggle took place between the colonial powers of Britain, France, Spain and the Netherlands, and was fought out in the Atlantic, English Channel, North Sea, Caribbean, Mediterranean and Indian Ocean. In addition, there were conflicts in more restricted areas, especially the Baltic and the Black Sea. There was a war between Sweden and Denmark in 1657–60, producing a major naval battle in the Sound in 1658; and another

Although the advantages of the broadside-armed sailing ship over the galley were clear by the early seventeenth century, the traditional galley fleets of the Mediterranean powers were maintained in decreasing numbers until the middle of the next century. They were supposed to have some use in amphibious warfare and could be dangerous when a sailing ship was becalmed, but as a demonstration of the relative powers of the two types in such conditions, in 1684 the French 50-gun Le Bon *fought a famous five-hour action against thirty-six Spanish galleys and escaped relatively unscathed when a breeze sprang up, allowing the French ship to make sail. (From Paris'* Souvenirs de Marine.*)*

(The Great Scanian War) in 1675–9, leading to the Battle of Øland in 1676, but the main eighteenth-century conflict in the Baltic was between Sweden and the expanding power of Russia. The Russians, under Peter the Great, began the century by building their first navy. They captured the port of Petrograd, and consolidated their hold in the area. Later in the century, af Chapman of Sweden produced his famous 'Skerries Fleet' of light draught gunvessels for use in the shallow waters, but Russian power continued to expand. The Baltic became involved in the general European power struggle during the Napoleonic wars – the British defeated the Danes at Copenhagen in 1801, and again in 1807, so that the Danish fleet was eliminated, except for gunboats.

Russia was also expanding into the Black Sea, and coming into naval conflict with Turkey. The Russians had no Black Sea fleet until the late 1760s, but over two wars they were able to create a naval base at Sevastopol, and take control of the Crimea and the north coast of the Black Sea.

The United States Navy had become a serious force by the end of the age of sail. It was born during the struggle for independence, but practically disappeared with the coming of peace. It was revived to fight Barbary corsairs from North Africa, and expanded to fight a war with the British from 1812 to 1815. It remained quite small, but its ships were of very high quality.

After the peace of 1815, naval warfare was comparatively rare, and the surviving fleets – especially those of Britain, France, the USA and Russia – had large stocks of ships left over from wartime. There was only one major naval battle in these years, when the combined fleets of Britain, France and Russia annihilated the Turks at Navarino in 1827. Nevertheless, advancement in naval architecture was greater than ever before. The new technology of the Industrial Revolution was spreading to naval shipbuilding, while the Seppings system of construction allowed considerable expansion in the size of ships. Steam was gradually applied to warships, beginning with the smaller ships in the 1820s, and ending with the ships of the line in the 1840s. By the time of the Crimean War (1854–6) it was recognised that the purely sailing warship had no place in action.

Ship design and national characteristics

In earlier ages, different countries and regions had built ships according to their own resources and traditions. The ships of the Spanish Armada were quite different from the English vessels which opposed them in 1588. Even sixty years later, during the First Anglo-Dutch War, the ships of the two nations were built in different styles, and for different needs; but the age of the line of battle caused a convergence between the various naval powers. Ships of one fleet could quite easily serve in another, and often did. Rigging and fittings were usually modified, but the hull remained unaltered.

This convergence was caused by the increased competition between nations, so that an idea produced by one was soon copied by all the others. It was facilitated by the fact that shipbuilding resources were international, and in general countries did not rely on a single region for their sources of timber and other stores. Thus Britain bought large quantities of naval stores, including timber, in the Baltic; all the Atlantic powers used large amounts of timber from America and the Caribbean. Shipbuilding was not restricted by the need to use local materials.

The actual interchange of ideas between the naval powers took place in several ways. One was by simple observation of an enemy fleet, in battle or otherwise. In 1673, for example, the French *Superbe* was seen by her English allies, and had considerable influence on ship design.

Another was by emigration of shipwrights. The Sheldon family went from England to Sweden in the mid-seventeenth century, and provided several generations of naval constructors; even the famous af Chapman was the son of an Englishman. In the mid-eighteenth century Spain received many men from France and Britain, and also developed a native system of design. Perhaps the most famous of the immigrants was Matthew Mullan, an Irishman who built the *Santisíma Trinidad* at Havana in 1769.

A third method was by the travels undertaken by the natives of one country, to study techniques in the leading shipbuilding powers. Such travellers could include the very highest in the land – Peter the Great of Russia undertook such a visit to England and Holland in 1697–8. Visits could be carried out by middle-ranking state officials, especially those trying to set up a major shipbuilding programme in the home country. Thus Arnoul of France reported on the Dutch and English in 1673, while Blaise Ollivier studied British shipbuilding in the 1730s when the French navy was beginning another revival. At a lower level, trainee Danish shipbuilders of the eighteenth century were routinely sent on study tours of France or England, and their brief included obtaining copies of ships' plans – the foundation of the great Danish plans collection which survives to this day. The great Swedish naval architect af Chapman travelled Europe on his own initiative in the 1740s, producing much of the material for his great work, *Architectura Navalis Mercatoria*; he was actually jailed in England for a short time, as a suspected spy. Indeed, the status of such information-gathering activities varied with the rank of the visitor. With Peter the Great it was little short of a state visit, while with men of lower rank it was close to technical espionage. The British themselves collected intelligence reports on foreign shipbuilding, though this was more to assess the strength of the enemy than to discover his technical secrets.

Of course, the ultimate way to learn from a

foreign navy was to capture an enemy ship and then reproduce its design. This was the chief influence on the British navy, from the mid-eighteenth century onwards. Beginning with the *Invincible* (captured in 1747 and copied in 1757), the British did this with the hull form of many French ships, though they took care to develop their own designs in parallel with these, and never relied solely on foreign prizes for their ideas.

It is notable that the transmission of ideas only went in particular directions, almost invariably from the two leading naval powers of the time – the Netherlands and Britain in the seventeenth century, France and Britain in the eighteenth – towards the smaller power. Both the Danes and the Spanish produced a kind of synthesis of British and French design; the Danes tended to lean towards the French, while the Spanish, with more overseas colonies to defend, tended to favour the durability of the British system of construction. Of all the naval powers, the late eighteenth-century French showed the least inclination to learn from abroad; they captured a number of British ships, but never copied them, nor even studied them very closely. The British copied many French hull forms, but never Spanish ones; even though some of the latter, such as the *Princessa* of 1730, were admitted to be very good indeed.

Warship development 1650–1840

Warships of all types tended to get larger over the years, though at a rather slow pace. The biggest ships, the three-deckers, were of around 1500 tons in the mid-seventeenth century. By the middle of the next century, they generally exceeded 2000 tons, and by 1800 they were of 2500 tons or more. In the middle of the range, frigates tended to increase in gun power as well as length; 32 guns was quite normal in the 1750s, 36 or 38 guns in the 1790s, and up to 44 guns thereafter.

Several factors combined to produce these increases. The wide-ranging colonial wars of the eighteenth century demanded that ships be more seaworthy, and therefore larger. By the 1750s it was known that large guns were more efficient in proportion to their size than smaller ones, and ships tended to be designed

Between 1650 and 1840 the sailing warship became larger, better constructed, more seaworthy and far more powerfully armed. This model of HMS Queen *(110 guns) depicts the ultimate achievement in the design of the purely sailing wooden warship and almost certainly the most powerful ship of her day.* (SM)

round weapons of a particular calibre. Conversely, a large ship had stronger scantlings, and could resist enemy gunfire much better than a small one. Shipbuilders gradually gained in confidence over the years and made their ships bigger; while the increasing wealth of some states, such as Britain, could be used to fund the new giants. The lesser naval powers had to keep up with this as best they could.

Throughout the age of the sailing line of battle, there was increased separation of the warship from the merchantman. The Dutch still used large numbers of merchantmen in their war fleets in the First Anglo-Dutch War, but this proved unsuccessful. After that, the occasional ship was still hired, bought or captured from merchant owners, and as late as the 1790s the British converted several East Indiamen into ships of the line; but this was highly unusual, and only a very good merchant ship, or dire necessity on the part of the navy concerned, could cause it to happen.

As the eighteenth century wore on, there was increased specialisation within the warships themselves. In 1700 the division between ships of the line and others was often rather arbitrary – in Britain, 50-gun ships were part of the line of battle, and 40s were not. By 1800 there was a clear difference between a small ship of the line of 64 guns and a large frigate of 40 or 44 guns; intermediate classes, such as the two-decker 50s, were very much out of favour

by this time. At the smaller end of the scale, the late eighteenth and early nineteenth centuries produced a proliferation of very small vessels – schooners, cutters, gunboats, brigs, and many other types were added to the more traditional fireships, bomb vessels, ketches and advice boats. By this time the rowing galley, dating back from classical times, had almost disappeared from the active fleets, and part of its role had been taken over by the rowing gunboat.

There is no doubt that there was a great improvement in seaworthiness during the two centuries of the ship of the line. In the period of the Anglo-Dutch Wars, the fleets fought in the summer only, in the southern end of the North Sea, and never more than about 100 miles from their main bases. A century later, warships were expected to sail anywhere in the world, to keep the seas throughout the winter, and to maintain their workaday station off ports such as Brest in all but the most difficult conditions. The age of the line of battle saw no great technological change to compare with the coming of steam and iron or, indeed, with the development of the three-masted sailing ship; nevertheless, there was great progress in design, and the sailing warship at the end of the period was a far faster, more weatherly and powerful weapon than its seventeenth-century predecessor.

Brian Lavery

1

The ship of the line

A SHIP of the line was simply a ship which was sufficiently strong and heavily armed to stand in the line of battle. Since such a tactical formation often demanded rigid station keeping, any ship of the line might be opposed by an enemy of greater force, but still had to maintain its position. Therefore there was an effective minimum size for a ship of the line – about 30 guns in the 1650s, 50 guns by the end of the century, 64 guns by the 1750s, and 74 guns (or perhaps 80) in the last days of the sailing battlefleet. Ships of the line were the biggest types of vessel afloat in the age of sail. The largest of their number, the great three-deckers of 100 guns or more, were the largest ships in the world; even the smallest ships of the line were larger than the vast majority of merchant ships, and only a very few long distance traders could match them for size.

The actual work of the ship of the line, apart from the few moments of battle, was often rather dull – endless patrols and blockades, or sitting in harbour forming a 'fleet in being' – but the ships themselves were given constant public attention. The strength of a great naval power was measured mainly by the number of effective ships of the line it could put to sea. Frigates and smaller vessels, while slightly more glamorous, were subsidiary in the calculation of the balance of power. A ship of the line, however, was far more versatile than a twentieth-century battleship. There was no threat from torpedoes and submarines, so it had no need for an escort of flotilla craft, and a ship of the line could sail alone without any great difficulty. Ships of the line were used as convoy escorts on many occasions – not always as a covering force against strong enemy forces, but as part of the actual escort. Occasionally they could be used as troop carriers, or take a direct part in landing operations. However these roles were also subsidiary; the real work of the ship of the line was to dispute command of the sea by forming part of a battlefleet which was ready to take on the main strength of the enemy navy. There is another

This van de Velde drawing of about 1648 shows one of James I's 'great ships', the Constant Reformation. *By this date the ship has much increased armament, including guns in the waist, but the upperworks are still relatively lightly armed.* (NMM)

striking contrast with the dreadnought battleship of the first half of the twentieth century, in that far more of them were built. The British navy had up to 180 ships of the line during the Napoleonic Wars, but never more than a couple of dozen dreadnought battleships in the First World War.

The ship of the line was either a two-decker or a three-decker – it had either two or three complete decks of guns, not counting the quarterdeck, forecastle and poop deck, which did not run the full length of the ship. Both of the main types, the two-decker and the three-decker, had their ups and downs over the centuries, and opinions on their relative merits varied. The three-decker provided a higher platform, and more accommodation; the two-decker was generally cheaper to build and fit

out, and it usually had better proportions and sailing qualities, unless the three-decker was very large indeed.

Before the line of battle

It is generally recognised that the line of battle, and the ship of the line itself, was an English invention. At the Battle of the Gabbard in 1653, the English fleet abandoned the last traces of the old kind of tactics, and fought in single line ahead. The result was devastating to their Dutch opponents. Of course this did not, in itself, create the ship of the line. In fact English ships were already, almost by accident, very suitable for the line of battle.

At the beginning of the First Anglo-Dutch War in 1652, the English fleet had two types of ship, the 'great ship' and the 'frigate'. The great ship had evolved in the early years of the century, out of the type of galleon which had fought against the Spanish Armada in 1588. It was given higher upperworks, greater gunpower, and a relatively low length:breadth ratio. According to the Commission of 1618 which did much to initiate this style of building, they 'should have the length treble the breadth, and the breadth near in like proportion answerable to the depth'.[1] They were of 650 to 850 tons, of 'middling size', and therefore 'best for sailing, and will also bear a very good sail, and are likewise nimble and yare [quick] for steerage.'[2] Such ships were suitable for the old style of turning and boarding tactics, where the ability to turn a ship was as important as any other quality. Initially they were not very heavily gunned for their size.

The hugely influential Sovereign of the Seas *of 1637 in the well known Payne engraving. With three full gundecks and 100 guns she set the pattern of heavy broadside fire, anticipating the needs of the line of battle. In the battles of the first Anglo-Dutch War, the 'Golden Devil' as she was known to the Dutch, was without a serious challenger.*

The *St George*, built in 1622, had 42 guns, weighing a total of 48 tons and firing a broadside of 604lbs, at her first commissioning. By the time of the First Anglo-Dutch War she was carrying 52 guns with a broadside of 710lbs, and by the 1670s she was planned to have 70 guns, weighing 112 tons and firing 1250lbs. The great ships had two complete flush decks, and initially they had little armament on the upper works.

In the first half of the seventeenth century progress in design came not through any real tactical developments but because the insecure monarchies of the age needed large ships to reflect their prestige. In England the class of 'ships royal' began as a natural extension of the great ship, and consisted of a few large Elizabethan galleons. However the *Prince Royal* of 1610 was something different. She was conceived by James I, and built by Phineas Pett, who to a certain extent stood outside the tradi-

tion of the craftsman-shipwright. She was almost a three-decker, though her upper deck did not yet carry a full tier of guns. Like most of her contemporaries she was under-armed – she had only 55 guns in her early years, but had 100 by 1660.

The next stage came in the 1630s, when Charles I built the *Sovereign of the Seas*, again employing the skills of Phineas Pett. This ship, launched in 1637, was indubitably a three-decker. Like the *Prince*, it was built against the protests of expert opinion: Trinity House commented that 'A ship of this proportion cannot be of use, not fit for service in any part of the King's dominions.'[3] This time the King was

1. A P McGowan, (ed), *The Jacobean Commissions of Enquiry* (1971) p289

2. W G Perrin, (ed), *Boteler's Dialogues* (1929) p256

3. W G Perrin, (ed), *The Autobiography of Phineas Pett* (1917) p214

determined to reach the magic number of 100 guns, and crammed them in to an unprecedented degree. Probably this was the beginning of the British practice of overloading their hulls. The French equivalent of the *Sovereign* was the *Couronne*, which had ports for only 68 guns, on a hull which was not very different in size.

One effect of ships such as these was to transfer a much greater proportion of the gunpower to the broadside, at the expense of the fore and aft guns. Another was the reduction in manoeuvrability. Sir Walter Raleigh believed that 'a fleet of twenty ships, all good sailers, and good ships, have the advantage, on the open sea, of a hundred as good ships and of slower sailing.'[4] According to Nathaniel Boteler, a fleet of nimble sailers, having 'bestowed one of their broadsides', would be able to 'speedily give the other', while a fleet of heavier ships 'can never use save one, the same beaten side.'[5] Although not designed with the line of battle in mind, the ships of the early Stuarts were already highly suitable for it. The *Sovereign* set the pattern for the three-deckers of the second half of the century. She survived until 1697, and no English ship was significantly larger than her until 1701.

The 'frigate' came from a different tradition altogether. In the English Civil Wars (1642–7), the fleet supported Parliament, but the great ships saw little action, as they were 'a royal fleet destinated to meet with another of the like'.[6] The main naval war was against royalist privateers and gunrunners, and for this small, fast ships were needed. Using examples of frigates captured from Dunkirk, the Parliamentarians began to build such ships of their own; the first of these was the *Constant Warwick* of 1645, originally a privateer but soon taken into the navy. The exact characteristics of these early frigates are difficult to determine, but they had a high length:breadth ratio, a long rake forward, and probably a single deck and no forecastle.

However such ships lasted only a few years. With the end of the Civil War, it became more important to build a navy to oppose the foreign powers of France, Spain and the Netherlands. The frigates were found to be weakly gunned and unseaworthy in heavy weather. New ones were ordered, with forecastles, larger dimen-

Three Commonwealth frigates in later life: in the foreground is the Fairfax *of the* Speaker *class, with the* Assurance *beyond (an early frigate, this ship has had a second tier of light guns added above her original single gundeck); astern is the* Elizabeth, *a later and larger two-decker. (NMM)*

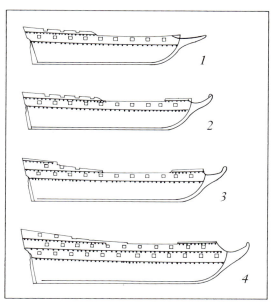

The development of the frigate layout, 1646–1660 (Brian Lavery)

1   *Early frigates, 1646–8. Single deck with armed quarterdeck but no forecastle.*
2   *Forecastle added, c1648–9.*
3   *Small poop added on some classes, 1649.*
4   *Fully developed two-decker layout, used on the* Speaker *and 'great frigate' classes.*

sions, and eventually with two full decks of guns. In 1649 an even larger frigate called the *Speaker* was begun. She was of 750 tons and designed for 50 guns, though she later carried 60. In size and power she was the equivalent of a great ship of the earlier epoch, though longer and narrower. Thus the frigates, like the three-deckers, tended to move away from the old turning and boarding tactics of the early part of the century, as they too had less room for forward firing guns, and were less capable of turning in battle.

The Anglo-Dutch Wars

Both the frigates and the three-deckers proved their worth in the battles of the First Anglo-Dutch War. Four new three-deckers were built in the 1650s, though all were smaller than the *Sovereign*. The largest, the *Naseby* (later *Royal Charles*), was of 1258 tons and carried 80 guns. The other three, the *Richard*, *Henry* and *Dun-*

4.   Quoted in Lavery, *Ship of the Line*, vol I, p11

5.   *Boteler, op cit, p253*

6.   *Ibid, p252*

In contrast to their opponent's three-deckers, the Dutch fleet flagship in the first war with the English was the Brederode, *a two-decker carrying fewer than 60 guns. This Van de Velde portrait, while reasonably detailed, does not give much sense of the ship's relative size. (NMM)*

bar, had 64 or 70 guns on about 1100 tons. The *Sovereign* herself had some of her extraneous upperworks cut down, and was rebuilt in 1660. The large frigates were ordered in substantial numbers – thirteen of the *Speaker* class were built, along with the *Antelope* of over 800 tons, and thirty-one frigates of slightly smaller classes, of 500 tons and upwards and 40 guns or more. When the monarchy was restored in 1660 in the person of Charles II, the English fleet consisted of 254 ships, of which 176 were of the Fourth Rate or above, and regarded as fit for the line of battle.

It is often suggested that the division of the fleet into Rates was a natural outcome of the line of battle, as certain ships had to be excluded because of their smaller size. In fact the early Stuarts had begun the process, and by 1633 the fleet was already divided into six ranks. In the 1650s, the First Rate included the very large ships – three-deckers of 80 guns or more. The Second Rate was made up of the old great ships, while the Third Rate comprised the frigates of the *Speaker* class, and a few other vessels. The Fourth Rate, made up of some of the smaller frigates of 36 guns or more, was the smallest to be included in the line of battle.

The Dutch, defeated in the war of 1652–4, did not stand still. Their ships at the beginning of that war had been small, and evolved from the long war of independence from the Spanish. The Dutch State was a federal one, and the navy was run by five separate admiralties, of Amsterdam, the Maas, Zeeland, Noorderkwartier and Freisland, each of which supplied ships for the national fleet. It was still common to use hired and requisitioned merchantmen, especially those of the large and powerful East India Company. The Dutch were producing excellent merchant ships at this time, economical of both timber and men; but such ships were not well suited to the line of battle, and were even less warlike than the English merchantmen, which were often designed for defensibility rather than economy. Furthermore, the Dutch had great problems with the depth of water in their ports and harbours, and this

was to impose increasingly severe limits on their naval efforts as time went on.

In June 1652, the Dutch were able to fit out a 'splendid' fleet under Van Tromp, with over 90 vessels, excluding fireships and pinnaces. Yet only the flagship, the *Brederode*, could compare with the English great ships and large frigates, much less the three-deckers. The *Brederode*, built in 1646, was 132ft long on the gundeck (122ft English) and 32ft broad (30ft English). She carried about 58 guns, and so was a match for the typical English ship of the *Speaker* or great ship type. The rest of the Dutch ships were much smaller – typically they had 26 to 38 guns, and a crew of 100 to 130.[7] The mobilisation orders of March 1652 demanded that the admiralties provide 'ships not less than 120 or 125ft in length, 27 or 28ft beam, 100ft from the top of the main mast to the deck, and at least 6ft under the half deck at the main mast.'[8]

Large shipbuilding programmes were instituted during the war. Sixty new ships were ordered in 1653, though not many of these were ready for the end of the war. Even so, the Dutch-pressed building programme did not slow up after the war, and several quite large ships were finished. Matters were accelerated when the next war with the English began in 1664. The new flagship was *De Zeven Provencien*, launched in 1665. She carried 80 guns, though only a two-decker, and was 163ft long and 43ft broad (nearly 40ft English). This made her broader than any English ships except the large three-deckers, and this was to prove something of an advantage. Unable to expand their ships downwards because of the

shallowness of their waters, the Dutch gave them greater breadth. This tended to increase their stability, which made them better gun platforms. At the Four Days Battle in 1666, the English fought in a strong wind with the weather gage; as a result, many of the ships could not open their lower deck ports because their ships were heeling towards the enemy, and the Dutch were given an important advantage.

More typical Dutch ships of this period were of around 60 guns, with a length of about 140ft, and a breadth of about 40ft. There was even less uniformity in the Dutch fleet than in the English, because of the five different admiralties, but Dutch shipbuilding retained many national characteristics. According to a French report of 1673, the Dutch ships were still more like merchant vessels, with large deep holds and relatively weak structures, built cheaply from imported timber, which was sometimes of poor quality.[9] However it was admitted that the method of construction gave greater stability, and certainly the new Dutch navy was good enough to take on the English in the war of 1665–7.

The French fleet and the Third Dutch War

The French began to build their own fleet of ships of the line after Louis XIV took effective power in 1661, and his great minister Colbert was in control of the navy from 1663. In order to rebuild the fleet, Colbert used the resources of Europe. He attracted shipwrights from Malta, Barcelona, Holland and other shipbuilding

7. S R Gardiner, (ed), *Letters and Papers Relating to the First Dutch War*, Vol 1, (London 1898) p261ff.

8. *Ibid*, pp120–1.

9. *Lettres, Instructions et Memoires de Colbert*, pp304–13.

The big French 70-gun Superbe *was typical of the impressive ships of Colbert's new navy. Far larger in relation to gunpower than either Dutch or English ships, they set a trend for large vessels that was to be a French characteristic down to the nineteenth century.* (NMM)

centres. Great shipwrights such as Anthony Deane of England were used as occasional advisers. A few large ships were built at Brest and Rochefort in the early 1660s, but the first real class of French ships of the line consisted of seven vessels built in Holland in 1666. They were two-deckers, of 1100 tons French measurement, and carried up to 72 guns each. The first large French three-decker, the *Royal Louis*, was completed at Toulon in 1668, and was registered at 2000 tons French. These ships were substantially larger than either English or Dutch ones of similar gunpower, and this made them good sailers, able to carry large quantities of stores for the crew. The process of expansion continued, culminating with ships such as the *Superbe* of 1671, registered at 1300 guns and carrying up to 76 guns on two decks. In 1674 Colbert produced his first regulations dividing the fleet into Rates. The First Rate comprised the three-deckers, from 80 guns upwards. It contained the subdivision known as the '*premier rang extraordinare*', which included such vessels as the *Royal Louis* and *Soleil Royal* of 120 guns, the *Reine* of 104, and the *Royal Dauphin* of 100. The Second Rate included two-deckers of 60–80 guns, and the Third Rate had ships of 50–60 guns, the other two rates being considered too small to fight in the line of battle.

The expansion of the English fleet continued through the late 1660s and early 1670s, partly in response to pressure from the Netherlands and France, and partly because of the natural tendency of English builders of this period to make ships bigger than planned. As a result, the old frigates of the *Speaker* class (re-

named *Mary* after the Restoration) developed into rather larger, more powerful and more seaworthy vessels. The first stage in the growth of the two-decker came in 1664, on the approach of the Second Anglo-Dutch War. Six new ships were ordered, initially to the same dimensions as the *Mary* and her sisters. All turned out rather larger – from 791 to 885 tons, instead of the 743 tons of the prototype. The contracts for the ships were soon amended, to give extra breadth and depth; one of the builders further claimed that the King himself had intervened in the affair, 'so much desiring breadth'. Meanwhile, news of the French ships being built in the Netherlands had filtered through, and this caused further increases. Despite the confusion, the new ships were highly successful. Two of them, the *Rupert* and *Resolution*, were built by Anthony Deane, who was the protegé of Samuel Pepys, the rising star of the naval administration.

The beginnings of standardisation

The two-decker continued to expand in an uncontrolled fashion. The next ship was the *Edgar*, ordered at 885 tons, the largest attained by the previous group, and completed in 1668 at 994 tons. By the time of the Third Anglo-Dutch War, the English were impressed by the new ships of their French ally, particularly the *Superbe*. Of this ship, Pepys commented with some exaggeration, 'She was 40ft broad, carried 74 guns and 6 months provision'.[10] Deane built two more Third Rates, the *Swiftsure* of 978 tons and the *Harwich* of 993. This ship was well approved, and Pepys wrote, 'The *Harwich*

carries the bell of the whole fleet, great and small'. The 1000-ton barrier was broken by the *Royal Oak* of 1107 tons, built by Jonas Shish of Deptford. In the fifteen years or so since the Restoration, the Third Rate two-decker had evolved into a ship of around 70 guns and 1000 tons. It is notable that English ships had increased in breadth since the days of the frigates, for this quality increased the stability of a ship which had to stand in the line of battle in any conditions.

The old three-deckers had seen a great deal of action in the second war with the Dutch, and many of them needed replacing. Three new 100-gun ships were built from 1670 to 1673, the first since the *Sovereign of the Seas* more than three decades earlier. There was always a tendency to overload such ships, and the *Prince* of 1670 and *Royal Charles* of 1673 both needed girdling to increase their buoyancy. Four slightly smaller three-deckers were also built in 1668–70, carrying 90–96 guns. The smallest of these, the *St Michael*, was of only 1100 tons, and was about the same size as the 74-gun *Royal Oak* of a few years later. Nevertheless she and her companions were considered as First Rates for much of their history. The Second Rate was largely reserved for the survivors of the old great ships, now fitted with up to 70 guns.

By 1677, after the Third Anglo-Dutch War, the English fleet was falling behind the French and Dutch, largely because of the mistrust between King and Parliament. In 1677, after several tries, Pepys finally persuaded the House of Commons that the navy was a national institution, not the property of the King alone; and that £600,000 was needed for thirty new ships of the line. He argued strongly, and largely successfully, for more three-deckers: 'The enemy having now very great ships, and many of them three decks, we need more of great ships to match them.'[11] In this case, the design process was even more confused than usual. Pepys had asked Parliament for one First Rate of 1460 tons, nine Second Rates of 1400 tons, and twenty Third Rates of 970 tons; instead he was allowed a First of 1400 tons, Sec-

10. J R Tanner, (ed) *Samuel Pepys's Naval Minutes*, (London 1925), p243.

11. Quoted in *Ship of the Line*, vol I, p43.

The ships were built over the next seven years, and as usual they emerged rather bigger than planned. The First Rate, named the *Britannia*, was rated at 1739 tons, being longer and narrower than the *Sovereign of the Seas*. The 90s averaged about 1450 tons, and the Third Rates, all of 70 guns, were between 1050 and 1164 tons. Due to political difficulties the programme was late, and many of the ships were allowed to fall into bad condition before they saw service; nevertheless it represents the culmination of British shipbuilding in the seventeenth century, and the three types of ship, the 100, 90 and 70, were remarkably similar to those which were to be used even in the 1770s, one hundred years later.

The 1677 building programme was combined with the first Establishment of Men and Guns, intended to be 'Solemn and Universal' and binding on the whole fleet for the future. In the past ships had been gunned without any regular system, and this had often resulted in overloading. In 1677, the *Britannia* was to have 'Cannon of seven', or 42pdrs, on the lower deck; the Second and Third Rates were to have 'demi-cannon' or 32pdrs, while the older ships of the fleet were to conform to this as far as possible. In fact the Establishment was far too ambitious, and tended to overload the ships yet further; by a revised Establishment of 1685, most ships were given somewhat lighter armaments.

Louis XIV's fleet continued to grow in strength, despite the death of Colbert in 1683. In 1689 an 'Ordonnance du Roi' was promulgated. The '*premier rang extraordinaire*' remained as before, and contained ships of up to 120 guns. The rest of the First Rate consisted of three-deckers of 80 guns or more. Both types carried 36pdrs (French weight) on the lower deck. The Second Rate also consisted of three-deckers, mostly of 60–70 guns, with 24pdrs as their largest guns; while the Third Rate had 50–60-gun ships, with two decks, carrying 24pdrs on the lower deck. The First Rates of ordinary class received much attention during this period – twenty-one ships of this type were built between 1689 and 1694. The French ships were large for the numbers of guns carried, and were predominantly three-deckers, which kept them high out of the water. Though the French had already begun

onds of 1100 tons, and Thirds of 900 tons. Clearly the biggest difference was in the Second Rates. Parliament probably saw them as an extension of the old great ship, but Pepys wanted something different – a smaller version of the 100-gun First Rate, able to carry 90 guns without undue strain.

The King intervened in the design process again, and at an Admiralty Board meeting he decided that the dimensions settled by Parliament were merely a minimum, and that he would make up any difference in cost from his own resources. After consultation with Deane and the Surveyor of the Navy, it was decided that the First Rate was to be of 1550 tons, the Seconds of 1307 tons, and the Thirds of 1008 tons.

A contemporary model of one of the 90-gun ships of the 1677 programme, possibly the Coronation *of 1685.* (Kriegstein Collection)

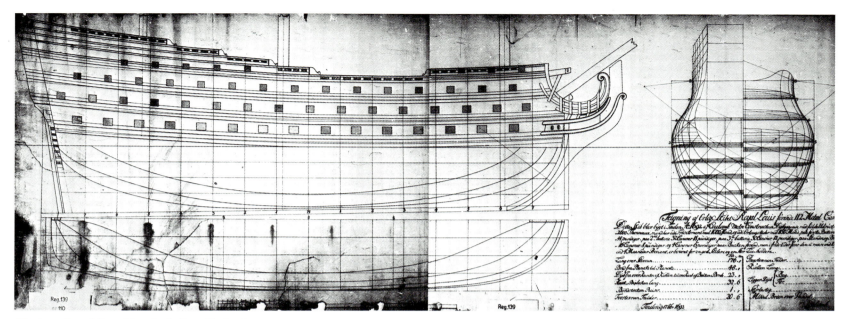

The huge French Royal Louis, *built at Toulon in 1692, carried 112 guns, the lower deck battery consisting of 48pdrs. This Danish draught is a copy, but judging by the style is probably based on a French original plan.* (Rigsarkivet, Copenhagen)

the scientific study of shipbuilding, there is no sign that their ships had particularly good sailing qualities; indeed, since so many of their ships of the line were three-deckers, they were mostly rather slow and clumsy.

The heyday of the three-decker

Nevertheless, the late seventeenth century was the heyday of the three-decker. The Dutch built three-deckers for the only time in their history – fifteen ships from 1683 to 1695. They carried around 90 guns, and tended to have less upperworks than the ships of other nations: they had no forecastle, a short quarterdeck with only a few guns, and a tiny poop. This was a layout which was to find much favour around 1670, but the Dutch ships were not a great success, and represent the last stage of the great age of Dutch naval power.

In England, the increase of the three-deckers came by a more roundabout route. In 1691, following the defeat at the Battle of Beachy Head, Parliament decided to vote money for twenty-seven new ships. The new building programme turned out to be a caricature of the 1677 programme. The tonnages voted by Parliament were too small, but this had not proved a problem in the past; however in this case the King, William III, was too busy conducting a great alliance to bother with the details of naval shipbuilding, and there was no-one else of sufficient authority to conduct the

programme. Thirteen two-decker 80s were built, with an average size of about 1200 tons; they soon proved to be weak and unstable ships, so the last four 80s were built as three-deckers. This was in accordance with the philosophy of the time, which preferred a high gun platform to a stable ship, but in the long term it proved to be a disaster. The three-decker 80s were only about 50 tons bigger than the two-deckers, and did not carry their guns well. But the defects were not immediately apparent, and over the next two decades all the two-decker 80s were converted to three-deckers. Originally they were three-deckers only in the sense that they had a deck connecting the quarterdeck and forecastle, but over the years they gained quarterdecks, poops, and armed forecastles, making them three-deckers in the fullest sense. Thus the small three-decker emerged as a major class of fighting ship, especially in Britain and France.

The 1691 programme also produced ten two-decked 60-gun ships. These were essentially a throwback to the old *Speaker/Mary* class of the 1650s, and were not a success as ships of the line, though they found some use as cruisers. Meanwhile, the English became more concerned about attacks on their trade after the enemy battlefleet was destroyed in 1692. The two-decker Fourth Rate of 50 guns, largely neglected since the 1650s, was revived. There was no great discussion about this, but it seems that it was seen as the ideal ship, able to serve in the line of battle or as a cruising and patrol vessel as required. In fact it was inadequate in either role, a typical attempt to reconcile impossible differences; but more than thirty were ordered in the 1690s.

The old and the new: English and French ship types

The beginning of the eighteenth century saw Britain established as *the* major naval power, largely because the others had withdrawn from the race. Yet the actual ships were often ill-conceived: the 100- and 90-gun ships were large and expensive; the three-decker 80s were unstable and poor sailers; the two-decker 70s were probably the best in the fleet, but were now quite lightly gunned, with only 24pdrs; while the 50s and 60s were essentially too small and weak for the line of battle. British ship design had passed out of its creative phase, and was almost frozen for most of the first half of the eighteenth century.

Three policies combined to create this epoch of stagnation. First, ships were now 're-built' when decayed, and as much as possible of the old timber was retained. The actual meaning of the term varied much over the years, but it certainly contributed to the atmosphere of extreme conservatism. Secondly, it was assumed that a ship, when lost or decayed, had to be replaced by another of the same type, except by special order. Thus the 80-gun ships were kept in service for over fifty years, despite increasing criticism of them. The only major change in the Navy List was that some of the 50-gun ships were replaced by 60s. Thirdly, 'establishments of dimensions' were drawn up from 1706 onwards, regulating the sizes for all ships of a given number of guns. In fact the dimensions were not immutable, and increases were allowed in 1719, 1733, 1741 and 1745; but such increases were small, and could only take place after some measure of agreement

By the end of the seventeenth century the smallest ships admitted to the line of battle were 50-gun ships, like this model of the St Albans *of 1687. However their value was already in doubt and their employment was largely confined to secondary theatres, and they were more often used as heavy cruisers and convoy escorts than ships of the line. (SM)*

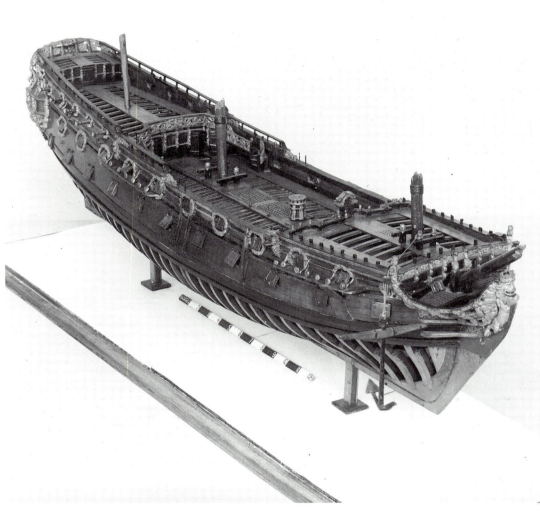

or a colonial expedition. In contrast to the European power struggles of the last century, a new age of colonial warfare was beginning. Maurepas needed ships which could be sent anywhere in the world – to India, North America or the Caribbean – with a minimum of preparation. Like his predecessors he sent shipwrights abroad to broaden their experience (notably Blaise Ollivier to England and Holland) although his ships remained of purely native design.

The new French navy avoided the three-decker almost totally. Only one ship of this type was laid down in this period, and it was accidentally destroyed by fire in 1742. Instead, efforts were concentrated on three main types of two-decker, the 64, 74 and 80. There was nothing new about the number of 64 guns; it went back as far as the *Princesse* of 1664. However the newer class of 64 can be said to date from the building of the *Eole* at Toulon in 1733. This ship carried twenty-six 24pdrs on her lower deck, and was somewhat larger than her predecessors, especially in breadth and depth. She was followed by many more ships of similar design.

The new class of 74 came next. Again, the 74 was quite an old type in a sense, and virtually the standard class in the French navy in the first quarter of the century. The innovation, as in the 64, was to increase the size of the hull, and to take guns off the upperworks and replace them with others, of a heavier calibre, on the gundecks. The old 74 had twenty-six 24pdrs on the lower deck, twenty-eight 18pdrs on the upper deck, and twenty light guns on the poop, quarterdeck and forecastle. The new type had twenty-eight 36pdrs on the lower deck, thirty 18pdrs on the upper deck, and no guns on the poop. The first of the new 74s was the *Terrible*, built by Coulomb at Toulon in 1737. The length was increased from the 152ft of the old type to 156ft, with breadth and depth in proportion, but the *Terrible* was not a complete success, despite her greatly increased gunpower. The next 74s built were the *Invincible* and *Magnanime*, constructed side by side at Rochefort in the early 1740s. The *Invincible* was 162ft long (by French measurement) and proved to be a very successful ship indeed. More 74s followed over the next few years, and

between the Admiralty and the ultra-conservative Navy Board. Establishments of guns were also put forward, but in practice these were far less restrictive than the Establishments of dimensions. In the case of the 1716 Establishment, for example, it seems that few ships were gunned exactly to the Establishment, particularly with regard to the guns on the upperworks.

French naval power reached its lowest point around 1720. Its revival began to accelerate from 1730, initially under Maurepas. There was a clear recognition that the French fleet would never again match the British in sheer size, but it was possible to construct a force which could strike anywhere, causing the British to fear an invasion of southern England, a campaign in support of Scottish or Irish rebels,

A model of a three-decker 80 of the 1719 Establishment, one of the most consistently criticised of all British sailing warship types. The relatively short, very high-sided layout is quite apparent. (SM)

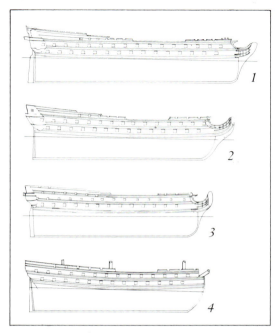

Mid-eighteenth-century French ships of the line: comparative profiles. (Brian Lavery)
1   *80-gun two-decker*
2   *New 74-gun ship, similar to* Invincible
3   *Old-type 74, with four guns on the poop*
4   *70-gun ship, superseded by the 74*

fifteen were launched between 1749 and 1756.

The 80-gun ships began with the *Tonnant*, built by Coulomb at Toulon in 1740. Four more had been built by 1748, including the *Soleil Royal*, which was 183ft long and 48ft broad by the French measurement. These 80s carried thirty 36pdrs on the lower deck, but the *Soleil Royal* introduced 24pdrs on the upper deck, making her a very powerful ship. The French navy had experimented with other types during these years, including ships of 72, 70, 66, 60, 56 and 50 guns, but by the mid-1740s the 80, 74 and 64 had begun to emerge as the ships with potential for development.

The period from 1730 to 1750 was a remarkably creative one for French shipbuilding, and it produced some of the classic warship types of the age of sail. Scientific training for shipbuilders had begun again but there is no real evidence that it had any great effect on the actual ships. The builders of the individual dockyards had great freedom of action, and there was no standard design or dimensions that had to be adhered to. They tended to concentrate on building ships of size and quality, rather than in large numbers, and the results were impressive.

In Spain there was a parallel revival. The Spanish, like the French, had no coherent plan to develop particular classes, and the results were more patchy than in France. But they too

concentrated on large vessels for a given gunpower. They built a few 70-gun ships, almost as big as the new French 74s, though less heavily gunned. One of these, the *Princessa*, surprised the Royal Navy in 1741 by putting up a tremendous resistance against three British 70s of nominally equal force, though of much smaller dimensions. They produced a major three-decker, the *Real Felipe* of 112 guns, launched in 1732. But the majority of their ships of the line were quite small, of 50 or 60 guns.

These were the dark ages of British shipbuilding. The Admiralty was generally aware of what was happening in foreign yards, but its attempts to get the British builders to produce bigger ships usually met with failure. In 1733 new dimensions were proposed, but the idea of designing ships to take higher calibres of guns was rejected by the Ordnance Board, on the grounds that sufficient supplies were not available. In 1741 there was yet another increase in dimensions, and some classes were given guns of a higher calibre, in return for reduced numbers – for example, the 70s became 64s, with 32pdrs instead of 24pdrs on the lower deck. In 1745 there was a major rethink, largely inspired by Admiral Anson at the Admiralty, but the conservative elements rejected plans to replace the three-decker 80s with 74s after the French model, and measured the depths of water in the main dockyards to prove that ships could not be made any bigger. The 1745 Establishment did result in a greater increase in size than ever before, and a restoration of traditional types such as the 70 instead of the 64. It also caused an even more rigid system, with the draughts as well as the dimensions of ships being fixed, and the orders being enforced by the King in Council, and not just the Admiralty.

The standard two-decker – the 74 and 64

The 1745 Establishment ships were not a great success, and the poor design of British ships was only emphasised by the capture of French masterpieces such as the *Invincible*; but it was ten years before anything could be done. Progress did not begin until the old officials of the Navy Board had retired or died, and in 1755 Anson was able to appoint his protégés Thomas Slade and William Bately, as joint Surveyors of the Navy. They immediately began on the design of a native British 74-gun ship. The first group, the *Dublin* class, was too small at only 1550 tons, but the type was expanded over the next few years until the *Bellona*

class of 1615 tons was produced. This size remained standard for British 74s over the next twenty years, though several different classes were developed, each with its own hull lines. Altogether, more than fifty 74s were built to Slade designs.

From the mid-1740s until at least the 1820s, the 74 was the most successful class in the line of battle. It was the ideal compromise, for its armament was kept lower than on a three-decker, but it could nevertheless mount a satisfactory armament of 32pdr guns, or their equivalent. It had lower topsides than a three-decker, but was better proportioned than a smaller two-decker, so its sailing qualities were good. The 74 was also considerably cheaper than a three-decker, even in proportion to its gunpower. Its advantage over the two-decker 80 was that it tended to need less maintenance – essentially the 80 was too long for the methods of construction then in use, and tended to hog badly after years of service (as did very large 74s). Thus the 80 found favour mainly with the French, who could afford such large ships, and whose fleets tended to spend less time in hard sea service than the British.

The 74 began to spread through all the main fleets of the world. The Spanish launched their

The British 74-gun ship of the late 1750s settled down to around 1600 tons and minor variations were worked on the hull forms for a number of related classes. This model of the Hercules *of 1759 represents one of the smaller Slade designs but is a good indication of the general appearance of these ships.* (NMM)

first in 1746, and had completed four more by 1750. A major building programme produced twenty-two between 1754 and 1756, and established the type as the main one in the battlefleet. The Dutch were still constrained by their shallow harbours, and they concentrated on the 64 as the main ship of the battlefleet. However they did produce a few 74s, mainly for use as flagships. The first was launched in 1759, and the second in 1763, but ten more were built in the early 1780s, because of Dutch intervention in the American War. The Danes built their first one, the *Sophia Frederica*, in 1773, and many more were to follow. The Swedes, operating in the confined waters of the Baltic, preferred ships of 62 guns, and did not produce their first 74 until near the end of the century. The Venetians, Russians and Turks all adopted it in some numbers later in the century, and the Americans built their first in 1782 – though it was immediately given to the French on completion, and no more were built for thirty years.

The 64-gun ship was essentially a smaller version of the 74, to be used where economy or geography precluded the larger vessel. It was always inferior in gunpower, and in most navies 24pdrs were standard on its lower deck. The British 64 developed just after the 74, using a variety of sources. Some were copied from the French, some from the scaled up lines of frigates, and perhaps it was also seen as a reduction of the old 70; but essentially the 64 was an enlargement of the old class of 60-gun ship. The British 64 had its heyday in the 1760s and early 1770s, when there was a large empire to defend, and the fleet had to spread itself rather thinly. The Spanish adopted it in quite large numbers, for similar reasons. The French abandoned construction of the 64 by 1780, regarding it as too weak for the line of battle. Smaller navies like the Dutch and the Danish continued it a little longer, but British officers had turned decisively against it by the 1790s, and it was only continued in the fleet because of dire necessity.

The revival of the three-decker

The three-decker had suffered an eclipse in the middle years of the eighteenth century. Its greatest exponents of the previous epoch, the French, completed none at all, while the Spanish built only one. In Britain it fell into severe

The famous Victory *of 1765 was one of the most successful British First Rates of the eighteenth century. Seen here during the American Revolutionary War, the painting shows her original appearance.* (NMM)

disfavour among progressive officers, largely because of the discrediting of the three-decker 80s. These were replaced by 74s in the Seven Years War, but even the more successful three-deckers, the 100- and 90-gun ships, where subjected to some redesign. Throughout the period of stagnation up to the 1740s, there were seven 100-gun First Rates on the Navy List (though not all of these were by any means fit for service at any given moment). One ship, the *Victory* of 1737, was lost in 1744, and there was no great enthusiasm to replace decayed ships, so that the number had declined to four in 1750. It rose again to five, but went down again to three by 1771. However the new ships which were built were of high quality: the *Royal George* and her sister the *Britannia* (which was to fight at Trafalgar in 1805) were among the few successful ships of the 1745 Establishment. The *Victory*, designed in 1759 by Sir Thomas Slade, was one of the most successful and famous ships of all time, and had excellent sailing qualities for a three-decker.

The 90-gun ship was affected by the same trends as the 74. Beginning with Slade's *Sandwich* class of 1755–9, the quarterdeck was left unarmed, and extra guns were placed on the gundecks. Thus windage and topweight were reduced, and the armament increased. In 1773 there was a further change of policy. Eight guns were to be fitted to the quarterdeck, making the ships into 98s. However they remained

quite different from the 100-gun ships; the 98s had 32pdrs on the lower deck, 18pdrs on the middle deck and 12pdrs on the upper deck, while contemporary 100-gun ships had 42pdrs, 24pdrs and 12pdrs.

For a brief time, there was convergence between the British and French in the building of three-deckers. The *Ville de Paris*, one of very few French 90-gun ships, was begun at Rochefort in 1757, and launched in 1764. Along with the *Royal Louis*, launched in 1759, she signalled the beginning of the revival of the three-decker in France. She took the reduction of the upperworks even further than the English 90s, and had no forecastle or poop, and only a small quarterdeck. Eventually she was built up to carry a much heavier armament.

In the French naval revival which followed the Seven Years War, funds were raised from the towns and provinces, and the names of the ships often reflected this. The *Bretagne*, launched in 1766, was the only other three-decker, and was a 100-gun ship. Again she followed the trend of taking guns away from the upperworks, for she had only six guns on the quarterdeck and forecastle. The real revival of the three-decker in France began with the renewed war against England, in support of the Americans. Four ships of 110 guns were launched in 1780. They were slightly longer than the *Bretagne*, but most had a similar gun arrangement on the three main decks; sixteen

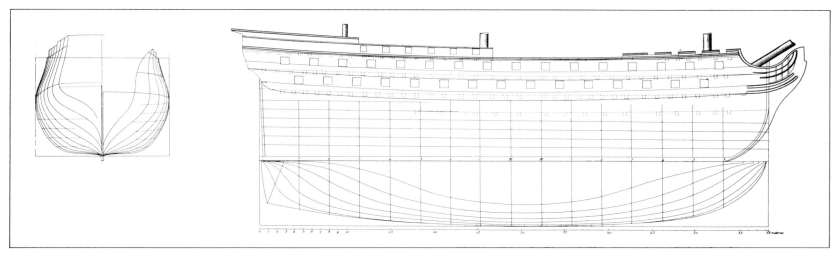

The draught of the French L'Auguste, *a two-decker 80 of 1811; this type was popular in the French navy, being more powerful than the 74, but its great length caused problems with 'hogging', and they were not much favoured by the British. (From Paris'* Souvenirs de Marine*)*

guns were now fitted on the upperworks, so that they were rated as 110-gun ships.

The Spanish also turned to the three-decker, though they built upwards rather than lengthwise. Their most famous ship of the post-Seven Years War period was the *Santisíma Trinidad*, launched at Havana in 1769. She was not particularly long at 186 Spanish feet, but carried a total of 120 guns, including twenty-six on the upper works. In later years she would be converted to a four-decker, with 140 guns, though she was always regarded as a clumsy ship, and a poor sailer. The French policy of lengthening ships, rather than heightening them, was eventually to prove more successful.

Late eighteenth-century developments

In France in 1786, the naval administration felt confident enough to impose a standard system of design – similar in many respects to the old British 'establishments', but much more successful, because they were based on much better principles, and because the ships were designed by one man rather than by committees. The man was Jacques-Noel Sané, who became Inspector General of Maritime Engineering, and was eventually known to the French as 'The Vauban of the Marine', after the great seventeenth-century fortress engineer.

For the line of battle, three main types were chosen – three-deckers of 118 guns, and two-deckers of 80 and 74. Standard draughts were drawn up and, with very few exceptions, all ships were built to them up to 1815. Sixteen 118-gun ships were built to Sané designs, along

with two 110s; thirty-five 80s and about a hundred 74s were also constructed. Yet the builders do not always seem to have followed the draughts in complete detail. Despite capturing numerous ships of the Sané type, the British seem to have regarded different ships as separate designs.

British ship design remained largely static from the 1760s up to about 1780. The Slade designed 74s were a great success, and new draughts tended to be slightly less successful. During the 1770s and early 1780s the main innovations in British ships concerned the fittings and construction – methods of seasoning and treating timber were improved, copper sheathing was developed and made standard, and the carronade was introduced to supplement the short range armament of ships.

Nevertheless the British were highly influenced by the French experience, and the vogue for copying the lines of French ships reached its peak in the last twenty years of the eighteenth century. The 64, which had been built in some numbers up to 1780, was largely abandoned (though many remained on the Navy List because of old stocks, captures from minor naval powers such as the Dutch, and conversion of East Indiamen). The 74 expanded slowly from 1780; the old Slade type, 168ft on the gundeck, was superseded by new ships which reached a maximum of 180ft in the mid-1790s. Many ships were based on French prizes, especially the *Courageux* of 1751.

It was becoming clear that longer ships, for a given number of decks, were better sailers than short ones. The 74 was better than the 64, and much better than the old 60s and 50s, because it could bear a full armament of 32pdr guns, and because its topsides were lower in relation to its length. Yet there were limits to this. Using the standard system of construction of the time, a very long ship would tend to 'hog',

or sag at the ends (where there was less buoyancy) and this was indeed a serious problem with the long 74s of the 1790s. Perhaps this is why the British did not adopt the two-decker 80 in any numbers; only two were built during this period – though again the numbers in the fleet were kept up by captured ships, this time from the French and Spanish.

Although the British 74 had reached an effective limit of size by the mid-1790s, the same was not true of the three-decker. Clearly the extra deck gave the hull greater girder strength, and a longer ship was possible. At the same time, the gunpower of the three-decker was reassessed. Such ships had invariably carried 42pdrs on the lower deck until the American War, when Admiral Keppel had complained that the shot was too heavy for a man to handle efficiently. After that there was a gradual programme of replacement with the 32pdr, though it was the 1800s before the last 42pdr went out of service.

The actual expansion of the three-decker began seriously around 1790. The *Queen Charlotte*, launched in that year, was the last 100-gun ship. The first British 110-gun ship was the *Ville de Paris* (named after the French ship, captured in 1782 but soon lost), completed the 1795. She was followed by the *Hibernia*, though that ship, ordered in 1790, was not completed until 1804. Meanwhile, development had turned to the 120-gun ship. The first was the *Caledonia*, designed by Sir William Rule and ordered in 1797. Again there were considerable delays; she was not begun until 1805, and launched in 1808. She was to prove a most successful ship, though the lateness of her launch meant that the lessons were not learned as well as they might have been.

In Spain, foreign influences competed with a developing native tradition, so that there were three schools of design. One was French, and

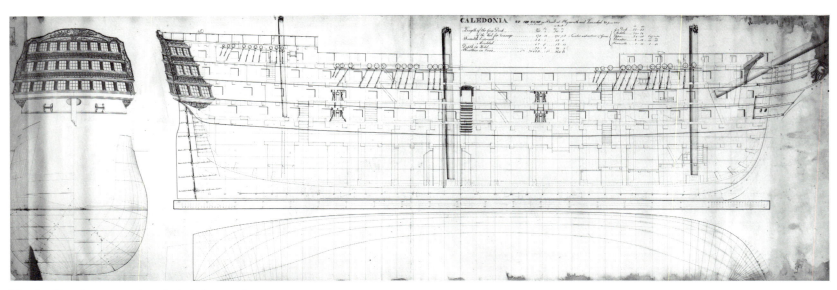

CALEDONIA

The first British 120-gun ship, the Caledonia, *of 2609 tons as designed. This ship was the largest vessel in the Royal Navy in her day, and formed the basis for postwar development, being regarded as superior to the succeeding* Nelson *class. (NMM)*

known as the '*Sistema Gautier*', after a naval architect of that name who had emigrated to Spain in 1765. The 'English system' was based on the traditions of various emigré shipwrights in the past. The native style was known as the '*Sistema Romera Landa*', after its founder. But in general Spanish ships followed the French in style and gun distribution. They built large numbers of 74s, especially after 1765; they constructed several two-decker 80s, mainly in the mid-1790s; and they bypassed the British 100-gun ship in favour of the 112 and occasionally the 120.

Stability and standardisation

As the nineteenth century began, all the major powers had conservative policies in building ships of the line, mainly because the system of construction did not allow any further expansion. In some of the secondary navies, there was some experimentation in detail. In Sweden, Chapman produced new types of gun carriages, and made some alterations in the layouts of ships. In Denmark, designers produced a new type of stern, as fitted on the *Christian VII*. But France was firmly committed

Following the success of the big 44-gun frigates in the War of 1812, the American attempts to produce far larger ships than the European norm culminated in the huge and ungainly Pennsylvania *of 1837. Nominally a 120-ton ship, a flush spar deck allowed the vessel a total of 132 gunports; however, she proved a poor sailer and too expensive for a peacetime navy to run. (NMM)*

to the Sané system, while Britain, having experimented with longer 74s in the 1790s, was now inclined to return to slightly shorter ships. The new vessels were about 176ft on the gun-deck, halfway between the 180ft of the longest ships of the 90s, and 168ft of the old Slade 74s.

In 1806 the British Surveyors, too, were asked to produce standard sets of draughts for the three classes of the line, to be known as the 'Surveyors' class – three-decker 120s and 98s, and two-decker 74s. Recognising that there had been little real development since the 1740s, when the 74 had been developed, Henry Peake and Sir William Rule based their draught for a 74 on the French *Courageux* of 1751, though with certain modifications. The

class was not a great success; it did not live up to the sea officers' expectations, and later the two score ships built to the draught became known as the 'forty thieves'. A draught for a 98-gun design was produced in the same way, but the type was already obsolescent, and only one ship, the *Trafalgar*, was built to it. The three 120-gun ships were constructed, forming the *Nelson* class; they too were unsatisfactory, largely because Rule's earlier *Caledonia* had finally been launched, and proved a very good sailer. Her hull form was to be the model for most three-deckers built in Britain from this time until the 1830s. Two-decker design reverted to other forms after the failure of the 'Surveyors' class; a Danish 80, the *Christian*

HMS Asia, *one of the two-decked 84-gun ships based on the captured French* Canopus, *showing the new round stern introduced by Sir Robert Seppings. Built of teak at Bombay and launched in 1824, she was Admiral Codrington's flagship at the Battle of Navarino, the last fleet engagement between pure sailing ships.* (NMM)

VII, was copied for four 74-gun ships, and an 80 was also built to the same draught.

The stagnation of ship design was ended by Sir Robert Seppings' improvements in construction, especially his system of diagonal bracing. First tried on the 74-gun *Tremendous* in 1810, it was used on a few more ships before the end of the wars with France in 1815. It almost eliminated the old problem of hogging on large ships, and made it possible to build ships with much greater length for a given number of decks. Seppings also gave the round bow to ships of the line. In the past, the upper part of this area had been protected only by a very weak beakhead bulkhead. Recent battle tactics, for example the bows-on approach at Trafalgar, had exposed this fault, and the bow was built up with frame timbers in the same way as the rest of the ship.

Much of the impetus for improvement came from the new United States Navy. The Americans had a policy of building the best individual ships possible, in contrast to the British who needed quantity rather than quality. The Americans had large virgin forests, and skilled and innovative shipbuilders. Their first successes against the British in the War of 1812 were with frigates, but they soon began to build ships of the line as well. Most were called 74s, but were quite different from the European concept of such a ship. Rather than dispute the control of the seas, each was intended to break the British blockade at a specific port, and to cause havoc among the squadrons outside.

The first American 74 (apart from the *America* given to the French on building in 1782), was the *Independence* launched at Boston in 1814; five more ships were ordered as part of the same programme, though only three were ever launched. The *Independence* was 190ft long, 14ft more than a typical British 74. She actually carried 82 guns, all 32pdrs, with long guns on the lower deck, medium length ones on the upper deck, and carronades on the quarterdeck and forecastle. Her broadside weight was 2624lbs, compared with 1964lbs for a typical British 74.

Her successors were even bigger. The *Ohio*, begun in 1816 and launched in 1820, was 197ft long, and part of a programme of eight ships of the line, of which six were eventually com-

pleted (though the *Alabama* was kept on the stocks for decades and not launched until 1864). The largest of all the American ships of the line was *Pennsylvania*, rated at 120 guns, and launched in 1837. The American ships were not all good sailers, as some were overloaded with guns; but they were enough to cause some rethinking in Britain.

Postwar developments

At the end of the wars with France in 1815, the British navy had large stocks of ships left over; but technological change was taking place, and the growth of the American fleet did not allow any complacency. The first task was to reorganise the rating system. Since the introduction of the carronade around 1780, the rating of a ship had no longer reflected the actual numbers of guns carried. This was remedied in 1816. The 80-gun ships (now regarded as 84s) were called Second Rates, while the 74s, in the guise of 76s, 78s or 72s, remained the backbone of the Third Rate. The American system of arming all decks with a single calibre was not entirely new in Britain – for example, several old 74s had been fitted out with a uniform armament of 24pdrs in 1807 – but it was adopted more extensively, with old 24pdrs being bored out to make light 32s for the upper decks.

It was time to take advantage of the pos-

sibilities offered by the Seppings system of construction. For new construction, the old 74 was virtually abandoned in favour of the two-decker 84. These were mostly based on the lines of the French *Canopus*, captured at the battle of the Nile in 1798, but using the new British system of construction. Nine such ships were built between 1819 and 1825. For three-deckers, the 120-gun ship, on variations of the lines of the *Caledonia* of 1808, became standard. Six ships were built postwar, being begun up to 1829 and completed as late as 1840. The only new type was the two-decker 90, a class which was made possible by the Seppings reforms, and indeed was designed by Seppings himself. These ships were planned specifically with the American threat in mind, but were intended to be more robust than the great American 74s.

In the postwar period, Seppings also developed the round stern. The old type of stern was weaker even than the bows, for it was very lightly constructed and broken up by windows and galleries. Seppings' new system was much stronger, and gave much more scope for mounting guns firing aft; but it proved very unpopular, because it reduced the comfort of the officers, and was considered ugly. In the 1830s it was replaced by the 'elliptical stern', similar in appearance to the old square stern, but actually much stronger.

The ultimate two-decker, the 90-gun Albion *of 1842. Designed by the controversial Surveyor Sir William Symonds, she was surprisingly fast and carried her guns at an unprecedented freeboard; on the other hand, she was not a good foul-weather ship, and rolled heavily. (NMM)*

France was still the second naval power in the world, and was capable of producing some very radical ideas. In 1822 General Henri Paixhans argued for small, steam-powered armoured warships firing shells, which would soon have eliminated British superiority. His ideas were only partly adopted, in that calibres were standardised on the different decks, and shell firing guns were provided. But the actual design of ships was no longer being improved in France. After a joint exercise in 1832, the French were forced to consider why their ships now seemed to be inferior to British ones.[12]

Seppings left office in 1832, as part of an overall reform of British society and naval administration, which abolished the old Navy Board and merged it with the Admiralty. His successor was Sir William Symonds, a former naval captain who had showed a talent for amateur ship design. He started with small yachts, and proved the advantage of a wide beam, and a sharp triangular underwater section. Before his appointment as Surveyor of the Navy he demonstrated this principle on brigs and

12. Fincham, *A History of Naval Architecture*, pp258ff.

The only French three-decker ordered after 1815 was the 120-gun Valmy, *eventually launched in 1847. She caused the French navy considerable trouble, being completed overweight and lacking adequate stability, which resulted in the ship being 'girdled' to increase her breadth at the waterline; she was never a satisfactory sailer. (By courtesy of Andrew Lambert)*

sloops, and after 1832 he was able to build frigates to similar lines. The first ship of the line built to his design was the *Vanguard*, begun in 1833 and launched in 1835. Eight more ships were built of this class, along with the *Albion*, a Second Rate two-decker of 90 guns, and the *Queen*, a First Rate of 110 guns. Symonds' ships seemed to demonstrate their sailing qualities in numerous trials during the 1830s and 1840s, but his critics pointed out that these proved very little, because ships performed differently in varying wind and sea conditions. The gravest fault of his designs was that the ships rolled very sharply, and therefore made unsteady gun platforms. He was always opposed by professional naval architects, and in the mid-1840s the naval administrators began to turn against him. He soon found that many of his designs were altered by the Admiralty, and he resigned in 1847. The ships building were modified, usually to make them more like the ships of the old construction.

By this time, the steam battlefleet was on the way. Paddle tugs had started to come into service by 1815, and their existence may have contributed to the fashion for longer ships, as it was no longer necessary for a ship to be able to short-tack into harbour. Paddle frigates were introduced in the 1820s, but the steam ship of the line had to await the invention of the screw propeller, for a paddle wheel would take up a great deal of space on the sides of the ship, and drastically reduce the armament. The first British screw ships of the line were four old 74s of the 'Surveyors' class, converted into 60-gun blockships between 1845 and 1852. Soon more modern ships were being converted to steam, or built as steamers from the first. By the time of the Crimean War it was clear that the pure sailing ship of the line was a thing of the past.

Brian Lavery

Ships of the Line: Typical Vessels 1650–1840

Name	Nationality	Launched	Built	Rate	Gundecks	Guns	Dimensions: Feet–inches Metres	Burthen	Fate	Remarks
SOVEREIGN OF THE SEAS	English	1637	Woolwich	First	3	90–100	127–0*kl* × 46–6 × 19–4 41.63*kl* × 15.25 × 6.34	1522	RB 1660, 1684; lost 1696	The first true three-decker
COURONNE	French	1638*	La Roche-Bernard	–	2	68	130–0*kl* × 44–0 × 19–0 40.0*kl* × 13.53 × 5.84		Stricken 1643	Largest French ship of her day
BREDERODE	Dutch	1646	Rotterdam	–	2	59	132–0 × 32–0 × 13–6 46.64 × 11.30 × 4.77		Lost 1658	The largest Dutch warship of the time
SPEAKER	English	1650	Woolwich	Third	2	50–62	116–0*kl* × 34–8 × 14–6 38.03*kl* × 11.36 × 4.65	727	Renamed *Mary* 1660; RB 1685; lost 1703	The prototype of the English two-decker
ZEVENWOLDEN	Dutch	1664	Harlingen	–	2		145–0 × 38–6 47.54 × 13.60		Capt by English 1665; recaptured 1666; stricken	Typical Dutch warship of the period
RUPERT	English	1666	Harwich	Third	2	64	119–0*kl* × 36–3 × 17–1 39.01*kl* × 11.88 × 5.60	791	RB 1703	Successful Third Rate of the period
ROYAL LOUIS	French	1668	Toulon	First	3	120	164–0 × 45–0 50.46 × 13.85	2000	Stricken 1697	The first 120-gun ship
SUPERBE	French	1671	Rochefort	Second	2	68–76	37–0 11.38	1300	BU 1687	Influential French large two-decker
NEPTUNE	English	1683	Deptford	Second	3	90	163–11 × 45–0 × 18–6 53.74 × 14.75 × 6.06	1497	RB 1710	Typical 90 of the 1677 programme
FOUDROYANT	French	1691	Brest	First	3	84	158–0 × 44–6 48.61 × 13.69	1600	Lost 1692	Typical large French ship of *c*1690
BOYNE	English	1692	Deptford	Third	2	80	157–0 × 41–3 × 17–3 51.47 × 13.52 × 5.65	1160	RB 1708	Typical 80 of the 1691 programme
WINCHESTER	English	1698	Rotherhithe	Fourth	2	50	130–0 × 34–4 × 13–7 42.62 × 11.25 × 4.45	673	RB 1717	Smallest viable ship of the line
PRINCESSA	Spanish	1730	Guarnizo	Third (in RN)	2	70	165–1 × 49–8 × 22–3 54.12 × 16.17 × 7.29	1709	Capt by British 1740; BU 1784	Large Spanish 70
NORTHUMBERLAND	British	1743	Woolwich	Third	2	64	159–1 × 44–2 × 18–11 30.52 × 14.48 × 6.20	1299	Capt by French 1744	Typical ship of the 1741 dimensions

Name	Nationality	Launched	Built	Rate	Gun-decks	Guns	Dimensions: Feet–inches Metres	Burthen	Fate	Remarks
INVINCIBLE	French	1744	Rochefort	Third	2	74 (in RN)	162 (French) 171–3 × 49–3 × 21–3 56.15 × 16.15 × 6.97	1793 (Brit)	Capt by British 1747; lost 1758	Inspiration of the 74 in France and Britain
SANDWICH	British	1759	Chatham	Second	3	90	176–1 × 49–1½ × 20–11½ 56.09 × 16.11 × 6.87	1869	BU 1810	First of the new type of 90
BELLONA	British	1760	Chatham	Third	2	74	168–0 × 46–11 × 19–9 55.08 × 15.38 × 6.48	1615	BU 1814	Standard dimensions for British 74s until 1780s
VILLE DE PARIS	French	1764	Rochefort	First	3	90–110	177–0 × 48–6 × 23–0 57.85 × 16.36 × 7.45		Capt by British and lost 1782	Later became a 110-gun ship
VICTORY	British	1765	Chatham	First	3	100	186–0 × 52–0 × 21–6 60.98 × 17.05 × 7.05	2142	Preserved 1922	Still in existence at Portsmouth
SANTISÍMA TRINIDAD	Spanish	1769	Havana	First	3–4	120	186–9 × 58–0 61.23 × 19.2	2153	Capt by British and lost 1805	Became a four-decker in 1796 (136 guns)
COMMERCE DE MARSEILLE	French	1788	Toulon	First	3	118	208–4 × 54–9½ × 25–0½ 63.86 × 17.00 × 8.10	2747	Capt by British 1793; BU 1802	Example of Sané 118-gun ship
POMPÉE	French	1791	Toulon	Third	2	74	182–2 × 49–0½ × 21–10 59.73 × 16.08 × 7.16	1901	Capt by British 1793; BU 1817	Sané 74; copied for two British ships 1796
MONTAÑES	Spanish	1794	Ferrol	Third	2	74	190–0 × 51–0 × 25–6 62.29 × 16.7 × 8.39	1500	Lost 1810	One of the Romero y Landa type of 74
AJAX	British	1807	Blackwall	Third	2	74	176–0 × 47–6 × 21–0 57.70 × 15.57 × 6.89	1761	BU 1864	'Surveyors' class 74; first steam blockship 1846
CALEDONIA	British	1808	Plymouth	First	3	120	205–0 × 53–6 × 23–2 67.21 × 17.54 × 7.60	2616	BU 1875	First British 120-gun ship
INDEPENDENCE	American	1814	Charlestown	–	2	74–86	190–0 × 50–0 × 20–0 62.30 × 16.39 × 6.56	2257	BU 1914	First American ship of the line in service
RODNEY	British	1833	Pembroke	Second	2	90	205–6 × 54–5 × 23–2 67.38 × 17.84 × 7.60	2598	BU 1882	First two-decker 90. Screw ship, 1860
ASIA	British	1824	Bombay	Second	2	84	196–1½ × 51–1¼ × 22–6 64.30 × 17.13 × 7.38	2289	Lost 1908	84-gun type intended to replace 74
QUEEN	British	1839	Portsmouth	First	3	116	204–2½ × 60–0½ × 23–9 66.95 × 19.69 × 7.79	3104	Screw ship 1859; BU 1871	Last British sailing three-decker completed
VALMY	French	1847	Brest	First	3	120	210–7½ × 57–5 × 26–1 69.10 × 18.82 × 8.55	5154 disp	Stricken 1891	Only French three-decker ordered after 1815

Notes:

Dimensions give the length of gundeck or the length of keel (indicated by *kl*) by the moulded breadth by the depth in hold.

Dimensions are given in native measures, in feet and inches, and then in metres (except after the metre was introduced in France in 1791). Tonnage is the original as measured by the navy concerned, except in the case of captured ships, where the captured tonnage is given. There were many variations in systems of measurement, even within the same country, especially in the seventeenth century, so the dimensions given provide only a rough comparison. Abbreviations: BU = broken up, RB = rebuilt, *disp* = displacement, RN = Royal Navy.

2

The Frigate

FROM earliest times war fleets have had their attendant small craft, but the emergence of a specialist cruising vessel had to wait on the development of the line of battle ship. This latter was the product of the mid-seventeenth-century Dutch Wars [see Chapter 1], whereas the cruiser only became clearly defined during the wars between England and France that began in 1689.

For the purposes of this chapter the 'frigate' is considered to be the largest vessel that was not meant to lie in the line of battle, but the smallest to warrant a rating – essentially the equivalents of English Fifth and Sixth Rates, although early Fifth Rates saw fleet action, and the latest frigates were large enough to be rated Fourths. It excludes what most navies called sloops or corvettes, but does make reference to small two-deckers, because this is essentially the history of a concept rather than a narrow chronicle of a naval architectural form (the so-called 'true frigate' which is popularly supposed to have been invented in the mid-eighteenth century). In fact, in terms of design, what was understood to be a 'frigate' changed many times during two centuries, as its chief functions developed.

The nature of the cruising ship's role[1] steadily expanded and the increasingly global nature of naval warfare meant ever more ambitious requirements laid down for frigate design. It is possible to see two trends developing in response to these factors:

1. Growth in ship size, both absolutely and relatively;

2. Increasing importance of the type in all major navies, again absolutely in terms of numbers but also relatively in the sense that the proportion of frigates in the fleet grows steadily.

The first is easily demonstrated: in the 1650s a single-decked Sixth Rate (16 guns) would measure about 150 tons, and a Fifth Rate of 32 guns about 290 tons; in 1850 the Sixth Rate would carry up to 28 guns on 1050 tons, while the biggest vessel still called a frigate would mount 60 guns and measure 2500 tons; firepower increased dramatically – broadside weight of shot went up from 100lbs to 900lbs respectively. What is more, from being about 20 per cent of the burthen of a First Rate in 1650, the largest frigate in 1850 was about the same length and nearly 60 per cent of the tonnage.

The second trend is quantified for some navies in Table 1, but available figures suggest that a similar movement applied to all the main naval powers, and even those in the second division – hence the inclusion of Denmark and Sweden. Table 1 in effect charts the history of the frigate, its relative decline in the 1660–90 period when it struggles to find a role, and then an inexorable rise in its significance in the fleet, to the point where it often outnumbers ships of the line.

From the design viewpoint, the history of the frigate is not a single continuous progression towards an ideal form; the changes in layout merely reflect the choice of one of a limited number of solutions to the same basic problem. A long but rigid hull for single-decker vessels was difficult to contrive, and so in practice for about a century after 1650, smaller ships had no more than ten or twelve ports per side. Single-deckers were thus about 20 guns and the smallest two-deckers 40-gun ships. To build a ship of around 30 guns meant a battery and a half, and almost every design in the early history of the frigate is a variation on one of two possibilities: the half-battery could go above the main, on the upperworks (on or under the quarterdeck and forecastle), or partially filling a lower deck. This latter arrangement had the advantage that if the upper deck battery is regarded as constant, for stability reasons any weapons on the forecastle and quarterdeck have to be lighter, whereas the lower deck guns could be heavier. Nevertheless, the former may seem the more logical, and it was the method in vogue in the 1650s, but the latter was to be more significant in the development of a specialist cruising ship.

---

1. Strictly speaking, in the age of sail the term 'cruiser' was applied to any ship on detached duties, but in this chapter it is understood to be synonymous with 'frigate' as defined above.

The Dutch Postiljon, *a 24-gun ship of the Amsterdam Admiralty, of about 1660, in a drawing by the Younger van de Velde. Apart from the lower deck battery, there are gunports under the forecastle and quarterdeck, the usual layout for the smaller ships of this period. This type of vessel was often referred to as a* pinasschip, *and a number of surviving draughts confirm the basic proportions and layout.* (NMM)

The English Sixth Rate Drake *of 1652 in a drawing by the Younger van de Velde. The simple single-deck layout with minimal superstructure was to remain essentially unchanged for Sixth Rates until the introduction of the new two-decked type with the 1719 Establishment. (NMM)*

topsides made this type of ship less weatherly. For vessels armed on the quarterdeck and forecastle, there was always the temptation to join them up to make a second full gundeck – as happened to the Cromwellian 'frigates' [see Chapter 1] and again 150 years later with the American spar-decked ships.

For a century designers worked variations on these themes, but by the mid-1700s cruising ships became large enough to justify both a lower deck and armed upper works. A more powerful upper deck battery nullified the doubtful advantages of a few lower deck guns, and so the classic frigate form came about as a logical and organic amalgamation of the two basic traditions. It was self-evidently successful, for it became the international standard for a century and was only challenged by a few spar-decked two-deckers in the largest category.

1650–1688: prehistory of the frigate

The origin and complex etymology of the term 'frigate' is beyond the scope of this chapter, but the name was always associated with speed and relative lightness of construction. How the

Because they had only one main battery, frigates had to be able to use their guns in all weathers, so the distance between the gunport sill and the waterline was of paramount importance, and this had implications for both arrangements. With no full deck below, the main battery was often too near the water; a lower deck elevated the main armament sufficiently, but it also allowed the fitting of a partial battery between decks. Unfortunately, the guns tended to be forward or aft (where the sheer gave them more freeboard) so these heavy weights were then best placed to cause 'hogging', while the two-decker height of the

Table 1: Growth in the Ratio of Fifth and Sixth Rates to the Battlefleet

Date	No of Ships Battlefleet: Cruisers	Cruisers as Percentage of Total Fleet	Date	No of Ships Battlefleet: Cruisers	Cruisers as Percentage of Total Fleet	Date	No of Ships Battlefleet: Cruisers	Cruisers as Percentage of Total Fleet	Date	No of Ships Battlefleet: Cruisers	Cruisers as Percentage of Total Fleet
Britain			**France**			**Denmark**			**Sweden**		
1651	54:43	44%									
1660	76:78	51%	1661	11:6	35%						
1677	76:24	24%	1674	95:33	26%						
1685	108:19	15%									
1688	100:8	7%	1689	112:33	23%						
1702	130:45	26%	1700	114:26	19%	1700	32:9	22%	1700	39:10	20%
			1720	27:10	27%	1715	36:14	28%	1715	29:13	31%
1739	124:51	29%				1745	28:8	22%	1745	24:8	25%
1753	132:78	37%	1750	50:26	34%						
1777	142:102	42%	1774	64:37	37%						
			1780	78:67	46%						
1783	197:175	47%	1786	67:77	53%	1785	32:18	36%	1785	26:17	40%
1793	78:98	56%									
1805	199:222	53%				1805	20:14	41%	1805	13:12	48%
			1814	50:36	42%						
1825	110:118	52%	1827	34:34	50%						
1849	68:89	57%	1847	21:31	60%						

Notes:
Cruising ships are considered to be Fifth and Sixth Rates plus those larger vessels that might be regarded as frigates in their day (*eg* English galley-frigates of the 1670s and large spar-decked 44–60s after 1815); for this purpose 50s and the like are considered battleships, even after they had been banished from the line.

Frégate a la Voile,

A contemporary illustration of the larger type of French frégate legérè of the 1675–80 period. Eleven guns a side (probably 6pdrs) are carried on a single deck, and although there seems to be a step-down aft, there is hardly room for a second deck below. The quarterdeck is armed and there is even a short poop. (Musée de la Marine, Paris)

frigates of the English Civil War became battleships has been outlined in the previous chapter, and the period of the Anglo-Dutch wars saw the rapid increase in the average size of line of battle ships. The Fifth Rates were rather left behind by this development, remaining the weakest units in the battle line – in the 1650s they did not exceed 290 tons and were armed with 16–20 demi-culverins (9pdrs) and 8–10 minions (4pdrs) – but without evolving an alternative role. In the Dutch fleet of 1654 57 per cent of all ships carried between 30 and 38 guns (69 out of 121 vessels), so the Dutch were even more dependant on small fighting ships. Both navies favoured ships with one full battery, sometimes with a partially armed deck above, plus quarterdeck and even a poop.

After 1660 the English built only a handful of Fifth Rates and to emphasise their unpopularity the four largest of the seven launched before 1689 were upgunned to fully two-decked Fourth Rates. Hired merchantmen were still tolerated in the battle line during the

Second Dutch War (19 out of a total of 106 English ships in 1665); most of these were equivalent to a Fifth Rate so they may have contributed to the growing dissatisfaction with ships of this force in the battlefleet while persuading the Admiralty that there were in any case more than enough available.

In France the 1670 *règlement* specified two-decked Fifth Rates with only 18–28 guns (presumably the upper deck carried guns only

under the forecastle and quarterdeck), but these were uprated to 30s in 1674, mounting 8pdrs or 6pdrs. Most European navies built similar vessels, a typical example being depicted in one of the earliest identified Danish plans, dated 1664, for the *Hummeren* of 32 guns (8pdrs).

Sixth Rates were usually single-decked ships in the navy of the English Commonwealth, without substantial upperworks, but since only six vessels were built in the 1650s, varying greatly from 60 to 150 tons and 8 to 16 guns, there was clearly no accepted form. After the Restoration, English Sixth Rates seem to be much influenced by royal yachts (many of which were formally rated as Sixths), producing low and elegant vessels of 140–200 tons mounting 16–18 sakers (5pdrs). French *frégates légères* were comparable in the 1670s but by the following decade had grown to around 300 tons, acquiring a large quarterdeck and poop on which they carried eight to ten 3 or 4pdrs to add to the upper deck battery of twenty 6pdrs. By contrast, the smallest Dutch cruisers, sometimes referred to as pinnaces, had always carried a forecastle, long quarterdeck and poop, producing a characteristically high stern – in fact a miniaturised version of larger warships.

A Danish draught dated 1664 for the Hummeren, *in layout typical of the smaller rates of the period, with a covered gundeck and armament under the forecastle and quarterdeck like an incomplete upper deck battery. This ship was not in fact designed as a blue-water cruiser but was intended as a coastal guardship – hence the relatively low freeboard and the oarports between the guns. (Rigsarkivet, Copenhagen)*

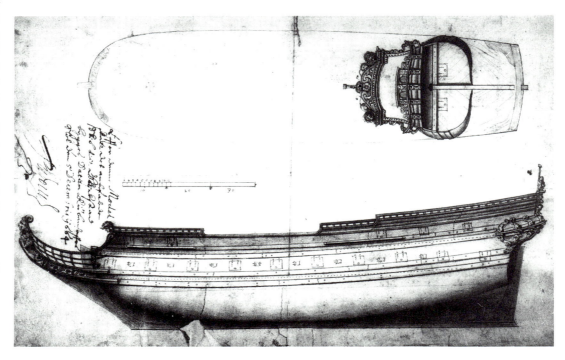

No navy built many ships of the smaller rates between 1660 and 1688, since they were palpably inadequate for service in the line of battle but as yet they had no clearly defined alternative role. This is demonstrated by an analysis of the traditional tasks of the frigate, which were either fleet support or independent cruising, as follows:

Fleet

1. Reconnaissance, the 'Eyes of the Fleet' so familiar from Nelson's time. In the seventeenth century this would usually fall to the fastest vessel, which in the era before copper sheathing would probably be the most recently cleaned, not necessarily the smallest.

2. Repeating signals. This did not evolve until the eighteenth century when fleet numbers were smaller and tactics more sophisticated.

3. Fireship duties. In a fleet action a fierce parallel battle might take place between fireships, their supporters and the anti-fireship forces, and the smaller rates were often dedicated to this; here manoeuvrability was prized above firepower, and since no full rigged ship of the spritsail era was particularly handy, small craft and boats were often preferred.

4. Advice boats and dispatch vessels. For the same reason, yachts and fore and aft rigged craft were preferred. In the 1690s the English introduced a new class of small advice boat specifically to keep an eye on French Channel ports because no larger vessel was expected to be able to get close enough and escape with its observations.

5. Inshore work. Shallow draught could be useful for shore bombardment and amphibious support, but these tasks only came to the fore during later wars.

6. Frontline reserve. In the Dutch wars the chief function of the smaller ships was to board damaged or secure surrendered vessels, while helping disabled or hard-pressed units of their own fleet. It might be argued that any ship powerful enough to intervene effectively should have been in the line to begin with, and it seems that often the decision to include a Fifth or even a Fourth Rate would depend on whether the admiral felt he had adequate forces at his disposal.

Detached duties

1. Trade protection. Convoys were widely used in the Anglo-Dutch wars, but the escort would depend on the size and value of the merchant fleet; it would not be thought unusual for Third Rates to undertake such duty, so it would rarely be entrusted solely to small ships.

2. *Guerre de course*. With the larger convoys well protected, frigates might be used against individual merchantmen, but whereas by 1800 a well manned frigate would be more than a match for any trader, the largest East Indiamen in the 1660s rated alongside contemporary 70-gun ships. At the other end of the scale, the

The galley-frigates of the Stuart navy represented one of the first specialist cruiser types. This fine portrait (probably by the Elder Van de Velde) shows the Charles Galley *with all her ports open.* (NMM)

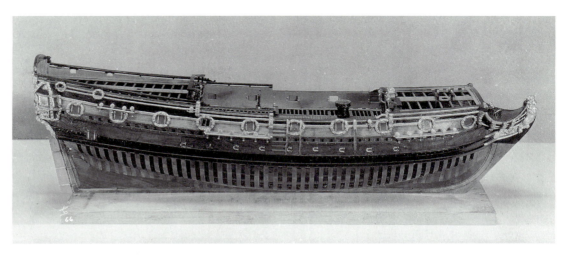

The English demi-batterie ships are almost unknown from visual sources, but this model which has always mystified its cataloguers almost certainly represents the ships as first proposed. As built they gained a few gunports fore and aft on the lower deck, but otherwise the model is probably representative of the early ships. (US Naval Academy, Annapolis)

Dutch had set a trend of very economical manning in the smaller merchant ships, so these did not even require Sixth Rates for their capture.

3. Independent cruiser. A frigate could perform securely in this role only if the likelihood of meeting battleships was reasonably remote (as it often was with the smaller fleets of the next century) or if she enjoyed a speed advantage. Neither could be relied on at this time, since all but the 'great ships' might be assigned detached duties, and as yet there had been no particular requirement for speed in Fifth Rates; Sixth Rates were better, but they were so small that they could often be overhauled by larger ships in even moderately rough weather.

4. Colonial flagship. The Fifth Rate was certainly employed as a 'battleship substitute' on overseas stations, but only *faute de mieux*; the role exerted no influence on design.

From the foregoing it seems that as yet there was no overriding strategic or tactical requirement for a specialist cruising ship. However, the 1670s saw one tentative step towards such a vessel, in the development of the galley-frigate. The marriage settlement of Charles II had included the North African territory of Tangier, and this was to bring the English navy into frequent conflict with the Barbary states. Apart from conventional warships, the corsairs of these states employed handy lateen rigged vessels and galleys which could be used with advantage against a slow moving or becalmed square rigger. The new galley-frigates therefore emphasised speed under sail, being long and lightly built, but a full set of sweeps was intended to allow them to row into or out of action. Sweeps were common enough on Dunkirk frigates earlier in the century and in the 1640s English Fourth Rates had carried them, but like a modern yacht's auxiliary engine, oars were meant for occasional or emergency use only. In the galley-frigates, however, performance under oars was an important design consideration, 160 unfortunate Thames Watermen being impressed to emphasise the point.

Structurally two-deckers, the galley-frigates

had the sweep ports on the lower deck between a couple of chase ports fore and aft, the main battery being on the upper deck. Although they mounted 30–32 guns, because they were large and heavily manned, they rated as Fourths; possibly regarded as too expensive and over-specialised, only three were built (the *Charles Galley* and *James Galley* in 1676 and the *Mary Galley* in 1687), despite having a high reputation in the fleet. They are supposed to have been inspired by similar French ships – the *Bien Aimée*, 24, built at Toulon in 1672 is one contender – but no firm design details are available for any such vessel. What is certain is that Denmark built a similar galley-frigate in 1687, and a smaller version the following year.

1688–1715: the birth of the specialist cruiser

The 'Glorious Revolution' of 1688 that brought William of Orange to the throne of England radically altered the pattern of European alliances and initiated more than a century of intermittent warfare with France. In the Anglo-Dutch wars both sides had been primarily naval powers with extensive merchant fleets which could only be adequately defended by defeating the opposing battlefleet; thus the engagements had been frequent, hard-fought and largely confined to the Channel and Dutch coast. A French war would be different, and those in England who had considered the matter feared that France would not commit its fleet to battle, but keep it well to the west as a screen for an all-out war on commerce (this was to be proved correct, but only after the major French defeat at La Hogue in 1692).[2] Furthermore, whereas geography had favoured England, which flanked all sea routes to Holland, the situation was now reversed in that most homecoming English trade was vulnerable to attack in the Mediterranean and from

French Biscay or Channel ports – and the waters of the Western Approaches and the Brittany coast were both rougher and more distant than the battle grounds of the Dutch wars.

Clearly there was an argument for a new type of cruiser, but the Royal Navy of 1688 also needed large numbers. William III faced opposition to his rule in Ireland and Scotland supported to varying degrees by French military intervention, so there was a sudden requirement for a multitude of small craft to intercept possible reinforcements, keep William's own supply line clear, and provide intelligence, besides the expected commerce protection duties. Very few small warships were in service, and desperate steps were taken to hire or purchase anything suitable, while a substantial building programme was put in hand immediately. It is worth noting that from this point onwards, whatever their design differences, British cruisers have one overriding characteristic in common: their scarcity. There were never enough to fulfil all the fleet, trade protection and colonial duties required of them and this had important implications for design policy. Quantity was more significant than individual superiority, which tended to result in the smallest possible ships for the armament, and robust, seaworthy vessels that could withstand the long periods at sea demanded by British strategy; it also produced an ingrained reluctance to increase the stakes by introducing larger, more powerful and consequently more expensive cruisers, a habit of mind that survived until the twentieth century.

This view was clearly taken for granted from the early eighteenth century so it is rare to find anything comparable to modern 'staff requirements' relating to British cruiser design. However, they do exist for the radical new Fifth Rates built as a response to the French war. The basic specification was devised by

William's chief naval expert, Lord Torrington, and reveals an intelligent appraisal of what was needed. The chief features were 'that they should have but one tier of ordnance flush and that to be on the upper deck whereby they will be able to carry them out in all weathers'; to have a light lower deck for the berthing of the crew, with ten oar ports a side; the lower deck to be at the level of the waterline when fully stored, when the ten upper deck ports would enjoy at least 7ft freeboard; as many guns on a large quarterdeck as convenient.[3]

They did not have the porportions of the galley-frigates, so handling under sail was paramount, but the small number of sweeps would give them useful manoeuvring power. However, 7ft freeboard for the guns was exceptional and not regularly matched until a century later. In concept this was a remarkable anticipation of the classic frigate form of the next century, but it proved impossible to resist arming the lower deck, so they were completed with two or three ports a side for demi-culverins with 20 sakers on the upper deck and 4–10 smaller guns on the quarterdeck, rating as 32–36 guns. The inspiration for this step may have been the

galley-frigates but it is more likely to have been mercantile practice, many of the hired merchantmen of this time having a low 'tween deck with a few guns fore and aft.

Appropriately, the first was called *Experiment* and proved a fast sailer, which is surprising given such top heavy proportions and a burthen of only 370 tons. About thirty were in service by the end of the war and although no two were entirely alike they did not grow much in average size.

The new Sixth Rates were more conventional, being single-decked vessels of about 250 tons designed in response to the urgent order of 1693 that 'some small light good sailing Frigotts of the Sixth Rate to carry about twenty guns each should be built as soon as conveniently may be . . .'[4] Their main battery of sakers was designed for 4ft 6in freeboard and they carried four smaller guns on the quarterdeck; about twenty were built before 1698.

The few French Fifth Rates built at this time were single-deckers rated as 30–36 guns, with heavy upperworks, including a poop. Slightly larger than their English equivalents at about 400 tons, they mounted a more powerful main battery (usually twenty 8pdrs) but carried it little more than 4ft from the waterline so would have to rely on quarterdeck armament in a seaway. These ships were phased out towards the end of the century, being replaced by enlarged *frégates légères*, whose twenty 6pdr main armament was augmented by 8–10 small guns added to their quarterdecks; little bigger than the English 24s, but also encumbered by a small poop, they cannot have been particularly good sailers.[5]

The damage done to British commerce by

this first clash with the French *guerre de course* was more a result of poor organisation and lack of strategic experience than inadequate ships. There was much contemporary carping, but the French certainly thought highly of their prizes, many a privateering squadron being commanded from a captured English cruiser.[6] However, the Admiralty thought that the *demi-batterie* Fifth Rates were not powerful enough and from 1700 a new class of two-decked 40-gun ships was introduced. With a lower deck battery of 12pdrs, on a burthen of 495 tons, they were hopelessly over-armed and only seven were built.

The design of Sixth Rates continued essentially unchanged in both navies, but mention should be made of one important oddity, the English *Peregrine Galley* of 1700. Designed by the same talented amateur, Peregrine Osborne, who had built the *Royal Transport* (see Chapter 4), she was described as 'the finest ship and swiftest sailer in England'.[7] Although she remained a 'one-off', the ship's form was immensely influential and was still being used as the basis for English fast-sailing ships into the 1760s.

When war broke out again in 1702 over the question of the Spanish Succession, France rapidly took up the trade war where she had left off – but with the added sophistication of properly disciplined squadrons. Ostensibly privateers, they chartered powerful warships from

---

3. Public Record Office Adm 1/3558. There are no known illustrations of the early ships, but a model at the US Naval Academy (Cat No 14) looks like the first stage of the design.

4. National Maritime Museum ADM A/1797.

5. The description of early French frigate development depends heavily on information supplied to the author by Jean Boudriot (letter of 1 October 1979).

6. See J H Owen, *op cit*, pp29–30.

7. Narcissus Luttrell in a contemporary diary (but not published until 1857), *A Brief Relation of State Affairs* . . .

The English continued to build demi-batterie *ships into the early years of the eighteenth century. This Danish draught – one of the few known plans of such vessels – represents one of the last, the* Sweepstakes *of 32 guns and 416 tons, built at Woolwich in 1708. (Rigsarkivet, Copenhagen)*

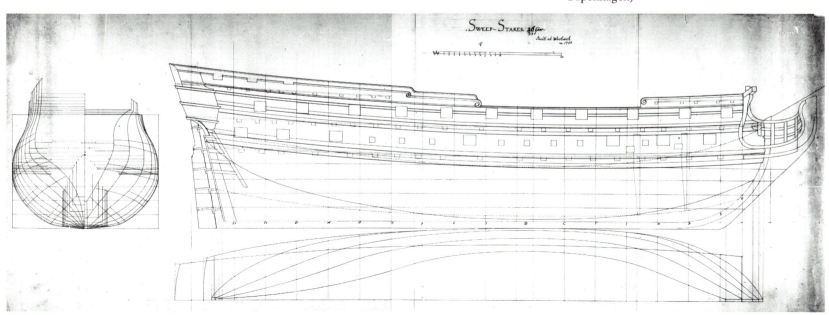

Table 2: Typical Armaments 1650–1715

Ship Type	Country	At Date	Lower Deck Armament	Upper Deck Armament	Quarterdeck/Forecastle Armament	Minimum Gunport Freeboard
Fifth Rate	England	1655 1666	18 × 9pdr 20 × 9pdr	4 × 6pdr 10 × 6pdr		
Fifth Rate	Netherlands	1655	16 × 9pdr[1]	16 × 6pdr		
Hummeren, 30 guns	Denmark	1665	No lower deck	20 × 8pdr	6 × ?4pdr/4 × ?4pdr	4.5ft
Delft, 34 guns	Netherlands	1667	14 × 12pdr	14 × 6pdr	2 × 4pdr, 4 × 3pdr	
Schakerlo, 28 guns	Netherlands	1667	8 × 8pdr, 6 × 6pdr[2]	12 × 6pdr	2 × 4pdr	
Sapphire, Fifth Rate	England	1677 1685	18 × 9pdr 16 × 8pdr	10 × 6pdr 10 × 4pdr	4 × 4pdr 2 × 3pdr	
Capricieuse, 30 guns	France	1688	No lower deck	20 × 8pdr	8 × 4pdr/2 × 4pdr	4ft
Demi-batterie Fifth Rate, 32 or 36 guns	England	1689 1703	2 × 9pdr 4 or 8 × 9pdr	20 × 6pdr 22 × 6pdr	8 × 6pdr/2 × 6pdr 6 × 4pdr	3.5ft 4ft
Sixth Rate, 24 guns	England	1694	No lower deck	20 × 6pdr	4 × 4pdr	4.5ft
Fifth Rate, 42 guns	England	1703	20 × 12pdr	22 × 6pdr		4ft
Demi-batterie 42 (*Amazone*)	France	1707	8 × 12pdr	26 × 8pdr	6 × 4pdr/2 × 4pdr	3.5ft
Demi-batterie '36' (*Gloire*)	France	1709	16 × 8pdr	24 × 8pdr	4 × 4pdr	3.5ft
Vita Ørn, 30 guns	Sweden	1711	Unarmed	20 × 12pdr	8 × ?6pdr/2 × ?6pdr	6ft
Illerim, 36 guns	Sweden	1716	?No lower deck	24 × 18pdr	10 × 8pdr/2 × 8pdr	5ft

Notes:

1. Probably Dutch 8pdrs. Before 1703 the English guns referred to above as 6pdrs were actually sakers firing a 5.25pdr shot; in the same period 9pdrs were actually demi-culverins.

2. Probably a mixed battery as shown, but exact disposition unknown.

the King to provide the firepower to overwhelm the escorts of all but the most well protected convoys while their smaller consorts played havoc with the merchantmen. The hired naval vessels were anything up to Third Rates, so the British employed squadrons of the smaller line of battle ships to hunt them.

Therefore French ships needed to be fast, to give battle only when it suited them, but strong enough to overcome quickly the Fifth or Fourth Rate convoy escorts. For this specific requirement the French developed a new and larger version of the *demi-batterie* ship, which was introduced in 1707. One of the first was

French demi-batterie ships were designed specifically for commerce raiding and were larger than their British equivalents. This plan from Admiral Paris' Souvenirs de Marine shows the Gloire, probably as designed, with the lower deck largely devoted to oarports; a draught of the ship as captured shows some variation, the most important being the addition of five additional gunports on the lower deck stretching as far forward as midships.

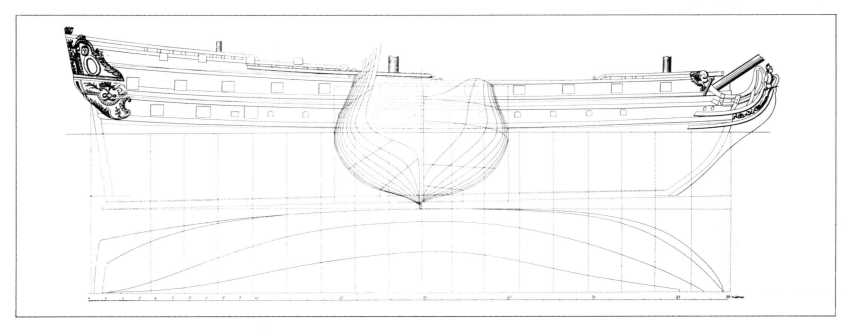

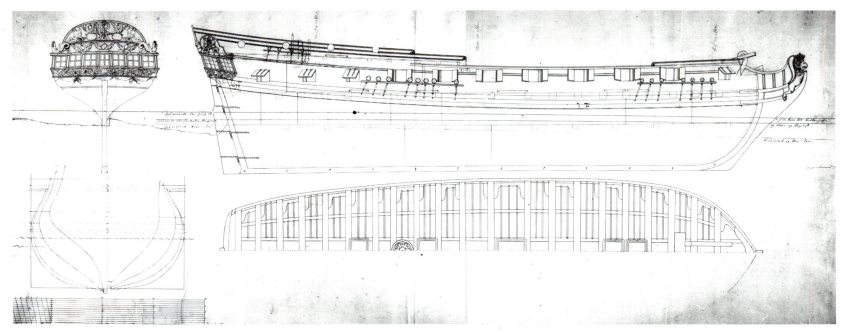

René Duguay-Trouin's famous *Gloire*, which originally had three lower deck ports a side aft for 12pdrs and a full row of sweep ports, but when captured in 1709 she had five extra ports reaching to just forward of the main mast and a homogeneous battery of forty French 8pdrs on two decks, plus four 4pdrs on the quarterdeck.

The British response to the squadronal war on trade was largely a matter of improved strategy, better intelligence of enemy movements, and an emphasis on frequent anti-fouling to retain cruisers' speed. Nevertheless, it was clear that British ships were very small for their rate and in 1706 a new Establishment of standard dimensions was laid down. It did not include Sixth Rates, but both the Fifth Rates were increased in size, the 40s to 530 tons – by way of comparison, the *Gloire* was measured at 657 tons as a 42 in British service. At sea the war was not going well and by 1709 the sense of frustration led the Admiralty to order a complete review of cruiser design. Very few of the *demi-batterie* 30s had been built after 1700, but they enjoyed a brief renaissance because, even when enlarged, the 40s did not sail well. Other measures included the removal of quarterdeck armament on Fifth and Sixth Rates, and a new version of the latter built to lighter scantlings. A few very small Sixth Rates of around 160 tons were also built at this time, probably as a result of the Admiralty's call for fast-sailing vessels to gain intelligence off Dunkirk.

While Britain and France were the principal naval powers of the period, innovation was by no means confined to the Channel. In the Baltic, the maritime side of the Great Northern

War was largely a cruiser conflict in its closing phase. The Swedes evolved a preference for large single-deckers and as early as 1711 the emigré English shipwright William Smith built a 12pdr-armed 30-gun ship, the *Vita Ørn*, with a complete unarmed lower deck, positioned just at or below the waterline as in the later so-called 'true frigate'. However, more radical was a class of four very large single-decker 36s of nearly 1000 tons armed with 18pdrs built during the same period; the *Illerim* of this type was captured by the British and handed over to Denmark. They had no obvious influence and there was to be nothing quite like them until the 1770s, but Sweden alone continued to build large single-deckers.

1715–1745: peace and stability

In Britain the 1719 Establishment heralded an era of stability in ship design, laying down dimensions and scantlings for every class of vessel down to Sixth Rates. It is often held responsible for stagnation in British design, but the real culprit was the complacency resulting from a long period of peace. For cruising ships, its provisions were sensible if not radical, but it did introduce a new type of Sixth Rate.

These were 'in the manner of the *Dursley Galley*', launched the previous year, and harked back to the 32s of 1689. The dimensions were virtually identical, but the new 20s preserved Torrington's original concept in a pristine form, having only oarports on the lower deck. The reasoning behind the revival is not clear, but may have been sponsored by the First Lord of the Admiralty who, as Lord Dursley,

The Swedish Vita Ørn *of 1711 had an unarmed lower deck placed below the waterline, thus anticipating the usual French claim to have 'invented' the form by more than 30 years. This Danish draught was taken off after the ship's capture in 1715. (Rigsarkivet, Copenhagen)*

commanded one of the *demi-batterie* Fifth Rates in his youth. As designed these ships had very light upperworks, only a short forecastle and quarterdeck and were big enough to carry their twenty 6pdrs without compromising their sailing qualities.

However, they were probably rather wet and had restricted accommodation, so there was a gradual move towards more substantial upperworks (not for the last time in peace, comfort was prized above fighting qualities). History was also to repeat itself, in that the unarmed lower deck was given a pair of gunports aft, and the enlarged quarterdeck also acquired guns.[8] Although they were broadened by 2ft from 1733, they were soon upgunned to carry twenty-two 9pdrs and two 3pdrs, further jeopardising their sailing qualities. Dimensions were increased slightly in 1741 and again in 1745, but so were the upperworks and the experience of war harshly exposed their deficiencies.

The 1719 dimensions provided for a 30-gun *demi-batterie* 30 of 114ft on the gundeck and 462 tons, but this type of cruiser had fallen from favour in the Royal Navy and for thirty-five years there was no British-built ship between the 20–24- and 40–44-gun classes.

---

8. These seem to have been introduced with the *Dolphin* of 1730 which had one lower deck port; 1733 Establishment 20s had two widely spaced, and 1741 ships had two close together.

Table 3: Typical Armaments 1715–1780

Ship Type	Country	At Date	Lower Deck Armament	Upper Deck Armament	Quarterdeck/Forecastle Armament	Minimum Gunport Freeboard
Establishment 20-gun Ship	Britain	1719	Unarmed	20 × 6pdr		7ft
Establishment 40-gun Ship	Britain	1719	20 × 12pdr	20 × 6pdr		4ft
Fregate – Deuxième Ordre	France	1730	6 or 8 × 8pdr	22 or 24 × 6pdr		4ft
Fregate – Troisième Ordre	France	1740	Unarmed	20 or 24 × 6 or 8pdr	2 or 4 × 4pdr	?5ft
Establishment 24-gun Ship	Britain	1741	2 × 9pdr	20 × 9pdr	2 × 3pdr	3.5ft
Establishment 44-gun Ship	Britain	1741	20 × 18pdr	20 × 9pdr	4 × 6pdr	4.5ft
8pdr Frigate	France	1740 on		26 × 8pdr	6 × 4pdr added from 1760s	4ft–5ft
28-gun Sixth Rate	Britain	1748		24 × 9pdr	4 × 4pdr added from 1750s	6ft
12pdr Frigate	France	1748 on 1790s on		26 × 12pdr 26 × 12 pdr	6 × 6pdr added from 1760s 10 × 6pdr/4 × 6pdr	5ft–6ft
32-gun Fifth Rate	Britain	1756 on		26 × 12pdr	6 × 6pdr	7ft–7.5ft
L'Abenakise	France	1757	8 × 18pdr	28 × 12pdr	2 × 6pdr	3ft
Hancock (in British service)	USA	1777		24 × 12pdr 26 × 12pdr	10 × 6pdr 4 × 6pdr/2 × 6pdr	6.5ft

Lineal descendants in size and layout of the demi-batterie *ships of the 1690s were the 20-gun Sixth Rates of the 1719 Establishment. This excellent model depicts the original form, with short quarterdeck and forecastle and only oarports on the lower deck. Later developments tended to increase the upperworks and added a couple of gunports a side to the lower deck, to the detriment of the ship's sailing qualities. (SM)*

For large cruisers, the British relied on small two-deckers of 40 and later 44 guns, although only fourteen were constructed in the twenty years preceding the outbreak of war with Spain in 1739. The 1719 design was 15 per cent larger than its predecessor, armed with twenty 12pdrs and twenty 6pdrs, with light and un-armed quarterdeck and forecastle. However, the same tendency as noted for the 20s was to manifest itself, with a slight increase in beam in 1733 being offset by the substitution of 9pdrs on the upper deck, and the addition of four 6pdrs to a built-up quarterdeck. Worse was to follow: a 4 per cent increase in burthen in 1741 was combined with the lower deck armament being increased to 18pdrs, in response to com-plaints from sea officers about more powerful Spanish opponents. As it turned out, the ex-perience of war was to demonstrate that the inadequacies of British cruisers was more a matter of sailing qualities than gunpower – more than anything else, they needed to be larger for their nominal rating.

If British design was at a low ebb during this period, the situation in France was little better, where a plethora of different types of cruising ship existed alongside one another. From the 1730s, *Frégates* were divided into three *Ordres*, the largest being two-deckers of 40–46 guns, usually armed with twenty or twenty-two 12pdrs on the lower deck and twenty-two or twenty-four 6pdrs on the upper, with no guns on the *gaillards* (a useful French term encom-passing both forecastle and quarterdeck). They were usually about 128ft on the gundeck but the last of the line, *Junon*, built at Le Havre in 1747, measured 145ft and was armed with thirty 12pdrs and twenty 6pdrs. Although larger than their English counterparts, they were also heavy sailers and had less than 4ft freeboard to their lower gunports – hardly acceptable in a deep-water cruiser.

Whereas the British had given up half-battery ships at the end of the Spanish war in 1712, France, who had only recently re-discovered their merits, went on building them for thirty years. Rated as the *2me Ordre*, they mounted 28–36 guns, in a variety of dispositions: ten to twelve 8pdrs or 12pdrs on the lower deck in the largest, and twenty-two to twenty-six 6pdrs or 8pdrs on the upper; some had 4pdrs on the quarterdeck. As an example of the smaller type, the 28-gun *Flore* built at Toulon in 1728 was armed with four 12pdrs, twenty-two 8pdrs on the upper deck and two 4pdrs on the quarterdeck, measuring 123ft on the gundeck. The last built in mainland France (two were built later in Quebec) was the *Etoile* at Le Havre in 1745, when the lower battery had graduated to eight 18pdrs, with thirty 12pdrs on the upper deck and twelve 4pdrs on the *gaillards*. As with all their predecessors the apparent advantage of a few heavier guns, was outweighed by the restrictions on their use (less than 4ft of freeboard would reduce them to using their upper battery more often than not in Channel conditions, but their two-decker height of topside would still hamper their sailing).

The *3me Ordre* were 6pdrs or 8pdrs armed vessels with a single battery, but the largest of these, at about 126ft in length, were structural two-deckers like the British 20s. Armed with twenty to twenty-four 6pdrs or 8pdrs on the upper deck, they had a forecastle and substantial quarterdeck (armed with two or four 4pdrs), plus a small poop, so their upperworks were anything but light. Needless to say, they were no better sailers than their British equivalents.

When war broke out between Britain and France in 1744 neither side was well equipped with cruisers, although the former should have benefitted from five years of war with Spain. In both countries, the next few years was to see radical change in cruiser design.

1745–1780: the classic frigate form

The way forward had already been indicated in France, where Blaise Ollivier had built a new light frigate called *Medée* at Brest in 1741. She was a two-decked ship, but Ollivier reduced the height below decks, restricted the twenty-six 8pdrs to the upper deck and kept both the scantlings and the upperworks very slight, resulting in a ship with sailing qualities that were a significant improvement on earlier French cruisers. This ship has been described as the first true frigate, but while she was an advance on previous cruisers, no single feature of the design was without precedent – and some, such as the unarmed quarterdeck, would never become standard frigate practice.

However, Ollivier was one of the most original of French constructors and in 1743 he

A comparison between the profiles of the new French frigates of the 1740s and the old style British Sixth Rate:

1. *A typical Sixth Rate of the 1741 Establishment, which is both relatively short and high-sided, as a result of giving the lower deck enough freeboard for gun- and oarports.*
2. *Panthère, the smallest of the new types and with only a 6pdr armament soon regarded as a corvette; the lower deck is below the waterline and the ship is so low that after capture by the British extra bulwarks were added to make the ship drier in a seaway.*
3. *Renommée, one of the finest frigates of the first generation, and similar in size to the Medée; there are no guns forward of the foremast because the fineness of her bow form gave little buoyancy, and also because the long lightly built hull could not stand heavy weights at the ship's extremities.*
4. *Embuscade, one of the largest 8pdr frigates of her day, was similar to Renommée in most respects; note that the extreme tumblehome required the channels to be set up below the gunports where they were vulnerable to damage in a seaway.*
5. *By way of contrast, the first British vessels of this form, Unicorn and Lyme, were not quite so low, although it was thought necessary to increase the height between the decks of later ships, incidentally improving the freeboard of the main gunports.*

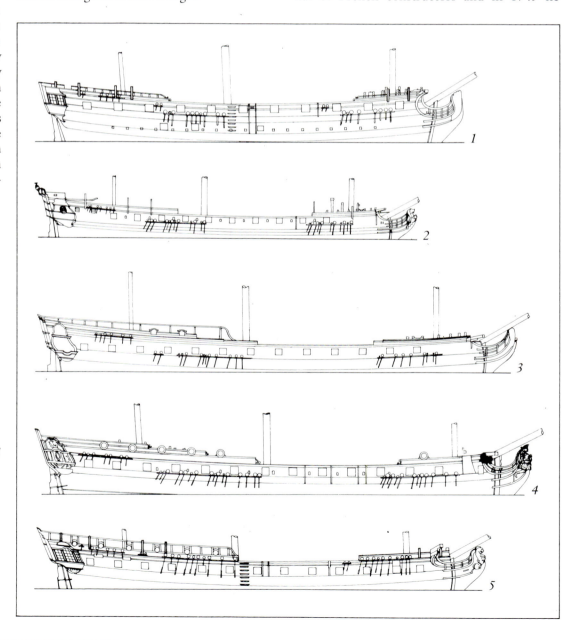

wrote an influential report in which he expressed grave reservations about the larger cruiser types, and advocated his own formula for the smaller designs. The 8pdr type rapidly became standard, with about thirty of them being built before the *Alcmene* and *Aimable* concluded the class in 1774. Even smaller frigates were tried, like Coulomb's *Panthère* of 1744, but the armament of twenty 6pdrs was soon regarded as fit only for corvettes.

As explained in the previous section, the construction of two-decker and *demi-batterie* ships had virtually ceased by the end of the war, but combat experience suggested that a larger version of the Ollivier frigate was necessary. The first of these, the *Hermione*, was built by Morineau at Rochefort in 1748, and this type was to become the standard French frigate for over thirty years. They were overshadowed by 18pdr ships from the 1780s, but just over a hundred 12pdr armed vessels were constructed up to the *Leoben* of 1797.[9]

In Britain, the material state of the Royal Navy contrasted poorly with its success in battle. The Admiralty, inspired by the reforming zeal of Anson, was trying to obtain much needed changes in ship design, but was being frustrated by a conservative bureaucracy at the Navy Board. Ironically, many of the new French frigates had been captured (including *Medée* and *Panthère*), so their qualities were well known. Contrasting their prizes with existing types, British sea officers argued that the 24s and 44s were too slow and unhandy for cruising ships, but nobody suggested that they were not well armed or robust; the Navy Board countered that French ships were not economical (they were very large for their gunpower), they were too lightly built (and so costly to maintain) and, with very slight upperworks, were vulnerable in battle.[10]

The Admiralty forced another Establishment in 1745, but although it increased sizes (44s to 815 tons and 24s to 508 tons) the basic designs remained unchanged, and before long there were complaints about the 1745 ships too. The need for a good Sixth Rate, in the face of the French war on commerce, was pressing and in 1747 the Admiralty cut the Gordion knot by ordering two 24s to the lines of a French privateer called the *Tygre*. Named *Unicorn* and *Lyme*, they were eventually rated as 28s in 1756 and were the prototypes of the 28-gun 9pdr frigate in the Royal Navy, some fifty being built up to the end of the American Revolutionary War. By way of comparison, the two aged Surveyors, Sir Jacob Acworth and Joseph Allin, were each allowed to build a 24 untrammelled by Establishment dimensions,

but the resulting *Seahorse* and *Mermaid*, although they eschewed lower deck guns, were of similar proportions to their predecessors and no match for the new type.

Unusually for peacetime, development work on cruisers went on after 1748. As fate would have it, both Surveyors were soon replaced by better men (William Bately, and the brilliant Sir Thomas Slade), and the Establishment was abandoned. With *Unicorn*, the Sixth Rate had reached 580 tons and a smaller, more economical, 20-gun ship of around 430 tons was deemed necessary. The first of these, the *Gibraltar* and *Seaford*, were ordered in 1753 and they introduced a new policy that was to influence warship procurement for over fifty years: each of the Surveyors produced competing designs to the same general specification, and if one proved particularly successful, it was then built in numbers. Slade chose to develop the *Tygre* lines, but Bateley followed those of the royal yacht, the *Royal Caroline*, herself derived from the Marquis of Carmarthen's *Peregrine Galley* of 1700 and representative of a very successful native fast-sailing tradition.

With war looming, the first British 12pdr armed frigates were ordered in March 1756. Although the French had only built three of the *Hermione* type to date, they had abandoned two-deckers, so a single-decked 32 or 36 was not only superior in speed and seakeeping to a 44, but was more economical (numbers were always a paramount consideration to the Royal Navy where cruisers were concerned). Bately scaled up the *Royal Caroline* for his *Richmond* class 32, whereas Slade produced a more independent design for the *Southamptons* and the similar but 36-gunned *Pallas* class. However, he soon reverted to the *Tygre* hull form for the following highly successful *Niger* class. All carried twenty-six 12pdrs, and six (or ten for the 36s) 6pdrs on the quarterdeck and forecastle.

For France's cruising ships, as with so many aspects of her maritime endeavour, the Seven Years War was an unhappy experience. Although she had taken the lead with 12pdr ships, France was rapidly overtaken in numbers of such ships afloat thanks to superior British shipbuilding capacity – a foretaste of the nineteenth-century situation where any French technological advance was rapidly nullified by Britain's larger industrial base. Only able to launch six 12pdr frigates before 1764, the French navy perforce relied on 8pdr ships, which suffered heavily at the hands of their opposite numbers. Attempts were made to increase their firepower by adding 4pdrs or 6pdrs to the upperworks in imitation of British practice, but it had little effect, except to compro-

During the Seven Years War the Royal Navy built most of its 32-gun frigates to one of three designs of similar specification, but also indulged in one or two larger vessels. One was the Lowestoffe, *depicted here in a particularly detailed contemporary model, based on the lines of the Quebec-built* L'Abenakise, *a hull form that was modified to provide the basis for designs ranging from Third Rates to sloops.* (NMM)

mise their sailing qualities and to strain their lightly built hulls. A few slightly larger ships with twenty-eight or thirty 12pdrs were built, but none saw action during this war.

By contrast, the first generation of Royal Navy frigates was very successful and made a significant contribution to the victory at sea. For example, during Hawke's blockade of Brest, the inshore detachments relied heavily on the rugged construction, seaworthiness and manoeuvrability of the new 28s and 32s. It is difficult to envisage the earlier types of cruising ship standing up to these exacting requirements for month after month – certainly no 44 was hazarded on this duty – and it is interesting that the one ex-French frigate so employed, the *Melampe*, was described as 'much shattered' by the experience. However, while British sea officers were less critical of their own ships during this war, admiration for certain French prizes continued. The 'star' was undoubtedly the *Abenakise*, a big 946-ton Quebec-built frigate taken into the Royal Navy as the *Aurora*. One of the last *demi-batterie* ships, her speed had vastly impressed her captors, and her lines formed the basis for a series of experimental designs, including the 32-gun *Lowestoffe* class and the 28-gun *Mermaids*.

9. Jean Boudriot, *La Belle Poule 1765* (Paris 1986).

10. PRO Adm 106/2183, 15 May 1747.

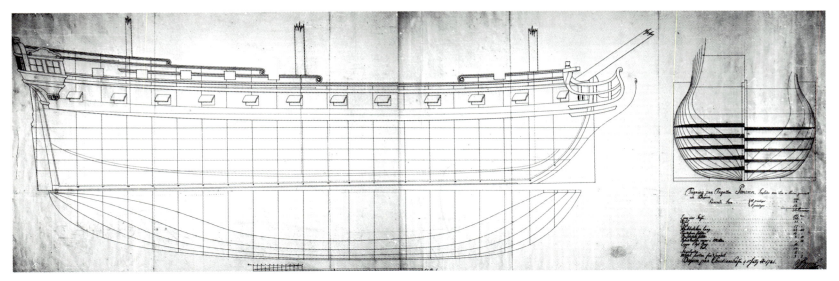

1780–1800: the era of the 18-pounder

By the third quarter of the century, a consensus had grown up among major navies that the larger cruising ships should have two flush decks, with the armament carried on the upper deck, quarterdeck and forecastle. Of the secondary powers, Denmark was quick to adopt this form when the French emigré constructor Barbé proposed it for the *Docquen*, launched in 1746, but as built the ship had a stepped series of platforms rather than a proper lower deck. Sweden had been designing ships which were outside the mainstream tradition since the beginning of the century and had anticipated Ollivier's formula by some thirty years. Preferring large single-deckers to two-decked ships, Sweden's frigates were unusual in that the great cabin with its quarter galleries was placed on, rather than under, the quarterdeck, a feature that persisted until the 1780s (Chapman's *Bellona* class shows it). Nevertheless, Sweden could also build a galley-frigate like the *Mercurius* of 1747 which was a direct descendant of seventeenth-century models; Holland, whose navy was moribund by the mid-century, also built cruisers very like British 20- or 24-gun ships of the Establishment period into the 1760s. When Spain adopted this form she continued her established preference for very large ships of modest armament: the *Santa Margarita* captured in 1779 carried only 8pdrs, but was the size of a British 38.

In Britain a general satisfaction with the ships of the Slade era made the new Surveyors reluctant to consider radical alterations, so the new 32s of Hunt's *Hermione* and Williams's *Amazon* classes were similar in overall specification to their predecessors. British design was again entering a period of relative stagnation,

but with sounder basic formulae than had been the case earlier in the century. Indeed, the lack of progress in cruising ship design was disguised during the American War of Independence by two developments outside the realm of naval architecture as such: the introduction of copper sheathing, which greatly retarded fouling; and the adoption of the carronade which gave frigates so equipped a close-range firepower way beyond their nominal rating. The former was probably more important, having two inter-related effects: in modern terms it acted as a 'force multiplier', since it significantly extended the period a ship could stay on station between cleaning (*ie* more ships were actually available at any one time); and since, other things being approximately equal, fouling had the greatest effect on speed, it increased the chances of a coppered ship being faster than an opponent.

Since the virtual extinction of the two-decker 44, both Britain and France had done without 18pdr cruisers, but the peculiar circumstances of colonial unrest in North America led the British to reintroduce small two-deckers in the 1770s. Sir Thomas Slade had designed a single example in 1758 and the larger *Roebuck* in 1769 which became the prototype for a class of twenty. As colonial flagships, they were cheaper than ships of the line but powerful enough to overawe any converted merchantman likely to be available to the Americans in the early years of the rebellion. However, their frontline role did not long survive the entry of France into the war and the introduction of 18pdr armed frigates; a class of seven was designed as late as 1782 but most 44s were soon relegated to ancillary tasks.

Following the Declaration of Independence in 1776, the American states rapidly estab-

Scandinavian frigate design went its own way for much of the eighteenth century. This Danish draught, dated 1741, depicts the Pommern *of 36 guns, which was built as the Swedish* Illerim *in 1716. She still shows the Swedish feature of a quarterdeck great cabin, but more significantly she was armed with twenty-four 18pdrs (and twelve 8pdrs), an unusually powerful armament for a single-decker of her era. (Rigsarkivet, Copenhagen)*

lished a frigate force of thirteen conventional, if highly competent ships (five each of 28 and 32 guns, and three 24s). They were generally slightly bigger than their British equivalents, but otherwise very similar in appearance and fittings. The design of many impressed their British captors, but having been built in a hurry the quality of their construction was found wanting. The independent spirit of American ship design had already manifested itself with the contract building of the 44-gun *America* and 24-gun *Boston* in the late 1740s, when the builders refused to follow the official Admiralty draughts and produced significantly bigger vessels.[11] During the Revolution original thinking was also to be seen in the 36-gun *Confederacy*, an updating of the galley-frigate concept on a far larger scale (160ft gundeck, 959 tons, twenty-eight 12pdrs on upper deck). Also prefiguring the later American obsession with monster frigates was the *South Carolina*, purchased in 1777, an odd French-designed but Dutch-built vessel somewhat resembling an East Indiaman; she measured about 154ft by 40ft, and mounted twenty-four 36pdrs and twelve 12pdrs of French manufacture.

The major advance in frigate development

11. See Daniel A Baugh, *Naval Administration 1715–1750*, NRS Vol 120 (London 1977) reproducing a letter of 27 June 1747 from Commodore Charles Knowles to the Admiralty.

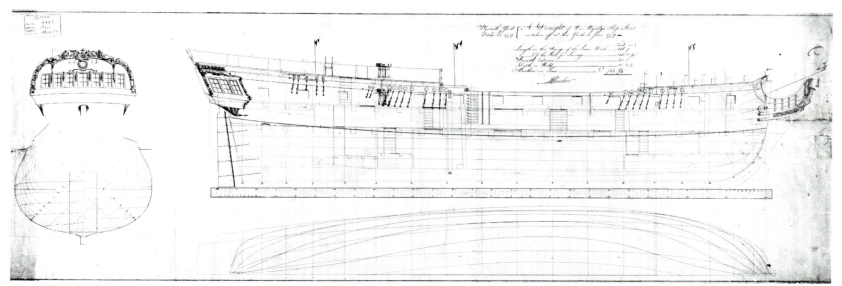

A new naval power was eventually to emerge from the struggle for American independence and the first native attempts at frigate design were impressive. Eschewing the more extreme hull form and building styles of French ships, the Americans tended to follow the British models with which they were already familiar but to somewhat enlarged proportions. Perhaps the best of these ships was the Hancock, which after capture served with great success as HMS Iris, *(NMM)*

during the American War was the adoption of an 18pdr main battery. With the exception of four Swedish ships in the 1710s, and the odd 44 razeed (cut down) to a single-decker, previous 18pdr cruisers had been two-deckers. A proposal had been put forward in France as early as 1762 for a big frigate with thirty 18pdrs to

replace the old 40–46-gun ships,[12] and a smaller design with twenty-six 18pdrs in 1775, but neither came to fruition. Despite the long-established Admiralty policy of resisting size escalation, it fell to the British to introduce the 18pdr as a regular frigate type in 1778, and may reflect the need for individual superiority since, unusually, the numerical balance of sea power was no longer in Britain's favour. Three designs were produced, the 36-gun *Flora* and *Perseverance* classes being distinguished from the 38-gun *Minerva*s by twenty-six rather than twenty-eight upper deck ports.

The first French 18pdr frigates were laid down in 1781 and five constructors built prototypes to a standard specification, and although some early ships had a 26-gun main battery, 28 soon became standard, along with six and later ten 8pdrs. In an effort to counter the close range advantage of the carronade – increasingly dominating the quarterdecks of

British frigates – France introduced small bronze 36pdr *obusiers*, based on army howitzers, but they were poor substitutes and a genuine iron carronade was eventually produced in 1807. However, the ships themselves were very successful, particularly those of Sané's *Hébé* class of 1781–2. A postwar ministerial decision of 1786 set the French frigate establishment at twenty 18pdr ships (plus forty with 12pdrs) and by 1790 there were thirteen in service with three more building.[13]

1793–1815: the era of the 24-pounder

A proposal for a huge 2000-ton frigate-built replacement for the 50-gun ship was put for-

12. Envisaged as a commerce raider that could outgun anything it could not outrun, and so in concept the ancestor of such otherwise diverse ships as the *Wampanoag*, *Rurik* and *Graf Spee*.

13. Jean Boudriot, *La Venus 1782* (Paris c1988).

Sané's Hébé, *a ship so highly regarded that her lines were used for the standard 18pdr frigate in both the French and British navies, large numbers of sisters being built well into the nineteenth century. (NMM)*

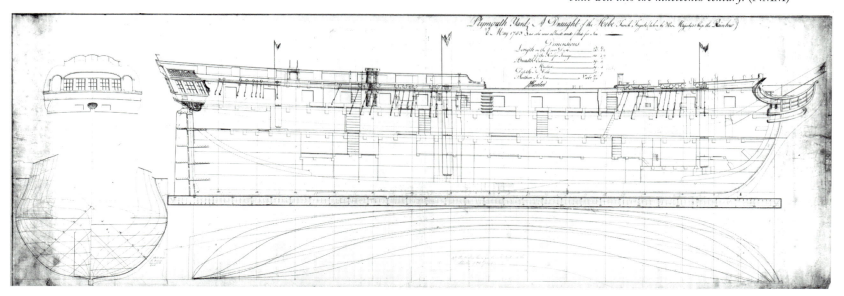

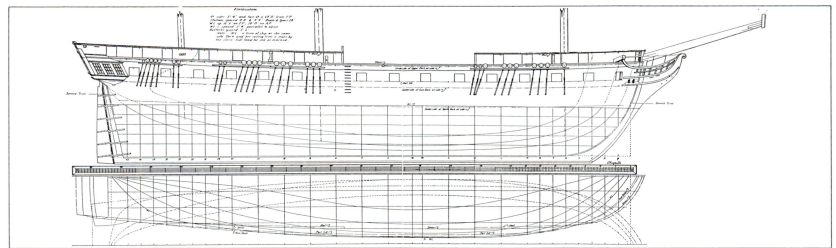

ward in France in 1768, but in the end the two vessels laid down under this scheme were completed as flutes (armed storeships), with the intended twenty-six 24pdrs replaced by 18pdrs.[14] It fell to the famous Swedish naval architect F H Chapman to complete the first 24pdr armed frigates in 1782. Because of Sweden's shortage of capital ships, Chapman designed these *Bellona* class frigates to fight in the battle line in an emergency, so although they were only the size of a British 38 and were completed with 18pdrs, they were always intended for a specially designed, and none too successful, short 24pdr.

After the Revolution, some standard French 18pdr 40s were given 24pdrs, but the Borda-Sané system of standardisation established during 1786–7, while admirable in administrative terms, was a powerful restraint on innovation in the 1790s. When 12pdr frigates were abandoned after 1797, the standard 18pdr vessels continued to be built – all sixty-five frigates launched between 1801 and 1814 were 40-gun ships of similar specifications, the vast majority of which followed the lines of Sané's *Hébé* of 1781. The only exceptions were the 24pdr frigates *Resistance* and *Vengeance*, designed by the radical young constructor Degay in 1793, and the even larger *Forte* (1794) and *Egyptienne* (1799), the product of a designer, Caro, whose previous experience was mercantile and consequently was less awed by Sané's reputation. Both classes mounted thirty 24pdrs, but at 160ft to the *Forte*'s 170ft on the gun deck, the first pair were somewhat overcrowded. However, these ships cost as much as a 64-gun

ship, which was considered the better investment, proving that even for a navy on the defensive there is a limit to the amount that can be paid for the nominal superiority of a few vessels.[15]

The experiment was not repeated in France but in 1794 the United States embarked on a frigate programme that included three huge 24pdr armed vessels, the famous *Constitution*, *United States* and *President*. Rated as 44-gun ships, as originally conceived they were virtually two-deckers with the flush weather, or spar, deck armed for the whole of its length – initially 12pdrs but soon converted to 42pdr carronades. Their intended mission and design history is confused, but they were certainly built to out-gun any frigate afloat and to outsail any line of battle ship. Although they had substantial scantlings, the complete upper tier of guns (a total of fifty-six could be carried) overstressed the hulls and there were many early complaints about their sailing qualities, leading to expensive refits and reduced armaments. After their victories in the War of 1812, there was a tendency to idealise these vessels, but an indication of the official opinion of their worth is the fact that while the US Navy went on building frigates that were very large for their rating, none was completed with a 24pdr main armament, and no new vessel of this type was ordered until after the first successes of the war. On purely technical merits, the big 38s like *Philadelphia* and *Constellation* were better ships, but it was the spar-decked 44s that were to influence future developments.

In Britain the outbreak of the French Revolutionary War found British ship design in one of its periodic crises of self-confidence. There was a general feeling that the previous generation of ships did not sail well because they were too short and so existing designs were lengthened by adding a section amid-

Although not the first to be armed with 24pdrs, the American Constitution *type were certainly the largest and most famous. This plan shows* President *as she appeared during the War of 1812, but as built they had continuous open rails and were armed along the complete length of the spar deck. The successes of these ships inspired the French navy to adopt large spar-decked frigates as commerce raiders, but genuine double-banked frigates were rare even in the mid-nineteenth century. (Smithsonian Institution)*

ships. This was followed in 1795 by a programme of experimental 'one-offs', some following the lines of French prizes and others of native inspiration. By an irony of history, the *Leda* class 38s, which was to become the standard large frigate, used the lines of Sané's *Hébé* (captured in 1782), so the two great antagonists adopted the same underwater body for their most numerous classes. By this period, even the smallest British 32 was being designed for twenty-six 18pdrs on the upper deck, so they were really more economical versions of 36s. In fact the widespread adoption of carronades meant that the nominal rating reflected only relative, not real, force.

The first 24pdr frigate to fall into British hands was the *Pomone* in 1794, and since it became clear that more French 40s now sported heavier metal, some remedial action was necessary. This took three forms: as an interim measure, three old 64s were razeed, making powerful cruisers of 44 guns nominal rating (*Anson*, *Magnanime* and Edward Pellew's famous *Indefatigable*); a straight copy of the *Pomone* was ordered as the *Endymion*; and the experimental series of 1795 included three particularly large frigates, although only the *Cambrian* was designed for 24pdrs (soon replaced by 18pdrs). After this flurry of activity, the '24pdr scare' seems to have passed, and even the capture of the very large *Forte* and *Egyptienne* occasioned no reconsideration.

14. *Pourvoyeuse* and *Consolante*, also intended for commerce raiding, particularly in the Indian Ocean where France had few bases. See J Boudriot, *Neptunia* 167 (3, 1987), pp37–44.

15. See J Boudriot, *Neptunia* 175 (3, 1989), pp10–16.

Table 4: Typical Armaments in the Carronade era 1780–1815

Ship Type	Country	At Date	Upper Deck Armament	Quarterdeck/Forecastle or Spar Deck Armament	Minimum Gunport Freeboard
Santa Margarita, 34 (in British service, 36)	Spain	1780	26 × 9pdr	6 × 6pdr/2 × 6pdr	5.5ft
		1780	26 × 12pdr	8 × 6pdr, 6 × 18pdr carr/2 × 6pdr, 2 × 18pdr carr	6ft
12pdr Frigate	France	1780	26 × 12pdr	10 × 6pdr/4 × 6pdr	6ft
		1786		4 × 8pdr, 4 × 36pdr ob*/2 × 8pdr	6.5ft
32-gun Fifth Rate	Britain	1780	26 × 12pdr	4 × 6pdr, 6 × 18pdr carr/2 × 6pdr, 2 × 18pdr carr	7ft
		1800	26 × 12pdr	4 × 6pdr, 4 × 24pdr carr/2 × 6pdr, 2 × 24pdr carr	
18pdr Frigate	France	1782	28 × 18pdr	4 × 8pdr/2 × 8pdr	6.5ft–7ft
		1794	28 × 18pdr (24pdr in some)	8 × 8pdr, 4 × 36pdr ob*/4 × 8pdr	
		1807	28 × 18pdr	6 × 8pdr, 6 × 24pdr carr/2 × 8pdr, 2 × 24pdr carr	6.5ft
36-gun Fifth Rate	Britain	1782	26 × 18pdr	8 × 9pdr, 4 × 18pdr carr/2 × 9pdr, 4 × 18pdr carr	7.5ft
		1794	26 × 18pdr	8 × 9pdr, 6 × 32pdr carr/2 × 9pdr, 2 × 32pdr carr	
		1799	26 × 18pdr	14 × 32pdr carr/2 × 9pdr, 2 × 32pdr carr	8ft
38-gun Fifth Rate	Britain	1780	28 × 18pdr	8 × 9pdr, 6 × 18pdr carr/2 × 9pdr, 4 × 18pdr carr	7.5ft
		1794	28 × 18pdr	6 × 9pdr, 6 × 32pdr carr/4 × 9pdr, 2 × 32pdr carr	
		1799	28 × 18pdr	14 × 32pdr carr/2 × 9pdr, 2 × 32pdr carr	8ft
Bellona Class, 40 guns	Sweden	1788	26 × 24pdr	10 × 6pdr/4 × 6pdr	7ft
Forte (In British service)	France	1799	30 × 24pdr	14 × 8pdr, 8 × 36pdr ob* (disposition uncertain)	7ft
		1800	30 × 24pdr	16 × 32pdr carr/2 × 12pdr, 4 × 32pdr carr	
44-gun Class (Design)	USA	1794	30 × 24pdr	2 × 24pdr, 22 × 12pdr	8ft
		1815	30 × 24pdr	16 × 42pdr carr/2 × 24pdr, 4 × 42pdr carr	8.5ft
Leander, 50 guns	Britain	1814	30 × 24pdr	4 × 24pdr, 26 × 42pdr carr	8ft

Notes:

*ob = Obusier, a type of howitzer used by the French as an interim substitute for the carronade.

The War of 1812 altered that. French 24pdr frigates had fallen to 18pdr ships, so the loss of three British 38s in a row to the big American 44s was a shock, and the massive building programme that followed was a reflection of the Royal Navy's mortification rather than a reasoned response to the threat. The British had already experimented with cheap softwood versions of existing classes – austere 'hostilities only' vessels of short expected lifespan, but rapidly built – and this experience was now put to use. To save design time, the one extant 24pdr draught (*Endymion*) was employed for five fir-built sisters, constructed together in the largest commercial yard on the Thames, and all were in the water by mid-1813. They carried twenty-eight 24pdrs but were still significantly smaller than the US ships, so two very large 'double-banked frigates', the *Newcastle* and *Leander*, were designed especially to match them. Although lightly built, they were armed

HMS Endymion *was built to the lines of the* Pomone, *the first French 24pdr armed frigate, and was regarded as a fine sailer even in the 1830s. She was the only British 24pdr frigate to meet one of the big American ships and played a leading role in the capture of the* President *in 1815. (SM)*

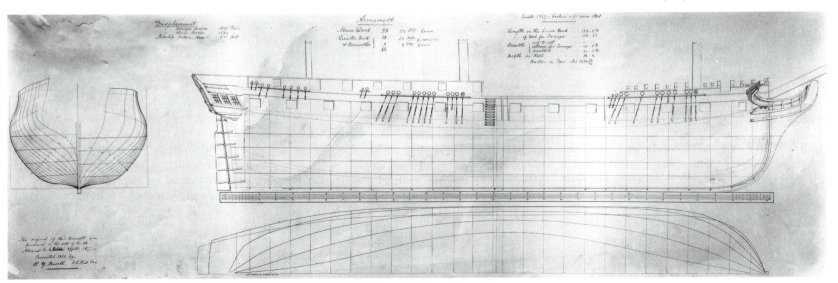

The Didon *of 1828, one of the more successful of the French 60-gun First Class frigates; note the complete spar deck battery and the austere round stern adopted by French warships of the period. In a common convention of ship portraiture, this illustration by F Roux shows the vessel from different angles.*

with thirty 24pdrs on what was still termed the upper deck with a further four 24s as chase guns and twenty-six 42pdr carronades on the spar deck; both were in service by the end of 1813. As in 1794, cut-down line of battle ships were also thrown in as stop-gaps: in this case, three small 74s (*Goliath*, *Sultan* and *Majestic*), which kept their lower deck 32pdrs, plus twenty-eight 42pdr carronades and two 12pdr chase guns on the now flush upper deck. An emergency programme of twenty-six frigates of the 18pdr classes was also put in hand, some ships being fitted with new medium weight 24pdrs, but as if to underline the superfluous effort, the only 24pdr to meet an American 44 was the old *Endymion*, none of the other designs being tested in action.

The new spar-decked type – effectively a flush two-decker without forecastle and quarterdeck – was much criticised at the time, and many would not accept such vessels as real frigates, but this form was to be the final manifestation of the cruising ship in the age of sail.

1815–1845: spar-decked frigates

The United States, as the originator of the radical spar-decked frigate, might have been expected to push forward development, but after 1815 far more design effort was devoted to very large sloops and corvettes. These were original concepts, generally as superior to their European counterparts as the big frigates had been in the previous decades, and obviated the need for medium sized frigates in the US Navy. Oddly

enough, the spar-decked ships were much more conservative: the three 44s ordered in 1813, *Java*, *Guerrière* and *Columbia*, were based on the dimensions of the 1796 ships, although the form was finer-lined. As built they were a foot broader, and with the addition of slightly more beam a new design of 1817 was also similar in size (nine ships of the *Brandywine* class, launched in leisurely fashion between 1825 and 1855). Apart from the mercantile-designed *Hudson* purchased in 1826, it was not until 1838 that a significantly bigger cruiser was designed, which emerged as the *Congress* in 1841, the last pure sailing frigate in the US Navy.

To be fair, it was only the size which was stagnating: armament increased from 24pdrs to 32pdrs and eventually included a few 8in shell guns; all the current structural alterations like the flattened sheer, wall sides, round stern and strengthened construction were incorporated; and no European navy had a noticeably larger frigate until the British *Vernon* of 1832.

The American big frigates exerted an influence out of all proportion to their numbers. In France, after the defeat of Napoleon, a new strategy evolved whereby the much reduced battlefleet would only take on the British as part of a coalition, but a renewed emphasis was laid on commerce destruction, for which a higher proportion of frigates would be needed.[16] Encouraged by American successes, France enthusiastically embraced the big frigate as a long-distance raider, but without giving enough thought to the details. The first eight ships of the *Jeanne d'Arc* type (1817 programme) fol-

lowed Caro's *Forte* of 1797 but having the waist filled up with carronades – for a total of 58 guns – they were generally regarded as over-gunned and poor sailers, with their height of ports reduced to some 5ft 8in.

A more balanced 52-gun design followed in 1826 with seven vessels of the *Artémise* class, but in the meantime a 74 had been successfully cut down into a razee 58. Retaining her lower deck 36pdrs, but carrying them some 1ft 3in higher thanks to reduced draught, the *Guerrière* was seen to possess the qualities that the earlier 58-gun ships lacked and a new type of 60-gun First Class frigate was proposed to a similar specification in 1822 but carrying the new standard 30pdr gun. Over twenty of these powerful two-deckers were laid down to a variety of designs in the late 1820s, initially armed on the upper deck with 30pdr carronades but later including a few shell guns; following the nineteenth century fashion, many spent a long time on the stocks and some were completed as steamers as late as the 1860s.

The earlier 1817 and 1826 ships became rated as Second Class frigates, and these adopted the 30pdr main armament after trials in the *Artémise* in 1838. The specification remained unaltered until 1844 when a slight increase in breadth was ordered, but the later ships completed as screw steamers. The old 18pdr frigates, now rerated as Third Class 44s were not built after 1823, and it was not until 1830 that new designs were prepared; the situation was then complicated by the desire to adopt the standard 30pdrs after 1838, but only two could be modified during building. A few ships were laid down to a revised design intended to accommodate the new armament, but all completed as steamers.

After 1815, Britain, which already had both the largest merchant fleet and the most far-flung empire to protect, also took on the role of the world's policeman. Maritime domination depended on the battlefleet, which would always have first call on resources, but the need for large numbers of cruising ships was greater than ever. In these circumstances, the advent of the big frigate was far from welcome to the Royal Navy's planners, whose response was re-

16. Andrew Lambert, *The Last Sailing Battlefleet* (London 1991).

Table 5: Typical Armaments 1815–1850

Ship Type	Country	At Date	Upper Deck Armament	Quarterdeck/Forecastle or Spar Deck Armament	Minimum Gunport Freeboard
Guerrière class	USA	1817	33 × 24pdrs[1]	20 × 42pdr carr	7ft
46-gun Fifth Rate	Britain	1817	28 × 18pdrs	14 × 32pdr carr/2 × 32pdr carr, 2 × 9pdr	7.5ft
50-gun Fourth Rate	Britain	1825	30 × 24pdr	2 × 24pdr, 20 × 32pdr carr	7.75ft
		1845	8 × 8in shell, 22 × 32pdr	20 × 32pdr	
52-gun Razee	Britain	1830	28 × 32pdr	16 × 32pdr/6 × 32pdr	8.25ft
60-gun First Class Frigate	France	1828	30 × 30pdr	28 × 30pdr carr, 2 × 18pdr	6.75ft
		1840	2 × 22cm shell, 28 × 30pdr	4 × 16cm shell, 26 × 30pdr carr	
		1850	4 × 22cm shell, 26 × 30pdr	As 1840	
58-gun Second Class Frigate	France	1821	30 × 24pdr	26 × 36pdr carr, 2 × 18pdr	5.75ft
52-gun Second Class Frigate		1830	28 × 24pdr	22 × 24pdr carr, 2 × 18pdr	6.5ft
		1847	4 × 22cm shell, 24 × 30pdr	4 × 16cm shell, 18 × 30pdr carr	
44-gun Third Class Frigate	France	1829	28 × 18pdr	16 × 24pdr carr, 2 × 18pdr	6.5ft
46-gun Third Class Frigate		1848	24 × 16cm shell, 4 × 30pdr	2 × 16cm shell, 10 × 32pdr carr	7ft
Brandywine Class	USA	1836	4 × 8in shell, 25 × 32pdr	22 × 42pdr carr	7.5ft
36-gun Class (*Castor*)	Britain	1832	22 × 32pdr	10 × 32pdr/4 × 32pdr	7.75ft
36-gun Class (*Pique*)		1845	4 × 8in shell, 18 × 32pdr	4 × 8in shell, 14 × 32pdr	
50-gun Class (*Vernon*)	Britain	1835	28 × 32pdr	14 × 32pdr/8 × 32pdr	9ft
50-gun Class (*Constance*)		1850	6 × 8in shell, 22 × 32pdr	4 × 8in shell, 18 × 32pdr	
Congress, 50 guns	USA	1850	4 × 8in shell, 24 × 32pdr	4 × 8in shell, 18 × 32pdr	7.5ft
Diamond, 28-gun Sixth Rate	Britain	1848	20 × 32pdr	1 × 8in shell, 4 × 32pdr/1 × 8in shell, 2 × 32pdr	

1. These vessels had a shifting chase gun that could occupy the most convenient empty gunport.

Despite the attraction of big frigates to countries like France and the USA, the British continued to build large numbers of standard 18pdr ships, although they were constructed with the structural improvements introduced by Sir Robert Seppings. The most noticeable of these was the round stern, an example of which survived on the Unicorn, *currently undergoing restoration in Dundee. (CMP)*

strained. Initially, enough 24pdr ships were laid down to match American construction (six ships based on the *Java* of 1814, a more considered design than the hasty *Newcastle* and *Leander*), but the required numbers were obtained by continuing to build the standard 18pdr ships of the *Leda* class and a slightly larger type based on the lines of the French prize *Piedmontaise* as late as 1830.

With the 1816 rerating, these old 38s became known as 46s, and later ships were to benefit from the radical structural improvements introduced by Sir Robert Seppings. With diagonally braced hulls, round (or later elliptical) sterns, flat sheers and berthed-up bulwarks, these ships were far stronger than their predecessors of the same nominal class. By the mid-1820s an establishment of 100 battleships and 160 frigates was being advocated, and since so many war-built frigates were worn out, the ongoing programme of construction could not be relaxed. Unfortunately, the same applied to battleships, a problem exacerbated by the 1826 decision to concentrate on 120s and 84s armed entirely with 32pdrs of varying weights in response to a perceived renewal of the French threat.

Luckily, this left a force of old 74s too weak for the battle line which could be razeed into powerful frigates, retaining their lower deck 32pdrs and a lofty rig. The selected ships had to be in reasonable condition to economise on repair effort and were only released when new battleships entered the fleet, but nine were found suitable in the late 1820s and four later.[17] These ships may have been seen as an emergency battlefleet reserve, but they allowed the Admiralty to avoid wasting resources matching the French 60s that so exercised many of the navy's amateur critics.

A new administration in 1830 reconsidered cruiser policy, all remaining 46s being cancelled along with other larger frigates. The 46s were replaced by a new 32pdr armed 36, three competing experimental designs by Seppings, Symonds and Hayes (*Castor*, *Pique* and *Inconstant*, respectively) being built. The *Pique* class and its derivatives was to become the standard British frigate until the end of the purely sail-

17. *Ibid.*

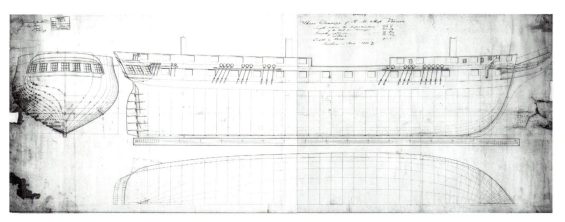

A full spar deck armament was regarded by the British as detrimental to sailing qualities and a strain on the hull, so even though later frigates had a structurally complete weather deck they usually carried no guns in the waist. This is Symonds' large and experimental Vernon; despite her sharp section, she carried 32pdrs at an unprecedented height of battery. (NMM)

ing cruiser. Symonds, shortly to become a very controversial Surveyor, was also allowed to test his ideas on hull form on a large frigate unrestricted by established dimensions. The resulting *Vernon* measured 2082 tons and carried fifty 32pdrs of differing weights, but was not universally approved of, even though she was fast and had unequalled freeboard to her gunports.

No 28s were built after 1785, Sixth Rates being confined to a small number of 'Post Ships'[18] of 20–24 guns. However in the post-war period, with frigates getting larger, a few ships were again rated as 28s. Not very different from the largest quarterdecked sloops, they were derisively known as 'jackass frigates', and cynics regarded them solely as a way of giving young Post Captains a taste of independant command without risking a valuable ship.

The British aversion to the big frigate had reasserted itself in the 1830s and it was not until another war scare in 1840 that the type was revived. Roughly the size of the *Vernon* but armed like the razees, the dozen or so new ships were built to six different designs, only Symonds' *Constance* class being built in quantity (four and one modified). Most were completed with or converted to screw propulsion and pointed the way towards the *Warrior*, the first iron-built seagoing armoured ship. Classed as a frigate, *Warrior* was nevertheless more powerful than any conventional battleship. In this respect, she closed the circle in frigate design: the type which emerged from the battlefleet in the 1650s was reabsorbed into it in the 1860s.

Robert Gardiner

18. So called because they were commanded by Post Captains, unlike sloops which were the province of the Master and Commander.

Frigates: Typical Ships 1650–1840

Ship or Class	Nationality	Launched	Built	Guns	Calibre	Dimensions Feet–inches Metres	Burthen	Fate	Remarks
ST PAULUS	Dutch	1652	Rotterdam	30	8pdr	84–0*kl* × 25–6 × 9–8 25.60 × 7.77 × 2.95	290	Capt by English 1655; sold 1667	Typical Dutch Fifth Rate of 1650s
HUMMEREN	Danish	1665	Copenhagen	32	8pdr	109–8 × 26–0 × 9–0 33.42 × 7.92 × 2.75	?	Capt by Swedes 1700	Earliest identified plan of a 'frigate'
CHARLES GALLEY	English	1676	Woolwich	32	6pdr	131–1 × 28–6 × 8–7 39.96 × 8.69 × 2.62	526	RB 1693; RB as new ship 1710	First identified 'galley-frigate'
EXPERIMENT	English	1689	Chatham	32	9pdr	105–0 × 27–6 × 10–6 32.00 × 8.38 × 3.20		Sixth Rate 1717; BU 1724	First 'demi-batterie' Fifth Rate
LIZARD	English	1693	Chatham	24	6pdr	94–3 × 24–4 × 10–8 28.72 × 7.42 × 3.25	250	Wrecked 1696	First of new Sixth Rates
GLOIRE	French	1707	Lorient	36	8pdr	122–0 × 35–0 37.19 × 10.67	657	Capt by British 1709; sold 1716	New French 'demi-batterie' commerce raider
GOSPORT	British	1707	Woolwich	40	12pdr	118–0 × 32–0 × 13–6 35.97 × 9.75 × 4.11	531	BU 1735	40-gun ship of 1706 Establishment
ILLERIM	Swedish	1716	Karlskrona	36	18pdr	130–0 × 33–6 42.68 × 10.98	?	To Denmark 1717; stricken 1765	Largest single-decker of her day
BLANDFORD	British	1719	Deptford	20	6pdr	106–0 × 28–9 × 9–2 32.31 × 8.76 × 2.79	375	Sold 1742	20-gun ship of 1719 Establishment
MEDÉE	French	1740	Brest	26	8pdr	125–5 × 33–9 × 16–8 38.25 × 10.29 × 5.08	c600	Capt by British 1744; sold as privateer	Prototype of French 8pdr frigates

Ship or Class	Nationality	Launched	Built	Guns	Calibre	Dimensions Feet–inches Metres	Burthen	Fate	Remarks
UNICORN	British	1747	Plymouth	28	9pdr	117–10 33–8 × 9–11 35.90 × 10.26 × 3.03	581	BU 1771	First British 28-gun frigate
HERMIONE	French	1748	Rochefort	26	12pdr	130–10 × 37–6 × 13–5 39.87 × 11.43 × 4.10	812	Capt by British 1757 and sold	First French 12pdr frigate
SOUTHAMPTON	British	1756	Rotherhithe	32	12pdr	124–4 × 34–8 × 12–0 37.90 × 10.57 × 3.66	652	Wrecked 1812	First British 12pdr frigate
BELLE POULE	French	1769	Bordeaux	32	12pdr	140–0 × 37–10 × 11–11 42.67 × 11.52 × 3.64	903	Capt by British 1780; sold 1801	Typical French 12pdr ship of the period
SANTA MARGARITA	Spanish	1770	El Ferrol	40	8pdr	145–6 × 38–11 × 11–9 44.34 × 11.87 × 3.58	993	Capt by British 1779; sold 1836	Typical large Spanish frigate of the period
HANCOCK	American	1776	Newburyport	32	12pdr	137–1 × 34–4 × 10–11 41.78 × 10.46 × 3.32	730	Capt by British 1777; by French 1780; blown up 1793	Best of the first generation of American 32s
FLORA	British	1781	Deptford	36	18pdr	137–0 × 38–0 × 13–3 41.76 × 11.58 × 4.04	869	Wrecked 1808	First British 18pdr frigate
HÉBÉ	French	1782	St Malo	40	18pdr	151–4 × 40–0 × 12–6 46.13 × 12.19 × 3.81	1071	Capt by British 1782; BU 1811	Classic Sané 18pdr design of great influence in French and British navies
BELLONA	Swedish	1782	Karlskrona	40	24pdr	152–0 × 39–0 46.33 × 11.88	1360 disp	Wrecked 1809	First 24pdr design to enter service
FORTE	French	1795	Lorient	50	24pdr	170–0 × 43–6 51.82 × 13.25	140–1	Capt by British 1799; wrecked 1801	Largest French frigate of the day
PRESIDENT	American	1800	New York	44	24pdr	175–0 × 43–8 × 13–11 51.82 × 13.31 × 4.24	1576	Capt by British 1815; BU 1817	Best of the famous US big frigates
UNICORN	British	1824	Chatham	46	18pdr	150–10 × 39–11 × 12–9 45.96 × 12.18 × 3.89	1078	Under restoration at Dundee	Standard British frigate type with Seppings' improvements
SURVEILLANTE	French	1825	Lorient	60	30pdr	178–6 × 46–3 × 21–7 max dr* 54.40 × 14.10 × 6.59	2558 disp	Stricken 1844	Largest class double-banked frigate
BARHAM	British	Conv 1826	Woolwich	52	32pdr	176–0 × 47–6 × 21–0 53.65 × 14.48 × 6.40	1761	BU 1839	Razeed 74-gun ship
VERNON	British	1832	Woolwich	50	32pdr	176–0 × 52–8 × 17–9 53.65 × 16.05 × 5.41	2082	Hulk 1863	Symonds' experimental frigate
CONGRESS	American	1841	Portsmouth	44	32pdr	179–0 × 47–8 × 22–8 54.55 × 14.53 × 6.91	1867	Sunk in action 1862	Last US sailing frigate design
DIAMOND	British	1848	Sheerness	28	32pdr	140–0 × 42–0 × 11–1 42.67 × 12.80 × 3.38	1051	Sold 1866	Smallest type rated frigate by the end of the sailing era

Notes:
Calibres are given in native weights; generally Continental pounds were heavier so the French 8pdr and 36pdr equated roughly with English 9pdrs and 42pdrs respectively. Dimensions are in English feet with metric equivalents. Wherever possible the dimensions are measured in the English fashion for consistency (those marked * are not) giving gundeck length, moulded breadth and depth in hold; but *kl* = keel length, *dr* = draught of water, and *disp* - displacement instead of tons burthen, which is simply calculated from the dimensions. In the Fate column, Capt = captured; RB = rebuilt; BU = broken up.

3

Sloop of War, Corvette and Brig

SLOOPS, corvettes and brigs, the square rigged small craft of every navy, are familiarly seen as miniature cruisers, below the rated ships in size but fully capable of independent action. While this is true for later periods, it belies their origins. Their earliest ancestors were not genuine warships and indeed many were not ships at all, but merely boats. The seventeenth-century rating systems included every vessel of fighting value, so anything unrated was necessarily an auxiliary – and since the warships themselves were relatively unhandy and spent more time at anchor than their descendants, they made much use of boats, some of which were very large.[1] Not only were they employed fetching and carrying but could also be used on occasions for towing the mother ship.

The regular attachment of tenders to the fleet introduced the second contribution to the ancestry of the sloop, with the hiring of the smallest merchantmen – inshore fishing craft and coastal trading craft – in times of need. This explains why there are so many type descriptions applied to early small craft, in contrast to the neat differentiation of warships by number of guns. The original duties of these vessels were essentially harbour-bound (to assist with manning in particular, the British fleet in 1690 having 112 hired tenders, for example); but enterprising captains began to use their tenders to extend the reach of their ships, to operate inshore, to act as miniature pickets, or even to cruise independently.[2] In the order of battle, 'tenders and fireships' came to be

The ancestors of naval sloops and corvettes were little more than boats. The barque longue *depicted here from a French work of 1679 shows an undecked boat pulled by eight oars a side or the simple two-masted Biscay shallop rig. Other sources suggest that* double chaloupe *would be a more appropriate designation. (Musée de la Marine, Paris)*

grouped together, demonstrating a further role for tenders in fleet engagements. This early association with the battlefleet lingered on and may explain why smaller navies had so few sloop-like vessels for most of the eighteenth century – the Dutch navy, an essentially trade protection force at this time, had none between 1712 and 1725 and only three in 1750.

The evocative, but much misunderstood, rating 'sloop' first appears in the English Navy List in 1656. Without entering into the complex etymology of the term, it is clear that it is related to shallop,[3] to the French *chaloupe*, Dutch *sloep* and Spanish *chalupa*. Despite many differences, what all these craft have in common is their decent from open boats, and although they were to become decked seagoing warships they remained true to their ancestry in certain respects – in particular their association with speed, light construction, and sail-or-oared propulsion. An eighteenth-century authority had claimed that sloops were built and rigged 'as men's fancies lead them'[4] but much

of the confusion arises because in English the term was applied to a wide range of craft from small boats to seagoing decked warships. A similar boat-or-ship dichotomy had arisen in the previous century with the 'pinnace' and was to happen in the next with the 'cutter'.

For the Atlantic navies the immediate ancestor of the sloop was very probably the double shallop, a large oared boat that was originally undecked but soon became completely covered; it could also set sails on lowering masts, the most common rig being that of the Biscay fishing shallops, which carried a large square main and smaller foresail, with a short bowsprit to extend the latter's tacks and bowlines when close-hauled. The use of these vessels was

---

1. The largest boats had to be towed at sea, and were frequently lost: see M Oppenheim, *The Administration of the Royal Navy 1509–1660* (London 1896), p339.

2. The *Bridget Galley*, hired tender to the *Resolution*, was actually owned by the *Resolution*'s captain, Lord Danby, and made him a small fortune in prize money in the early 1690s.

3. In 1652 two 'shallops to row 20 oars' were among the smallest craft on the list and as late as 1692 there were plans to build 40 'sloops or shallops' for fleet duties – 45–57ft long, they were not ship's boats.

4. T R Blanckley, *A Naval Expositor*, 1750 (but written about 1732).

The next stage in the development of the double chaloupe *into the* barque longue *proper is demonstrated by this Gueroult de Pas engraving: the vessel is now decked, carries a few small guns and is rigged with bowsprit and topsails. (Musée de la Marine, Paris)*

widespread for fishing and coastal trading in the Channel, North Sea and Atlantic seaboard, and even in the American colonies. Their use as naval auxiliaries is also attested (on Admiral Rainborowe's expedition of 1637 against the Sallee Rovers, the longboats of his squadron were replaced by Biscay shallops, propelled by sixteen oars as well as their sails, intended to watch the channels at the river mouth at night).[5] W A Baker has demonstrated that in late seventeenth-century England the term

---

5. Kenneth R Andrews, *Ships, Money & Politics: Seafaring and Naval Enterprise in the Reign of Charles I* (Cambridge 1991), p172.

6. W A Baker, *Sloops and Shallops*, Ch III.

7. The clearest are probably the younger Van de Velde's painting of the *Mary Rose* action, 1669 showing the *Roe*; and Sailmaker's portrait of the *Britannia* in William III's day with a naval ketch.

8. See M Oppenheim, *op cit*, p336.

sloop gradually took over from shallop, and equally in France it is associated with *barque longue*, which was itself to be replaced by corvette in naval usage.[6]

The first aggressive employment of the shallop/sloop can be traced to the ports of the Low Countries, and especially Ostend and Dunkirk. Because this was the much fought over 'Cock-pit of Europe', most maritime nations had experience of its privateers, whose ships being faced with more powerful adversaries were necessarily nimble and speedy. As early as 1636 the captured Dunkirkers *Swan* and *Nicodemus* were regarded in the English navy as the fastest ships afloat and a prime model for imitation; not surprisingly, the first sloop in the Navy List, captured in 1656, was named *Dunkirk* after its port of origin. When the French navy began acquiring *barques longues* in the 1670s, the vast majority were built in Dunkirk and virtually all were built on the Atlantic coast.

1650–1688: ketches, sloops and barques longues

In the rapidly expanding navy of Cromwell's England, the first distinct new class of small craft to emerge was the ketch. Eight were built between 1654 and 1657, ranging in length on the keel from 37–47ft and 47–90 tons, and with 8–14 small carriage guns they were obviously serious warships despite their diminutive size. A few similar but slightly larger ketches were built or purchased after the Restoration, and since these were reliably depicted by some of the best marine artists of the period, their appearance is in no doubt.[7]

The hull form, which was probably derived

from small merchantmen, was relatively stubby (a length:breadth ratio of about 2.5) with a round stern and narrow transom like a Dutch fluyt and a plain curved stem. Deep-waisted, they seem to have had a short quarterdeck, and some even sported the 'big ship' features of quarter badges and gunport wreaths. The rig is consistently shown as: a short bowsprit with at least one triangular headsail but apparently no square spritsail; a tall main mast with topmast carrying a square course and topsail, plus a topgallant in some later examples; and a relatively short mizzen with the usual lateen sail.

It is unlikely that they were very fast, but they appear to emphasise seaworthiness. In fact, their careers did not confine them to coastal waters, and indeed two, the *Blackmoor* and *Chestnut*, were specifically designed for service in the Virginia colonies.[8] Besides convoy escort and fishery protection, ketches also saw some fleet action in the usual support and fireship warfare roles [see chapter 2], and although their rig would make them handier than three-masters, oared craft and fore and aft rigged vessels would have been more useful. Perhaps it is significant that ketches fell from favour in the later 1660s when the qualities of the new sprit rigged yachts were becoming widely admired. Given the expanding commitments of Commonwealth England, these ketches probably represent an attempt to produce the smallest viable warship for secondary duties and out-of-the-way theatres.

The foreground of the van de Velde drawing of the Battle of Schoonevelt (1673) reveals the fleet role of the early English sloops and ketches: two sloops can be seen to the left, while a ketch is in the centre; a gaff rigged yacht is visible on the extreme right. The oarports along the sides of the sloops are very prominent. (NMM)

A closely related type was the pink, four of around 55 tons being built in the mid-1650s. A few ketches were later rated as pinks with the same dimensions, which suggests alterations to the rig only. It seems that at this time the English referred to small fluyts as pinks[9] and one of the few identified portraits shows the *Portsmouth* pink – rerated from a ketch in 1670 – with the usual three-masted ship rig carried by fluyts.[10] Certainly, contract specifications from the pinks and ketches of the 1690s suggest no obvious structural differences between the types.[11]

The first purpose-built sloops were four launched in 1666–7, but eighteen were added during the Third Dutch War period in the 1670s. They mostly ranged from about 35–60ft on the keel and 30–68 tons and carried four guns and a couple of swivels. Not only were they significantly smaller than ketches (with only 3pdrs compared with the latter's sakers), but their proportions were strikingly different, producing a very long, low hull with a length: breadth ratio of around 4.0 (a few even reached 5.0).[12]

There is reasonable consistency in the evidence, both visual and documentary, as to their rig. Many were two-masted, with the Biscay shallop rig augmented by a main topsail and occasionally a square spritsail under the bowsprit. However, some van de Velde pictures of sloops show a small mizzen mast with short gaff sail in addition. *Spye, Emsworth* and *Fanfan*, the earliest constructed, definitely had three masts, each with a topmast, and topsails on fore and main; the mizzen may have been a lateen but is unspecified in the most telling document. *Fanfan* – admittedly often classed as a Sixth Rate – even crossed a square mizzen topsail. The van de Velde drawing of *Bonetta*'s hull shows deadeyes for a fore and main but there is a tall pole (possibly a flagstaff) of the proportions and position of the gaff mizzen in other pictures.

Since these vessels were virtually all built in the Royal Dockyards by prominent shipwrights – including Sir Anthony Deane, Jonas Shish and two of the Petts – they were obviously the product of conscious policy. It is known that *Spye* and *Fanfan* were built at Harwich by Deane '. . . of small draught of water, to clear the sands before this harbour, then much infested with Dutch Picaroons [privateers]'.[13] They could be handled under sweeps (long oars) so would be useful in confined waters, and some were employed in the suppression of smuggling. However, they also had a fleet role, acting as tenders to the fireships and as dispatch vessels, but despite their speed they were probably too weakly armed and deficient in seakeeping qualities for long range scouting (six were lost to stress of weather, two were captured, and one sunk in action).

In Colbert's great expansion of Louis XIV's navy, at first little consideration was given to new types of small craft. However, the French navy operated galleys – including a squadron in the Channel – and various galley-derived vessels like the *brigantin* and double chaloupe, so it was a while before the particular needs of northern waters became apparent. The earliest vessels below the five official *Rangs* (Rates), were classed initially as *frégates d'avis* (with connotations both of information gatherer and of dispatch carrier). These were then reclassified as light frigates (*légère*), and in 1671 a new type was introduced in the form of the *barque longue*, which was probably intended to take over some of the original *d'avis* fleet roles, plus inshore patrol and pursuing the coastal *guerre de course*. Although generally shorter, more beamy, and more ship-like than English sloops, they were roughly the same size, and armed with four 4pdrs. Of the twenty built in 1671–78, the most powerful, with eight 4pdrs, was called *La Corvette*, and hereafter the term corvette (a word suggesting Breton, Basque or Provençal origins) gradually supplanted *barque longue* as a description of vessels below the rated warships but above the unrated *bâtiments interrompus*; by about 1750 the term had disappeared altogether.

They were almost certainly two-masted, with square courses, topsails and a spritsail, although one view indicates that they had only a large square course on the main.[14] The northern *barques longues* should not be confused with the Mediterranean usage of the term, which was applied to a form of half-galley or *brigantin*, albeit square rigged.

Considering its justifiable claim to have been the foremost sea power of its day, the Dutch navy's small craft are very poorly documented. This is partly the result of its unique organisation whereby the constituent states each contributed ships to the national fleet, leading to duplication of names, and the inevitable confusion of decentralised records; it is also partly a reflection of the Dutch navy's heavy dependence on taking up ships from trade, with the lower end of any navy list reflecting the Netherlands' rich variety of local ship types.

In the first war with England, most ships with less than 10–12 guns are listed as *jachts*, although this should not be automatically associated with the gaff rigged yachts of Restoration England, since in Holland the term denoted a sharp-lined hull form rather than a rig. The largest *jachts* carried 24 guns and were probably ship rigged with the conventional

9. Michael Robinson, *Van de Velde Drawings*, Vol I, Glossary, p245.

10. The van de Velde painting of the action in Bugia Bay, May 1671 (one of a trio in the Queen's Collection, Buckingham Palace).

11. PRO Adm 106/3070. It is possible that the pink rig was preferred for overseas deployments, being regarded as more seaworthy. See also Note 15 below.

12. Interestingly, Sir Anthony Deane's sloops were all built to exact length to breadth ratios; his were also the longest in relation to breadth.

13. Quoted by L H St C Cary in 'Harwich Dockyard', *The Mariner's Mirror* IX (1927), p170.

14. See Jean Boudriot, 'Les Barques Longues', *Neptunia* 117, pp13–16 for publication of the most relevant visual evidence.

lateen mizzen. During the second war (1665–7) the Dutch employed substantial numbers of *fluyts* – over twenty were captured in two years – of large tonnage (150–350 tons) but limited firepower (4–8 guns). These were typical merchant ships of the period, and apart from two *advis-jachts* (dispatch vessels), there is no hint of specialist small craft equivalent to English sloops or ketches.

This was to change in the 1670s when the Dutch were on the defensive, heavily outnumbered by the Anglo-French alliance. A series of over twenty *advis* vessels were built, presumably to give the fleet the intelligence it needed to fight its skilful defensive campaign. These vessels were armed with 6–12 guns and were probably similar to earlier *jachts* but, regretably, nothing is known for certain about them.

1688–1700: brigantines and advice boats

As explained in more detail in the previous chapter, in 1689 the new English government of William III faced the novel strategic problem of a maritime war with France, at the very time it had lost much of the experience and continuity of the previous regime's naval administrators. As far as ship design was concerned, this was manifested in a somewhat schizophrenic policy: on the one hand, unthinking perseverance with obsolete types, while on the other, radical experimentation with new.

At this time the shortage of small craft was acute, and the particular circumstances of William's campaign to retain his new throne required many such vessels to patrol Scottish

No illustration of a brigantine or advice boat of the 1690s has ever been identified with any certainty. Most earlier research has concentrated on the rig – which was not characteristic (they were rigged like earlier sloops) – as in this reconstruciton of a late seventeenth-century brigantine by W A Baker. (From Sloops and Shallops*)*

and Irish waters to isolate the Jacobites from French supplies, reinforcements and intelligence. The first move was to hire merchant ships, vessels of 60–100 tons and 4–12 guns being specified, but the supply of suitable vessels was soon exhausted. Perhaps lacking the time to think out requirements, the new Admiralty's first purpose-built small craft were eight ketches and three pinks of very similar dimensions to those last built in the early 1660s. With one exception they were constructed between 1691 and 1694 in merchant yards and were armed with 10 guns.[15]

However, at the same time as these very conservative vessels were being built, a new type entered the Navy List under the heading brigantine. As with so many terms that later came to denote rigs, at this time it was more descriptive of a hull type – in this case a lightly framed vessel designed to be rowed as well as sailed. The name may have been adopted by mental association with the Mediterranean *brigantin* (or *galiot à rames*), a fast oar-and-sail hybrid that one contemporary authority described as a kind of quarter-galley. They were designed for 24 oars, 'to attend the fleet for towing off ships and cutting off fireships in battles', acting as precursors of nineteenth century paddle vessels. They had an outrigger, or 'bank', to facilitate rowing and so important was the towing function that the later craft were deepened to give them a better grip on the water.

As with the Restoration sloops, which they resembled in size (75–80 tons), all nine were constructed in the Royal Dockyards, and were capable of other fleet tasks besides that of tug – for example, the first of them, *Shark*, rowed in the van of the boat attack on the stranded French ships at La Hogue. Thanks to a study of the log of the brigantine *Dispatch*,[16] the characteristics of these vessels are reasonably clear. Armed with six 3pdrs and two or four swivels or falconets, they were square rigged with two masts, each with a topmast and topsails, and later two jibs could be set; the main was a 'buss' sail, lowered for reefing, and there was no gaff or fore and aft sail on the main. *Dispatch* could pull thirty oars, but when not in use the long sweeps were undoubtedly an encumbrance and at one point fourteen were landed because 'they make us crank [unstable]'. Despite her small size, *Dispatch* accompanied Russell's fleet to the Mediterranean in 1694–5, where she ran the kind of errands suggested by her name, but much of her career was spent chasing small privateers. Usually described as sloops or shallops, these could also operate under oars, and were all too often able to escape, for the brigantine was decidedly slow under

both sail and oar. This was undoubtedly the principal shortcoming of the design, and from 1694 a new class, called advice boats, began to supersede them. Initially advice boats were hired and discharged as occasion demanded, for carrying dispatches as quickly as possible to and from fleets and distant stations, but once the French *guerre de course* got under way, fewer owners were willing to sail without convoy, negating the purpose of advice boats. Thus the Admiralty was forced to build its own, and requested small seaworthy fast-sailing vessels. The Navy Board recommended Lord Danby's tender, the *Bridget Galley*, described by Cloudisley Shovell as 'an incomparable sailer', but she was too expensive a model and eventually a Dockyard-designed boat of 71 tons was chosen.

They were often listed with brigantines, and in *The Naval Expositor* T R Blanckley accords them the same rig; furthermore, another eighteenth century antiquarian[17] claims that these craft were first employed to gather intelligence at Brest before La Hogue in 1692, whereas none was completed before 1694, but they were certainly employed for reconnaissance, where their speed would be a vital asset. The first six advice boats were built in 1694–5 by the Royal Dockyards to the same specification and armament (4 minions and 6 swivels), but they were followed by a far smaller 38-ton craft simply referred to as *Scout Boat*, proposed by the Commissioner at Portsmouth as a Solent patrol craft 'to gain intelligence of what vessels come within reach of Portsmouth, which will likewise be useful in carrying off pacquets to the ships at Spithead and St Helens in bad weather' – a brief which neatly combines the two roles of the advice boat. In 1696 two much more powerful vessels were built by merchant builders (150 tons, 10 guns) in response to an Admiralty requirement for craft 'fit for foreign voyages upon occasions'.[18]

In sharp contrast to the variety of English types, the French navy built nearly forty basically similar *barques longues* in the first five years of the war. Reviving the type after a lapse of a decade on the threat of war, France again

15. The first eight were built to identical contract specifications, although *Talbot* was completed as a pink, confirming that only the rig differentiated the pink from the ketch (PRO Adm 106/3070).

16. L G Carr Laughton, 'HM Brigantine Dispatch, 1692–1712', *The Mariner's Mirror* IX (1923), pp354–9.

17. Charles Derrick, *Memoirs of the Rise and Progress of the Royal Navy* (1806), p113.

18. The official quotations in the brigantine and advice boat paragraphs are from PRO Adm 106/3570 *et seq* and Adm 2/173 *et seq*.

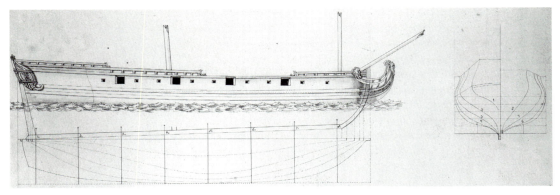

One of the earliest known draughts of a sloop-type vessel is this unidentified French barque longue of the late seventeenth century in the Danish archives. The hull form suggests emphasis on sailing qualities but the oarports are very much in evidence. (Rigsarkivet, Copenhagen)

entrusted this extensive programme largely to the builders of Dunkirk, although a few other Atlantic ports were also involved. The usual armament was six or eight 4pdrs but some carried as many as ten and, in three cases, twelve. As far as can be judged by dissimilar methods of measurements, they were relatively longer and a little deeper than English brigantines and would have come out around 60–80 tons by the English formula.

The appearance of these vessels can be gauged from a surviving plan in the Danish Archives (one of the last of the Dunkirk-built ships but not identified), while a contemporary masting specification gives a precise deliniation of the rig.[19] The ship that emerges is a miniature *frégate legère* with four gunports a side and nine oarports on the same level; the deck is cut down aft with the great cabin over and there may be a small forecastle platform forward. She carried a two-masted square rig with topsails on both masts, a spritsail under a steeply steeved bowsprit, and an unidentified item on the main which may be some sort of fore and aft sail. Thus, apart from this mysterious '*brajart*' the *barque longue*/corvette is similar in rig to English brigantines.

Corvettes appear to have been designed primarily for fleet duties (Tourville had the relatively high proportion of thirteen, and only four frigates, to eighty-seven ships of the line in his 1693 order of battle) and none was built after France turned seriously to the *guerre de course*. However, resources were short so very few warships of any type were built in this period, and corvettes were certainly employed in both the attack and defence of trade.

Although any battlefleet would have required tenders, in most other navies they do

not seem to have evolved into fighting ships to quite the same degree, and certainly not in the same numbers. The Netherlands built only five 10–18-gun vessels of the smallest 'Charter' [Rate] in the 1680s, and a further five in the next decade, the number in service having declined to two by 1700. In the eighteenth century when Holland maintained a fleet predominantly for the defence of her trade, numbers did not exceed two or three before 1780 and at times the class was completely extinct.

Regarding the Baltic navies, the position is somewhat similar, with many and varied types of small craft listed. In Sweden before 1700 the navy operated an extensive transport service around the country's Baltic empire using a multitude of typical Northern European merchant types – *flojt*, *pram*, *jakt*, *katt*, *kreiare*, *skuta*, *galiot* – and some were lightly armed but only the *jakt* and the *galiot* were genuine small combatants. The most common type of light warship was the *bojort* (from the Dutch *boyer*), carrying six to ten guns, which could be square rigged rather like the contemporary ketch; and there was also a handful of 14- to 20-gun ves-

sels described by the Swedish term *pinass*. By the end of the century, a corvette equivalent had appeared in the guise of an 8-gun vessel of about 65ft length bp, of which both a brigantine and a snow rigged version was listed. The former was preferred and about a dozen were built in the first decade of the eighteenth century for service in the Great Northern War, when they carried up to fourteen 3pdrs and as many swivels or the short howitzers so popular in skerries warfare.

Many of the same types existed in the Danish navy, but the French influence can be seen in the construction during 1679–84 of nine *barca longaer*; the first pair were about 75ft long bp and armed with eight guns, but they quickly grew to 100ft and carried twenty guns. They were superseded by a few small ship rigged frigates of similar size and power, the designation *snauer* being used for some of the smaller craft. This became an administrative term with the English sloop, and although the early vessels were probably two-masted (like a snow), their larger successors were almost certainly ship rigged. The Danes had about fourteen in 1700 and built or captured at least seventeen during the Great Northern War, but after about 1720 Denmark never possessed more than a couple of snows and brigantines

---

19. Both published and analysed by Jean Boudriot, *La Creole* (Paris 1990), pp7–10.

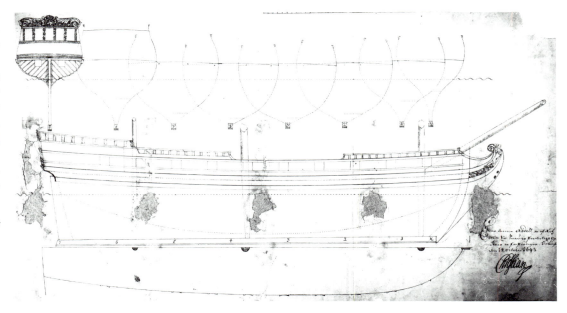

Although larger, the Danish Maagen of 1694 resembles the French barque longue in layout. The plan designates the vessel a snaw (snow) despite the ship rig, and in size and function the Maagen is closer to an English Sixth Rate than a sloop. (Rigsarkivet, Copenhagen)

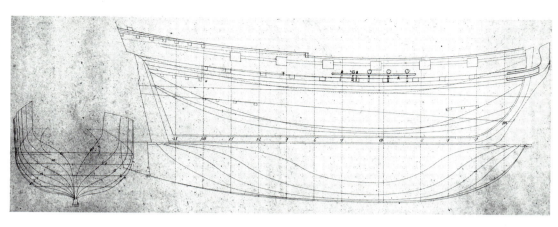

The original Admiralty draught of the Ferret, *the oldest identified British sloop plan. Howard Chapelle reconstructed the rig of this vessel as a single-masted gaff sloop, which seems reasonable from the sheer draught but the deck plan seems to suggest a second mast; she certainly had two masts by 1716. (NMM)*

(usually about 70ft length and eight to twelve guns).

For other navies, little is known beyond names. The Russian fleet had small numbers of 'snows' in the early eighteenth century, but thereafter a few rather large *jachts* of about twelve guns were the only real warships smaller than frigates. Portugal rated her small craft, in descending order of size, *fragata*, *fragatinha* and *patacho*, but Spain seems to have had very few square rigged small craft until the 1760s.

1700–1750: standardising on sloop and corvette

After the conclusion of the French war, the Royal Navy revived the sloop category for eight small 66-ton vessels built in the Royal Dockyards in 1699 and a slightly larger 83-ton pair the following year. Armed with only two falconets of 1½pdr calibre and two swivels (although the larger two had double the armament), they were intended to replace vessels hired to enforce the government ban on the export of wool. With a peacetime concern for economy, they had to be as small as possible, although the Admiralty recommended that they be decked and fitted to row about a dozen oars.[20] These were not real fighting ships, and when war again loomed, the next sloops, ordered in 1704, were twice the size (125 tons) and armed with at least ten guns–minions or 3pdrs.

Hereafter, all the other categories of small fighting ships disappeared, their functions presumably taken over by the new sloops. However, the ships themselves, while not built in large numbers, displayed considerable variety, perhaps indicating that the separate roles continued even if the rating was now the same.[21] For example, the three 125-ton craft of 1704 were followed by a large but peculiar vessel, the *Drake*, which carried fourteen 3pdrs on two decks – the ship measured only 175 tons and if it had not been built in a Royal Dockyard it would suggest a purchased merchantman.[22]

In fact there was a hiatus in small craft construction in the early years of the War of Spanish Succession and the Admiralty was ill-prepared for the French return to their 'piratical war', as the *guerre de course* was derisively termed. The year 1709 was the watershed: for

three years the Admiralty had pursued a policy of relying on purchased or hired small craft (none bigger than 120 tons and 12 guns) against considerable opposition from the Navy Board, who felt that better ships could be built in the Dockyards by using up the small timber unfit for larger ships. Because it was no longer possible to obtain such vessels to 'guard the coasts from enemy privateers', the Admiralty was compelled to change its policy and build the necessary ships.[23] The first attempt was a series of seven ships constructed in 1709–10, despite the Navy Board's views, largely by contract. Although only around 160 tons and armed with fourteen minions (4pdrs), they were classed as Sixth Rates because they were ship rigged – right down to a minuscule spritsail topmast. Their sailing qualities left much to be desired and as early as January 1710 the Navy Board was pressured into suggesting methods of lightening the rig.[24]

At the same time the Admiralty was enquiring about small ships to reconnoitre Dunkirk, and how to improve their sailing, so the old requirement that had produced the advice boat was still alive. What was actually built was a class of six moderate sized sloops, carrying ten guns and two swivels on 113 tons. The armament was rather makeshift, consisting of 3pdr or 4pdr minions, but two carried sakers making them as powerful as the ketches of fifty years earlier. In general concept the sloops of 1710–11 were to form the basis of steady development for the next half century, so it is possible to see them as a satisfactory general purpose small warship that would perform all the more specialist tasks of its predecessors.

None of the sloops built from 1699 revealed the extreme boat-like proportions of their Restoration predecessors, and their length:breadth ratio averaging about 3.5 suggests a scaled-down version of a big-ship hull. They were able to use sweeps but no compromise was made to make them particularly fast or handy under oars. Oddly enough, their appearance is

less certain than their predecessors', although a bare lines plan survives of the *Ferret*, one of the 1711 sloops. It is unwise to be dogmatic about their rig, but the position is confused by Howard Chapelle's confident reconstruction of this vessel with a single mast published in a number of his books. It is not impossible but the burden of evidence makes it very unlikely: in an age when smaller vessels could be ship rigged, the navy was clearly reluctant to place all a warship's propulsive assets on one mast, and both earlier and later sloops had at least two; even the *Ferret* had two by 1716 (although Chapelle interprets this as a modification), so it seems safe to assume that if any were ever single-masted, the survivors would have been re-rigged later.[25]

Needless to say, the position in France was less complicated, where in any case few corvettes were built during the war (nine in 1701–3 and seven in 1706–8). This reinforces the impression that they were for fleet duties, the navy's contribution to the *guerre de course* being the larger vessels that privateering *armateurs* would be less likely to finance for themselves. The first group were somewhat smaller than earlier *barques longues* (50–56ft long between perpendiculars compared with 60ft or more for

20. PRO Adm 2/180.

21. 'Sloop' was actually a rating, applied equally to bomb vessels, fireships, frigates *en flûte* and also to Admiralty yachts: in essence it signified that the ship was captained by a Master and Commander.

22. There is a model in the Rodgers Collection at Annapolis, Maryland that might be relevant (No 2). The brigantine rigged vessel has 10 oarports amidships between 2+4 gunports and at least 4 on the upper deck.

23. The correspondence can be found in PRO Adm 1/3611.

24. PRO Adm 1/3613, printed in R D Merriman, *Queen Anne's Navy*, NRS CIII (1961), p86. Their mast and spar dimensions are to be found in an anonymous manuscript of c1716 in the National Maritime Museum.

25. The draught is ambiguous, showing only one obvious set of channels, but the deck plan seems to indicate positions for two masts.

the 1690s vessels) and with two 2pdrs three of the Brest-built craft were no more powerful than the English 1699 sloops. By way of contrast, the last six were larger than standard (64–66ft) and armed with eight 4pdrs, but there is no evidence of any other significant differences. Unlike earlier programmes, the construction was more dispersed, with only four being built in Dunkirk.

No more corvettes were to be built at that port for the rest of the century, construction being largely concentrated in the naval arsenals. France added a mere thirteen corvettes to its forces between 1710 and 1750 and it is noticeable that no major navy built sloops and corvettes in large numbers before the middle of the eighteenth century. Admittedly, an English merchant shipbuilder could turn out a sloop in six months, so there was little reason to spend scarce peacetime resources on such craft, but their sparse numbers compared with even the smallest Sixth Rates suggests that there was very little that was uniquely the province of the sloop. As the command of a Master and Commander they could not even keep a Post Captain off the half-pay list.

While the gun calibre of French corvettes generally remained at 4pdr, the number was increased to 14–16 with the two built in 1727–8, but 10–12 was the norm. This pair was rather larger than any predecessor at 80ft on the deck and 20ft broad, and may herald the introduction of the three-masted ship rig which was certainly standard by mid-century. Five slightly smaller vessels were launched in 1734, but surprisingly the War of Austrian Succession provoked only a modest programme of six more (all constructed at Brest in 1744–7). As with frigate design [see chapter 2], Blaise Ollivier expressed strong views on the best layout for corvettes, insisting that the frigate-style lower deck produced a hull which was too lofty to sail well; in his view, if the upper deck were cut down fore and aft so that the quarterdeck and forecastle built over them were kept low, then there was no need for a deck below. This made sense with the relatively small corvettes of the 1740s, but as their dimensions increased there was a tendency to include what the French called a *faux pont* below the upper deck.

In Britain the period of the Establishments

A model of an early eighteenth-century English sloop. She is about the size of the vessels of the 1720s, although she cannot be identified with a particular ship. The built-up upperworks suggest a more 'naval' layout than the mercantile appearance of the Otter *and* Swift *(for which draughts survive). (NMM)*

(approximately 1719–50) is often represented as a time of stagnation in naval technology, but strictly speaking it was one of *stability*. The numbers of sloops on the Navy List remained at about twelve to fifteen until the next European war but as their dimensions were not established there was great variety in size and design. The usual pattern was for a common specification to be issued to a number of Master Shipwrights in the Royal Dockyards, each to produce a separate design. For such small ships there were few economies of scale to be derived from series construction in peacetime, whereas comparative hull forms encouraged constant improvement.

The eight built in 1721, for example, consisted of two pairs of 66 tons and 91 tons approximately and four of just over 100 tons; most carried eight guns, but the smallest two were fitted for four or six. Draughts survive for the middling pair, the *Otter* and *Swift*, which although not exact sisters were obviously built to the same specification. By the standards of later sloops, they were unusual in that they had virtually no weather deck protection for the crew; the rises fore and aft forming quarterdeck and forecastle were very shallow and the guns fired over low bulwarks beneath flimsy rails. In fact, the ships have the appearance of contemporary small merchant ships.

The two-masted rig was described as a snow,

but because the *Swift* was reported to be over-canvassed in 1738, we know that in 1722 she had been refitted with a 'boom mainsail' (presumably a fore and aft sail like the later spanker) in lieu of the standard square main. This was regarded as dangerous in heavy weather and in defending his decision to re-rig the ship the Surveyor of the Navy, Sir Jacob Acworth, underlined the importance of speed to these craft: '. . . if they are designed to sail fast, they must have a quantity of canvas to assist them, and in a gale of wind care must be taken to hand or shorten sail in time, and in my opinion such vessels, especially small ones, that do not sail fast, should not be employed, but laid up as quite useless'.[26]

In fact, in the 1720s and 1730s the Navy Board waged periodic campaigns against peacetime excrescences like awnings and built-up bulwarks that made for more comfort but poorer fighting qualities. Frequent orders enjoined the dockyards to keep the masting and rigging of sloops as light as possible and from 1728 they were established with a crossjack and main topsail 'with proper yard' (previously set flying). This must imply the abandonment of the square course and the substitution of a fore and aft main. According to one list of spar dimensions, the *Fly* of 1732 had a gaff main but no boom,

26. PRO Adm 91/3.

The new British 200-ton sloops of the 1730s were something of a throwback to seventeenth century concepts: long and low, they emphasised rowing but were also built for speed under sail. This model, although unidentified, displays the main features of the type. (NMM)

whereas a bomb ketch of the mid-1740s had both, so *Swift*'s boom main was by no means standard.[27]

From 1728 a far larger and more warlike 200-ton sloop became the norm; pierced for up to fourteen guns, they were long and low, some having a continuous sheer line that hid the short quarterdeck and shallow forecastle platform. There was a renewed emphasis on rowing with the provision of up to thirty-four sweep ports between the guns on the upper deck. Not only were they designed to the same general specification, but in February 1732 *Wolf* and *Grampus* of the new type were tested at sea against the older *Hawk* and *Otter* and the 24-gun *Experiment*. The new ships were significantly faster, *Wolf* being the star with a speed of 10kts in a fresh quartering breeze. Following this gratifying success, about eight similar vessels were laid down in 1732, including three of the *Cruizer* class by the *Wolf*'s builder (Stacey, the Deptford Master Shipwright) which are probably the first sloops built to a common draught. As with the majority of sloops, most were snow rigged, only the *Sharke* being demonstrably a ketch.

The outbreak of war with Spain in 1739 did not bring any sudden upsurge in sloop construction. Three 200-tonners of the *Drake* class were ordered from merchant yards in 1740, but from 1742 a new contract-built 14-gun class of about 245 tons was introduced. Apart from the 4pdr carriage guns, their bulwarks bristled with

twelve to fourteen swivel guns and the search for more firepower inevitably led to an increase in gun calibre to 6pdrs; this was probably occasioned by the threat of French entry into the war, and certainly from 1743 the number of sloops grew dramatically: only fifteen were in service in 1739, but between 1743 and 1746 over twenty of the new 270-ton 6pdr type were built. Like many medium sized navies, Spain had little need for sloop-type vessels, and even France had less than ten in service in 1744, but the prospect of the coasts swarming with small French privateers was enough to stimulate this relatively large British programme.

The new sloops of the *Swallow* class, with ten and later twelve 6pdrs, were a step towards big-ship characteristics, having a fully flush upper deck and structural quarterdeck and forecastle instead of being little more than roofed-over cabins. Wheel steering under the quarterdeck soon replaced the very exposed tiller position on top, and perhaps most significantly, the majority were built to one basic design, like any other war emergency programme.

1750–1793: The miniature frigate

The Royal Navy ended the War of Austrian Succession with thirty-five sloops, but there was to be none of the usual retrenchment since the peace was widely perceived as little more than a truce. There were still thirty-four on the Navy List in 1753, but by the outbreak of the next war in 1756 there were already forty-two. Given the short life of sloops, this meant considerable new construction, and for sloops – as for all other British warships – this was to be a time of dramatic change, with a plethora of hull forms being tried, the adoption of the ship rig, and further increases in size.

However, the first requirement was for a specialist class 'to draw a small draught of water to cruize against the smugglers', for which competing designs were requested in January 1749. This approach was being introduced for larger craft but was far from unusual for sloops, except in this case the specification allowed more scope, since it gave only an outline of function, intended armament, and tonnage without recommending any dimensions, but insisting that they be 'good sailing vessels'. Four were built initially to the 140-ton limit, to carry eight 3pdrs and ten swivels, and although Allin's *Peggy* was officially the competition 'winner', Benjamin Slade's *Hazard* was more

---

27. The *Drake* of 1729 set a loose footed spanker extended by a boom. See R C Anderson, 'Some Additions to the Brigantine Problem', *The Mariner's Mirror* VIII, pp111.

The smallest corvette of her day was the Badine, *built at Brest in 1745. Armed with six 3pdrs, and although only 60ft long, she had a full ship rig. The plumb stem and sternpost was fashionable in the 1740s with constructors influenced by Blaise Ollivier (they can be seen for example in the designs for the Danish navy by the emigré Frenchman Laurent Barbé). (Musée de la Marine, Paris)*

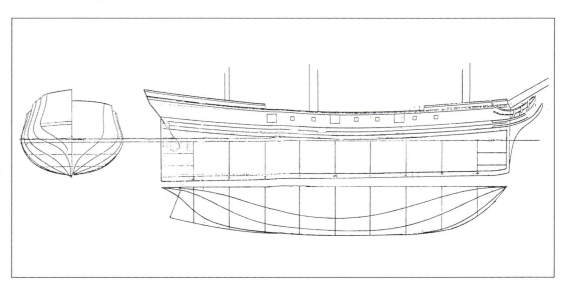

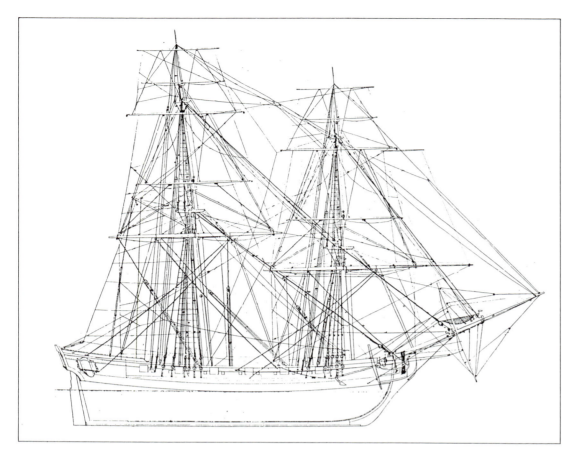

A spar and rigging plan of the Cruizer *of 1752, signed by F H Chapman, the famous Swedish naval architect. Some of the class were ketch rigged but this vessel had what was then called the snow rig; it is noteworthy that the gaff main is loose-footed, no boom being shown.* (Krigsarkivet, Stockholm)

highly regarded in the long run.[28] Structurally they were a return to earlier forms, the latter for example having a cut-down upper deck aft for the cabin and a low step up forming a forecastle platform.

In 1752 more small sloops were required and the same specification was issued, but 'to make an experiment' one class was to use the lines of the fast-sailing yacht *Royal Caroline* and the other the hull form of a captured French 74, the *Monarche*. The experimental spirit continued with units of the resulting *Cruizer* and *Fly* classes respectively being rigged as ketches and snows by way of comparison; furthermore, in 1753 *Cruizer* was modified to test a full ship rig. There had been a few ketch rigged sloops earlier, but most were snows and it is perhaps significant that following a few years of trials, not only was the ketch rig abandoned for sloops but bomb vessels adopted the ship rig as well (in fact the three-masted rig would also dominate the sloop classes for a generation until the snow staged a comeback in the guise of the brig).

The limited size and firepower of the 140-tonners marked them out as the equivalent of Victorian masted sloops and gunboats, whose role was essentially that of peacetime policeman. When war became inevitable, substantial increases in dimensions and armament quickly

followed: 220 tons and ten lightweight 6pdrs in 1755; 309 tons and sixteen 6pdrs by 1757. A few smaller slooops of less than 250 tons were built to carry ten or twelve 4pdrs, but the short 6ft 16½cwt 6pdr rapidly became the norm. However, there was never a standard design and the inspirations for the various hull forms were amazingly diverse: *Hawk* (1755, 220 tons, lines of the *Royal Caroline*); *Bonetta* class (three ships 1755, 220 tons, to the lines of the French privateer *Tygre*); *Druid* class (two ships 1760, 208 tons, same as the *Cruizer* of 1732); *Beaver* class (three ships 1760, 283 tons, based on the lines of the French frigate *Abenakise*); *Vulture* class (two ships 1762, 263 tons, to the lines of the French privateer *Epreuve*); there were also *ab initio* designs by the Surveyors Slade (*Hunter* and *Viper* 1755, 238 and 223 tons; *Favourite* class, two ships 1757, 309 tons; *Ferret* 1760, 286 tons; *Nautilus* 1761, 314 tons; *Otter* class, three ships 1766–9, 302 tons) and Bately (*Alderney* class, three ships 1755–6, 230 tons).

At first sight the absence of a preferred war-standard design looks like a failure, but sloops were developing rapidly and the comparative value of small batches must have been great – apart from different rigs, the *Viper* and *Hunter* tested the relative merits of square and pink sterns, for instance. If anything, the continuation of a peacetime-style design policy at a

wartime rate of procurement, reflects the superiority of the Royal Navy in this war – there was time and resources for continuous improvement. At first, the smaller sloops tended to follow earlier forms with a cut-down aft and short quarterdeck and forecastle, but the introduction of the ship rig encouraged the extension of the quarterdeck to facilitate the handling of the mizzen sails. The new 16-gun class, introduced with Slade's *Favourite* in 1757, were the first ship rigged sloops designed as such from the outset, and it is significant that they and the slightly smaller 14-gun ships were officially referred to as 'frigates' in their early years: like their French counterparts they had become miniature frigates in all but rating.

France's corvette force had dwindled to a pair of ships by 1755, but a wartime programme produced eleven new vessels in 1756–7. Mostly designed by J–L Coulomb, these were all 4pdr ships, but one was never completed, five carried sixteen guns and the rest twelve. The larger ships were built to one design and measured about 385 tons by English calculation, but no dimensions of the smaller corvettes seem to have survived. They were probably all frigate-built with a lower *faux pont* and were large for their armament – as an example, the *Guirlande*'s sixteen 4pdrs were replaced with eighteen 6pdrs in British service.[29]

All were lost in the course of the war and a major replacement programme was necessary. Three were launched in 1762–3, including the first 6pdr armed ship, the *Isis*, but these were the only serving corvettes until seven were built in 1767–71. An order of 1763 had established two ranks (one with twenty 6pdrs and the other with twelve 4pdrs) but in practice no more 4pdr ships were added and those commissioned carried twelve, sixteen or eighteen guns on much the same displacement as their ill-fated predecessors. Flush-decked with a *faux pont* below, these were not entirely satisfactory ships, the constructors at Brest complaining that the dimensions of both the nominal 18-

---

28. At the end of 1749 the Admiralty requested specimen draughts of the most favoured ships in each class and of the sloops selected the *Hazard*. NMM Adm/B/141.

29. Oddly, the draught of this ship as captured suggests she had a two-masted, presumably snow, rig; however, there is room for a mizzen, even though neither the mast, its step, nor a channel are shown.

Swallow, *built at Dover in 1779, one of the Royal Navy's first purpose-built brig sloops. This contemporary model demonstrates the heavily sheered open upper deck that suggests cutter rather than naval sloop ancestry; this ship was even clinker-built like so many South Coast small craft.* (NMM)

and 12-gun classes of 1767, which were supposed to stow six months' stores, would not allow the usual corvette qualities of speed, stability, seakeeping and height of battery. By comparison, Coulomb's *Calypso* of 1757 – usually regarded as the paragon – was only required to carry sixteen 4pdrs and four months' stores on much the same tonnage as the 18-gun class.

To underline her limited requirement for corvettes, as France prepared for intervention in the American struggle for independence only four vessels were built during 1777–9. Two were enlarged versions of the standard 6pdr type but carrying twenty guns, whereas the other pair were to be the prototype 8pdr corvettes, taking over that calibre when 8pdr frigates were no longer built. *Coquette* and *Naïade* were to have six sisters built to the same draught in 1780–1 (unusually, for corvettes, the products of Toulon), and one to the same specification from Rochefort in 1782, so France fought the American War with fewer than twenty corvettes all told. All around 640 tons, the 8pdr ships were actually superior to British 28-gun frigates, and the captured *Naïade*, for example, was established with twenty-two 12pdrs on the upper deck, six 12pdr carronades on the quarterdeck and two 18pdr carronades on the forecastle – more than twice the original weight of broadside.

In the circumstances, a reversion to a smaller type was almost inevitable, and France at first tried cutters, although her relative inexperience with the type quickly became apparent. Possibly inspired by a memorandum of

1762 claiming that seven could be built for the cost of one corvette, the first group in 1771 were reasonable 67-ton craft with an appropriate armament of six 3pdrs. However, at the beginning of the American War there was an ill-conceived attempt to grossly enlarge them – initially to 212 tons and fourteen 6pdrs and then to 300 tons and eighteen 6pdrs.[30] The huge areas of canvas made them unhandy and dangerous, so of the nineteen big cutters, ten were re-rigged as brigs (and one as a schooner) during the war. Actually, smaller two-masted vessels were already entering service, two 'snows' with ten 4pdrs and two ketches with eight 8pdrs being constructed in 1776, following limited experience with a few snow rigged transports and a pair of fast pacquets. The snows had a cut-down aft, with cabin roof forming a short quarterdeck, like the earlier corvettes for which they were almost exact replacements.

Brigs were first built in substantial numbers after the war with two classes, each of eight vessels: a very sharp *aviso* or dispatch vessel built at St Malo by Forfait in 1786–8, armed with twelve 4pdrs; and a smaller brig of war, armed with six 4pdrs, designed by Haran at Bayonne and constructed in 1787–8. A class of five 20-gun 6pdr corvettes was also added postwar, following a proposal by Baron Bombelle, a naval officer and enthusiastic amateur ships designer. With very short upperworks covering breaks in the deck fore and aft, they might be

considered a throwback to earlier layouts, but the large expanse of uncluttered upper deck actually looked forward to the genuine flush-decked ship of the near future.

For the British navy, the American War was a period of unprecedented adversity, with its huge battlefleet significantly outnumbered for the first time since the 1690s. Cruising ships were in particular demand, and the quarter-decked ship sloops came to represent a cheap frigate substitute. There was little time and less inclination to fine-tune designs and at the outbreak of colonial fighting, the existing 300-ton 14-gun *Swan* class (first built in 1767) was mass-produced, eventually reaching twenty-six ships by 1779. A 360-ton 18-gun prototype, the *Ceres* (based on the lines of the French privateer *Chevert* captured in 1761, but with no cut-down and a long quarterdeck), had been designed in 1774, but the preference was for more economical ships. A few 16-gun ships, slightly enlarged over the *Swans*, were also built, but no other design found particular favour.

For a generation, all new-built sloops for the Royal Navy were three-masted quarterdecked ships, but as in France a new class developed to replace the smaller rates. The brig category was introduced in 1778 for the *Childers* class of six 200-ton flush-deckers armed with ten, and later fourteen, 4pdrs. Along with two larger vessels, this group soon became rated as brig sloops on the Navy List. The exact difference between a snow and a brig at this time is still a matter of debate, but although the mast dimensions make it clear that the ships set a gaff and boom mainsail, for what it is worth, the draught calls them 'brigantines'. In size and

30. See Jean Boudriot, *The Cutter Cerf* (Paris 198?) for fuller details.

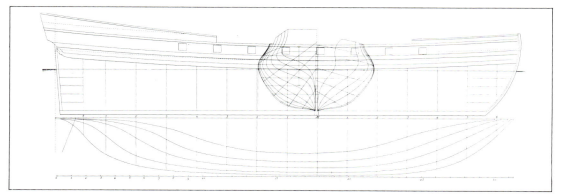

France began to build 6pdr-armed corvettes in the 1760s, although not in large numbers. This draught, from Souvenirs de Marine, *purports to represent a 16-gun ship built by Rolland in 1765, although no completed vessel matches these details. Nevertheless, the draught is typical of the corvettes of the period which did not carry guns very far forward or aft.*

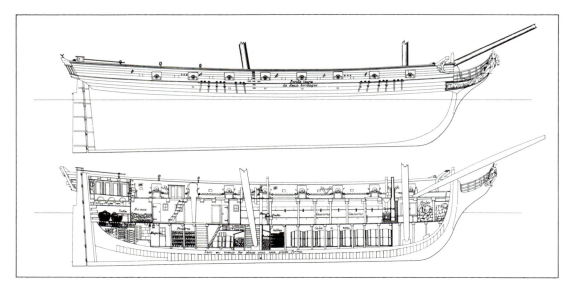

function they were a return to the two-masted sloops of preceding years, but structurally their sharp lines, steep sheer and tiller steering give them the appearance of enlarged cutters, unlike the more ship-like sloops of the 1740s and 1750s.

As with previous conflicts, there was immediate postwar retrenchment, but the British peacetime sloop establishment was now stabilised at around fifty: there had been forty-five listed in 1764, only reduced by one in 1775, and although at the height of the war in 1782 many captures and purchases had pushed the total to ninety-eight sloops and eleven brigs, by 1786 these had been reduced to forty-five and six respectively. At no time previously had they exceeded frigates in quantity but the gap had been closing – in the great struggle with Napoleon's European empire, they would become the most numerous warship on the Navy List.

1793–1815: innovation versus standardisation

For other navies, as already noted, the sloop or corvette was never particularly popular. Although virtually nothing is known about her earlier small craft, even Spain – the third largest naval power – kept less than a dozen of such ships for most of the latter half of the

eighteenth century; and the secondary powers, like Denmark, Sweden and Russia maintained only a handful. The one exception was Holland, which suddenly espoused the type in the 1780s (there were about thirty corvettes in service by 1785) at the same time as she was expanding her trade protection navy into a genuine battlefleet; both were the result of going to war with Britain after nearly a century when her commerce was not exposed to British attack.

The paucity of corvettes is partially explained by the fact that for most navies they were small frigates (like British 20- and 24-gun ships) rather than sloops, and liable to be overpowered if used for the recognised duties of a frigate. Navies of small numbers preferred fewer, larger cruisers, but took up genuine small craft, like brigs, schooners and cutters, for dispatch vessels and coastal patrol, where speed and manoeuvrability might offset inferior gunpower. The timing of the European adoption of the naval brig seems to be remarkably consistent: the first Danish brig dates from 1770; the first Spanish *bergantino* is listed in 1771; a Dutch brig was built in 1772; and the Russian and Portuguese Navy Lists have similar vessels from the 1770s; the major naval powers, as outlined earlier, were only a little behind.

Twenty brigs of 12–16 guns formed one-third of the proposed French corvette establishment under the massively ambitious Borda construction programme of 1786; there would also be twenty ship rigged corvettes armed with twenty-four 8pdrs and the same number armed with twenty 6pdrs (119ft and 113ft length bp respectively, approximately 535 and 510 tons burthen). Unlike the approved Sané design for frigates, the constructors were to be allowed a free hand with hull form and detail dimensions, but the Revolution intervened before more than a few could be completed. Nevertheless, the basic specification survived, with at least eight 6pdr and nine 8pdr corvettes being built before 1800, but some more powerful 22-gun and 24-gun 8pdr ships were also added; the records for this period are fragmentary, reflecting post-revolutionary turmoil, but there were at least four of the former and eight of the latter, a conventional quarterdecked 580-ton design.

New ideas flourished after the Revolution, but one of the most curious was the *corvette-canonnière*, a frigate-sized ship armed with fourteen 48pdrs, a 12in mortar, and a red-hot shot furnace. Five of the 1000-ton *Incorruptible* type were eventually completed with twenty-four 24pdrs; they retained the 12in mortar, which was also fitted to three smaller 600-ton vessels with sixteen 18pdrs, another large 900-tonner with fourteen 24pdrs, and the *Bacchante* class of four 640-ton ships, two armed with twenty 18pdrs and two with twenty-four 12pdrs. These might all be regarded quite legitimately as frigates, but the concept was also applied to a few ships of genuine corvette proportions: *Fraternité* with six 24pdrs and two sisters with twenty 12pdrs, *Torche* with eighteen 12pdrs and *Bergère* with sixteen 12pdrs. This almost desperate search for more firepower in the mid-1790s was a total failure, since the mortar was useless for anti-ship use

A typical French 20-gun corvette of the 6pdr class from the Revolutionary period. By this time the battery was longer, but the foremost port was still for chase purposes and did not regularly house a gun. The larger classes of corvette had extended quarterdecks and built-up bulwarks but were otherwise similar (there was also a flush-decked type). From Souvenirs de Marine, *the vessel is described as built at Le Havre in 1793 by Forfait.*

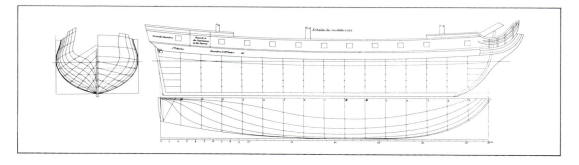

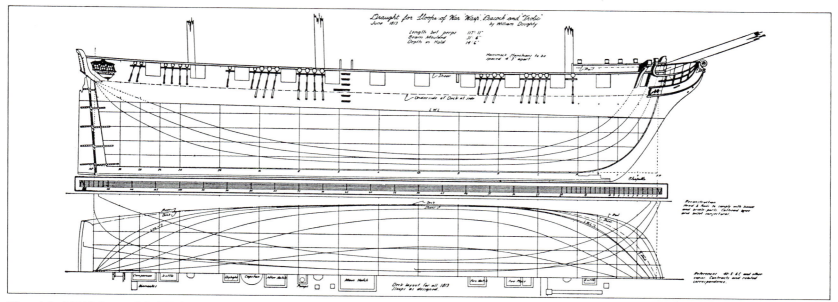

The original 1813 design of the US flush-decked ship sloops Wasp, Peacock *and* Frolic *as redraughted by Howard Chapelle. Although larger, they are very similar in layout to the British* Hermes *of 1810, herself based on the French* Bonne Citoyenne. *They were very successful in the War of 1812, giving considerable impetus to the development of the flush sloop/corvette. (Smithsonian Institution, Washington)*

The British reaction to the big US sloops was more muted than the feverish attempts to match the big frigates. A large flush-decked sloop of 507 tons, the *Hermes*, had been built in 1810 and three more were added after 1812; they carried two less 32pdrs but were not noticeably inferior. However, a reduced design was built in a hurry, and the sixteen 454-ton vessels of the *Levant* class were armed with the same number of 32pdr carronades as the US vessels, although the long guns were only 6pdrs.

1815–1850: the era of the corvette

From 1815 there was a tendency for the flush-decked ship sloop to take over from the quarterdecked version, perhaps influenced by the success of US ships of this configuration, and gradually the term corvette became a universal description. The Americans retained their formula for most of the remaining period of sail, merely expanding it to 600 tons for ten 24-gun sloops in 1824, and to 792 tons for the *Cyane* and *Levant* in 1837. These were not as highly regarded as their predecessors, but since they were mostly employed on distant stations representing US interests, it is likely that the large establishment of guns, boats and equipment that gave them independence also hampered their sailing.

Some US naval officers came to believe that the changing nature of ordnance would give a large corvette armed with a small number of the most powerful long range guns a distinct advantage over the traditional frigate. Seven such vessels were ordered in 1841, the largest of which was over 1000 tons, and *Plymouth* and *Jamestown* of this group introduced complete spar decks above their battery of eighteen medium 32pdrs and four 8in shell guns; although they had full length solid bulwarks, happily for their sailing qualities the spar deck carried no broadside armament.

In postwar Britain the subject of naval architecture had become a matter of fashionable

The final configuration of the big sloop/corvette was a complete but empty spar deck above the main battery, represented by this Chapelle plan of the USS Jamestown *of 1844. The spar deck sometimes carried a shell gun on a pivot mounting fore and aft on similar vessels, but the essentially empty deck made sail handling very much easier. (Smithsonian Institution, Washington)*

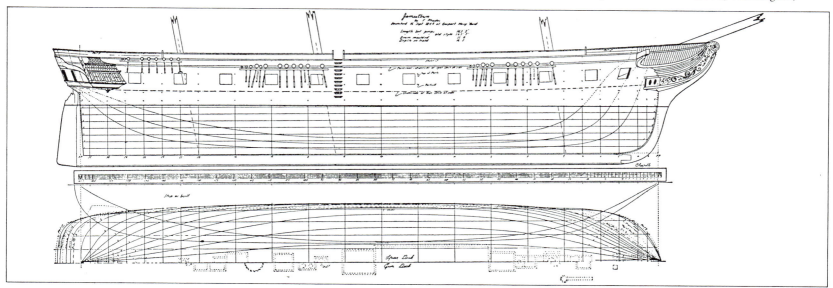

concern – and inevitably controversy – but the experiences of a war largely spent in pursuit of a numerically inferior and therefore reluctant enemy led to an over-emphasis on speed. For small ships, the effects were potentially less damaging but some officers felt that the 'yacht-like' speed of the new brigs and corvettes was achieved at the expense of their fighting qualities. In the early 1820s, the Admiralty cast its net wide for a series of experimental flush-decked sloops, designed by the official Surveyors, the Dockyard Apprentices, the School of Naval Architecture, a merchant shipbuilder, and a couple of amateur but talented naval officers, Captain John Hayes and Commander William Symonds. The vehicle for comparison was the sailing trial – effectively a series of races – and while the results were never very scientific, the experimental squadrons were widely employed.[32] The trials also involved a few 28-gun ships (the old quarterdecked ship sloops rerated; often nicknamed 'donkey frigates'), and led to the progressive increase in the size of both classes (the flush-decked ships from about 400 to 560 tons, and the 28s from 500 to 600 tons by 1825).

In 1832 the Navy's administration was radically overhauled, and the Surveyorship was awarded to Symonds (now promoted to Captain), largely on the strength of several fast-sailing designs. Throughout his controversial tenure there would be an emphasis on speed, and more sailing trials, but the old restraints on size were also overthrown, and Symonds' unrated craft were marked by large tonnage for their armament, a complete reversal of traditional British policy. Symonds' sloops – now increasingly referred to as corvettes – reached

A Danish draught of the French Volage, one of a large class of brigs of the Gazelle class built between 1822 and 1841. Designed by Marestier and heavily influenced by American pilot boat hull forms, they were initially known as 'schooner-brigs' and rigged as brigantines, but were later rated as brick-aviso and rigged as brigs. (Rigsarkivet, Copenhagen)

730 tons with the Dido of 1834, but thereafter settled down to around 600. From about 1830, the usual 32pdr carronades were replaced with Dixon's 25cwt short 32pdr guns on corvettes, so the new ships had to carry a greater weight of metal.

The one exception to the dominance of the flush-decked corvette was France. Some naval officials led by Baron Tupinier favoured giving up quarterdecked corvettes altogether, since the existing designs were such poor sailers, but nevertheless a class of about twenty-five 32-gun batterie couverte ships were built right down to 1850. Miniature spar-decked frigates with heavily armed upperworks, they fully vindicated Tupinier's opinion in their lacklustre performance against British flush sloops in the sailing trials of the early 1830s. A few 24-gun open battery ships were constructed in the late 1820s to the dimensions of the old 20-gun corvettes but the other popular type was the 18-gun corvette-aviso, based on the fast-sailing Diligente of 1801, some of which were barque rigged.

After 1815 most of the smaller navies found the corvette increasingly useful, perhaps as a reaction to the cost of the new style spar-decked frigate, but never in great numbers. A high proportion were sent to distant stations, and their relative economy and good seakeeping led to their employment on long voyages of scientific or geographical discovery; for similar reasons they were often the preferred type for cadet training. Development tended to follow trends in the major navies, towards larger and more heavily armed ships: Spain, for example, acquired two 600-ton vessels from France in 1816 and after making do with corvettes of moderate proportions for decades, built two 1100-tonners armed with 32pdrs and shell guns based on the British Spartan of 1841.

If anything, the brig was even more popular, becoming the standard small all-purpose vessel in virtually every navy, except the American where the schooner regained its popularity

after 1815. Although brigs varied considerably in size, they were virtually all open flush-decked designs, perhaps with small topgallant forecastle and poop platforms. Alterations to the rig included the introduction of auxiliary spencer masts, and the brigantine (with no square canvas on the main) also made a limited appearance as a good compromise between the brig and the schooner.

In France there were three types of brig: the large brick de guerre of 18–20 guns, inspired by the ever-popular Diligente; a smaller 10–16-gun brick-aviso, heavily influenced by American hull design and often brigantine rigged, introduced in 1821; and a small canonnière-brick of 10 guns for coastal waters. As with the corvettes, later development tended to replace carronades by the new 30pdrs, and a limited number of shell guns, but from the mid-1840s new designs featured all-shell gun armament (retaining only a pair of solid shot chase guns). The largest of the first type displaced around 500 tons, the second a more moderate 250 tons and the gun-brigs about 200.

Britain finally abandoned the construction of small Cherokee class brigs when Symonds took over as Surveyor. His reputation had been enhanced by the performance of his large brig Columbine (492 tons) in the 1827 trials, and not surprisingly he turned his attention to more powerful vessels than those previously contemplated. Unlike the corvettes, which were largely built as one-offs, some of his brig designs were constructed in reasonable numbers. They were initially divided into First and Second Class (roughly above and below 500 tons) but in the 1840s a 12-gun Third Class was added for those below 450 tons. Paralleling developments elsewhere, the armament turned from carronades to lightweight long guns in the 1830s, but there was never any real movement in favour of dependence on shell guns.·

32. Full details can be found in John Fincham, A History of Naval Architecture (London 1851), pp220ff.

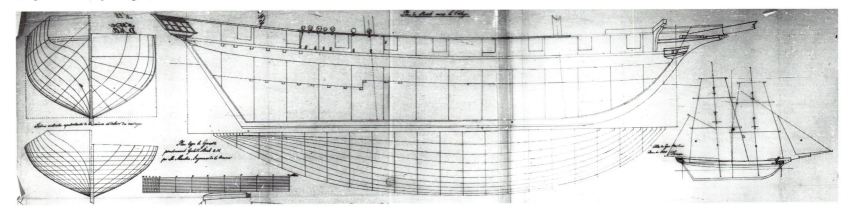

In 1846 a Third Class brig called the *Recruit* became the first – and only – iron-hulled sailing warship built for the Royal Navy. In sharp contrast to this technological audacity, it is worth noting that the same navy continued to build wooden-hulled brigs for sail training purposes down to 1890, the last descendants of literally thousands of 'unrated' small craft that served every significant navy in the world.[33]

Robert Gardiner

33. There were even later training brigs, such as USS *Boxer* of 1903, but these were 'modern' merchant ships in hull form, whereas the British brigs were effectively replicas of earlier brigs of war.

Acknowledgements
The definitive history of the sloop and brig have yet to be written, and the above survey could not have been attempted without access to two very important but as yet unpublished works: David Lyon's 'Sailing Navy List' provided a skeletal outline of British development from 1688, with basic data on all classes, while Jan Glete's 'Navies and Nations' contains very full statistical data on the size and constitution of fleets in the sailing ship era.

Sloops, Corvettes and Brigs: Typical Ships 1650–1840

Ship or Class	Type	Nationality	Launched	Built	Guns	Calibre	Dimensions Feet–inches Metres	Burthen	Remarks
EAGLET	Ketch	English	1655	Horsleydown	8	?saker	40–0kl × 16–0 × 7–0 12.19kl × 4.88 × 2.13	54	A Commonwealth ketch
DUNKIRK	Sloop	Dunkirker	capt 1656	Dunkirk	2	?3pdr	40–0kl × 12–6 × 4–6 12.19kl × 4.88 × 2.13	33	First sloop in English navy; taken 1656
YOUNG LION	Ship	Dutch	capt 1665	Holland	10	?3pdr	42–0kl × 14–0 × 5–0 12.80kl × 4.27 × 1.52	44	Smallest type of Dutch ship rigged warship
BONETTA	Sloop	English	1673	Woolwich	4	3	61–0kl × 13–0 × 5–0 18.59kl × 3.96 × 1.52	57	A Restoration sloop
UTILE	Barque longue	French	1689	Dunkirk	8	4pdr	58–8 × 13–10 × 6–0* 17.88 × 4.23 × 1.82	c50	Typical early 'corvette'
MAAGEN	Snaw	Danish	1691	Copenhagen	20	?3pdr	82–4 × 21–7 × 10–9 dr* 25.10 × 6.59 × 3.29	c160	Despite designation, probably ship rigged
DESPATCH	Brigantine	English	1692	Deptford	6	3pdr	63–3 × 16–9 × 6–3 19.28 × 5.11 × 1.91	80	One of the first brigantines, enlarged over prototype
FLY	Advice boat	English	1694	Portsmouth	4	minion	61–6 × 16–1 × 6–0 18.75 × 4.91 × 1.83	73	The first purpose-built advice boat
SEAHORSE	Sixth Rate	British	1710	Limehouse	14	4pdr	76–0 × 22–1 × 9–3 23.17 × 6.73 × 2.82	161	Small ship rigged Sixth Rate
FERRET	Sloop	British	1711	Deptford	10	3pdr	64–6 × 20–8 × 9–1 19.66 × 6.30 × 2.77	113	One of the first of the new larger sloops
NYMPHE	Corvette	French	1728	Toulon	14	4pdr	85–4 × 22–2 × 10–3* 26.00 × 6.76 × 3.12	c180	Typical French corvette
WOLF	Sloop	British	1731	Deptford	14	4pdr	87–0 × 25–0 × 6–0 26.52 × 7.62 × 1.82	244	Successful snow rigged sloop; good performance under oars
FAVOURITE	Ship sloop	British	1757	Shoreham	16	6pdr	96–4 × 27–0 × 8–6 29.36 × 8.22 × 2.59	309	First British ship sloop class
CALYPSO	Corvette	French	1757	Brest	16	4pdr	111–0 × 28–6 × 14–0 33.83 × 8.68 × 4.62	386	Best corvette of the Seven Years War period
SWAN	Ship sloop	British	1766	Plymouth	14	6pdr	96–7 × 26–9 × 12–10 29.43 × 8.15 × 3.90	300	Standard ship sloop of the American War period
CHILDERS	Brig sloop	British	1778	Thames	10	4pdr	78–7 × 25–0 × 11–0 23.95 × 7.62 × 3.35	202	First British brig sloop

Ship or Class	Type	Nationality	Launched	Built	Guns	Calibre	Dimensions Feet–inches Metres	Burthen	Remarks
NAÏADE	Corvette	French	1779	Toulon	20	8pdr	126–8 × 33–8 × 10–2 38.61 × 10.26 × 3.09	640	An eight-ship class of big quarterdecked corvettes
CORMORANT	Ship sloop	British	1793	Rotherhithe	16	6pdr	108–4 × 29–7 × 9–0 33.12 × 9.00 × 2.74	422	Standard quarterdecked sloop; actual armament 26 guns by 1805
BONNE CITOYENNE	Corvette	French	1794	?	20	8pdr	120–0 × 31–0 36.57 × 9.45	511	Corvette '20 de 8'; very influential hull form in Royal Navy
CRUIZER	Brig sloop	British	1795	Ipswich	18	32pdr carr	100–0 × 30–6 × 12–9 30.48 × 9.30 × 3.89	335	Prototype of the most numerous class of wooden warships
DILIGENTE	Corvette	French	1801	Brest	18	6pdr	110–11 × 27–9 × 15–0* 33.80 × 8.45 × 4.57	472 disp	Very fast; influential on post-1815 designs
ARCHER	Gun-brig	British	1801	Deptford	12	18pdr carr	80–0 × 22–6 × 9–5 24.38 × 6.86 × 2.87	177	Prototype of most numerous gun-brig class
CHEROKEE	Brig	British	1808	Blackwall	10	18pdr carr	90–0 × 24–6 × 11–0 27.43 × 7.47 × 3.35	235	Standard British class of small brigs, built 1808–30
FROLIC	Ship sloop	American	1813	Charlestown	22	32pdr carr	119–5 × 31–5 × 14–2 36.32 × 9.58 × 4.32	539	Successful US sloop of 1812 War
LEVANT	Ship sloop	British	1813	Chester	22	32pdr carr	115–6 × 29–8 × 8–6 35.20 × 9.04 × 2.59	454	Flush-decked sloop of War of 1812
GAZELLE	Brig-aviso	French	1821	Bayonne	18	18pdr carr	98–9 × 26–3 × 12–7 30.11 × 8.00 × 3.85	268 disp	Prototype of the 'brick-aviso' type built 1821–40
CYGNE	Brig of war	French	1824	Lorient	20	24pdr carr	109–11 × 26–3 × 15–1* 33.50 × 9.00 × 4.59	537 disp	'Brick de guerre' of Paris Commission built 1823–30
COLUMBINE	Brig sloop	British	1826	Portsmouth	18	32pdr carr	105–0 × 33–6 × 7–11 32.00 × 10.21 × 2.41	492	Symonds' experimental brig
BERCEAU	Corvette	French	1834	Lorient	32	30pdr carr	141–1 × 35–1 × 15–10* 43.00 × 10.70 × 4.83	1057 disp	'Batterie couverte' type
DIDO	Flush-decked corvette	British	1836	Pembroke	18	32pdr	120–0 × 37–6 × 18–0 36.58 ×11.43 × 5.49	730	Largest British flush corvette
VILLA DE BILBAO	Spar-decked corvette[?]	Spanish	1845	Thames	28	32pdr	179–0 × 47–8 × 22–8* 54.55 × 14.53 × 6.91	1189	Largest Spanish corvette
CONSTELLATION	Spar-decked corvette	American	1855	Norfolk, VA	24	8in shell	176–0 × 41–0 × 21–3 53.65 × 12.50 × 6.48	1265	The last US sailing warship to be designed and built

Notes:

Calibres are given in native weights; generally Continental pounds were heavier than English, so the French 8pdr and 30pdr equated roughly with English 9pdrs and 32pdrs respectively. Dimensions are in English feet with metric equivalents. Wherever possible the dimensions are measured in the English fashion (those marked * are not), giving gundeck length, moulded breadth and depth in hold; but *kl* = keel length, *dr* = draught of water, and *disp* = displacement; burthen, which is simply calculated from the dimensions, make up the remainder, *carr* = carronade.

4

The Fore and Aft Rigged Warship

ALL the principal fighting ships of the major sea powers between 1650 and 1850 were square rigged, the only exception being the surviving galley fleets (dealt with in Chapter 6), which were primarily oared craft and were in any case declining in both numbers and importance by the beginning of our period. Vessels employing any one of the many fore and aft rigs were essentially small and auxiliary craft, and in every case represented the naval adoption of an existing mercantile rig – and occasionally of the hull form as well. While ocean-going warships faced much the same conditions across the world, which gave them a broad similarity, the design of small craft was particularly sensitive to local requirements and was subject to a process of gradual evolution and adjustment. This means that the vessels covered in this chapter are particularly diverse and their development cannot be adequately described without some reference before 1650. Furthermore, the single chronological sequence of previous chapters cannot be followed for so many types, and so separate descriptions by rig have been employed.

Lateen

The lateen sail, probably the oldest European fore and aft rig, dominated most Mediterranean fleets from at least the thirteenth century. The origins of the lateen rigged naval galley are beyond the scope of this volume, but besides the smaller *galeota*, or half-galley, there were a number of galley-related Mediterranean sail-and-oar hybrids that used lateen sails, not-

A convincing portrait of a brigantin *or* bergantino *can be seen in the foreground of this painting by Van Wieringen of Heemskerk's defeat of the Spaniards off Gibraltar in 1607. Its resemblance to Furttenbach's description is evident in hull form, the lateen rig and the oared propulsion. (NMM)*

ably the *brigantin* (brigantine, *bergantino* or other variant forms) and felucca.

Brigantin

Contemporary descriptions are usually very general but Furttenbach's *Architectura Navalis* of 1629 gives their length as 60 *palmi* (c14.6m, 48ft) without the *sperone* or beak and a breadth of 16 *palmi* (3.8m, 13ft). Although sometimes regarded as a quarter-galley, the *brigantin* was more of an open boat in appearance. Unlike the galley, they had no centreline *corsia* or walkway but instead a 6ft wide opening in the deck left only about 3ft covered at each side; the oarsmen, one to each oar, stood or sat in this space, and various commentators credit the craft with between eight and fifteen oars a side.[1]

In the seventeenth century they carried a two-masted lateen rig, with two small guns on the *proda* or fore deck; the quarters were frequently shaped like a galley but without the roof covering. They were popular for the free-booting kind of warfare practised in the Mediterranean at the time, but were severely limited in their seakeeping so were only fair-weather craft. The type was adopted by the French navy in 1669 for a vessel called the *Subtile*, and seven more were built (mostly at Toulon) before 1700 but no dimensions seem to have survived.[2] This may have been a response to corsair attacks on French shipping – meeting fire with fire – or they may have had a more limited coast defence role.

There seems to have been some connection

1. Contemporary illustrations by Jauve de Marselha and C Randon are reproduced in M Vocino, *La Nave nel Tempo* (Rome 1942), p103.

2. P le Conte, *Lists of Men of War 1650–1700, Part II French Ships* (Greenwich 1935).

between the southern *brigantin* and the northern brigantine but the relationship is by no means clear. As used in northern Europe, the term was obviously associated with rowing, since the English brigantines of the 1690s were effectively oared tugs (see Chapter 3), while the Scandinavian navies listed a few brigantines along with their galley forces.[3] The Danish navy introduced *galejer* for the defence of the deeply indented Norwegian coastline in 1654, and although these need not have been exactly of the classic galley type, it is likely that they were at least influenced by Mediterranean technology, as were the Baltic navies in the eighteenth century (see Chapter 6). One vessel, the *Naesvis* of 1688, was distinguished by the description 'brigantine' and was much the same size as Furttenbach's *bergantino*. A couple of brigantines were also built by Sweden in the 1690s, while their forces defeated by the Russians on Lake Ladoga in 1701 consisted of three galleys, three brigantines and two small boats. The appearance of these vessels is uncertain, but later draughts survive for similar craft, namely two Danish 'skerry boats' (*skaerbåde*) of 1769;[4] their length of 54ft by 11ft 6in (Norwegian) was not too far from early seventeenth century measurements and the design showed similar characteristics, except for the quarters, where a small cabin gave more shelter for the commanding officer. Skerry boats were armed with two 2pdr and six ½pdr swivels, and carried ten pairs of oars. Only the rig was radically different, the lateen being supplanted by a more modern fore and aft schooner rig.

American 'galley'

The quasi-war between the USA and France produced a peculiar new class of small naval craft, described as a 'galley'. This term was used very freely in various navies for oared fighting vessels not fitting the mould of the classical full or half-galley and in fact more closely related to the original *brigantin*. A Congressional Act of May 1798 authorised the US Navy Department to build or purchase up to ten galley-type vessels for river and harbour defence, to be manned with naval militia.

3. P Holck and H J Börjeson, *Lists of Men-of-War 1650–1700: Part III Danish/Norwegian Ships and Swedish Ships* (Greenwich 1936).

4. The *Beaveren* in the Rigsarkivet, Copenhagen, and the *Elgen* in the Marinemuseet, Horten, Norway.

5. M Vocino, *op cit*, p103.

6. J H Röding, *Allgemeines Wörterbuch der Marine* (Hamburg 1793), Vol I, p571.

7. Reproduced in W zu Mondfeld, *Die Schebecke und andere Schiffstypen des Mittelmeerraumes* (Bielefeld and Berlin 1974), Pl 23.

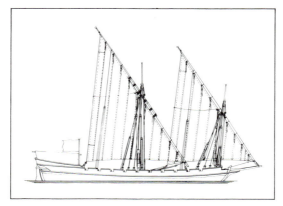

The French felucca with ten pairs of oars from Chapman's Architectura Navalis Mercatoria. *Her relationship to the* brigantin *is clear, and although this vessel appears to be unarmed, there is evidence for craft with swivel guns along the gunwales and even small carriage guns in the bow.* (K H Marquardt)

Joshua Humphreys was commissioned to design the first galley, a vessel of 50ft 6in length bp and 14ft 4in extreme breadth. Armed with an 18pdr in the bow and four 3pdr howitzers mounted along the sides and stern, the draught followed the general concept of the Danish skerry boats from 1769, except for being slightly wider and deeper and carrying a two-masted lateen rig. Similar designs for the use on the Mississippi and western rivers varied from 45ft to 56ft in length. The US Navy considered the galleys as useless and the coastal vessels were disposed of in 1801–2.

Felucca

Feluccas, frequently two-masted and lateen rigged, formed the next group down in size among southern European vessels, and were employed equally in trade and war. Furttenbach described a double-ended craft of six or seven oars to a side with one rower each, no large gun, no *sperone* and the crew doubling as fighting men. An etching by Randon (around 1690),[5] depicting a small Genoese felucca being pursued by a brigantine, reveals a similar beak as for the brigantine, but not the usual two-masted lateen rig. Her rig is single-masted with a spritsail and a jib set to an outrigger. The felucca in Chapman's great work, *Architectura Navalis Mercatoria* of 1768, was designed to carry ten pairs of oars, had a length of 42¾ft and a breadth of 8¼ft. The US Navy bought a felucca in 1814 at New Orleans; she was named *Bulldog* and was armed with two guns. Other contemporary sources suggest slightly larger dimensions, ten to sixteen pairs of oars and a two-masted lateen rig with both masts raking forward by 3 degrees. Röding's detailed description of a felucca equipped for war claims

that such vessels were very strongly built for their size;[6] they carried two 2pdr guns in the bow and thirty-two swivel guns along the broadsides. In the deck were twelve small hatches for the twelve rowers, who sat not on benches as in other vessels but on the hatch coamings, with their feet against foot-rests at half the tween deck height. In the middle of the tween deck was a small passage leading to twelve small cabins on each side for the rowers. The captain's accommodation was at the rear under an awning, stretched over a frame of strong curved timbers. The sides were boarded-in with planks extending far aft, being joined by a small timber displaying the felucca's name. The helmsman stood behind the rudder, with the tiller facing aft, so that its movement did not interfere with the after accommodation.

Tartane

In his short description of a tartane or *tartana* Furttenbach quotes a length of 60–70 *palmi* (14.6m, 48ft–17.0m, 56ft); all other aspects of construction were considered similar to the slightly larger polacre, which was armed with six iron guns. An excellent artistic impression of a seventeenth-century tartane is provided by J Jouve in 1679.[7] Described as a trading vessel, this craft mounted ten swivels and two guns and had a two-masted lateen rig with a fore mast raking forward sharply. More modern vessels, like the French tartane armed with eight 4pdrs and four swivel guns in Chapman's work, had a length of 61ft and a breadth of 17ft.

Generally single-masted with a large lateen sail and a triangular headsail, two-masted tartanes also existed, either in fore-and-main or in main-and-mizzen mast configurations. The latter rig can be noted on models of a French and an Albanian tartane from 1810 at the Musée de la Marine in Paris. Furttenbach attributed the tartane's popularity in the Mediterranean to its easy handling (mercantile versions needed a crew of only ten) and swiftness – qualities which inevitably led to the vessel's adoption by corsairs, privateers and in naval service.

Parancelle

Attacks on American ships and the humiliation of paying tribute to the Barbary coast regents forced the United States to go to war in early 1802 and send a squadron of two frigates, two brigs and three schooners to the Mediterranean. Lacking the support of smaller cruising vessels, the ensuing blockade of Tripoli was not very effective; the frigate *Philadelphia* ran

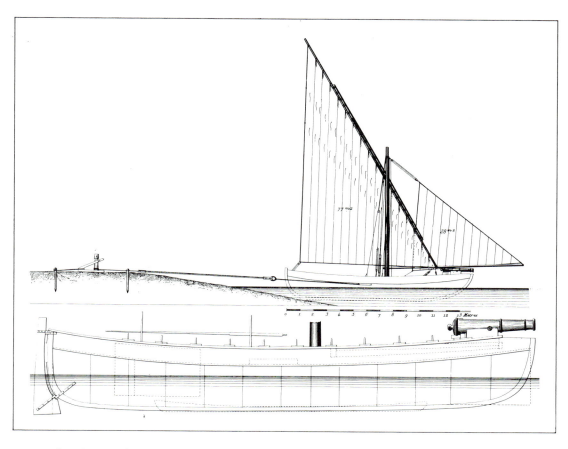

A Neapolitan parancelle rigged gunboat with a single 18pdr gun dating from about 1800. The row of thole pins along the gunwale indicate that the boat was as frequently rowed as sailed. (From Paris' Souvenirs de Marine)

famous *Souvenirs de Marine*. The period 1801 to 1812 in the US Navy has been characterised as the gunboat era, and numerous designs were produced with single- or two-masted lateen rigs but without the hull forms being influenced by Mediterranean types. Commodore Edward Preble himself provided gunboat designs based on enlarged longboat lines with a sliding gunter and a gaff rigged sail plan (see below).

Xebec

For the general reader the term xebec (zebec, chebec or any of a number of forms) is close behind galley as the archetypical description of a Mediterranean sailing craft. The xebec's origin is still very uncertain: legend associates its development with Ali el Uluji (Uluch Ali or Ali the Apostate) who was a Calabrian slave who rose to become supreme commander of the Ottoman navy and Viceroy of Algiers, dying in 1587; but descriptions of xebecs by name have not been found earlier than the eighteenth century. Nevertheless, only a few decades after Ali el Uluji's death Furttenbach described a Turkish vessel he called a *caramuzzal*, which in action and shape could have been an early xebec. He reported that those vessels were nothing but higher sided and more strongly built tartanes – swift sailing vessels, used largely by Turks and Barbary corsairs in the Mediterra-

aground and was subsequently captured by the Tripolitans with more than three hundred American sailors taken prisoner, whereupon the lack of bomb vessels and gunboats for an attack on the city and its harbour became really apparent. Despite Stephen Decatur's daring raid on Tripoli harbour which burnt the frigate, the American Commodore, Edward Preble, was still forced to acquire six gunboats and two 'bombards' (mortar vessels) from the Government of the Two Sicilies for an assault on the harbour to force the Pasha into freeing his prisoners. The Tripolitans had eleven gunboats in position when it finally came to battle on 3 August 1804 and these six Sicilian vessels, known in the US Navy as the Messina gunboats, made their claim on history with Decatur's attack against overwhelming odds.

The rig of these boats was listed as parancelle (or *paranzello*), a Neapolitan version of the tartane. They had a long 24pdr mounted in the bow and the official length of keel was 56ft 6in, with a beam of 18ft 5in. Single-masted and lateen rigged, these vessels carried a large jib

on an outrigger and could be rowed with ten pairs of oars. Similarly rigged but shorter in length were the three captured Tripolitan gunboats taken into American service and numbered, following on from the purchased six, 7, 8 and *9*. *No 9* had a length of keel of 31ft 1in and a beam of 14ft and compares closely with another eighteenth-century Sicilian gunboat of parancelle type reproduced in Admiral Paris's

Chapman's Algerian xebec from Architectura Navalis Mercatoria *shows the obviously galley-derived hull forms of the early versions – furthermore, the ship's heaviest weapons, four 12pdrs, were equipped to fire forward in galley fashion. The xebec retained the ability to employ nine pairs of oars when necessary.*

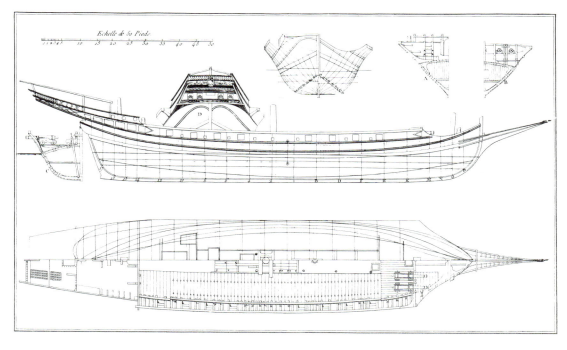

A polacre rigged xebec privateer of 22 guns dated 1784 from Paris' Souvenirs de Marine. By this date the hull is more ship-like, and the lateen mizzen is the sole survivor of the original fore and aft rig.

nean to prey on Christian shipping during the summer months when the sea was generally calm. Armed with eighteen (and often more) guns and manned with fifty to sixty well-equipped corsairs (probably in addition to the sailing crew), those vessels were superior to most contemporary merchant ships.

When comparing plans of eighteenth-century xebecs with those of their smaller relatives, a definite family resemblance can be found. With the long beak-like prow and the overhanging rear platform the appearance was that of a stretched tartane. Early xebecs had a considerable flare above the waterline, which may suggest a development from the *apostis* or outrigger of the galley. In his *Marine Dictionary* of 1769, Falconer described a xebec as being similar to a polacre in rig, but very different in hull shape from that and almost every other type of vessel. Generally equipped as a corsair, the xebec was constructed with a narrow floor for swiftness and considerable breadth to enable it to carry a great press of sail. As these vessels were very low-built, their decks had a much larger camber than normal to help the water to run off. Since a deck of such convexity made it difficult to walk on, gratings extended from the centreline to the gunwales.

Depending on wind and weather, xebecs were sailed in one of three different modes: very wide square sails were set on the main and sometimes also on the fore mast in a quartering or following wind; when the wind was further forward, the square yards and sails were replaced with large lateen sails; heavy weather would see them lowered again and shorter yards with proportionally sized lateen sails hoisted on all masts. These methods of changing sails instead of reefing were common to nearly all Mediterranean lateen rigged vessels. When Falconer said that the sails of the xebec are in general similar to those of the polacre, he must have had in mind some of the French xebecs from after the mid-eighteenth century; these were polacre rigged for easier handling, but with the change these vessels lost a lot of their flexibility.

Xebecs were added to every naval power in

8. Vice-Admiral E Paris, *Souvenirs de Marine* (Paris 1884), Vol II, Pl 78.

9. *Ibid*, Pl 90.

10. *Ibid*, Vol I, Pl 25.

the Mediterranean during the eighteenth century, not only to fight piracy but also as well armed and fast-sailing cruisers. Details of a Spanish xebec from 1735 point to a length between stem and sternpost of 103ft 9in, a moulded breadth of 22ft and a depth in hold of 8ft 2in. In armament and shape this vessel was very similar to the very well known and slightly larger Algerian xebec published in Chapman's work from 1768. Chapman's drawing documented the xebec as it was in the first half-century, with widely projecting sides, a steeply turtlebacked deck and guns in the bow. He probably obtained these draughts during his period of study in France (1755–6).

French xebecs appeared as part of the navy around 1750 and a draught titled 'Chebec de 1750 à 1786'[8] as well as the similar draught of *Le Requin* from 1752 reveal not only a reduction in the flared sides of the former, but also the disappearance of the bow chasers. The *Mistique* (about 1750–86),[9] a smaller xebec, had no additional flare and the sheer line ran uninterrupted to the stem; the deck camber was also reduced to a slightly exaggerated rounding up of the beams. The lateen rig of the previously mentioned xebecs was replaced on this vessel with an early form of polacre rig. Another two xebecs, the *Caméléon* and the *Séduisant*, armed with twenty 8pdrs, were built in 1762. A further development of the trend is visible in Jouvin's 22-gun xebec of 1784.[10] Here the deck had a normal rounding of beams and the mast plan was changed to a more developed square

rigged polacre with the shrouds fitted to channels. There were never large numbers in service (two in 1780) and xebecs began to disappear from the French naval scene after the peace of 1815 and none survived after about 1840 (according to Paris). Their principal place of construction was always Toulon.

A draught at the Museo Maritimo, Barcelona, reveals a different line of evolution.[11] This Spanish xebec from 1765–70 with thirty guns and twenty swivels still retained the long stern overhang and the long beak (*sperone* or, in French, *berthelot*), but the hull followed the general shape of a frigate. The main frame was no longer flared but had a tumblehome of about 10 per cent of its extreme breadth, a decked forecastle and a quarterdeck from the main mast aft. The forward raking main and fore mast indicate a lateen rig. Approximate dimensions for the 1765 xebec (English measurements) were: length bp 113ft 11in, breadth moulded 30ft 10in, depth in hold 11ft 1in.

The building centre for Spanish xebecs was the island of Majorca, but presumably expertise also existed on Minorca for the only xebec actually constructed for the Royal Navy was built at Port Mahon in 1778 when the island was under British occupation. Although lateen rigged, the appropriately named *Minorca* had a hull form similar to a contemporary British sloop of war. She measured 96ft 9in on the gundeck by 30ft 6in breadth for 388 tons, and was armed with eighteen 6pdrs and twenty swivels.

Reports of naval action between Russian ships and the Turkish fleet in the latter half of the eighteenth century repeatedly mention the use of numerous xebecs in the Turkish navy. Generally listed after frigates, these reports point to a strong reliance on xebecs as fast reconnaissance vessels in the Turkish fleet. They were also acquired in greater numbers as part of the rebuilding of the Turkish navy after the defeat at Chesma (1770) and for the second Russo-Turkish war of 1787–94 several reports of xebec involvement in naval actions exist. The Turkish main battlefleet, for example, in its 1788 engagement with the Sevastopol squadron of Count Voinovich, had twenty-one xebecs in its order of battle.[12]

Russia's Baltic galley fleet adopted a few xebecs about 1760 for warfare in the Gulf of Bothnia (Chapman's new 'skerries frigates' can be seen as a response to those Russian efforts), and some were still available during the second battle of Svensksund in July 1790. The Swedish navy, with Chapman's innovative craft available, considered xebecs unsuitable for the harsher weather conditions of the Baltic. Denmark, however, had one or more built at Toulon in 1771 as a response to others in the Baltic. A draught of the Danish naval xebec *Lindormen* exists in the Rigsarkivet, Copenhagen. She was laid out for twenty-two guns on the main deck and had a quarterdeck of similar proportions to that of the Spanish xebec from 1765 mentioned previously. Her measurements in English feet were: 127ft 2in bp by 31ft 8in moulded. Her mast arrangement, with the mizzen mast stepped relatively far forward, suggests the proposed rig must have been that of an earlier polacre, or as Steel called it, a polacre-settee rig.

A few xebecs were even built in North America during the Revolution and one in 1812 at Baltimore as a privateer.[13] Howard Chapelle regarded the *Champion* and the *Repulse* as the most important; they carried two long 24pdrs, two 18pdrs and four 9pdrs and were part of the Pennsylvania State Navy gunboat flotilla. Both were employed when the British forces moved against Philadelphia and destroyed to prevent capture. Nothing is known of their measurements or their appearance.

Xebec armament generally ranged from sixteen to thirty guns (usually 6pdrs or 8pdrs in French vessels), although late examples might carry as many as forty. Chapman gives a most detailed account of the twenty-eight guns in an Algerian xebec, with four 12pdr bow chasers, sixteen 6pdrs on the broadsides, eight 3pdrs on the quarterdeck and thirty musketoons (large calibre muskets fitted on swivels). Estimates of manning levels varied from the grossly exaggerated (Falconer spoke of 300 to 450 men, two-thirds of them soldiers) to Furttenbach's 50 to 60 corsairs, although he may not have been counting the pure seamen of the crew. The truth is probably in between, at around 130 to 150, which would compare with similarly armed sloops of war. Indeed, in Mediterranean navies xebecs seem to have been the rough equivalents of Northern sloops or corvettes, although privateer and corsair vessels probably carried a larger complement to provide prize crews.

Barks

A familiar sight off the French Mediterranean coast from about 1670, naval barks were three-masted, lateen rigged broad-beamed vessels, normally built for mercantile ventures, but serving in the French navy in a coastguard role. They ranged from about 22.1m (72½ft) around 1670 to 31.85m (104½ft) in 1770 but always had a length:beam ratio of approximately 3.5:1. Differing from xebecs in being broader, square sterned with a more pronounced quarterdeck and built with tumblehome, naval barks were usually armed with 6pdr guns, increasing in number from ten in 1670 to eighteen in the last vessels. Rigs were similar to xebecs, with the exception of having a long outrigger protruding over the stern for the mizzen sail sheet; barks could also have been polacre rigged.

There were never many of these vessels in French service – usually not more than two to four at a time – and all operated from Toulon. A navy list from 1669 includes two unnamed 'barques'; in 1675 there were four and a 1719 report mentioned two by name, *La Conception* and *Le Saint Jean-Gaetan*. The building of

The French privateer bark Fileuse *built at Marseille in 1778 by a navy* ingénieur–constructeur *Victor Jouvin, a protégé of the great Coulomb who had built a number for the French navy at Toulon.* Fileuse *was armed with sixteen 4pdrs and had a crew of forty.*

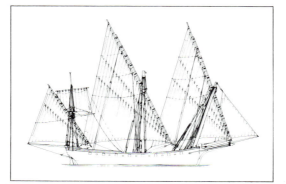

barks for naval service was abandoned in 1775 in favour of corvettes, the last bark being *L'Eclair*, launched in 1771.

Spritsail and half-sprit

Dutch smak

Turning away from the Mediterranean to northern waters, the earliest fore and aft rig with naval applications was probably the spritsail. Perhaps the starting point for the fighting career of the spritsail was the makeshift force of the Dutch 'Sea Beggars' during their late sixteenth-century struggle for independence from Spain. These were simple river and coastal craft, converted into fighting ships, known to Dutch history as 'the small fleet of smak sails', a name deriving from the rig on the larger of those vessels (a main spritsail and a mizzen [smak] lateen sail). Armament usually consisted of two forward-firing larger guns and some smaller weapons on the broadside. The Dutch developed these small craft during their wars of independence into formidable fighting machines, known in the Elizabethan English navy as cromsters, where they served as coastal guardships. Cromster may have derived from *kromsteven* or *cromsteven* (*crom* = bent, concave; *steven* = stem), a name given to an earlier Dutch craft.

Also known as *watt-convoyers*, similar craft were employed after about 1665 (first known date) by the City of Emden to accompany merchantmen to Bremen, Hamburg or other harbours along the Lower Saxony coastline, known as the Watt or Wadde; during the last years of the seventeenth century the City of Bremen also had such a craft (armed with four guns) in its service. Nothing is known about their size, but the Dutch artist Reinier Nooms produced an etching around 1650–60 of a smak rigged armed vessel he described as an *uytlegger* or *Watte Convoyer* (guardship or Wadden convoy ship).[14] The only real difference between

11. Reproduced in Howard I Chapelle, *The Search for Speed under Sail* (New York and London 1983), p137.

12. D W Mitchell, *A History of Russian and Soviet Sea Power* (London 1974), p75.

13. Howard I Chapelle, *The Search for Speed*, p132.

14. Reproduced in I de Groot and R Vorstman, *Sailing Ships: Prints by Dutch masters from the sixteenth to the nineteenth century* (Maarssen 1980), p83.

A Dutch smak rigged naval auxiliary attending a warship during the Battle of Scheveningen, 1653 (detail from an engraving by the Elder van de Velde). The mizzen sail is furled but its mast is visible before the ensign staff. (NMM)

(1647–1728) of the River Orwell with Landguard Fort provides a missing link in regard to these early English Revenue smacks. Probably dating from the late seventeenth century, this drawing depicts a man of war, two brigantines and a small Customs smack, recognisable by the jack flown at the end of her long bowsprit; her rig was that of a half-sprit and a lateen mizzen, with no square topsail visible. The vessel clearly shows Dutch influence and suggests that the early English smack had more in common with its Continental namesake than just the name.

Between 1660 and 1702 the Royal Navy employed seven smacks, ranging from the purchased *Royal Escape* (the collier *Surprise* in which Charles II escaped after the battle of Worcester) to Dockyard-built craft of 16 to 30 tons. They were all tenders and most were unarmed; a van de Velde illustration of the *Royal Escape* makes it clear that she carried a single-masted half-sprit rig and the others were probably similar.

Brief mention should also be made of the mysterious *patache*, sometimes associated with the guardship and coastal convoy duties of the *Watt-convoyer*.[15] It may be Portuguese in origin – that country's Navy List indicated that the *patacho* was smaller than the *fregata* – but very little else is known of them. Falconer (1769) defined *patache* in his French index as an armed tender, or vessel which attends a ship of war or fleet; also a packet boat. A quarter of a century later in 1794 Röding referred to a *patache* as a Portuguese two-masted merchant vessel, but understood in France to apply to small armed vessels which guarded the entrance to harbours and examined incoming and outgoing merchant ships.

Yacht

When first employed the Dutch term *jacht* had no automatic connotations of a pleasure craft but merely implied a swift sailing smaller ship; certainly there were *speel-jachts* for sport, but equally there were *oorlog-jachts* for war. The *oorlog-jacht Neptunus*, built in 1595 for Prince Maurice of Orange, was the warring Dutch leader's flagship. She was rigged in similar fashion to the *watt-convoyer*, with a main sprit-

this and earlier cromsters or *oorloge convoyerts* was a cutwater with figurehead, a topsail and a standing gaff (or half-sprit) rig on the main mast of the later vessel. Nicolaas Witsen described these ships as fitted out for war and operating in shoal waters; they had a flat transom stern and sometimes carried leeboards. Their sail plan comprised a main mast with a gaff sail and a mizzen (lateen) sail.

In England the larger vessels in the employ of seventeenth-century Revenue (Customs) Service were known as smacks. How far these

smacks resembled the cromsters of earlier years cannot be ascertained, but there were similarities in their coastal and estuary work, and possibly also in their rig. A smack's rig differed from that of a catch or ketch by having the main mast sprit rigged instead of square. The second half of the seventeenth century saw a change on both sides of the North Sea from a sprit to a half-sprit sail (a long standing gaff without a boom) and English smacks came to be characterised by a single mast. However, a small topographical drawing by Francis Place

15. Anon, *Der Geöffnete See-Hafen* (Hamburg 1705).

The van de Velde painting of the Royal Escape, *a small collier purchased by Charles II on his Restoration. Despite the decorated gunports, the mercantile build is evident.* (NMM)

sail and a smaksail on her mizzen mast. A second yacht, armed with 10 guns and built in 1614, was portrayed in Vroom's well-known painting 'The arrival of the *Prince Royal* at Flushing, 8 May 1613'; she was single masted and can be seen as the forefather of all subsequent state or naval yachts.

In the early years of the Netherlands *jachts* provided transport for officials and dispatches, reconnaissance and scouting for the battlefleet but were also a mainstay of inshore defence. Until about 1660 they usually carried a single-masted sprit rig, mostly with a bowsprit but in some cases without, gradually changing to a half-sprit, or standing gaff, rig. Their armament consisted of six to twelve 3pdrs in most cases. Yachts were a formal part of the Dutch fleet until 1843, when the navy minister of the day, J C Rijk, ordered their abandonment. However, long before their demise yachts had provided a fertile inspiration for the development of a number of other naval craft.

The employment of yachts in other fleets became widespread in the early decades of the seventeenth century. The large numbers of yachts in Danish-Norwegian and Swedish naval service make it clear that the lessons learned by the Dutch in inshore attack and defence did not go unnoticed in maritime nations with similar defence problems. Of the fifty-six yachts in Swedish service before 1700 little more is generally known than the name and the year of their first appearance in lists. The earliest notice of a 'jagt' was the *Duvan* in 1633, and several of the later yachts are known to have been built in Stockholm or Karlskrona.

A review of Dutch yachts before Czar Peter the Great. This painting by Abraham Storck reveals the main features as well as the rigging variety of Dutch yachts at the end of the seventeenth century. Some have the long half-sprit or standing gaff, while others set their main sails from a much shorter hoisting spar. For such a prestigious occasion, these would be the largest yachts the Dutch states could muster, the equivalent of the royal yachts of other countries. (NMM)

The royal yacht *Lejonet*, the second of that name, was built in Amsterdam in 1669 and her dimensions have been preserved by Nicolaas Witsen; her stern also features in a drawing by van de Velde the Elder.

Fifty Danish-Norwegian *jakt*s were listed between the *Jomfrusvend* of 1633 and 1700 but it is not known if they were built in the Dutch Style. Norwegian 'jekts' derived from their own native shipbuilding tradition and were square rigged, whilst the slightly different term *jakt* seems to have described a fore and aft rigged vessel. The earliest vessel for which some data survives was the *Papegoejen* from 1657; she carried four to eight guns, had a length of 46ft 6in Danish (47ft 10in English) and a breadth of 10ft 9in (11ft 1in).

Yachts became popular with the ruling aristocracy all over northern Europe during the seventeenth century. The Elector of Brandenburg had his first yacht built in 1652 in Amsterdam, a vessel with ten guns used mainly as a personal transport and pleasure craft. The Elector's second yacht, known only as the 'Elector's Large Yacht', was built in Kolberg in 1678 and carried eight to ten guns. Her dimensions were: length bp 70ft Dutch (65ft English), beam 21ft (19ft 6in); she was broken up in 1721. Three other smaller yachts were later added to the Brandenburg fleet. Another

The English royal yacht Mary *arriving with Princess Mary at Gravesend, 1689. Although most English yachts carried the same half-sprit rig of their Dutch predecessors, the hull form was more ship-like. In fact, many were formally regarded as Sixth Rates and played an active part in many of the wars of the late seventeenth century.* (NMM)

yacht, built in 1707 in Amsterdam for the Elector's son, King Frederick I of Prussia, is worth mentioning for her *watt-convoyer* rig.[16]

A small Dutch state yacht, presented by the Burghers of Amsterdam in 1660 to England's returning King Charles II, formed the nucleus of an ever extending English fleet of pleasure craft. The *Mary* was of 52ft in length, 19ft in beam and 100 tons, carrying eight guns. Besides the *Mary* and the *Bezan*, both given to the King, twenty-four yachts were built in England during the reign of Charles II – though some were for official Admiralty use rather than for the royal court – and Sir Anthony Deane also built two similar yachts for the French king. Sailing was greatly enjoyed by Charles II and his brother the Duke of York, so English yachts were generally built for pleasure; the court also enjoyed gambling so that sailing soon became highly competitive, and from their numerous races the modern sport of yachting is ultimately derived. Experimentation with hull shapes and rigging in pursuit of this rivalry led to faster sailing small craft to the advantage of the Royal Navy as a whole.

Royal patronage of the great father-and-son team of marine artists, the van de Veldes, ensured that these are among the most heavily depicted craft of all time. They were originally rigged with the half-sprit main (although the smallest had the short-gaff bezan rig – see 'Sloop' below), a couple of jibs and, in favourable conditions, a square topsail set flying. Later vessels were ketch rigged, with square main and topsail and a lateen mizzen – the *Fubbs* of 1682 was probably the first, and Charles, taking credit for applying the rig to

yachts, regarded her as the fastest of his yachts. Later craft carried main topgallants and even crossed a square mizzen topsail. Hull development tended towards greater length and lower topsides, while only the original Dutch gifts carried leeboards.

In the contemporary confusion between what belonged to the king and what belonged to the nation, the status of yachts was ambiguous since they were partly paid for out of the king's privy purse, but naval manned and actively employed in wartime as scouts, advice boats and even small cruisers. Conversely, certain small Sixth Rates, like the *Greyhound*, *Saudadoes* and later the *Peregrine Galley*, regularly saw service as yachts, so the gradual shift to a ship rig is understandable. After 1688 the number of royal yachts was reduced but the craft themselves became larger. However, something of the original Stuart style was carried on in the yachts built for use by Admiralty and government officials; most of these craft were single-masted and fore and aft rigged but in general did not see service as warships.[17]

Gaff

Sloop

'Sloop' is one of the most confusing of all ship

16. An etching by J L v Wolfgang depicting this vessel is reproduced in G C E Crone, *De Jachten der Oranjes* (Amsterdam 1937).

17. G P B Naish, *Royal Yachts* (London 1964).

type definitions in English: it was used by the Royal Navy as a generic classification for ships below the usual six Rates whose captain was a Master and Commander (see Chapter 3), but it also came to denote a rig, although there was no consensus on its precise characteristics until modern times.[18] For the sake of this section the sloop is regarded as a single-masted vessel with a gaff (and sometimes boom) main sail, in combination with a standing bowsprit, triangular headsails and possibly a square topsail. This can be considered a creation of the late seventeenth and early eighteenth centuries.

The fore and aft sloop rig evolved from the bezan rigged yacht, of which the earliest known draught is dated 1657, with the earliest bowsprit rigged example ('Yacht of the Prince of Orange') appearing in a painting by Verschuier depicting Charles II's arrival at Rotterdam in 1660; this carried what was known in eighteenth century England as the Bermudes (or Bermudian) rig. The origin of this name is obscure and it cannot be established when the associated rig (raked mast, short gaff and long boom, as well as overly long bowsprit) appeared first, but the rig, without an obvious mast rake, was known in England from at least 1661, when a second Dutch yacht, named *Bezan* after her rig, was given to Charles II. This yacht type was considerably smaller than the state yachts and at least six other yachts of similar size to the former (35 tons) carried that rig during his reign. The use of this single-masted short gaff/boom rig was already widespread in Dutch merchant shipping, and could have been as easily transplanted to the Bermudian sloop as the two-masted Dutch *speel-jacht* rig was to earlier Bermudian boats. Captain John Smith explained in his 1619–21 *Generall Historie . . .* that a skilled Dutch boatbuilder shipwrecked at Bermuda was forcibly detained by the Governor, since the colony was in great need of boats.

The bowsprit also appeared in a painting by Sailmaker, 'The East India Company yard in the Thames' of about 1670 and in a van de Velde the Younger painting from 1686. Thereafter most of the iconographical evidence for the naval employment of sloops emanates from North America. E P Morris[19] points to another bowsprit rigged sloop in a crude sketch from the *Journal of a Voyage to New York* (1679–80) by Danckaerts and Sluyter. This sketch probably represents an English bezan yacht, since it carried not only an ensign but also a jack, the usual sign of a naval vessel. One of the earliest (probably the first) well presented illustrations of fore and aft rigged sloops is a print by William Burgis, 'View of New York'

W A Baker's interpretation of Burgis' 'Sloop off Boston Light' (c1725) reveals a loose-footed main sail with a short gaff and long boom; the square topsail yard is fitted with footropes. Howard Chapelle argued that this vessel resembled the British sloops of the Ferret class (1711), and his version of this drawing has a naval stemhead with figure, but the prominent quarterdeck is not a feature of this class (see Chapter 3).

from 1717, showing about twenty sloops of which nine are flying a jack or sporting a jack staff. Ten guns can be counted on one and others are firing guns; none has a square topsail. Another British sloop with twelve guns in a second print from about 1725 by the same artist, 'Sloop off Boston Light', also has the typical Bermudes rig, and no topsail yard.

There is not much evidence that the purpose-built Royal Navy sloops of war were ever single-masted (see Chapter 3). For vessels of naval design, the sloop rig was confined to tenders and auxiliaries, some of which saw frontline service on occasions – the tiny 35-ton *Culloden* of 1746, for example, was employed in Scotland in support of the anti-Jacobite 'Pacification' policy; in 1759 a Portsmouth hoy was converted to serve as the local guardship/ floating battery *Goree* in West Africa; and two 42-ton craft were built for service in Newfoundland in 1789. However, many visual sources show sloop rigged vessels with naval pendants, particularly in American waters. One possible explanation of the apparently naval jack and pennant is that the craft depicted are revenue cruisers: the early vessels were described as sloops and although there was lively debate about the authority to wear a pendant, many craft did so whether legal or not.[20] However, many mercantile vessels were hired or purchased in wartime by both the Royal Navy and the American colonial governments so the sloops represented in these illustrations were presumably taken up from trade. As an

example, the first documented American-built sloop in British service was the *Mediator*, a vessel of 105 tons constructed in Virginia in 1741–2, and armed with ten carriage guns and eighteen swivels. She was purchased in the West Indies early in 1745 but served in Europe, being sunk at Ostend. The vessel was very similar in measurements and shape to the Bermuda sloop in Chapman's work.

Armed sloops operated by the Americans during the War of Independence, some of which were formed in the Bermuda mould, included the *Hornet* (ten guns), *Providence* (six to twelve guns), *Sachem* (ten guns), *Independence* (ten guns) and *Mosquito* (four guns). A few additional vessels were purchased or captured, but after its early popularity in the American colonies, the sloop rig was not widely adopted by the newly formed US Navy. Soon after independence the US Revenue Cutter Service was founded and among the first ten vessels commissioned in 1791 were two sloops. The *Argus* was launched as a 35-ton schooner at New London, but her size was later increased to 48 tons and the rig changed to a sloop. The *Vigilant*, built at New York, was also a 35-ton schooner whose rig was altered to that of a sloop before she was sold out of service in 1798. The first *Massachusetts*, a schooner of poor sailing qualities, was replaced in 1793 by a small sloop of the same name built at Cohassat. She was the only vessel built as a sloop for the Revenue Service, a marked preference being shown for the schooner.[21]

By 1794 Röding could speak of this rig as being used mainly in England and America but to a lesser extent by the Baltic nations. Chapman provided a draught and dimensions of a 72-ton privateer sloop of 62ft 9in length and an armament of eight 3pdr carriage guns on the broadsides and two 6pdr bow chasers; seven pairs of sweeps served for extra manoeuvrability. Chapman widely employed the sloop rig for many of the vessels he designed for the Inshore Fleet[22] and one may note that by this point, in common with so many ship type descriptions, sloop now defines a rig as much as a hull form.

18. See Blanckley's exasperated comment in his *Naval Expositor* of 1750 that sloops were 'sailed and masted as Men's Fancies lead them, sometimes with one Mast, with two, and with three . . .'

19. *The Fore and Aft Rig in America* (New Haven 1927), p70.

20. G Smith, *King's Cutters: The Revenue Service and the War against Smuggling* (London 1983), pp17–18.

21. I H King, *The Coast Guard under Sail: The US Revenue Cutter Service 1789–1865* (Annapolis 1989), p13.

22. Daniel G Harris, *F H Chapman: The First Naval Architect and his Work* (London 1989).

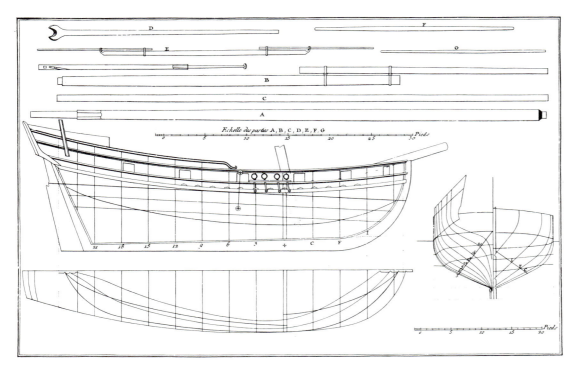

Chapman's plans from Architectura Navalis Mercatoria *of a Bermudian sloop, which he regarded as a warship (ten 4pdrs and twelve swivels). The spars shown are: A. mast; B. bowsprit and jibboom; C. boom; D. gaff; E. crossjack with studdingsail booms; F. square topsail yard; G. topgallant yard. His comment is 'a vessel often used in West Indian waters'.*

there were several with a sloop rig. The Tripolitan gunboats captured in 1804 and added as *Nos* 7, 8 and 9 to Preble's gunboat flotilla were re-rigged by the Americans as sloops. Josiah Fox designed several gunboats with two large guns on a circular traversing mounting (24pdrs) and the gunboats *13* to *16*, built in 1805–6 for service at New Orleans, are known to have been sloop rigged. Their length bp was 71ft; usually double-ended they were also equipped with fifteen pairs of sweeps.[23]

23. Howard I Chapelle, *The History of the American Sailing Navy* (New York 1949), p209.

The rig became common on a variety of naval small craft from the late eighteenth century. Admiral Paris, in his famous work, provided drawings of a number of Dutch vessels, described as gunboats, landing-boats and coastal guardships, usually in the shape of the flat-bottomed, full-bodied coastal craft with leeboards, rigged with a shorter boom (not extending beyond the sternpost). These craft were built at Amsterdam in 1803–4, measuring about 40 to 50ft bp and usually armed with one or two forward-firing carriage guns. They may all have been associated with Napoleon's planned invasion of England, but as late as 1835 there were two classes of single-masted gaff rigged gunboats listed in the Dutch navy; their armament consisted of one or two 18pdrs forward, two 8pdrs aft and three swivels. The last of these gunboats was built in 1855 at Amsterdam.

Twenty British gunboats on Lake Champlain in 1776–7 during the American War of Independence were gaff rigged. They were small open double-ended craft with only one forward mounted long 18pdr, a length bp of 37ft and were additionally propelled by seven pairs of oars. Among the vessels in the American gunboat fleet during the period 1801–12,

A contemporary model of a British cutter showing all the principal sails carried by these vessels, including the square course hoisted inside the deeply roached topsail. The model has eighteen guns and sixteen swivels, rather more than was usually carried, and although it bears the inscription 'The Hawke cutter', it does not seem to represent an actual naval vessel. (NMM)

This drawing by Admiral Paris almost certainly represents the Puce, *the prototype French cutter built by Denÿs at Dunkirk. She was armed with six 3pdrs and is very similar to English models in hull form.*

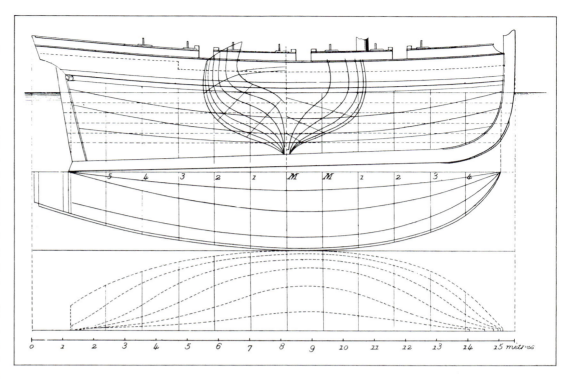

Cutter

The cutter was a uniquely English development, traceable back to at least the second quarter of the eighteenth century. The description originally applied to a hull form, so although the rig resembled that of a sloop, the vessels would have been clearly differentiated in the mind of a seaman. Closely associated with the Channel ports of Kent and Sussex, the original characteristic of a cutter was its light clinker-built hull. The sloop had a ship-like hull form, often with stepped decks and an elevated rear cabin and an ornamented cutwater, in conjunction with a length:breadth ratio of approximately 3.3:1; the cutter, by contrast, showed an uninterrupted deck, a plain stem without embellishment, a length:breadth ratio of 2.5 to 2.8:1, a deeper and sharper midsection compared with a sloop of similar size, and she was built for speed – despite being wider she had finer lines than a sloop and less freeboard, enabling her to set a larger area of sail. Cutters often trimmed substantially by the stern (they drew far more water aft than forward), and later vessels were of carvel construction or clinker up to the wales and carvel above.

Besides hull differences, the cutter also carried a rig which was a distinct variation on the sloop as understood at the time. Whilst a cutter mast had an integrated topmast section but a separate topgallant mast, later sloops tended to have fidded (separate) topmasts. The sloop's bowsprit was usually permanently fixed on the centreline at a relatively steep angle, whereas the cutter had a near-horizontal running bowsprit to one side of the stemhead that could be housed (brought inboard). The cutter's lower mast was also taller in relation to its full height, making for a larger gaff main sail; consequently, the higher fore stay meant that the square topsail needed a deeply roached (cutaway) foot, producing a characteristic appearance in eighteenth-century cutters. To fill the large gap between the foot of the topsail and the spread yard, a comparatively small square sail would temporarily be hoisted to a horse on a short yard at the level of the hounds. After 1800 the stay was rigged at a lower position, with the result that the topsail roach became more conventional. A square sail was then only taken up to the spread yard, sometimes hoisted without its own yard.

From the beginning the cutter's speed made it a favourite with illicit traders. The expression 'smuggling cutter' was already general currency by 1747, but on the right side of the law, cutters served in the Revenue (Customs and Excise) Services on anti-smuggling duties, being first mentioned in June 1744, when the twenty-four vessels of the Service were described as 'Yachts, Wherries, Sloops and Cutters'.[24] The last named had a crew of about thirty, six to eight guns and some swivels. Such was the potential nuisance of cutters in the wrong hands that those used for trade were forbidden by law to carry as tall a rig as revenue vessels, so that they would be unable to escape. From the Revenue Service to the Royal Navy was a short step, and cutters were soon employed in war as coastal cruisers, inshore scouting vessels and dispatch boats.

A letter of 20 September 1745 from Horace Walpole mentioned that the Royal Navy had hired 'Folkstone Cutters', the usual official description of these craft, although they were built in other ports as well.[25] Hired cutters were augmented by purchased vessels from 1762 and by October 1764 there were thirty-eight cutters on the Navy List. One of these early vessels was *Fly*, bought into the Royal Navy in 1763; she had an overall length of 51ft 6in, an extreme breadth of 20ft 10½in and a measurement of 78 tons, armed with twelve carriage guns and fitted with eight sweep ports a side.[26] With the usual peacetime resolve to suppress smuggling, the Navy began to design its own in 1763, with four constructed in the Royal Dockyards and three by specialist builders in Folkestone and Broadstairs; they varied in detail but all were about 85 tons and measured around 48ft–55ft on the deck and carried four to six small carriage guns. The cutter was also attracting attention abroad, and the first experiments with that type of vessel on the other side of the Channel took place in 1756 when Sieur Denÿs, a Dunkirk boatbuilder, constructed a small clinker cutter, the *Tiercelet*, as a coastguard vessel. Nothing is known of her dimensions, but she carried six 4pdrs. Prior to this, in 1747, the Amsterdam Admiralty had already ordered two cutters to be purchased in England, with more vessels to be built in Holland.[27]

The French navy was singularly short of small craft suitable for northern waters and in 1770, nearly a decade after cutters became part of the Royal Navy, a decision was taken by the French Court to direct the navy to construct their first eight cutters at Dunkirk and Bordeaux, following the successful methods of the British, and therefore clinker-built. One was built by the experienced Denÿs at Dunkirk, but the others were constructed by naval *ingenieur-constructeurs* at St Malo and Bordeaux. They were all about 48ft bp, measured around 67

24. G Smith, *op cit*, p50.

25. Howard I Chapelle, *The Search for Speed*, p75.

26. Draught reproduced in D MacGregor, *Fast Sailing Ships 1775–1875* (Lymington 1973), pp30–1.

27. W V Cannenburg, *Beschrijvende Catalogus der Scheepsmodellen en Scheepsbouwkundige Teekeningen 1600–1900* (Amsterdam 1943), p28.

A Baugean engraving of a large Dutch cutter of the Napoleonic Wars period. Note the topgallant yard; the main sail furl suggests that it was not lashed along the length of the boom but merely extended loose-footed by it.

tons and were armed with six 3pdr carriage guns, ten swivels and were equipped with eighteen oars.

The draught of an early English cutter but of a slightly larger size than *Fly* appeared in *Architectura Navalis Mercatoria*, and it is not surprising that Chapman designed a few cutters for the Swedish navy. These followed a trend towards greatly enhanced size and they were not regarded as successful. The British naval cutters of the 1770s reached 180 tons and a 70ft length on deck; the armament of ten or twelve 4pdrs were strong enough for *Alert* and *Rattlesnake* to be rated as sloops for a period. Unfortunately, the sails and gear of a single-masted vessel of this size become very difficult to handle, so even for strongly manned naval craft the rig is not very efficient.

The French took the process to extremes. Despite very little native experience with cutters, a series of four of the *Pilote* class built by Denÿs in 1779–80 were 212 tons and carried fourteen 6pdrs. A second group of nine, the *Levrette* class, measured an enormous 300 tons and were armed with eighteen 6pdrs. This new class was inspired by the capture of the British cutter *Wasp* in 1778, taken into the French navy as *Guêpe*. Dissatisfaction with these unhandy giants was quick to manifest itself, and of the six cutters built by Segondat between 1780 and 1781 at Lorient, only one was completed as a cutter, one being schooner rigged and four rigged as brigs. After complaints in 1779 from *Chevreuil's* and *Hussard's* commanders about their vessels' mediocre speed and their inability to catch small British privateers, a conversion to brig rig was granted for four of Denÿs' 300-ton cutters. Two of the 212-ton cutters were also re-rigged as brigs in 1782. A protest at this treatment from Denÿs claimed that his cutters sailed well and their being not equal to British cutters was caused by being overloaded with netting on the upperworks, by being over-manned and by having too much tophamper of every sort. He also cited the ex-British cutter *Frélon*, an excellent sailer before she came to Calais in 1778, but after her upperworks had been heightened and the number as well as the calibre of her guns increased, she turned out to be very mediocre. Two cutters of the *Levrette* class, the *Espion* and the *Fanfaron* were built in 1781, these being the last, whereupon the short French love affair with the naval cutter came to an end.[28]

The rig survived for the occasional tender: a list of French ships afloat on 1 April 1850 still included an unarmed cutter of 134 tons, the *Favori*, built by Allix in 1842.

Revenue cutters also grew in size and numbers. By 1780 the British Revenue Service numbered forty-two vessels with an average of 120 tons, with another six cutters being operated by the Excise Service. Some of the largest British revenue cutters ever built date from this period, but it is noteworthy that none reached the size of the French 300-tonners. They included the *Repulse* of Colchester, of 180 tons with a crew of forty-one, mounting sixteen 3pdr or 4pdr carriage guns plus twelve swivels, built in 1778; the *Rose* of Southampton, a 190-tonner; the *Tartar* of Dover (194 tons); and the *Speedwell* of Weymouth, of 200 tons; all had a similar armament and crew. These large cutters were privately built by the Collectors of various ports and then contracted to the Revenue Service. During wartime it was not unusual for these individually owned revenue cutters to become involved in privateering. The *Repulse*, for example, was wrecked in 1780 during the pursuit of French vessels near Calais and her crew captured.

Despite the order of 1747 (see above) the first cutter known to have been built in the Netherlands with the *Kemphaan*, launched in 1781 at Rotterdam and lengthened in 1787; she was armed with eighteen guns. Another cutter of eighteen guns and four carronades, represented by a model in the Nederlandsch Historisch Scheepvaart Museum in Amsterdam, is probably the *Mercuur*, purchased in 1782. Other cutters of larger dimensions can be seen on Dutch prints from 1781, one named as the *Spion* showing twenty guns; another probably with fourteen guns was identified as *De Vlissinger*, a very successful privateer of 1782. The Dutch obviously followed the trend towards larger cutters, because the Scheepvaart also holds plans of the two separate 92ft designs dating from 1781. Another cutter draught from 1797 marks a return to more modest proportions.

Although primarily English in inspiration, cutters were not only accepted into navies across the Channel, but also saw limited service further afield. However, the cutter received very little attention across the Atlantic, although at least five cutters were employed in the US Navy. Three cutters, the *Dolphin* and *Surprise* of ten guns, and the *Revenge* of fourteen 6pdrs and twenty-two swivels, were purchased in 1777 in France as dispatch vessels, but only the last reached America and served for a short time in the Continental Navy. Another of these early American cutters was built at Skenesboro, Lake Champlain in 1776. The *Lee* was only 43ft 9in long, measured 48 tons, and was armed with one 12pdr, one 9pdr and four 4pdrs. After sinking during the Lake Champlain action of 13 August 1776, she was raised and taken into the lake flotilla of the Royal Navy in 1777, where her draught was taken off. An English-type cutter (73ft long by 23ft 8in broad) was built between 1806 and 1808 by Josiah Fox at Norfolk and first named *Ferret*,

28. J Boudroit and H Berti, *Cutter Le Cerf 1779–1780* (Paris 1982).

but she did not retain the rig for long; in 1809 it was planned to re-rig her as a schooner but she was finally fitted out as a brig and received the name *Viper*.

The growing size of cutters made it inevitable that the huge areas of canvas would have to be divided over a two-masted arrangement eventually. Some cutters already carried a mizzen mast which was stepped temporarily during long reaches when the overhand of the main boom would not interfere; a lug sail was set from this, giving the cutter a 'dandy' rig. This was not popular with navies and a number of purchased cutters were converted to brig or schooner rig. The cutter hull form was still distinctive and this gave rise to confusing terms like 'cutter-brig', which was in common use for about thirty years after 1780. One of these vessels, the *Cameleon*, was bought in 1781; she was 85ft on deck, of 268 tons and armed with fourteen guns. Schooner rigged examples included the *Helena* of 1778, a 215-ton cutter-built vessel of fourteen guns. The mast construction of cutter-built schooners was similar to that of cutters, with integrated topmasts but fidded topgallants. The association of cutters with speed was so strong that eventually 'cutter-built' came to mean little more than fine-lined, and the term was as loosely applied as 'clipper-built' was to be in the nineteenth century.[29]

The numbers of cutters in naval service tended to fluctuate wildly between peace and war, because of the widespread hire, purchase and capture of mercantile craft. The Royal Navy built only seven cutters in 1763–4 and the same number between 1776 and 1780 but there were forty-three in service by the end of 1782; France at the same time had twenty-two. If the experimental *Trial*[30] of 1788 is excluded, the British built no more naval cutters until ten were produced during 1804–11; three of the latter were re-rigged as schooners and it is clear that during the Napoleonic wars the Royal Navy preference was for two-masted small craft. Nevertheless, the numbers on the Navy List grew from twenty-two in 1790 to fifty-three in 1814, a big increase occurring after the invasion scare of 1804 and the imposition of Napoleon's Continental System. By this time the French employment of cutters was minimal.

In 1816 the Royal Navy was made responsible for Revenue cruisers, and consequently in the decade that followed sixteen vessels based on a variety of existing Revenue cutter designs

A model, thought to be contemporary, of the Royal Transport. *The gaffs are missing, but other details suggest a primitive schooner rig, the first identifiable as such.* (Central Naval Museum, Leningrad)

were ordered. A few were quite small at 70–80 tons, but the majority were medium sized vessels in the 150/160-ton range. Later a few naval-designed cutters were built, but they were mostly intended for the usual peacetime roles in support of the civil power: for example, the little 70-ton *Sylvia*, designed by Symonds, was intended to protect the Jersey oyster beds from illegal fishing. The final batch of sailing cutters built for the Navy (eight in 1827–30 and two in 1836) were rated as tenders, and although they carried a few guns, they were not really cruising warships.

The total number of cutters employed on revenue duties continued to grow. Between 1777 and 1815 one of the more successful cutter-builders, John Gely of Cowes, alone built at least fifty-two known cutters for the Revenue Services of Great Britain; and during the period from 1822 to 1838 sixty-nine Revenue cutters were constructed at several shipyards around the country. One was even built for service off the Australian coast (the *Prince George*, a 72-ton cutter launched at Hastings in April 1833 which arrived at Sydney at the end of August; she had a length of 55ft and a beam of 18ft). In 1844 the fleet of Revenue cutters reached its peak with seventy-six in service.

Cutter building costs became excessive and in 1838 a Committee of Enquiry was set up to investigate. Its main recommendation, to construct all future Revenue cutters to uniform standards, was accepted and three classes of cutter and one tender were established. The first class included craft above 100 tons, the second above 60 tons and the third below that figure; tenders were below 30 tons. Four vessels were selected in 1839 as prototypes and sent to Portsmouth Dockyard for detailed survey: these were the *Stag* of 130 tons, the *Royal George* of 150 tons, the *Active* of 99 tons and the *Neptune* of 42 tons. Standard specifications were developed from these vessels and all future Revenue cutters built accordingly.[31] By the 1850s steam launches were beginning to replace sailing cutters, but so strong was the old association that vessels in Revenue (and later Customs) service continued to be called cutters, whatever their type – and the curiosity still applies in the US Coast Guard, the lineal descendant of the US Revenue Cutter Service.

Schooners

For so many types covered in this chapter, the first naval adoption of a rig is a matter of some uncertainty, but for the schooner a single identifiable vessel has recently been advanced as the prototype.[32] This vessel, the English yacht *Royal Transport*, was designed by a gifted amateur, Peregrine Osborne, Marquis of Carmarthen, to act as a fast and safe method of

29. D MacGregor, *op cit*, pp33.

30. This 121-ton vessel had three sliding keels and was the prototype for the system devised by Captain Schank that was later applied to a sloop and some of the gunbrigs.

31. G Smith, *op cit*, p112.

32. W F Ryan, 'Peter the Great's English Yacht', *The Mariner's Mirror* 69 (1983), pp65–87.

The Dutch speel-jacht *rig, reconstructed from an illustration dating from 1629. The very short gaffs, absence of headsails and lack of standing rigging are features of the type.* (K H Marquardt)

conveying King William III to and from his Dutch domains. Largest of the yachts for the English Royal household, the ship was launched on 11 December 1695 at Chatham Dockyard; considered a Sixth Rate, the 220-ton ship carried eighteen guns. She was a great success and often described at the time as the fastest ship in the Royal Navy, on one occasion easily outrunning two French privateers. During Peter the Great's visit to England in 1698 the vessel was made a royal gift to the Russian Czar and sailed in May 1698 to Archangelsk (she served the Russian fleet until wrecked in 1715). Carmarthen's involvement was obviously very detailed, because before the ship was transferred he petitioned the King that 'he may be permitted to put her in a better sailing condition than he supposes her to be at present, by the alteration of her foremast and otherwise'.[33]

Although the ship was fine lined, it was essentially the rig which was revolutionary, and this is well documented not only in letters but also in a contemporary model in the Central Naval Museum at St Petersburg. It is essentially a two-masted schooner, and the model has a boom on the main; a late painting by Willem van de Velde the Younger (died 1707) of 'English Yachts at Sea in a Fresh Breeze' shows a similar rig with short gaffs to both courses. The yachts in that painting were of a similar size to the *Fubbs* of 1682 and the *Isabella* of 1683, both of which were originally ketches

The American-built St Ann, *whose lines were taken off in 1736 making her the earliest schooner depicted in an accurate drawing.* (K H Marquardt)

but were rebuilt in 1701 and 1703 respectively. It is possible that the next yachts to be refitted after the success of the *Royal Transport* received the new efficient rig. Nothing is known of further schooner rig applications in early eighteenth-century England or on the Continent, but as mentioned in the 'Sloop' section, the Burgis view of Boston from about 1720 shows a schooner rigged naval vessel, recognisable by a pendant; there is still no square canvas and the gaffs are relatively short but there is now a boom.

Although the traditional American claim to the invention of the schooner has long been abandoned, the popularisation of that rig was undoubtedly an American achievement. The earliest recorded use of the word 'schooner' certainly comes from America: it was used in the *Boston News-Letter* of 4–11 February 1717, yet the same publication mentioned in a later issue of the same year that a London-owned schooner was captured by pirates off the North Carolina coast,[34] which is proof of European mercantile employment of that type at a time when the schooner had just earned its first mention in the American colonies.

The Burgis view of Boston revealed that these early vessels were simple fore and aft schooners, very much like the van de Velde English yachts. This rig actually has earlier precedents for small boats in the Dutch *Speel-jacht* of the first half of the seventeenth century and many similar English small craft of the same period. However its application to sea-going vessels was a novelty, which was to be subject to development and refinement for two

centuries; the next stage was the introduction of square topsails, which were already familiar by the 1730s.

The first known draught of a schooner, the *St Ann* from 1736, is preserved in the archives of the Sjöhistoriska Museum in Stockholm. American-built and sailing under the Portuguese flag, she arrived with dispatches in England, where her lines were taken off. Her principal dimensions were 58ft 2in on deck, 11ft 10in moulded beam, depth 6ft 10in for 36 41/94 tons. The ship had square fore topsail and topgallant yards and could probably have set a square fore course in addition.

There is little evidence of the schooner's use as a warship in the early eighteenth century. The first recorded appearances of armed schooners do not antedate the French and Indian war of 1755–63 (the Seven Years War to Europeans), when the combatants made use of North American merchant schooners in warfare and the Admiralty built the schooners *Vigilant*, *Lively* and *George* in 1755, as well as *Huron*, *Brunswick*, *Michigan*, *Charlotte* and *Victory* between 1763 and 1771 on the Great Lakes and Lake Champlain. Others like the *Sir Edward Hawke*, *Marblehead* and *Earl of Egmont* were constructed on the eastern seaboard at the same time, with further schooners being purchased into the service. One of these purchases was re-

---

33. Carmarthen was interested in fast sailing ships for the whole of his life and he was later to design the *Peregrine Galley*, another Sixth Rate/yacht that was to be highly influential (see Chapter 2).

34. M A Edson, Jr, 'The Schooner Rig: An Hypothesis', *The American Neptune* XXV/2 (1965).

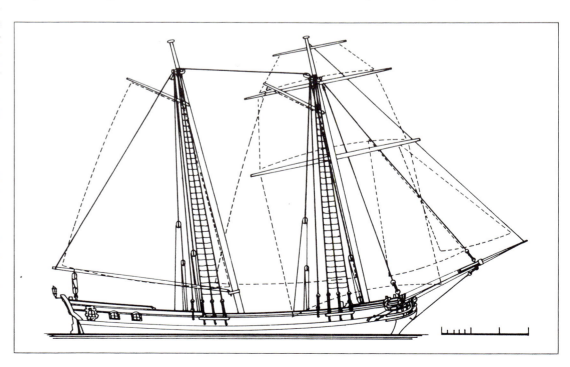

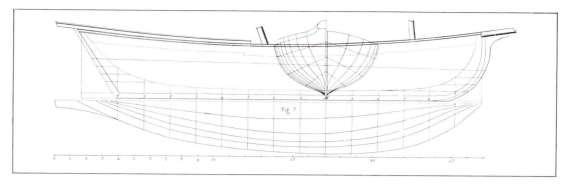

Admiral Paris' plans of the French schooners Agile, Biche *and* Decouverte *built around 1799. With dimensions of 26.0m (85ft) bp by 6.55m (21ft 6in), they were regarded as too narrow but otherwise were fine vessels.*

corded as being completed by Commodore Moore at Antigua, West Indies on 15 March 1757. The vessel was the *Barbadoes*, a Virginia-built schooner of 130 tons. Considered a fast sailer, she was sold out of service on 15 March 1763. No draught of the vessel has been found.[35]

The naval schooner's usefulness was proved during the St Lawrence campaign when they performed a range of duties from troop and livestock transport to scouting. One of the purchased schooners, the *Grenville*, ex-*Sally*, a 68-ton craft built in Massachusetts in 1754, was James Cook's first independent command, in which for five years he carried out surveys on one of the wildest coastlines in the world, that of Labrador and Newfoundland. In his tiny vessel he crossed the stormy North Atlantic every winter to carry on his meticulous chart work and surveys.

During the war the control of central government over the shipowners and merchants of the American colonies had been inevitably loosened, and new taxes to pay for the war were very unpopular; smuggling and the evasion of duties became endemic. To reduce these great losses in customs dues, the British government decided to employ naval ships and personnel in the revenue service, but traditional warships were not really suitable for the shallow and indented coastline, so the Admiralty decided to adopt local craft. This Admiralty decision was conveyed on 7 January 1764 to 'Rear-Admiral Lord Colvill, Commander in Chief of His Majesty's Ships and Vessels in North America, to cause Six Marblehead Schooners or Sloops to be purchased for His Majesty . . . and to cause the said Vessels to be registered on the List of the Royal Navy by the following names: *Chaleur, Gaspee, Magdalen, Hope, St John* and *St Lawrence*.'[36] As an indication of their size, the *Chaleur* was 70ft 8in on deck, 121 tons and was armed with six 3pdrs and seven swivels. Although schooners had served in the Royal Navy previously, this marked their first formal appearance on the Navy List.

The 1760s was the decade in which armed schooners are first noted in other European navies. The *Afrique*, a vessel armed with eight 4pdrs was built by Chevaillard the Younger at Rochefort in 1767 and some dimensions of an armed schooner from Brest by Ollivier (1769) are reproduced in metric measurements in *Sou-*

venirs de Marine: length bp 15.727m (51ft 7in), breadth 3.330m (11ft), depth in hold 1.853m (6ft 1in); armament six 4pdrs. The vessel was fore and aft rigged, no indication of square topsails being given.

The outbreak of the American War of Independence in 1774 saw the employment of some schooners on Lake Champlain, as well as seagoing vessels acting as packets or dispatch vessels; of the latter, *Fly* and *Wasp* were Baltimore schooners, with the former carrying six 9pdrs, and *Warren* was a Marblehead schooner. The vessels fitted out by General Washington are known to have been *Hancock, Harrison, Lynch* and *Hannah*, the last named being regarded as the first ship of their navy by many Americans. Blockade running and privateering during the war more than ever required the building of fast schooners on a large scale, resulting in the creation of the clipper schooner (also known as the Baltimore clipper). The Royal Navy built no schooners of its own during the war, but captures and purchases kept up the numbers on the Navy List (thirteen in 1777 and eleven in 1782).

After the Revolution all Continental naval forces were disbanded and the ships sold. The ensuing predatory attitude of even the smallest European and Mediterranean powers towards the unprotected American shipping lent further impetus to the development of fast merchant ships from the Chesapeake river and Marblehead and, in particular, to an expansion in the size of schooners. The earliest known draught (dated 5 August 1789) that might be regarded as a Baltimore clipper is the *Berbice* of 100 tons, an armed schooner of eight carriage guns (six 4pdrs and two 12pdrs) and four swivels, bought into the Royal Navy in 1793. With her sharp lines and extreme rake in stem and sternpost, she can be seen as a prototype of the new American schooner; by 1796, these vessels had already developed a very low freeboard and the raised quarterdeck was beginning to disappear. Schooners were more and more often built flush-decked with a continuous sheer line; bulwarks were low and sometimes only a single plank. They were modelled on the small pilot-boats of the American east coast ports and were therefore generally known as pilot-boat schooners.

When the United States Revenue Cutter Service was founded in 1789 it was natural that schooners were the first choice for the fleet. The earliest ten vessels taken into service were schooner rigged, although two were converted to sloops later. Those first revenue cutters of 35 to 70 tons were on the whole too small and too lightly armed to be useful. The approaching quasi-war with France led to the construction of ten larger vessels, six of which were 187-ton schooners (length bp 77ft, moulded beam 20ft, and depth in hold 9ft). One of them, the *Virginia* built in 1797 at Norfolk, is known to have carried six 6pdr carriage guns and four 4pdr howitzers.[37] The schooner became a characteristic American warship, and in the sixty years following its establishment in 1794, the US Navy, together with the Revenue Cutter Service, employed a large number of schooners of varying sizes (120 are named by Chapelle, but many of these were schooner rigged gunboats rather than cruising vessels).[38]

By the end of the eighteenth century the schooner was well established in most navies. As well as two sophisticated privateer schooner designs offered in *Architectura Navalis Mercatoria*, Chapman also designed a schooner rigged yacht for King Gustav III of Sweden in 1777. The *Amphion* was 110ft long, and although her armament was reduced by order of the King to swivels and saluting guns only, she served as Gustav's 'field' headquarters during the 1788–90 war with Russia and was present at several battles. Other naval schooners designed by this shipbuilding genius include a pair for the Inshore Fleet in 1790 and a further ten unnamed schooner rigged gunboats brought

35. Howard I Chapelle, *The Search for Speed*, p154.

36. H M Hahn, *The Colonial Schooner 1763–75* (London 1981), p20.

37. I H King, *op cit*, p23.

38. *American Sailing Navy*.

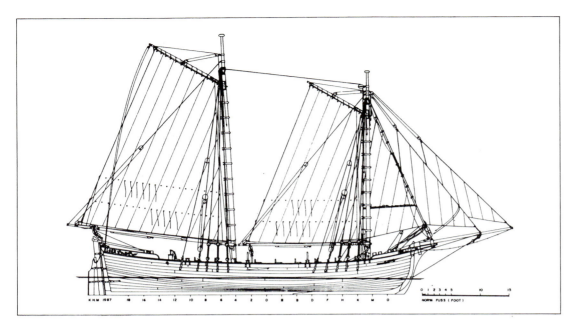

The Danish schooner rigged 'skerry boat' Elgen of 1769; these vessels could also be rowed as evidenced by the thole pins along the gunwale. (K H Marquardt)

into service between 1776 and 1808.[39] The newly built American merchant clipper schooner *Experiment* arrived at Karlskrona in 1812 and her construction and sailing abilities attracted Swedish naval attention. Purchased for the Swedish navy in 1813, her lines were taken off and the plans used to build the naval schooners *Falk*, *Puke*, *L'Aigle* and *Activ*. These vessels were 71ft 6in long bp, of 23ft 1in extreme breadth and were armed with two 4pdr carriage guns and six 12pdr carronades.

In Denmark the use of the fore and aft schooner rig on naval craft goes back to at least 1769 – possibly further – with the first schooner rigged 'skerry boats' *Elgen* and *Beaveren* (see 'Brigantin' section above). However, cruising

A Dutch schooner rigged gunboat built at Amsterdam in 1803. Armament consisted of two long guns firing forward, one on the centreline aft, and two carronades on each broadside. (From Souvenirs de Marine*)*

schooners were always few in number: Gerner built one in 1776, and Hohlenberg two in 1799–1800, but there were never more than a handful. A Dutch armed topsail schooner first appeared in one of Groenewegen's etchings in 1789,[40] described as a gunboat and very similar in design to the draught of a schooner rigged gunboat from 1803 in *Souvenirs de Marine*, which also contains a draught of a Dutch *cannonière galère* of 1800 rigged as a topsail schooner. A group of six schooners (the *Zwerver* class) was built in 1799 at Amsterdam and Rotterdam. Armed with seven guns, they measured 74ft 4in by 19ft 6in. Another group of eight schooner rigged 1-gun gunboats was built in the same year, but the following decades saw the building of several seagoing schooners for the Dutch navy after the American model, of which a few are known from models or drawings.[41]

Despite considerable experience with the schooner rig in the Americas, the Royal Navy was in no hurry to employ the rig for its mainstream operations. The first British-built examples were not launched until 1796–7 and these were far from conventional craft. Samuel Bentham, the newly appointed Inspector-General of Naval Works, was allowed to apply his highly original mind to the design of small experimental warships. The result was some of the strangest ships of the day: the ship sloops *Dart* and *Arrow* are best known (see Chapter 3), but his principles were also extended to four schooners, the 158-ton *Eling* and *Redbridge*, the 125-ton *Milbrook* and the 176-ton *Netley*. There was considerable confusion surrounding their rating, the first pair being designated advice boats initially, but they were eventually listed with the gun-brigs, whereas the other two were regarded as gun-vessels from the start. They were very sharp in section, almost double-ended, had a number of innovative fittings, and carried a heavy carronade armament (twelve/sixteen 18pdrs or 24pdrs) mounted on Bentham's 'non-recoil' principle. They were widely regarded as curiosities by the conservative, but more technically minded contemporaries saw virtue in their sea-kindly hull and remarkable sailing – the *Netley*, in particular, was said to have shown great superiority, especially in working to windward in heavy

39. D G Harris, *op cit*, p88.

40. G Groenewegen, *Verzameling van Vier en tachtig Stuks Hollandsche Scheepen* (Rotterdam 1789), P1 G8.

41. W V Cannenburg, *op cit*.

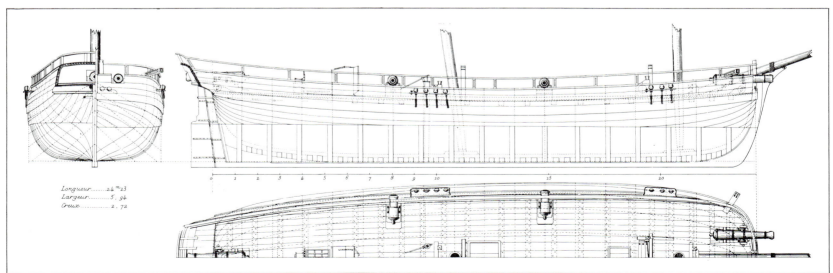

Longueur 26ᵐ23
Largeur 5,96
Creux 2,72

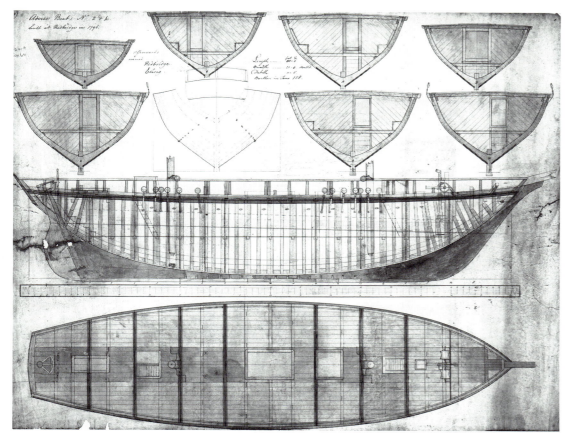

The sheer draught of HMS Redbridge, *one of Bentham's innovative schooners. Original features included solid bulkheads and external iron ballast.* (NMM)

weather.[42] One particularly significant innovation was the external ballast – the first documented example in history – placed in 4ft lengths below the keel and in section widening out from the keel downwards (a crude anticipation of the winged keel which helped *Australia II* break the US monopoly of the America's Cup nearly two centuries later). Somewhat ahead of their time, Bentham's concepts exerted no lasting influence on the Royal Navy.

However, it was a time of rapid advances and other inventions, like Captain Schank's drop keel and the pivoting centreboard of Henry and Swain, soon found their way into schooner construction; the first American schooners with a drop keel were in use as early as 1806, while the pivoted centreboard became more common after 1820. New ideas for the mounting of guns – principally, the pivot-mounting of a single large calibre gun, traceable back to some of Chapman's designs in the 1760s – gave schooners a long range punch, while the lightweight carronade enabled them to carry a good short range broadside as well. The combination made privateer schooners formidable opponents.

The Royal Navy's first series-built schooners were designed and constructed in Bermuda, based on a local dispatch boat model. During 1804–6 sixteen *Ballahoo* class, built of pencil cedar in Bermuda, were followed by eleven similar *Cuckoo* class built in Britain. At 71 tons and armed with only four 12pdr carronades they were very weak fighting ships, and a contemporary historian roundly condemned them as 'a disgrace to the British navy',[43] claiming that they were crank, unseaworthy and poor sailers (only eight of the whole class escaped capture or shipwreck). However, Bermuda continued to enjoy a reputation for its fast-sailing small craft, and a larger 142-ton class was inspired by 'the Bermudan sloop *Lady Hammond*'; the eleven schooners of the *Adonis* class carried the more respectable armament of ten 18pdr carronades.

Though most of the schooners of this period were two-masted, the later eighteenth century also saw the appearance of a variant with three masts, sometimes called tern schooners. Through naval reports we know of their existence from at least the 1790s – a French tern schooner, the *Pandour* was listed in 1796 and another unnamed vessel in 1800 – but their certain employment as warships begins with the *Revenge*, built at Baltimore in 1805. This 150-ton vessel was purchased into the Royal Navy as the *Flying Fish* and her draught taken off in 1806; she was armed with ten 9pdr guns or 12pdr carronades, and was 78ft 8in long on deck. Regarded as uncommonly well built and a remarkably fast sailer, her lines were used to build a further six of these schooners in Ber-

muda between 1807 and 1808 (the *Shamrock* class).

The apogee of the schooner's development as a fighting ship must be the large privateers of the Napoleonic wars, and especially those of the United States. A great shortage of cruisers and privateers led the French revolutionary government to the United States in search of such vessels and the subsequent capture of some of these American-built schooners led to a protest by the British Government. Not many purchases were made by the British themselves in America, but most of the captured vessels were taken into the Royal Navy; however, besides the *Flying Fish* the usual practice of taking off the lines of worthwhile prizes did not greatly influence the relatively small numbers of schooners designed for the Royal Navy. Other European nations, as we have already seen, bought American-built schooners and also made a habit of recording the lines, a practice which gives us today such a rich insight into the construction of smaller craft at this time.

Large privateers taken into the Royal Navy included the French *Duc de Wagram* of 203 tons (which became HMS *Dominica* in 1810); the *Lynx* of 225 tons (becoming *Mosquitobit*), and the 243-ton *Pictou* (ex-*Zebra*). However, one of the very largest and most famous was the American *Prince de Neufchatel*. Designed and built by Noah and Adam Brown in New York in 1812–13, she was 110ft 8in long on deck and measured 328 tons. Her armament consisted of sixteen 12pdr carronades and two long 6pdrs. In her short but illustrious career she cruised mainly in European waters and did great damage to enemy shipping. An impressive turn of speed once prevented the vessel from being captured by an overwhelming British force of seventeen men of war and on another occasion she fought off an attack by the boats of the British frigate *Endymion*. Luck finally ran out for the big schooner during a winter gale in December 1814 when she could not outrun three British frigates and had to surrender.[44]

In 1815 the Royal Navy still had about

42. J Fincham, *A History of Naval Architecture* (London 1851), pp130–2.

43. W James, *The Naval History of Great Britain* (London, rev ed 1837), Vol III, p510.

44. Howard I Chapelle, *The Search for Speed*, pp226–31.

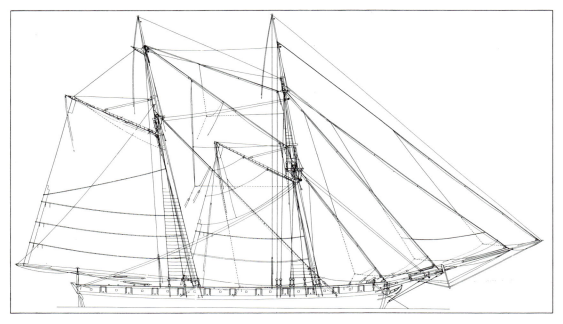

Howard Chapelle's drawing of the big American schooner Prince de Neufchatel, *a noted fast sailer and a successful, if short-lived, privateer.* (Smithsonian Institution, Washington)

Other fore and aft rigs

Lugger and chasse-marée

During the Seven Years War the French navy had experienced a shortage of fast reconnaissance and dispatch vessels which also could be useful as small cruisers against the enemy's merchant fleet. This eventually led to the adoption of the cutter but was also instrumental in bringing another major fore and aft rig, the lug, on to the naval scene. The lug rig is not, as it is so often considered, a typically French rig; it has been in simultaneous use on both sides of the Channel for fishing and trading vessels, and also often in illicit trades. The typical French type was the small, round sterned and open *chasse-marées*, up to 50ft in length, two-masted and rigged without a bowsprit. The British equivalent was the lugger, usually a vessel larger in size (around 75ft in length), decked, square sterned and also two-masted, but rigged with a bowsprit and often carrying a third mast, known as the jigger.

The first known naval use of the rig was for two *chasse-marées*, the *Bellislois* and *Oiseau*, built in 1768 at Lorient by the Company of the Indies. They were armed with two 2pdrs and four swivels and served a few years later as coast-guard vessels during the American War. Seven *chasse-marées* were used by the French navy at Brest for port and other services. About a year after the French adoption of the cutter, a French naval officer, Monsieur de Keavney, following a voyage up the Channel to Dunkirk, advocated the naval use of 'a sort of vessel called the lugger, which the English esteem greatly and even prefer to cutters, by reason of superior speed'.[46] In the same year an English lugger, known for its fine lines, called at Dunkirk and beached for several days to do certain repairs. A Monsieur d'Anglemont used this opportunity to take the lines off for Sieur Denÿs, (the Dunkirk builder of small craft so closely involved with the French cutter), who then converted these lines into a design for the first

twenty schooners in commission, the majority on the North America station.[45] Those at home were mainly doing duty as dispatch vessels, fleet tenders and advice boats. It was one of these tenders, the schooner *Pickle*, which achieved lasting fame by conveying Admiral Collingwood's despatches and the news of Nelson's death to England after Trafalgar. The name was preserved for one of a trio of ships built at Bermuda in 1827 that were among the last schooners designed for the Royal Navy. There were one or two later, but in general the Navy had always preferred the brig rig, which it regarded as superior in combat, and later ships attempted to compromise with the windward qualities of the schooner by adopting a brigantine rig – in effect, a brig fore mast combined with a schooner main.

In other navies, after a brief decline in the first postwar years, armed common, as well as tern, schooners continued to be built but at a slower rate. The Central and South American countries, then involved in an independence struggle with their Spanish colonial masters, provided a new market for surplus wartime schooners and brigs, which formed the nucleus of these new navies.

Lacking suitable small armed vessels, the US Navy returned to schooner construction in 1820–1 in order to fulfil the government's pledge to suppress piracy in the West Indies. The new group of five vessels was required to be of moderate size to keep down manning and maintenance costs. Four of these schooners, the *Alligator*, *Dolphin*, *Shark* and *Porpoise*, were of Baltimore clipper design, had a length of 86ft bp, measured 177 tons and were designed

for eleven or twelve guns – initially, ten 6pdr short guns and one 18pdr long gun on a midships pivot but later the pivot gun was replaced with two 18pdr carriage guns and the 6pdrs with 12pdr carronades. The fifth schooner, named *Grampus*, was launched in 1821; she was longer at 92ft 6in bp, for 171 tons, and her armament was one 18pdr pivot gun and eight to ten 12pdr carronades. Another eight smaller schooners for the West Indies were bought in 1822 and a number of US Revenue Cutter Service schooners of varying sizes were built.

The French navy began to build a new class of eleven schooners for service in the Colonies in 1823. Designed by the *constructeur* F J Delamorinière, the best known of that class was *La Jacinthe*. At 68ft 10in bp, she was a small vessel in the pilot-boat schooner mould, launched in 1823 at Toulon and armed with two 12pdr carronades. These schooners remained in service for a long time, the last being stricken only in 1844. Two more schooners were launched in 1841 and 1842. The first, named *La Jouvencelle*, was a vessel of similar size (102 tons) and she was armed with four guns; the second, *La Fauvette*, was also armed with four guns, but was only 54 tons. There was also a successful class of larger (157-ton) schooners armed with six 18pdrs: beginning with the *Iris* of 1818, fourteen were built up to 1824; the design was then repeated in 1835 and 1842 for two further groups of four. In total there were twenty schooners in French service in 1820, and by 1850 the miscellaneous small craft (which included schooners) numbered: (six to eight guns) eight active and nine laid up; (four guns and less) sixteen on active service, one in port and seventeen laid up.

45. D Steel, *List of the Royal Navy, 1 March 1815* (London 1815).

46. J Boudroit, 'The Chasse-Maree and the Lugger', *Nautical Research Journal* 26/2 (1980), p63.

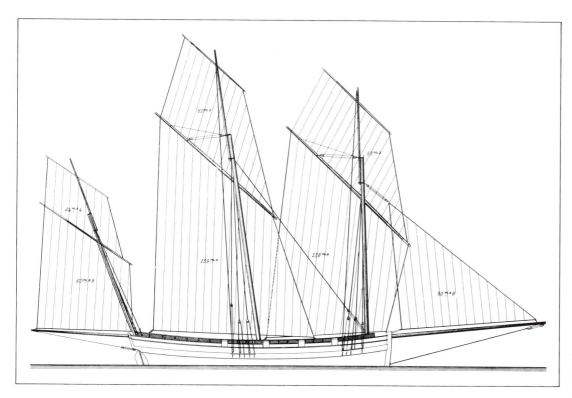

French naval lugger. Approved by the Naval Council on 11 December 1772, *L'Espiegle* was laid down at Dunkirk in 1773. Being of 60 French feet in length (64ft English on deck), she had a displacement of 113 tons and carried eight 4pdrs.

L'Espiegle was followed by more than fifty luggers before 1815, many of them built by Denÿs. The second lugger, built in 1776, was *Le Coureur*, which is particularly well documented thanks to the survival of her original draught from 1775, its copy with a sail plan included in *Souvenirs de Marine*, and a British Admiralty draught taken off in 1778 after her capture. Her measurements according to the latter were: length on the deck 69ft 10in, keel for tonnage 52ft 5¾in, breadth extreme 22ft 7¼in, depth in hold 9ft 10½in, burthen in tons 134 ²⁰⁄₉₄. She was clinker-built and carried lug and lug topsails on all three masts and additionally a jib with a total sail area of 551m² (5900sq ft). Her armament consisted of eight 4pdr carriage guns, plus six swivels, and a crew of fifty men. The exceptionally detailed Admiralty draught makes clear many details of the fittings, including the windlass position beneath the bowsprit – the latter horizontal like a cutter's spar on the port side of the stem and foremast – of sky-

lights and a covered companionway among other deck furniture.

The larger *Chasseur* was launched in the same year (she was 76ft 9in long on the deck and carried ten 4pdrs), but thereafter there was a reversion to smaller dimensions for a class of eight luggers built in 1782; this was probably a reaction to the unsuccessful large cutters of the period, which were then in the process of being re-rigged. Their displacement was the same as *L'Espiegle* but the armament was reduced to four 3pdr guns. Luggers were employed on much the same duties as small sloops and cutters, and many armed luggers acted as privateers during these Revolutionary and Napoleonic war years. However, after the war luggers all but disappeared from the French navy.[47]

Fast sailing English luggers may have inspired the French navy to convert them into warships, but the Royal Navy itself did not greatly indulge in these craft. A lugger was first mentioned in a Royal Navy List of 1783, and there was usually one on strength over the next 25 years, but the only purpose-built naval lugger was launched by a Plymouth boatbuilder in 1783. The Navy's attitude to this craft is probably summed up by its name, *Experiment*, its draught reveals sharp lines and extreme deadrise, indicating a good turn of speed. Nominally armed with ten 12pdr carronades and twelve swivels, she had seven gunports cut a side, was 71ft 8in long on deck, and measured 111 tons burthen.

However, luggers were popular as small privateers, and a surviving draught of the English lugger *Lark* of eighteen guns, taken into the Royal Danish Navy in 1790 as *Larken*, may be one of these. The approximate dimensions are 72ft 6in bp, 24ft 8in moulded beam and 8ft 2in depth in hold. Chapelle also notes that two luggers are known to have been in American hands during the Revolution, while a list of the Spanish navy at the beginning of 1813 includes fourteen 'polacres, luggers &c' in their service.[48]

The lug rig was also carried by warships not rated as luggers or *chasse-marées*. Dutch gunboats reproduced in *Souvenirs de Marine* dating from the 1790–1800 period have a three-masted lug rig, while some of Chapman's artillery landing craft and gunboats for the Swedish Inshore Fleet were rigged with the two-masted variant. The gunboats in particular were successful craft and both the Danish and Russian navies adopted a similar *kanonjoller* and *kanonerskia lodki* respectively.

Sliding gunter and periagua rigged gunboats

Making up a large contingent in most of the major late eighteenth-century fleets, gunboats were rigged to innumerable sail plans, from the relatively seaworthy British gun-brigs to schooner, sloop, lateen, and lug rigs. However, during its 'Gunboat Period' the US navy rigged a number of craft according to Commodore Edward Preble's ideas. His two gunboat designs, with two midships mounted guns, had two masts of which the main was gaff/boom rigged, whilst the fore had a sliding gun-

A US periagua rigged gunboat. (K H Marquardt)

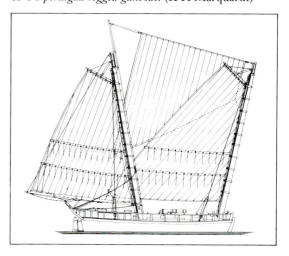

47. J Boudroit and H Berti, *La Belle-Poule – Le Coureur* (Paris 1986). The second part of this dual monograph, covering *Le Coureur*, provides a short history of the type in French service.

48. Burney edition of Falconer's *Marine Dictionary* (London 1815), p315.

ter sail with an additional jib extended by a bowsprit. Another fourteen gunboats were even more unorthodox in their rig. Designed by Christian Bergh in 1806, they had a 24pdr or 32pdr gun amidships and were rigged like a schooner without a bowsprit. However, the fore mast was stepped right up in the bows and raked forward at about 15 degrees, whilst the main raked aft at a similar angle. Both masts had a sail laced to a short gaff, with the fore sail remaining loose footed but the main was extended by a boom. The rig was known as a periagua – or perry-auger, as it was pronounced among American sailors – and was popular in New York harbour and other restricted waters along the East coast, being considered more weatherly than a sloop.

Barquentine

This rig is usually associated with later nineteenth-century merchantmen, but in a primitive form it was used on one experimental warship, the British *Transit* of 1808. Designed by Captain Gower of the East India Company, who built more than one vessel with this name, the 262-ton 'advice boat' was very long in relation to breadth (130ft by 22ft 6in), had a tapered midsection with hollow 'V' floors, and four masts – square rigged on the first and fore and aft rigged on the others, the sails being set from horizontal 'gaffs'. Designed to sail closer to the wind than conventional craft, the relative simplicity and labour-efficiency of the rig was of no particular advantage on a warship,

which in any event needed large numbers of men to man the guns, so the experiment was not repeated.

With the advent of steam, some fore and aft rigged warships had the new motive power added as an auxiliary, but the balance between steam and sail was soon inverted; fore and aft canvas was retained on many steamers to provide economical cruising or a steadying effect (employed on British motor launches as late as the Second World War) but ships no longer fought under canvas, leaving the historical names like cutter and sloop to develop new meanings.

Karl Heinz Marquardt

Fore and Aft Rigged Warships: Typical Vessels 1650–1840

Ship or Class	Type	Nationality	Launched	Built	Guns	Calibre	Dimensions Feet–inches Metres	Burthen	Remarks
Not known	Brigantine	Italian	1629		2	½–2pdr	47–10 × 12–9 14.58 × 3.90		First known measurements of brigantine
PAPEGOEJEN	Yacht	Danish	1657		4–8		47–10 × 11–1 × 4–6 14.58 × 3.38 × 1.37	28	Early Danish jagt
MARY	Yacht	English	?1660	Amsterdam	8		52–0kl × 19–1 × 7–7 15.85kl × 5.79 × 3.31	100	Presented to Charles II
ROYAL ESCAPE	Smack	English	p1660		4		30–6kl × 14–3 × 7–9 9.30kl × 4.34 × 2.36	34	Mercantile smack purchased in 1660
BEZAN	Yacht	English	1661	Amsterdam	4		34–0kl × 14–7 10.36kl × 4.27 × 2.13	35	Presented to Charles II
LEJONET	Yacht	Swedish	1669	Amsterdam	6?		54–4 × 15–5 16.56 × 4.70		Royal yacht
Not known	Yacht	Dutch	1678		6		57–7 × 16–8 × 6–3 17.55 × 5.08 × 1.91	85	First known draught of a Dutch yacht
MARY (2nd)	Yacht	English	1677	Chatham	8		66–4kl × 21–6½ 20.22kl × 6.57	155	RB 1727
Elector's Large Yacht	Yacht	Brandenburg	1678	Kolberg	8–10		65–0 × 19–6 19.81 × 5.94		Second yacht of the Brandenburg Elector
NAEVIS	Brigantine	Danish/Norwegian	1688	Copenhagen	4		51–6 × 10–3 × 4–1 15.68 × 3.14 × 1.25	29	Listed under 'Galleys'
ROYAL TRANSPORT	Schooner	English	1695	Chatham	18		90–0 × 23–6 × 9–9 27.43 × 7.16 × 2.97	220	First schooner; present to Peter I of Russia
LA SIBYLLE	Bark	French	1728	Toulon	14	4pdr	81–0 × 24–9 × 8–7 24.69 × 7.54 × 2.59	237	Typical French bark
Not known	Xebec	Spanish	1735		30	12, 6, 1pdr swivels	103–9 × 22–9 × 8–2 31.62 × 6.93 × 2.49	247	Early type xebec

Ship or Class	Type	Nationality	Launched	Built	Guns	Calibre	Dimensions Feet–inches Metres	Burthen	Remarks
ST ANN	Schooner	Portuguese	1736?	America			58–2 × 11–10 × 6–10 17.73 × 3.61 × 2.08	36	First known schooner draught
MEDIATOR	Sloop	British	1741/2	Virginia	10 18	swivels	61–4 × 20–1 × 9–9 18.69 × 6.12 × 2.97	104	Early Bermuda type sloop in the Royal Navy
MISTIQUE	Xebec	French	1750		18		91–2 × 25–3 × 9–2 27.80 × 7.70 × 2.80	279	Smaller new type xebec; early polacre rig
BARBADOES	Schooner	British	p1757	Virginia	14	?3pdr	80–0 × 21–6 24.38 × 6.55	130	Earliest known American-built schooner in Royal Navy
FLY	Cutter	British	p1763		12		51–5 × 20–10½ × 8–1¼ 15.67 × 6.36 × 2.47	78	An early purchased naval cutter
CHALEUR	Schooner	British	p1764	Boston	6 7	3pdr swivels	70–8 × 20–4 × 7–9 21.54 × 6.20 × 2.36	120	First schooner on Royal Navy list
Not known	Xebec	Spanish	1765		30		113–11 × 30–10 × 11–1 34.72 × 9.40 × 3.38	505	Early Spanish xebec frigate
BAEVEREN	Skerry boat	Danish/ Norwegian	1769	Frederik-svaern	2 6	2pdr howitzers ½pdr swivels	55–6 × 11–10 × 5–2 16.92 × 3.61 × 1.57	38	One of the first Danish skerry boats
L'ECLAIR	Bark	French	1770	Toulon	18	6pdr	104–6 × 28–9 × 12–9 31.85 × 8.76 × 3.89	394	Last French navy bark
LA PUCE	Cutter	French	1770	Dunkirk	6 10	3pdr swivels	48–6 × 11–10 × 8–6 14.78 × 3.61 × 2.59	67	One of the first French navy cutters
LINDORMEN	Xebec	Danish	1771	Toulon	22		127–2 × 31–8 × 11–4 38.78 × 9.65 × 3.45	554	For skerry defence
L'ESPIEGLE	Lugger	French	1773	Dunkirk	8	4pdr	64–0 × 22–0 × 11–2 19.5 × 6.71 × 3.40	113	First French navy lugger
LEE	Cutter	American	1776	Skenesboro	6	12, 9, 4pdr		47	First known American cutter
AMPHION	Schooner	Swedish	1777	Djürgard	? ?	saluting swivels	107–2 × 21–8 × 8–6 32.66 × 6.60 × 2.59	240	Royal yacht; 1779 brigantine
LEVRETTE	Cutter	French	1779	Dunkirk	18	6pdr	86–2 × 27–9 × 12–2½ 26.27 × 8.45 × 3.72	300	Very large type
Not known	Cutter	Dutch	1781		24		92–10 × 30–2 × 12–9 28.30 × 9.19 × 3.89	400	Very large design by J Vlaming
PIGMY	Cutter	British	1781	Dover	10	4pdr	69–4 × 25–7 × 10–9 22.75 × 8.39 × 3.53	181	Largest British naval cutter of the period
EXPERIMENT	Lugger	English	1783	Cawsand	10		71–8 × 18–11 × 9–0 21.84 × 5.77 × 2.74	111	Only purpose built British lugger
Not known	Xebec	French	1784	Marseille	22		129–6 × 34–0 × 9–7 39.47 × 10.36 × 2.92	670	New type with new polacre rig

Ship or Class	Type	Nationality	Launched	Built	Guns	Calibre	Dimensions Feet–inches Metres	Burthen	Remarks
BERBICE	Schooner	British	?1789	Virginia	8 4	12, 4pdr swivel	72–9 × 20–6 × 8–6 22.17 × 6.25 × 2.59	100	First known draught of 'Baltimore clipper'
ARGUS	Sloop	American	1791	New London			47–9 × 16–3 × 6–2 14.55 × 4.95 × 1.88	48	One of the first US revenue cutters
REDBRIDGE	Schooner	British	1796	Redbridge	14	18pdr carr	80–6 × 21–6 × 11–3 24.54 × 6.65 × 3.43	158	Experimental vessel by S Bentham
Gunboat	Parancelle	Neapolitan	?1798	Naples	1	18pdr	44–8 × 14-6 × 4–1 13.61 × 4.42 × 1.25	40	Typical Mediterranean gunboat
ZWERVER	Schooner	Dutch	1799	Amsterdam	7		74–4 × 19–6 × 8–4 22.66 × 5.94 × 2.54	125	Class of six schooners
LA SUPÉRIEURE	Schooner	French	1801	America	16		86–4 × 23–6 × 9–5 26.31 × 7.16 × 2.88	196	American built; sold to France 1802
BALLAHOO	Schooner	British	1804	Bermuda	4/6	12pdr carr	55–4 × 18–0 × 9–0 18.15 × 5.90 × 2.95	71	Small naval schooner to local design
FLYING FISH ex-REVENGE	Schooner	British	1805	Baltimore	10	9, 12pdr carr	78–8 × 21–7 × 7–10 23.98 × 6.58 × 2.39	150	Early three-masted schooner draught
FERRET	Cutter	American	1806/08	Norfolk			73–0 × 23–8 × 7–6 22.25 × 7.21 × 2.29	205	One of a few US cutters
DUC DE WAGRAM	Schooner	French			16		91–0 × 22–9 × 9–3¾ 27.74 × 93 × 2.83	203	French privateer; capt 1810 (HMS, Dominica)
EXPERIMENT	Schooner	Swedish	1812	Virginia	2 6	4pdr 12pdr carr	71–6 × 23–1 × 8–10½ 21.79 × 7.04 × 2.71	164	Purchased for Swedish navy; model for four vessels
PRINCE DE NEUFCHATEL	Schooner	American	1812	New York	2 16	6pdr 12pdr carr	110–8 × 25–8 × 11–6 33.73 × 7.82 × 3.51	328	Large US privateer
ALLIGATOR	Schooner	American	1821	Boston	10 1	6pdr 18pdr	86–0 × 24–7 × 10–4 26.21 × 7.50 × 3.15	177	US Navy postwar schooner type
LA JACINTHE	Schooner	French	1823	Toulon	2	12pdr carr	68–10 × 19–1 × 6–6 21.00 × 5.80 × 1.98	100	French postwar schooner type
PRINCE GEORGE	Cutter	British	1833	Hastings			55–0 × 18–0 16.74 × 5.49	72	British Revenue cutter for Australian station
LA JOUVENCELLE	Schooner	French	1841				65–7 × 20–4 × 6–8 20.00 × 6.20 × 2.03	102	Late French naval schooner

Notes:
Dimensions one in English feet with metric equivalents and are usually gundeck length, moulded breadth and depth in hold, but *kl* = keel length. In launched column *p* = purchased; in the Remarks column RB = rebuilt; in the Calibre column *carr* = carronade.

5

Fireships and Bomb Vessels

ONE of the most feared occurrences at sea in the days of sail was a fire aboard ship. Whilst accidents were plentiful, deliberately causing such an event proved a lot harder and this was as true for red hot shot as for fireships, and later for shellfire.

Fireships

The beginnings of fireship warfare

The first fireships were not purpose-built but were either merchant vessels or minor warships converted to the role. Perhaps the best known exploit of fireships was their employment by the English against the Spanish Armada in Calais Roads in 1588. There several small vessels which had been part of the English fleet harrying the Armada up channel were hastily prepared for the attack. Barrels of pitch and faggots of wood were stowed in holds and crude fireworks, used as fuses, were also set aboard. The same basic technique of expending them was used at Calais and for the next two hundred years. The vessels were manned by skeleton crews who sailed the vessels to within one or two cables' length (200–400yds) before setting off the fireworks and securing the helm so that the fireship fouled the intended target. To aid this, grapnels were fixed to the end of the yards. The crew of the fire-

ship had then to make good their escape in a longboat towed astern.

That at least was the theory. The Calais Roads attack was successful in a way which pointed up the limitations of the fireship as a type. The Spanish cut their cables and ran on the flood tide, and though subsequently brought to battle by the English none of their vessels was lost directly to the fireships. Targets which had not been crippled by gunfire and which still had the power to manoeuvre and whose crews were not demoralised could more often than not either fend off or move out of the way of the fireship. Thus a basic necessity for a successful attack by a fireship was a target which was stationary or nearly so, probably with a thoroughly demoralised crew. For success the attack normally had to be made inshore or in confined waters rather than the open seas, so the room for manoeuvre of the intended target was diminished. This was to be proven many times when these vessels were used in action.

By the late sixteenth century the use of fireships was becoming one of the options which

could be used in a fleet action, as much as for its shock value and the creation of disorder and panic amongst the opposition as for any damage that might be caused. The vessels themselves were more often than not merchant vessels converted for the purpose. For example, five of the vessels expended at Calais Roads were between 140 and 220 tons and cost the Exchequer no less than £5100 in compensation to their owners.[1]

The Spaniards were also quite adept at the use of fireships having panicked the crew of one of Hawkins vessels, *Jesus*, at San Juan De Uloa. However, during the long struggle for Dutch independence, they were more often on the receiving end of the tactical employment of fireships, and a related weapon, the explosion boat. Devised by an Italian engineer called Federigo Gianibelli, these 'infernal machines' were dumb barges filled with gunpowder and incendiaries, and were launched against the bridge built to blockade Antwerp during the

1. *Calender of State Papers Domestic*, CCXVI, 18, ii.

The fireship was an early 'terror weapon' whose success depended to a large extent on the panic it could induce in an enemy. In fact, it was difficult to succeed in open water when the target was underway and had sea room. One of the greatest of such successes was the burning of the 100-gun Royal James at the Battle of Solebay in 1672, depicted here, but the English ship was surrounded by Dutch opponents and was not free to manoeuvre. Note the terrified crew abandoning ship from the bowsprit despite the fact that the fire has yet to take hold; the Dutch boat in the right foreground has presumably taken off the personnel of the fireship. (NMM)

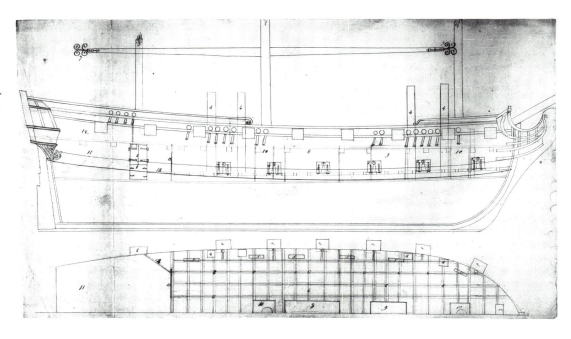

The earliest known draught of a fireship is this Danish plan of about 1700. It may represent an English ship and was obviously intended to demonstrate the special features of a fireship, all of which are numbered. These include the port-side sallyport for the crew to escape from [1]; the downward opening port lids [2]; the chimneys for additional draught [4]; a lattice work false deck on which the combustibles were stacked [6]; grappling irons on the yardarms; coffer dams around the masts below deck to prevent the fire bringing them down prematurely. (Rigsarkivet, Copenhagen)

Spanish siege of the city in 1585. One machine exploded with such force that 200 Spaniards were killed. Machines as such would reappear from time to time during the period under review. Usually they were small coastal craft – hoys or barges – converted for the purpose after being purchased into the service. They were used on a limited number of occasions, and with a varying amount of success, throughout the seventeenth century. They reappeared in the English service in the assaults on Napoleonic France and its fleet.

The heyday of the fireship

If the sixteenth century had been a period of experimentation in the use of fireships, as part of the general ferment surrounding the development of naval tactics, ordnance etc, the seventeenth century could be called the heyday of the fireship as a weapon of war. Several factors joined forces to make it so. Whilst the great gun was taking its place as the arbiter of battles at sea, fleet tactics and command were still in their infancy. Fleets could quickly loose coherence and a general mêlée ensue. A commander could take advantage of this if he had vessels fitted as fireships; or if an individual vessel became cut off from the rest of the fleet and was battered into a defenceless state she could be finished off with a fireship. This lack of tactical flexibility available to the commander of a fleet was compounded by the very nature of navies at this period. They were not led at the highest level by professional seamen but by the nobility and gentry, who also formed the core of the army. Their attitudes to fighting at sea were those bred in land battles.

For the first quarter of the seventeenth century there were few large fleet actions between the major powers. However, later in the English Civil War fireships were used, despite the fact that the navy as a whole had gone over to Parliament. Neither of the two incidents in which they were used was conventional. In the first case, at the siege of Weymouth, both sides used commandeered merchant vessels to try

and set fire to the opposite, enemy-held side of the harbour. In the second case, at the siege of Newcastle a small coracle (the smallest ever fireship?) was fitted out with a mortar shell, carcass and other combustibles and floated down river. In both sieges the attempts to use fireships were unsuccessful.

The dimensions and rig of these early fireships is difficult to ascertain. Many were conversions of small warships, others were merchant vessels brought into service for the task. A list of ships in English service in 1670 gives some idea of overall dimensions. The largest fireship listed had a length on the keel of 90ft, a breadth of 30ft and a depth in the hold of 11ft 6in. This vessel, had been captured from the Dutch; of 405 tons burthen she was classed as a Fifth Rate. The next largest vessel on the list was also captured from the Dutch and had a length on keel of 80ft, a breadth of 22ft 10in, a depth of hold of 10ft and a tonnage of 206. She was also classed as a Fifth Rate.

The earliest vessel on the list was built at Limehouse on the Thames in 1653, was classed as a Fourth Rate and had a length on the keel of 90ft, a breadth of 27ft 2in and a depth in hold of 11ft. From this it can be seen that the type of vessel converted to use as a fireship was between 60ft and 90ft in length and had a length:breadth ratio of approximately 3:1. This was also true for the vessels the Dutch used, as their policy was very much akin to the English on the conversion of old warships for use as fireships.

Size and the similarity of these vessels to their conventional sisters meant that they spent much of their service careers carrying out the duties that any small vessel would be assigned

to, whether or not she was serving with the fleet. First, there was always a chronic shortage of small vessels to carry out the myriad tasks which are necessary in both peace and war. Second, the very nature of the fireships' role meant they were only fitted with the fireworks and combustibles when there was a likelihood of their being expended.

This highlights the truism that individual specialist craft are rarely, if ever, called upon to perform the function for which they were designed. For example, three of the English fireships used in 'Sir Robert Holmes' Bonfire' (8 August 1666) had all seen at least ten years' service with the Royal Navy before being expended. They were, in addition, all prizes: two had been taken from the Dutch, the other from the Royalists under Prince Rupert. The *Fox*, captured in 1658, saw service off the Irish coast in 1660 then went down to the Mediterranean, came home to go into Ordinary (reserve), before being expended in 1666. The service of the two others, the *Gift* and the *Greyhound*, was very similar, the former being part of the 'winter guard' and then protecting the North Sea fisheries for seven years until she was sent to the coast of Guinea. The *Greyhound* spent most of her career in the Mediterranean. All three were classic cases of small ships expended at the end of their useful lives. Their career pattern is mirrored by that of most, if not all, fireships. The need for small cruisers and the limited number of opportunities to expend fireships meant that relatively few were built as such – and those which were spent most of their careers on conventional small ship service.

While the Spanish Armada is the best

known, if not the most successful, example of the use of fireships, the last half of the seventeenth century saw the greatest number of successful attacks by such craft. Mention has already been made of Sir Robert Holmes' attack in 1666; here all the elements were in favour of such a tactic. His attack on the Dutch in the Vlie was against vessels which were moored in a buoyed channel, and against an enemy whose fleet had been decisively beaten in a major engagement not long before, giving the English command of the sea. Each of the five fireships successfully grappled her target and set it ablaze. The harbour was so thronged with merchant ships that no less than 170 were destroyed,[2] making this perhaps the most successful fireship attack of all time. The Dutch for their part also scored some notable successes. The most striking was the attack on and destruction of the *Royal James* in 1672. The *Royal James*, a 100-gun First Rate, was attacked by no less than three Dutch fireships; she sank two and only later in the action when partially disabled and with no other English vessel to support her was the final attack crowned with success.[3]

All three engagements showed up the limitations of the incendiary when used at sea. Tactically they should have been a weapon of opportunity, yet they needed deliberate and careful preparation before action. This inherent contradiction, between the need for surprise and the need to prepare both vessel and attack deliberately was never fully resolved throughout the life of the fireships as a type.

From the English *Sailing and Fighting Instructions* it is quite clear what role was foreseen for these vessels, and that after the close of the seventeenth century tactical thought on the subject begin to ossify.[4] As an example, in the Duke of York's instructions to the fleet of 1673 article XXI stated that 'The fireships in the several squadrons are to endeavour to keep the wind: and they (with the smaller frigates) to remain as near the great ships as they can, attending the signal from the admiral, and act accordingly'.[5] This and the preceding article, which enjoins the frigates and smaller vessels to take the same station and identify and fend off the enemy fireships by all means possible, readily illustrates the tactical thinking on the employment of the type in the eighteenth century. The additions to the fighting instructions which were made in the next fifty to a hundred

years did not substantially alter the nature of the tactical control or the position in the fleet of the fireships during a general action.

Although it was the larger purpose-built or converted vessels which are recorded, it should not be forgotten that most navies carried aboard their larger vessels equipment and incendiary devices to be carried by the ship's boats. It was often the ship's boats and not the fireships which were sent in to finish off a stricken enemy. Swung out on the disengaged side of the ships, with crew ready to man them, they would be fitted with firechains and grapnels as ersatz fire vessels. They would then have to row up to the intended victim, attach the firechains and other incendiaries and, having lit them, withdraw. This was the method by which many of the French vessels were destroyed at La Hogue in 1692, after the running fight which left the French fleet embayed, or in shoal water, where more conventional fireships could not operate.

If tactical thought in the Western navies stood still, design and construction of the fireships themselves mirrored that of Fifth and Sixth Rate vessels. Their lines grew a little finer and usually they had the rig of a three-masted ship. The only real difference came in the layout of the deck, as funnels to draw the fire were fitted, and port lids were hinged at the bottom instead of the top so they would fall open when the retaining ropes burnt through. Both of these features would increase the through draught to make the fire burn more fiercely.

The fireship in eclipse

As the seventeenth century gave way to the eighteenth the use of fireships in action went into a steady decline. As mentioned above the fighting instructions for their operation in battle hardly changed at all over the century. As on land, where armies increasingly resorted to manoeuvre rather than head-on clashes so the increasing formality of sea battles gave little scope for the weapons of terror and opportunity. The indecisive nature of many of the set piece battles, whether or not brought on by strict adherence to the doctrine of the line of battle, meant there was little opportunity to exploit these vessels. Also the social fabric of the navy was such that sea officers could gain more in prize money if an enemy vessel were captured rather than sunk. This also combined with a certain abhorrence for the barbarity of such attacks, forming a strong and as yet under-explored obstacle to the use of these vessels in action.

Neither the Seven Years War – with the exception of the unsuccessful French attack on the English below Quebec in 1759 – nor the War of American Independence, saw fireships

2. W Laird Clowes, *History of the Royal Navy*, Vol 2, pp283–4.

3. W Laird Clowes, *op cit*, pp303–4.

4. J S Corbett, *Fighting Instructions 1530–1816*, (London 1905). Navy Records Society.

5. *Ibid*, p160.

The destruction of the embayed French ships at La Hogue by the Anglo-Dutch fleet was an example of the use of ships' boats in a makeshift fireship role. Painting by the Younger van de Velde. (NMM)

play any significant role in the war at sea. In the Royal Navy Lord Howe was a believer in the potential of the fireship and may have been instrumental in the ordering of the first purpose-built British fireships since the 1690s. However, although the combatants wrestled for control of the sea, none seemed to want to encompass the total destruction of the enemy's fleet, which, given the right conditions, fireships could help to bring about. It was the coming of the wars of the French Revolution and Napoleon which saw the swansong of the type. In these wars many have suggested that the total destruction of the enemy was the object of any engagement, as personified by Nelson in the Royal Navy. The vessels were by this time, more often than not, purpose-built and had very fine lines. The English vessels were built on the lines of a French sloop taken in the War of the Austrian Succession half a century earlier – and by the end of the first decade of the new century had been reclassed by the Admiralty as sloops. The vessels themselves were used in a manner not dissimilar to a century earlier, except that at the most famous incident, at Basque Roads, in 1809 Lord Cochrane used fireships as a type of 'machine'. This meant that the holds were loaded with explosives rather than combustibles, the object being an explosion rather than just a conflagration. To assist in this effect the explosives were tamped down with bricks to make the explosion vent through the side against any nearby ship rather than skyward as was normally the case. This was a reversion to an earlier idea of what was in basic essence a floating bomb.

Another type of floating bomb was Fulton's Catamaran – but this was not a ship turned into a weapon but a swimmer-propelled device reminiscent of the later 'human torpedo' packed with explosives and set off by a primitive time fuse. Fireships, explosion vessels and catamarans were all used, with partial success only, against Napoleon's invasion barges at Boulogne and elsewhere.

It should be remembered that the Chinese, as befitted the nation which brought the world gunpowder, also used fireships and explosion vessels. The major use in wars against the encroaching Westerners was after our period – and probably the last use of the fireship concept in the age of sail and wooden hulls. On

Despite the continued building and conversion of fireships during the eighteenth century, not many attempts were made to employ them. One such was the French attack on English shipping massed for the assault on Quebec. However, even in the relatively restricted waters of the St Lawrence, the fireships passed through their target's lines without damage. (NMM)

more than one occasion the ingenious Chinese filled barges full of human excrement over charges of powder, and then sailed the barge down onto its intended targets, with more than the usual unpleasant consequences for the victims!

In retrospect the fireship was at best a limited success, the few startling successes being more than balanced by many more failures. The reliance on wind, tide and current for propulsion was of course a handicap to this method of attack. The increasing formalisation of the line of battle plus the social and financial constraints enumerated above took away the *raison d'etre* of fireships throughout most of the eighteenth century. In its heyday in the seventeenth century the fireship was operating in a period of doctrinal flux where exploitation of

A well-documented model of the British 20-gun Dolphin of 1731. The other side shows the ship as built, but this side demonstrates the features of the vessel as converted to a fireship in 1747. The two-deck arrangement of these ships was ideal, since ports could be opened along the lower deck to provide a fierce draught. The ports were fitted with downward-hinged lids so that they could not be closed by fire burning through the port tackles; what appears to be a larger port aft is a sallyport to allow the crew to escape into a boat at the last minute. (NMM)

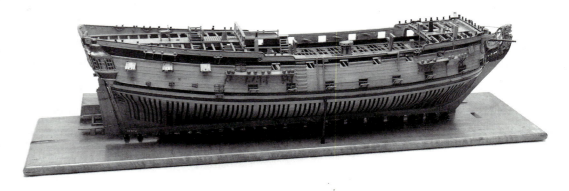

surprise or terror was more frequent. When this period passed the fireships were used to fill the places of small general purpose vessels (especially sloops) which were always in demand for a thousand and one duties either with the fleet or on detached service.

By the time there was a new doctrine abroad which espoused the total destruction of the enemy fleet, the gun and not fire was supreme at sea. The development of the shell gun and the extensive use of heated shot supplanted the need for a once and for only weapon such as the fireship. Although wooden ships would again show their vulnerability to fire, particularly during the Crimean war, it was to heated shot and shellfire not fireships or machines. The coming of iron construction and steam propulsion, not to mention that of rifled guns, sounded the death knell of these unusual craft. Whilst fire was to remain one, if not the principal, enemy of ships in action, the crude use of one vessel to destroy another, always so wasteful of material, was no longer either practical or necessary. Other weapons, especially underwater ones such as the mine and the locomotive torpedo were in their infancy, and would pose a much deadlier threat to the future capital ships than could the fireship and the variety of infernal machines devised throughout the nearly two hundred years under review.

Bomb vessels

If the fireship's antecedents are shrouded in the mists of antiquity, those of the bomb vessel are more certain. At the same time that artillery was becoming dominant at sea, on land the art of fortification was reaching new levels of sophistication. Built to resist artillery as well as infantry assault, this type of fortification became increasingly common not just as landward defence but also to protect the principal harbours in western Europe.

Ships versus forts

Ships had an inherent disadvantage in attacking any land target, in the elevation of that target above sea level and hence the need for greater elevation of the ship's guns, which in turn was restricted by size of the gunport. Since the heaviest pieces would always be carried below the upper deck, large angles of elevation were impossible, so that a solution to the problem had to be found.

On land one of the weapons used to overcome the new defences was the mortar, a short but large calibre gun designed to fire shell, *ie* hollow projectiles filled with gunpowder and a fuse, at high angles over the top of the defences. This combination of high angle of fire (which also gave range) and explosive projectile meant that, theoretically at least, there was a potent weapon which might be used. There were problems, however. Not only were mortars heavy, but they had a huge recoil force, which meant that if some such weapon was to be used at sea it would have to be given a substantial mounting to take the strain. Because of this the internal structure of the vessel had to be altered, which in turn, allied with the size of the projectiles, meant that the size of, and space available for, a magazine would be somewhat limited.

The first bomb vessels

It was the French – or more particularly one engineer Bernard Renau d'Elicagary – who were first to take the mortar to sea. This was in 1682 when the first of a revolutionary new type of warship was commissioned; this so-called

This well-known engraving by Randon is often used as an archetypal representation of a 'bomb ketch' but actually represents one of the early French 'galiotes à bombes', possibly the Ardente of 1692. The mortars, side by side, are invisible behind the waist cloths forward of the main mast.

galiote à bombes had a hull which was based on the Dutch galliot, strong and heavy, to take the stress of firing. The vessels themselves were built to be ketch rigged, had a hull length of 70ft stem to stern and a beam of 24ft and measured between 120 and 150 tons. Their principal armament was two mortars fixed both in traverse and elevation mounted either side of the centreline to discharge over the bows.

From the surviving evidence the mortars were of a similar type to those used for land service, of approximately 13in bore, which sat on a bed of earth which in turn was laid on a strong frame of timber, the whole to absorb the recoil. These early French vessels also had three small guns a side mounted below the quarterdeck with which to defend themselves. The mortars were placed in pits which were in the fore part of the waist. The placement of the main armament, itself dictated by

The English attempted to improve the seakeeping of bomb vessels by adopting the ship rig for a few built in 1693. One of these was the Mortar *for which this Danish draught survives. Only one mortar is shown and when combined with the evidence of a sketch by the ship's captain, it seems likely that the* Mortar *had a long quarterdeck from the main mast aft; therefore, if this ship had two mortars they must have been positioned side by side, French fashion. (Rigsarkivet, Copenhagen)*

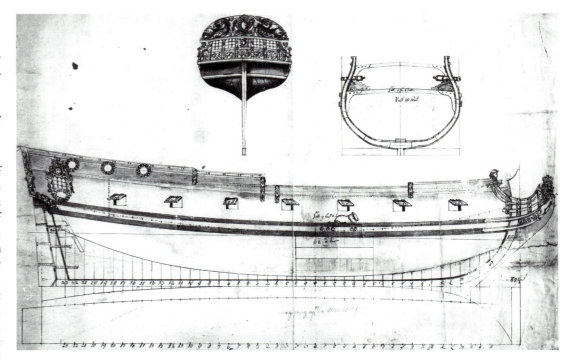

the weight and recoil, also dictated the rig of this type of vessel. Although these early vessels were normally ketch rigged, the main mast was stepped abaft the halfway point in terms of length and the mizzen was crowded on to the quarterdeck. The asymmetry of the rig, which in itself went against all the rules of balance for sailing vessels, meant that when fitted as mortar vessels the craft were usually poor sailers. At this time they also had tiller steering which would have made them heavy to handle in bad weather. The main disadvantage with the early French vessels was that to take aim the whole vessel had to be trained at the target, which could be a complicated procedure, especially if under enemy fire at the time; on the other hand the bow profile offered the smallest target to counter-fire.

The Royal Navy was not long in introducing

*Although this illustration was taken from a French work published in 1698 (*Memoires d'Artillerie *by Pierre Suriry de St Remy), it probably represents the English bomb ketch* Thunder *of 1695, which was captured by the French in the following year. It certainly depicts the main English innovations, the swivelling mortars placed on the centreline fore and aft of the main mast.*

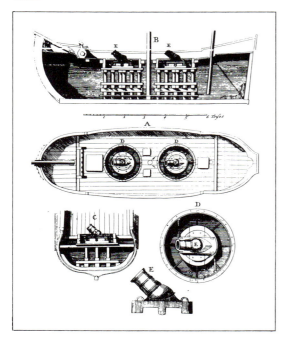

similar vessels into service. The *Salamander*, the prototype, was built at Chatham 1687 and her dimensions were very similar to those of the French vessels: length 64ft 4in, beam 21ft 6in, 134 tons. At first these vessels, like their French counterparts, were ketch rigged. The mortars were both before the main mast, but a slightly heavier secondary armament of ten guns was carried for self defence.

However the three English vessels which were built up to the end of the reign of James II were not thought to be totally satisfactory. Eventually the services of a Frenchman, Jean Fournier, were acquired to infuse new life into progress in England. The call of war is always a great spur to invention and innovation and the English, once embroiled in the wars with France, started to use a large number of bombs, as they became known, to attack French coastal towns, and privateering bases. This was a strategy that would be contiued throughout the eighteenth century.

Not only did the English use increasing numbers of these vessels, but they also made two important innovations to the type. First they developed a swivelling mounting which could be fired on a wide arc of bearings; and second, they shifted the position of the mortar beds so that one was before and one abaft the main mast. The next group of vessels that the English built had very similar dimensions to one another: length 85–87ft, beam 24–26ft, and a burthen of between 203 and 279 tons. There were four in the group which diverged from the French model in replacing the ketch rig of the earlier types with a three-masted ship

rig. Concern had been expressed over the limited seaworthiness of Fournier's French-style designs and the ship rig was almost certainly an attempt to produce a vessel capable of the overseas deployment British strategy required. From surviving evidence it seems that the fore mast was stepped well forward to leave a clear space in the waist of the vessels for the mortar beds to be sited. This rig must have been experimental as it was not seen again in British vessels until the late 1750s. The War of the League of Augsburg (1689–97 between William III and his allies and Louis XIV) saw an expansion in the building of most types of warship and this included the bomb vessel. For instance, in 1694 eight vessels were ordered to be converted to bomb vessels; these were smaller than their purpose-built cousins, being of between 65 and 135 tons burthen. This upsurge in interest in the type in England had much to do with William III's Continental commitments.

The strategy partially alluded to already, attacks on coastal towns, was to become a common thread of British policy throughout this and subsequent wars against the French. The idea was that a threatened descent on the coast, or an attack against a port such as Dunkirk, would induce Louis to withdraw troops to defend the coast and thus ease the pressure on William's field armies in Flanders and Germany. The bomb vessel was the ideal adjunct to this kind of operation; having been designed to lob mortar shells and carcasses (a hollow projectile similar to a shell filled with incendiary material) into heavy fortified structures, they were to see a great deal of use throughout this war. In 1695 nine new bombs were ordered from yards on the Thames which, along with one built in the next year, were the last of this type to be built in England until the late 1720s. Their dimensions were similar to the earlier types; *ie* length 66–72ft, beam 23ft and a tonnage of 143–163 tons burthen. They reverted to ketch rig.

The Baltic and Mediterranean 1700–1740

The end of the War of the League of Augsburg saw all the major belligerents financially exhausted, which had much to do with the ending of hostilities. The peace also brought retrenchment in the navies of the major powers – in fact, the French battlefleet had been partially laid up since the middle of the war due to that country's shortage of money. There was no new building until the turn of the century, surviving bomb vessels being stripped of their mortars and used to supplement the other small vessels in commission, undertaking such duties as protecting the North Sea and Newfoundland fisheries, and operating against the 'owlers' (smugglers of wool) in the English Channel. In this they closely mirrored the fireships in the duties they undertook to supplement the small number of sloops which were usually assigned such duties. Both fireships and bomb vessels were usually rated as sloops while employed on cruiser service.

War and the weather cut into the number of bomb vessels which remained on the establishment so that by the conclusion of the next war, of the Spanish Succession, there were just seven bombs left in the English service and no new vessels built to replace them. With the coming of peace England turned her attentions, after the accession of George I, to the Baltic, important to George by reason of his interest in the Electorate of Hanover and to Britain for the supply of naval stores such as hemp and Stockholm tar. The Great Northern War between Sweden and Russia was also of concern to Britain through the newly acquired Hanoverian interest and the early decades of the eighteenth century saw regular British deployments to the Baltic.

Whilst Britain sent fleets into the Baltic to restrain various states and to protect what she saw as her interests, the new Russian navy operated against Copenhagen in 1720, using mortar vessels to attack the city and its defences. The size and type of these vessels has not been possible to ascertain but given their heavy dependence on outside help to build and, in some cases, officer their ships, it is more than likely that the Russian bombs followed the French pattern closely.

Throughout the 1690s the French had also continued to build bomb vessels at a steady rate. Compared with the prototypes, the hull form remained much closer to British bombs, at least until the middle of the eighteenth century, and they also kept the mortars two abreast, rather than fore and aft; like the English they still kept the ketch rig, but there were refinements to the internal layout of the hull.

These vessels were employed to a great extent in the Mediterranean, often for attacking the Barbary corsairs in their strongholds. In 1683, for instance, seven French bombs are supposed to have fired off no less than 10,200 bombs in an assault on the city of Algiers. The results of this can be judged by the fact that the operation was repeated in 1688 when ten vessels took part and discharged the staggering total of 20,220 bombs against the town and its port. Although the British were to use this weapon against the French during the War of the Spanish Succession (1702–14), the French also attacked both the Spanish mainland (Alicante in 1691 and Barcelona again in 1691) and

overran Carthagena, in Spanish South America, with the help of bomb vessels. The French were active in employing their bomb vessels outside major wars, particularly against the Barbary states, but they did not build any new vessels until the late 1720s. At much the same time, the British started to take a renewed interest in constructing these vessels.

It was, however, the French who were the first to restart construction with three vessels laid down at Toulon: *Ardente*, *Tempête* and *Foudroyante*, all of which carried twin mortars, still mounted abreast and eight small cannon for self defence. The *Ardente* and *Foudroyante* did not survive the War of the Austrian Succession, the former disappearing from the lists in 1743, the latter in 1746. By contrast the *Tempête* was to survive until 1780.

Although the English did not build any new bomb vessels until 1730 they did convert a Spanish vessel, taken in 1720, during one of the periods of tension between England and Spain which marked the 1720s and 1730s. She was renamed *Thunder* and was unusual in that she was allocated only one mortar as well as the six 9pdr cannon. *Thunder* was ordered to be broken up 1734, by which time the first new bomb vessel to leave an English yard was already four years old. This was the *Terrible*, built to a draught prepared in 1728. She was launched in 1730 and had a length on the deck of 83ft, a beam of 27ft 4in and a depth in hold of 11ft. She was to carry two 13in mortars and six 4pdrs and eight swivels. Despite the earlier experiment with square rig, *Terrible* was rigged as a ketch although the main mast was stepped

This magnificent modern model of the British bomb ketch Granado *of 1742 was built by R A Lightley for the National Maritime Museum. It divides horizontally to reveal the internal structure and fittings of a bomb vessel, and represents a significant achievement of original research as well as an outstanding feat of craftsmanship.* (NMM)

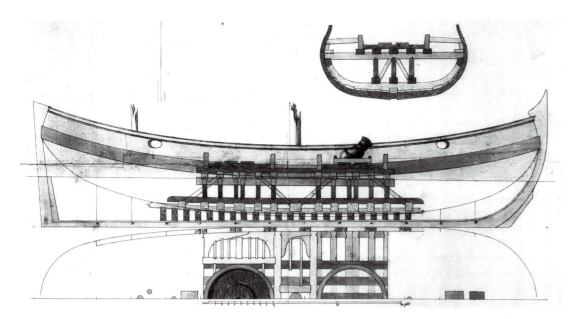

This eighteenth-century Danish draught of a hukkert *('bomb hooker') demonstrates the massive structure of supports needed for the mortar beds, enhanced by the relatively small size of the hull. The hull appears Dutch inspired, with some form of ketch rig, but the layout of the mortars follows English practice. (Rigsarkivet, Copenhagen)*

somewhat forward of the usual position which had some advantages both from the point of view of the sail plan and the siting of the second mortar.

Technical details

One innovation which came in during the early years of the eighteenth century was the use of mortars with adjustable elevation, previously set at 45 degrees for maximum range. With

trunnions cast at the breech end of the piece there was greater flexibility in the use of the weapon and more importantly in the positioning of the bomb vessel relative to the target. In practice, however, the main advantage of trunnions was that they allowed the mortar to be stowed horizontally when at sea, improving the stability of the vessel.

Another innovation which was of even greater importance to the development of the bomb vessel had first been seen in the vessels built during the War of the League of Augsburg. This was to have the mortar beds on turntables so that they could be traversed and the mortars fired on the beam, instead of over

the bow which had been the case previously.[6] Although at first mortars, as discussed above, were of fixed elevation the union of the two innovations prefigured the idea of the barbette and turret as the most effective means of mounting artillery, and this was some considerable time before Chapman and his first tentative ideas on the subject. This marriage was not just a technical innovation: it had tactical implications also as it allowed those commanding the bomb vessels in action a greater freedom to place their vessels either to engage the target more effectively or avoid the return fire of the enemy. However it is really only in retrospect that these two developments can be seen for their true importance to the future of seaborne artillery.

This discussion of the *raison d'être* of the mortar vessel moves us on to the technical details of internal fittings of these vessels which have thus far not been mentioned. This was

This early nineteenth-century Dutch ship rigged bomb shows the final development of the internal arrangements. The magazine is on the lower platform aft with the filling room directly below the capstan; the shells are stowed in shell rooms under the mortar pits. (From Paris' Souvenirs de Marine)

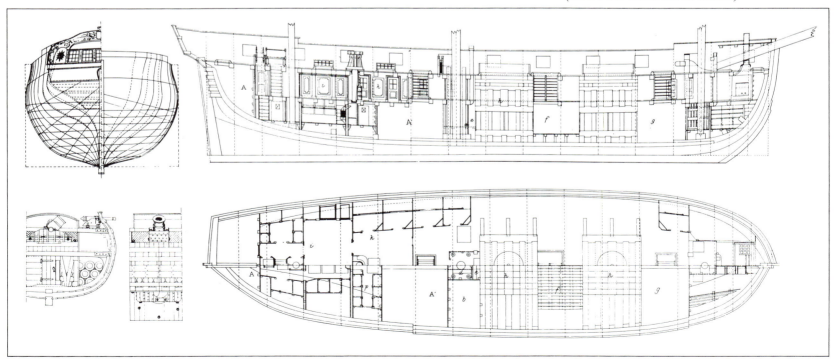

---

6. I am most grateful to David Lyon for bringing to my attention his note on this subject in Vol 2 of the Ordnance Society Journal.

dominated by a massive structure below the mortars which had the dual purpose of taking the weight of the mortars – upwards of 4 tons for a 13in mortar, and absorbing the recoil of the discharge. The mortar bed rested on a huge construction of timber somewhat akin to railway sleepers stacked in a grid pattern, which took the weight of the mortar and recoil down through the hull. On top of this sat the mortar bed, constructed of oak, with a smaller disk, also of oak, set into it and protruding below it. By means of an iron pintle and fore-lock the bed of the mortar could be traversed and then wedged in place for firing. In a similar fashion the mortar was elevated then kept in position either by a wooden block, set into the mortar bed, or by a metal chock below the barrel. In the earliest vessels, the French had tried both earth and thick cables as a method of absorbing the shock of firing.

Below all of this was the bomb room which, because of the size of the projectiles, took up a great deal of space. There was no continuous deck on these vessels, only platforms fore and aft of the mortar beds, the men being housed forward, above the cable tier, with the officers aft, above the bread room. The lack of space below meant that bomb vessels were cramped even by the standards of the eighteenth century for officers and crew alike. It should be mentioned here that in the English service the firing crew for the mortars was drawn from the Royal Artillery (ie the Army) and they were accommodated aboard a tender, along with many of the stores necessary for firing the mortars in action. The French had a special corps of naval bombardiers for the task.

The actual operation of firing a mortar was cumbersome. The decks were wetted, a special pump with an inlet through the bottom of the hull being used. Heavy curtains were erected between decks and in the captain's cabin (these were also drenched), and the charges were made up in the captain's cabin. If firing was to take place at night, all charges needed for that night's shoot were prepared during daylight, to preclude any accidents with either oil lamp or candle. Having prepared the charge, then rammed it home, a wad was placed in and rammed home also. The shell itself, with the fuse cut to explode at the right time, was lowered home. The act of firing was an adventure as the shell fuse had to be ignited by one

person whilst another, a split second later, discharged the mortar. The placement of the shell in the mortar so that this operation could be undertaken was itself no easy matter although it was facilitated by lugs on the shell. Later it was found that the flash from the firing of the powder charge would ignite the fuse, no doubt much to the relief of the Royal Artillery gunners!

This seeming digression, via the interior of the hull and firing procedure, is necessary to the understanding of the development of the type, which in essence was to change little in the next hundred years – with one exception, and that was the question of rig.

The advent of the ship rigged bomb

Not surprisingly, it was the spur of war which brought the next bout of new construction. In this war, that of the Austrian Succession, no less than twelve new bombs were built in English yards between 1740 and 1742. On average they were 91ft 1in in length on the deck and had an extreme breadth of 26ft 4in, dimensions for the *Granado*, built in 1742. The overall dimensions of the vessel changed only slightly in the fifty-odd years since the introduction of the type; although *Granado* had a square stern the rest of those built at this time retained the lute

stern which was one of the hallmarks of the type – ironically, in hull form the English bomb bore a closer resemblance to the Dutch galliot than the French *galiote à bombes* ever did.

The War of the Austrian Succession (1739–48) was not one of the most glorious in the annals of the Royal Navy and the bomb vessels played their part in the failures and success. One accompanied the ill-starred fleet under Admiral Vernon set to attack Cartagena in Spanish South America in 1741. Three others sent in 1742 as part of a squadron to pressure the King of Naples into keeping his treaty obligations to the British by threat of bombardment of the city of Naples itself were more successful, albeit without firing a shot, or shell. Once again with the coming of peace most of the surviving bombs were paid off and no new construction was undertaken.

However, peace was not to last long before hostilities between France and England were renewed. The outbreak of the Seven Years War (1756–63) once again found both navies short of specialist vessels. This is not surprising since the overwhelming need in peacetime was for cruising vessels, hence the adaptation of both fireships and bomb vessels to this service. There was no money in the slim peacetime estimates for such specialised vessels, but the coming of war changed all that. Those vessels

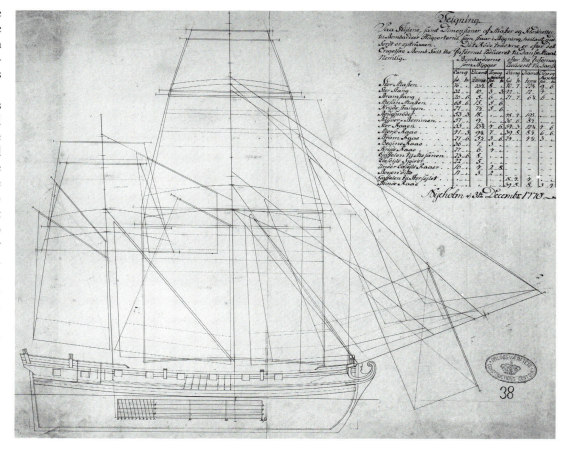

Rigging plans of bomb ketches are rare but this interesting Danish draught shows the spars of the British Infernal *of 1757 and the proposed reduced dimensions for a Danish* hukkert *of the 1770s. (Rigsarkivet, Copenhagen)*

from the preceding war which survived were brought forward into service (only three of the twelve), and as a stopgap six other vessels were converted to bombs; all were sloops, mostly built towards the end of the previous war.

One at least of these conversions was to find fame outside wartime; *Racehorse*, as an Arctic exploration vessel in 1773, along with the *Carcass* in which a certain midshipman Horatio Nelson was serving. This was not the first time that bombs had been used for this purpose, nor would it be the last. In 1741 an expedition under Middleton had been sent out to search for the North West Passage and the new bomb vessel *Furnace* chosen as one of the two vessels involved. It is not difficult to see why they should be chosen for such a task. The broad beam and rounded hulls built to withstand the shock of mortars discharging were also close to the ideal for withstanding the encroachment of pack ice and the pounding of the Arctic seas. Towards the end of the period under review the bomb vessel was to enjoy a renewed life in this role.

Returning to 1758 when the next class of bombs was ordered, the overall dimensions were not increased by much over the preceding class, but it was with these vessels that a change of rig was introduced. Although three remained ketch rigged, the other three were to be ship rigged and from then onward all bombs in English service would be ship rigged, the experiment having been judged a success. Also introduced at this time was wheel steering which along with the change in the rig no doubt alleviated the poor sailing characteristics of the type to some degree.

The Seven Years War saw Britain return to its strategy of descents on the coast to distract the French and take the pressure off Britain's Continental allies. During the war several bombardments were undertaken, with varying degrees of success. At Rochefort two bombs attacked the outlying works on the Isle of Aix. The rest of the attack did not proceed and there was much public disquiet about the policy of attacking the French coast in this manner. It was during this operation that a bomb vessel was used for close infantry support. A party of French dragoons were spotted approaching a British position and the bomb fired carcasses to exploded in the air and drive off the French with great success. The new bomb vessels were also to see service in the West Indies, as for example at the reduction of Havana in 1763.

Whilst there were to be further refinements the bomb vessel can be said to have come of age in the Seven Years War, but like so many other weapons having reached its apogee its demise was not far away. The next two wars, the American War of Independence and the French Revolutionary and Napoleonic Wars, were to be different in character from those which had gone before. Whereas the previous wars had been dynastic or related to subtle adjustments in the balance of power, those which were to follow were ideological, ushering in a new era in warfare. Before, the capture of territory was used as part of the bargaining process; thereafter this was less so and the nature of wars radically altered. The total destruction of an enemy's means to fight was attempted for the first time since the Thirty Years War. In this atmosphere fleet and single ship actions took on new earnestness and although Britain retained a policy of attacking French possessions overseas it was becoming increasingly difficult to justify the classical attack with bomb vessels on ports and towns.

The American War in particular gave little scope for the operation of bomb vessels, since American towns were not heavily defended and mortar attacks might well be psychologically counter-productive. When France and Spain entered the conflict Britain lost command of the sea, and having no Continental allies, diversionary attacks on the enemies' territory would have been risky and pointless. As a result the Ministry only slowly expanded the Royal Navy throughout the 1770s and into the 1780s. However two were built in 1776 and two in 1778–79 similar to those built in the 1750s but with an extended quarterdeck, the capstan moved and the position of the after mortar moved before the main mast.

With the coming of the French Revolutionary War bomb vessels were, to start with, converted rather than purpose-built. At least six vessels underwent conversion in 1797. One of these vessels was fitted with folding screens and channels in the deck so that the mortar could be fired at a lower angle of elevation. The next two classes to be built were not radically different from one another although they were a departure from previous vessels in that they were almost indistinguishable from any small ship built at this period, excepting of course the armament. They retained the bluff bow and square midship section although the stern was by now conventional instead of lute-shaped.

British bomb vessels in action during Nelson's attack on Copenhagen in 1801. In the left foreground ship rigged bombs, at anchor with backed mizzen topsails to steady them, are firing into the city and its fortifications, beyond the ships of the line and floating batteries fighting it out in the centre of the channel. (NMM)

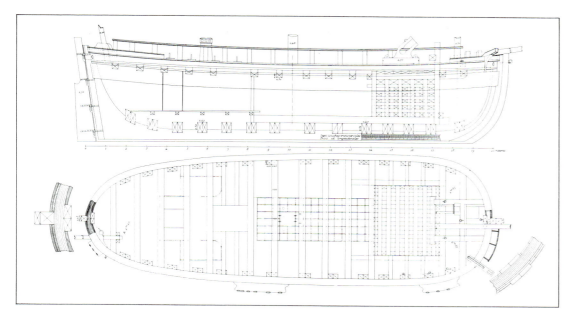

The French mortar boat Infernale *built at Le Havre in 1804 was an example of the carriage of mortars by small craft. Presumably built to support the intended Napoleonic invasion of Britain, the craft would have required no more seaworthiness than the ability to cross the Channel in the fair weather required for such an operation.* (From Paris' Souvenirs de Marine)

Thus the bomb vessel rejoined the mainstream of ship development.

Vessels of these two classes were to find fame in the role of Arctic exploration, in particular the *Erebus* and *Terror* which were to be used by such luminaries as Ross and Franklin. They were both fitted with steam engines, bought on the cheap from the London and Greenwich Railway. Both were to be abandoned in the ice in 1848 when Franklin made his last, and fatal, expedition to find the North West Passage. However, the immortality of the bomb vessel was ensured not by Arctic exploration but by the War of 1812 – even if it is unknown to most people today – for one of the bomb vessel's last operations is celebrated in a line of the American national anthem: 'the rockets' red glare and the bombs in the air'.

Other mortar vessels

This chapter has concentrated on the two main sea powers of the eighteenth century, who between them were responsible for the invention, improvement and construction of the vast majority of bomb vessels. However, other navies took up the type as and when necessary – Sweden, for example, built her first bomb ketch, the *Åskedunder*, at Karlskrona in 1698; she was very similar to the English *Thunder* and in general most navies chose to follow the English pattern of revolving mortars on the centreline rather than the original French paired arrangement.[7]

Smaller navies, with little need for operations much beyond their own coast, employed mortars on smaller craft. The American force sent to deal with the Barbary powers borrowed a pair of Neapolitan 'bombards' in 1804 (they had a form of ketch rig but with only a gaff on the mizzen); the following year two trabaccolos – a type of Adriatic lugger – were purchased for conversion into bombs.[8] Provided that they were to be used in sheltered waters, mortars could be installed in craft little bigger than boats. A French proposal to do just that was put forward at the same time as the first bomb vessels were under discussion and at various times in the eighteenth century French *prames d'artillerie* (c1759), *chaloupes carcassières* (1740s) and *cannonières bombardes* (1790s–1800s) carried mortars. During the period of the great Napoleonic invasion scare, Britain did the same, many of the post-1800 gun-brigs being fitted with 10in or 8in mortars.

There were also occasional instances of mortars being deployed from larger ships. During the War of American Independence France had only two purpose-built bombs in service and as an interim measure two *flûtes* (armed transports) were converted to *transports bombardes*. This formula was revived in 1825 when eight such vessels were built, replacing the traditional *galiote à bombes* with a 300-ton ship that served as a transport in times of peace. From time to time the French had used mortars from more conventional warships (a frigate at the siege of Rio de Janiero in 1710, for example) but during the Revolutionary War period a concerted effort was made to widen their employment. A number of frigates were converted during the 1790s and a bizarre class of *corvettes à bombes*, armed with 48pdr guns and a 12in mortar as well as a red-hot shot furnace, were built from 1794 (see Chapter 3).[9]

The traditional bomb vessel fell from favour in the 1820s and 1830s as horizontal shellfire appeared to offer conventional warships most if not all of the advantages of the more specialist vessels. However, the swansong of the naval mortar was provided by the Crimean War, for which a number of small craft were converted to mortar boats. A British example is the *Sinbad*. She had been a dockyard hoy and there is a draught of her conversion in the Admiralty collection of draughts at the National Maritime Museum. This shows *Sinbad* with a single mortar amidships and, as might be expected, smaller dimensions than a typical bomb vessel of the earlier period.

The bomb vessel was an ingenious solution to the problem of attacking fortification on shore in the age of gunpowder. Like the fireship they were to be replaced by other weapons, in this case by shell-firing guns: when mounted either in barbettes or turrets, and in combination with steam propulsion and iron hulls they were to bring about a revolution in the design of fighting ships. Bombs had the strengths and weaknesses of all specialist vessels – they performed their one task to perfection but spent more time on other service for which they were not wholly suited. However, the need for a bombardment vessel did not entirely disappear and one can perhaps see more than a faint resurgence of the type in the monitors built in the First and Second World Wars, not least of which was the resurrection of such names as *Erebus* and *Terror*.[10]

Chris Ware

7. G Halldin, *Svenskt Skeppsbyggeri* (Malmo 1963), p159.

8. H I Chapelle, *The History of the American Sailing Navy*, pp193–9.

9. J Boudriot, 'L'Artillerie de Mer de la Marine Français 1674–1856', *Neptunia* 98–99 (1970).

10. This section on the bomb vessel is based on the study of the draught collection at the National Maritime Museum, Greenwich; also the unpublished *Sailing Navy List*, by David Lyon, which I hope will soon be available to a wider public. Of great assistance were: the articles of D Wray in *Model Shipwright*, Nos 19, 25, 26 and 27; the *Catalogue of the Tower Armouries*, by H L Blackmore and Granado (Anatomy of a ship series) by P Goodwin. Lastly I am indebted to A W H Pearsall and David Lyon for useful suggestions and points of detail.

Fireships: Typical Vessels 1650–1840

Name	Origin	Nationality	Launched	Built	Guns	Dimensions Feet–inches Metres	Burthen	Remarks
YOUNG PRINCE ex-JONGE PRINS	Fourth Rate	English ex-Dutch	1634	Noorderkwartier	38	90–0*kl* × 28–0 × 10–2 29.53*kl* × 9.19 × 3.34	375	Capt 1665; fireship 1666 and expended
LITTLE VICTORY	Fifth Rate	English	1665	Chatham	28	75–0*kl* × 21–0 × 10–0 24.61*kl* × 6.89 × 3.28	176	Converted 1671 and expended
FIN	Purpose-built	French	1671	Rochefort	12	105–3 × 29–7 × 11–11 32.08 × 9.02 × 3.62	300	Expended 1673
YOUNG SPRAGGE	Sixth Rate	English	*p*1673		10	46–0*kl* × 18–0 × 9–0 16.08*kl* × 5.91 × 2.95	79	Converted 1677; hulked 1693
FLAME	Purpose-built	English	1690	Rotherhithe	8	91–7 × 25–4 × 9–8 30.05 × 8.31 × 3.17	273	One of 20 built in early 1690s; 6 were expended as fireships
SOLEBAY	Sixth Rate	British	1711	Portsmouth	24	95–10 × 25–2 × 10–8 31.44 × 8.26 × 3.50	272	Bomb vessel 1726–34; fireship 1734–5; Sixth Rate until hulked 1742
STROMBOLO ex-MOLLINEAUX	Merchant ship	British	*p*1739		8	88–0 × 24–6 × 11–6 28.87 × 8.04 × 3.77	217	Purchased Sept 1739; sold 1743
INFERNAL	Merchant ship	British	*p*1778	Thames	8	82–6 × 28–10 × 13–2 27.07 × 9.46 × 4.32	307	Purchased on stocks; sold 1783
TISIPHONE	Purpose-built	British	1780	Dover	12	108–9 × 29–7 × 9–0 35.68 × 9.01 × 2.95	422	To the lines of French corvette; 9 built 1780–81 and 6 in 1805–6
INCENDIARY ex-DILIGENCE	Merchant ship	British ex-French	*p*1804		14	53–6 × 17–4 17.55 × 5.69	62	Sold 1812
PHOSPHORUS ex-HAASJE	Merchant ship	British ex-Dutch	*p*1804		4	55–7 × 19–9 × 12–6 18.24 × 6.48 × 4.10	115	Sold 1810

Notes:
Dimensions are in English feet with metric equivalents, by the naval method, giving gundeck length, moulded breadth and depth in hold; but

kl = keel length. In the Launched column
p = purchased.
  Although nearly all the examples are from Royal Navy service they demonstrate the usual sources for

fireships: prizes, purchased merchantmen, and converted small warships, with a limited number of purpose-built vessels that served mainly as cruisers.

Bomb Vessels: Typical Ships 1650–1840

Ship	Rig	Nationality	Launched	Built	Guns	Mortars	Dimensions Feet–inches Metres	Burthen	Remarks
BOMBARDE	Ketch	French	1682	Dunkirk	4	2–12in	74–3 × 25–2 22.68 × 7.68	120	One of the first group (of four) bombs
ARDENTE	Ketch	French	1682	Toulon	6	2–12in	80–7 × 30–7 24.56 × 9.32	150	Largest of 1682 bombs
BELLIQUEUSE	Ketch	French	1683	Toulon	8	2–12in	83–2 × 27–9 25.35 × 8.45	140	One of second group (of four) bombs
SALAMANDER	Ketch	English	1687	Chatham	10	2–12¼in	64–4 × 21–6 × 8–4 19.61 × 6.55 × 2.53	134	First English bomb

Ship	Rig	Nationality	Launched	Built	Guns	Mortars	Dimensions Feet–inches Metres	Burthen	Remarks
FIREDRAKE	Ketch	English	1688	Deptford	12	2–12¼in	85–9 × 27–0 × 9–10 26.14 × 8.23 × 3.00	279	Larger English bomb
PORTSMOUTH	Ketch	English	RB 1688	Deptford	10	2–12¼in	59–0 × 21–4 × 9–0 17.98 × 6.50 × 2.74	143	Yacht of 1673 converted to a bomb in 1688
MORTAR	Ship	English	1693	Chatham	12	2–?13in	86–0 × 26–0 × 9–10 26.21 × 7.92 × 3.00	260	One of four ship rigged bombs
CARCASS	Ketch	English	1695	Rotherhithe	4	2–13in	66–6 × 23–2 × 10–0 20.26 × 7.06 × 3.05	143	Class of eight bombs of more moderate dimensions
VULCAIN	Ketch	French	1696	Toulon	6	2–12in	84–0 × 27–9 × 10–8 25.59 × 8.45 × 3.25	170	Larger second-generation French bomb
SALAMANDRE	Ship	French	1696	Toulon	12	2–12in	101–3 × 29–4 30.88 × 8.94	200	Only French ship rigged bomb until 1820s; 'English' layout
ARDENTE	Ketch	French	1725	Toulon	8	2–12in	85–0 × 26–11 × 11–7 25.92 × 8.21 × 3.54		Class of three bombs, first since 1690s
TONNANTE	Ketch	French	1734	Brest	8	2–12in	83–5 × 26–7 × 11–11 25.43 × 8.10 × 3.62		One of a pair
BLAST	Ketch	British	1740	Deptford	8	1–13in 1–10in	90–6 × 26–0 × 11–0 29.41 × 7.92 × 3.35	265	Class of six, similar to *Alderney* of 1734; five more built in 1741
ETNA	Ketch	French	1754	Toulon	8	2–12in	86–4 × 26–8 × 11–9 26.32 × 8.12 × 3.57		One of only three bombs in service in 1780
BASILISK	Ship	British	1758	Deptford	8	1–13in 1–10in	91–6 × 27–6 × 12–1 27.89 × 8.38 × 3.68	198	Class of six, three testing the ship rig; four more built 1776–8
HECLA	Ship	British	p1797		8	2	92–9 × 26–8 × 12–5 28.27 × 8.13 × 3.66	300	Converted merchantman
AETNA	Ketch	American	1806	Portland, ME	10	1–13in 2–8in how	83–6 × 24–0 × 8–0 24.45 × 7.32 × 2.44	140	First purpose-built US Navy bomb
No 13	?Schooner	Danish	1808	Kiel		1	51–6 × 13–5 × 8–9 15.69 × 4.08 × 2.67		Typical Scandinavian *morterchalup* or mortar boat built in quantity
BEELZEBUB	Ship	British	1812	Bideford	10	1–13in 1–10in	102–0 × 27–0 × 12–6 31.09 × 8.23 × 3.81	325	Class of three; modified for *Hecla* class 1813 (three, plus five in1820s)
VÉSUVE	Ship	French	1825	Bayonne	8	2–32cm	108–3 × 27–11 × 12–1 33.00 × 8.50 × 3.68	300	Class of eight transport-bombs; served as transports in peacetime
ETNA ex-WALCOTT	Brigantine	American	p1846			1–10in shell gun	80–0 × 22–8 × 10–0 24.38 × 6.91 × 3.05	182	'Bomb brig'; one of three merchant ships purchased for the Mexican War

Notes:
In the Launched column RB = rebuilt and *p* = purchased. Mortar calibres are given in native units, the French 12in being equivalent to the English 13in; *how* = howitzer. Dimensions are in English feet with metric equivalents, but the native methods of measurement apply.

6

The Oared Warship

ARED warships in the age of the large battlefleets were mainly built to fulfil purposes for which sailing warships were unsuitable. Their main tasks were to provide mobile seaborne firepower in areas where calm weather, shallow water or narrow passages prevailed and to combine gunfire with amphibious capability. Compared to sailing warships, the ratio between firepower and manpower was very unfavourable in oared warships and this made them expensive to maintain in service unless the oarsmen were soldiers who used the oared craft for amphibious warfare. The two principal areas for oared warfare in this period were the Mediterranean and the Baltic, where permanent oared flotillas of considerable size were maintained. In other parts of Europe and in America, oared warships were built only as temporary forces when rivers, lakes or certain coastal waters became strategically important during a war.

The survival of the Mediterranean galley

The Mediterranean galley type in the seventeenth and eighteenth centuries has received little attention in the literature of the period. As far as the available evidence shows, the galley had by the mid-seventeenth century developed into its final form. Standard galleys were vessels with 25–26 pairs of oar-benches with five oarsmen on each, that is with 250–260 oarsmen. The crew of such a galley usually also consisted of 50–100 sailors and a similar number of soldiers. Around 400–450 men were

Admiral Paris' drawing from a model probably representing La Dauphine, *built 1735–6, the last French* galère extraordinaire *or flagship galley ever built. With twenty-nine pairs of oars this vessel served as* Patronne *or second flagship during the last decades of the French galley fleet. Being reduced to harbour service in the 1760s the hull survived until 1792.*

cramped into a hull of about 300 tons displacement – sailing warships with such a crew were four to five times larger. The galleys were armed in the bow with one gun of the heaviest type in use (24–36pdr) flanked by two or four lighter guns (4–12pdr). Along the sides between the oars and on the platform above the guns there were several light swivel guns for use against enemy crews in close combat. The length from stem to sternpost of such galleys was 45–47m (148–154ft) while the beam of the hull was around 5–6m (16–20ft). A length:beam ratio of 8:1 was normal. The rig normally consisted of two masts with one large lateen sail on each – a third mizzen mast with a small sail could be fitted but it is seldom shown on plans.

Apart from the standard (or 'main battle') galleys, most navies also had one or a small number of flagship galleys with a few additional pairs of benches (up to 30) and six or even seven oarsmen on each bench. Small galleys, either with the traditional type designations galeota and brigantin or with the more recent French designation *demi-galère* (half-galley)

were very few in numbers in the state navies but more numerous in the North African corsair fleets. Some of these vessels had a considerably shorter hull in proportion to the beam than standard galleys and may have been closer to sailing ship designs. Galeasses – the hybrid type of warship developed from the medieval merchant galleys – were only used by Venice where the type was finally abolished in 1755.

The permanence of the sailing battlefleets was primarily determined by the need to keep a force of specialised warships with a large number of guns in serviceable condition in peace as well as in war. Except for officers and a nucleus of sailors and specialists, few men saw service in peacetime. The Mediterranean galley forces were different. They were primarily permanent personnel organisations where forced labour – slaves, convicts and prisoners of war – was the most numerous group. The galley hulls were cheap to produce and a lost or discarded galley was normally quickly replaced, often from a reserve of more or less ready hulls in the arsenal. The galley fleets were normally in ac-

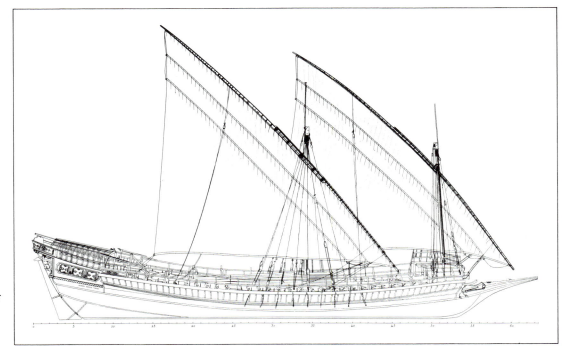

Table 1: The Mediterranean galley fleets 1650–1800

	1650	1670	1700	1720	1740	1760	1790	1800
Venice	(70)	(60)	(50)	(40)	(30)	(20)	(20)	–
The Ottoman empire	(70–100)	(60)	(30)	(30)	(15)	(15)	5	(0)
France	36	25	42	15	15	10	0	0
Spain	(30–40)	(30)	30	(7)	7	0	4	2
The Papal state	5	5	4	6	4	5	5	0
Malta	6	7	8	5	4	4	4	–
Genoa	10	(10)	(6)	6	(6)	(6)	(6)	–
Tuscany	5	4	3–4	2–3	(2)	0	0	0
Savoy/Sardinia	(2)	(2)	(2)	4	4	(0)	0	0
Austria	0	0	0	(4)	0	0	0	4
Naples	–	–	–	0	4	3	0	0
Approximate total	(220–260)	200	170	120	90	60	45	6

Notes:
The table includes standard galleys and flagships but not galeasses and smaller types of galleys: demi-galères, galeotas, brigantins. – indicates that the state did not exist as an independent political unity at the time. Figures within parentheses are uncertain or approximate, especially those for Venice and the Ottoman empire.

tive service in summer, while they spent the winters in harbours. They usually patrolled only a limited area of the Mediterranean, a fact that was determined by the limited endurance of the galley: they often had to replenish their water supply and give the crew some opportunity to rest from the extremely cramped conditions on board.

The galley fleets of this period no longer functioned as battlefleets: that is, as concentrated forces acting in strategically important areas. In fact, no large galley fleet battles took place in this period. In the 1630s Spain and France had introduced sailing battlefleets to Mediterranean warfare and from the time of the Cretan war between Venice and Turkey (1645–69) the sailing battlefleets also became the main fighting force in the Levant. Galleys were now used only as cruisers, patrolling the lines of communication and along threatened coasts as well as acting as scouts. In battles, they supported the sailing battleships from behind the line, just as frigates did in the Atlantic fleets. Up to the mid-eighteenth century few cruisers (frigates, corvettes, sloops) of the type developed in the Atlantic and Baltic were based in the Mediterranean. The galley with its independence of wind was obviously for a long time regarded as the best Mediterranean cruiser, even in a country like France which used many frigates in its Atlantic fleet. Concentrated galley fleets were mainly used for troop transports and amphibious warfare during full-scale wars between France and Spain in the west, Venice and the Ottomans in the east.

There were three basic conflicts in the Mediterranean which determined the operational pattern of the galley forces. In the east, Venice and the Ottoman empire were involved in full-scale wars during a long period up to 1718. In the 1720s and 1730s the tension between these two powers faded away. In peacetime these navies used their galleys as police forces in the Adriatic and the Greek archipelago respectively. In the western Mediterranean, the old conflict between Bourbon France and the Habsburg empire in Spain and Italy gave the galley fleets a continuing purpose. The Spanish–Italian galley fleet provided the main transport force for troops and their supplies within the Habsburg sphere of influence and the French galleys were mainly built to attack these Habsburg lines of communication. The Bourbon inheritance of the Spanish throne in 1700, and the subsequent separation of Italy from Spain, radically reduced the need for galleys. Finally the north-south conflicts between Christian powers and the North African corsairs continued throughout the seventeenth and eighteenth centuries. However, it is significant that by the early seventeenth century the North Africans had already changed to sailing warships supplemented by xebecs (a Mediterranean sailing vessel – see Chapter 4) and light galleys while their Christian adversaries from Spain, Italy and France continued to use large galleys as patrol and escort vessels against corsairs into the eighteenth century.

The gradual pacification of the Mediterranean and the winding up of the traditional conflicts in east and west is reflected in Table 1 in a declining number of main battle galleys. The four great galley fleets of Venice, the Ottoman empire, France and Spain were much reduced and the latter two powers, together with Tuscany in the late 1740s, decided to abolish their galley fleets entirely. Sardinia and Naples soon took the same decision and the Turkish galley force gradually dwindled into insignificance. With the exception of a small resurrected Spanish galley force, only Venice, Genoa, the Papal State and Malta retained large galleys by the 1790s. These states were now in themselves becoming archaic and in a few years they were destroyed as political powers by the French revolutionary forces. The galley fleets disappeared with these states, a fact that suggests that they had been retained as traditional institutions rather than as useful naval forces. From the mid-eighteenth century onwards most of their traditional cruiser tasks had been in fact transferred to xebecs and Western-style frigates and corvettes.

The question of the extent to which Mediterranean galleys in this period were retained for reasons of prestige, tradition and institutional inertia rather than utility has never been fully investigated. Galley forces were usually run by socially and politically influential men and already in the seventeenth century a certain nostalgic romanticism seems to have flourished around the galley type. There is little doubt that the almost total lack of change in the basic galley design and the final abolition of the type show an increasing inability to adjust to changed conditions, including an increasing lack of forced labour in an area that gradually became more peaceful. But it was the type of warship and its connection with forced labour that became obsolescent, not oared warfare. Until the advent of steam there was still a considerable need for muscle power to provide mobility in calm weather. But the large galleys had originally been intended for main fleet combats – they formed the line in such battles while smaller galleys acted as cruisers. After the mid-seventeenth century such combat became a thing of the past but the galley fleets continued for a century or more to spend large amounts of money on maintaining large galleys serving a cruiser role which might have been better fulfilled by smaller oared vessels or sailing craft with auxiliary oars.

Oared warships in the Baltic

Oared warfare in the Baltic was the result – and to some extent the cause – of the Russian conquest of Sweden's empire in the east which gave this continental power access to the sea. During the war with the Ottoman empire in the 1690s

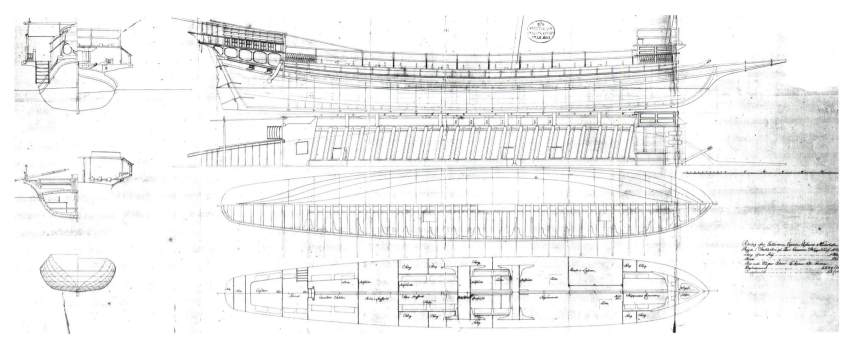

Drawing of the three Swedish galleys Upsala, Upland *and* Västerbotten *built 1749 at a private yard in Stockholm. Somewhat shorter than Mediterranean galleys but otherwise similar to them, forty-four of this type were built 1784–9 in two versions, one with twenty-two and one with twenty pairs of oars. Armed with one 24pdr and two 6pdrs forward the offensive firepower of the galleys was small by eighteenth-century standards.* (Krigsarkivet, Stockholm)

Russia had already built a considerable galley force for service in the Sea of Azov. The Mediterranean technology was thus readily available when the thrust towards the Baltic began in 1700. Originally Russia mass-produced small galleys for riverine and lake warfare and larger types of galleys became common only in the 1710s. Russian galleys showed their value first when they supported and protected Russia's conquest of the shallow innermost part of the Gulf of Finland (the present-day Kronstadt–St Petersburg area) and later during the conquest of Finland when the coastal archipelago was a key area. Sweden's response was largely dictated by the high command's (ie King Charles XII's) reluctance to release army manpower for a

Udema Torborg, *designed by Fredrik Henrik af Chapman in early 1770 and launched 1772. Nine 12pdrs (only six shown on the drawing) are placed on pivotting mounts on the centreline and could be fired from both port and starboard gunports in the narrow superstructure. There were also four 12pdrs in conventional broadside fashion fore and aft while two 18pdrs and two 12pdrs were mounted forward. Primarily a sailer, the vessel could be rowed with twenty pairs of oars with four men to each oar. Note the diagonal stiffenings in the hold.* (Krigsarkivet, Stockholm)

maritime counter-balance to the Russian offensive, although the battlefleet-orientated naval leadership did little to argue for such a change. Consequently few galleys were built until after the death of the king in 1718 when large-scale Russian amphibious attacks on the Swedish coasts with galleys became a serious threat. The Swedish galleys were of various domestic designs with a length:beam ratio around 5:1 compared to 8:1 for standard Mediterranean galleys.

From the 1720s, Sweden began to study Mediterranean galley technology and in the following decades both Russia and Sweden built very similar galleys – vessels with 20 or 22 pairs of oars with five men to each and with a length:beam proportion between 6.5:1 and 7:1. Thus they were somewhat shorter than Mediterranean standard galleys but with the same beam and armament. This reflected the fact that galleys in the Baltic were archipelago warships where manoeuvrability was more important than speed. Primarily the type was built for the control of the Kronstadt–St Petersburg

area and the Finnish skerries, which in a war between Sweden and Russia became the main east-west route for army logistics as well as the key area for flanking amphibious attacks on army positions in Finland. In sparsely populated Sweden the galley type was never popular since it had a high manpower requirement and because the crews were exposed to weather far less clement than the Mediterranean conditions which made it possible for the crew to sleep on deck. However, Swedish attempts to produce heavily-armed floating batteries as an alternative resulted in vessels with very low mobility. Russia continued to build galleys until the 1770s but in Sweden no more were built after 1749. By that time the two Baltic powers had galley fleets far larger than any Mediterranean state: Sweden had eighty units and Russia about a hundred, including some smaller craft.

From 1760 the naval architect Fredrik Henrik (af) Chapman in co-operation with the senior officers of the newly constituted Inshore Fleet began to experiment with new solutions to the

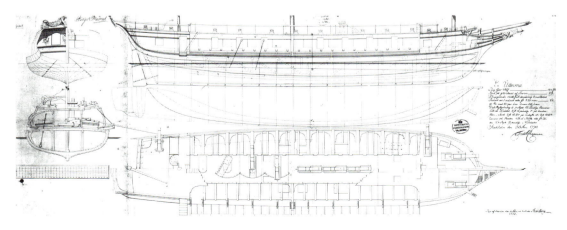

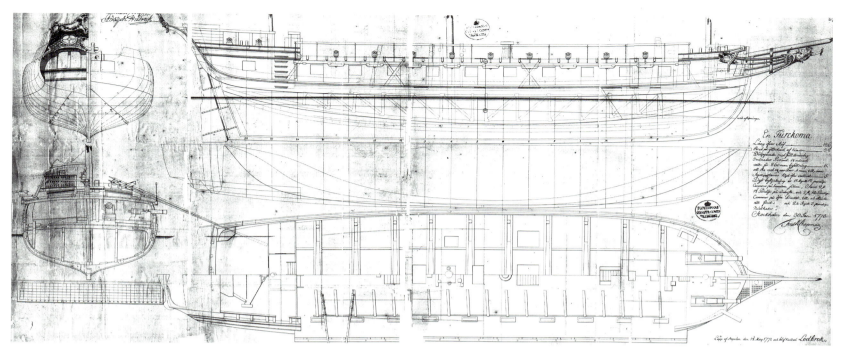

Drawing of the turuma Lodbrok, *launched 1771 and followed by four similar archipelago frigates launched 1773–4. A conventional broadside armed shallow-draught sailing vessel with benches for nineteen pairs of oars (four men to each oar) on the upper deck. Note the diagonal stiffenings in the hold which gave longitudinal strength to a heavily armed vessel.* (Krigsarkivet, Stockholm)

problem of combining firepower, manoeuvrability, protection, habitability and amphibious capacity in oared warships. First he tried to design larger hulls which provided sheltered accommodation for the crew (possibly a reflection of the great problems with disease which the galley crews had encountered during the war with Russia 1741–3). The result was essentially two types: broadside-armed vessels (called *turuma* and *hemmema*) and an unconventional design with guns placed on the centreline on pivoting mountings which might be fired on both sides (called *udema*). Both types were originally mainly armed with 12pdrs although two 18pdrs were mounted in the bow on most of them. The chief innovation was hidden in the hull in the shape of a new system for longitudinal strength, including diagonal stiffenings. That made it possible to combine a heavy armament with a light, low and shallow hull which could be rowed with reasonable speed.[1] However, the new types of warships could not be rowed and fire their broadside armament at the same time as the oars masked the guns and as the same men were oarsmen and gun crews. The broadside type in particular was somewhat deep-draughted for the Finnish archipelago and none could beach on shores as amphibious assault craft.

Therefore, these new types were soon found to be less suitable for offensive tactics. Such tactics required mobility and firepower directed forward to support an advance. In the mid-1770s af Chapman designed a radically new type (originally conceived as two different types, one with a landing gun) which proved to be able to mount heavier armament than first expected. It was a gunboat (*kanonslup*) armed with two heavy guns, one at each end. The gun mountings were placed on wooden rails on which they could be moved to the hull bottom amidships when they were not used. This minimised longitudinal stress and made the guns into ballast when the boats sailed. On a displacement of about 60 tons an armament of two 24pdrs could be carried. With a draught of only 1.2m (4ft) the boat could easily act as an amphibious assault craft and even land a gun on a field carriage if required. As a complement an even smaller type (*kanonjolle*) with one gun firing aft was introduced in 1778. It was mainly intended for defence of harbours and narrow positions. In order to minimise hogging the gun was mounted amidships fastened to two longitudinal bulkheads which stiffened the hull. Aft of the gun a 'tail' gave additional buoyancy and facilitated loading. As the gun was mounted directly on the hull the whole craft recoiled when it was fired. Both types could easily take down their masts in preparation for combat. The basic innovation in both types of gunboats was the combination of heavy guns in a small hull, something which was achieved by a systematic study of how the stress from gunfire could be absorbed in a

wooden structure and judicious solutions to the problem of providing end-on gunfire without creating serious hogging problems by placing permament heavy weight in the end of the craft.[2]

These two types of gunboats were manned by about 60 and 25 men respectively, most of them usually soldiers. The larger had 14–15 pairs of oars with two men to each oar, the smaller usually 7 (post-1815 boats 10) pairs with one man to each oar. As they were undecked and cramped the crews had to be accommodated on shore in tents (sails might be used as tents) and gunboat flotillas had to be followed by a fleet train of small craft: hospital boats, boats for cooking, ammunition boats, etc. A gunboat flotilla in *mobile* archipelago warfare had to be organised along army lines in order to keep the crews in good health, a type of organisation which was radically different from that of a sailing ship, which was fighting platform, storeship and accommodation combined in one hull and in which sailors could live for years without ever going ashore. Naturally

---

1. To the best of my knowledge no modern author has explained that the most important innovation in af Chapman's larger oared warships was his system for longitudinal strength. This is lucidly explained by af Chapman himself in *Försök till en theoretisk afhandling att gifva at linieskepp deras rätta storcek och form* (Karlskrona 1804), pp147–149. His diagonal support system is shown on drawing XXXVI in his *Architectura Navalis Mercatoria* of 1768 (there have been several modern reprints).

2. The same solution was reintroduced in the Armstrong-designed gunboats from the late 1860s (the Rendell gunboats) where hydraulic power was used to lift a heavy gun from the bottom of the hull to the firing position.

This kanonslup *of Fredrik Henrik af Chapman's design was mass-produced in Sweden in 1808–9 and was very similar to contemporary Danish and Russian copies of Chapman's designs. Note that the guns can be moved down to the bottom of the craft when not in use. To facilitate mass-production a standard drawing was printed and distributed to small yards along the coast. (Statens Sjöhistoriska Museum, Stockholm)

only volunteer crews could be used and officers had to be experienced in army-type bivouacs – hence the need for a separately constituted Inshore Fleet.

The war between Sweden and Russia in 1788–90 to a considerable extent became a test of the new technology for skerries warfare. During the war the Russians very rapidly built a new archipelago fleet of vessels which at least roughly equated to the new Swedish types and the last large-scale battles with oared vessels took place during 1789–90. The results were clear-cut: the galleys were no longer suitable for frontline warfare – a Russian galley force was massacred in 1790 when it made a frontal attack on a line of Swedish gunboats and broadside-armed vessels. The galley was too lightly armed, but large enough to be easily hit, and the crew was very exposed to gunfire. Much of the front of a galley fleet formed in line was used by the broad sweeps of oars, not by guns. On the other hand, broadside-armed vessels provided powerful gunfire when anchored in a defensive formation but were vulnerable in their slow approach during an attack and they were often lost in retreats. Therefore by 1790 Sweden was already minimising the use of such vessels and had concentrated building efforts on gunboats, a policy that proved successful in combat.

The gunboats proved to be the best offensive and defensive weapon carriers in the archipelago. They had high mobility and manoeuvrability and needed little tactical sophistication – relatively untrained crews could easily form long lines of gunboats to provide relatively concentrated gunfire. Acting individually or in

A Swedish kanonjolle *design of November 1789, used for mass-production during the winter 1790 when Sweden prepared an early spring assault on Russian bases. This small single-ended gunboat was essentially a floating gun mount. Note the two longitudinal bulkheads which extended from the gun mounting to the stem. These were made of 3¾in oak and were intended to diffuse the stress from the firing of the 24pdr along the small hull. (Krigsarkivet, Stockholm)*

small groups, they could attack larger vessels from shallow waters or from angles where these could not manage much defensive fire and they could penetrate into narrow and shallow waters where neither galleys nor broadside-armed vessels could act. Their low hulls made them difficult targets and they easily escaped during retreats. As they were also cheap to build and easy to maintain on shore under cover, the small gunboat proved to be the final solution to the problem of oared warfare.

The oared gunboat

Gunboats were not unknown outside the Baltic before 1788–90 but little is known about such vessels. Algiers and Spain used gunboats in their contests in the 1770s and 1780s and Spain used such craft during the siege of Gibraltar in 1779–83. France built various types of *chaloupes-cannonières* in the Channel area during the war of 1778–83. These latter seem to have been primarily sailing craft for harbour defence and coastal escort duties, the larger being armed with three guns (18pdrs or 24pdrs), two forward and one aft. Turkey built a large number of gunboats during the war with Russia in 1787–92, Venice built gunboats from the 1770s and Austria from 1788. These latter were somewhat

larger than the Swedish (about 80 tons), shorter, with more beam and draught and armed with only one 24pdr. This was a sailing gunboat design with auxiliary oars, suited for open water, which reflects the different requirements in the Baltic and the Adriatic.

During the long war period 1793–1815, large numbers of flotilla craft of gunboat types were built around Europe and also in North America. The most spectacular of these was the French Boulogne flotilla which was intended to lift a large army to Great Britain. Thousands of specially built or requisitioned small craft suitable for amphibious warfare were massed in the Channel area during 1798–1801 and 1803–06. These forces included several hundred *chaloupes-cannonières* of the three-gunned French type and *bâteaux cannoniers* of smaller types (armed with one 24pdr and a landing gun) which at least partially was copied from the Swedish designs. The Dutch navy also used gunboats for coastal defence, apparently an indigenous design which was primarily intended for sailing. In Italy, the French forces built gunboat flotillas of considerable size in Venice and in the south. All these forces were short-lived *ad hoc* creations and they disappeated when peace reduced the military and naval efforts.

The Danish-Norwegian navy, by tradition a sailing battlefleet, had used a limited galley force and shallow-draught broadside vessels with considerable skill during the Great Northern War. After 1720 only a few galleys were maintained. From the 1780s systematic experiments with various gunboat designs were conducted. The problem was that the open waters around Denmark required a craft with

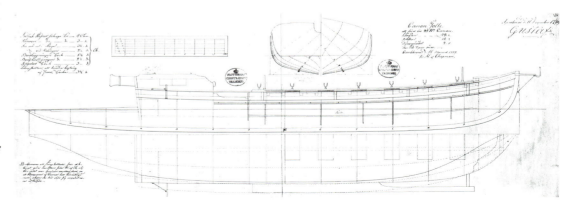

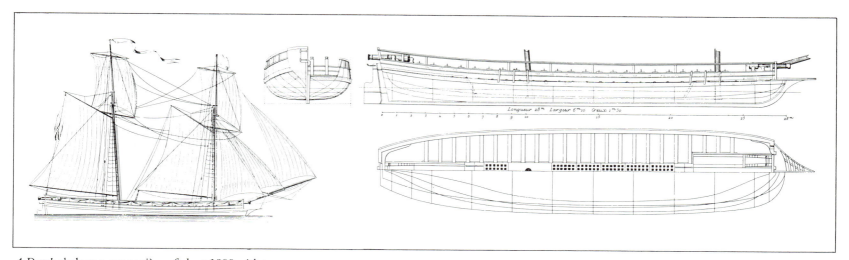

A Dutch chaloupe-cannonière *of about 1800 with two guns forward and one aft. Unlike many native designs primarily intended for sailing, this is a French-style galley, although it could set a primitive schooner rig. (From Paris'* Souvenir de Marine*)*

some sailing abilities while the strategically important archipelago in the Norwegian-Swedish border zone required a craft that was primarily an oared vessel. In the end a Swedish design was chosen based on drawings acquired from Russia. This type went into series production when Denmark-Norway had to recreate some naval defence after the British capture of almost all their sailing warships in 1807. In spite of the fact that these gunboats were intended for sheltered archipelago waters they proved able to fight with some success in the open sea against British brigs and merchantmen in several small actions from 1807 to 1813. As Russia built most of its early nineteenth-century gunboats to exactly the same dimensions as Denmark-Norway and as the type was practically identical with the Swedish af Chapman-designed gunboats which were built 1788–90 and 1808–09, the Baltic powers had achieved what must have been the most complete international standardisation of warships ever in the pre-industrial age. The small Swedish *kanon-jolle* type was also copied although not in large numbers.

The young navy of the United States made an attempt to build a gunboat force as an alter-native to the sailing fleet during the presidency of Thomas Jefferson (1801–09). Jefferson was opposed to the very idea of a permanent sailing navy with a large professional officer corps and possible entanglement in European power politics. To him and his party coastal defence gunboats manned by the militia was a solution to the maritime defence problem in line with their view of America's future. In practice the large number of gunboats built (around 200) to several designs proved to be disappointments, possibly because there was little systematic testing of prototypes before series production begun. The problem with these gunboats reported in the literature indicate that the European experiences were not properly digested and that traditional sailing navy requirements were allowed to dominate over the special requirements of oared warfare.

The American gunboats were primarily built as short and broad-beamed sailing craft which made them difficult to handle under oars. The idea of mounting the gun on a rotating turn-table amidships – an attempt to produce broadside fire typical of a sailing warship – proved impracticable. Such small vessels almost capsized from the recoil of the heavy gun and it was very difficult to aim such a gun accurately in any other direction than forward and aft. However, firing in these directions damaged the rig as the boats fought under sail. The successful European craft had fought under oars alone (with the rig dismantled) and they essentially aimed their gun with the rudder. Finally, oared craft could only be used against broadside-armed vessels in shallow or narrow waters or during calms. The large American harbours in general did not offer favourable conditions for gunboats to operate as a defensive force against attacking sailing ships. America's cities were founded from the seaward side, and were placed where the early colonists found convenient harbours for their sailing ships.

After 1815 large permanent gunboat forces were primarily maintained by the Baltic states

Despite its reliance on the deep-sea dominance of its fleets, the Royal Navy also built coast defence gunboats at various times. This model depicts one of Commissioner Hamilton's designs, of around 50 tons dating from 1805. The first six were employed at Gibraltar but a further eighty-five were built from 1808 and these saw action in the Danish skerries as well as around the coast of Britain. This is a late example with a long gun on a slide mounting and a pivotting carronade aft. Note the frame-like thwarts for the rowers. (NMM)

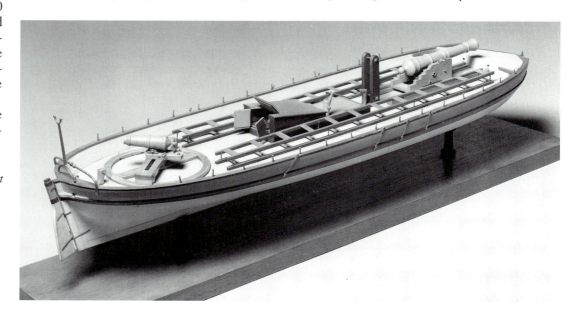

(Sweden-Norway, Denmark, Russia, Prussia) although Austria continued to use gunboats of a sailing craft type in the Adriatic. Most of these gunboat forces used vessels that were based on the ideas developed in Sweden in the 1770s and the basic types changed only marginally in design. Small forces of gunboats existed in other navies. From about 1830 shell guns introduced the possibility of enhanced fighting power gunboats against larger ships. Gunboats saw some action during the war between Denmark and Germany in 1848–50 and in the Anglo/French-Russian War of 1854–56, but the experiences were limited. Russia mass-produced oared gunboats as late as 1854 but that year also saw the introduction of the small steam-powered screw gunboat (in the British navy known as the 'Crimean gunboats'). With two heavy guns in a small shallow-draught hull there was a considerable similarity in the concept but as the steam gunboat had a small crew of sailors only it was no longer a potential landing craft. In fact, the old combination of heavy gunfire and amphibious assault capability which galleys and oared gunboats had provided since about 1500 has never been recreated in the machine-powered navies. Machinery can do a lot which muscular power cannot but it is unable to turn a landing force landed from a small warship into an infantry. Landing craft were of course reintroduced on a large scale during the Second World War but none has been produced that at the same time can give fire support to troops and alternatively act as a coastal defence craft.

Jan Glete

Oared Fighting Ships; Typical Craft 1650–1840

Ship or Class	Type	Nationality	Launched	Armament	Dimensions Feet–inches Metres	Banks	Remarks
Standard type	Galley	French	c1670		140–6 × 19–0 42.8 × 5.8	25	
Flagship type	Galley	Venetian	c1690		170–0 × 22–6 51.8 × 6.9		
Standard type	Galley	French	1691		153–6 × 19–0 × 7–6 46.8 × 5.8 × 2.3	26	Standard design fixed 1691
Not known	Small galley	Russian	1704		72–0 × 10–2 × 2–6 21.9 × 3.6 × 7.6		Early Russian small galley, *skampavej*
SV PETR	Galley	Russian	1704		128–4 × 16–4 × 6–11 39.1 × 5.0 × 2.1	16	Early Russian galley, probably Mediterranean type
GRIPEN	Small galley	Swedish	1713	2–18pdr	97–4 × 19–6 × 5–10[1] 29.7 × 5.9 × 1.8[1]	15	Early Swedish-designed galley
CAROLUS	Galeass	Swedish	1717	3–36pdr, 2–18pdr, 4–12pdr, 44 swivels	155–9 × 31–2 × 9–9[1] 47.5 × 9.5 × 3.0[1]	30	Super galley or galeass
HORN	Galley	Swedish	1720	1–24pdr, 2–6pdr, 2–4pdr, 14–3pdr swivels	126–6 × 19–8 × 7–6[1] 38.6 × 6.0 × 2.3[1]	20	An early Swedish Mediterranean-type galley
Standard type	Galley	Tuscan	c1725	1–24pdr, 4 lighter and swivels	155–3 × 20–3 × 7–3 47.3 × 6.2 × 2.2	26	
Standard type	Galley	Venetian	c1725		146–0 × 18–6 × 6–8 44.5 × 5.6 × 2	25	
Standard type	Galley	French	c1725	1–36pdr, 2–8(?)pdr, 2–6pdr and swivels	152–0 × 19–6 × 7–8 46.3 × 5.9 × 2.3	26	
BODRAJA	Half-galley	Russian	1739		100–0 × 17–6 × 4–5 30.5 × 5.3 × 1.35	16	Typical small Russian galley of the 1730s and 1740s
UPSALA	Galley	Swedish	1749	1–24pdr, 2–6pdr, 19–3pdr swivels	126–6 × 19–6 × 6–6[1] 38.6 × 5.9 × 2.0[1]	20	Swedish standard galley, short Mediterranean type
ACHILLES	Floating battery	Swedish	1749	20–24pdr, 6–6pdr	118–0 × 33–0 × 11–3[1] 35.9 × 10.1 × 3.4[1]	7	Typical Swedish *pram*, broadside-armed, heavy hull
Standard type	Galley	Maltese	c1749		155–10 × 21–5 47.5 × 6.5	26	One under construction 1749

Ship or Class	Type	Nationality	Launched	Armament	Dimensions Feet–inches Metres	Banks	Remarks
Not known	Galley	Turkish	c1749	1–30pdr, 2–12pdr, 2–8pdr, 22 swivels	160–6 × 20–7 49.0 × 6.3	27	A galley based at Rhodes c1749
Flagship type	Galley	French	c1749	1–36pdr, 2–8pdr, 2–6pdr, 2–2pdr, 24 swivels	174–0 × 22–6 × 10–7[1] 53.1 × 6.9 × 3.2[1]	29	Late French galère extraordinaire
Not known	Brigantin	Maltese	c1749	4–3pdr, 8–3pdr swivels	55–3 × 11–5 16.8 × 3.5	12	Brigantin or half-galley
LODBROK	Turuma	Swedish	1771	2–18pdr, 24–12pdr, 26–3pdr swivels	122–9 × 30–2 × 10–9[1] 37.4 × 9.2 × 3.3[1]	19	Broadside armed archipelago frigate
TORBORG	Udema	Swedish	1772	2–18pdr, 15–12pdr, 24–3pdr swivels	117–10 × 28–3 × 8–3[1] 35.9 × 8.6 × 2.5[1]	20	Centreline armed archipelago frigate
PERNOV	Galley	Russian	1773		140–0 × 20–0 × 6–6 42.7 × 6.1 × 2.0	22	One of the last mass-produced Russian galleys
Standard type	Gunboat	Swedish	1776	1(later 2)–18pdr, 4–2pdr swivels	61–10 × 13–2 × 2–6[1] 18.9 × 4.1 × 0.8[1]	10 (14)	First Swedish gunboat type
EKATERINA	Oared frigate	Russian	1790	2–24pdr, 20–18pdr, 2–12pdr, 14–6pdr	130–0 × 32–0 × 11–0 39.6 × 9.8 × 3.4	?	One of 8 built in 1790
Kanonslup	Gunboat	Swedish	1790	2–24pdr 4–3pdr swivels	66–3 × 14–6 × 4–0[1] 20.2 × 4.4 × 1.2[1]	14–15	With small variations built in large numbers 1789–90
Kanonjolle	Small gunboat	Swedish	1790	1-24pdr	48–4 × 9–11 × 2–4[1] 14.7 × 3.0 × 0.7[1]	7	With small variations built in large numbers 1789–90
Standard type	Gunboat	Venice	1795	1-24pdr, 2-1pdr	57–8 × 16–1 × 5–3[1] 17.6 × 4.9 × 1.6[1]	12	Several built 1774–95. Later an Austrian standard type
Standard type	Gunboat	French	1803	3-24pdr, 1-6pdr howitzer	82–0 ×18–4 × 6–6[1] 25.0 × 5.6 × 2.0[1]	?	Chaloupe cannonière
Standard type	Gunboat	French	1803	1-24pdr, 1 landing gun	65–6 × 15–1 × 4–11[1] 20.0 × 4.6 × 1.5[1]	?	Bâteau cannonier
JUPITER	Gunboat	Swedish	1803	2-24pdr, 6-12pdr carr, 4-3 swivels	75–0 × 17–6 × 5–8 22.9 × 5.3 × 1.7	14	Special decked gunboat type for open water operations
No 50	Gunboat	American	1806	1-24pdr or 32pdr, 2-12pdr carr	48–3 × 18–0 × 5–4 14.7 × 5.5 × 1.6	?	One of several US gunboat designs
Standard type	Gunboat	Russian	1806	2-24(?)pdr	66–3¼ × 14–7½ × 5–9¼ 20.2 × 4.5 × 1.8	15?	Based on Chapman's gunboats. 199 built 1806–09
KALLUNDBORG	Gunboat	Danish-Norwegian	1807	2-24pdr	66–3 × 14–8 × 3–9[1] 20.2 × 4.5 × 1.1[1]	15	Based on Chapman's gunboats. 168 built 1807–14, 11 more 1825–33
VON SYDOW	Gunboat	Swedish	1830	1–72pdr shell gun, 1–24pdr, 4–3pdr swivels	63–0 × 13–10 × 4–0[1] 19.2 × 4.2 × 1.2[1]	13	Prototype for the last series of Swedish gunboats
No 1	Gunboat	Prussian	1848	1-24pdr, 1-25pdr carr	63–0 × 11–0 × 4–0[1] 19.2 × 3.4 × 1.2[1]	13	First of 36 Prussian gunboats built 1848–49. Some had composite-built hulls

Notes:
[1] Draught of water. Banks relate to the number of oars per side.

7

Support Craft

SUPPORT craft of various kinds were used by the British navy far more than any others, for several reasons. First, the British fleet operated much further and longer away from its main bases, and needed transports, hospital ships and other craft to supply it. Second, the British Parliament, while reasonably generous in providing money for warships, was rather more parsimonious about dockyard buildings. As a result, old warships became hulks, and were adapted for many purposes. For a parallel political reason, the British Admiralty preferred to keep its seamen afloat in hulks where its authority was absolute, rather than ashore where it might be disputed by local magistrates and other officials. Finally, the British dockyards were all in strongly tidal waters and certain operations, such as the fitting of masts, were better done from a base which was itself floating – hence the lack of mast cranes in British naval yards, and the prevalence of sheer hulks.

The Dutch also employed many support craft, though for entirely different reasons. Their waters were proverbially shallow, so they pioneered the use of dredgers to clear channels into their ports. They also developed the 'camel' to lift a large ship over a sandbank. The Venetians, with their difficult lagoon, were not far behind.

Support craft can be divided into three main categories. The first group consisted of purely static vessels, especially the various types of hulk which were used within the British dockyard ports. Secondly there were harbour support vessels, such as dredgers, buoy boats and towing vessels. These were essentially mobile, but remained within the vicinity of a particular harbour to service the harbour itself, or the vessels entering or leaving it. Finally, there were completely mobile ships and vessels, able to follow a fleet at sea, or to carry out miscellaneous transport duties.

A sheer hulk in action, raising the lower masts of a ship of the line, the power being derived from the men at the capstan at the stern of the hulk. From an engraving of 1805 by J T Serres.

Static vessels

Sheer hulks

A sheer hulk was defined as 'an old ship of war, cut down to the gun or lower deck, having a mast fixed in midships, and fitted with an apparatus consisting of sheers, tackles and co, to heave out or in the lower masts of His Majesty's ships.'[1] The ship to be fitted with its masts was brought alongside the sheer hulk, which was permanently moored off one of the main dockyards. The sheers formed a kind of crane by which the mast was lifted from a lighter, and then lowered through the holes in the deck of the ship to be fitted. Sheer hulks were not universal; merchant ships were usually masted by a system of sheers fitted aboard the vessel to be rigged, and in the tideless ports of the Mediterranean and Baltic it was far more common to have the sheers fitted on the dockside.

The sheer hulk appears to have originated in

1. W Burney, *Universal Dictionary of the Marine* (1815, reprinted New York 1970).

Despite the fact that Port Mahon, Minorca, had a dockyard (and a purpose-built naval hospital), as the main Mediterranean fleet base for the British in the eighteenth century it still required a large number of hulks for accommodation and storage. Most are clearly superannuated ships of the line, but a few frigates are also visible. Many of Britain's home bases were similarly cluttered, and present day shore establishments (known as 'stone frigates' to seamen) often owe their names to the hulked ships that formed their first homes. (NMM)

England in the late seventeenth century, and in 1694 the *Chatham Hulk* was purpose built for the role. This was extremely rare, and it was far more common to convert an old warship, usually a two-decker. One such was the *Guernsey*, rebuilt in 1740 as a 40-gun ship, and converted to a hulk for service at Woolwich in 1769. She retained her lower deck and orlop, and the remains of her upper deck formed a kind of quarterdeck and forecastle. She was equipped with a large mast amidships, supported by nine shrouds on her starboard side, and only four to port. Like most sheer hulks, she was equipped to operate on one side only, and her port side was fitted with heavy wooden fenders to protect the ships coming alongside. She had two large capstans in the waist, for operating the sheers, and smaller ones on the quarterdeck and forecastle, mainly for manoeuvring the ships coming alongside. Internally, she was equipped with a few cabins, and many storerooms. In 1807 each British sheer hulk was manned by a boatswain, mate and six seamen, though presumably more were brought on board for heavy work.

The sheer hulk spread after its inception in the 1690s, and each of the six main English dockyards had at least one for the remainder of the age of sail. It also spread to France, and one was in use at Rochefort by the 1740s, under the name of 'Machine à mâter'. However it was not needed in the tideless seas, and remained mostly a British device.

Prison hulks

The prison hulk was one of the types of vessel which was almost unique to the British. Originally prisoners of war had mostly been kept in old fortresses and castles, with the officers being given parole in inland towns. In the Seven Years War the British took an unexpected number of prisoners, and began the practice of keeping them in harbour hulks. The prisoner of war hulks became even more common during the French Revolutionary and Napoleonic Wars; by 1814 there were eighteen ships at Portsmouth, sixteen at Plymouth and ten at Chatham. All were old men of war, and many were prizes. The division at each port was commanded by a captain, and most ships had a first and a second lieutenant.[2] Men were crammed into the ships, even more than on a warship in commission. Unlike hospital ships, there were no doubts about using the orlop deck for accommodation, though holes were sometimes cut near the waterline to allow ventilation. Prison hulks, like other static vessels, soon acquired extensive and ramshackle upperworks; their gunports were barred to prevent escape, and washing lines often reduced the seamanlike appearance even further. One witness reported just after the wars with France had ended,

> The Medway is covered with men of war, dismantled and lying in ordinary. Their fresh and brilliant painting contrasts with the hideous aspect of the old and smoky hulks, which seem the remains of vessels blackened by a recent fire. It is in these floating tombs that are buried alive prisoners of war – Danes, Swedes, Frenchmen, Americans, no matter. They are lodged on the lower deck, on the upper deck, and even on the orlop deck.[3]

The use of hulks for civilian convicts began in 1776, as the American revolt ended the practice of transportation over the Atlantic, and caused the jails to become grossly overcrowded. An Act of Parliament was passed to allow convicts to be kept in old warships, and they were to be landed in the daytime to carry out labouring work in dockyard construction, often in dredging.

The Mediterranean powers had condemned criminals to service in the galleys, and as late as 1780 there were still five French galleys at Toulon serving as static prison-hulks.

Other hulks

The British dockyards were reasonably well equipped with buildings and other facilities up to the middle of the eighteenth century. After that, despite some large scale building programmes, the supply never quite met the demand. Furthermore, it was politically impossible to consider building barracks for seamen ashore. Instead, they had to be kept afloat, even when they were awaiting allocation to a ship. From about 1740 onwards, dozens of old warships were laid up and converted to hulks and storeships for various purposes. Receiving ships were moored at the main anchorages, such as Spithead and the Nore, and used for the accommodation of seamen recently recruited by the press gang, or being transferred from one ship to another. Naturally the largest warships, especially three-deckers, were most suitable for this role. Although not resorting to the same methods of impressment, other navies found receiving ships useful for the temporary accommodation of seamen.

The guardships were similar to receiving ships in wartime, but served a slightly different function in peacetime. They were kept at the

---

2. Navy List, 1814.

3. Dupin, quoted in F Abell, *Prisoners of War in Britain 1756–1815* (London 1914).

The hoy was a common naval support craft, either hired or specially built and employed as both fleet tender and dockyard auxiliary. There was little to differentiate a mercantile hoy from a naval one, and this contemporary model of about 1730 shows the main features of hull and rig. (NMM)

main ports, partly manned, armed, rigged and stored, and ready to be fitted for sea very quickly if war threatened. Unlike the receiving ships, they were in good condition and often highly favoured vessels. Hulks were also used for miscellaneous stores – gunpowder, clothing (slop ships), rigging hulks for storing cordage and blocks, and numerous others.

Harbour service craft

Hoys and lighters

Ships could rarely come alongside in ports, due to difficulties of manoeuvring, depth of water, and often fear of desertion. Supplies needed to be brought out to them – whether in the main dockyard ports, or in anchorages such as the Downs, Torbay or the Ile d'Aix (near Rochefort). All ports needed small craft to take

The Admiralty draught of a large 104-ton sailing lighter for service at Chatham Dockyard. The first was built in 1785, but the draught was used for two further vessels in 1798. She has both a large and a small davit over the bow so may well have been intended for maintaining the many moorings in the Medway. (NMM)

supplies out to ships, either in the harbour itself or in a nearby anchorage. Many were single-masted, gaff or lug rigged sailing craft, and in Britain these were generally known as hoys. The actual definition of this term varied, but in most cases it was a craft of rather round cross section and bows, often with a 'pink' stern. In 1783, Portsmouth Dockyard had two of these: the *Forrester* of 112 tons, with a crew of six men and a boy, built in 1748 and used for taking stores to ships at Spithead, and for ships being built by contract elsewhere in the area; and the *Old Truelove* of 58 tons, with a crew of six, built in 1720 and used mainly for supplying ships under repair.[4] By 1813, Woolwich had two transport craft.[5] In other navies, similar craft followed local rig types, some French auxiliaries carrying the *chasse-marée* (lugger) rig so popular on the Atlantic coast.

Normally a 'lighter' was an unrigged vessel, propelled by large oars or by towing. However the term 'sailing lighter' was quite common, and Portsmouth had one in 1783, for example. A sailing lighter launched at Gillingham (near Chatham) in 1785 was of 306 tons, with heavy bows and a wide flat stern. She had a certain amount of accommodation for master and crew in the bows and stern, a large hold amidships, and was well equipped with heavy capstans and windlasses, to help move anchors or serve as a buoy boat when required.[6] However, 'dumb' lighters, without any mast or sails, were more common; Portsmouth had nine small ones in 1783, ranging from 29 to 91 tons, and used for carrying stores to and from ships. In addition, the yard had four mooring lighters, of 108 to 120 tons, to service the chains and buoys which were used for the ships of the Ordinary; and two chain lighters of 54 and 58 tons for similar work. Such a vessel, built at Deptford in 1787,

was of 43 tons. It had no crew accommodation, and was open amidships. It had a very large davit over the bows, and two windlasses in the hold.[7]

Other craft were rather more specialised. Pitch boats were used for supplying tar and pitch to ships; one built at Plymouth in 1806 was of 42 tons.[8] Each yard had at least one buoy boat, used by the Master Attendant for shifting and repairing navigational and mooring buoys. That at Portsmouth in 1783 had been taken from the French three years earlier, and was of 35 tons. The *Tamar*, used at Plymouth a few years later, was rather like a hoy in shape, with two windlasses and a capstan.[9]

Personnel transport

Because of the large number of ships in any dockyard port or its neighbouring anchorages, there was a constant movement of personnel to and from them. At the higher end of the scale, the dockyard officers had a yacht to take them to outlying parts of the harbour, or to go on board ships to supervise the payment of the seamen. Workmen such as riggers or shipwrights were taken out to work on ships afloat, and other craft were used to patrol the yard at night, to look out for smugglers and petty thieves as much as to guard against enemy in-

4. R J B Knight, *Portsmouth Dockyard Papers 1774–1783, The American War* (Portsmouth 1987).

5. B Lavery, *Nelson's Navy* (London 1989), p224.

6. NMM Draught No 4630.

7. NMM Draught No 4505.

8. K V Burns, *Plymouth's Ships of War* (Greenwich 1972).

9. B Lavery, *op cit*, p224.

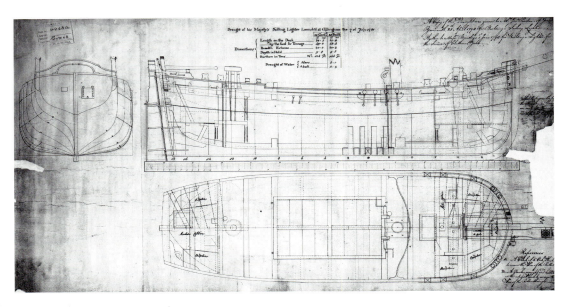

The Admiralty draught of the Trinity Lighter, *a simple grab dredger of 1786 for use at Deptford Dockyard.* (NMM)

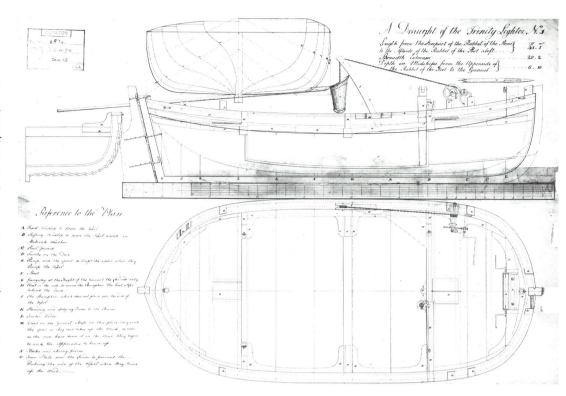

cursion. Every yard had a full range of vessels to carry out these duties. In 1783 Portsmouth had three yachts; one for training the young men of the Royal Naval Academy, one for the Commissioner, and one for the Governor of the Isle of Wight. The Commissioner also had a pinnace, yawl, cutter and wherry. The two Master Attendants, who spent much of their time inspecting the ships laid up in Ordinary, had three boats between them. The other officers of the yard had thirteen boats between them, mostly yawls and wherries. There were ten more yawls and workboats, used by the workers of the yard for various tasks.[10] The yachts were simply a scaled-down version of the royal yachts which had served with the navy since 1660. The wherries were light rowing craft, as used on the Thames and other rivers, while the yawls were probably fitted for either rowing or sailing. There was a certain amount of interchange between ships' boats and dockyard craft. The launch, as adopted as a standard ship's boat by the British Navy around 1780, had originated as a heavy workboat in the dockyards. By 1813 the complement of boats at Woolwich included gigs and cutters, and these had possibly been first brought to the yard in the form of ships' boats.[11]

Dredgers

Shallow water presented a problem in many dockyards, particularly those of Britain and the Netherlands which faced onto the North Sea. Yards such as Deptford, Chatham and Woolwich were on sites well up river. Ships tended to get larger and deeper over the years, while the rivers began to silt up. Surprisingly little was done about the problem in Britain, and until very near the end of the eighteenth century, methods were primitive. The most common type of craft used was the 'spoon dredger', originally invented by the Dutch in the Middle Ages, but still in use throughout the age of sail. Around 1800 it was described as follows:

> The common method of dredging is performed by men in a barge; the gravel, or ballast, is taken up in a leather bag, the mouth of which is extended by an iron hoop, attached to a light pole, of sufficient length to reach the bottom; in the small way, two men are employed to work each pole. The barge being moored, one of the men takes his station at the stern, with the pole and bag in his hand, the other stands in the head, having hold of a rope, tied fast to the hoop of

the leather bag. The man at the stern now puts them pole and bag down, over the barge's side, to the bottom, in an inclined position. The hoop being farthest from the man in the head of the barge, and having a rope, one end of which is fast to the gunwale of the barge, he passes it twice, or thrice, round the pole, and then holds it tight; the man in the head now pulls the rope, fastened to the hoop, and draws the bag and hoop along the ground, the other allowing the pole to slip through the rope as it approaches the vertical position, at the same time causing such friction, that the hoop digs into the ground, the leather bag receiving whatever passes through the hoop; both men now assist in getting a bag into the barge, and delivering its contents.[12]

This system could be improved in small ways. In 1786, for example, a vessel known as the *Trinity Lighter* was constructed at Deptford yard on the Thames, fitted with a crane and windlass to help raise the bag; it was 47ft 7½ins long, 20ft 1in broad, and of 61 tons.[13] Around this time convicts were often employed in dredging work, especially at Deptford and Woolwich. Yet more sophisticated was the ladle dredger, which used a battery of spade-like devices, each at the end of a long pole. The pole-men operated from small boats, and the ladles were drawn towards the broadside of a large barge, by means of winches. This system was invented at Leiden by van Wesel in 1627; it was revived by the French in the eighteenth century, and used at Brest and Toulon.[14]

Clearly the bucket dredger, in which a continuous chain fitted with a series of buckets was

rotated, would be far more efficient for large scale work. Such a system had been proposed as early as the sixteenth century, by Leonardo Da Vinci among others. The first practical machine is believed to have been produced by Muys at Delft in 1589. It became quite common in Dutch waters, especially at Amsterdam. It could be powered by men operating a treadmill, a series of wheels, or a capstan. Alternatively it could be driven by a horse-gin. But until the development of the steam engine it was difficult to find enough power to operate the machine at its full efficiency. As a result, steam power was applied to dredgers before it became common as the main propulsion of ships. The first steam dredger was built in 1796, for use in Sunderland harbour. The British continued to lead at this type of machine, and in 1804 another version was used by John Rennie at Hull.[15]

Camels

When it was not possible to deepen a harbour entrance by dredging, the Dutch sometimes

10. R J B Knight, *op cit*, pp166–7.

11. B Lavery, *op cit*, pp224–5.

12. *English Encyclopaedia* (London 1802), vol, p195.

13. NMM Draught No 6894.

14. G Singer, *A History of Technology*, Article by G Doorman in vol 4, pp632–3.

15. G Doorman, *loc cit*, p641.

A contemporary engraving of a Venetian 74-gun ship lightened with the aid of a pair of camels for crossing the lagoon. The bracing timbers through the lower deck ports are clearly visible, while the cables that secured both halves of the camels run over seven chocks that were probably fitted with sheaves to allow the cables to be more easily tightened up.

instead of the rectangular exterior form of the Dutch camel.

Pressing tenders

The 'pressing tender' was another craft peculiar to the British navy, for it alone used the crude means of conscription known as 'impressment'. The press gang always preferred to get its victims afloat as soon as possible, partly because the legal power of the Admiralty was much greater at sea, and partly because sea transport provided a convenient and relatively escape-proof way of getting men to the fleet. Pressing tenders first appeared during the Second Dutch War in the 1660s, when they were used to carry men from the Tower of London to the fleet at the Nore. Typically they were small merchant ships, such as hoys. By the 1690s the methods of hiring them had become established; they were 'hired by the ton for wear and tear; King to victual and man; owners to find guns and necessaries, but not powder and shot'. By this time, the tenders were equipped to hold men for somewhat longer periods. 'Formerly the pressed men had no conveniencies of bedding, but lay on the ballast, or the cask, which proving prejudicial to their healths, the masters are now supplied with bedding for them. . . . The ships allow hammocks out of their stores.'[17] Even so, the hold of a pressing tender remained very unpleasant: 'Gracious God, what a place! It was somewhere in the bowels of the ship. There was a kind of platform where several persons were sitting, reflecting seriously on their state, and some swearing furiously.'[18] The press room was in the hold, and its sides were constructed of stout timbers. Its hatch was heavily barred, and guarded by marines.

By 1704, each large warship was allocated a number of tenders. While manning for the first time, a three-decker had three tenders, and while replenishing with men it had two. A Third Rate ship had two or one tender, and a Fourth Rate had one, only during its first man-

reverted to another method: raising a ship further out of the water by attaching vessels known as 'camels' to the hull. In earlier periods it had been normal to raise a ship over a shoal by fixing casks to the hull. Around 1690, the camel was invented for raising ships over the shoals in the Ij near Amsterdam. A British authority described it as follows:

A camel is composed of two separate parts, whose outsides are perpendicular, and whose insides are concave, shaped so as to embrace the hull of a ship on both sides. Each part has a small cabin, with sixteen pumps, and ten plugs, and contains twenty men. They are braced to a ship underneath, by means of cables, and entirely enclose its sides and bottom; being then towed to the bar, the plugs are opened, and the water admitted until the camel sinks with the ship, and runs aground. Then, the water being pumped out, the camel rises, lifts up the vessel, and the whole is towed over the bar.[16]

Much of the weight of the ship was taken by large timbers inserted through the gunports of the lower deck. Models suggest that many camels were much larger, with more than sixteen pumps her side. As well as the Dutch, the Russians used camels at St Petersburg, and the Venetians used them for getting large ships into the lagoon; in this case, the two halves seem to have been shaped more like lighters,

16. W Burney, *op cit*, p66.

17. Corbett Ms, Admiralty Library.

18. W Mark, *At Sea with Nelson* (London 1929), p65.

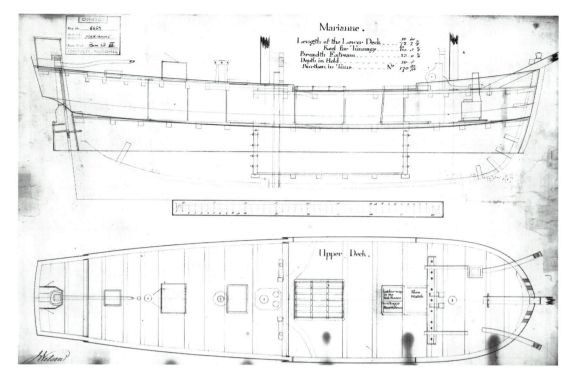

Marianne.

Length of the Lower Deck ....
Keel for Tunnage ....
Breadth Extream ....
Depth in Hold ....
Burthen in Tons .... N° 170

At 170 tons the Marianne *was relatively large for a pressing tender but the claustrophobic nature of the 'press room' in the hold is all too apparent.* (NMM)

ning. After 1755, tenders tended to be operated by the Impress Service rather than by individual ships, and to be attached to ports where the permanent shore-based press gangs operated.

The type of vessel used is illustrated by a report of 1742,[19] which describes seven tenders hired in the Portsmouth area. Typical was the *William and Margaret* brig, tender to the Second Rate *Duke*. She had a crew of eight men, carried four carriage guns, four ½pdr swivels, and was of 74 tons. She had three anchors, one boat, and sailed 'indifferent well'. She had been built in New England, but now belonged to Teignmouth in Devon. Like her companions, she was poorly equipped for defence – 'open and no shelter'. The other six vessels were of 70 to 96 tons, rigged as snows, sloops or brigs; on average they accommodated one man per ton.

Seagoing auxiliaries

Transports

Transport ships were needed to carry troops overseas, either as part of an invasion force, or merely for normal troop movements. Transport ships also carried the supplies of food, ammunition and other stores needed by armies and navies. The great majority of transport ships were hired merchantmen, and were indistinguishable from their sisters in the general

trade, except for certain interior fittings. However the warship armed *en flûte*, without its full complement of guns, was also used in certain circumstances.

Several large invasion forces were assembled in the seventeenth century, and as an example of the numbers involved, for his 'Descent on England' in 1688, William of Orange needed 125 vessels, 'smacken, roeyers, galioots, boots and fluyten'.[20] By the following century the British were the main users of troop transports. Colonial warfare became predominant, and transatlantic movements were not uncommon. From the War of Jenkins' Ear (1739–48) onwards, a large amount of naval effort was put into amphibious warfare, especially in the Mediterranean and West Indies. In the American War of Independence the problem reached new proportions, and a great army had to be transported across the Atlantic, and kept supplied in hostile territory. During the wars that followed there was little let-up, for there were dozens of amphibious operations, and from 1808 another army had to be transported and supplied in the Iberian peninsula. The French also used great numbers of transports, though less regularly; Napoleon's expedition to Egypt in 1798 required over one hundred vessels.

In 1711, an unsuccessful British expedition to Canada used thirty-one troop transports, ranging from 66 to 530 tons.[21] Each carried one man for every 1½ tons. By the Seven Years War, it became normal to allow 2 tons per man, and this remained the figure for the rest of the age of sail. The American War of Inde-

pendence was fought across the Atlantic, and involved a vast transport effort. At this stage vessels were still hired by the Navy Board, among its many other duties. In the French Revolutionary and Napoleonic Wars the system was changed, and a separate Transport Board was set up. Apart from expeditions to the West Indies and other areas of imperial expansion, the Peninsular War was a major commitment after 1808. In 1810, 77,400 tons of shipping were used for troopships; 17,617 for horse transport; 3690 for army victuals; 16,534 for navy victuals; and 32,574 for transporting stores to the overseas dockyards. In addition, the Ordnance Board hired its own transports for carrying heavy guns and ammunition.[22]

A typical troopship was a medium sized merchant ship, of 300 to 400 tons. She was fitted between decks with cabins for the troops, and they were issued with hammocks and bedding to sleep in. As passengers, they were only entitled to two-thirds of the victualling allowance of seamen. The ships were expected to have at least 4ft 8ins height between decks, and in 1762 the *Prosperous Armilla* of 382 tons was rejected as a trooper for the expedition against Havana, precisely because she was 'too low between the decks for soldiers'.[23] Some shipowners built their businesses largely on supplying ships for government service. Henley's of Wapping was a notable example:

Between 1793 and 1802 and from the end of 1804 until October 1815 Henley's always had ships in the transport service. They accompanied and reinforced major expeditions; they victualled and watered major fleets; they supplied armies in Scandanavia, Germany, the Low Countries, France, Spain, all parts of the Mediterranean, North and South America, the West Indies, Cape of Good Hope and America. . . . They moved troops, horses, equipment and stores round the coast of Britain and Ireland, backwards and forward across the Channel and Atlantic. They remained as storeships for weeks and months on end, sometimes in hostile environments, sometimes in uncomfortable and even dangerous anchorages. Their boats and

19. NMM POR/H/5.

20. J Carswell, *The Descent on England*, (London 1969), p169.

21. D Syrett (ed), *The Siege of Havana, 1762*, Navy Records Society (London 1970), pp178–9.

22. B Lavery, *op cit*, p273.

23. D Syrett, *op cit*, p5.

The British landings that led to the capture of Havana, Cuba in 1762. The troopships are to the left of the painting with landing boats full of soldiers heading for the shore. The British had considerable experience of amphibious operations, but because opposed landings were not usually attempted, there was no impetus to develop the specialist assault ships of the twentieth century. (NMM)

crews helped land soldiers and their equipment on enemy shores.[24]

Arming *en flûte* was typically a French way of carrying troops. A naval ship with its main guns removed, or stowed in the hold, could carry a large number of men, and still be fit for operations after they had been discharged. It could even pretend to be an active warship, and perhaps deter an attack in this way. In the Bantry Bay expedition of 1796, the French transports carried mostly horses and stores, while seventeen ships of the line, thirteen frigates and a flotilla of smaller vessels carried troops about their decks.[25] In Napoleon's invasion of Egypt, two ships of the line and seven frigates were armed *en flûte*, as well as 100 transports. The British used this system occasionally, and sometimes in peacetime; for example, the *Tiger* and *Invincible* carried a regiment of infantry to Gibraltar in 1752, having their lower deck guns taken out. Later, obsolete ships, particularly small two-deckers of 44 or 50 guns, were also used for carrying troops.

As well as hired and purchased craft, most major navies had at least a few purpose-built storeships and transports at various times in their history, but only the French navy regularly designed significant numbers for naval service. Generically known as *flûtes*, the largest – about 900 tons burthen by the end of the eighteenth century – had the proportions and layout of small frigates but with a much fuller hull form; the smaller versions of 200–500 tons were closer to corvettes. In 1780 there were twenty in service, of which seven were larger than 400 tons.

In general appearance they resembled warships, and were masted on similar proportions, but they had fewer gunports, which were usually disposed on the upper deck amidships without extending to the ends of the deck. Armament was only 4pdrs, 6pdrs or occasionally 8pdrs and only the largest would carry more than about eighteen guns. Nevertheless, they were occasionally employed, as in the French navy, as makeshift cruisers and a few were converted to bomb vessels and other special duties; one or two of the larger type, such as the *Ménagère* captured during the American War, even served as frigates in the Royal Navy.[26]

Hospital ships

Like other support craft, hospital ships could be either static or mobile. Some naval ports, especially in Britain and her colonies, had no hospital ashore, and an old vessel was used in-

stead. One such was an old 90-gun ship, the *Blenheim*, fitted out as a hospital ship in 1743. Her middle and upper decks were used for the accommodation of patients, and each was divided into areas described as 'ague ward,' 'itchy ward,' 'flux ward' and 'fever ward', with cabins for nurses in the corner of each. There were 255 cots for patients on board. On the upper deck were cabins for the lieutenant in command, the surgeon and his mates. The orlop deck was difficult to ventilate, and was 'thought unwholesome for the sick'.[27] Static ships became less necessary after the mid-eighteenth century, when naval hospitals were built to serve the fleet at Portsmouth and Plymouth. Nevertheless Chatham still had no hospital, so an old 74, the *Arrogant*, was used as hospital ship for most of the Napoleonic Wars. She was commanded by a lieutenant, with a purser, gunner, boatswain and carpenter, but no master. She had a total crew of sixty-seven, plus twenty-five marines to prevent desertion.[28] Falmouth, which was not a regular naval port,

24. *Henley's of Wapping*, National Maritime Museum Monograph, pp16–7.

25. E H Jenkins, *A History of the French Navy* (London 1973), p222.

26. Jean Boudriot, *The Seventy-Four Gun Ship* (Rotherfield 1987), Vol 3, pp258; 264.

27. Lloyd and Coulter, *Medicine and the Navy*, Vol III, p67, 1961.

28. B Lavery, *op cit*, p216.

also had a static hospital ship in this period, the *Chatham*, an old 50-gun ship. Quarantine ships were also employed at many ports. These were generally old men of war, and were known as lazarettos.

Mobile hospital ships became increasingly important throughout the eighteenth century, as fleets operated ever further from their home bases, and large fleets of troop transports were fitted out. Even in 1688–90, the English navy was hiring four ships, ranging from 240–400 tons, to follow the Channel Fleet.[29] The *Reward* hospital ship of 399 tons followed the abortive expedition to Quebec in 1711. In 1762 the Admiralty ordered the Navy Board 'to cause three ships of about 400 tons each (and one of 300 tons for the smallpox only) to be fitted for hospital ships for the troops to be employed on the same service [*ie* the assault on Havana], and the said four hospital ships to be fitted with ventilators and awnings'.[30] Aside from the ships which followed the fleets of

In the French navy the term flûte *referred to a specialist naval storeship. In the eighteenth century they were to become rather frigate-like but their origins show that the name was originally purely descriptive. This storeship for the galley fleet, dated 1684, confirms that the original vessels were indeed very similar in form to capacious Dutch fluyts. (From Paris'* Souvenirs de Marine)

transports, some hospital ships were dedicated to the main fleets, and carried the Physician of the Fleet on board. One such was the *Charon*, used by Dr Thomas Trotter with the Channel Fleet in the late 1790s; she was an old 44-gun ship built in 1783.

Exploration craft

In the second half of the eighteenth century, the maritime powers began to fit out ships with naval crews, and send them to the unexplored areas of the world, mainly in the Pacific, to conduct scientific research, and to find new territory which could be annexed. Such ships count as naval vessels, though many were converted merchantmen of various types which had been taken into naval service. For the British, the wave of exploration began soon after the end of the Seven Years War, when Captain John Byron carried out a circumnavigation in the 24-gun Sixth Rate *Dolphin*, built at Woolwich in 1751 according to the 1745 Establishment of Dimensions. The same ship set out again in 1766, commanded by Samuel Wallis and accompanied by a smaller vessel, the *Swallow*, commanded by Phillip Carteret. In fact the two vessels separated during the voyage, and the *Swallow* carried out a good deal of exploration on her own. Meanwhile, the French

had sent out an expedition in 1766, under Louis de Bougainville. Again a standard naval ship was used, the 26-gun 'frégate de 12' *Boudeuse*, built near Nantes in 1762, to a design by Rafeau. She too was accompanied by a smaller vessel, the flute *L'Etoile*.

By this time it was becoming recognised that regular warships, however well they might reflect the majesty of the state, were not really suitable for exploration. They were not designed to spend years away from home bases, so their holds tended to be too small; their powerful armament was largely superfluous; they needed large crews, which were not always easy to find; and they tended to be deep draughted, which was a serious disadvantage. When James Cook was chosen to lead the British expedition into the Pacific in 1768, he chose the type of ship on which he had begun his career – the sturdy, roomy, square-hulled but unglamorous Whitby collier. The *Earl of Pembroke* of 366 tons was purchased for the Royal Navy, re-named *Endeavour*, and fitted with much more extensive accommodation below decks. Even so her officers' cabins were comparatively cramped, for she carried a team of scientists led by Sir Joseph Banks. However

29. British Library, Sloane Mss 1815.

30. D Syrett, *op cit*, p6.

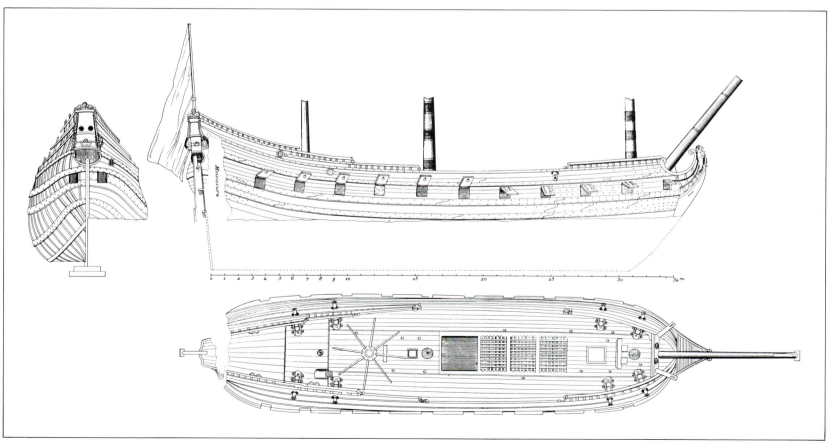

of the voyage was to transplant samples of breadfruit rather than pure exploration. As a result, the internal fittings of the ship were rather different, and for the return voyage most of the great cabin was to have been given over to plant pots.

Converted warships could still be used for certain purposes. In 1773 Constantine Phipps set out to look for the North East passage, using the converted bomb vessels *Racehorse* and *Carcass*. The former ship, of 385 tons, had been captured from the French in 1757; the latter was built at Rotherhithe in 1759. Both had their bow planking doubled against the Arctic ice, with strong bracing inside the hull. (The strong hulls of bomb vessels made them particularly suitable for ice navigation and a number were used for Polar exploration, the most famous being the *Erebus* and *Terror*, which took part in Ross's Arctic expedition of 1839 and were later lost during Franklin's disastrous attempt on the North West Passage.) In 1790 the Spanish explorer Malaspina began a circumnavigation with two small, specially built ships, the *Descubierta* and *Atrevida*. In 1791 George Vancouver reverted to an earlier practice for his voyage in the Pacific. He sailed in a new *Discovery*, built privately in 1789, bought by the navy soon afterwards, and rated as a 10-gun sloop. After her return she was converted to a bomb vessel, and became a prison ship at Deptford in 1799. As such she was drawn by E W Cooke in the mistaken belief that she was Cook's old ship.

Brian Lavery

the *Endeavour* served Cook well during the three-year circumnavigation; she grounded on the Great Barrier Reef, but was careened and repaired by her crew.

For Cook's second voyage, the idea of using the Whitby collier was retained, but experience suggested that two vessels were needed in case one was damaged. The *Resolution* (ex-*Marquis of Granby*, 462 tons) and the *Adventure* (ex-*Marquis of Rockingham*, 336 tons) were converted in a similar way. The *Resolution* was retained for his third voyage, but the *Adventure* was replaced by the *Discovery* of 299 tons. The fashion for converted merchant ships lasted after Cook's death, though the Whitby collier was not always used. In 1788 William Bligh set sail in the *Bounty*, a ship of 215 tons, built at Hull four years earlier. This time the purpose

Fleet Support: Typical Craft 1650–1840

Name	Type	Nationality	Launched	Built	Dimensions Feet–inches Metres	Burthen	Remarks
Not known	Towing galley	English	1658	Chatham			A rowing 'tug' to manoeuvre ships in the constricted waters of the Medway
CHATHAM	Towing galley	English	1683	Chatham	76–0*kl* × 9–6 × 4–0 24.93*kl* × 3.12 (×2) × 1.31	73	Twin-hulled towboat for the Medway
PROFOND	Storeship	French	1685	Rochefort	127–6 × 29–9 × 13–10 38.88 × 9.07 × 4.21	450	Early French *flûte* or large transport, 6 guns (40 as warship)

Name	Type	Nationality	Launched	Built	Dimensions Feet–inches Metres	Burthen	Remarks
BLENHEIM	Hospital ship	British	Woolwich (RB)	1709	162–3 × 47–2 × 18–10 53.23 × 15.47 × 6.18	1418	Converted from 90-gun ship
FORTUNE	Transport	British	1709	Deptford	126–3 × 31–2 × 13–6 41.42 × 10.23 × 4.43	545	Dockyard-built transport, 24 guns
GUERNSEY	Sheer hulk	British	Chatham (RB)	1740	134–0 × 38–8 × 15–9 43.96 × 12.68 × 5.17	863	Converted from a 50-gun ship in 1769
ROYAL ESCAPE	Lighter	British	Limehouse	1743	63–2 × 20–0 × 8–4 20.72 × 6.56 × 2.73	106	Typical dockyard lighter
CULLODEN	Smack	British	1746	Plymouth	43–0 × 14–0 × 5–6 14.11 × 4.59 × 1.80	36	Transport/guardship for duties off the Scottish coast
ESTURGEON	Transport	French	1746	Brest	116–3 × 21–6 × 11–4 35.42 × 6.55 × 3.46	360	French *gabare* (small transport), 10 guns
MEDWAY	Receiving ship	British	Deptford	1755	140–4 × 42–10 × 18–6 46.04 × 14.05 × 6.01	1204	Converted from a 60-gun ship in 1787; renamed *Arundel* 1802
TRINITY LIGHTER	Dredger	British	Deptford	1756	41–1 × 20–2 × 6–10 13.48 × 6.62 × 2.24	62	Fitted with davit and winch for dredging
BOUDEUSE	Exploration ship	French	Indret, nr Nantes	1766	132–10 × 34–9 × 10–7 40.50 × 10.58 × 3.24	960	Used by Bougainville in the Pacific
ENDEAVOUR	Exploration ship	British	Whitby	*p*1768	100–0 × 29 32.80 × 9.51	366	Used by Cook on his first voyage
MÉNAGÈRE	Storeship	French	1775	Rochfort	153–6 × 34–8 × 14–4 46.80 × 10.56 × 4.36	650	French *flûte* or large transport, 28 guns
BELLEROPHON	Prison hulk	British	Frindsbury	1786	168–3 × 47–4 × 19–9 55.20 × 15.53 × 6.48	1644	Converted from a 74-gun ship in 1815.
DISCOVERY	Exploration ship	British	Rotherhithe	1789	96–0 × 27–0 31.50 × 8.86	337	Used by Vancouver; bomb vessel 1799; prison ship 1818
MARIANNE	Pressing tender	British		*c*1795	72–2 × 23–0 × 10–5 23.68 × 7.55 × 3.42	171	Typical hired pressing tender, with secure 'press room' below decks, and strengthened hatches
TAMAR	Buoy boat	British	Cowes	1795	64–10 × 21–0 × 9–1 21.27 × 6.89 × 2.98	121	Fitted with capstan and davits; also rated as a storeship
Chatham sailing lighter	Hoy	British	Brindsley, Lynn	*c*1800	60–3 × 20–0 × 9–5 19.77 × 6.56 × 3.09	106	Fitted with a capstan, two winches and three davits for work in the river.
INVESTIGATOR	Survey vessel	British	1811	Deptford	75–0 × 19–10 × 10–11 24.61 × 6.51 × 3.58	121	Purpose-built survey vessel
Not known	Lighter/ water tank	American	1816	Charlestown	62–9 × 18–0 × 4–6 20.59 × 5.91 × 1.48		Schooner rigged vessels for dockyard work and watering ships
Not known	Rowing barge	British	Plymouth	1823	35–0 × 8–½ × 3–33 11.48 × 2.64 × 1.09		Typical yard rowing craft
CONSORT	Exploration ship	American	1836	Boston	78–9*bp* × 25–4 25.84*bp* × 8.31	230	Barque rigged vessel for Wilkes' expedition to South Seas
SOUTHAMPTON	Storeship	American	1845	Norfolk, VA	152–6 × 27–0 × 16–0 50.03 × 8.86 × 5.25	567	Converted from paddle steamer

Notes:
Dimensions are usually length on moulded breadth and depth in bold, but *kl* = keel length, *bp* = between perpendiculars. Units are English feet and inches and unit metric equivalents. RB = rebuilt.

Design and Construction

NAVIES were potent, but expensive, instruments of national power and prestige, so even in the age of autocrats building warships could only be justified to defend and promote a nation's most vital interests. National policy aims dictated the strategy under which the fleet would operate and these factors determined the procurement policy – the numbers, types and sizes of warships to be built. Thus warship design in the age of sail could never be a purely abstract exercise of the naval architect's skill. The designer worked to a specification constrained by the tonnage, cost or gunpower stipulated, and behind every order for a new ship was a framework of assumptions – strategic, tactical and financial – laid down by the navy, and ultimately the government, that employed him.

National policy and warship procurement

This can be demonstrated in the broadest terms for all the major navies of the age of sail. The navy of the United Provinces in the mid-seventeenth century was intended to protect and encourage the country's immense foreign trade, and initially comprised relatively small warships and a high proportion of armed merchantmen, which were able to deal with pirates and small local squadrons. These vessels were at a disadvantage in action against the genuine battlefleets of England and France, and so larger ships were built (including a few three-deckers), but it is noteworthy that the Netherlands reverted to its small-ships policy for most of the eighteenth century when an English alliance freed her from a battlefleet threat. By contrast Cromwellian England began with small fast 'frigates' suitable for hunting down Royalist privateers, but soon traded speed for gunpower when faced with the Dutch, who made little attempt to evade battle unless grossly outnumbered. The rationale for the sudden development of French naval power under Louis XIV has always been something of a mystery, but the very large size of its ships suggests an attempt to wrest command of the sea from the existing naval powers by means of superior quality if not quantity (an attitude perhaps reflected in the extensive programme of very large three-deckers, the most powerful ships of their day).

By the end of the War of Spanish Succession (1713), England was established as the leading naval power and thereafter France gave up any concerted attempt to compete in numbers. She developed a doctrine of the use of naval power which emphasised the primacy of the 'mission'; this allowed an admiral to refuse battle if it would jeopardise the task for which he had been sent to sea, and this tended to favour speed over gunpower in warship design. This also encouraged the traditional French concern for individual quality (most obviously manifested in large size for any given Rate), in complete contrast to the British, who believed that sea control depended first and foremost on numbers, and always preferred the smallest, and hence cheapest, individual unit (the highest practical firepower-to-tonnage ratio was regarded as the most cost-effective).

Not only relative size but also the type of vessel reflected national priorities. Spain, for example, when rebuilding her navy after the War of Succession, opted for the 60-gun ship as a standard type. Spain's empire was still the most far-flung of her day and she needed ships of great range and staying power, which would be large enough to operate independently and embody considerable firepower on distant stations, but small enough to possess good all-round sailing and seakeeping qualities; they were not really battlefleet units but more akin to large cruisers, for colonial policing and showing the flag. Naturally, radical changes to national policy and strategy usually produced new types of ship – the English cruisers of the 1690s developed in response to the novel difficulties of war with France, for example – but the relationship is not always so obvious: the introduction into the Royal Navy of both the 74-gun ship and the frigate in the late 1740s is probably a reaction to the improved seakeeping required by the new strategy of the Western Squadron, with its emphasis on all-weather

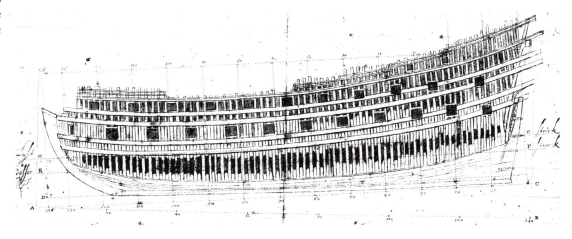

By 1650 the use of plans in the construction of large ships was already well established but few examples survive from this period or earlier. One that does is this mid-seventeenth-century Dutch framing plan of one of the typical moderate sized warships of 46–50 guns favoured by admiralties of the Netherlands; a matching internal profile also exists for this ship. Although the draughtsmanship is crude and freehand, it is convincing as to accuracy; the keel line is angled down to represent the position of the ship on the launchway (the Dutch employed the bow-first method of launching). (Scheepvaart Museum, Amsterdam)

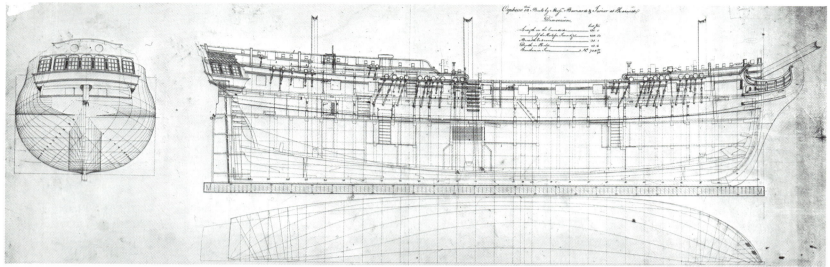

A typical British Admiralty draught of the later eighteenth century (the 32-gun frigate Orpheus *of 1773). To the left is the body plan, with lines defining the shape of vertical sections at regular intervals along the length of the hull; the lefthand side represents sections aft of midships and the righthand side those forward of it, although the stern is drawn in full. The elevation is a combined sheer (external view) and profile (internal), which on the original are drawn in black and red ink respectively; alterations were indicated in green. Below is the half-breadth plan, giving the waterlines (sections in the horizontal plane). This draught is an 'as fitted', made after the completion of the ship; it dates from a short period in the 1770s when such plans were mandatory, and is consequently slightly more detailed than the average design draught. (NMM)*

blockade. However, it should be remembered that technological innovation was relatively slow in the age of sail, so the apparent leaps forward in design were little more than steps in a process of gradual, if constant, improvement.

The shaping of design requirements

The mechanics whereby national priorities were refined into the specific requirements for a ship, class or building programme have not been much studied,[1] but the decision-making was always in the hands of a political body rather than the navy itself – the Admiralty Board in England or the office of the Minister of the Marine in France. These organisations decided the numbers, and in general, the types to be built, handing down broad specifications to an executive arm of the service. Thereafter, the systems differed radically: in France the orders would go direct to a *Conseil de Marine* (a naval council) at each dockyard, but in Britain there was an intervening Navy Board, a more or less permanent bureaucracy of civil servants and sea officers who administered the material side of the Royal Navy's affairs. Since it included the chief expert on shipbuilding – the Surveyor of the Navy – the Navy Board was always able to exert a powerful influence on design matters and at times completely dominated decision-making on the size and characteristics of warships built, sometimes to the frustration of the Admiralty's good intentions. By contrast, in France the Surveyor's equivalent, the *Ingénieur-Constructeur-General*, served with the Ministry and was available at all times to advise the Minister.

This led to a very different system of design in France, whereby individual dockyards (or more precisely, individual *constructeurs*) might produce their own designs to meet a centrally

decided specification; the design was always vetted by the *Ingénieur-Constructeur-General*, but it meant that the French navy could encourage new ideas, give young talent an opportunity, and produce a number of basically similar designs which could be evaluated against one another. At first glance the system operated in England during the period of the Establishments (roughly 1706–50) resembled that of France, in that the ships were designed by the individual Master Shipwrights at the Royal Dockyards, but the effectiveness of the English procedure was compromised by two factors: first, the dimensions were laid down in great detail and were considered immutable (they *were* altered from time to time, but not substantially, and only after considerable argument); second, if the surviving letters of Sir Jacob Acworth are any indication, the Surveyor regularly interfered with the design process, imposing his own views and suppressing any residual individualism allowed by the tight Establishment specifications.[2]

As a result of Admiralty dissatisfaction with Navy Board obstruction, from 1755 the design of all except small craft was concentrated in the hands of two Surveyors (three during 1813–22), whose appointment became a matter of vital importance to the Admiralty Board. Design variations on each specification, therefore, were usually confined to one from each Surveyor and large 'classes' of identical ships resulted; but if the specification was considered anew for each class there was still a possibility of steady improvement. This did not happen in the 1770s and 1780s, but at other times changes were frequent and large building programmes of numerous classes allowed variation. However, the Navy Board continued to exert a conservative influence, particularly constraining the growth in size of British ships,

and it is significant that it was not until after the abolition of the Board in 1832 that Royal Navy warships were built larger than those of rival powers. Paradoxically, after 1782 France made a concerted attempt to standardise on a few designs – mostly those of the brilliant Sané – but in practice, variations by particular *constructeurs* were still allowed.

Warship design

The designer's conundrum

Warships were not designed entirely *ab initio*, development being largely a matter of gradual modification, so the starting point was usually a

1. An honourable exception is Andrew Lambert's *The Last Sailing Battlefleet*, which covers British naval procurement policy in the 1815–50 period from Cabinet level to the minutiae of ship design.

2. PRO Adm 91/2–3, Surveyor's Office Letter Books, 1738–40 and 1742–5.

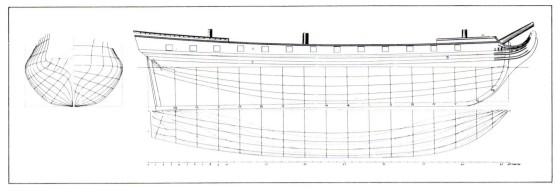

By contrast to British draughts, the French official plan is very austere indeed: the constituent parts are the same but the external details are confined to the most basic features like gunport positions and wales. Comparing design draughts with those taken off after capture, it is clear that the design plans do not even represent the final configuration of topside details like rails. No quarter galleries are indicated but it was French practice until late in the century to produce separate drawings for the heavily decorated extremities of the ship (see Chapter 12). This plan of the frigate Medée is from Souvenirs de Marine but was obviously traced by Admiral Paris from an official original.

'previously successful ship'. This might be a consciously chosen prototype, or the many such ships represented by the designer's accumulated experience. Every design had to take account of ships it might meet in combat, so there was always mutual influence among opposing forces, but some navies found specific inspiration in the ships of the enemy. In the second half of the eighteenth century the British navy built many ships 'to the lines of' French prizes, but this should not be construed as crude copying; it was usually just a starting point, and the resulting ships might exhibit markedly different design emphases. All the second rank powers were influenced by the great navies of their day (the Dutch in the seventeenth century, and the English and French in the eighteenth), not just through employing foreign nationals to build their ships but by conscious evaluation of different approaches to design and construction: the Swedes, Danes and Spaniards all tested British and French style ships on their way to establishing a national design policy that suited their own particular requirements. Most navies knew as much as they desired about each other's ships, and there were no technological secrets in the modern sense;[3] this made ship design a common European (and later American) heritage, which left the designer to choose how best to resolve the competing requirements of a good warship.

The qualities of a sailing warship might be summarised as:

1. *Firepower* – this encompassed not only the number and weight of guns, but the space to fight them, the height of gunports to allow the heaviest (always the lowest for stability reasons) to be fired in heavy weather, and the characteristics of a good gun platform – slow, steady rolling (also an aspect of requirements 2. and 5.).
2. *Good sailing qualities* – speed is the most obvious, but was not always the priority it might seem; ideally, it should be on every point of sailing, and the advantage might be lost if the ship was not weatherly. Stability was also important – neither too stiff, which would induce rapid and violent rolling, nor crank which would prevent the carriage of sufficient sail; the ability to carry sail well (without strain on hull or rigging) was the object.
3. *Manoeuvrability* – to be able to steer well, and to go about (both tacking and wearing) quickly and with certainty, since the safety of the ship might depend on it.
4. *Range* – for a sailing ship this was largely a matter of the ability to stow enough ammunition, water, victuals and stores for long cruises; navies with distant colonies usually insisted on stowage for a minimum of six months at sea.
5. *Seakeeping* – in essence this meant that the ship should be able to meet the worst extremes of wind and waves without losing its ability to fight; a 'sea-kindly' hull was one whose motions (particularly rolling and pitching) were not too violent, which could rise to a head sea, and which did not ship too much water. Subsidiary characteristics were the ability to lie-to or scud under reduced canvas and to ride at anchor safely in heavy weather.
6. *Economy* – possibly the least obvious, this included capital (*ie* building) costs and running costs (frequency of repair); the size of ships was the main determinant of the first, while durability affected both, since poorly built ships cost more to maintain and had to be replaced more frequently.

None of these characteristics was absolute – 'good' could only describe performance in relation to a similar ship – but many features were actually at odds with one another. Speed required a long hull, manoeuvrability a short one; stowage implied a full hull shape, speed a sharp one; a shallow hull might be faster, but a deep hull would be more weatherly; a good height of battery made stability more problematical; a good reserve of stability would allow more sail to be carried, but would make the ship roll too quickly to be a steady gun platform. Similar contradictions can be found in the subtle variations of hull shapes: fine bow lines enhance speed and manoeuvrability, but could lead to the ship pitching and not rising to a head sea, particularly when weighed down with heavy armament forward; similarly, fine stern lines made the ship responsive to the helm, but ran counter to the requirements to carry guns far aft and rendered the ships vulnerable to being 'pooped' by a following sea.[4] All designers were aware that their profession was an art rather than a science, an inevitable compromise between competing requirements (the few that attempted extreme forms, like Sir William Symonds, were usually amateurs operating outside the mainstream of professional experience). Different nations chose to emphasise certain characteristics over others, and these inevitably reflect the policy concerns briefly outlined above.

The only relief from the incompatible requirements of the ideal warship lay in increased size, although even this could not entirely square the circle. French ships were traditionally bigger than those of their enemies and much of the superiority of French ships is a product of the greater scope offered to their designers by enlarged dimensions for a given weight of armament. An extreme example of this, from late in the history of the sailing warship, is the British battlefleet of the 1830s and 1840s which, in a break with long-standing tradition, abandoned previous size restrictions; by the admission of the French themselves, the ships designed during Symonds' Surveyorship were generally bigger, faster and carried their guns higher than those of their traditional foe.

3. The draughts of highly regarded ships often survive in the archives of many navies: for example, the plans of the French *Ambuscade* of 1746 exist as Danish, Swedish, Dutch and English ('as taken') copies.

4. An accessible outline of these factors is given by Jean Boudriot in *The Seventy-Four Gun Ship*, Vol 1, pp19–22.

However, to underline that even size is not a universal panacea, the ships tended to be too stiff and were not ideal gun platforms, their form making them prone to rapid and 'uneasy' rolling.[5]

The process of design

With the exception of small craft, the sailing warship was first and foremost a floating gun platform. Therefore, the starting point for any design brief was usually the number and calibre of guns to be carried, combined with a basic notion of dimensions. Although not all would need articulation, other characteristics would form a mutually understood set of 'staff requirements', as modern navies term them: height of gunports from the waterline; fighting space between guns; the thickness of the hull scantlings; ability to stow the necessary water, victuals and ammunition, as outlined above. Matters of seaworthiness and sailing qualities were important, if secondary, considerations, although they would be given a higher priority in a frigate, for example, than a ship of the line.

Armed with the outline requirements the designer began preparing a set of plans or draughts. Although medieval warships may have been built without plans, the practice was

5. The rationale for these ships is covered in great detail by Andrew Lambert in *The Last Sailing Battlefleet*. The technical reasons for their 'dipping oscillations' are quoted by William White in the 1877 edition of his *Manual of Naval Architecture*, pp118–120.

6. For example, J Boudriot, *The Seventy-Four Gun Ship*, Vol 1; B Lavery, *Ships of Line*, Vol II and *Deane's Doctrine*; David White, 'Understanding Ships' Draughts', *Model Shipwright* 46–56 (1983–85).

well established by the commencement of our period. Large ships whose shape was defined by pre-cut frames could not be easily altered so it was essential to 'prove' a well formed hull on paper first. To achieve this the draughtsman usually needed three views, each corresponding to a dimension: the sheer elevation was a side view; the half-breadth was a top view (only half was necessary because the ship was symmetrical about the centreline); and a body plan, which combined a bow-on and stern-on view (the bow usually to the right of the centreline and the stern to the left). On these were drawn the contour lines which defined the shape of the hull, which is why the shape of a ship came to be described as its 'lines'; these had to match in all three dimensions if the hull was to be 'fair'.

Besides those delineating the shape, other plans might be employed, such as a profile (a longitudinal elevation of the internal works, in some cases combined in a second colour with the sheer) and the layout of decks. These were necessary for fitting out the ship, but in the second half of the eighteenth century additional structural plans became more common; a framing draught would show the precise disposition of the main structural elements of the hull, while internal and external planking might be laid out in a two-dimensional form known as an expansion. Draughts were intended to convey the designer's intentions to the shipbuilder, and in most navies were quite austere (the French navy in particular), although some services produced separate sketches for carved work and decoration. Masting and rigging usually followed standardised rules and procedures, so outside the smaller navies spar

or rigging plans were rare before the nineteenth century, when ships began to receive more individual treatment.

Models were often used in the design process, but only relatively simple block models – called 'solids' in England – or half-models. The elaborate so-called Navy Board or Admiralty models took too long to build (indeed some are known to have been completed long after the real ship), so in most cases they can only have been for display purposes. Block models, on the other hand, would have been a useful three-dimensional draught, allowing the designer to demonstrate the hull form to the technically illiterate who could not read a conventional plan.

The main set of draughts would be accompanied by some form of highly detailed written specification, setting out precise requirements in terms of species and sizes of timbers, nature of fittings and exact quality of finishing. For a privately built vessel this would be part of the contract document, while those destined for the navy's own yard might simply follow existing conventions or a formalised 'establishment', although a simpler list of scantlings (timber dimensions) might be necessary. The employment of standardised conventions as well as specifications relieved the draughtsman of the necessity to depict every last detail on the plans.

Calculations and theory

Drawing up the plans was largely a matter of geometry, and although it was sometimes invested with a pseudo-scientific cloak, it was essentially empirical and highly dependent on the skill and experience of the designer. The mechanics are too complex to be outlined here but there are a number of readily available accounts in print.[6] For much of the sailing warship's history, the process of design involved little more than the draughting of the plans, but gradually some elements of calculation began to be included. The late seventeenth-century English designer Sir Anthony Deane was credited with a system that allowed him to work out his ships' draught of water before launching, but much of the contemporary effort – especially in France – was devoted to highly theoretical studies of hydrodynamics,

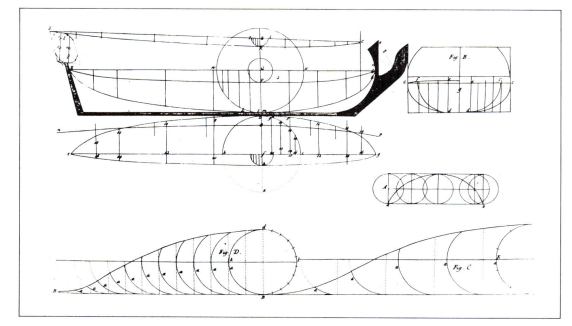

Early ship design was hampered by its insistence that all shapes should be derived from geometry, and relatively simple geometry at that. This plate from Sutherland's early eighteenth-century treatise The Shipbuilder's Assistant *shows how to develop curved shapes from circles.*

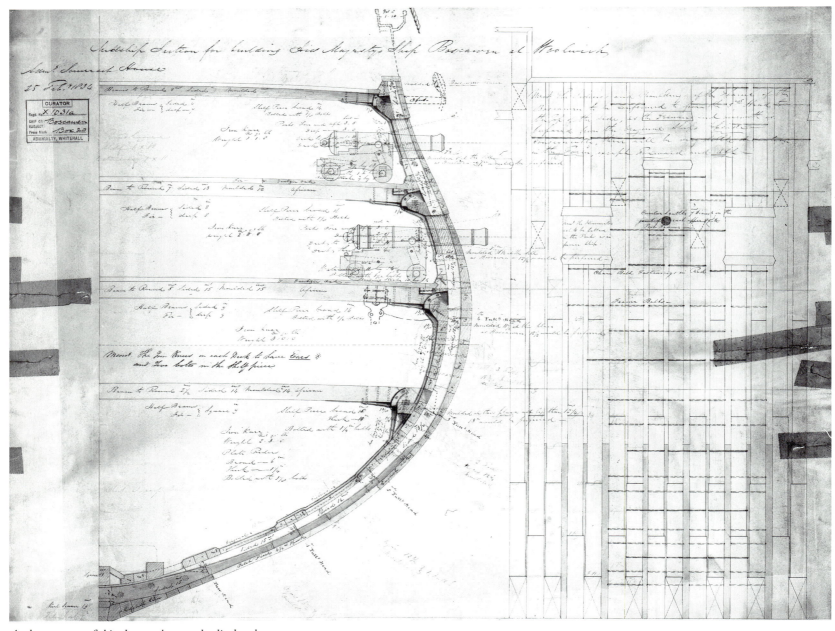

As the structure of ships became less standardised and more complex – a process that gathered momentum in the nineteenth century – the standard three-view drawings were no longer sufficient so additional sketches of detail were often provided. This Admiralty draught, dated 1834, represents the midship section and a length of framing of the battleship Boscawen. *The annotaion amounts to a minutely detailed specification of the fastenings – the type, size, number and position of bolts, iron knees and riders, all of which were being employed in ever increasing quantities.* (NMM)

which were not only inapplicable to practical shipbuilding but actually wrong.

Bouguer's *Traité du Navire* of 1746, which first expounded the concept of the 'meta-centre', offered a step forward in the under-standing of ship stability, but the calculation of the ship's centre of gravity was so long-winded that it is by no means certain that it was much used in practice. Indeed, the famous case of the French 74-gun ship *Scipio* of 1779, the cause of whose instability defeated all the contemporary experts, suggests that it was not.[7] Actually, cal-culating a vessel's stability *after* completion was relatively easy, and an inclining experiment to quantify this was formulated by Jean-Charles Borda, who became France's Inspector of Naval Shipbuilding in 1784.

The man who has been called the first naval architect,[8] the Swede F H af Chapman, pub-lished a number of important works on theo-retical aspects of ship design from the 1760s onwards, and gradually his influence spread as his books and papers were translated into the major European languages. As a practising shipbuilder his studies had a utilitarian dimen-sion missing from earlier work, and as late as the 1830s,[9] in the absence of anything better, these formed the basic textbooks of the Royal Navy's School of Naval Architecture. Unfor-tunately, in a pre-computer age the usefulness of calculation was devalued by the sheer length of time needed to carry them out: the scien-tifically trained 'Chatham Committee' was criticised in the 1840s for taking four months to design a ship, and it was far from obvious that the result was a better vessel.[10]

7. C N Romme, quoted in Fincham's *History of Naval Architecture*, pxliii and plxxiii.

8. Daniel G Harris, *F H Chapman: The First Naval Architect and his Work* (London 1989).

9. D K Brown, *Before the Ironclad* (London 1990), p21.

10. Andrew Lambert, *op cit*, p80.

This model of Woolwich Dockyard in the 1770s demonstrates how the sheer bulk of large timbers dominated the site of a shipbuilding yard. In the foreground 'unconverted' trees are piled up as delivered, but most of the other stacks consist of roughly shaped 'great timbers' awaiting employment as frames. They have been carefully wedged to allow air to circulate around them to aid seasoning. On the nearest slip the keel of a ship has just been laid and a few floor timbers are crossed, while the framing of the frigate beyond is almost complete. (SM)

Design mistakes and remedial action

Given the limitations of contemporary theory, it was inevitable that some ships, however well formed on paper, would be unsatisfactory. The high proportion of displacement given over to moveable weights – armament, stores, ballast – often meant that careful restowage might improve stability and even sailing qualities, but a permanent reduction in firepower or stowage would be regarded as a serious failure. It was also easy to modify the rig, and a reduction in sail area might improve stability or an increase provide more speed.

However, the most common design fault, especially in the seventeenth century, was inadequate stability and related difficulties like lack of sufficient freeboard for lower deck ports. Assuming that the problem was too radical for any of the relatively minor adjustments outlined above, then an increase in breadth would add stability and buoyancy. To achieve this the designer might have recourse to one of two methods: the ship could be 'girdled', with extra layers of planking added to the exterior of the hull; or a more extreme measure would be to strip off existing planking and add timber to increase the width of the frames (known as 'furring'). As the major navies became more experienced, these crude modifications became less common, but there are isolated examples even in the nineteenth century. At the same time ship design was becoming less experimental, so total failure was rarer; this allowed modifications to be reserved for later ships, and was one reason why design tended to become a process of gradual alteration of existing models.

Construction

Sources of supply

For all major navies, securing adequate sources of naval supplies was important enough to influence, if not dictate, the country's foreign policy.[11] Only the United States, with a comparatively small navy and a huge forested hinterland, was never short of suitable timber, but even America depended on some imported naval stores. The Baltic was the main source of cheap softwoods for planking (as well as some hardwood), pine for masts, hemp for rigging and Stockholm tar, which was widely used as a preservative. The principal shipbuilding timbers were hardwoods, of which oak was generally the most highly regarded, but elm had some specialist employment, particularly for keels.

The sheer bulk – and hence shipping cost – of the great timbers that comprised a ship's skeleton, made importation unattractive, if not actually impossible. For these reasons, even within a country transportation had to be kept to a minimum and most large shipbuilding timbers were locally obtained wherever possible. The amount of timber required for a major warship was astounding: in England, where the unit was called a 'load' (50cu ft or the equivalent of one large tree), by the 1750s a 100-gun First Rate would take up 5750 loads, a 74 about 3500, and even a 50-gun ship would consume 2450.[12] Given the huge building programmes provoked by the maritime wars of the seventeenth and eighteenth centuries, it is not surprising that local timber was often in short supply. Furthermore, the problem was exacerbated by the particular difficulty of growing the

The structure of a traditionally built wooden warship was complex and sophisticated, as shown by this model of the midship section of a British 74 of about 1795. By this time there was a growing shortage of large scantling timber for the frames and particularly the naturally formed 'grown' knees (the brackets that support and tie the ends of the beams to the hull sides) so moves were already afoot to reduce the requirement by the introduction of new techniques and technology – especially the use of iron for supports and fastenings. (SM)

11. R G Albion, *Forests and Sea Power* (Harvard 1926) and P W Bamford, *Forests and French Sea Power* (Columbia 1956).

12. Brian Lavery, *Building the Wooden Walls* (London 1991), pp56–7.

naturally curved 'compass' timber that was essential for frames and knees.

If timber could not easily be brought to the shipbuilder, then some navies sent their shipbuilders to the timber. France built a number of ships in Quebec before the province was lost to the British;[13] the British themselves had a few warships constructed in North America in the 1690s and 1740s, albeit reluctantly, but they were more enthusiastic about the teak-built products of Bombay which were gradually introduced after 1800. However, the most concerted and highly developed exploitation of colonial resources was by the Spanish, whose great arsenal at Havana in Cuba built nearly a hundred warships in the eighteenth century, more than any mainland dockyard.[14] Usually employing teak, Havana-built ships were among the largest, best finished and longest lasting in the Spanish navy.

An alternative response to the paucity of appropriate timber was to modify the methods of construction, and as the eighteenth century drew to a close there were more and more experiments directed to this end. The British had used softwoods for war emergency frigates in the 1750s (a tactic employed in later wars as well) but while the ships could be constructed quickly, they were rapidly worn out; softwoods were out of the question for ships of the line, which was where the shortages were most acutely felt, so the approach was no answer to the overall problem. (The Russians built softwood battleships in times of emergency but

they were very short-lived.) More careful husbanding of existing resources, particularly with regard to seasoning, became the norm from the 1770s and there were attempts to construct frames of more but shorter timbers or timbers of reduced scantlings. A more radical, and ultimately more successful, direction was to consider other materials; the Industrial Revolution made iron relatively cheap and plentiful in Britain by the late eighteenth century and its first novel application in shipbuilding was to be found in the gradual replacement of wooden knees with iron brackets of various patterns. The new approaches to hull construction and the increasing use of iron are inextricably linked with efforts to improve the structural strength of ships, and as such are dealt with in more detail below.

The structure of wooden warships

Since timber was not available in limitless lengths or sections, the wooden ship was fabricated from many pieces, and this placed the most fundamental restrictions on its size and shape. The stempost-keel-sternpost structure that formed the ship's 'backbone' was made up of several sections, as were the 'ribs' or frames (strictly speaking, these were 'framed bends' and comprised paired units of overlapping timbers called floors, futtocks and toptimbers). The essentially transverse nature of the framing meant that wooden warships were always deficient in longitudinal strength; the shape of the bow and stern with less buoyancy than amidships meant that in a seaway the ends tended to droop, distorting the hull, breaking the sheer and producing a condition known as 'hogging' (there were other destructive stresses

that shortened the life of a wooden hull but this was the most common).

To combat hogging ships had thickened strakes of planking known as wales and internal reinforcements called riders, but they were never very effective. As warships became larger the problem became more acute, and more effort was expended on finding a solution. Eventually, towards the end of the Napoleonic Wars the British Surveyor, Sir Robert Seppings, perfected a system of diagonal bracing that not only reduced the problem to manageable proportions, but also allowed the construction of ships which were far larger and stronger than their predecessors. Seppings compared conventional structures to a five-bar gate with the diagonal missing, and his system provided the diagonal, first in the form of wooden riders and then in a much improved iron pattern. Combined with the ever increasing use of iron knees, the diagonal system was first applied as an emergency measure to keep much needed but worn-out British ships of the line at sea in the final years of the Napoleonic Wars, so to some extent it was also a response to the timber shortage outlined earlier.

Seppings went on to introduce radical new timbering schemes for the vulnerable ends of the wooden warship. At the bow the cant frames were extended upwards to eliminate the filmsy beakhead bulkhead, and the frames themselves were rearranged. However, it was at the stern that his innovation was at its most radical: the highly vulnerable multi-level glazed stern windows were replaced by his so-called 'round stern', which was stronger and allowed all-round gunfire. Although a distinct improvement in fighting qualities, it was regarded as unsightly and difficult to build, and was gradually replaced by more conventional looking modifications, but the principle of a more solidly defensible stern was retained. Others also developed Seppings' basic structural ideas, with the result that the final generation of wooden warships were able to adopt longer and more efficient hull forms, to carry far more powerful armaments,

13. Jacques Mathieu, *La Construction Navale Royale á Quebec 1739–1759* (Quebec 1971).

14. John Harbron, *Trafalgar and the Spanish Navy* (London 1988), Ch 3.

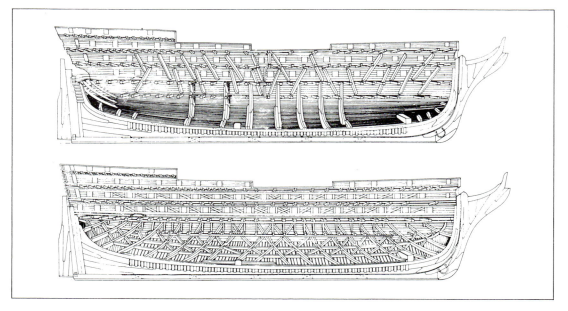

The biggest breakthrough in the structural design of wooden ships was achieved by Sir Robert Seppings who introduced a new pattern of diagonally bracing hulls; this allowed them to become both stronger and longer. He also pioneered the round stern, which contributed to the strength as well as the defensibility of the stern. These two drawings contrast (top) the traditional form of internal reinforcement, with its rather ad hoc pattern of riders and a stern structure that was not integrated with the rest of the framing, with (bottom) the original Seppings' system of wooden diagonal riders; these were later replaced with iron braces and trusses which were stronger and lighter.

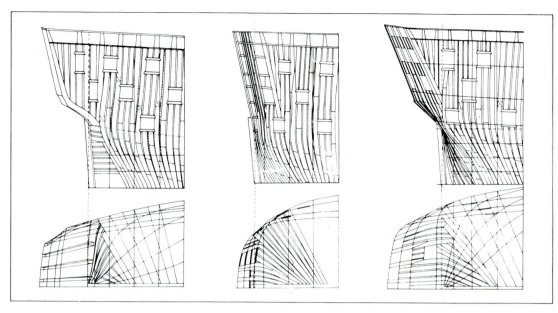

The nineteenth-century development of the stern progressed from the square stern (left), via Seppings' strong but aesthetically unpopular round stern (centre) to the elliptical stern (right). The square stern had only a flimsy framework, rendering ships highly vulnerable to raking fire; the round stern made the ship as well protected from aft as on the broadside, except that it left the rudderhead exposed; it was also difficult to construct, so aesthetics apart, the elliptical stern represented the compromise of a simpler but still defensible framing scheme. There were a number of improvements to the elliptical pattern during the 1830s and 1840s.

and to enjoy longer active careers – indeed, it is unlikely that the steam screw line of battleship would have been practical without this structural revolution.

The sequence of construction

The first step in the translation of a design on paper into a warship in wood was the process known as 'lofting'. To construct an accurate hull shape involved scaling up the outline of each of the ship's 'ribs' or frames and constructing a full size pattern or 'mould'; this was then used to cut the timber to shape. This process required a large area on which the lines could be scribed, preferably uninterrupted by supports or pillars. In England the top spaces of buildings came to be used, giving rise to the term 'mould loft' from which the activity became known as 'lofting'.

Before the advent of iron and steel, shipyards did not require very elaborate infrastructure and quite large wooden warships could be built almost anywhere with access to raw materials, labour and enough water into which to launch the completed hull. On the other hand, the state dockyards of the major navies were among the largest industrial enterprises of their day, and were usually in the forefront of technological development Britain's, for example, were quick to employ steam-driven machinery for labour-intensive activities like pumping, sawing and blockmaking. The usual method was to construct the ship on an in-

clined slipway, but some of the largest ships were built in drydocks and floated out, since this was less risky. However, the value of drydocks for maintenance ruled out their use for too many vessels. English vessels were usually launched stern-first while most European countries preferred the bow-first method.

The actual process of wooden ship construction has been well covered in print,[15] but it is important to remember that while the essential principles remained the same until the last generation of wooden warships, there was both a gradual development of techniques and a variation from country to country in detail

practice. In outline, the keel laying would be followed by the installation of the floor timbers and then the raising of the frames; the elaborate timbering of bow and stern came next, the whole structure being held together with temporary internal bracing and external strakes of ribbands (presumably derived from rib-bands) and the sharper angled harpins at bow and stern. For most of the history of the wooden warship a major problem was rot and decay in the great timbers, and the only agreed solution was the use of well seasoned timber. Therefore, if time permitted, the ship might be allowed to 'stand in frame' to season for at least a year, before the decks, planking and fittings were added. In the nineteenth century many navies left ships on the stocks for years, if not decades, as a form of ready reserve, but by this time it was felt that exposure to the elements could do more long term harm than good, so

15. See, for example, works by Lavery and Boudriot.

A demonstration model of the British 74 Bellona of 1760, exposing the framing and deck beams. The only planking applied are the wales and lower ribbands. (NMM)

A model of Deptford Dockyard in the 1770s. Because of competition for labour and dock space, maintenance and repairs could only be conducted at the expense of shipbuilding. In wartime this was an especially pressing problem, which the Royal Navy sought to solve by directing those like Deptford which did not also function as fleet bases to concentrate on construction and fitting out. (SM)

the practice arose of roofing over the hull on the slipway to keep rainwater out of the hull.[16]

Unlike modern ships, wooden warships were almost complete when launched so the fitting out period could be very short – a few weeks at the most in the full swing of a war effort, although this was extended somewhat after the introduction of copper sheathing, since this required docking the ship. The biggest task was to step the masts and yards and rig the ship, but it was also necessary to ship the ballast (in the form of iron 'pigs' and shingle), to take in the armament and stow the provisions and stores. Formal trials of a new ship were rare, but most major navies had a system of reporting on the sailing qualities of a ship and the best disposition of ballast and set-up of rigging to achieve optimum performance; since this experience could only be established over time, such reports often date from the end of the first (and sometimes later) commissions.

Refits, repairs and rebuilding

The almost organic nature of the wooden warship ensured that it required regular attention to keep it fit for sea. The hull was under continuous stress from the motions of the sea, which racked, distorted and damaged the structure; there was a perennial battle against rot and decay; marine borers might attack the underwater body, while weed growth would gradually reduce the ship's speed. On the other hand, wood was relatively easy to replace and everyday maintenance could be carried out by the ship's carpenter and his crew.

Various methods of cleaning the underwater hull – graving, paying and sheathing – were

16. A contemporary roof survives on the British frigate *Unicorn* of 1824, currently undergoing restoration at Dundee.

17. Roger Morriss, *The Royal Dockyards during the Revolutionary and Napoleonic Wars* (Leicester 1983), pp22–3.

18. Brian Lavery, 'The Rebuilding of British Warships 1690–1740', *The Mariner's Mirror* 66, 1 and 2 (1980).

probably the most frequent reasons for docking a ship, but this was reduced after the widespread introduction of coppering in the 1770s. In the Royal Navy it became the norm to give each ship a 'triennial trimming', which was a regular survey and refit, but the pressure of war inevitably extended the period between attention. Rapid wartime construction and the use of inferior or improperly seasoned timber made the need for serious repairs more frequent and further reaching. It is difficult to generalise about the longevity of wooden warships, because so many factors had a bearing, but it is clear that regular and extensive attention was essential for a long life.[17]

Even without battle damage, the cost of maintenance was very high – a ship might have more than three times its initial cost spent on it during an active career of a dozen years – but in a world where warships became obsolescent only slowly there was more incentive to preserve existing vessels. This lead to the practice of 'rebuilding', an elusive concept that encompassed everything from a major reconstruction without substantial change of design to a purely administrative fiction that allowed the construction of a totally new ship. During the period of the Establishments in England, the numbers of ships of the major Rates were considered fixed, so instead of building replacements, ships began to receive very considerable reconstruction, eventually culminating in the ship being entirely demolished and another built 'with the serviceable remains'; from here it was a short step to constructing a genuinely new vessel, and there are examples of ships existing for years only as a name on the Navy

List, while others were 'rebuilt' in different yards from where they were taken to pieces.[18] A variation of this situation pertained in early nineteenth-century America, where government parsimony prohibited funds for new ships, so they were provided out of the repair and maintenance budget under the cover of 'rebuilding'; one subject of this process, the corvette *Constellation* preserved at Baltimore, is still believed by some to be essentially the frigate of 1797.

It is commonly believed that warships developed very little between 1650 and the coming of steam, and compared with later nineteenth-century progress it is true that advances were not revolutionary. However, the old idea that the *Sovereign of the Seas* of 1637 would have been fit to fight at Trafalgar (1805) is facile: in the interim, the line of battleship had become larger, far more robustly constructed, was faster, more manoeuvrable and more seaworthy, and fired a greater weight of broadside at a rate that would have reduced the *Sovereign* and her contemporaries to total wrecks in short order. Better technology helped – improved gunfounding or a more efficient rig are examples – but much of the gain was the result of the gradual refinement of design and vastly improved methods of construction. By 1840, after the full application of the latest structural advances, the last generation of sailing warships were as superior to those of 1805 as the Trafalgar ships were to the *Sovereign*.

Robert Gardiner

9

Rigs and Rigging

THE 'machinery' of the sailing warship was provided by its masts, yards, sails and rigging, generically often referred to as its top hamper. In normal seaman's language the *rig* was understood to describe the design of that top hamper – the number, type and position of masts and the orientation of the yards and/or sails – whereas the term *rigging* was reserved for the constituent elements of the sail plan, but particularly the system of cordage and blocks that supported the masts and controlled the sails.

In early usage the definition of a ship type usually related to its hull design or employment, but during the eighteenth century it became more common to make the rig the characteristic aspect of a ship, giving rise to a kaleidoscope of possible meanings for traditional terms like 'brigantine' and 'bark'. The problem is largely confined to the lower end of most orders of battle, but some navies compounded the confusion by employing idiosyncratic meanings for standard terms – the Royal Navy's 'sloop' is the best known example, but there are others. As sail was challenged by steam in the nineteenth century the tendency to describe sailing ships by their rig increased, to the point where those meanings became formalised and static. These relatively late definitions are the ones understood by modern yachtsmen and seafarers but they are often misleading or even incorrect when applied to earlier periods.

In general rigs fall into one of two categories: square rigged, where the sails are carried on athwartship yards; and fore and aft rigged,

where the sails are disposed along the longitudinal centreline on yards or stays. Many types set canvas of both descriptions, in which case the category was decided by the orientation of the primary driving sails; in the vast majority of cases the rig name also implied the number of masts (unlike in the nineteenth century when more than three masts became so common that the definitions had to be stretched to take in the new types), the only significant exception being 'schooner' which could have two or three masts. All the largest vessels in this period were square rigged, which was reckoned the best all-round deep sea sail plan, but fore and aft rigs could sail closer to the wind and did not require so much manpower so were regarded as more handy for small craft in confined waters; they were less effective before the wind but some types like cutters carried large areas of square canvas to be set in favourable conditions.

The ship rig

As its name implies, the most widely employed of square rigs was the full or ship rig, effectively the norm for large vessels and used by all navies for their rated warships. After some late sixteenth- and early seventeenth-century experiments with four-masted ships, the rig settled down to three – reading from forward, the fore, main and mizzen (the fourth had been known as the bonaventure mizzen). Above those were separate topmasts, prefixed by fore, main or mizzen, with further masts – called the topgallants – above them (strictly speaking, the mizzen topgallant was a later development). Except for the mizzen lower mast, each of these masts had an equivalent 'square' (*ie* athwartship) yard and sail, called in the case of the first mast the fore yard, fore top (or topsail) yard and fore topgallant yards; the sails were known as the fore course (or fore sail), fore

A spar plan for an English three-decker of the 1670s from Anthony Deane's Doctrine of Naval Architecture. *The yards are shown in two positions – down on the caps (on deck for the lower yards) where they were carried when sail was not set; and hoisted to their positions under sail. The main features of the rig at this time are the spritsail topmast at the bowsprit end, absence of royals (and no mizzen topgallant, although the ship has a fidded flagstaff at the mizzen topmast head), and a long lateen mizzen yard.*

topsail and fore topgallant sail. The main was similar in nomenclature, but the mizzen set a fore and aft sail on a long lateen yard, with a square topsail above. Above the bow at an angle of roughly 45 degrees a further short spar called the bowsprit set a small square 'spritsail' below it.

This sail plan was to undergo a number of changes over the 200 years from 1650, but the improvements largely altered the extremities of the rig and added to the existing suit of sails. The seventeenth-century ship tended to have very large extensions to the uppermost masts for use as flag staffs, and it was common to carry extra fair weather sails on these. These 'poleheads' were not rigged as separate masts and the sails, lacking some aspects of permanent rigging, were said to be 'set flying'. The first mizzen topgallants were of this kind, while the sails carried at the top of the fore and main masts were originally known as topgallant roy-

1. Early pictorial evidence for the sprit topmast is provided by H C Vroom's painting 'Return to Amsterdam of Cornelis van Houtman from the East Indies in 1599'.

2. J Davis, *The Seaman's Speculum or Compleat Schoolmaster*, published in 1711 but referring to his service in the *Degrave*, East Indiaman, in 1676.

3. J Lees, *The Masting and Rigging of English Ships of War 1625–1860*.

4. This may have been inspired by the revolutionary yacht the *Royal Transport* of 1695, which was schooner rigged and featured a jibboom. See the section on Schooners in Chapter 4.

als, which was soon shortened to royals. Separate royals were carried by the *Sovereign of the Seas* of 1637, but it was nearly the end of the eighteenth century before this feature became common naval practice; mizzen topgallants were regularly issued in the French navy from at least the 1690s, but the British preferred a larger topsail and the occasional 'flying' topgallant until the middle of the next century. Other fair weather sails, with exotic names like skyscraper and moonraker, became increasingly popular from the late eighteenth century but they were never permanent and were not officially countenanced.

The head underwent the most dramatic of alterations to the ship rig. The small spritsail under the bowsprit was useful in levering the ship's head around when tacking (see Chapter 13), and so very large ships attempted to enhance the effect with a second sail, the sprit topsail, which was carried on a tiny mast precariously stepped on the end of the bowsprit (a few sources even mention a spritsail topgallant, presumably set from the jackstaff above the sprit topmast).[1] Sails at this time were not shortened by reefing in bad weather; on the contrary, the lowest were extended by the addition of bonnets to their bottom edges in light winds. The spritsail did not alter its position and shape very much after the 1650s, except for replacing the bonnet around 1700 with a horizontal (English), or diagonal (French) reefband in the upper part of the sail, with the English

horizontal band soon becoming a diagonal, covering nearly the whole of the sail.

Fore and aft sails could be useful to a square rigger in certain wind conditions and these began to appear in the form of staysails from the 1660s. As their name implies, these were set between the masts on the stays that supported the masts from forward. The first were the fore top staysails, main and main top staysails, and the mizzen staysail, but one source also mentions a fore topgallant staysail and a mizzen topsail staysail by 1676.[2] These latter sails were not formally introduced into the Royal Navy until 1709,[3] although canvas was often provided for light weather sails to be made up on board long before the Establishment issued such sails (royals are a case in point). Staysails up to 1760 were triangular and in British ships thereafter, with the exception of the staysails before the fore mast, quadrangular. Most Continental navies preferred triangular staysails into the nineteenth century. The final generation of sailing warships adopted trysails (gaff-and-boom sails set on auxiliary masts abaft the fore and main masts like a contemporary snow), which were more efficient than the staysails they largely replaced.

The last years of the 1600s saw the introduction of another novelty, an extension of the bowsprit called the jibboom.[4] The jibboom made possible an extention of the fore topgallant staysail, now called a jib, beyond the extremes of the bowsprit. By 1711 this was well established, Sutherland's *The Shipbuilder's Assistant* of that date declaring, 'There is another Sail, call'd a flying Gib, a Sail of good service to draw the Ship forward, but very prejudicial to the Wear of the Ship forward'. The official introduction of the jibboom to small ships in the Royal Navy took place in 1705, but on large vessels for a few decades of transition, the jibboom was stepped beside the bowsprit, with a spritsail topmast still being carried. The latter's size was then reduced to that of a jackstaff, either fixed to the bowsprit cap, or fastened to a standard at the head of the bowsprit like the topmast had been previously.

With the demise of the sprit topmast, the sprit topsail yard was relocated beneath the jibboom, disappearing all together after the introduction of the martingale and its stay. The spritsail yard survived as a spreader for the jib-

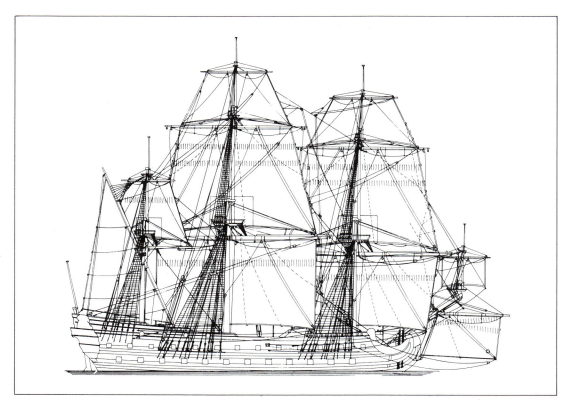

A French Second Rate of about 1700. The sail plan is identical to the slightly earlier English vessel, but differs in some details of rigging; the shape of the tops and caps, and the relatively wider upper sails would give the ship away as a French vessel to the trained observer. (K H Marquardt)

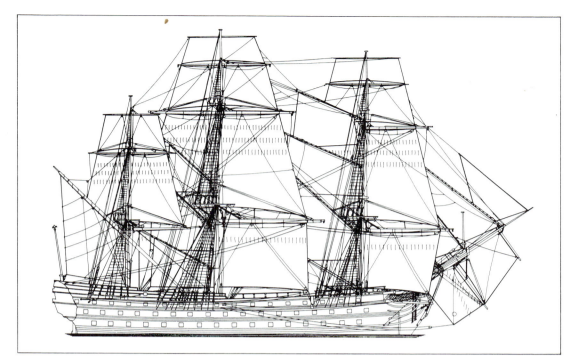

A French three-decker of the 1780s. Compared with earlier ships, the sprit topmast has gone and for most practical purposes the triangular headsails have replaced the square spritsails, although these can still be set if required; fore and main royals and a mizzen topgallant have been added; there is a full suit of staysails between the masts; and the lateen mizzen sail is cut off at the mast (by this time most British vessels were being fitted with gaff-and-boom mizzens). Studding sails are not shown. (K H Marquardt)

boom shrouds, until about 1800 when it began to be replaced by two spreaders.

A second extension to the bowsprit was officially introduced into the Royal Navy in 1794. The flying jibboom, like the jibboom before, was probably an English innovation and only arrived on the Continent some years later. In connection with the flying jibboom the Royal Navy officially approved the martingale, a vertical spar fitted at the lower end of the bowsprit cap. Its first appearance in English ships goes back to the mid-1780s, when it was used to stabilise the jibboom. First mentioned by David Steel in 1794,[5] one martingale stay was set up to the spar, to counteract the flying jib's upward pressure on the jibboom. Only in later years, from the turn of the century onward, did martingales carry more than one stay.

Of all the major sails in a ship, the mizzen course underwent the greatest modification. Originally a fore and aft lateen sail (and not altered in most Continental ships for the duration of the period under review), by the early seventeenth century in English and Dutch ships it had acquired a bonnet to its foot, which gave the sail a four-cornered look. Around 1680 the bonnet was integrated into the course and, strictly speaking, the sail was then a settee rather than a lateen sail. After 1730 the large mizzen course's part before the mast was gradually dispensed with and the new fore edge, or luff, was laced to the mizzen mast. The change came first to smaller ships and was progressively extended to all, with the last of the larger ships being altered during the 1780s.

Small craft had carried a short gaff rather than the more unwieldy mizzen yard from early in the century, but the sail usually had a vertical leech and a clew which belayed inside the taffrail (or a little outside it on fixed outriggers). The gaff can trace its ancestry to the 1620s, with the first gaff rigged vessels being Dutch *boeiers*; evolved from the diagonal sprit yard, for a time it was also known as a half-sprit. During the American Revolutionary War, the relatively small mizzen began to be replaced with a larger gaff-and-boom sail 'in the form of a brig's main sail'. The new sail came to be called the spanker, and gradually took over from both the loose-footed gaff and the truncated sail set from the long mizzen yard. Nelson's flagship during the Battle of the Nile in 1798, HMS *Vanguard*, was the only ship of the line still carrying a mizzen yard during that action.

Preceding the spanker, and often confused with it, was the driver, at first an additional fine weather square sail, hoisted to the peak of the mizzen yard. After about 1780 in English merchantmen it became a mizzen's fore and aft extension, but in the Royal Navy the term was applied to a larger temporary fore and aft sail of brig main sail shape hoisted to the gaff instead of the small loose-footed mizzen. An ancilliary boom was essential to extend the clew of the driver, but the sail disappeared when the permanent spanker rendered it redundant. Continental ships seem to have carried the square driver for much longer.[6]

Other evolutionary developments in a ship's rig relate to studding sails and boomkins. Stud-

ding sails – usually pronounced 'stunsails' – were additional fine weather sails set outside the regular sails on extensions called boom irons or their own small yards were secured to yardarm jewel blocks. There is reference to these temporary sails as early as 1620–25,[7] and thereafter their employment becomes more common. Boomkins – two booms diagonally protruding from the head – developed out of the need to hold the fore course's clews into the wind when close-hauled. Because the fore mast was stepped very far forward, it was always difficult to achieve an efficient lead for the fore tacks. As a result the fore course's leeches were diagonally cut toward the clew over several widths of cloth, to prevent the latter from being pulled inward by the tack. According to Captain John Smith, writing in 1627, a temporary boom or long pole was the initial response, but the gradual introduction of boomkins (also called bumpkins or bomkins) to all ships during the first half of the eighteenth century provided a permanent solution to that dilemma. Fore tack boomkins disappeared again in the early nineteenth century, when the fore mast's position shifted aft and iron cathead extensions took their place.

Other three-masted square rigs

Purpose-built warships rarely deviated from the ship rig, but a few variations are worth mentioning since they were carried by auxiliaries and vessels originating in the merchant service. The closest relation to a ship rig was the bark rig. Bark was originally a generic term for several types of vessels of divers shapes and rigs in northern and Mediterranean waters. However, the more modern definition of bark rig was described by William Falconer as early as 1769 as 'peculiarly appropriated by seamen to those which carry three masts without a

5. D Steel, *Elements of Mastmaking, Sailmaking and Rigging*, 1794 edition.

6. See, for example, A Roux's watercolour of the French battleship *Wagram* in 1811.

7. In the anonymous *Treatise on Rigging* printed by the Society for Nautical Research in 1958 (edited by W Salisbury and R C Anderson).

mizzen topsail'. As the 'barque' rig, it found some naval following in the mid-nineteenth century for a number of sloops and smaller vessels; a particular use was in re-rigging the larger brigs, whose main sails had become too big to be handled efficiently.

If a barque can be seen as a ship with no square canvas on the mizzen then the barquentine, with no square canvas on the main either, is a logical development. It was not much used for naval vessels before the era of auxiliary steamers, but Darcy Lever's *The Young Sea Officer's Sheet Anchor* of 1811 describes an unnamed rig with boom sails on the main and mizzen mast (but with main topsails) as common in the Baltic and coasting trade and the earliest evidence of that type is from around 1785.

The simplest three-masted square rigs, with only one sail to each mast, deserve mention. One of the earliest (already in use around 1600) was that of the Dutch herring buss. That rig had not changed much when Steel recorded it 200 years later as having three short masts, each in one piece. On each was a square sail, and sometimes a topsail above the main sail. In fine weather they added a sort of studding sail to the lower sails, and a driver. Occasionally they also set a jib forward, on a small bowsprit or spar.[8] A few saw naval service during the Anglo-Dutch wars but it was never a proper naval rig.

8. D Steel, *op cit*.

Scandinavian skerry boats in naval service were usually schooner rigged but rigging plans exist for an alternative three-masted square rig. Closely related to the single-masted Norwegian inshore craft rigs, these also had no topsails. The masts were short and their sails were cut to a trapezoid shape; the mizzen mast set a gaff sail.

Two-masted square rigs

Ketch

The ketch rig is peculiar in that it has both square and fore and aft rigged forms, the characteristic feature being the 'absence' of a fore mast. In its square form it is strongly associated with northern waters, a basic version being used for mercantile doggers and hookers, fishing vessels of mainly English and Dutch origin in the coastal regions around the North Sea. Early English 'catches' and Dutch *vischhoekers* usually had square sails on both masts, but the mizzen could be a lateen sail. In naval service it is the most clearly attested of all non-ship rigs, being used by the English navy from the 1650s, the original form having a square main course and topsail, balanced by a lateen mizzen and at least one headsail (a square spritsail is possible but the earliest illustrations show a triangular

jib, which since the ketch's main is set nearly amidships, would be more efficient).

A topgallant was one of the first developments and more headsails and a mizzen topsail were quick to follow. Apart from small craft, the rig became popular for the new bomb vessels from the 1680s, since the large space forward of the main mast was an ideal position for the mortars. French bombs were referred to as 'galliots', but the rig was very similar to the English ketch (although they seem to have set a mizzen topsail from their inception). From the early eighteenth century the ketch rig was applied to yachts and limited numbers of English sloops carried the rig from about 1720 to the 1750s. The principal improvement was to replace the lateen with a gaff sail, known examples dating from at least the 1740s. France persevered with the galliot rig until the early nineteenth century, by which time the mizzen carried a gaff-and-boom spanker. Mercantile ketches and hookers developed a gaff-headed wing sail, set abaft the main mast, from about 1750 onward, and English naval ketches adopted this feature at about the same time.

Sloop and shallop – ancestors of the snow and brig

Mid-seventeenth-century naval small craft were rigged with a number of similar sail plans that reflected their derivation from boats. The simple Biscay shallop rig of square fore course and larger main, without headsails, is probably the forerunner of all these. A square topsail was soon added, along with a spritsail under the bowsprit, but although the topsail might be carried by fore, main or both, there was as yet no after sail. The English sloop and French *barque longue* of the 1660s and '70s were rigged in this fashion, as were English brigantines and advice boats. A difference may have begun to manifest itself between those with a deep 'buss' style main (which had to be lowered for reefing) and those with a conventional standing course. At some as yet undetermined time, the square main was augmented (or replaced) by a fore and aft sail, perhaps temporarily to begin with, but eventually leading to what was called the snow rig.

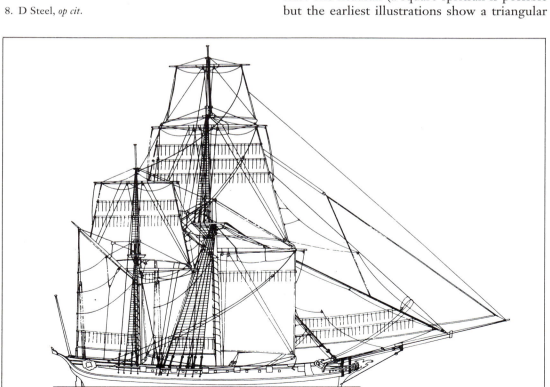

The fully developed eighteenth-century ketch rig. Earlier ketches had no topgallant and some contemporary illustrations even lack a mizzen topsail, but they seem always to have triangular headsails (jibs) rather than square spritsails. In English bomb ketches the main mast was often stepped further forward to allow the mounting of a mortar fore and aft of it, the result being a better balanced rig with less need for such very large headsails. (K H Marquardt)

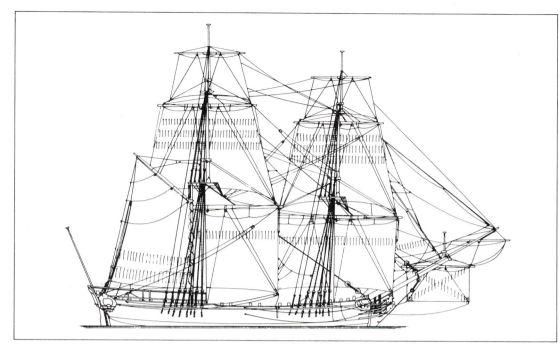

The snow as understood by the 1750s. Naval vessels often had the luff of the gaff main laced to a rope horse rather than a separate trysail mast, as shown here. Trysails (and their associated masts) were widely employed in the nineteenth century as a replacement for staysails. The naval brig rig was similar to this, but the foot of the main was extended by a boom and the sail was laced to hoops around the mizzen mast itself.
(K H Marquardt)

Snow and brig

All contemporary sources agree that the snow was the most common two-masted merchant vessel type in Europe. The sails and rigging of main and fore mast were similar to those of ships, except that directly abaft the main mast was an auxiliary trysail mast with a gaff-headed sail hoisted to it. The foot of the trysail mast was stepped on deck with its head fastened between the rear ends of the mast top's trestle-trees. The related *snau* or *snaw* suggests a Scandinavian origin for this rig but its first naval employment is unknown.

By the early eighteenth century English sloops of war were described as snow rigged, although they may not have had a trysail mast, preferring a vertical rope horse instead. The snow rig originally set a small loose-footed mizzen (and retained the use of a square main course), but a boom was used to extend the foot beyond the taffrail from at least the 1720s.[9]

The snow was replaced by the ship rig for British sloops from the 1750s, but in the 1770s a similar rig was reintroduced under the name of brig. This rig undoubtedly came from the merchant service, and was adopted by a number of navies at much the same time. Its main

difference from the snow was its large fore and aft rigged main sail, its foot spread by a boom, in contrast to a snow's square main sail. The fore and aft main sail of a brig fastened to hoops round the main mast with its foot extended by a long boom, whilst a crossjack yard was substituted in a brig for the main yard in a snow. From around 1800 the crossjack yard was often replaced with a proper main yard, giving the possibility of setting an additional square main sail; this tendency to confuse the features of a snow and a brig continued in the nineteenth century when naval brigs began to set their spanker on a trysail mast, although they usually continued to be rated as brigs.

The term brig may be derived from brigantine and as such the rig may be descended from the late seventeenth-century vessels of that description but influenced by the mercantile snow and the bilander. The latter may be something of a 'missing link', being a two-masted square rigged vessel but with a settee main sail; this may be the first application of a fore and aft after sail to the late seventeenth-century two-masted rigs, there being some visual evidence for it in naval service.[10] As a description, brigantine died out in naval usage until the early nineteenth century when it was re-adopted for vessels conforming to the current mercantile definition – a brig-like two-master but with no square canvas on the main, a triangular topsail replacing the square topsail and topgallant. In the Royal Navy the rig had a brief vogue in the 1830s and 1840s, possibly inspired by the experience of the Surveyor, Sir William Symonds, as a yacht designer.

Fore and aft rigs

Compared with square rigs, the variety of fore and aft sail plans is far larger since there are many more ways of carrying the canvas and almost an infinity of small-craft types on which to develop them. However, traditionally fore and aft rigs have been categorised by the method used to extend the sails: a lateen yard balanced against the mast, a diagonal sprit yard across the sail, or a short yard called a gaff at the head of the sail, sometimes with a boom at its foot (sails were also set from forestays, but canvas abaft the mast needed one of the preceding methods).

Lateen rigs

Historically the oldest fore and aft rig with its origins traceable to classical antiquity, the lateen was a large triangular sail, bent (secured along its length) to a yard of extreme length and hoisted diagonally to a relatively short single-piece block mast. Lateen rigs could be one-, two- and three-masted and were primarily at home in south-west Europe, the western part of the Mediterranean, and the North African coast. The largest three-masted lateen rigged types in the Mediterranean was the galleasse of Venice and Genoa, followed by the xebec, the barque and pink. The rig was exported to the Baltic when Russia and Sweden adopted Mediterranean style galleys for inshore warfare around 1700.

The most prominent two-masted lateen rigged craft in the Mediterranean were the galley, followed by the felucca and the tartane, with the latter being often also single-masted. Similarly rigged Arab vessels like the sambuk, the baghla, bhum (or boom), ganja, kotia etc had a settee rather than a lateen sail. The difference between the two was a straight forward edge (luff) on the settee sail, as if a rectangular cloth had been added to the bottom of the triangular lateen sail.

A related type was the polacre, which was another example of a hull designation being transferred to a rig. Originally the polacre was a Mediterranean trading vessel, described as early as 1629 by Furttenbach as second in size to only the *nave* or ship.[11] The plate of a 'pol-

9. See Chapter 3; snows obviously played a major part in the development of the lateen mizzen into the spanker.

10. A van de Velde drawing of what looks like a bilander in naval service is commented upon by R C Anderson in *The Mariner's Mirror* XX (1934), p371.

11. J Furttenbach, *Architectura Navalis* (reprinted Hamburg 1968).

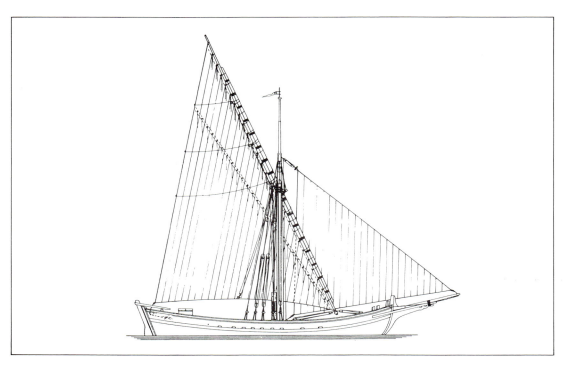

The lateen rig, carried here in a single-masted form by a Mediterranean tartane. The short mast reduced the standing rigging and the lateen was considerably more efficient before the wind than many fore and aft rigs. (K H Marquardt)

top-mast nor top-gallant-mast; neither have they any horses to their yards, because the men stand upon the top-sail-yard to loose or furl the top-gallant-sail, and on the lower-yard to reef, loose, or furl the top-sail, whose yard is lowered sufficiently down for that purpose.'[12]

'Polacre' came to denote pole-masted and was applied to northern European types like cats and crayers which were otherwise conventionally square rigged. With neither tops nor caps (except occasionally for the mizzen mast), the advantage of the rig was its light weight and its ease of handling by a small crew; but the commensurate disadvantage was the pole mast itself, which needed replacing *in toto* when damaged in the upper section.

Sprit rigs

The sprit was another ancient rig, which was very simple and familiar all over the northern European maritime scene, where it dominated the rigging of riverine and coastal craft on the Continental North Sea shore. However, sprit rigged vessels could also be found in the eastern Mediterranean, mainly in Greece and Turkey, and even as far distant as China where fishermen employed the rig.

Common to all was a quadrilateral sail, spread diagonally by a strong boom called the sprit, usually confined at its lower part to the bottom of the mast by a snotter. A snotter was made of two or more turns of rope to the loose circumference of mast and sprit, the ends being spliced together. It was then tightly marled, served all over and covered with leather. A seizing close to the mast was clapped on and

aca' in his work depicts a two-masted vessel without a bowsprit with a main and fore mast similar to a *barca*; they were rigged with lateen yards and block masts. Later in the seventeenth century the polacre's main mast stepped a top-

The curious polacre rig found some limited employment for fighting ships in the Mediterranean. It was an attempt to combine the windward advantages of the lateen rig with the superior downwind performance of the traditional square rig. Eventually, 'polacre' came to be applied to vessels with single-piece lower masts and topmasts, irrespective of rig. (K H Marquardt)

mast and a flag staff and had square sail yards hoisted. A mizzen mast with a lateen sail and sometimes a square topsail were also added and for about a century that plan defined the polacre rig. However, in 1780 Falconer described a new trend: some polacres now carried square sails on all three masts, particularly ships from Provence. 'Each of their masts is commonly formed of one piece, so that they have neither

12. W Falconer, *An Universal Dictionary of the Marine* (1780 edition).

A two-masted sprit rigged ship's boat, probably a more common naval employment of the rig than for larger craft. However, a number of seventeenth-century Dutch auxiliaries were sprit rigged. (K H Marquardt)

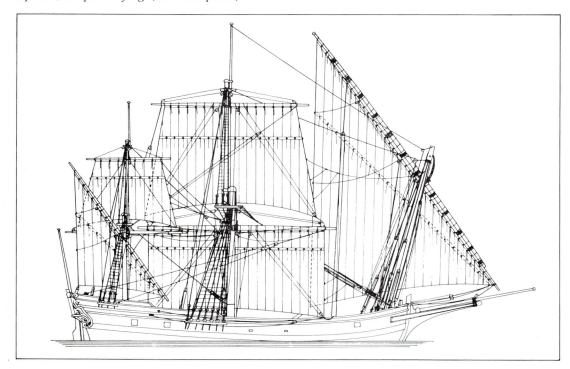

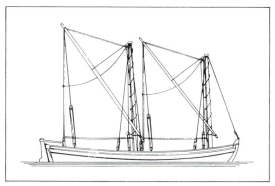

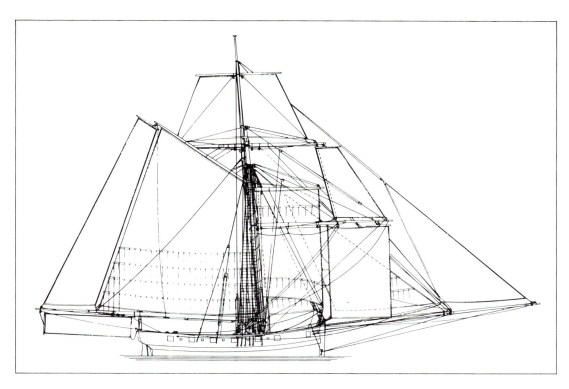

The English cutter rig about 1800, showing all the sails that could be carried. Later cutters set the square main directly from the crossjack yard instead of hoisting it on a separate yard as shown here. (K H Marquardt)

the sprit's foot came to rest in the remaining small eye. Continental vessels varied from English craft by often having a 'greelband' fitted to the mast and a small tackle to the sprit's foot, whilst the Chinese snotter was only a rope fastened to the mast, running along a notch in the sprit's foot and belaying round the mast and sprit. Southern European sprits also differed in rigging a standing topping lift between the peak and the masthead to which the spritsail head was hanked.

Vessels with a ketch-like main and mizzen mast, but fore and aft rigged, were variously known as galliots, Dutch galeasses, koffs, crompsters or Wadden convoy ships; and if the mizzen mast stepped at the stern, as Dutch smacks or Levantine sacolevas. The earliest configuration was a sprit rigged main sail, set to a mast stepped forward of the later main mast position, a lateen mizzen, a spritsail on the bowsprit (late sixteenth century), and later spritsails on both masts, although the sacoleva set a 'shoulder of mutton' shape sail instead of a lateen mizzen. These rigs in naval service were generally confined to auxiliaries, and in the eighteenth century tended to adopt gaff sails in place of sprits, as well as square topsails in some cases.

Gaff rigs

The gaff rig, whereby the sail was hoisted by a short yard at its head called a gaff, showed two different lines of development. The short hoisting gaff was usually found in connection with a boom of far greater length to spread the

sail's foot and during the seventeenth century neither bowsprit nor topsail were part of that rig. It belonged mainly to pleasure craft but was also used for small mail packet boats, etc. In parallel, a longer, standing or slung gaff emerged, from which was set a sail with a near vertical leech which did not require a boom. In its early days it was more commonly known as a half-sprit, a suggestive name pointing to its spritsail ancestry. There were also distinct similarities in the rigging: the cut of the sail was derived from that of the spritsail, and only a few tackles needed to be shifted to other positions. Unlike the short gaff (sometimes called the bezan rig), the half-sprit rig, like the earlier sprit rig, was usually accompanied by a bowsprit and square topsail.

While the difference was still clear during the seventeenth century, during the eighteenth a bowsprit with more headgear, and later square topsails, was introduced to single-masted boom rigged craft. This tended to be called the sloop rig, but there were many subtle variations, with no universal agreement on terminology. The clearest departure was the cutter, which was originally a term denoting hull form but came to refer to the rig as well. A cutter rig was basically a larger sloop rig with a running bowsprit – whereas a standing bowsprit was usually steeved directly above the stem at an angle of about 20–25 degrees to the horizon and permanently fixed to the vessel, a running bowsprit lay in a near horizontal position alongside the stemhead and could be taken in. Simpler versions of single-masted gaff rigs

continued to survive; the English hoy, for example, had fewer headsails than a sloop, no topsails, and a loose-footed main sail.

The earliest two-masted gaff rig is the seventeenth-century Dutch *speel-jacht* and this may be seen as the forerunner of the schooner, since it set a small gaff sail on a fore and main mast. A recently suggested contender for the position of prototype schooner is the English yacht *Royal Transport* of 1695 (see Chapter 4). Designed by Peregrine Osborne, Marquis of Carmarthen for King William III, the ship seems to have introduced a rig that would later be known as the fore and aft schooner. A particular innovation was the jibboom, its shrouds and related rigging, which soon after their first introduction began to revolutionise the headsails in all European ships, large and small.

Although the early history of the schooner is unclear, it seems to have been adopted with some fervour by settlers in England's North American colonies for fast sailing coastal vessels. The first recorded use of the word 'schooner' is a reference from 1717, and before long mercantile schooners had adopted square topsails. The schooner soon virtually became America's national rig and it was not until the latter half of the eighteenth century that it found much favour in Europe. The acceptance of schooners into European navies did not occur before the 1770s (although the Royal Navy had a few earlier, naturally enough for use in North America) and the rig was not employed in large quantities until the nineteenth century.

A British armed schooner of about 1780. The earliest schooners had no square canvas – and some vessels continued to be built without any – but in naval use the value of square topsails was too great to ignore: they gave greater power downwind, and could be backed, allowing a war schooner useful powers of manoeuvre. (K H Marquardt)

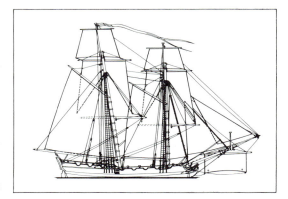

Other rigs

The naval employment of the lug rig was another development of the eighteenth century. It progressed from the simple ancient lug sail of small one-masted fishing craft like the *ewer* of the Lower Elbe and the *chasse-marée* from Brittany to the two and sometimes three-masted luggers of the second part of the century, with their additional lug topsails and topgallants fitted to temporary spars.

Lug sails were quadrilateral and bent to yards, known as sprits, slung at a point one-third of their length and not, like square sail yards, in their centre. As explained by David Steel, 'The yards have haliards, lifts and braces. To the lee-clue of the sail is a sheet, and to the windward-clue a tack, which is occasionally shifted as the vessel goes about'.[13] Luggers were mainly at home on both sides of the English Channel, but the lug rig was also part of the Eastern Mediterranean shipping scene, where its main representative was the *trabaccolo* of the Adriatic.

Another Mediterranean rig adopted by northern navies (principally for boats) was the sliding gunter rig. It originated as the *houario*, a small two-masted coaster or pleasure craft with sliding topmasts and triangular sails. The upper part of the luff of the sail was laced to the sliding topmast, whilst the lower part was bent to mast hoops.

---

13. *Elements of Mastmaking, Sailmaking and Rigging* (1794).

Masting and rigging

This short outline of the most common naval rigs cannot be concluded without considering the main principles of rigging common to most, if not all, sail plans. The rigging of any sailing craft was usually divided into a standing and a running element. Standing rigging mainly supported the masts and had both ends fixed in position, so as to be more or less permanent. Running rigging was employed for the moving of yards and handling of sails, and usually ran through blocks or made up tackles etc; each line normally had a standing and a hauling or running part, the standing being attached to a fixed point like an eyebolt, the becket of a block or similar, with the moving end belayed (temporarily fastened) to a cleat, pin or any other belaying point. However, before going into further detail it is necessary to give a brief description of the main features of masts and yards.

Masting

Far from being the simple wooden cylinders seen on so many crude ship models, masts and yards were complex in shape, subtly tapered and rarely properly circular in cross section.

Lower masts were widest at the partners (where they passed through the deck), narrowing down to the heel and upwards in stages of increasing taper to the hounds – the supports for the tops – above which was the head, of further reduced section. Long strengthening

pieces called fishes were added to the sides and front and further reinforced with rope lashings called woolding at intervals (rope was replaced with iron bands from the end of the eighteenth century). The head corresponded to the overlap, or doubling, with the heel of the topmast, and was topped with a mast cap, which also contained a hole through which the topmast passed. Lower masts could rarely be constructed from a single timber and so-called made-masts involved the elaborate and skilful longitudinal scarphing together of numerous pieces. Although different in shape and proportion, in principle the bowsprit was similar to the other lower masts.

Topmasts and topgallants, although usually made from a single stick, were even more complex in shape and section, not only tapering but also having square and octagonal sections, rebated heel and head, and a number of built-in blocks. These upper masts were locked in position ahead of the mast below them by a bar of wood or iron called a fid; thus separate topmasts were usually referred to as fidded masts.

At the hounds the lower masts supported a broad platform called a top; this helped to spread the shrouds of the mast above, but also provided a position for sharpshooters in action. Originally round, British tops developed a squarer shape from about 1700, with straight rear and sides combined with a curved front. The tops were constructed on a framework of timbers called trestletrees (in the fore and aft direction) and crosstrees athwartship; topmasts and topgallants usually had only the trestle- and crosstrees, without a top.

Although nowhere near as complicated as masts, yards were also tapered in the arms and after about 1690 had octagonal centre sections; in the later eighteenth century the yards were sometimes made up of two pieces with a long scarph joint in the centre, when the eight-sided section would be made up by nailing on battens. The yards variously required cleats, fixed blocks and studding sail boom irons by way of fittings.

The dimensions, proportions and ratios of taper for all spars were usually laid down in formal tables. These were related to the size of the ship, but in detail the practice not only varied from navy to navy but also developed with every other aspect of rigging during the period under review. Further information can be found in the books quoted in the relevant section of the Bibliography.

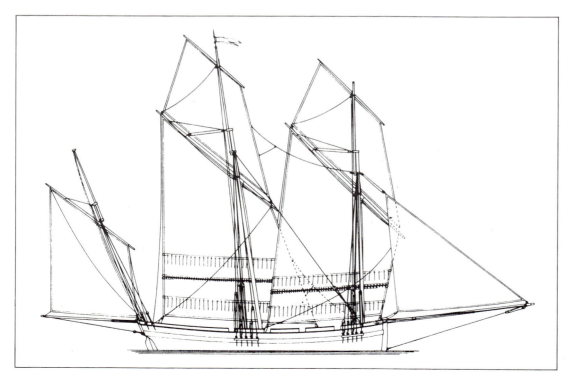

The lugger rig, as employed by a number of French naval chasse-marées. *It was also popular with British privateers (as well as smugglers). (K H Marquardt)*

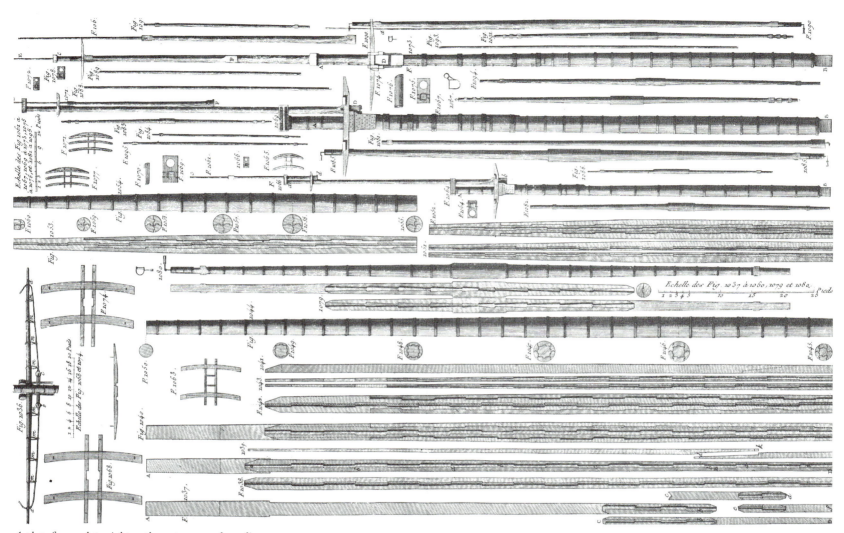

A plate from a late eighteenth-century encyclopaedia showing the construction of masts. Note the elaborate scarph-joints in the sectional views of the lower masts.

Standing rigging

The standing rigging, like the guy-ropes of a tent, supported the mast in each direction: from aft and athwartship (against the all-important pressure of the sails) tension was provided through shrouds and backstays; stays provided the counterbalancing strength from forward. Each mast, and each constituent part (topmast, topgallant, etc), had a full array of shrouds and stays.

The order of 'dressing' a mast was as follows. The first step was to drive a grommet over the masthead down to the hounds or trestletrees, to prevent any rope fitted subsequently from chafing on timber. When bolsters were part of a mast, their surface had to be covered with several layers of old canvas and tarred. Only then did the first ropes go over the masthead with an eye; these were the mast tackle pen-

dants, with large blocks in their lower end, though in later years these were often replaced with spliced-in thimbles to accommodate the hook of a tackle block.

Shrouds followed next, the first pair being the starboard forward, the second the port side forward, the third pair again to starboard, and so on. A single shroud always came last, sometimes coupled with the rearward pointing mast tackle pendant. 'By this method, the yards are braced to a greater degree of obliquity, when the sails are close hauled, which could not be, were the foremost shrouds last fitted on the masthead.'[14] The number of shrouds depended on the mast's size and that of the sail carried. English as well as some French men of war and large English merchantmen had their shrouds cable-laid – that is, three strands of pre-formed hawser-laid rope, totalling nine strands laid up against the twist – whilst smaller merchant vessels and most Continental naval craft preferred them to be simple hawser-laid rope of three strands.

Shrouds were usually tensioned using dead-

eyes – discs of timber with three holes (they were originally more triangular in shape, more closely resembling a skull from which the name was presumably derived). Deadeyes were seized into the lower end of the shroud, set up opposite deadeyes in the channels (or 'chain wales', platforms outside the hull that gave the shrouds greater spread) for the lower masts; those on topmasts set up to deadeyes in the tops and those on the masts above to crosstrees. A line (called a lanyard) running back and forth through the holes in the dead-eyes was used to get the required degree of tension into the shroud. As an alternative to deadeyes, it was quite common in Mediterranean lateen rigged vessels to have blocks toggled into eye-splices at the ends, with the lower block of each tackle toggled to an in-board span. Since the masts were shorter no channel was necessary for those rigs.

For easier access to the yards, tops etc, ratlines were hitched across the shrouds about

14. David Steel, *op cit.*

The standing rigging of a late eighteenth-century British Sixth Rate. The principal elements are the forestays which brace the masts from forward, and the shrouds (identifiable by the ratlines that allowed the crew to climb them) and backstays which support the masts from aft and to the sides. (John McKay)

fore stay and the mizzen stay. Main and fore stay were duplicated for extra safety, with the second one being the preventer stay; preventer stays date from the end of the seventeenth century, but a mizzen preventer stay did not appear until a hundred years later. Lower stays usually had a spread of crowsfeet between the upper end and the rim of the top, to prevent the topsail from chafing. There were topmast stays and topgallant stays above, the main and fore topmast stays being doubled with a preventer stay. Royal stays were also carried when there was a separate royal mast. With the introduction of the jibboom, some of the fore mast stay nomenclature altered. The stay outside and above the topmast stay became the jib stay in English usage, while in Continental rigging it was called the inner jib stay or the standing jib stay.

With the fore stay reaching out to the middle of the bowsprit, the last decades of the seventeenth century saw a bowsprit stay evolving, designed to neutralise this upward pressure. Probably a French invention, this bobstay was set up between a hole in the cutwater or stem and the middle of the bowsprit. Initially only single, the bobstay was to double and triple during the next century. Martingale stays prevented the jibboom from lifting upward. They came on the scene about one hundred years after the bobstay and were fitted to the jibboom head and the jib's traveller. They were set up over a spar called the martingale or dolphin striker that was angled down from the bowsprit cap.

Beside the rigging of ordinary and preventer stays, additional staysail stays were needed where staysails could not be hoisted to the former. Finally, before moving on from stays, it should be noted that stays are mainly associated with square rigs and northern European fore and aft rigs. Lateen, settee, and frequently also lug rigs did not require stays.

Other standing parts of the rigging were the horses, which had a number of separate meanings. The term applied to ropes which allowed work to be carried out on yards, booms and the bowsprit (footropes and lifelines); it also applied to a vertical rope behind a mast on which to hoist a trysail, or one before the mast for guiding a temporary square sail yard in fore and aft rigged vessels; finally it was a synonym

13in apart. Futtock staves were lashed across the upper section of the shrouds where they crossed the futtock shrouds coming down from the deadeyes of the topmast shrouds. These allowed catharpins to be set up between the futtock staves to tension the shrouds and to allow the yards to be braced round more obliquely when close-hauled. Preventer shrouds were additional shrouds, used in bad weather to ease the lower rigging and were set up like ordinary shrouds.

Backstays acted as additional lateral support for topmasts and topgallant masts. They were rigged as standing, shifting or breast backstays. Standing backstays led from above the hounds downward to the rear of the shrouds on the channels or to separate backstay stools and fastened to deadeyes. Similarly set up, but to the centre of the channels, were the breast backstays, but after 1730 in English ships the deadeyes were replaced with blocks and they then became running backstays. Shifting backstays were not synonymous with running backstays,

but only came into being in later years when they acted like preventer shrouds; they were set up via a luff tackle to the most effectively placed eyebolt in times of strong winds or heavy rolling.

One of the innovations associated with the *Royal Transport* was the bowsprit shroud. Coming into general use in 1706 these shrouds supported the bowsprit, by now extended by a jibboom. In English ships they hooked laterally to eyebolts in the wales and were lashed by deadeyes or hearts in the fore end to a shroud collar round the bowsprit. Continental bowsprit shrouds came as a pair, its bight seized to the bowsprit and the ends set up with tackles to the wales. Jibboom shrouds or guys were introduced at the same time to offset the pull of the jib.

Stays were last over the mastheads; they provided support to the mast from forward and a vessel usually had one for each separate mast. A seaman identified stays according to their position; the lower ones were the main stay, the for the jackstays across the yards to which the sails were bent (introduced in the 1820s).

Running rigging to the yards

To comprehend more clearly the multitude of ropes that constituted the running rigging, the following outline is divided into those lines controlling the yards and those used to manage the sails.

Yards were swayed into place either by an assemblage of tackles, known as jears or jeers, or by a tye, a thick rope passing through a block at the masthead or a sheave in the hounds, then through a block, stropped to the yard, to fasten to the masthead, or simply fasten without a block to the yard. A tackle was attached to the lower end of the tye. With the lower yards in position, from about 1770 the jeers were relieved by slings around the mast; however, crossjack yards were always slung. To balance a yard or for topping it, lifts were needed. Depending on the size of the yard, lifts

might be either single or double. Single lifts went over the yardarms and passed through blocks at the mast cap; double lifts formed tackles between the yardarms and mast cap. Ropes or tackles to suspend or top a boom's end or a gaff's peak were called topping lifts.

Braces swung a yard horizontally and also had single or double forms, with double braces having a pendant, or a brace block directly attached to each yardarm. Braces usually ran aft, the exception being those on the mizzen mast which had to run forward; likewise, its topsail yard and topgallant braces ran forward when there was a hoisting mizzen gaff or yard, but otherwise they led to the peak of the gaff or yard. Braces of a gaff or mizzen yard were known as vangs and were only employed on a standing gaff; the hoisting yard was usually associated with a boom where vangs would have been more of a hindrance than a help. Preventer braces were part of a warship's preparation for action, being rigged forward to counteract damage to braces in battle.

To keep the yard close to the mast, a parrel was employed, consisting of several ribs separating rows of beads called trucks. During the later years of the eighteenth century lower yards used trusses instead. To prevent the lower parrels or trusses from jamming on the mast when swaying or striking the yard, a nave line was hitched to them and led through a block beneath the top, keeping the parrel from fouling.

Sails and their rigging

Like masts, sails were more complex than they appear on some models. They were made up of a number of cloths, tailored to a complicated shape, with reinforcing pieces (called lining or doubling) added to prevent chafing and boltropes and cringles sewn into the sail. Sails also had their own terminology. In a square sail, besides the head and foot the sides were called leeches and the lower corners clews or clues; in a triangular sail, the leading edge was the luff, the after the leech and the bottom was the foot, the corners being head, tack (forward) and clew (aft); in a four-sided 'shoulder of mutton' sail the two forward corners were called the nock (upper) and tack; a gaff sail's upper corners were the throat (nearest the mast) and the peak, but was otherwise similar to triangular sails.

The boltrope was sewn into the perimeter of the sail but was actually divided and named after whichever edge it encompassed. Loops were formed in each corner and cringles spliced into the foot- and leechropes; the loops formed with the ends of the headrope were called earings, and were essential to stretch a square sail towards the yardarms. The lower, clew, cringles were used to secure the sheets, tacks, clewlines and clew garnets, while those in the footrope were for buntlines, and those in the leechropes for bowlines, leechlines and reef tackles. On fore and aft sails cringles were employed for brails and mast lacings.

Originally sail was not reduced in bad weather but conversely extra sail was set in favourable conditions. To achieve this bonnets were attached to the feet of the lower sails. Sometimes a second, called the drabbler, might be added. Bonnets were very much part of the seventeenth-century shipping scene, but dur-

With the running rigging added the top hamper appears maze-like to the uninitiated eye, but running rigging could be further divided into lines that controlled the yards and those that controlled the sails (the sails are shown in dotted lines in this drawing). (John McKay)

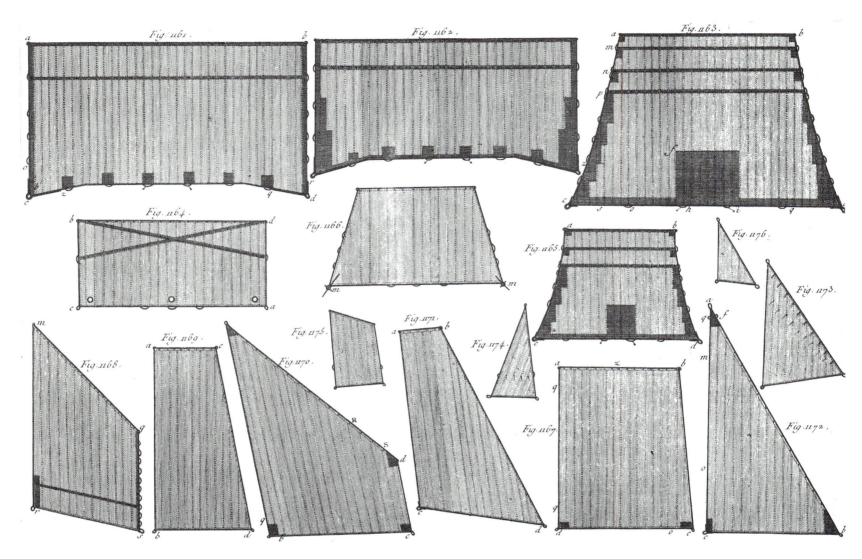

The shape and details of sails from an eighteenth-century French encyclopaedia. The darker areas represent strengthening in areas of particular stress or potential chafing; boltropes and cringles are also apparent, as are the seams of the individual bolts of cloth. Note the spritsails' diagonal reefbands.

ing the next century they were only employed in smaller vessels. They usually accounted for one-quarter of the sail's total area and were a quick approach to shortening sail. However, from the last decades of the century, reefing of courses began to replace the removal of bonnets as a method of shortening sail (it had been employed on topsails since at least the middle of the century); reefing involved folding a section of the upper sail to the yard and securing it using a row of reef points, visible as horizontal bands of cloth across the upper part of the sail. Sails were normally attached to yards or gaffs with robands or lacings.

The lines for the control of sails consisted of halyards for hoisting sails, downhaulers for lowering them, sheets for holding the sail's clew into the wind, and tacks for counteracting the sheet and keeping the clew steady. Bowlines fastened with bridles to the lower half of the leech and prevented the windward leech from shivering when close-hauled. Clew garnets and clewlines were placed to the rear of a sail and trussed the clews up to the yard; and the former only applied to courses and the latter to all other sails. Brails were lines with the same function in fore and aft rigging and ran on both sides of the sail.

Buntlines on the face of a sail, fastened to their cringles, drew the foot up to the yard. Leechlines functioned similarly for the sail's vertical edges and fastened to cringles in the middle of a leech. To facilitate the reduction of sail reef tackles lifted the leech far enough toward the yard to enable seamen to shorten the sail with reef points. A slab line trussed up the foot of a main and fore course when required for the convenience of the helmsman.

Other specialist gear like the fish tackle and cat tackle were necessary for getting the anchors in. Mast tackles, yard tackles and garnet tackles were needed for hoisting stores, boats, etc in and out of a ship. Mast tackles in larger ships were positioned forward and aft of the main and fore lower shrouds, those facing the waist being for the heaviest loads. Yard tackles, being set up to the yardarms, helped in that task and garnet tackles or stay tackles were directly placed over the main and fore hatches for straight lifting. Burton tackles were originally part of the topmast rigging but were found useful for lifting.

In such a concise essay on rigs and rigging, naturally not every aspect can be fully explained, and some have not even been addressed. However, most of the important principles and many of the most significant terms have been touched upon. Any reader seeking deeper insight is directed to the relevant section of the Bibliography.

Karl Heinz Marquardt

10

Ships' Fittings

THE stern rudder was universal for warships of the seventeenth, eighteenth and nineteenth centuries. It had begun to replace the steering oar in the thirteenth century, and had superseded it completely by 1500. Rudders for galleys might be curved, but this meant that only two hinges could be used on each. The sailing warship had a straight rudder, hinged to an equally straight sternpost. This type of rudder, though a great improvement on its predecessors, was not without its disadvantages: in particular, it was not 'balanced' like a steering oar or a modern rudder, – ie the whole area of the blade was behind the axis on which the rudder turned, so it took a considerable force to move it.

Steering gear

Rudders

The position of the rudder had important effects on the design of the ship. The straight sternpost meant that ships could no longer be double ended; furthermore, the hull lines aft of midships had to be carefully designed to allow an easy flow of water to the rudder for maximum effect. The rudder itself was high, quite thick, and relatively narrow in its fore and aft dimension. It was high so that its top end could be carried up to the level of the upper deck, under which the tiller was usually fitted. Its thickness matched that of the sternpost, and it was thicker at its head than at its foot. It was rounded on its foremost edge to allow it to rotate, but there was little attempt to taper it aft of that, to present a more streamlined form. Seen from the side, the rudder was at its widest at its lower part, at the level of the bottom of the keel. From there it tapered to just above the waterline, where its width was reduced more drastically by a step, or hance. More steps were added over the years, so that a British warship had three by the end of the eighteenth century. After that, the steps were replaced by a curved shape. In any case, the thickness increased towards the head, and the width decreased; as a result, the rudder was approximately square in cross section at its head, where it received the tiller.

The rudder was held to the sternpost by a series of hinges – perhaps six or seven on a ship of the line – which came in two parts, known as gudgeons and pintles. A gudgeon was bolted to the hull, by means of arms which were shaped to fit round the sternpost at the appropriate point, and held a ring in position just aft of the post. A pintle was bolted to the rudder in the same way, and was fitted with a pin which fitted into the ring of the gudgeon. The forward face of the rudder was cut with grooves for the pintles. The rudder could be fitted lifting the ends of the pintles over the gudgeon rings, and then lowering it into place.

Tiller and whipstaff

The tiller was the universal means of moving the rudder from side to side, and of providing enough leverage to turn it against the effects of the sea. In general the tiller was a straight piece of timber, extending almost as far forward as the mizzen mast. On British ships it was fitted to the rudder by cutting a hole through the head of the latter; other nations, such as the Dutch, often preferred to reverse the situation and have a broader tiller, with a hole to fit it over the rudder head. On ships of larger size

The changing shape of the rudder:

A. A large ship of about 1690: note cutaway for skeg and decorated head.

B. A rudder of about 1780 with two hances; iron bound head.

C. Large ship, early 1800s, with three hances and more elaborate ironwork.

D. The 'round' rudder as fitted to a British First Rate, 1808.

E. Detail modifications to this rudder of about 1815 include washers between gudgeons and pintles, squared off scores, and a heel which is both angled and extended no lower than the main keel (to avoid unshipping the rudder in the event of grounding).

The final development of this era, the so called 'plug stock' form involved joggling the rudder head forward so that its axis was an extension of the line of the pintles, which reduced the aperture in the counter to a small radius circle. These are British examples but changes in other navies were parallel. (Brian Lavery)

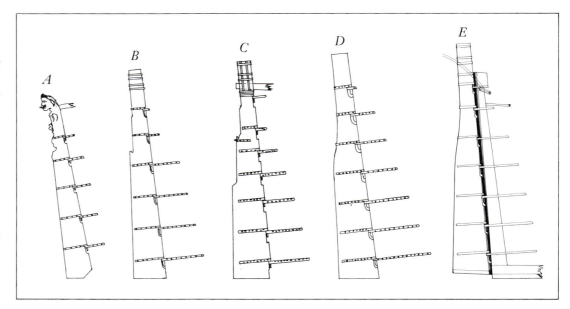

The best contemporary illustration of an English whipstaff (from the Phillips print of the 1690s). Although raised a deck by this device, the helmsman still had no sight of the sails. (NMM)

the tiller was fitted just under the lower deck, but on the smallest vessels this option was not always available. On the very smallest, it was fitted above the level of the only deck. On larger ships, for most of the seventeenth century, the forward end of the tiller was supported by a straight piece of timber placed under it, and hung from the deck beams above. By the end of the century a more sophisticated system was coming into use, with a round piece of timber known as a sweep fixed directly to the beams above, and a projection from the tiller, known as the gooseneck, holding the tiller to the sweep.

Often the tiller did not provide enough leverage for steering a large ship. Furthermore, its position was far from ideal, since it was buried below decks, where the helmsman could not look at the set of the sails, or indeed have any idea of the effects of moving the tiller, unless instructions were shouted down to him. The seventeenth century answer to this was the whipstaff. This was a vertical lever attached to the end of the tiller by an iron fitting (also known as a gooseneck), and pivoted by means of a 'rowle' fitted between the planks of the upper deck. The whipstaff provided a little extra leverage, and it raised the helmsman's position by one or two decks. However it allowed only a very limited movement of the tiller, before the mechanical advantage was lost. Because the whipstaff could slide through the rowle, it was possible to move the rudder rather further, though only by losing a good deal of leverage.

The steering wheel

Until near the end of the seventeenth century, the head of the rudder remained outside the hull of the ship. Around 1700 there was a subtle change in the stern of British ships, and the counter of the stern was altered to include the rudder head. In the long term, this allowed the rudder head to be extended up through the upper deck, to provide room for a spare tiller fitting at that level. More important, it allowed the possibility of much greater movement for the rudder, and it is perhaps no coincidence that it was not long before the whipstaff began to be replaced.

It had long been the custom to disengage the whipstaff in heavy seas, and steer by means of tackles leading from the tiller end to the side of the ship. It was a relatively short step to extend the tiller ropes upwards through the decks, and lead them to a winch on the quarterdeck. This system appeared very briefly, and can be seen on a model of the early 1700s, with the winch fitted with its barrel athwartships, and operated by crank handles. The windlass was soon turned round to run fore and aft, and the handles were replaced by a wheel with spokes. There is still some controversy about the exact date of the fitting of the wheel, and no written orders on the subject have ever been found; nevertheless it is generally agreed that it was invented by the British navy between 1700 and 1710.[1]

The steering wheel spread quickly to other

nations, though there is evidence that the French were still using the whipstaff on some ships in the 1720s. By the 1730s the wheel was being fitted forward of the mizzen mast, which suggests a slightly more sophisticated method of rigging the tiller ropes. It was soon found that a wheel could be fitted at both ends of the barrel, so that more men could apply their strength to it if necessary. Only the very smallest warships still relied solely on the tiller, and the whipstaff was completely superseded. An important improvement in the fitting of the

Typical double wheel under the poop of a large late eighteenth-century ship of the line. Note the triple-compartmented binnacle, with the helm indicator on the break of the poop above (the tiller ropes activated a 'tell-tale' which moved in the slot to indicate how far over the rudder had been put). (NMM)

1. See D H Roberts in *The Mariner's Mirror* 75 (1989), pp272–3; and John Franklin in *The Mariner's Mirror* 76 (1990), pp171–2 for the latest contributions to the debate.

wheel came in the 1770s, when Pollard, an official of Portsmouth Dockyard, invented a system of 'sweeps and rowles' by which the tiller rope was led round the forward edge of the sweep. Before this, the geometry of the system had demanded that some slack be left in the tiller ropes, and this could be dangerous in intricate manoeuvres. Pollard's system was soon copied by the French and other navies, though drawings in the Chapman collection suggest that the Swedes were rather late in taking it up.[2]

A plate from a late eighteenth-century naval architectural treatise demonstrating the main features of an Admiralty pattern anchor and aspects of its manufacture. This 'angle crown' type was later replaced by a round version in which the arms were formed by an arc of a circle; it was adopted in Britain in the 1820s but was common in other navies rather earlier.

Certain fittings were used as an aid to navigation and steering. The binnacle normally held two compasses, with a light between them. In the days of the whipstaff, two binnacles were needed, one at the steering position and one on the quarterdeck for the pilot or officer of the watch. After the invention of the steering wheel, only the latter was needed. One disadvantage of the steering wheel was that it gave no easy indication of the position of the rudder. By the 1740s the French were fitting a kind of helm indicator, linked to the tiller lines, which gave a reading on a scale at the break of the poop. This was adopted by the British soon after the capture of the *Invincible* in 1747.[3] It was not suitable for frigates and smaller ships, which had no poop; another type of indicator was evolved, with a dial in front of the wheel itself.

Ground tackle

Anchors and cables

The anchor was probably subject to less variation through the ages than any other feature of a ship. Its best known form originated in classical times, and this can still be seen in use today. It is known as the 'Admiralty pattern', or 'fisherman's', anchor. It consists of a long, straight piece of iron, known as the shank; two arms extending from one end of the shank, each fitted with a spade-like piece known as a

2. Statens Sjöhistoriska Museum, Stockholm, Chapman collection, ÖR 2920.

3. B Lavery, *The Royal Navy's First Invincible* (Portsmouth 1988), p43.

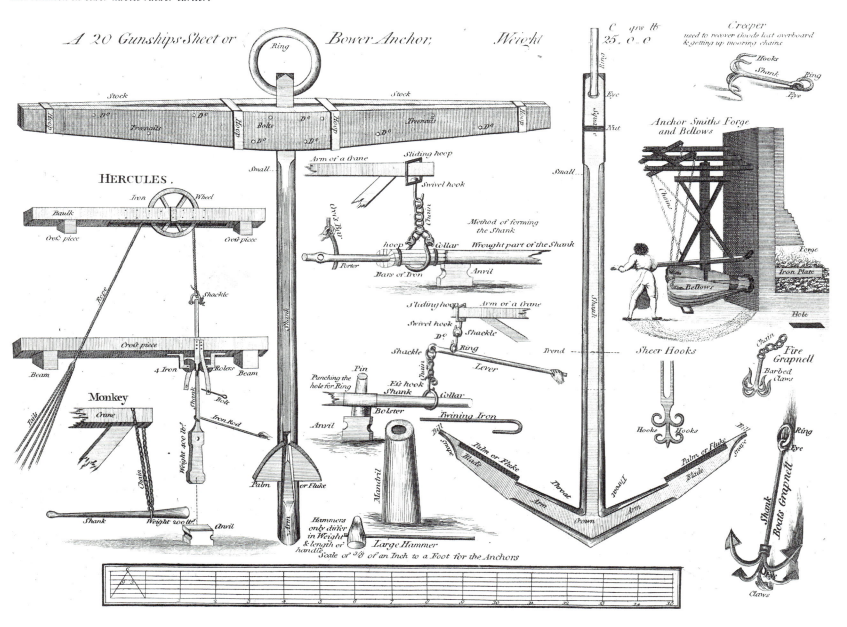

palm; a stock, which was fitted at the opposite end of the shank, and in a plane at right angles to that of the arms; and a ring, fitted through a hole at the stock end of the shank, to which the cable would be attached. The stock was made of wood, except in the smallest anchors, where it was of iron. The rest of the anchor was iron, made up from small pieces of metal heated and forged together.

Within the pattern, there was some development. The point where the shank met the two arms was known as the crown, and on early anchors the two arms formed a distinct angle. By the eighteenth century the Dutch and French were using the 'round crown' anchor, in which the arms were shaped to form a stronger and smoother join. The British remained very backward in this respect, and continued to rely on the 'angle crown' anchor until after the defeat of Napoleon in 1815. The British wooden stock was invariably straight, tapering to its ends, and made of two pieces bound together with iron hoops. Other navies, particularly the Dutch, often used a stock in which the ends curved upward and outwards from its centre.

The largest ships carried up to nine anchors, but the average was about six. Typically there were four large anchors, carried from the bows and used for normal anchoring. One, known as the sheet anchor, was often slightly larger than the others and was reserved for use in a serious emergency; the others were the bower anchors, so called from their position. Smaller anchors, such as the stream and the kedge, were used mainly for moving the ship in a calm or an unfavourable wind. One could be slung under a boat and rowed out ahead and dropped in the water. A British 74-gun ship of the late eighteenth century had four main anchors weighing from 57cwt to 69cwt each, a stream anchor of 16cwt, and a kedge of 9cwt.[4]

Anchor cable consisted of very thick rope, up to 22in in circumference. 'Cable laid' rope was made up of nine strands – that is, three normal three-strand ropes twisted together. The standard British cable was 120 fathoms, or 720ft long, allowing the ship to lie at anchor in up to 40 fathoms of water. On British ships the cables were stowed amidships on the orlop deck, or on a special platform in that position on frigates which were too small to have an orlop; or on planks on top of the casks in the hold on even smaller ships. In general, other navies preferred to keep their cables lower down, usually forward in the hold.

Details of the construction of a large double capstan from a naval architectural treatise of 1805.

Lighter tackle was needed for lifting the anchor directly out of the water, using a kind of crane known as the cathead to keep it away from the side of the ship. This was a stout piece of timber which had sheaves cut into it for the tackle, and was supported by a strong knee. It was fitted above the beakhead bulkhead (except of course in ships with a round bow), but its exact position varied slightly in different periods and navies.

When in use, the anchor cable was attached to the bitts. These were solid vertical pieces of timber, arranged in pairs on the lower deck (or wherever the cable might enter the ship through the hawse holes) and fixed to the timbers of the ship in the hold. A strong cross piece was fitted between the pair of bitts. British practice was to have two pairs of bitts, one behind the other; most other navies made do with one pair.

Capstans

The very smallest warships, such as schooners, gunboats and cutters (as well as most merchantmen), used windlasses, with the barrel set horizontally, to raise their anchors. Others had capstans, with the barrel set vertically. Apart from the spindle which formed the core of the machine, the capstan had whelps, which projected from the barrel and gave it a greater diameter, and perhaps created more friction with the cable; pawls, which could be lowered or set to prevent the capstan from surging back and injuring the crew; and a head, through which the bars could be fitted when it was in use. The earliest type of capstan, known retrospectively as a crab, simply had holes cut in the upper part of the barrel, and bars which passed right through. The difficulty with this, of course, was that all bars had to be at different levels, and their number was limited to about four. The major innovation was the drumhead capstan, which was invented around 1675 by Sir Samuel Morland.[5] A much larger and more circular head was now fitted to the capstan, with holes for about twelve bars. These no longer went all the way through so that all could operate at the same level.

It was rare to have a capstan which operated on a single deck. The simplest ones, as used on the smaller vessels, had a spindle which extended from one deck to the one below, giving a much greater rigidity. It was more common to have the lower part of the capstan fitted with whelps, so that it could operate from two deck levels; this was called a double capstan. From about 1740, the trundlehead was also fitted. This was another drumhead, fitted just above the whelps on the lower deck, so that if necessary men could push on two sets of bars at once; using these, up to 200 men could apply their strength to a capstan.

The typical British drumhead capstan had a large recess in each whelp, known as the surge,

---

4. B Lavery, *Anatomy of the Ship: The 74-Gun Ship Bellona* (London 1985), p15.

5. A Bryant, *Samuel Pepys, the Saviour of the Navy* (London 1938, reprinted 1949), p185.

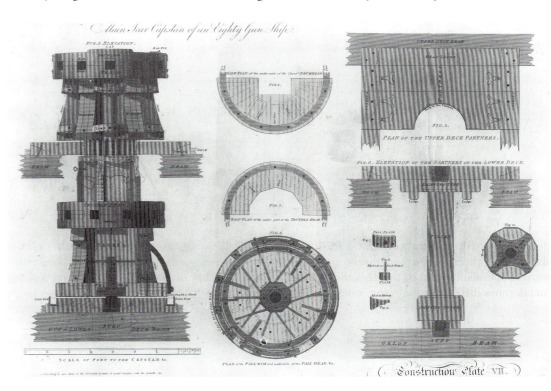

Section and elevation of a set of chain pumps, as fitted to a Danish 50-gun ship of 1736. Although the principles remained the same, numerous detail improvements later in the century made the pump more robust and more mechanically efficient. (Rigsarkivet, Copenhagen)

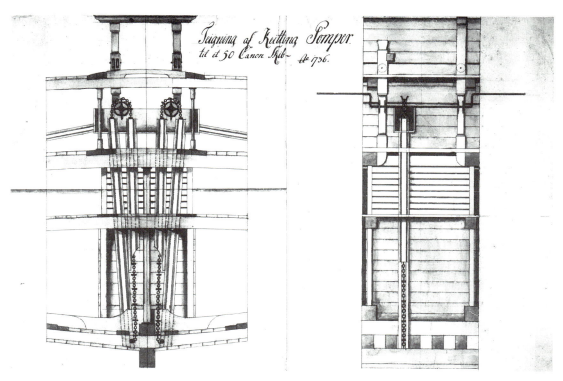

which was intended to take the cable, and a projection above intended to prevent it from riding up too far. It had a head which was rather larger than the whelps. The French capstan was closer to a cylinder in form, with a slight concave on the whelps and a head which was no larger than them. The Spanish capstan was different again, with a curved surge and no projection, but a large head.

The actual numbers and positions of the capstans varied with time and place. For example, a British three-decker of the 1690s had three double capstans: one between the main and mizzen, on the lower and middle deck; another, on the same decks, forward of the main mast; and a third on the upper and middle deck, just aft of the break of the forecastle. A French three-decker of the same period had a double capstan on the forecastle, as well as a double halfway between the main and mizzen masts, on the lower and middle decks.[6] By the 1740s, British two-deckers were fitted with two identical capstans, so that they could be interchanged if one was broken. Both were sited on the upper and lower decks, with one between the main and mizzen and the other in the waist, between the main and fore mast. The French, however, had different capstans for different purposes. A 74 of the late eighteenth century had a double capstan between the main and mizzen, on the lower and upper deck; and a smaller, single capstan on the forecastle with its spindle reaching down to the upper deck.

Pumps

Wooden ships always take in some water, either through the gaps between the planks or from above, in the form of rainwater and spray. A simple drainage system was incorporated in the design of the ship. Decks were cambered to cause water to drain towards the sides of the ship, while the sheer would direct water towards the midships part of the deck. Scuppers – metal pipes fitted through the sides at deck level – allowed a certain amount of water to drain out of the ship. The rest was allowed to

6. Vice-Admiral E Paris, *Souvenirs de Marine*, Vol II, plan of the *Royal Louis*.

find its way into the hold, and the hull structure was arranged to collect it in the area of the main pumps, so that it could be raised to the lower deck, and then run out through the scuppers.

In most ships, the pumps were sited amidships, around the main mast, which was stepped in the lowest part of the hold. The peculiarities of Dutch ship design, however, caused other arrangements to be made. Some ships were trimmed very much by the stern, and the pumps were sited well aft. The same situation was found with some English gunboats around 1800. The flat-bottomed Dutch ship also needed the true bilge pump. Because of the shape, it proved impossible to drain all the water from the turn of the bilge while the ship had any heel, and some pumps were fitted to angle outwards from the main mast, to meet the bilge.

Most navies used the simple suction pump – sometimes known as a brake pump because it was operated by a lever, or brake. The lever caused a cylindrical 'box' to move up and down inside a tube. The box had a hole drilled through it from top to bottom, with a leather flap on top. As the box moved upwards the flap closed, so that water moved with it. As it moved downwards the flap opened, so no water moved in that direction. A second box was fitted at a lower level in the tube, to cause more pressure on the water during the downward stroke; that box was fixed.

The British navy used a rather different mechanism – the chain pump, invented in Elizabethan times. The chain itself was endless, and

fitted with saucers at intervals. It travelled up through a tube, drawing some of the bilge water with it. It passed over a wheel, and then down again through another tube, and round a smaller wheel set in the bottom of the ship. The main advantage of the chain pump was that it operated through a rotary action, rather than an up and down one like the suction pump. It proved relatively easy to fit extensions to the handles, so that large numbers of men could work at once. Nevertheless work on the pumps remained very gruelling, and the chain pump did not deliver water under pressure. As a result, the British often fitted brake pumps as well, for use in firefighting. There were numerous attempts to improve the chain pump, and many inventors sent their ideas to the Navy Board. The most successful was the Coles-Bentinck pump, which became standard in 1770. Among other changes, it used a system rather like a bicycle chain, instead of the more conventional chain. In the 1800s pumps were also adopted for other purposes, such as raising drinking water from barrels in the hold.

Underwater protection

Sheathing and antifouling

The underwater hull of a ship was affected by two main problems. Weeds and barnacles could attach themselves to the planks, and drastically reduce the speed of the ship. Even more serious was *teredo navalis*, or ship worm. This flourished in the tropics, and could eat its way along the planks of the hull, making the ship totally unsafe.

Until the late eighteenth century, the two problems were generally tackled separately. For protection against the worm, ships on the way to the West Indies or India were sheathed. A noxious composition, usually a mixture of hair and tar, was put over the underwater hull. This was covered with light planks, usually ¼in thick on British ships, but thicker on French. It was hoped that the worm would confine itself to the sheathing planks, and not attempt to penetrate the tar.

For protection against weed, other antifouling compositions were used, and put on top of the sheathing if that had been applied. In the seventeenth century the most common was a mixture of train oil, rosin or sulphur. This gave a white appearance, and so was known in Britain as 'white stuff'. Around the middle of the century some ships were tallowed as well, though this was probably a way of getting a smooth, frictionless surface, rather than for the protection of the hull. A cheaper alternative to white stuff was 'black stuff', made from pitch and tar. Though the work of modelmakers and marine artists suggests that white stuff remained prevalent, most British ships of the first half of the eighteenth century were in fact coated with black stuff. In the 1740s, 'brown stuff' became standard for British ships; it was black stuff mixed with sulphur, and was said to have some of the advantages of both compounds.

Metal sheathing

The idea of covering the bottom with metal was not a new one. Clearly weed would find it difficult to attach itself to metal, especially one such as copper or lead, which formed a slightly poisonous surface. Moreover, the worm would find it impossible to penetrate. In the 1670s the British navy experimented very seriously with lead sheathing, and at one point it looked likely to become standard. However this took no account of electrolytic action, and several ships were put in serious danger because their rudder ironwork decayed.

The coppering pattern for a British 32-gun frigate as laid down in November 1779.
A. The thickest copper of 32oz per square foot.
B. Medium copper, 28oz.
C. Thin copper, 22oz.
Note the strake of wood sheathing immediately below the waterline. (Brian Lavery)

Copper sheathing was first suggested in 1708, but rejected on the grounds of expense. However, small scale experiments began in the late 1750s. It seems that the false keel of the 74-gun *Invincible* was coppered as an experiment, and in 1758 several more ships had their keels coppered. This had some success, and in 1761 a frigate, the *Alarm*, was fully coppered with very thin plates. This was generally successful, but by 1766 the problem of electrolysis had begun to reappear – the iron bolts under the copper were in a state of serious decay. The Admiralty tried lead sheathing again on two 74-gun ships, the *Marlborough* and *Egmont*, but soon found that lead could be worn away very quickly. By 1769 the Admiralty had found that the best solution was to fit the underwater hull with copper bolts, but this was too expensive for general adoption. However the problem of decay of the rudder irons was solved, by replacing them with a cuprous alloy.

In 1775 the struggle for American independence became open war, and in the following year it was decided to copper some small ships, despite the risks. In 1779, after the war had become general and the British navy was outnumbered, it was decided to copper ships of the line as a matter of policy. There was not time to drive out the old iron bolts, so efforts were made to keep the copper from the iron by covering the hull with tar and brown paper before coppering. This was enough as a temporary wartime measure, but after the war ended in 1783 it was decided to re-fasten the whole fleet as ships came into dock for repair. The French, who had never been far behind in the development of coppering, adopted it at the same time, and it became universal in other navies.

Copper was applied to the hull in the form of thin sheets, 4ft by 14in. They were of 32oz, 28oz or 22oz per square foot, with the thickest plates being put in the bows. The plates were nailed to the hull, arranged in strakes like the planking, with a small overlap between the plates. In some of the early experiments the plates were laid in rows, both fore and aft and up and down. In the developed form, they were arranged like brickwork.

Ships' boats

Ships' boats had many uses, often undreamed of in the days of powered vessels. Since ships of war rarely came alongside except for dry-docking, boats were needed to ferry men and supplies out to the ships. They could help to move a ship in a calm or an unfavourable wind, by warping, kedging or towing. They could take officers to a conference aboard the flagship, or be rowed round a ship in harbour to prevent surprise attack or desertion. They could land troops on a hostile shore, or carry out independent patrols. They could be used to take the surrender of a captured ship, or in a 'cutting-out expedition' on an enemy vessel. They were used in the inhumane punishment known as 'flogging round the fleet', and for taking wounded to the hospital ship. They could also be employed in the rescue of the crew of a sinking ship, but this was not regarded as a primary function, and they were not designed as 'lifeboats' as such.

Because of the variation in duties, most ships carried more than one boat. Some boats, such as launches, were specifically designed for heavy work such as moving anchors and stores. Others, such as barges and pinnaces, were intended for fast rowing, to carry officers about in relatively calm waters. Yet others, such as cutters and yawls, were designed for good performance under sail.

Until 1780 the main English boat was the longboat. In the earliest period it was half the length of the keel of the ship, but it declined in

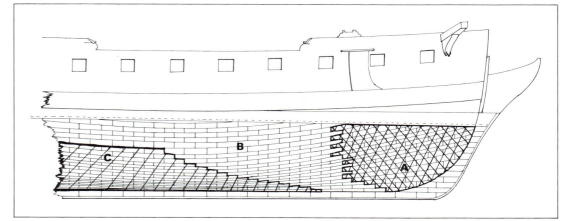

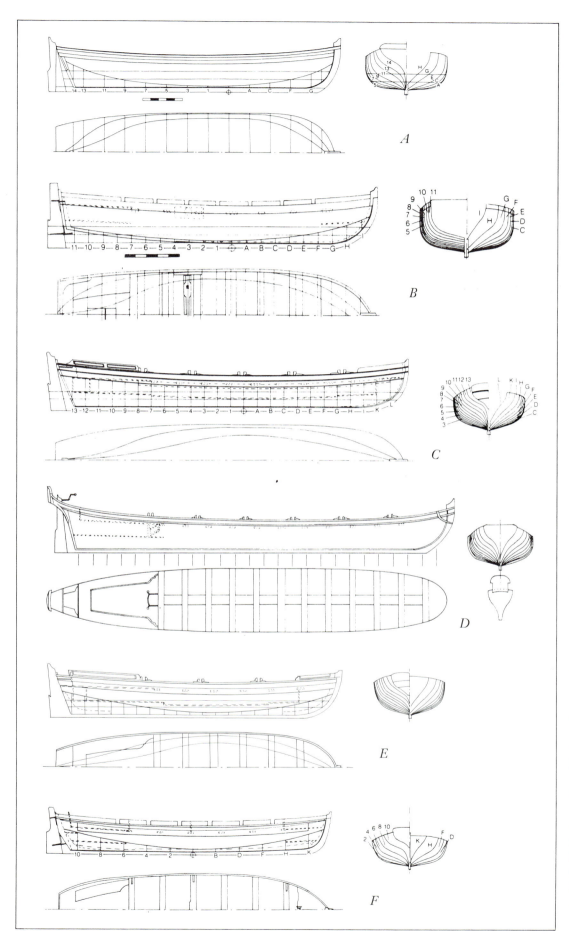

Typical eighteenth-century Royal Navy ship's boats.
A. *A 26ft longboat, 1758.*
B. *A 29ft launch, 1779.*
C. *A 32ft 10-oared pinnace, 1798.*
D. *A 36ft 12-oared barge, c1750.*
E. *A 26ft yawl, 1798.*
F. *A 25ft cutter, c1790.*
(Brian Lavery)

relative length, and by the early eighteenth century it was often shorter than the barge. Despite its name, it was quite broad in proportion to its length, and was designed for heavier work, and for good sailing. The French *chaloupe* was similar in form, though with a broader transom. In 1780 the British longboats were replaced by launches, which also had a broad transom, and were better for carrying heavy loads, but less good at sailing. For her second boat, a ship generally carried a rowing vessel, long and narrow and with some decoration in the stern. In England this was known as the pinnace, and in its larger version, reserved for flag officers and later for captains, as the barge. In the seventeenth century most ships up to the Fourth Rate had two boats, but larger ones had a third, usually known as a skiff, shallop or jollyboat in English. Three boats per ship were to suffice for most navies throughout the eighteenth century, but the British had a constant tendency to add more boats, of different types, to the complement. The first was the yawl, which was established in 1701. The cutter, perhaps the best sailing boat of all, was taken up in 1740, and a smaller version, known as the jollyboat, was adopted later in the century. Other types, such as wherries, gigs, dinghies and galleys were adopted for personal or local use. By 1805, a British ship of the line had six boats. For a 74, these were a launch or longboat of 32ft, a barge of 32ft, a pinnace of 28ft, two 25ft cutters, and an 18ft jollyboat. In contrast, a French ship of 1768 had a *grand canot* 11.6m long, and a *petit canot* of 8.45m.[7]

Most ships' boats were carvel-built – that is they were constructed in the same way as the ship itself, with the frame erected first, and the planks put onto it. There was no direct join between the planks. Some types, especially the British cutters and jollyboats, were clinker built. The planks overlapped one another, and were nailed or 'clenched' together. The planks were erected first, and the frame, which was much lighter than in carvel build, was put in later as a stiffener. Clinker building tended to produce a stronger hull for a given weight, but it was difficult to repair, and did not find gen-

7. *Ibid*, Vol II, p105.

eral favour. Boats were of course fitted with thwarts as seats for rowers, to brace the hull and to help support the masts. Heavy boats, such as longboats, usually had windlasses and davits to help with anchor work.

Many different types of sail were used on boats, though of course it was always fore and aft rig. Lug, gaff and sprit rigs were probably the most common. Masts had to be removable, in order to stow the boats. Those which were mainly intended for sailing, such as cutters, were rowed 'single banked' – one man sat on each thwart, on the opposite side from where his oar entered the water. Boats designed mainly for rowing, such as pinnaces, were rowed 'double banked', with two men on each thwart. Some barges at the beginning of the eighteenth century were rowed by as many as twenty oars. Boats were issued with other gear, such as grapnel anchors and boathooks.

In the early seventeenth century boats were normally towed behind the ship in all circumstances. This of course involved some risk of loss, and in the second half of the century it became more common to hoist them inboard and stow them in the waist. This involved a complicated tackle rigged from the main stay and from the ends of the lower yardarms. On British ships the boats were stowed at quarterdeck level, on spare spars fixed between the quarterdeck and forecastle, to keep them clear of the capstan. The French tended to stow them directly on the upper deck in the waist, as they did not have a capstan in that position, and this was the practice adopted by other nations such as the Spanish. They favoured the practice of nesting – of removing the thwarts from a large boat so that a smaller one could be stowed inside it, and often all three boats could be stowed so that they only took up the space of one. This was less common in Britain, perhaps because removable thwarts could be a source of weakness. However it was possible to turn the smaller of two boats upside down to stow it inside the larger.

As the British added new boats to their ships, they had to find ways of stowing them. From the 1740s, gangways were built along the sides of the waist to link the quarterdeck and forecastle, and booms were placed between them to support the boats. This structure became more permanent over the years. In the late eighteenth century wooden davits were added to ships, to hang the cutters over the quarter galleries, and other davits were put in the stern, for the jollyboats.

The standard layout of cabins of British 74-gun ships from the 1750s onwards. (Brian Lavery)

Accommodation

Aside from its qualities as a fighting machine, a warship had to act as home for a large number of men, often for years at a time. It had to carry food and drink, and provide them with bedding, with clothes, and with tables and utensils for eating. It needed some kind of medical accommodation, offices, and cooking facilities. In addition it needed a powder magazine, and store rooms for spare parts for the hull and rigging of the ship. Though there was some variation in ships' accommodation over the years, there were certain constants. Stores had to be kept in the hold, with the heaviest items, such as liquids, at the very lowest level. The officers' cabins were always placed in the stern, to give them more space, comfort and light. The crew always had their main living space on the lower deck, whether or not that area was fitted with guns. To solve the accommodation problem, it was necessary to use many spaces for multiple purposes. On a ship of the line the gundeck served as dormitory and dining room for the crew, and in battle as the main fighting strength of the ship. On British ships the cockpit, aft on the orlop deck, served as junior officers' accommodation in normal times, and as the surgeon's operating theatre in battle.

Officers' cabins

The captain's cabin on a ship of the line was usually placed aft on the upper deck in the seventeenth century, for that deck was wider, and was fitted with windows or an open gallery. By the 1740s it tended to move upwards to the quarterdeck; reduction in tumblehome made that deck wider than before, and now it was fitted with galleries like the upper deck. On French and Spanish ships the area was kept free of guns, but this was not so in other navies. On three-deckers, the cabin aft on the upper deck was now for the use of the admiral. The number of lieutenants tended to increase over the years, and in the British navy around 1745, they combined with the marine officers and certain warrant officers such as the purser, surgeon and master, to form the wardroom, aft on the upper deck of a two-decker, or the lower deck of a three-decker. Single cabins, usually made from canvas curtains, were fitted round the sides of the wardroom, each containing a gun. In the Spanish navy the junior officers used the same area, but had small cabins erected near the centreline, with others on the poop deck. In the French fleet, the wardroom for the officers was similar to that on British ships.

In the seventeenth century, battleships,

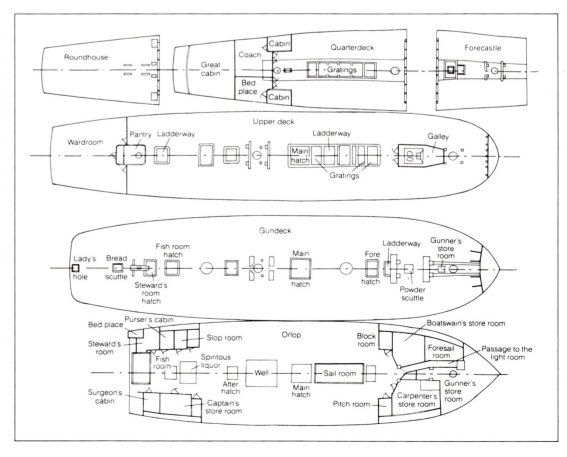

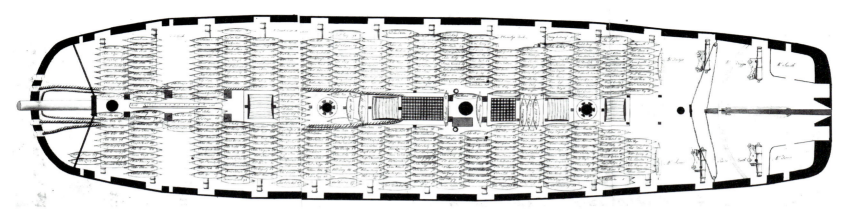

especially three-decker flagships, had been clogged with numerous cabins erected between the guns, and used for the courtiers and gentlemen volunteers who followed an admiral. These were largely abolished by the beginning of the eighteenth century. The gunroom, aft on the lower deck, was used by the gunner, and also had cabins for some of the junior officers and space for young men training to become officers. This area was known as the *St Barbe* on French ships, after the patron saint of gunners. On frigates there was usually no poop, so the captain lived on the upper deck, with closed stern galleries. The lieutenants and other officers were obliged to go one deck below, to the gunroom, which had no galleries and was rather less comfortable. On British ships, some of the wardroom officers lived aft on the orlop, including the purser and surgeon who had their store rooms and cabins there. The midshipmen and the master's and surgeon's mates were also berthed there, and by 1800 they had messing areas set aside.

Officers were expected to furnish their own cabins. Junior officers had room only for a hanging bed, and perhaps a sea chest, a table and a stool. Captains had a much larger area to furnish, and admirals had even more: in 1756 it took five hours to transfer Admiral Boscawen's furniture from one flagship to another, and the inventory of Admiral Rodney's furniture in 1781 occupies several pages.[8]

Crew accommodation

The common seaman was of course much less well provided for. In the British navy he was allowed 14in in which to sling his hammock, and presumably not much more in any other fleet. The hammock itself was the universal answer to the problem of accommodating large numbers of men in a confined space. It was simply a strip of canvas fitted with ropes to allow it to be slung from the deck above. The seaman also provided himself with bedding, including a mattress for use inside the hammock, blankets and a pillow. Hammocks were generally slung on the lower deck, though some might be found on the middle deck of a three-decker, and on the orlop deck on larger ships, often in the cable tier of British ships.

At mealtimes, tables were slung from the deckhead on the lower deck. In the case of a ship of the line this meant a table between each pair of guns, but a frigate had no guns on this deck, and there was more space. It is difficult to see how all the men could be given space aboard a ship of the line, even if extra tables were slung amidships. Wooden benches were fitted up to serve the tables, and half barrels could also be used for the men who sat at the head. The seamen were provided with wooden spoons and bowls, but often preferred to buy their own at the first opportunity.

The food itself was prepared in the cook room of the ship, often known as the galley. In the early part of the seventeenth century this had been sited in the hold, but it soon moved up to the space under the quarterdeck, or one deck below, on the middle deck on many three-deckers. The earliest cooking stove was simply a cauldron suspended over a brick furnace. By the second half of the seventeenth century this had been replaced by a copper 'kettle' built inside a brick furnace. From the 1750s the British began to fit all-metal stoves, constructed of iron round a copper kettle. This allowed boiling of the crew's provisions in the aftermost part of the stove, with capacity for grilling, roasting and other activities in the forward part, where the officers' cooks worked. As might be expected, the French galley of the late eighteenth century was more sophisticated, with a copper in an iron firehearth, a separate bread oven made from brick, and a hanging charcoal stove.

The crowded condition of the crew's sleeping arrangements can be gauged by this mid-eighteenth century hammock plan of a British Third Rate's lower deck. (NMM)

Before 1801, there was no fixed place for the sick bay on British ships; sick men were merely accommodated wherever was convenient among the tiers of hammocks on the lower deck. After that date, a new kind of sick bay was established under the forecastle. An area was partitioned off, and fitted with cots, and a dispensary for the surgeon. Being close to the galley stove, it could be warmed as required; conversely, it was easy to cool or ventilate, and gave easy access to the toilet accommodation of the 'round house' near the beakhead.

The surgeon's operating theatre was much longer established, and was placed on the orlop deck, away from the effects of enemy shot. By the early eighteenth century, the orlop deck of British ships of the line was fitted out in quite a well established way. Aft of it was the bread room, holding ships' biscuits in bags, away from the bilge water in the hold. Next came the cockpit, with several cabins grouped around it, for the steward, surgeon and purser, and store rooms for marine clothing, seamen's slop clothing, and for the personal belongings of officers.

Forward of the cockpit were the cable tiers, one on each side of the ship, and with pumps and other store rooms down the centre. In the bows were store rooms for the boatswain, carpenter and gunner, filled with numerous spares and supplies. The subdivision of this area was quite complex, and it included passages to the magazine, and to the light room below the orlop. On French ships, the arrangement below the gundeck was completely different. Cables were stowed forward in the hold, rather than on the orlop. Store rooms and magazines were generally placed aft, with the cockpit amidships, and with bread rooms aft of that.

Brian Lavery

8. B Lavery, *The Arming and Fitting of English Ships of War, 1600–1815* (London 1987).

11

Guns and Gunnery

THE sailing warship was, above all else, a floating gun battery and its effectiveness was a function of the number, calibre and efficiency of its 'great guns'. Like the ships themselves, the smooth bore muzzle-loading gun had already reached a plateau of development by 1650 and thereafter development was subtle but steady and significant.

or continuous fire and engagements were not expected to be very lengthy (English ships of the 1650s carried about thirty-five rounds per gun, whereas by the 1760s ships of the line were allocated sixty rounds for Channel service and eighty for Foreign).[2] The supply of guns never met all requirements and ships were often forced to take whatever was available;

even where there was a choice, it was felt necessary to have different types of gun for each function – long range disabling fire, medium range battering, and anti-personnel

1. B Lavery, *The Ship of the Line*, Vol I, p15.
2. B Lavery, *The Arming and Fitting of English Ships of War 1600–1815*, pp84–5, 279.

The warship as gun platform

The development of ships' armament

In 1650 the armament of the most advanced warship was moving towards a disposition in which guns of a uniform calibre were carried on each deck (the deck itself being flush, without steps up or down), with the heaviest guns lowest down for reasons of stability. This situation applied almost universally to large ships in the eighteenth century and with hindsight its simple logic is so obvious that it seems obtuse not to have adopted it sooner.

However, there were good reasons why it was so slow to become the norm. Primarily there was the nature of the tactics of the time, which placed emphasis on almost individual combat, with a ship manoeuvring to fire in succession the guns of one broadside, followed by the chase guns as she turned away, and then the other broadside; sheer firepower was unlikely to force a surrender, the *coup de grace* having to be administered by boarding.[1] The methods of handling the guns and the metallurgy of the guns themselves made them incapable of rapid

English ships at the Isle de Rhé in 1627. Note the relatively few guns on the broadsides, frequent half batteries, and some evidence of stepped-down decks. (NMM)

Many of the English Fourth Rates built during the 1650s did not have complete upper deck batteries – indeed, as originally built, they did not have many guns on the upperworks, but this example from a Van de Velde drawing of the 1670s shows an early stage in the relentless up-gunning of these ships, with quarterdeck and forecastle extended to form a complete upper deck, although she still carried no guns in the waist. The line of battle placed increased emphasis on broadside firepower and eventually most of these ships became genuine two-deckers. (NMM)

'murderers' to clear the decks prior to boarding. Consequently ships tended to have a large and disparate range of weaponry: as late as the 1640s English ships might have seven calibres, which inevitably meant mixed batteries even on the principal gundecks.

The relative importance of turning tactics kept the ships short, and their steep sheer lines made flush decks too acutely angled fore and aft for chase batteries, so stepped decks were preferred; this also helped to avoid cutting into the wales which provided the main longitudinal strength of the ship. Also the persisting influence of boarding can be perceived in the desire for a deep fall in the waist which was regarded as more 'defensible' (having gained a flush deck a boarding party would face no obstacle beyond the opposing crew).

The largest ship of her day, the *Sovereign of the Seas*, had flush decks but the old ideas persisted in the division of the armament into 'luffs, sides and quarters', as well as chase guns. A fifth of the ship's 102 guns did not point on the broadside, and these were mostly of a different calibre from the rest of the guns on their deck; ostensibly there were four calibres but two also had 'drake' variants (see below) which would have had different powder charges.[3] The French seem to have persevered with stepped decks longer, although the *Sovereign*'s contemporary, *Couronne*, was not so heavily armed.[4]

The First Anglo-Dutch War was to exert a powerful influence on the way capital ships and their armament developed (see Chapter 1). The introduction of the line-ahead tactics placed particular emphasis on broadside rather than chase batteries, but the hard fought close combats of the war also stressed the value of heavy firepower. In the 1650s English ships were progressively up-gunned, not only with extra weapons but, more significantly, with heavier calibres. As new ships to standard specifications were added to the fleet, there was a gradual move towards single-calibre batteries on each deck, and these of the largest size that could be carried.[5] Other navies were soon following suit,

and by about 1670 the newly developed 'line of battle ship' was almost universally defined by this pattern of armament.[6]

In some cruising ships, a part-battery of a few heavier guns was regarded as useful as late as the mid-eighteenth century (see Chapter 2), and of course the few remaining galleys continued to emphasise the forward-firing weaponry that reflected their ancient ramming tactics; but the battlefleet became a more homogeneous collection of broadside-armed ships which could be meaningfully categorised by the number of guns carried. Attempts at standardisation became more effective as ship design stabilised but there was always a need for periodic revision. In France, for example, gun establishments were promulgated in 1674, 1689, (with minor revisions in 1721 and 1733), 1758, 1766, 1778, 1786, 1820, 1824 and 1829; in Britain similar rules were laid down in 1677, 1685, 1703, 1716, 1733 (but not really implemented until 1743) and 1745, after which armament was more closely tailored to individual designs. Needless to say, the standardised ideal represented by the establishments could rarely be achieved in practice.

The guns were of the same basic type – a relatively high velocity smooth bore muzzle-loader – and although the calibre would be reduced the higher up the ship they were placed, all had the same ship-smashing function. A few dedicated anti-personnel weapons might be carried (usually light swivel guns), but these were more widely employed on cruisers, and were not usually reckoned in the ship's rating. In essence this disposition survived until the development of the carronade by the British in the 1780s. This otherwise novel design in effect reintroduced the old concept of specialist weaponry: it was short-barrelled and light, firing a large calibre shot at low velocity, which at short range could actually do more damage than an equivalent long gun (the high velocity gun would punch a smaller and less jagged hole

whereas the early nickname of the carronade, the 'smasher', bears witness to its effect).[7] Its light weight allowed it to be mounted high up in the ship, either replacing the small calibre long guns or taking up positions where guns had not previously been mounted; in either case there could be a considerable increase in the weight of broadside. For this reason at first it was more widely applied to the superstructures of frigates and sloops, while some small craft had all but a couple of chase guns replaced by carronades; battleships were not much affected until after 1800.

Despite its anti-ship potential, initially no carronade was included in the ship's rating so it may have been regarded as an anti-personnel ancillary weapon, like the old swivel gun it rendered obsolete. Given its range restriction, it was always a controversial weapon and its popularity waxed and waned for fifty years. It is perhaps significant that it was first employed by the Royal Navy, which always favoured close action; it made less sense for any service whose inferior numbers dictated defensive tactics. As secondary armament it was effective, but some navies made the mistake of arming cruising ships entirely with carronades and paid the price in action.[8]

By the end of the Napoleonic Wars many

3. G S Laird Clowes, *Sailing Ships: Their History and Development as illustrated by the Collection of Ship-Models in the Science Museum* (London 1932), Part II, p29.

4. C H Hancock, *La Couronne, A French Warship of the Seventeenth Century*. The evidence is by no means conclusive.

5. B Lavery, *Arming and Fitting*, pp112–4.

6. Even in 1689 some French Third Rates had mixed lower deck batteries: J Boudriot, 'L'Artillerie de Mer de la Marine Français 1674–1856', *Neptunia* 103 (1971).

7. S Tucker, *Arming the Fleet: US Navy Ordnance in the Muzzle-Loading Era*, p12.

8. A famous example is the American frigate *Essex*, whose 32pdr carronades could not reply to the long range fire of HMS *Phoebe*'s long 18pdrs, forcing her surrender (1814).

battleships carried carronades of the same calibre as their main batteries, which inevitably led to the questioning of the value of the intermediate calibres. In the 1820s and 1830s a new principle evolved whereby a ship would carry guns of only one calibre, but differentiated by weight; this involved designing guns of medium length or reduced thickness of metal (and hence weight) to be mounted between genuine long guns and carronades. The usual calibre was 32pdr (or 30pdr in France) and in Britain after 1826 some 1600 24pdrs were bored up to make the required numbers. They were less powerful than purpose-designed medium guns, suffered from a fierce recoil, and could not be double-shotted at close range, but were an essential temporary expedient.[9]

One further development of the postwar period was the shell gun, whose perfection is usually attributed to the French Colonel Paixhans in the late 1820s. Explosive shells should have spelt the demise of wooden warships, but the unreliability of the ammunition and the inaccuracy of the early guns tended to restrain their employment. Early steamers and small craft often mounted a few of large calibre, but before the late 1840s the standard ship of the line carried very limited numbers, usually disposed at the ends of the battery decks. They were formally adopted by the French navy in 1837, although a few had been in service since 1824, and by the British in the following year (again, experiments had been underway since 1824). In the USA an early interest in shell guns during the War of 1812 had evaporated and it was not until the late 1830s that development work revived; it was to be the late 1840s before any number were at sea in US Navy ships.

Ship design and armament

Before the concept of the ship of the line crystallised in the late seventeenth century, armament was not the overriding influence on design that it was to become. The main striking power of the ship certainly lay with its heavy guns but as with a land fortress the size and number of these might well depend on what was available, while weight restrictions could be met by mixing heavy and lighter guns in each battery. The gunport configuration could not be altered easily, but it seems that early seventeenth-century ships did not always fill every port, and the upperworks provided much scope for altering the smaller calibres. Thus armament was something of an afterthought in the design process.

This was to change with the increased

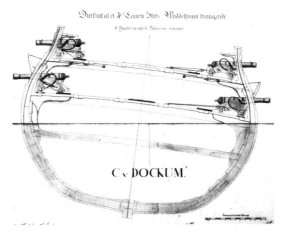

The midship section of a Danish 70-gun ship, showing the guns run out. The 7-degree angle of heel shown in this drawing is the maximum to be expected of a ship of the line sailing close-hauled in moderate weather; in this condition there is only 3ft freeboard between the waterline and the lee lower gunport sill, which with any kind of sea running would mean water breaking through the gunport. Thus, ultimately, problems of stability and seaworthiness were closely allied to the requirements of gunnery. (Rigsarkivet, Copenhagen)

weights of the 1650s and 1660s, which affected both stability and structural strength. As long as naval warfare was largely confined to coastal waters and the summer months, the extra weight was acceptable, but from 1660 the Royal Navy was obliged to adopt a reduced scale of gunning for foreign service in wartime (which also applied in peacetime). Hereafter armament weight became critical, so that the number and calibre of the gun batteries was usually the starting point of the design specification.

The armament would be decided by the function and rate of the ship, usually with some tacit reference to international standards (the armament of the ship's likely opponents). This would set the number of gunports, from which the ship's length would ultimately derive, while the weight of the battery would dictate the structural strength of decks and constitute the most significant element in the calculation of its stability. As requirements came to be more consciously formulated, the height of battery (distance of gunport sill from the load waterline) and the space between guns would also be stipulated, and from all these armament-related factors the dimensions of the ship would be derived. Of course in a design system where changes were rarely radical (see Chapter 8), in practice the dimensions and the armament could be specified simultaneously, but the impact of armament on design was real nonetheless, even if it did not require calculation anew for each class. Sailing qualities and

seaworthiness were decidedly secondary, but although different navies might well give one or both greater priority, it was never at the expense of gunpower (navies requiring more speed, like the French, or better seaworthiness, like the Spanish, would build larger ships for their rate). The Americans also built very large ships for their rate, but they tended to carry heavier metal as well, in an attempt to compensate for their very small numbers.

The design of ships not intended for the line of battle was less dominated by armament considerations. Advice boats, cutters and small craft, for example, where performance under sail was paramount, might well have their armament decided by what they could carry without detriment to those qualities. Frigates and sloops were compromises, where speed and seaworthiness were as important as gunpower; the number and calibre of guns might well be the design starting point, but the significance of the height of battery in single-gundeck ships points to an emphasis on the ability to use them in all weathers.

Ship design also influenced the nature of the guns themselves. Barrels needed to be long enough not to endanger the shrouds with their muzzle blast; this was a constant problem with carronades but in earlier days the extreme tumblehome of ships also encouraged longer barrels. On the other hand, guns could not be so long that there was no room for some energy-absorbing recoil, a particular difficulty on narrower upper decks encumbered with hatchways, capstans, boats etc. There is some evidence that early guns were reloaded from outboard for this reason, which would have considerably retarded the rate of fire.[10]

The muzzle-loading smooth bore

The standard ship gun for the whole period covered by this volume was a muzzle-loading smooth bore – in effect a large hollow tube closed at the breech end, manufactured by casting and then bored out. For the largest calibres these had replaced built-up breech-loaders in the previous century and although small breech-loaders survived into the late 1700s they were normally cast.

9. A Lambert, *The Last Sailing Battlefleet*, p104.

10. Recoil was originally believed to reduce range, so attempts were made to constrict if not prevent it altogether. (S Tucker, *op cit*, p27).

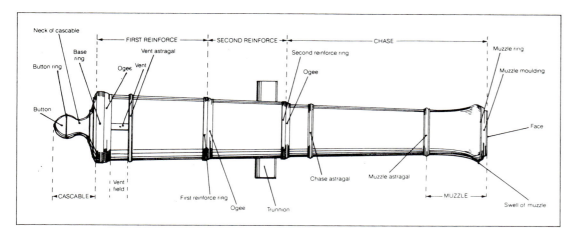

The parts of a gun, a British Armstrong pattern used from c1725 to the 1780s. The terminology applied to most long gun types. (Brian Lavery)

Gunfounding and gun development

The casting of cannon was a time-consuming,[11] highly skilled and consequently expensive operation (which is why navies rarely had enough guns for their perceived needs). In the seventeenth century a full size pattern for each gun was built up around a wooden core or spindle representing the bore (a clay mixture applied over a rope armature was one early technique); the pattern represented the external form of the finished gun and from it a female mould, usually in sections, was constructed in clay. The mould was then assembled, breech downwards, with a spindle for the bore, and filled with molten metal. Once cooled the mould was broken and the gun would be finished with hand tools and the rough bore reamed as smooth and true as could be achieved. The gun was then subject to 'proofing', which involved firing with an abnormal charge, followed by close inspection for cracks or casting faults.

Since it was such a lucrative business, gunfounding was subject to constant attempts at improvements. Brass spindles for more accurate bores were introduced in England from at least 1730, while standard patterns of hardwood or metal were employed in an attempt to improve accuracy and uniformity. From about 1750 moulds of sand replaced clay which again contributed to improved quality.[12] However, the biggest step forward came from Switzerland where in 1715 a gunfounder called Johan Maritz perfected a technique for casting the gun solid and boring it out when cold. The casting method made for denser, more homogeneous metal and consequently stronger guns, while his technique of turning the gun (on its

Diagram illustrating equipment for boring out cannon, from a late eighteenth-century French encyclopaedia. Note that the gun is revolved on its axis with the cutter remaining stationary, following the Maritz principle.

horizontal axis) rather than the cutter ensured a smoother and more accurate bore. Maritz's sons took his technique to France and Spain, but it was the Dutch Verbruggen father and son who greatly improved the approach and by the 1780s the foundry they established in England, at Woolwich, was reckoned to be the best in the world.

The inadequacies of early methods of casting, where the pattern was broken after the casting of each gun, made it virtually impossible to produce genuinely standard weapons; poor tolerances were also inherent in the process, while early iron was difficult to cast because it cooled rapidly and was relatively brittle when cool, so iron guns tended to be cast very thick-sided for safety. These factors produced a preference for what in England was usually called brass (but was actually bronze): it was stronger, rustfree, less prone to bursting, could

be re-cast, and was amenable to the most elaborate decoration that appealed to the pride of captains and kings. Its drawback was that it was far more expensive than iron (£150 versus £18 per ton in 1670). As battlefleets became larger and individual ships more powerfully armed, there was a rapid decline in the employment of brass *vis-à-vis* iron: in France in 1661 the navy had 570 brass guns to 475 iron and in 1699 1246 to 7136, but by 1768 only 186 of 7774 were bronze;[13] in England in 1698 only 11 of 323 ships had any brass guns. Bronze guns continued to be 'high status' weapons, issued to flagships and royal yachts, but by 1782 only the *Royal George* in Britain carried any. Oddly, although France abandoned the manufacture of bronze naval guns in the first quarter of the eighteenth century, she revived the art in 1781 for a batch of special light guns for her first 18pdr-armed frigates.[14]

The decline of brass was driven as much by changing tactics as by relative costs. The line of battle, with its implication of heavy and continuous firing, required improved metallurgy.

---

11. Even in the nineteenth century it was reckoned to take 3–4 weeks to make a 24pdr (S Tucker, *op cit*, p55).

12. S Tucker, *op cit*, pp53–4.

13. J Boudriot, 'L'Artillerie de Mer de la Marine Français 1674–1856', *Neptunia* 90 (1968).

14. J Boudriot, *op cit*, p25.

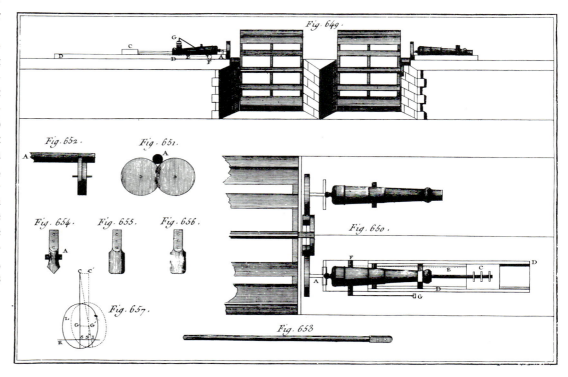

Bronze would not usually burst but overheated relatively quickly when it would bulge, rending it equally useless. The quality of iron improved dramatically during the eighteenth century, and the burgeoning industrial revolution gave Britain a distinct advantage in this area (in 1812 some British 24pdrs were calculated to have been fired 3000 times without accident; even the norm was 1000 firings).[15] Thus the superior rate of fire often attributed to Royal Navy gun crews during the Napoleonic Wars probably reflects superior technology as much as better training.

Types of gun

The seventeenth century inherited an almost medieval system of categorising guns, and in England the quaint and exotic names survived until the first years of the following century, whereas other countries were quicker to adopt the simpler method of categorising guns by their weight of shot. The plethora of type names disguised the division of gunpowder artillery into four very basic categories depending on their function and identifiable by the ratio of their length to calibre.

The longest, at about 32–34 calibres as originally manufactured, was the culverin type; with the slow burning powders of the sixteenth century, length was believed to equate with range, so these guns were widely used on ships in the era of 'manoeuvre-and-board' tactics. The 'whole' culverin proper was a precursor of later English 18pdr and the demi-culverin of the 9pdr, but there were also sakers (firing shot of roughly 5–7 pounds) and minions (4pdrs), but the smaller falcons, falconets and robinets were not very numerous after 1650.

Cannon were shorter – 18 to 28 calibres long in early forms – but of greater bore than culverins; they were medium range battering pieces and with the line of battle concept came to dominate naval artillery to the point where any muzzle-loading smooth bore was loosely referred to as a 'cannon'. The largest seagoing

calibres were of this type: in English service the 'cannon of seven' or 42pdr (named for its 7in bore) and demi-cannon or 32pdr; France mainly employed a 36pdr (approximately 39 pounds English) until the new 30pdrs of the 1820s, but bronze 48pdrs were carried by a very few First Rates from the *Royal Louis* of 1692.[16] After 1815 the USA tried 42pdrs in its battleships, but other navies found the 30–32pdr to be the heaviest calibre that could be handled with enduring rapidity in a crowded battery; this view persisted until nearly the end of wooden fighting ships, the 1840s seeing a 50pdr adopted in France and a 56pdr and 68pdr in Britain, but these guns needed pivot mountings and were mostly deployed aboard steamships.

There were also perriers, which were very short (6–8 calibres) and originally intended to fire stone shot at low velocity for a splintering impact. In larger sizes, like the cannon perrier, they were virtually obsolete by 1650 but some smaller types survived longer firing iron shot in anti-personnel roles – variously called murderers, port-pieces, petreroes, slings and fowlers.[17] They were the direct ancestors of swivel guns (see below) and it is significant that in the French navy such weapons continued to be called *pierriers*. In some respects it is possible to see the carronade of the 1780s as a revival of the principles and role of the original perrier.

Although not strictly naval 'guns', mention should be made of howitzers and mortars, which were very short (as little as 1½ calibres for mortars); these fired explosive shells at high trajectories and their inherent inaccuracy confined them to large and fixed targets like fortifications, or fleets at anchor. Heavy mortars required special ships for their deployment, these 'bomb vessels' being a French invention of the 1680s, although rapidly adopted by other navies shortly after. Howitzers were longer (8–10 calibres) but generally smaller and not much employed in naval service, although they were occasionally mounted to fire at the rigging of their opponents. Since it was intended to fire on a horizontal trajectory, it was not a true howitzer, but the initial French response to the British carronade was described as such (*obusier de vaisseau*).

French bronze mortar of 1683 with fixed elevation and integral base-plate. (David Wray)

Proportions and weights of guns

In the course of the seventeenth century there was a tendency for culverins to get shorter and cannon to get longer. Furthermore, new intermediate calibres introduced into English service from the Netherlands (24pdrs, 12pdrs, 6pdrs and 3pdrs) enhanced this movement towards more homogeneous gun proportions, and filled the gaps in the spectrum of calibres. Slowly a new principle was emerging whereby varying lengths (and hence weights) of the same calibre would be used according to where the gun was to be employed (the mid-eighteenth century Royal Navy, for example, had five different 9pdrs, varying from a 7ft 23cwt weapon for Sixth Rates to a 9ft 26cwt gun for the upper decks of 80-gun ships).

However, in the previous century the principle was confused by the existence of 'drakes' and 'cutts', lighter and/or shorter versions of the standard guns of the time. Drakes were a Dutch invention of the 1620s, whose lightness was achieved by reducing the thickness of metal and the length of the barrel; they were low velocity, short range weapons, originally used in anti-personnel roles. However, the principle – like the later carronade – allowed large calibre guns to be mounted aboard ship when ordinary 'fortified' guns could not be carried, and like the later weapon could be handled by a small crew (two to three instead of four to five). However, they also had many of the

15. S Tucker, *op cit*, p50.

16. J Boudriot, *op cit*, p21.

17. Lavery, *Arming and Fitting*, p103.

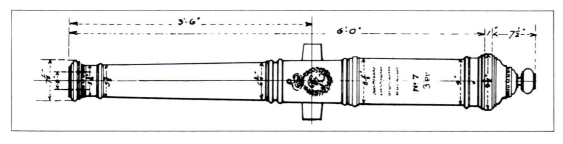

A Danish bronze culverin-type weapon dated 1633. These were proportionately the longest style of gun and tended to get shorter as the seventeenth century progressed.

carronade's disadvantages (like a tendency to overheat and to recoil violently) and cautious observers felt that their lack of range made them suitable as secondary armament only. Nevertheless, they formed the principal armament of the *Sovereign of the Seas* in order to increase the designed complement from ninety to a hundred guns. The other characteristic of drakes was that their bores were tapered from muzzle down to chamber, which may have facilitated quick firing but only at the expense of range. Drakes went out of fashion during the later Anglo-Dutch wars and none was manufactured for English naval service after about 1670, guns thereafter being 'home' or 'whole' bored (*ie* straight).

As English drakes began to be made in the same lengths as fortified guns, a new category of 'cutts' emerges. These were short, or very short, versions of long gun calibres and were in vogue from the 1630s to about 1680. The length and weight could be as little as a half of the full length fortified version. It was originally thought that these guns were physically cut down from long guns with casting faults in the muzzle, but although a few may have originated from this process, the majority were cast as cutts.

By the eighteenth century, guns of different calibres tended to be similar in overall design but, effectively, scaled up or down in proportion to calibre. This drawing from the Danish archives seems to be a British original depicting iron guns of the Armstrong pattern, but a reference to Dutch pounds and the inclusion of an 8pdr suggest an export order. Besides the 8pdr, the other guns are of 24pdr, 18pdr, 12pdr and 6pdr calibres. (Rigsarkivet, Copenhagen)

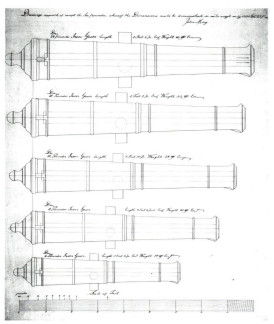

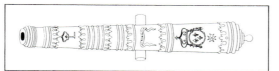

A typically heavily decorated bronze gun of the mid-seventeenth century. This example was a French 36pdr used as the main forward-firing armament of a galley. (From Paris' Souvenirs de Marine*)*

The shape and appearance of guns

The development of guns was a gentle progression towards a more streamlined appearance: in general, the earlier the gun the more complicated its shape. Apart from the heavy heraldic decoration and elaborate lifting handles called 'dolphins' on bronze guns, all seventeenth-century ship's guns had a large number of narrow external rings – a skuemorphic holdover from the days when guns were stave built and needed bands to strengthen them; they also featured a swelling at the muzzle end of the barrel and a complicated pattern of mouldings and 'cascable' or button at the breech.

In the eighteenth century the rings tended to become simpler in section and were eventually replaced by 'steps' in the diameter of the barrel, which in the nineteenth century were further smoothed into 'knuckles' at each swelling. The cascable became larger and from the late 1780s in England guns of the Blomefield pattern were cast with a breeching ring above the button (adopted in 1820 in France). Trunnions (the elevating 'axle' of the gun), which had been tapered, became parallel and were generally placed below the axis of the bore; this was believed to reduce the 'kick' of the gun on firing, but others felt that it also increased the strain on the carriage. The basic proportions also changed with relatively more metal being cast around the breech end and less in the 'chase' (the section between the trunnions and muzzle), although in general guns became heavier. The other great change was invisible: the 'windage' or difference between the diameter of the bore and the shot (as much as 1/20th in eighteenth-century British guns) was reduced, allowing a smaller charge to do the same work but placing a greater emphasis on accuracy in casting the shot and on keeping it free from rust. These changes were not cosmetic but were intended to cast stronger guns in order to cope with more powerful gunpowders and the increasing need for rapid and continuous firing.

Decoration was never as elaborate on iron guns as bronze, mostly for reasons of the value

of the latter but also because decorative reliefs complicated an already difficult process of casting in iron. Nevertheless, early iron guns usually had a simple coat of arms or monogram forward of the vent field although this became much smaller and more austere in the nineteenth century. Casting marks (denoting maker and manufacturing details) were usually chiselled into the ends of the trunnions and sometimes the weight was added to the barrel.

Other weapons

In terms of numbers and importance the heavy muzzle-loading smooth bore dominated naval gunnery in the seventeenth and eighteenth centuries, but there was always a variety of ancillary weapons, and by the early nineteenth century new developments began to threaten its monopoly of the main gundecks.

Mortars and howitzers

Designed to lob explosive shells at high trajectories, these were not really naval weapons in that they could not be used for ship-to-ship combat. They were essentially land warfare siege weapons taken to sea in special ships to improve the effectiveness of fleets in shore bombardment roles (see Chapter 5 for fuller details of bomb vessels). Nevertheless special mortars, optimised for sea service, were manufactured from the earliest days of their naval employment in the 1680s.

Very short at about two to four times the bore diameter, mortars were initially cast with an integral base plate and consequently at a fixed elevation of about 45 degrees to give the greatest range. French practice was to mount a

A British 'trabucco' type sea service mortar of the 1790s; the trunnions at the breech allowed the mortar to be stowed horizontally when at sea. (From Falconer's Marine Dictionary*)*

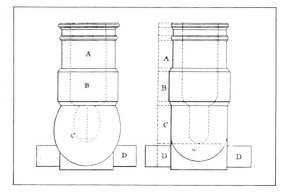

A Danish elevation and section showing the fitting of swivel guns along the quarterdeck rails of a frigate; dated 1763. (Rigsarkivet, Copenhagen)

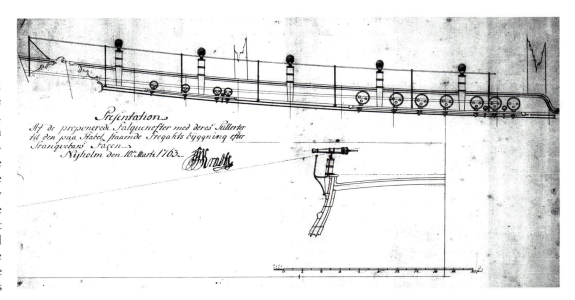

pair of mortars side by side before the main mast pointing over the bow so as to present the smallest target to defending counter-fire. However, the English rapidly introduced a pivoting mounting that could fire on any bearing unmasked by rigging; this encouraged the fitting of mortars on the centreline, one before and one abaft the main mast.[18] In the early eighteenth century the English took to sea the land service 'trabucco' type with trunnions cast at the breech of the mortar, which was still fired at the same angle, but when not in use could be stowed horizontally to improve the stability of the bomb vessel. At first range was determined by varying the powder, which was poured loose into a chamber, which could be one of various profiles – conical, spherical, cylindrical or elliptical – but the last generation of mortars were given mountings in which elevation could be varied.

The standard calibre was fixed very early: France adopted the 12in mortar from the beginning, and after some trials with 12¼in and

The Baltic navies were the principal exponents of the naval howitzer, which was widely employed by their inshore flotillas. On the left is a 3pdr on a pivot mounting, fitted just inside the bulwark rails; the larger weapon on the right also fired over the bulwarks but required a reinforced platform and carriage. Both mountings, on the non-recoil principle, were devised by the innovative Swedish naval architect F H Chapman. Not surprisingly, the Scandinavian navies regarded the carronade as a natural development of these weapons. (K H Marquardt)

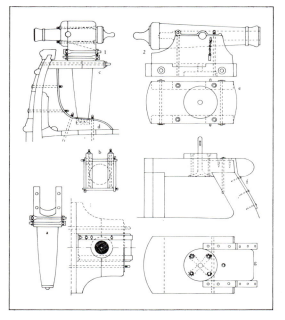

12¾in the English settled on 13in (because the French unit was larger the two calibres were virtually identical at around 325mm); from the mid-1700s the English also employed a 10in weapon as the second mortar on most bomb vessels, and the US Navy came to follow British practice from about 1800. Smaller calibres were not uncommon on gunboats and various forms of inshore specialist craft, but not on purpose-built bomb vessels. Apart from their very squat proportions, mortars originally resembled long guns in the details of their appearance and decoration, but had become much plainer and utilitarian by 1800; being made in very much smaller quantities they were less standardised, the majority continuing to be cast in bronze until the end of the eighteenth century.

Howitzers differed from mortars in being longer and having trunnions cast in the conventional position as for long guns. Their employment at sea was never extensive nor indeed regularly countenanced for seagoing warships, but they were used on some specialist inshore craft and occasionally were unofficially added to larger vessels. Like small mortars, they were fitted in tops and on upperworks (as well as for boat work), and were used for dismantling fire; they were not counted in the ship's rating.

Swivels and anti-personnel weapons

The sole survivors of the perrier genre of cannon described above were the various forms of small anti-personnel weapons used by most navies. Some early style breech-loaders of the type described in the Royal Navy as petreroes may have survived to the end of the seventeenth century, but thereafter the swivel gun became in effect a miniature muzzle-loading

cannon cast in either bronze or iron. Breech-loading guns continued in mercantile usage for some time and there is evidence of their employment as late as the American Revolution.[19] The Royal Navy settled on a standard ½pdr calibre but larger swivels were used by the French (up to 2pdrs) and a Dutch 4pdr breech-loader has been recovered from a ship lost in 1727.

All these guns were mounted in much the same way. Their trunnions fitted into a Y-shaped iron crutch which could be mounted in the ferrule of a wooden stock, allowing the piece to be swivelled. To aid pointing, an extension (called a tiller in English) was fixed to the gun or its crutch. The swivels were easily removed and were not considered part of the ship's rated armament.

Principally used for firing grape or canister, swivels could be backed up in a man-killing role by large shoulder-arms, called musketoons in the Royal Navy and *espingoles* by the French. Strictly speaking, the former resembled a large flintlock musket and was used by many navies, whereas the latter was developed from it and as a replacement specifically by the French navy. Although early *espingoles* of the American War period resembled musketoons, they quickly took on the form of a swivel gun and by about 1800 even the trigger mechanism had disappeared; they were usually of ¼pdr calibre. Musketoons continued to be issued to even

18. One such French vessel, the ship rigged *Salamandre*, was built in 1696, but otherwise the pivoting mounting was not used in French service before 1815. J Boudriot, 'L'Artillerie de Mer', *Neptunia* 97 (1970).

19. S Tucker, *op cit*, p8. Anson also noted 3pdr breech-loaders when he captured the Spanish 'galleon' *Nuestra Señora de Covadonga* in 1744.

large Royal Navy ships until 1806,[20] but all these anti-personnel weapons were rendered obsolete by the progressive introduction of the carronade from the 1780s.

Carronades and obusiers

As outlined above, the principles of a light-weight short gun were understood from the seventeenth century heyday of 'drakes', but were largely forgotten in the drive towards uniformity and firepower. In 1778 the Carron Iron Company in Scotland refined these principles for a new weapon that was to carry its name. The precise reasoning behind the carronade is not clear but the company was banned from supplying long guns to the Royal Navy following a series of casting faults and may have been looking for a weapon of particular attraction to the merchant marine – because it was light it was also relatively cheap and could be handled by a very small crew, an important consideration in lightly manned merchant ships.

Lightness was not achieved solely by cutting the barrel length: the gun was optimised for short range work, so a reduced diameter chamber would be sufficient for the small charge of powder, which kept the thickness of metal below that of an equivalent long gun. On the other hand, the windage was reduced, making the charge more efficient. The weapon could

---

20. PRO Adm 7/677.

21. The Tower of London possesses an early Carron weapon of 1778, a swivel-mounted 4pdr that resembles a howitzer; it may be the carronade's immediate ancestor. H Blackmore, *The Armouries of the Tower of London*, p144.

trace its ancestry from the howitzer, which influenced its shape, and it may well have been regarded as a replacement for the swivel gun (early small calibre 'monkey-tailed' carronades had a tiller like swivels).[21]

Hard pressed during the American War of Independence, the Royal Navy was quick to adopt the carronade as a potentially large increase in short range firepower. Initially they were purely additional but soon began to replace the smaller long guns. Although a 68pdr was one of the prototypes, the smaller calibres were adopted first, with 12pdrs, 18pdrs and 24pdrs being followed by 32pdrs and a few 42pdrs after 1780. The gun itself underwent rapid if not fundamental change, growing slightly in length (to offset the blast effect on shrouds and bulwarks) and replacing the conventional trunnions with a cast loop under the gun and a breech that allowed a screw elevating device; from about 1790 a nozzle extension of the muzzle solved much of the blast problem. Thereafter the form of the carronade barrel did not alter radically for the rest of its active employment.

At first the carronade was a British monopoly and its exact principles were not understood at all clearly. The first French response came in 1787 with the 36pdr *obusier de vaisseau*, a bronze howitzer-like weapon of simple tubular appearance, but given a carronade style slide mounting; it was originally envisaged as firing explosive shells but the idea was soon abandoned as too dangerous. In 1804 it was replaced by a more precise imitation of British practice, cast in iron to 36pdr and 24pdr calibres. Baltic navies, whose inshore forces had a tradition of relatively heavy bulwark-mounted

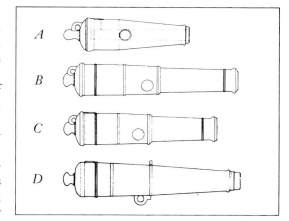

British short guns.
A. Sadler's 32pdr.
B. Gover's 24pdr.
C. Blomefield's short 24pdr.
D. Congreve's short 24pdr.
(Brian Lavery)

anti-personnel weapons, were also quick to adopt a form of carronade, but they too eventually developed a British-style gun. The nascent US Navy followed the British pattern from the beginning.

Short and medium guns and 'gunnades'

The difference in relative weight between carronades and long guns of the same calibre (18cwt–55cwt for an English 32pdr) inevitably led to experiments with intermediate types. Again Britain took the lead with a 24cwt 32pdr to Sadler's patent being tested in 1796. This was unsuccessful but in 1805 Captain Gover's medium 24pdr found favour and as early as 1806 was used to give some old ships of the line a uniform armament of 24pdrs. However, the real impetus for change was the Anglo-American War of 1812, when medium 24pdrs were in great demand to up-gun British 18pdr frigates in an attempt to give them some chance against the huge US frigates of the *Constitution* class. The Gover gun was found to be dangerous if double-shotted and a new and more satisfactory type, looking like an enlarged carronade, was developed by William Congreve.

In the postwar period France developed the concept further by introducing a new 30pdr gun in short and long forms, which when combined with 30pdr carronades allowed battle-

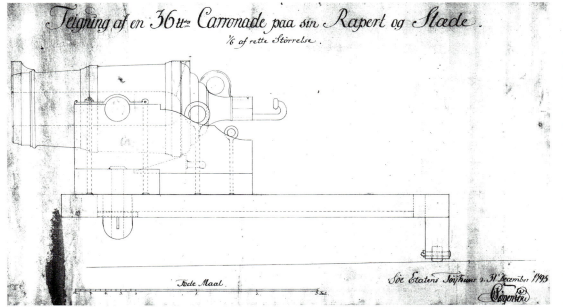

The early form of carronade, with no muzzle extension (nozzle), trunnions and a tiller. This Danish draught is dated 31 December 1795 and is one of a pair contrasting this gun with the improved type 'in the English fashion'. (Rigsarkivet, Copenhagen)

ships a powerful single-calibre battery. Other navies followed suit in the 1820s and 1830s, the British standardising on 32pdrs, the lighter marks being initially bored up from short 24pdrs; the only exception to this approach was the US Navy which strove for extra firepower with long guns and carronades of 42pdr calibre combined with 32pdrs. Most navies found the 30–32pdr the best compromise between weight of fire and ease of handling and a spectrum of sizes evolved, allowing 32pdrs to be carried even as main deck armament on the last sailing frigates and sloops. Some of these short guns were referred to as 'gunnades' (a cross between a long gun and carronade) but the term had different connotations in various navies.

Shell guns

The final alteration to the established armament of wooden fighting ships was brought about by the perfection of shell guns in the 1820s. Explosive and projectiles had long been employed by mortars and howitzers and during the siege of Gibraltar (1779–83) the British fired mortar shells from long guns. Building on this experience Lieutenant Shrapnel of the Royal Artillery devised his famous 'spherical case', which exploded a parcel of musket balls above an enemy concentration.[22] It had only limited use at sea during the later years of the Napoleonic War because it was most effective at ranges beyond that at which naval battles were usually fought.

There were other examples of shell being fired at low trajectories, unlike in mortar fire, in both experiments and battle.[23] However, it was the systematic work of the French artilleryman Colonel Henri Paixhans that led to the development of a practicable shell gun. It was a large, chambered weapon of distinctively austere external form and capable of long range (over 4000yds was achieved during

The very plain original model of Paixhans' 22cm shell gun, seen here on a late double pivot slide carriage used as the weather deck bow and stern chase guns of steamers. (From Douglas's Naval Gunnery)

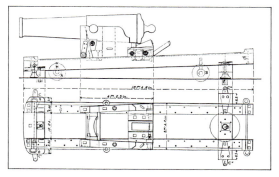

trials) but the spherical shell was not as accurate as equivalent solid shot. The first naval pattern adopted in 1827 was an 80pdr (in later practice shell guns were to be categorised by their bore diameter, in this case 22cm); this was in service by 1830 but there was no formal establishment until 1837. Even then, only four (ten from 1849) were carried by battleships and two by large frigates.

Britain was not slow to follow this lead and had an experimental 10in undergoing tests by 1824 and an 8in shortly afterwards. The 10in became a pivot gun for steamers – they were armed with a small number of large guns – whereas by 1838–9 a satisfactory 8in (68pdr) shell gun was assigned to the ends of battleship gundecks; they could also fire solid shot so were regarded as more suitable for the close action favoured by the Royal Navy and by the late 1840s were making up the complete lower deck batteries of new ships.

After some pioneering efforts in the 1812 period the Americans lost interest in shellfire and it was not until the visit of a French warship in 1838 that the US Navy restarted experimental work. An 8in gun was contrived from bored-up 42pdrs while a purpose-designed Paixhans type of the same calibre was ordered in 1841; a 10in gun followed a year later. The 8in guns were nominal 64pdrs but were not strong enough to fire solid shot of that weight; later guns had the heavier breech metal necessary for shot.[24]

Congreve rockets

All navies used firework-type rockets for signalling but the British made the most concerted attempt to use rockets for naval warfare. At the beginning of the nineteenth century war rockets were still used by local warlords in India; these were brought to the attention of the ingenious William Congreve, who was able to improve such rockets to the point where they became a serious bombardment weapon, even if they were never accurate enough for ship-to-ship engagements.

Comprising a thin metallic case and a long stabilising stick, Congreve rockets came in

various weights – there was a large 42pdr model with a range of 3500yds, but the standard size was a 32pdr of 2000–3000yds depending on payload. Warheads could be explosive shells, carcasses (incendiary devices) or shrapnel; for projecting the first two, rockets compared well with mortars and carrying the last could achieve double the range of field artillery, although their accuracy was always suspect.

For naval employment the great advantage of rockets was the total absence of recoil effect and so even small boats could fire an explosive shell that had previously required a heavily built bomb vessel. The carcass-carrying version went into action first in the naval attack on Boulogne in 1806 but really distinguished itself at Copenhagen the following year. From then until the end of the Napoleonic War rockets were used by the British in virtually all set-piece coastal assaults as well as by special Rocket Troops on land. Their effect on craft (mainly fireships and gunboats) earmarked to carry them was negligible so no purpose-designed rocket vessel was ever needed; for this reason, they may have contributed to the declining popularity of the bomb vessel, in eclipse since the introduction of horizontal shellfire.[25]

Small arms for boarding tactics

Besides the ship's armament, the crew was trained to some degree in the use of shoulder arms (muskets, in later days usually used by the ship's force of marines), pistols, hand grenades and edged weapons – cutlasses and swords, poleaxes, pikes and tomahawks. The last were the particular preserve of boarding tactics, the long-staffed weapons like pikes being used to repel would-be boarders, while the others were

Cutlass drill as depicted in a contemporary manuscript. The use of small arms continued to be important even after steam replaced sail and boarding became less likely because naval brigades were often employed ashore in numerous colonial campaigns. (NMM)

22. O F G Hogg, *Artillery: Its Origin, Heyday and Decline* (London 1970), p179.

23. S Tucker, *op cit*, p176, lists a number of recorded occasions. The early American efforts of Bomford and his 'Columbiad' of 1811 are also chronicled in this book (pp182–3).

24. S Tucker, *op cit*, pp186–190.

25. W Burney, *Falconer's New Universal Dictionary of the Marine* (London 1815), pp408–12.

all useful in the desperate mêlée that often developed once a boarding party had a footing on the enemy deck; axes might be needed to hack a passage through anti-boarding netting and could also be used to disable a ship by cutting important rigging or to clear away fallen top hamper. All warships carried substantial numbers of small arms and cutlass drill was practised by many navies well into the steam era.

Gun mountings

Just as the muzzle-loading smooth bore was the dominant naval weapon for the whole period under review, so the standard mounting was a relatively simple wooden wheeled carriage that proved surprisingly adaptable to even the technological innovations of the nineteenth century.

The truck carriage

In 1650 the standard truck carriage was already a century old, although it had undergone minor development. Basically it consisted of a wooden platform called the bed, two side brackets (their tops stepped down in profile towards the rear of the gun) and four small

A Danish gun carriage of about 1675. The design and proportions are typical of the earlier flat-bed form of truck carriage. (F Howard)

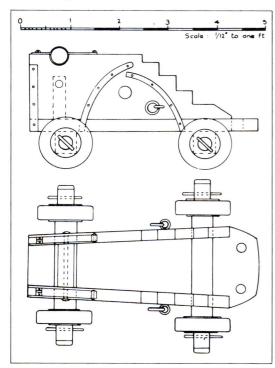

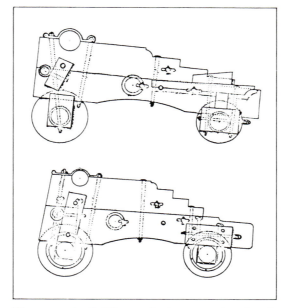

There were detail differences in the construction of truck carriages from country to country: this draught compares British practice (top) with Danish and is dated 1766. (Rigsarkivet, Copenhagen)

wheels known as trucks from which the carriage took its name; the gun was balanced by its trunnions in recesses on top of the brackets, retained by capsquares, and elevation was provided by one or more wedges called coins or quoins jammed under the breech end of the gun. The proportions varied from navy to navy (and according to period), as did details – the front trucks were sometimes larger than the rear ones, for example – but in essence this design of carriage was scaled up and down to suit the largest 42pdr or a tiny 3pdr. The British evolved a lighter version about 1730 in which the solid bed was replaced by a short 'stool bed',[26] but this was not adopted by other navies until later (about 1760 for the French navy).

The advantages of the truck carriage were simplicity, ease of maintenance (it could be repaired on board with relatively unskilled labour and simple resources), economy and efficiency in action; this last encompassed ease of movement (running in or out as well as from port to port if necessary), speed of elevation with quoins, and a simple recoil system using a breeching rope to stop the backward motion on its trucks. Its main disadvantage was the difficulty of traversing the mounting (it required handspikes and lots of muscle), but this did not become a problem as the ship itself was

26. B Lavery, *Arming and Fitting*, p127.
27. J Boudriot, 'L'Artillerie de Mer', *Neptunia* 98 (1970).

manoeuvred to face the enemy. Later developments only affected the fittings and ironwork and were largely in response to advances in techniques of handling the guns.

The final version of the truck carriage replaced the rear wheels with a block of wood sometimes called a 'dumb truck'. It was primarily used for shell guns in gundeck batteries, which rather like chase guns were intended for particular rather than broadside fire and so had more need to be pointed accurately. The dumb truck helped to suppress the fierce recoil, but paradoxically the mounting was also easier to traverse thanks to the employment of handspikes with small rollers that could be thrust under the dumb truck to act like a castor. This mounting was introduced into the French navy in 1838 and adopted by the US Navy as the Marsilly carriage. Similar 'rear-chock' carriages were also used by the Royal Navy for shell guns and the final generation of big smooth bores.

Mortar beds

Bomb vessels required entirely different mountings for their mortars, which were fired at a high trajectory so that the mounting – and the ship underneath – had to absorb a large and repeated recoil. Early French mortars were cast with an integral bed but the 'trabucco' type had trunnions which were retained by capsquares; the first French bomb vessels used layers of large hemp cables under the mortars to cushion the impact of firing,[27] but ultimately all bombs needed a massive structure of supporting timbers to absorb the shock.

Because they could pivot, British mountings were more elaborate than the fixed type, with a bed of oak baulks revolving on a wooden disc set into a recess. The turntable was moved using screw jacks in early vessels but later ones seem to have depended on handspikes (a 13in mortar alone weighed over 4 tons) so it must

A nineteenth-century sea service mortar and bed. (David Wray)

A detailed plan of the mounting of a quarterdeck 32pdr carronade on the British frigate Latona, *dated 1802. Notable features compared with earlier practice are: the wheels at the end of the slide for easy traversing; the pivot on the gunport sill, allowing the gun to be run out well clear of the ship's side; a lug replacing the trunnions, thus simplifying the bed; screw elevating gear; and a gunlock for firing. (Rigsarkivet, Copenhagen)*

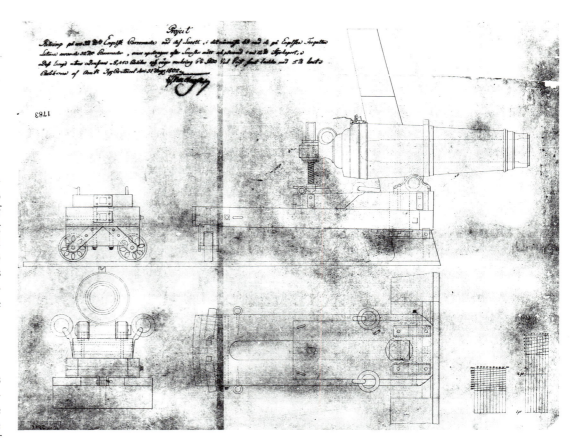

have been a laborious operation. The 'trabucco' type mortar lay flat when not in use so had to be propped up for firing with a chock of wood or iron like a quoin; when an elevating mounting was developed the chock was fitted with a ratchet so it could be moved in or out to add or decrease elevation. With their emphasis on worldwide operations, the British soon developed hatch covers that could protect the mortar when the bomb vessel was in transit.[28]

Pivot and slide mountings

The truck carriage was satisfactory as long as no real traversing was necessary and the somewhat erratic recoil could be contained. There were a few specialised naval applications where this was not the case and a different type of mounting ensued. The obvious example was the small vessel with only one large gun which for reasons of space and stability could not be broadside mounted. Most of the smaller sailing gunboats had a gun on the centreline firing over the bow or stern, and this tended to be fitted on a slide mounting (rather like a conventional carriage with the trucks removed whose recoil was suppressed by the friction of sliding along a wooden bed fitted with some form of flange that prevented the slewing that sometimes afflicted truck carriages).

This type of mounting – which could trace its ancestry back to the forward-firing guns of seventeenth century galleys – allowed no traverse at all so was only practical for manoeuvrable small craft, where the helm could do the pointing. However, it was not long before the whole slide was made to pivot, either from one end, which would give the gun a wide arc of fire, or from the centre where in theory it might have 360 degrees of traverse. The precise origin of the pivot mounting is unclear but Frederik af Chapman certainly experimented with versions for the Swedish Inshore Fleet in the 1770s and in 1778 designed the new 60-gun ship of the line *Wasa* with a lower deck battery of pivoting slide mountings.[29] Although the slide mounting reduced the size of crews needed, it had no real advantage to battleships: without a system of centralised fire

control accurate directed fire was impossible from broadside batteries, while the mounting was less able to withstand the rigours of rapid firing in fleet engagements.

The pivot came into its own as a mounting for guns intended to be fired independently and with a relatively high degree of accuracy. In the Anglo-American War of 1812, for example, many small American privateers carried one large gun on a centreline pivot that could be fired on any bearing not masked by rigging. This allowed the privateer to overawe any potential mercantile victim with a long range shot across the bows, thus shortening the chase; when the hunter became the hunted the gun would give the privateer the chance of disabling a pursuing warship from a distance. This philosophy was developed in the early nineteenth century with the introduction of shell guns; small numbers of large calibre guns were employed rather like chase guns on the weather decks of battleships for long range precision fire and a pivot was the obvious mounting for these. (Although it is outside the scope of this volume, pivot-mounted shell guns were also used on early paddle warships, to compensate for the relative paucity of broadside weapons and to allow them to inflict damage outside the range of retaliation.)

The best known employment of pivoting slide mountings was for the carronade. Although both pivot and slide predate Carron's novel weapon – indeed, the early small carronades had trunnions and truck carriages – slides and carronades were closely associated. The exact rationale for the mounting is not clear, although the Carron Company originally supplied one with each gun, so presumably gave it conscious thought.[30] It may have been seen as a successor to previous short range weapons like swivels which had always allowed some pointing; being light, the carronade also suffered from a fierce recoil so the slide may have helped contain this; furthermore, there was originally an emphasis on economy of manpower and speed of fire, both of which were assisted by the pivoting slide.

The mounting developed rapidly in detail in the first twenty-five years of its service and varied according to application, but the essentials remained unchanged. It had two main features: a bed to which the gun was secured, and a slide or training bed on which it recoiled. The slide was pivoted at the outboard end, on the 'outside principle' if the pivot pin was outside the gunport (used on early short carronades to re-

---

28. David Wray, 'Bomb Vessels', *Model Shipwright* 27 (1979), pp25–6.

29. D G Harris, *F H Chapman: The First Naval Architect and his Work*, p69.

30. B Lavery, *Arming and Fitting*, p130.

duce the chance of muzzle blast damage to the shrouds), or on the 'inside principle' if within the port. Early mountings did not allow much traverse and a chock was fitted to support the inboard end of the bed; later models had a pair of rollers. The bed had a long slot cut down its centre; a bolt from the bed secured the two parts together, with the slot acting as a guide when the gun recoiled. Once the carronade had developed a mounting lug, the bed became a relatively simple baulk of timber, but for a carronade with trunnions it looked more like a normal carriage without trucks. Early models used conventional quoins but from about 1790 the British introduced elevating screws, which passed through the breech end of the gun to bear on the bed.

Radical variations from this form were mostly experimental or designed for highly specialist employment: Bentham's non-recoil mountings of the 1790s are an example of the former; moveable chase carronades on trucks an instance of the latter. Most navies adopted similar mountings to the pivoting slides of the British but from about 1811 France introduced a limited-recoil mounting with a short slide resting on chocks at its front and rear; most of the restraint was provided by a powerful breeching rope which passed through the side of the ship to form a complete loop.[31]

Ammunition and equipment

Solid shot

For the whole of the period covered by this book the most important projectile was the simple cannon ball or round shot (so pervasive was its influence that ammunition is still counted in 'rounds'). It was cast in solid iron using clay moulds and had replaced the lighter but more expensive stone shot in the sixteenth century. It was the densest material easily available and thus had the greatest range and penetrating power of contemporary projectiles. However, its effect on thickly timbered ships was limited (very few warships were actually sunk in combat in the age of sail) and this had two implications for the development of wooden fighting ships: first, they needed to carry large numbers of guns to batter the enemy into submission; and secondly, they required a lot of shot to achieve it. As a result, the allocation of shot per gun rose steadily in all navies. In an English warship of the

1650s it was about thirty-five, about fifty-five in the early eighteenth century, and by the 1760s the Foreign Service allowance was eighty for ships of the line and a hundred for frigates; French ships of the line carried sixty by the 1780s;[32] figures for American frigates and smaller vessels were generally about seventy-five per gun in peacetime and a hundred in wartime.[33]

This steadily increasing demand for shot led to improved methods of casting, while the gradual decrease in the windage of guns inspired greater manufacturing accuracy. Reduced tolerances also meant that efforts to keep shot free from rust and damage had to be stepped up and so cannon balls tended to be painted or lacquered.

There was a brief vogue for hollow shot in the 1830s and 1840s. Designed to maximise the splintering effect at short range of a lighter round striking with reduced momentum, they were regarded as particularly suitable for the weaker bored-up versions of large calibre guns since they could be fired with reduced charges. Hollow shot was relatively inaccurate at longer ranges and fell from favour as shellfire became more widely adopted.[34]

Dismantling shot

Besides solid shot, warships carried specialist ammunition for use against rigging. The oldest, and always the most common pattern, was double-headed shot, although the exact form of this varied – it could be a bar connecting either a simple pair of shot, cylinders of iron, or hemispheres; the single bar could be replaced with interlocking pairs to make expanding shot. Somewhat similar was chain shot in which a chain replaced the bars for even greater spread of damage (said to have been invented by the Dutch about 1665),[35] and star shot which was a more elaborate version with four or five bars folded around a ring that flew out to form a whirling star when fired. The very simplest form was bar shot, a single length of iron wrapped in wood strips to bulk it out to the bore diameter of the gun. Langrel (langridge or langrage) might also be used; this consisted of jagged pieces of scrap iron packaged into a cylinder, and was equally effective against personnel. It was frowned upon by traditional navies but much used by privateers and the less hidebound, like the Americans.

The proportions of dismantling shot varied from navy to navy depending on tactical philosophy. Since it was only effective at close range it could not be used to slow a fleeing enemy and in practice was more useful to facilitate escape from superior force. In the Royal Navy the allowance was three rounds per gun in the latter half of the eighteenth century;[36] the equivalent figure for the French was ten;[37] while a US warship might give over 25 per cent of its ammunition to dismantling shot.[38]

Anti-personnel shot

These worked on the shotgun principle of large numbers of small projectiles and were essentially of two kinds. The larger was called grape shot, in which a number of small round shot were trussed together in a canvas bag roughly equal to the calibre of the gun, the result resembling a bunch of grapes; this burst on firing, forming a deadly cone of shot. This pattern was replaced in the late eighteenth century by tiered shot, which consisted of three layers each of three shot separated by perforated iron plates or 'stools' and kept together by a central spindle, all encased in canvas. The principle was understood from the earliest days of gunpowder artillery but it does not seem to

Shot and gun equipment to the same scale:

1. *Round shot*
2. *Chain shot*
3. *Bar shot*
4. *Expanding shot*
5. *Tompion and lanyard*
6. *Sponge*
7. *Rammer*
8. *Worm*
9. *Flexible rammer and sponge combined.*

(Peter Goodwin)

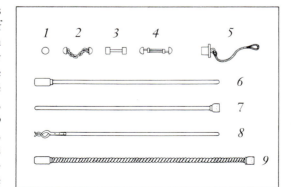

31. J Boudriot, 'L'Artillerie de Mer', *Neptunia* 94–5 (1969).

32. J Boudriot, *The Seventy-Four Gun Ship*, Vol 2, p172.

33. S Tucker, *op cit*, p97.

34. Sir Howard Douglas, *A Treatise on Naval Gunnery* (1855 edition), p70.

35. O F G Hogg, *op cit*, p158.

36. Lists in PRO Adm 95/66–7 suggest that this was the standard figure. Ships of the line carried them for all guns but frigates were allocated double-headed shot only for their main batteries.

37. J Boudriot, *The Seventy-Four Gun Ship*, Vol 2, p172.

38. S Tucker, *op cit*, p95.

have been employed at sea until the beginning of the eighteenth century.[39]

Individual grape shot were quite large (3lbs for a British 32pdr tiered round) but case or canister shot was smaller, packing a thin iron or tin can which shattered on firing producing a denser pattern at short range than grape. Used at sea from at least the early seventeenth century, it was originally known as bace, burr or burrel. Like dismantling shot, grape and canister was carried in relatively higher proportions by French (ten rounds per gun) and American (twenty-five) ships than British (three to seven). Grape and canister also made up a high proportion of ammunition for swivel guns and, later, carronades.

Explosive and incendiary devices

The first explosive projectiles regularly taken to sea were the shells fired by the mortars of bomb vessels. These were hollow iron cylinders cast in one piece and sometimes having a neck around the fuse hole and carrying lugs. Filled with gunpowder, they were detonated by a time fuse, which was originally a burning slow match inserted in the bung of the fuse hole, but by the eighteenth century hollow tubes containing a portfire composition were being used. The fuse was obviously the key to accurate detonation and many types of paper, wood and iron tubes were developed. By the 1760s the British had settled on a beech or willow fuse, calibrated to represent a set proportion of burning time (the fuse was sawn off at the required time mark, based on calculated range). In early practice the fuse was lit before the mortar was fired but this was fraught with danger and eventually a safer system was adopted whereby the muzzle flash of the mortar ignited the shell's fuse.

Even if a mortar could achieve accurate range and bearing, it was always difficult to get

A general view of a shell (note lifting lugs and fuse hole) and a carcass, with an enlargement of a typical beechwood fuse, which was filled with a gunpowder-based even-burning composition; the horizontal lines mark timing divisions, the fuse being sawn off at the chosen point to equate with the time of flight to the calculated range. (Peter Goodwin)

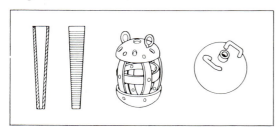

a shell to explode at the right moment. One answer against certain targets was the incendiary or carcass shell which did not explode at all but on detonation burned intensely for anything up to ten minutes. Its invention is attributed to a German gunner in 1672 and was originally an iron skeleton bound in canvas – hence its name. The composition was devised to be difficult to extinguish, and vents in the shell casing ensured that the flaming mixture had the widest possible effect.

Mortar shells were relatively fragile so could not be fired with substantial powder charges. To obtain range with a small charge, a high trajectory was necessary which added a dimension to the problem of accuracy (at short range bearing was the most significant factor, but as distance increased elevation became more important). In a mortar, with fixed elevation, range was determined by varying the powder charge, an unreliable technique given the inconsistencies in the performance of contemporary gunpowder. As such mortar fire was virtually useless for ship-to-ship engagements.

In the circumstances, therefore, it was inevitable that attempts would be made to harness the destructive properties of explosive shells to the short range flat-trajectory firing that dominated naval battles of this period. Eighteenth-century experiments along these lines are well documented,[40] but much of the effort seems to have been anti-personnel rather than anti-ship in purpose ('spherical case' or shrapnel shells were mainly used against massed troops ashore). Paixhan's work in France in the 1820s made shellfire practical from long guns, although he designed special chambered ordnance to fire them. The shells themselves were developed from those fired by mortars and were basically cylindrical in shape but seated on a recessed wooden base or 'sabot' to protect the thin-skinned shell from the shock of firing and to ensure that it sat tightly against the powder cartridge; a rope grommet or hollow wad around its fuse end kept the shell correctly orientated in the bore of the gun.

The earliest fuses were of the timed burning variety with the slight improvement of being iron with a screw safety cap (the French persevered with wood), but otherwise suffered all the uncertainties familiar from mortar fire. In ideal conditions the shell exploded after it had lodged deep in the target ship's timbers for maximum damage, but this was very difficult to achieve and in practice many shells broke up without exploding or had their fuses extinguished by grazing the water. The British made some progress with percussion mech-

anisms but these tended to explode the shell before it could penetrate the hull and a satisfactory fuse was not perfected during the period covered by this book.

As well as its dubious effectiveness, the progress of shellfire was held back by its lack of accurate range (the last generation of solid shot guns had a greater 'first graze' range). There was little test of shells in battle to back up its supporters, whereas peacetime practice made clear the danger of shells to the ships carrying them and despite strenuous efforts to prevent misadventures – including keeping shells in individual boxes and not uncovering the fuses until they were about to be loaded – there were a number of serious accidents.[41]

Red-hot shot had been tried at sea from time to time but again the dangers seemed to outweigh any advantage. A furnace was required and a gun had to be run out and fired very quickly after the shot was loaded; the shot needed to lodge in the target ship's timbers to stand a chance of setting the ship alight and even in these circumstances the fire was often quickly extinguished. Conventional wisdom confined the use of hot shot to coast defence fortifications.

Propellant

Gunpowder, a mixture of saltpetre, sulphur and charcoal was the sole propellant in use during this period. By 1650 the earliest forms of loosely mixed and hence variable, serpentine, powder had been replaced by the more powerful and consistent corned powder in a range of grain sizes. Towards the end of the eighteenth century a far more powerful cylinder[42] powder was introduced, and although it required stronger guns to make the best use of it, range and striking power was increased.

Powder charges were generally proportional to shot weight, windage and length of gun, a shorter gun requiring a smaller charge; reduced versions of standard charges were generally used when the gun heated up and for close range. As powder became more powerful, the size of all charges was reduced. Powder was loaded in prepared cartridges made from paper or canvas in the seventeenth century and flannel from about 1755 (parchment was tried for a short while in the 1720s). Although heavier and

39. B Lavery, *Arming and Fitting*, p137.

40. S Tucker, *op cit*, pp176–7, 182–3.

41. Sir H Douglas, *op cit*, p268–70.

42. So called because the charcoal was charred in containers called cylinders rather than in a pit; this increased its consistency and hence its effectiveness.

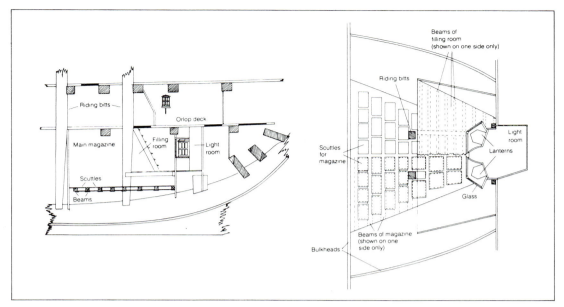

The magazine arrangements of the 70-gun Dorsetshire *of 1757 (longitudinal section and plan view). The pallating system was well developed by this time.* (Brian Lavery)

more expensive than paper, flannel shared its advantage of being entirely consumed by the explosion (leaving no dangerous burning embers to set off the next cartridge prematurely) but was more water resistant than paper.

Powder was obviously the most dangerous of all the ship's stores and from the earliest employment of guns at sea special precautions had to be taken to keep it cool, dry and away from naked flames or even sparks. A separate magazine in the hold or on the orlop deck for the bulk storage in barrels was an early development, followed by a filling room to make up and store the ready-use cartridges. They were usually lined with fire-resistant material (a lime and hair mixture was one primitive formula, while the magazine was separated from the rest of the hold by an earth-filled cofferdam in French practice);[43] and from the first decade of the eighteenth century a separate sealed light room illuminated both magazine and filling room. To keep the powder dry and to contain any stray powder, a false floor, or pallating, was introduced and even a layer of charcoal as a moisture absorbent was tried.[44]

Ships of the line soon acquired a second powder room (and the largest a third) to deal with the increased rate of fire of eighteenth-century artillery. From the 1830s further demands on internal volume were made by the

necessity for shell rooms; because shells were stowed in individual boxes they required twice the space of round shot and for safety in battle that space had to be below the waterline, compounding the difficulty. Powder itself came to be stored in metal cases and the magazines were fitted with flooding arrangements in case of fire.

Round shot, by contrast, was simple to store, needing only lockers, although for stability reasons these tended to be on the centreline and low down. Ready-use shot rounds were carried on deck in racks called garlands, though their shape and position varied from navy to navy. The French also kept supplies of grape and bar shot on hooks driven into the ship's side around each gun.

Gunners' stores

Besides its powder and ammunition a gun required various items of stores and equipment for its proper service. The charge and shot were driven home by a rammer (most commonly a wooden staff about a foot longer than the bore of the gun and marked to indicate the position at which the various weights of charges were properly seated); this was followed by the insertion of a wad, usually of oakum, to hold the shot tight up to the charge against the rolling of the ship. A priming wire or iron cleared the vent and pricked open the cartridge, priming powder was added from a horn and the gun was ready to fire; in late eighteenth-century practice priming tubes and gunlocks were used for firing, but earlier a match held in a 'linstock' was applied to the vent.

After firing, the gun was wormed to remove any burning residue and sponged; originally

this required two implements but they were combined so the woolly sponge head incorporated a bronze worm extension. A further improvement was a flexible rammer/sponge, with the staves replaced with stiff rope and a different head on each end (introduced in the 1660s). A separate worm or wad hook was still provided to remove cartridges if firing had ceased, as was a long ladle (since loose powder was no longer heaped into the gun it was presumably used to remove powder from torn cartridges). The loading implements were usually stowed against a deck beam adjacent to their gun.

Other equipment included handspikes to point the gun, match tubs, cartridge passing boxes, battle lanterns, and fire buckets. When not in action the muzzle of each gun was stopped with a wooden tompion, sometimes tallowed, to keep out salt spray and rainwater.

Shipboard gunnery

Crew numbers and gun handling

Although there is some evidence of the survival of loading guns from outside the port into the 1650s,[45] the usual method thereafter was to load from within-board. This meant running out the loaded gun, perhaps 'uphill' if the ship was heeling, for which tackles at either side of the gun carriage were provided. Even with the mechanical advantage of tackles, this made gun handling with the truck carriage a labour-intensive activity.[46] The numbers involved remained remarkably consistent for most of the period under review: the Royal Navy's 1674 gunnery establishment fixed the crew of a 32pdr at five or six (effectively ten or twelve since the crew of the opposite gun on the disengaged side would be combined when only one broadside was being fought); in 1817 the first formal instructions for gunnery stipulated twelve men for a 32pdr, ten of whom were employed heaving on the gun tackles during run-out. Numbers were virtually identical in other major navies.

On firing, the recoil returned the gun inboard, although its run was limited by a stout breeching rope which ran from ringbolts in the

43. J Boudriot, *The Seventy-Four Gun Ship*, Vol 2, p57.

44. B Lavery, *Arming and Fitting*, Ch 27 outlines British developments in some detail.

45. P Padfield, *Guns at Sea*, pp62–3.

46. The carronade and pivot mountings needed smaller crews. Most of the generalisations in this section relate to gunnery with the truck carriage, exceptions for other mountings being noted where applicable.

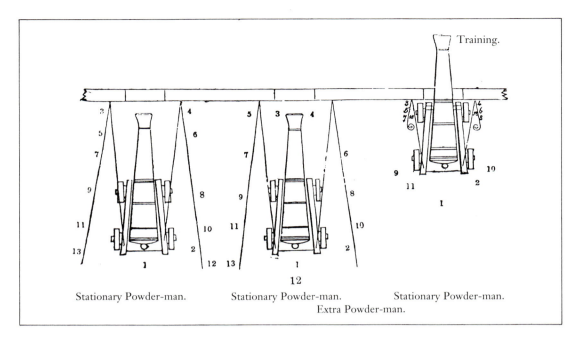

Training.

Stationary Powder-man.   Stationary Powder-man.   Stationary Powder-man.
                          Extra Powder-man.

The positions of a 14-man crew of a 32pdr as exercised by HMS Excellent *the British gunnery training ship, in the 1840s: before loading (left); loading (centre); and training (right). When fighting both sides, with the numbers halved, there was a reorganisation of duties. Nine commands were recognised: Prime; Point; Elevate; Ready; Fire; Stop the vent; Sponge; Load; Run out. (From Douglas's* Naval Gunnery*)*

ship's sides via eyebolts in the carriage sides to be secured at the gun's cascabel (in French practice the breeching went through the carriage brackets and did not attach to the gun itself). To keep the gun from running itself out during loading, a train tackle was fitted between the inner end of the carriage and the deck near the centreline of the ship.[47]

After firing, the gun had to be wormed and sponged to clear the bore of any smouldering remains of the previous round; a made-up cartridge was rammed home (for reasons of safety they were never stored near the guns but brought up from the powder room as needed inside cases or cartouches by a 'powder monkey'); the shot followed, sometimes separated by a wad, but it was important to seat the shot or wad tight up against the cartridge since a slack fit might cause the gun to explode; a final wad rammed down held the shot in place.

The gun was then primed by pricking the cartridge through the vent and laying a trail of fine powder to it. (In earliest practice it was ignited with a slow match and a slight delay was necessary to prevent the match being extinguished by the flash of the gun going off.) Before firing the gun was aimed by the gun captain; elevation was a relatively easy matter of moving the quoin in or out, but any degree of traversing needed much effort with handspikes and crowbars to lever the carriage around. There were no sights and aiming was very approximate; the motion of the ship had a significant effect on where the gun was pointing when it went off, so battles had to be fought at close range to have any chance of frequent hits.

Constant firing made the gun hot, which would heat up the powder charge making it more efficient, so reduced charges were employed at this stage; recoil also increased, although relatively less with heavier guns, which was another reason to reduce the charge. At close range guns were often double-shotted or charged with ball and grape or case, which also required reduced charges.

With a well drilled crew the guns could be fired in a number of modes. A full broadside, or simultaneous discharge, was potentially very damaging to the enemy, but imposed great strain on the timbers of the firing ship. Guns could be fired in groups, by quarters (divisional batteries) or by deck, or might be fired in succession to give a ripple effect – if the ship was manoeuvring the order 'fire as you bear' would allow each gun captain to fire when the target came into sight. Finally, there was independent firing as each gun was ready, and in battle firing often degenerated into this mode as damage, smoke and noise broke down command and control.

Gunnery improvements 1650–1840

The rate at which shipboard great guns could be fired increased roughly sixfold in the period covered by this book. This was partly the result of better training, and could only have happened with the improved metallurgy of the guns themselves, but it was also facilitated by a number of specific developments which speeded up the handling of the guns. Most related to the priming and ignition of the gun, which incidentally also improved accuracy on a rolling deck by shortening the delay between decision to fire and actual detonation.

The first was the late seventeenth-century introduction of quickmatch or portfire, an inflammable composition strong enough to be applied directly to the touch hole, removing the need for a train of powder. A further step forward was the priming tube which replaced priming powder altogether; loose powder was slow to apply, tended to enlarge the touch hole and was liable to potentially dangerous spillage. The first tubes, of tin, were introduced into the Royal Navy in 1755, but at the Battle of Quiberon Bay in 1759 Admiral Hawke complained of the tubes flying out as the guns fired, endangering the crews. They fell out of use in the peacetime navy, but Sir Charles Douglas, a noted gunnery innovator, introduced goose quill tubes in the late 1780s and these gradually found official favour. Filled with a paste-like gunpowder composition, tubes could be ignited by quickmatch, but Douglas fired his with the spark of a flintlock. These had also been tried in the 1750s and abandoned but Douglas was able to get them officially adopted by the Royal Navy in 1790 and other navies followed shortly after.

The flintlock was similar to the device used on muskets, although the trigger was a lanyard. This gave a more nearly instantaneous ignition and offered the possibility of superior direction of broadside or firing by quarters. The lock itself was improved in the nineteenth century but the biggest step forward was the introduction of the percussion cap as a primer; based on fulminates of mercury, it could be ignited by a sharp blow. Incorporated into a primer detonated by the hammer of a gunlock, this was the final method of firing large guns in the era of sailing warships.

Efforts were also made to improve the accuracy and effectiveness of naval gunfire by introducing sights and methods of concentrating fire. Sir Charles Douglas was again a leading proponent (and a practical innovator) but most of his ideas of the 1780s were not taken up until the 1820s and later, when longer ranged guns and shellfire made such matters important.

47. The exact date of its introduction is uncertain; the *Wasa* of 1628 has no fittings on carriages or ship, but it was used on British ships in the early eighteenth century.

Elaborate methods were pursued to prevent guns breaking loose in heavy weather, since such heavy objects were then highly difficult and dangerous to re-secure. This is the Danish navy's method of dealing with its heaviest weapon, the 36pdr. (Rigsarkivet, Copenhagen)

Tactics and training

Apart from the technological shortcomings of early guns and the inherent difficulties of firing from a moving platform, naval gunnery was hampered by a generally unscientific attitude to training. France instituted a special corps of naval gunners in 1666 (abolished during the Revolution which may explain the dismal performance of French ships in the ensuing war), but other navies relied on training ordinary seamen while at sea.

Although the maximum theoretical range of a long gun might be 2500yds or more, its point blank range[48] was about 10 per cent of that and so fighting distances tended to be smaller still. From at least the 1650s the English made a virtue of necessity by concentrating on close action and training crews to serve and fire their pieces with speed rather than directed accuracy. A seventeenth-century writer calculated that a demi-cannon (32pdr) could be fired

every six minutes and a falcon (3pdr) every four, allowing time for the bronze gun to cool;[49] by 1805 Collingwood's *Dreadnought* could achieve three co-ordinated broadsides in three and a half minutes, and a round a minute in independent firing was not uncommon in the British fleet.

At fighting ranges the penetrating power of long guns was impressive: an experiment of 1813 showed that a 24pdr ball could penetrate 2ft 6in of ship's timbers. To utilise this power the British fired at the hull, usually on the 'down roll' (as the ship began to heel towards the target). This was noticed as early as the First Dutch War[50] but the effect was enhanced by the English preference for the 'weather gage' (see Chapter 13) which tended to heel the firing ship towards the target. The Dutch were among the few navies to meet the English on their own terms, relishing close action despite often being outgunned in their early encounters.[51] With a more theoretical approach to sea warfare, France tended to emphasise the advantages of long range fire for disabling an

opponent (hence the greater allocation of dismantling shot issued to ships of the line) but in practice it was not very effective against an enemy determined to close, though it often aided the escape of inferior squadrons. The American position was different in that the US Navy never had a real battlefleet so tended to concentrate on the tactics of single ship engagements; very well trained crews allowed fast and accurate fire, following the British preference for hulling fire discharged on the down roll.[52]

The final generation of sailing warships saw no action that tested the latest gunnery developments, but if they had lived up to expectations fighting range would have been greater; the weight of metal would have been considerably heavier; and although firing might have been slightly slower,[53] it would have been more deliberate and, with better methods of concentrating fire, more accurate and even more devastating.

Robert Gardiner

48. Defined slightly differently in various navies but essentially the distance a shot fired at zero elevation will reach before hitting the water. See S Tucker, *op cit*, p37.

49. Sir James Turner, quoted by P Padfield, *op cit*, p64.

50. P Padfield, *ibid*, pp81–2.

51. The attitude persisted: the Battle of Camperdown (1797), relatively speaking, was the bloodiest fleet engagement of the wars of 1793–1815.

52. S Tucker, *op cit*, p47.

53. *Excellent*, the British gunnery training ship, achieved 43 seconds per round for a 32pdr and 46 seconds for an 8in shell gun but it is unlikely that this rate was possible in action. (S Tucker, *op cit*, p207).

Naval Guns: Typical Ranges 1650–1840

Gun	Date	Nationality	Point blank Yards	Maximum Yards	@ Elevation Degrees	Remarks
Cannon of seven	c1650	English	185			Range quoted in 'paces', but assumed to equate roughly with yards
Demi cannon	c1650	English	162			As above
Culverin	c1650	English	460	2650	10	From W Eldred's manual of 1646
Demi culverin	c1650	English	400	2400	10	As above
Saker	c1650	English	360	2170	10	As above
Minion	c1650	English	125			From T Venn's manual of 1672

Gun	Date	Nationality	Point blank Yards	Maximum Yards	@ Elevation Degrees	Remarks
13in mortar	c1750	British	690	4200	45	Range controlled by varying the powder charge from 2lbs to 20lbs
10in mortar	c1750	British	680	4000	45	Charge varied from 1lb to 9lbs 8ozs
36pdr long gun	1767	French	711 (650m)	3609 (33300m)	16	J Boudriot, *The Seventy-Four Gun Ship*
8pdr long gun	1767	French	547 (500m)	2743 (2500m)	16	As above
68pdr carronade	c1800	British	450	1280	5	From R Simmons manual of 1812

32pdr long gun
  Double-shotted
  Grape
  Case
  Double-headed
	c1800	British	350
			100
			90
			40
				2900
				500
				1450
				1150
				800
					10
					2
					2
					0.5
					2
						From H Douglas, 1820 edition
						
						Collated from Simmons and Douglas, 1855

32pdr carronade	c1800	British	330	1087	5	R Simmons, 1812
12pdr carronade	c1800	British	230	870	5	R Simmons, 1812
9pdr long gun	c1800	British	300	1800	6	H Douglas, 1820
24pdr congreve	c1812	British	c575*			H Douglas, 1855
30pdr No 1 long gun	1820	French	230	2648	9	H Douglas, 1855
Canon obusier de 80	1827	French	460	2830	13	H Douglas, 1855; for comparison with US gun, @ 5 degrees range was 1640yds
8in Shell gun	1839	British	330	2910	13	H Douglas, 1855; range @ 5 degrees was 1700yds
8in Shell gun	1841	American	332	1769	5	Quoted by S Tucker from official US sources

Notes:
The 'point blank' quoted by Boudriot equates with 1 degree of elevation in other navies; the equivalent ranges for British 32pdrs and 9pdrs would be 750yds and 863yds. The 16-degree elevation is not practical at sea but indicates a theoretical maximum.
* In 1813 trials the gun reached between 505yds and 640yds point plank compared with 370yds for a standard 50cwt gun; up to about 5 degrees range was roughly equal but beyond that the standard gun had a distinct advantage, although Douglas does not quantify this.

Naval Guns: Typical Characteristics 1650–1840

Gun	Date	Nationality	Calibre Inches Millemetres	Length Feet–Inches Metres	Gun weight Cwt Kilos	Shot weight Pounds Kilos	Powder weight Pounds Kilos	Remarks
Cannon of seven	c1650	English	7 (177.8)	10–0 (3.05)	62.5 (3175)	47 (21.3)	34[1] (15.4)	Iron gun; ancestor of the 42pdr
Demi cannon	c1650	English	6 (152.4)	10–0 (3.05)	53.5 (2722)	27 (12.2)	25[1] (11.3)	Iron gun; ancestor of the 32pdr
Culverin	c1650	English	5 (127)	11–0 (3.35)	35.7 (1814)	15 (6.8)	18[1] (8.2)	Bronze gun; ancestor of 18pdr
Demi culverin	c1650	English	4.5 (114.3)	10–0 (3.05)	32.1 (1633)	9[1] (4.1)	9[1] (4.1)	Bronze gun; ancestor of 9pdr
Saker	c1650	English	3.5 (88.9)	9–0 (2.74)	22.3 (1134)	5.25 (2.4)	5[1] (2.3)	Bronze gun; replaced by 6pdr after 1703

Gun	Date	Nationality	Calibre Inches Millemetres	Length Feet–Inches Metres	Gun weight Cwt Kilos	Shot weight Pounds Kilos	Powder weight Pounds Kilos	Remarks
Minion	c1650	English	3 (76.2)	8–0 (2.44)	13.4 (680)	4 (1.8)	3.5[1] (1.6)	Bronze gun; replaced by 4pdr c1715
36pdr long gun	1689	French	(6.88) 174.8	(10–0) 3.04	(65) 3300	36 (38.8) (17.6)		Bronze gun; iron equivalent weighed 3700kg
Demi cannon	1691	English	6.5 (165.1)	10–0 (3.05)	55 (2794)	32 (14.5)	17.5 (7.9)	Iron gun for 1691 programme
Culverin	1691	English	5.25 (133.4)	9–0 (2.74)	39 (1981)	17.25 (7.8)	11.4 (5.2)	Shortest of three iron culverins for 1691 ships
13in mortar	c1750	British	13 (330.2)	5–3 (1.60)	81.4 (4135)	193 (87.5)	32 (14.5)	Standard large sea service mortar, brass
10in mortar	c1750	British	10 (254)	4–8 (1.42)	32.8 (1666)	86 (39.0)	12.5 (5.7)	Smaller sea service mortar, brass
36pdr long gun	1767	French	(6.88) 174.8	(9–7) 2.925	(71.7) 3643	36 (38.8) (17.6)	12 (13) (5.9)	Largest standard gun in French service
8pdr long gun	1767	French	3.9 (4.17) 106	(7–3) 2.221	(23.6) 1198	8 (8.6) (3.9)	3 (3.2) (1.5)	Smallest regularly used gun, although there were 6pdrs and 4pdrs for small craft
68pdr carronade	c1800	British	8.05 (204.5)	5–2 (1.57)	36 (1829)	68 (30.8)	6 (2.7)	Largest carronade in Royal Navy service
32pdr long gun	c1800	British	6.41 (162.8)	10–0 (3.05)	55.5 (2820)	32 (14.5)	10.7 (4.9)	Largest regularly used long gun
32pdr carronade	c1800	British	6.25 (158.8)	4–0.5 (1.23)	17.1 (869)	32 (14.5)	4 (1.8)	Most widely used carronade
12pdr carronade	c1800	British	4.5 (114.3)	2–2 (0.66)	5.8 (295)	12 (5.4)	1.5 (0.7)	Smallest carronade
3pdr long gun	c1800	British	2.913 (74)	4–6 (1.37)	7.25 (368)	3 (1.4)	1 (0.5)	Smallest long gun; cf 12pdr carronade
24pdr long gun	c1812	American	5.8 (147.3)	9–4 (2.84)	48 (2439)	24 (10.9)	8 (3.6)	Upper deck armament of big frigates
24pdr congreve	c1812	British	5.825 (148)	7–6 (2.29)	42 (2133)	24 (10.9)	8 (3.6)	Lightweight short gun, used to up-gun 18pdr frigates
30pdr No 1 long gun	1820	French	(6.48) 164.7	(9–3.4) 2.829	(58.9) 2992	30 (32.3) (14.7)	10 (4.5)	Replacement for 36pdr; three shorter models
Canon obusier de 80	1827	French	(8.79) 223.3[2]	(9–3.8) 2.84	(73.88) 3753	(58.5) 26.5	(10) 4.5	First French shell gun to see service
8in shell gun	1839	British	8.05 (204.5)	9–0 (2.74)	65 (3302)	56 (25.4)	10 (4.5)	Standard shell gun for battleships
8in shell gun	1841	American	8 (203.2)	9–3.5 (2.83)	63 (3200)	51.5 (23.4)	9 (4.1)	First standard US shell gun

Notes:
Converted figures are given in (parentheses); original figures without.

Pre-metric French shot weights are given first in French Poids (with equivalents in English pounds following)

[1] Charge of serpentine powder; corned powder ⅔rds for larger calibres to ⅓ths for smaller.
[2] Nominally 22cm.

12

Ship Decoration

IN this modern age of stark functionalism, uniformity of design, and lack of individuality, it seems astonishing that warships of the sailing era should have been so heavily decorated with a mass of sculpture and embellishment of every kind. But the reasons are not hard to find. Principally there was the prestige of kings and powerful states, a reflection of their wealth and national pride, designed to impress and awe the opposition. A no less valid reason was that it reflected the artistic spirit of the age. The construction of a large wooden ship was the supreme technological achievement of the time, equalled only by the raising of a great building, and it would have been unthinkable *not* to lavish on it the most elaborate ornamentation – in neither case was it structurally necessary but it was part of the overall design. There was also the national pride of craftsmanship, and a degree of rivalry between the Master Shipwrights, with each one wishing his ship to be the most beautiful ever built, was probably a contributory factor in the escalation of decoration in the late seventeenth century.

General appearance 1650–1840

Before embarking on a description of decorative details it is worth outlining the major changes to the appearance of warships in this period. The most obvious difference between a ship of 1650 and one of 1840 was that of proportion: the later ship was longer in both absolute and relative terms (the average number of gunports per deck rose from 10–12 to 15–16). Seppings' structural reforms (see Chapter 8) allowed ships to be constructed far longer than ever before, but when combined with a much flatter sheer line and reduced superstructure, the appearance of length was greatly enhanced.

Very big ships continued to carry a poop and even a topgallant poop well into the eighteenth century (the *Victory* of 1737 was the only British ship to have four levels of stern galleries), but being longer they did not seem as lofty as their seventeenth-century predecessors. After 1800 there was an increasing tendency to join up the quarterdeck and forecastle into a flush 'spar deck', replacing the old stepped profile rising from the waist. A parallel development was the replacement of the old inward-curving topside, called tumblehome, with a more wall-sided cross section. The relatively light structure of rails around the weather decks began to be replaced with solid bulwarks – along the quarterdecks from about the 1750s and extended to the forecastle from the 1780s (possibly influenced by the spread of carronades); later spar-decked ships often had continuous bulwarks, apart from an entry port.

The shape of bow and stern also developed significantly. The bow profile was altered by the gradual reduction in the projection of the stemhead, the raising of the headrails, and a generally lighter appearance brought about by greater integration of the various elements of the head; during the eighteenth century the athwartship beakhead bulkhead was slowly replaced by taking the bow planking up to forecastle level, the ensuing 'round bow' being applied to frigates from the 1750s and ships of the line from about 1800. The total height of the stern tended to reduce in the eighteenth century and projecting balconies disappeared towards the end of the century, but the greatest change was the introduction of Seppings' round stern in the 1820s; Britain then developed a more traditional looking elliptical stern but both France and the US opted for a very utilitarian round stern with no visible galleries for the officers' quarters. Decoration is dealt with in more detail below, but ships became notably more austere as the eighteenth century drew to a close and by the 1820s most navies had adopted a black and white chequerboard colour scheme that offered little opportunity for decorative work.

As well as the hull the top hamper underwent various improvements. The principal changes are covered in Chapter 9, but apart from specific additions and alterations it should be remembered that the proportions of the sail plan were more subtly modified: early topsails and topgallants narrowed radically from foot to head, but the eighteenth-century tendency was to broaden the heads of these sails, producing a much squarer look. Gradual reduction in tumblehome also affected the rig, allowing the channels to be placed higher up the hull, where they were less vulnerable to wave damage; the British took the lead here in the early eighteenth century, but the greater tumblehome of French ships meant that, in order to maintain the necessary spread for the shrouds, the channels had to be retained in the lower position for longer.

These generalisations apply to most navies but it is worth emphasising that there were also national characteristics in appearance that allowed the seaman's experienced eye to guess the probable nationality of any warship at some distance. Much of this was a matter of decorative style, detailed below, but there were aspects of the build that would also give them away. It is impossible to summarise these in a few sentences – and indeed illustrations are far more effective – but a few examples will suffice to make the point. The greater tumblehome of French ships has already been mentioned, but those built around 1700 were also marked by a sheer line that seemed to run down towards the bow without rising again; the sternposts of French ships also tended to be more upright, and they did not usually carry gunports as near the bow and quarter gallery as British ships. Some differences were the result of social or administrative factors: the French navy traditionally allowed officers more space, so many French frigates had a poop or cabins on the quarterdeck, whereas British ones never did; conversely the early American navy had no admirals so the first ships of the line had only one level of stern gallery. Masting and rigging also displayed subtle variations of national preference: most European navies persevered with round tops instead of the squarer ones intro-

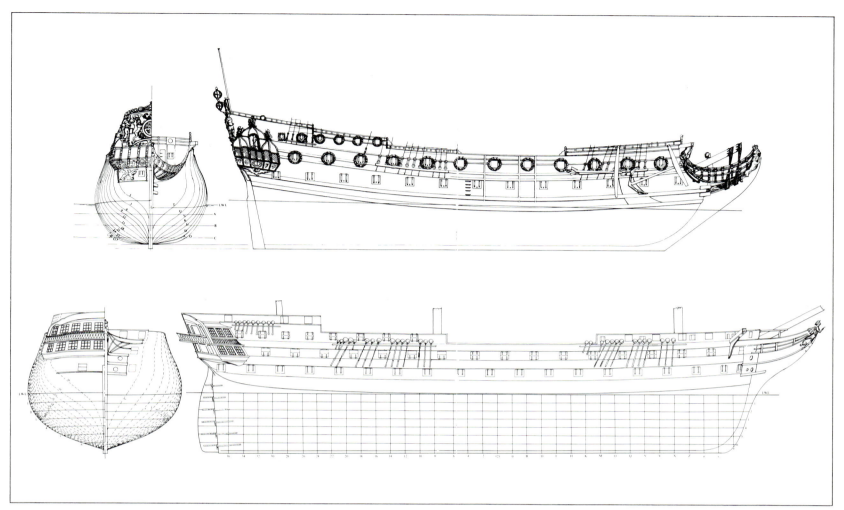

Ship decoration

We can discover the nature of ship decoration from several sources. Manuscripts, books, manifests of carved work, and contract specifications are all important, as are the many thousands of contemporary drawings, paintings, and ship draughts. For more precise details in three dimensions, the many official 'Admiralty' or 'Dockyard' models made from around 1650 are perhaps the most valuable for their superbly executed carvings, and much other information in perfect miniature.

duced from about 1700 by the British, while in the early eighteenth century it was possible to tell British ships by their taller, narrower topsails. However, some features can only be attributed to style – stem profiles, for example, or the horseshoe-shaped stern associated with the Sané era in France – so at this point it is appropriate to turn to the details of ship decoration.

Sources of artistic inspiration

The men responsible for design – whether they were shipwrights, the craftsmen engaged in carrying out the work, or the central authority – drew heavily for their inspiration from three main themes: civil architecture, classical Greek or Roman mythology, and heraldry. All were influenced by the great artistic movements of the day, although the designers or decorators of ships built in different countries mostly superimposed their national characteristics on, for example, the Baroque style. The influence of the French Court on the arts during the reign of Louis XIV in the seventeenth century was considerable, and there was little similarity between the decoration of French and English ships; of all the national styles they were the least alike. In one important respect, however, in the practice of fitting open stern galleries or balconies, the English did follow French design. In 1672 the eminent shipwright Anthony Deane was directed by Charles II to build his new ships along the lines of the French *Superbe*, which had galleries. Although there was little similarity between Deane's ships and the *Superbe*, they did

The changes to the general appearance of warships between 1650 and 1840 can be represented by these comparative profiles of the British two-deckers Resolution *(1667, 70 guns, 148ft) and* Albion *(1842, 90 guns, 204ft). The longer, lower and generally more austere appearance of the later ship is obvious, but there are some perhaps surprising survivals – notably the projecting stern gallery, the headrails and figurehead. (Brian Lavery)*

incorporate open galleries. They first appeared in 1673 and became increasingly common in English ships, and indeed in other nations' ships.

Designers of decoration were educated men well versed in the arts and in classical subjects and they would have been familiar with the works of Palladio and other classical architects. Some, no doubt, would have been on the Grand Tour and experienced the classical world at first hand. Many of the carved figures on tafferals were evidently taken from the friezes of Greek or Roman temples and the influence of classical architecture can be found in the broken arch pediments on sterns, the design of gallery balustrading, and in the staircases between decks, many of which would be entirely at home in a

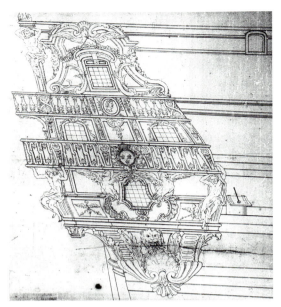

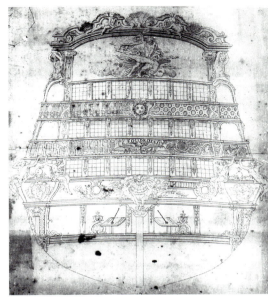

Up until the late eighteenth century, France favoured a distinctly architectural style for the stern design of her ships. Particularly during the reign of Louis XIV, the decoration was closely associated with Court artists and so its iconography was often more elaborately developed – these drawings of the Foudroyant (Thunderer), *for example, are unified by the theme of Jupiter (or Zeus) the Thunderer, and besides the portrait of the god on the taffrail, incorporate many of his legendary attributes (particularly the eagles and thunderbolt motifs). The drawings themselves, although Danish copies, are typical of French practice; there are no surviving British equivalents.* (Rigsarkivet, Copenhagen)

country house. Indeed, the adoption of the predominant architectural style of any period was commonplace. The large quarter galleries of seventeenth-century ships often resembled the jutting oriel windows of an Elizabethan building and the many mouldings about a ship closely followed the style of those in contemporary buildings and furniture, from the rather heavy, simple designs generally favoured in the mid-seventeenth century to the elegant patterns of the Queen Anne and Georgian periods.

Greek or Roman mythological subjects were commonly used for figureheads, quarter pieces, tafferals (or taffrails), and friezes. Quarter pieces were often carved to represent an individual god or goddess, and many can be identified on models, particularly when they are accompanied by their particular attribute. Figureheads and tafferals on large ships sometimes depicted a whole narrative and Zeus and Ganymede, Europea and the Bull, and Hercules engaged in his labours are just a few that can be identified on models. There were also motifs from a more obscure mythology, or superstition, such as fabulous sea monsters and grotesque mask heads.

During the most flamboyant period of decoration in the seventeenth century heraldic symbols and royal devices were widely incorporated in the carvings of the stern and head. In later times the practice declined, but the monograms of monarchs and small royal arms on figureheads were common. The Coats of Arms of towns and cities after which ships were named are sometimes found on English models, and the arms of individuals are occasionally seen.

The most conspicuous form of heraldry appeared on the flags which were not, of course, mere decoration but functional. The

beautiful Royal Standard at the main mast was quite spectacular. A silk one of 21ft by 15ft is recorded for a yacht in the mid-eighteenth century.

The stately splendour of a seventeenth-century three-decker must have been a magnificent sight, and it is sometimes difficult to remember that concealed behind its exquisite facade the crew suffered a life of comparative squalor.

Generally speaking, the French style of decoration had few imitators, but this Swedish First Rate (the Kronan *of 1660), although built by the emigré English shipwright Francis Sheldon, is clearly influenced by French taste.* (Rigsarkivet, Copenhagen)

The artists

Design, in England at least, was very much the responsibility of the Master Shipwrights. The Navy Board might have given general guidance in contracts or specified the figurehead for important ships but even when an item was specified the designer had considerable freedom. This is particularly evident in the contract for the *Yarmouth* (1695) which called for a '. . . complete pair of the Kings Arms' in the stern, 'or other ornament of like value'. Specifications were sometimes issued by the Navy Board, such as that for the *Victory* (1765), which were masterpieces of detailed instruction, and left the carver in no doubt as to exactly what was required.

In France the approach to design was more formalised than in England. A school of carving was established in the latter half of the seventeenth century, and the sculptors trained there executed the fantastic ship decoration designed by Pierre Puget and other artists. The craftsmen who carried out the work in England were mostly independent of the dockyards and, like gilders, painters, and other artists, were in business on their own account.

Much of the simpler inboard work was probably carried out by ordinary carpenters and joiners, and they would have brought with them their experience in house building and contributed to the architectural details of the elaborately balustraded staircases, the panels and mouldings of bulkheads, and in the design of belfries and other structures.

The development of decoration

The difference in appearance between a ship built in 1650 and one built 200 years later was vast, and the general trends were much the same in all countries although detailed stylistic differences were quite marked.

Change was sometimes due to the need for economy, or for the need to conform with a particular style; change was forced on design-

These two heads from English models dating from c1702 and c1710 respectively show well the dramatic reduction in carved work during the early years of Queen Anne's reign. The later ship still has a carved cat-supporter and pierced trailboard in the earlier style but this was very old fashioned by 1710. Supplementary figures of various forms abaft a lion figurehead had been very common in the seventeenth century, and these are just about the last survivors of the fashion. (John Franklin, by courtesy of the Kriegstein Collection)

ers by variations in hull form, such as the round and elliptical sterns of the early nineteenth century. Change could be sudden, as in the early 1700s, or slow and gradual, as it was for much of the eighteenth century. The marked changes which occurred in the early 1700s roughly corresponded with the end of the Stuart period and the apogee of the Baroque style. By that time the carved work on ships had reached such splendour (and cost) that the Navy Board decided to impose a measure of restraint. In June 1703 an Admiralty order was issued: '. . . the carved work be reduced only to a lion and trailboard for the head, with mouldings instead of brackets placed against the timbers; that the stern have only a taffrail and two quarter pieces, and in lieu of brackets between the lights of the stern galleries and bulkheads, to have mouldings fixed against the timbers'.

It seems clear that this was effective, for the differences in decoration of models representing ships built in 1700 and 1710 is remarkable, and well illustrates the intent of the order. But there was a distinct transitional period in those ten years, when what can be called the Queen Anne style emerged and then declined. This was not so much a reduction in the *extent* of decoration, as a difference in style, where the brackets of the head, stern, and bulkheads were lighter and carved with fruit, foliage, and flowers instead of the old-type figures.

The parts of the ship

The head

The head of most ships of all nations throughout the period was made up of a complex arrangement of vertical timbers supporting a variable number of curved moulded rails which concealed what was a rather ungainly bluff bow. The uppermost rail, or main rail, commenced with a carved human head, an ornament of some kind or just a plain timber head at the outermost corners of the forecastle. From there it swept down in an elegant curve to about the level of the beakhead platform and then up again to unite with its opposite number

Detail of the head from an English Fourth Rate of 1684. Carved items seen here from left to right are part of a port wreath, cathead and cat-supporter, head of the main rail, and two of the four brackets on the head timbers. Two of the large sculptures on the beakhead bulkhead can also be seen. (John Franklin)

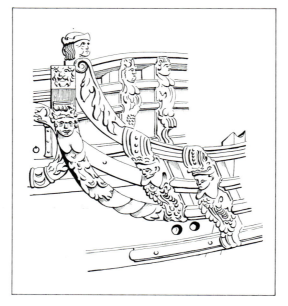

abaft the figurehead. Many French ships were distinctive for having a pair of main rails in parallel which curved up to the top of the side where they were joined by a rosette or badge abaft the cathead. Between the main rails and the cheeks of the head were one, two, or three intermediate rails depending on the class of ship, which followed much the same curve as the main rails.

In general, the ornament applied to the vertical timbers consisted of carved figures in the seventeenth century, and mouldings or elongated panels later. In contemporary jargon, the carved figures were known as brackets or terms, the latter probably deriving from Terminus, the Roman god of boundaries. The term on an English ship was typically an armless torso on a fanciful pedestal with female breasts, though mostly with male heads. Most seventeenth-century Dutch ships were notable for having no carvings on the head timbers, and the only concession to decoration in this area was the trailboard. The trailboard on most ships was between the pair of cheeks uniting the bow with the knee of the head, and was usually pierced with elaborate carving in the seventeenth century and in relief later.

The beakhead bulkhead, which closed off the foremost part of the forecastle, was a much decorated area. A model of the First Rate *Prince* (1670) shows that every square inch of the bulkhead was covered with figures, heraldic emblems, and lion mask heads. This was exceptional, but most early ships had at least a row of full length figures, terms, or other ornament. Applied mouldings were usual in the eighteenth century, often combined with painted designs, until the bulkhead disappeared with the introduction of the round bow around 1800.

The catheads protruding from the hull at each end of the beakhead bulkhead, were usually decorated on the fore and aft sides with carved or painted scroll work in the seventeenth century, and either left plain or given panels later. A cat's face or other ornament such as a star was often carved or painted on the end. Beneath the cathead was the cat supporter, which provided another subject for carving. This was a heavy knee, the lower end of which continued down and around the bow until it met one of the head rails. On seventeenth-century English ships the supporter was carved in an almost standard form, and represented the god Pan, or a satyr. As with most other features, the carved supporters were displaced by moulded ones later. Hawse holes were sometimes surrounded by carved work in the seventeenth century but this practice was not widespread.

The design for a standardised form of figurehead intended for French ships of the line after 1785; not unnaturally, the French Revolution made radical changes to the iconography of ship decoration, Republican imagery replacing the mythology of Monarchy, so it is unlikely that this design gained much currency. (From Souvenirs de Marine)

Figureheads

Figureheads were one of the glories of sailing warships. Mostly carved from pine or elm, the figure on a large ship could attain enormous proportions. A lion could, for example, be up to 16ft in height. First Rates had elaborate individual creations, but by far the most common type was the lion which appeared on most Second Rates and Third Rates and below. The lion was almost universal and only the French did not adopt it. It lasted until around the middle of the eighteenth century on English ships, and a late example can be seen on a model of the Third Rate *Lion* of 1777. A fine original example of a lion from a Sixth Rate dating from around 1715 is preserved at the National Maritime Museum, Greenwich. A rare example of an early eighteenth-century English two-decker having a figurehead other than a lion is a Third Rate of about 1710 which has St George fighting the dragon.

The figureheads on First Rates were more various, though the equestrian motif was common on English, Swedish and Danish ships for much of the period. It was at first arranged as a

Left: A typical English lion figurehead from the Second Rate Coronation, *1685. This carving would have been some 13–14ft in height. (John Franklin)*

Right: This figurehead of a peer in his robes is supposed to represent the Earl of Egmont, who was First Lord of the Admiralty 1763–6. Individual figureheads were common in the latter part of the eighteenth century after the disappearance of the lion. (John Franklin)

single rider astride a prancing horse, usually trampling over his enemy, as in the case of the Second Rate *Marlborough* (1706), where the Duke is depicted crushing the luckless Marshal Tallard. In the eighteenth century, the horse sprouted two heads and acquired a heraldic device in between, such as the Royal Arms or a monogram, and the decoration became much more elaborate. Generally of an allegorical nature, the equestrian figures often depicted the monarch in classical garb, with his monogram on the saddle cloth. Mythological figures also appeared as figureheads. The old *Naseby* of 1655 was renamed the *Royal Charles* at the Restoration in 1660, and her figurehead of Cromwell on horseback was removed amid scenes of public rejoicing and replaced by Neptune. The god is depicted in a van de Velde drawing as seated in a shell and towed by a pair of seahorses.

Elaborate figureheads appeared throughout the eighteenth century on three-deckers, but the lion on smaller ships gradually gave way to individual figures, often of mythological sub-

jects – these sometimes represented the name of the ship – or senior figures at the Admiralty. In 1796 an order was issued by the Admiralty to minimise carved work, and it directed that a scroll or billet-head was to replace figureheads. This created uproar among the shipwrights, and it seems that little notice was taken of the order, and whole figures continued for a while much as they were previously. Half figures and busts became common in the early nineteenth century, and many fine examples of this type are still preserved.

The broadside

The broad flanks of a ship offered much scope for decoration, the principal features of which were the gunports, the entry ports of three-deckers, hances, various moulded rails, and the painted or carved friezes on the topsides. In England, until the early eighteenth century, the gunports of the upper deck, quarter deck, and poop and forecastle were surrounded by carvings. At first they were more or less rectangular, resembling picture frames, but after the 1660s they became circular wreaths; this was very much an English practice. These wreaths were sometimes of a simple design based upon laurel leaves, but more often they were carved with elaborate designs of stylised foliage, fruit and flowers, and some incorporated a cherub on either side. The upper deck wreaths vanished first, around 1703, followed by those on the decks above about fifteen years later.

The steps, or hances, formed along the topsides by the varying levels of the planksheer were treated in a number of ways. On English ships, for much of the seventeenth century, there was typically a vertical carved figure planted outboard of the step with a crouching

English port wreaths were carved in an infinite variety of styles. This small selection is taken from contemporary models. A and B. Third Rate, c1655; C. Fourth Rate, c1710; D. Fifth Rate, c1660; E. Third Rate, c1702; F. Fifth Rate, c1685. (John Franklin)

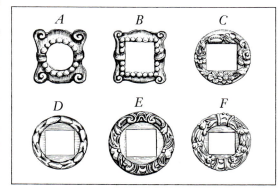

The stern of a late seventeenth-century English Third Rate. Every part is covered in carvings, and the influence of heraldry can be seen in the design of the tafferal. The practice of placing the full Achievement of Arms of the Stuarts on sterns had largely ceased in the 1670s, mainly because there was no longer room for it, but in this case it was not abandoned altogether as the designer took separate elements from the Arms and incorporated the lion and unicorn supporters at each end of the tafferal, with each holding one Quarter of the Arms. (John Franklin)

dog or occasionally a little lion against it. In the Queen Anne period, the hances were often decorated with a rosette or flower, but from then on the classical volute was universal until around 1800 when the square steps were simply left plain. French practice involved the use of carved architectural style brackets, planted on top of the planksheer against the step. The hances of other countries were broadly similar to English fashions, but not in general so ornate, at least in the seventeenth century.

The various fore and aft mouldings applied to the topsides to define the friezes and black work were usually classical, and often ornate. A plain astragal was common in the seventeenth century, particularly for the first rail down from the gunwale which was usually called the waist rail. On a draught by William Keltridge of c1684 the waist rail is actually named the 'astricall rail'. In his book William Sutherland illustrates some mouldings of the early eighteenth century, but models, with their fine detailing, are the best source. The ogee, either cyma recta or cyma reversa, and the ovalo were commonly used on their own, and many complicated patterns can be found made up of two or more of the main shapes in combination with flutes, beads and hollows.

Entry ports were a prominent feature on large ships and were mostly a feature of English vessels. Except for one known example on a Third Rate, entry ports only occurred on three-deckers where the usual position for it was on the middle deck amidships. At first there was only one, located on the port side, but from about 1670 it became the practice to fit an entry port on the starboard side as well. One model of c1702 is remarkable for having four entry ports, two on the middle deck and two on the upper deck. A typical form was a balustraded platform, which was often an extension of the main channel, with a canopy supported by pillars or cantilevered brackets. Entry ports were always handsome affairs, and were sumptuously enriched with carved work in the seventeenth century.

Decorative friezes on the topsides, running the full length of the ship, were common until towards the end of the eighteenth century. It is not easy to detect from paintings or drawings whether they were painted or carved in relief. Models show both, and it is reasonable to suppose that this was the case on the ships themselves. In the seventeenth century, and occasionally later, war-like trophies of arms were popular designs, while later mythological subjects and pastoral scenes combined with scroll work in the narrower friezes predominated. Minor items of the broadside decoration were the channel ends which were returned with fancy shapes similar to the section of a moulding, such as an ogee, and the port lid straps, the ends of which were forged in decorative styles. The scuppers of seventeenth century ships were sometimes fitted with a gargoyle in the form of a carved lion mask, and the slender gutters placed above gunports, known as rigols, were decorated. They were moulded, and the usual forms were an arch, a gable, or a double ogee; sometimes they were alternated so that an arch was fitted on one deck and a gable on another.

The stern and quarter galleries

There were so many changes in the evolution of decoration in these complex structures that it is only possible here to discuss the more important aspects. The appearance of a stern was really decided by how many tiers of stern lights there were. Around the middle of the seventeenth century two-deckers normally had one tier, and three-deckers two, which left a large area of the upper part of the stern available for decoration, and much decorated it was too. On English ships the massively carved royal arms of the Stuarts predominated after the Restoration, and the use of heraldic devices was also widespread on the ships of other nations. The Dutch in particular, were fond of quite complex painted scenes surrounded by highly ornate carved work. The *Gouda* of the 1650s, for example, had a huge panoramic view of the town of that name painted on her stern while a drawing of a Spanish ship dating from the 1660s shows her stern painted with a religious scene.

A second and third tier of lights on two- and three-deckers respectively began to appear in the 1670s, and with the addition of open galleries on many ships the area available for decoration was greatly reduced and the appearance of sterns was transformed in the upper part, though the tafferal itself was still richly carved. Until the end of the seventeenth century the whole stern was a mass of carved work, with figures and hideous grimacing mask heads on the counter, terms or putti between the lights, elaborate quarter pieces and much other embellishment.

During the eighteenth century sterns became plainer, more dignified and quite beautiful and only the tafferal, quarter pieces and ornamental brackets were carved. Moulded pilasters were placed between the lights which were sometimes arched above, but the counter was left plain or simply painted. Elaborate balustrading surrounded the open galleries when they were fitted. By the early 1800s little remained in the way of decoration to the stern, but the influence of late Georgian and Regency architecture in the design of bow windows and cast iron balustrading to galleries is apparent.

The quarter galleries, fitted each side of the hull close to the stern, were appendages to the hull and housed the captain's and officers' latrines. But despite this mundane function, they provided the designers with an opportunity for lavish decoration. The galleries were also important in enhancing the visual appearance of a ship from the broadside for they provided a balance with the mass of decoration at the bow.

In general, the number of tiers of lights in galleries on any ship corresponded with the stern; thus in the mid-seventeenth century, the galleries with only one or two tiers of lights were low on the side, and although they were topped with fanciful turrets, the upper parts were unconnected with the stern itself and this contributed to the narrow and tall appearance of the upper part of the stern. As the galleries migrated up the side with more tiers of lights, they had a tendency to lean aft and were integrated with the stern which appeared lower and broader as a result, and the quarter pieces, formerly on the corners of the hull, were placed on the corners of the quarter galleries. The quarter pieces were massive carvings and were only exceeded in size by the figureheads. They usually took the form of a single figure and mythological subjects were common; on seventeenth-century English ships a Roman warrior was popular. The upper parts of quarter galleries were decorated with crowns, heraldic devices, monograms, figures, and all manner of other ornament. On seventeenth-century English ships the galleries were often supported by the winged heads of cherubim, but later an infinite number of beautiful and elegant designs appeared which are worthy of a minor study in themselves. Early small ships with a single deck usually had one or two small windows in the side of the hull which were surrounded by quite large carved work known as a badge; later in the eighteenth century, single-deckers had a small projecting single-

An English 'quarter badge' from a Fifth Rate of 1685. On small ships, elaborate carvings such as this were planted directly on the ship's side and were merely a surround for the windows. (John Franklin)

tier gallery similar to those on larger ships.

There were many stylistic variations between the different countries but most were of basically similar form except for the French designs which had a distinctly rococo appearance and were asymmetrical in form.

Inboard work

For information on inboard decoration models are the most important source. There are few contemporary illustrations which show any significant detail except for some eighteenth-century draughts which include elevations of bulkheads. The most decorated areas were the bulkheads at the forecastle, quarterdeck, and poop. Until around 1700 there was generally a row of up to eight carved terms or brackets planted on the bulkheads combined with horizontal moulded rails. The terms were usually of figures, often grotesque, reaching the full height of the bulkhead, but towards the end of the seventeenth century they tended to be shorter and commenced at the middle moulded rail. The centre pair on the forecastle bulkhead were much larger, up to 9ft high and often carved in the form of caryatids to support the belfry. At the quarterdeck, the bulkhead was usually taken up past the deck itself to serve as a support for the breast rail, and the upper part was either decorated with the Royal Arms or sometimes the Arms of an individual or a town, and often with scroll devices. As the quarterdeck lengthened in later years, so the bulkhead disappeared beneath it, and the carvings were replaced by

pilasters and mouldings surrounding fielded panels, as on all the other bulkheads.

On seventeenth-century ships there was a profusion of heads carved on the upper ends of bitts, the newels of staircases, and on the various rigging fittings on the bulwarks. Although generally referred to as knightheads they were rarely recognisable as such; most were given a sort of cap, or sometimes a turban, while others had elaborate hair and no headgear. There was also a row of carved heads all round the forecastle on the fiferail on many ships, and this is illustrated by a model of a galley-frigate of *c*1702 where every other head is wearing a cap and the remainder left apparently bald. All these carved heads disappeared in the eighteenth century and were replaced by plain timber-heads.

The wonderful curved and winding staircases and the narrow gangways connecting them to the various decks were notable for their balustrading. It seems that only the largest ships were fitted with balustrading to the stairs in general, but on most classes in the seventeenth century there was highly ornate carved work beneath the gangway handrail. This was commonly stylised foliage which might sometimes incorporate the monarch's monogram; this gave way in later years to turned balusters or pilasters.

In the ornamentation of belfries, the ingenuity of the designers knew no bounds. The belfry simply housed the ship's bell but it became a most elaborate structure. From the fantastic creations favoured on large ships in the

Most of the decoration was purely for its own sake and served no useful purpose, but very many of the functional parts of a ship were also carved or moulded into elegant and attractive forms. This is the bitts and gallows from a late eighteenth-century Fourth Rate. (John Franklin)

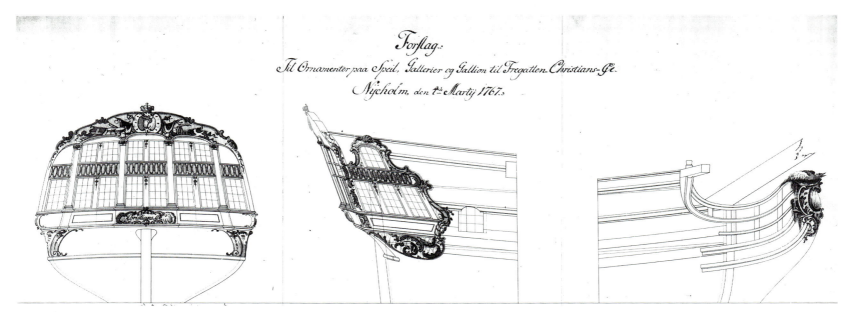

The cool, restrained classical spirit of the later eighteenth century was manifest in many navies. This is the decorative scheme for the Danish frigate Christians-øe, *dated 1767. (Rigsarkivet, Copenhagen)*

seventeenth century to the cool and elegant styles as typified on the *Victory* of 1765, there was a vast number of different types. The canopies of seventeenth century belfries were mostly carved with foliage and dolphins which was supported on further decorative work. On one late seventeenth-century Fourth Rate, the canopy is intriguingly adorned with a pair of crouching male figures, apparently in prayer with their naked buttocks thrust in the air. Later belfries were much plainer and had no carved decoration. A crossed arch with moulded edges on four turned or square pillars was common on large ships, while on other vessels the canopy was most often a single arch supported on two, or sometimes four, pillars.

Painting and gilding

Much of a seventeenth-century ship was painted black. This was usually the case with the wales, planksheer and fiferails, the head timbers and knee of the head, bulkheads, and the counter and panels of the stern and quarter galleries. The topsides above the waist rail were also black, or occasionally red, and provided a ground for any frieze designs. Red was also widely employed for the inboard sides of bulwarks and gunport lids, a practice which was continued throughout much of the eighteenth century.

From early in the eighteenth century it became the fashion to paint the topsides between the main wales and the waist rail, which had previously been 'bright' or varnished, yellow. Blue became fairly common for the friezes and counter, but there were many variations. Some English ships were all black above the waterline, and many vessels of other nations were also all black except for a broad red band corresponding to the lines of gunports. Late in the eighteenth century the so-called 'Nelson fashion' appeared whereby the ship's side was painted in distinctive bands of black and yellow though this evolved into black and white later.

From at least as early as 1678 the French and Dutch had painted the ship's name on the stern as a regular practice and this was soon followed elsewhere. However, it was not until 1771 that names were ordered officially in England and it is possible that it may have been optional long before then; a number of English models dating back to the early eighteenth century have names on the counter, although this might just have been to identify the model itself. Lion mask heads or other devices were usually painted on the red inner sides of gunport lids until the fashion slowly declined in the first half of the eighteenth century.

The practice of gilding with gold leaf was common in the seventeenth century, although not generally to such a great extent as depicted on many models where all the carved and moulded work is gilt, even on the edges of channels and other unlikely areas. But as the shipbuilders had ignored instructions to reduce carved work, it is reasonable to assume that real gilding was more widespread than generally realised today. On royal yachts, at least, the entire decorative surfaces must have been laid with gold and the famous *Mary* given by the Dutch to Charles II in 1660 had '983 little books of gold' lavished on her. Assuming that a book was made up the same as today, this amounts to more than 24,000 leaves of about 3in square, or enough to cover very approximately 1500 superficial feet. Nearly a century later, the decorations of the *Caroline* (1749) were laid with the enormous quantity of 120,000 leaves of fine gold. All in all, it seems probable that the extent of gilding on large ships declined very slowly from the time of the great *Sovereign of the Seas* (1637), nicknamed the 'Golden Devil' by the Dutch, to the last decade of the seventeenth century when contracts call for 'the gilding work being intended to be only the lion in the head and the King's arms in the stern'. Even if this was strictly adhered to, the quantity of leaf required for a large lion, with all its deeply cut contours, would have been enormous.

There are various accounts of carved work being painted 'gold colour' or 'fair colour', but what this paint actually was is a matter for speculation. One authority has suggested a transparent yellow varnish over white paint, and it is probable that yellow ochre was also used. Exactly when the use of gold ceased is unclear. Models as late as around 1750 show gilt decoration, but it seems likely that only the figurehead of important ships was gilt and then only in the earlier years of the century. Instead, there was much use of polychrome decoration, which oddly enough, is rarely evident on models, and many brightly painted examples of figureheads still exist from around 1800 to the end of the sailing era.

John Franklin

13

Seamanship

ALTHOUGH good seamanship will always be important to the efficient operation of navies, in the mechanical and electronic age it is unlikely to endow any one navy with a major advantage over another. This was not so in the sailing era, where what individual ships, squadrons and whole navies could achieve was strictly limited by the skill of their crews in the mechanics of shiphandling. It is probably no exaggeration to say that, whatever their other virtues, none of the great sailing navies could have had much impact on history if they had not first excelled in the art of seamanship.

In the right hands, the square rigged ship – and virtually all major warships were so rigged – enjoyed advantages unknown to its powered successors. It could go virtually anywhere that wind and depth of water allowed and stay at sea for months, if not years. Not only did it require no fuel, but much of the supplies it did need, like food, water and wood for the galley stove, could be obtained without recourse to a formal dockyard. Furthermore, the ship was almost self-sustaining, since even quite major repairs could be carried out by its own crew – the famous circumnavigations and voyages of exploration were magnificent achievements but differed only in degree, not kind, from what any well-found ship could do.

To exploit the advantages of wind and tide also put the ship at their mercy, so the art of seamanship was both active and passive: a matter of moving the ship to its destination as efficiently as possible, while avoiding all the potential dangers. Since conditions of sea and weather are almost infinitely variable, it took much of a lifetime to master the subtleties of seamanship, and most of its greatest exponents went to sea at an early age. Today the sophistication of square rig seamanship is almost entirely lost, although a few training ships are attempting to keep it alive. The yachtsman has inherited some of these skills, but the fore and aft rig is less demanding (and less flexible) than square rig, while the advanced technology of the modern yacht is constantly reducing the level of dependence on basic human capabilities.

In the short summary that follows, only the most basic aspects could be addressed in the space available, but it does emphasise those essential to an understanding of other aspects of the subject – the inter-relationships between performance, ship design and tactics, for example. An art which was both complex and arcane naturally developed its own language, only some of which is familiar to today's sailor. Since paraphrase can be cumbersome and inaccurate, in the brief descriptions that follow the proper terminology has been employed, allowing the description to define its meaning and context. Those seeking greater detail are directed to the works in the relevant section of the Bibliography.

The principles of sailing

The art of moving a square rigged ship was based on a number of relatively simple principles, although the variations on their employment were much more complicated. The mariner's compass was divided into thirty-two points, each amounting to just over 11 degrees, and in the descriptions following the angles are given in points as would have been understood throughout the age of sail.

Points of sailing

To fill a square sail, it was necessary for the wind to come from at least three points abaft the yard (F in the diagram), but it could be thrown aback – plastered against the mast and rigging – when the wind lay just one point ahead of the yard (A); between those angles the sail would shiver. Since the wind needed to be three points abaft the sail in order to fill, and the yard could be braced up to no more than three points (35 degrees) off the keel line, a square rigged ship could come no closer to the wind than about six points. This means that there was a sector of twelve points where the wind was contrary. (Fore and aft rigged vessels could sail closer but had disadvantages as warships – see below – so this description is largely confined to the square rig.)

The mariner's compass of 32 points. (Mark Myers)

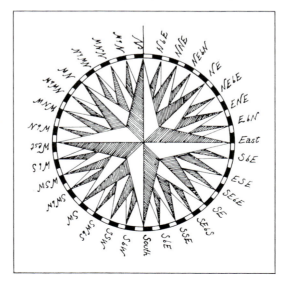

Square sails aback (A) and filled (F). (All uncredited illustrations in this chapter by Denys Baker after originals by John Harland)

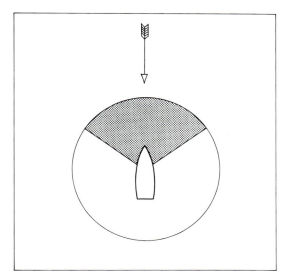

The shaded portion represents the area into which a square rigged ship could not sail.

If the ship was sailing as close to the wind as possible – about six points from the wind – it was said to be by the wind or close-hauled. As the wind drew aft it was said to be so many points free: thus, with the wind abeam, the ship was two points off the wind or two points free. As it drew further aft, to the quarter, the ship was said to go large, and when it had a following wind, the wind was more or less directly aft. If the ship wished to proceed generally in the direction from which the wind was blowing, it was necessary to follow a zig-zag course, sailing as close to the wind as possible in one direction, and then turning the bow through

Points of sailing:
A. Close-hauled or by the wind
B. Two points free
C. Sailing large
D. Following wind.

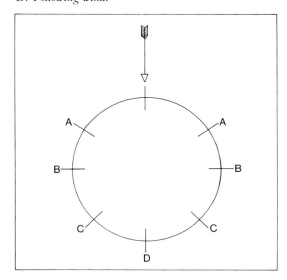

the wind and sailing close-hauled at about 90 degrees to the previous course. This was called tacking (see section below).

In relation to the ship itself, everything towards, or on the side of, the direction of the wind was described as windward or 'weather'; anything downwind was leeward or 'lee'.

Making best use of the wind

It was important to distinguish between true and relative wind. The relative wind was the strength and direction of the wind, as felt by the ship, and it might be greater or less than the true wind. In the diagram below, where the ship's speed is S, and the speeds of true (T), and relative (R), winds are shown, it is clear that when the wind is aft, the relative speed of the wind is least. For instance if a 20kt wind drove a ship running before the wind at 12kts, the relative wind was only 8kts. In the same conditions, a ship managing 8kts sailing by the wind, would experience a relative wind of about 25kts. The greater the relative wind strength, the less the amount of canvas set, and hence in the same conditions, a vessel running before the wind could carry more canvas than one close-hauled.

True and relative wind.

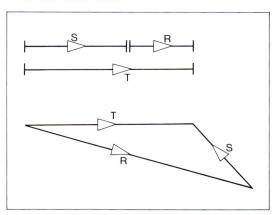

Effect of wind on loftier sails (top); ship under reefed fore and main topsails (bottom).

In general, lofty sails, like the topgallants and royals, were taken in first. They were set on the less well supported upper masts, and being at the upper end of the lever, caused the greatest heel. The old weather rhyme put it:

Mare's tails and mackerel scales,
Make lofty ships carry low sails

Exceptions to this rule were the reefed fore

Below: Fore and after canvas, backed and full.

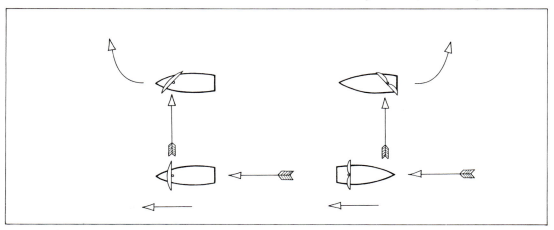

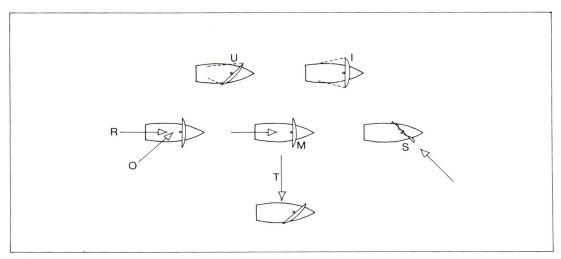

The effect of wind on sails:
R. *Striking the sail at right angle*
O. *Striking obliquely*
M. *With yard squared*
S. *Sail shivering*
U. *Yard braced up sharply*
I. *Yard braced in square*
T. *Yard trimmed at 45 degrees.*

and main topsails, which could be set in almost all weathers.

Forward canvas, whether full or aback, pushed the bow off the wind. After sail, whether full or aback, pushed the bow into the wind. A sail which was full, pushed the ship ahead; a sail which was aback, pushed the ship astern. A square rigger, unlike a fore and aft rigged vessel, could sail backwards, albeit not for any great distance, and it was this potential manoeuvrability that made square rigs more popular for warships since it could be used to effect in battle.

The wind had the greatest effect when it struck the sail at right angles (R in the diagram above) and less when hitting it obliquely (O). The 'push' contributing to forward movement of the ship was maximised when the sail was at right-angles to the keel, that is to say, with the

'Corkscrew' trimming of upper yards.

yard squared (M). A sail which was shivering, with the wind blowing along the yard, had no effect (S). The sail exerted the greatest twisting moment, turning the bow or stern towards or away from the wind, when the yard was braced up as sharply as possible. There was no torque of this kind when the yard was square. The yard was trimmed by hauling on the braces. If the weather brace was eased off, and the lee brace hauled, the yard could be swung round (U), so that it was braced up, as sharp as possible. Bracing in was the opposite manoeuvre, the yard ending up in the square position (I).

With the wind dead aft, the yard was square, in the best position both for making headway, and in its orientation to the wind. If close-hauled, the yard would be braced up as sharp as possible. On other points of sail, the yard was trimmed to some intermediate position, in the hope of maximising the push and making the best use of the available wind. As a rough rule of thumb, it was best if the yard bisected the angle between the wind and the keel-line. For instance, with the wind abeam, the yard would be trimmed so it was at about a 45-degree angle to the keel (T).

Rather than being trimmed 'over', the upper yards were commonly trimmed a fraction less sharply, as they ascended, so that the yards were placed in a sort of spiral configuration. Even with a fore and aft sail the same thing is true – the foot is trimmed sharper than the peak. One explanation for this, is that the wind aloft was faster, and therefore the apparent wind was 'fairer', as compared with the surface wind.

Although usually the fore and after yards were trimmed alike, the after yards might be braced up a little sharper; first, because they were not working in clean air, and second, if the wind was well free, so they would not take the wind out of the forward sail. On the other

hand, if the vessel was carrying weather helm [see below], bracing the fore yards up a bit, relative to the after yards, helped ameliorate the tendency to run up into the wind.

Centres of effort and lateral resistance

A paper boat, launched on a pond will drift helplessly downwind (to leeward). A sailing ship does not behave the same way because the water resists the movement of its hull. The shape of the hull ensures that, when squeezed between the force of the wind above, and the resistance of the water below, it tends to move either ahead or astern, but relatively little to leeward. For convenience, we can think of each of these forces as concentrated at a single point, the wind at a Centre of Effort (CE), and the resistance at a Centre of Lateral Resistance (CLR). If the CE is ahead of the CLR, the pivot point, the bow will be pushed off the wind, and if astern of the pivot, the bow will be pushed into the wind. To maintain course, it will be necessary to correct for this with appropriate helm. When the tendency is for the bow

Centres of effort (CE) and lateral resistance (CLR).

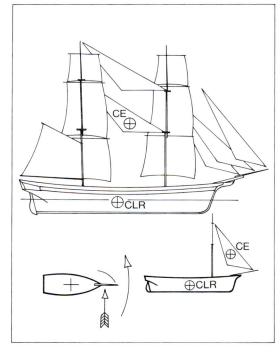

to run up into the wind, the vessel is said to be ardent and, as a corrective measure, she will have to carry weather helm. In the opposite case, she is said to be slack, and will have to carry lee helm. If the rudder were other than amidships, it caused increased drag, and hence anything other than minimal weather helm was undesirable.

In a three-masted ship, the CE lies somewhere between the fore and main masts, meaning that the forward sail (shaded in the diagram below) includes the sails on the fore mast, and everything forward of this, while the after sail includes everything set on the main and mizzen. The position of the CLR was affected by the trim of the hull. If 'down by the head', it moved forward, and if trimmed by the stern, it moved aft. The trim of the hull was affected by the stowage of heavy weights in the hold, and also by what sail was being carried. All the square sails, with the exception of the fore course, tended to push the bow down. The fore topgallant was particularly aggressive in this regard. Lifting sails included the staysails on fore and main, and the fore course. The vessel might also become too ardent because lofty sail unduly increased the angle of heel, and moved the CE out to leeward of the keel.

Measures to avoid excessive ardency, and carrying weather helm, included:

Taking in some after sail.
Decreasing rake of the masts particularly the fore mast.
Setting more forward sail, or bracing the fore yards sharper.
Shifting weight aft or taking in the fore topgallant.

Slackness could be cured by:

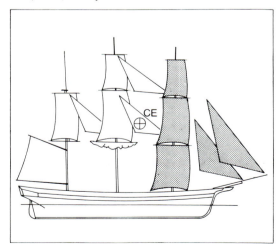

Centres of effort and lateral resistance for a three-masted ship. The sail plan can be divided into forward sail (shaded) and after.

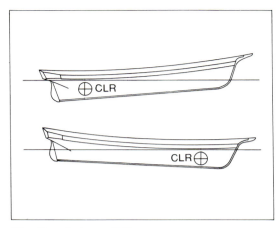

The effect of trim on CLR.

Taking in forward sail, or bracing the fore yards in somewhat.
Setting more after sail, or bracing up after yards a bit.
Shifting weight forward in the hull.
Increasing the rake of the masts, particularly main and mizzen.

Steering

If the ship was making headway, the ship's head turned the same way as the rudder; if the ship were making sternway, the stern turned in the same direction as the rudder. It is worth remembering that the tiller (or helm) and rudder pointed in opposite directions. When going ahead, if the helm were a-weather, the bow would fall off the wind; if the helm were a-lee, the bow would turn up into the wind; if the helm were a-port, the bow would turn to starboard, and so on. Thus, in British ships until 1933, the order 'Port your helm!' meant 'Turn the ship's head to Starboard!'

The rudder performed well up to an angle of about 35 degrees or so, beyond which it exerted so much drag that it diminished headway. In small vessels, the helmsman could manage this range by pushing directly on the tiller, but with a tiller exceeding 10ft or so in length, it was necessary to gain some mechanical advant-

Effect of rudder in ship going ahead (left) and astern.

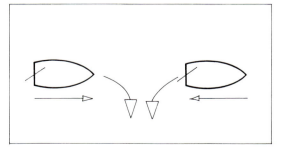

age. Up to the early 1700s, this was managed by prying the tiller from side to side with a lever called the whipstaff [see Chapter 10]. This functioned – or in any event worked well – only over a few degrees of tiller movement, either side. The introduction of the steering wheel was a great improvement, allowing the tiller to be readily shifted over its full useful range.

In larger vessels, the man at the helm could not see what was going on, and was instructed or conned by someone on deck. With the wind free, he steered by compass. Having been given a course, he kept the ship steady on that compass point. When working to windward, on the other hand, the ship was steered by the wind, the man at the conn watching the sails. At any time, the wind might change direction by a point or two, and the ship was kept in a particular relationship to the wind, with a concomitant change in compass course. She could be kept, for example, full and by, that is to say the sails well full, not trying to 'pinch' or get too close to the wind, the steersman judging the amount of helm needed by watching the weather leech of the sails. If the leech flapped, he was too close to the wind. The actual sail chosen as a guide varied – perhaps the main course, perhaps the mizzen topsail, or a weather fore topmast studdingsail.

Speed and leeway

Other things being equal, speed was related to wind speed and the amount of sail set. It also depended on the point of sailing. At first thought one would imagine that the best speed would be achieved with the wind directly aft but practical experience (confirmed by modern wind tunnel tests) indicate that the best speed should be reached with the wind on the quarter. Under these conditions, there is less blanketing of the forward sail by the after canvas than is the case with the wind directly aft.

Surviving reports suggest that by the mid-eighteenth century speeds of 12–13kts were possible for the best line of battleship designs, and the occasional frigate was logged at 14–15kts. This usually required the somewhat unusual combination of strong winds (Force 6–7 by the modern Beaufort Scale) so that the maximum canvas could be set, with relatively smooth water so as not to slow up the ship by pitching. The ship would also have needed to be free from underwater fouling, which was very detrimental to speed, although this was alleviated after the introduction of copper sheathing in the 1780s.

Besides pure speed, it was important that

warships did not make too much leeway. With the wind anywhere except more or less aft, there was a tendency for a square rigged ship to lose ground downwind – the ship did not go exactly in the direction she was pointing, but made good a course a point or two further from the wind. This was known as leeway, and a ship with a marked tendency in this regard was said to be leewardly, the much-prized opposite being weatherly. Ships could have their speed advantage cancelled by leewardliness, so that in a chase to windward, for example, ground lost to leeward on one tack would have to be made up on the next; the end result might well be a slower, but more weatherly ship catching a faster but leewardly one.

Ship handling

Making and shortening sail

If wind strength were not the major consideration, the point of sailing determined which sails were set. A less important sail was not allowed to blanket a more useful one. Thus, as the wind drew aft, the weather clew of the main course and the tack of the mizzen were pulled up. By the time the wind was on the quarter, the main course was brailed up or taken in completely, and with the wind almost due aft, the mizzen was also taken in, so the wind would have the best shot at the fore course. The weather fore topmast and topgallant studdingsails were set with the wind a point forward of the beam, and lee main topmast and topgallant studdingsails could be set with the wind abeam. The weather lower studdingsail was set with the wind on the quarter, and lower studdingsails set both sides – often one on the main and one on the fore, if the wind were almost due aft.

When setting or taking in sail, it was best if the wind helped rather than hindered the operation. When taking in a topsail, the yard would be braced so that the sail was a-shiver, the wind spilled out of it as far as possible. Although in blowing weather square sails were usually got in one side at a time, there was substantial division of opinion among eighteenth-century writers as to whether it was best to take in the lee or weather clew first. Falconer's lines 'And he who strives the tempest to disarm, will ne'er embrail the lee yard-arm' were not the last word on the subject.

In shortening sail, a sail could either be taken in (or handed), being furled completely,

or alternatively reefed. In general, taking a sail in was less complicated than reefing it. The topsails were reefed most commonly; courses, spritsail, and mizzen, less often; topgallants and royals, never. To take in, the sail was clewed up in its buntlines and clewlines and then secured to the yard with gaskets. A topsail commonly had four reefs, which were taken in one after another, and secured to the yard with reef-points. During the reefing process, the upper part of the sail was made slack, by hauling up on the reef-tackle. At the yardarm, the reef-band was secured with a strong lashing called the reef earing.

When the ship was close-hauled, the yards braced up, the tacks (or lower weather corners) of the fore and main course on the weather side were hauled down, and the sheets on the lee side were hauled aft. If the port tacks were down, the vessel was said to be on the port tack, and if the starboard tacks were boarded, she was said to be on the starboard tack.

Manoeuvres

Going about could be achieved either by tacking – taking the bow through the eye of the wind – or by wearing, turning away from the wind, and taking the stern through the wind.

For tacking, the best way possible was got on the vessel, if necessary bearing away a little, and when ready, the helm was eased down, and the ship run up into the wind. When the wind was about a point on the weather bow, or almost dead ahead, the sails on the fore mast were thrown aback, and with luck this, together with the ship's forward momentum, acted to push the bow through the wind, and the success of the manoeuvre was assured. At

The sequence of tacking:
1. *Building up speed by bearing away*
2. *Turning into the wind; sails shivering*
3. *Forward sail backed; after sail braced round*
4. *After sail filling on new tack, gaining steerageway*
5. *Forward sail braced round and filling.*

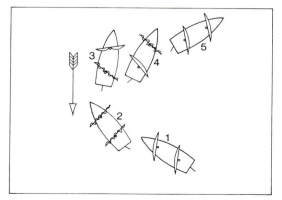

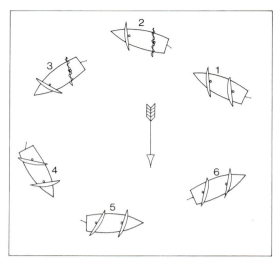

The sequence of wearing:
1. *Starboard tack*
2–3. *After sail brailed and yards braced in*
4. *Fore sail squared; after sail braced up for new tack*
5. *Fore sail braced up for new tack*
6. *Port tack.*

this point, the sails on the main and mizzen masts were braced around and filled on the new tack, giving the ship headway, and bringing her again under the control of her helm. Finally, the fore yards were now braced around for the new tack, allowing the foresail and foretopsail to fill.

The alternative was to put the helm up and bear away. The turn was accelerated by brailing in the mizzen and brailing up the main sail, bracing in the after yards to shiver the sails on the main and mizzen, and cause the bow to fall off as rapidly as possible. When the wind was almost due aft, the yards on the fore were squared, and the after yards braced up for the new tack, and once the after sails filled, they pushed the stern in the proper direction. When the wind was roughly abeam, the foreyards were braced up on the new tack, the helm being kept over until the ship was full and by on the new tack.

Boxhauling might be treated as a manoeuvre in its own right, or as a means of recovering from a failed attempt at tacking. In the second case, let us imagine that the ship, which had been on the port tack, has run up into the wind, but has failed to pay off on the new tack. The main sail and mizzen are taken in, and the headyards are hauled around for the other tack. The backed fore course and fore topsail push the bow off to starboard, and the vessel starts to make sternway. The helm is kept a-starboard and the ship travels back in an arc. By keeping the sails on the after yards lifting, the stern is encouraged to come up into the wind. When the wind is almost due aft, the headyards

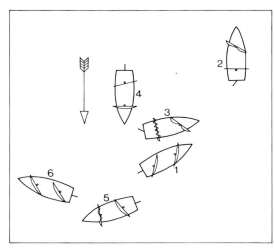

The sequence of boxhauling:
1. *Original port tack*
2. *Failed attempt to tack; after sail brailed*
3. *Ship sailing astern, fore sail backed, after sail shivering*
4. *Fore sail squared as ship comes up stern to wind*
5. *Ship making headway; after sail filled*
6. *Head sail braced up for a new tack.*

are squared, the afteryards braced up for the new tack, and the helm reversed. The ship now starts to make headway, and when the wind is about abeam, the headyards are braced up on the new tack, and the ship luffed up to the proper point.

Wearing round short:
1. *On port tack, rocks sighted ahead*
2. *Fore sail backed; after sail shivering or taken in*
3. *Bow falling off rapidly, fore sail squared*
4. *After sail filled*
5–6. *Ship luffed up to desired new tack.*

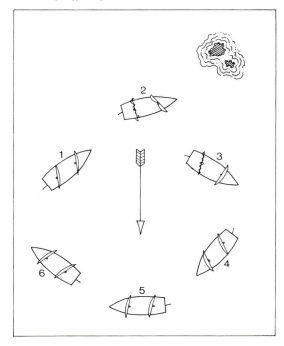

Wearing round short was a variation on box-hauling, and was used in an emergency, such as the case of a ship on the port tack unexpectedly coming upon a ship on the starboard tack, and being in imminent danger of collision, or the lookout sighting breakers ahead. The helm was put up, the headyards were braced around to throw them aback, and the sails on the after yards shivered or taken in. These measures resulted in the bow falling off briskly, and when the wind was abaft, the foreyards were squared, and the manoeuvre followed that described for boxhauling.

The advantage of tacking was that it lost no ground to leeward, and the manoeuvre had every prospect of success when there was a relatively smooth sea, and a good working breeze – the situation found when a breeze was freshening. If the vessel were a dull sailer, or if the bow was knocked back by waves, the manoeuvre might fail. Wearing inevitably lost some ground to leeward, but unlike tacking it never miscarried, besides which, it was easier on the rigging, because nothing was thrown aback, and on the rudder fastenings, because at no point was the ship sailing backwards.

By shortening sail, and trimming the yards appropriately, it was possible to balance those sails tending to push the ship ahead with those tending to cause sternway, and keep the vessel more or less stationary – called heaving to. This would be done, for example, when picking up or lowering a boat, and could be employed as a tactic in battle. It is true that the vessel drifted steadily downwind while this was going on, but because the length of the hull was broadside to the wind, this tendency was not excessive. The vessel could be hove to fore topsail to the mast (A in the diagram), or main topsail to the mast (B). A study of contemporary paintings, suggests that in the 1800s, the latter was the common method, although the reverse appears to be preferred in some modern training ships. Whalers, when cutting in, commonly hove to with the fore topsail partially struck, and backed. The full aftersail made the vessel forge slowly ahead, keeping the tail-chain taut, and the whale in the proper position in relation to the flensing platform, on the starboard side (C). For warships the ability to back square canvas was a major advantage over the fore and aft rig, which explains why it was confined to small craft whose roles were more related to speed than fighting qualities.

Heavy weather

In a storm, the ship's master had two options: to scud (or run before the gale), that is to say

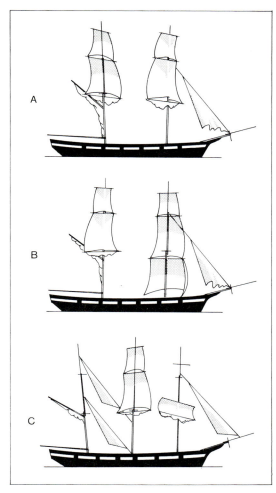

Methods of heaving to:
A. *Fore topsail to the mast*
B. *Main topsail to the mast*
C. *Whaler-fashion, fore topsail partially struck and backed.*

head directly downwind; or alternatively to lie to, or try, that is, to lie heading seven or eight points from the wind, with just enough canvas set to keep headway on, and make as little leeway as possible.

Scudding was resorted to when there was sufficient sea room to leeward, particularly if this would take the ship in the desired direction. The reefed fore course, or the reefed fore or main topsails were suitable canvas for this purpose. If the wind was so violent that even these sails would not stand, the ship could scud under bare poles. In this sort of situation, heavy following seas might cause the vessel to wander from its course, or yaw. The danger was that the ship might fly up into the wind, or broach to, have the square canvas thrown aback, and be in danger of having the beam seas fling the ship on her beam ends, or damage her rudder fastenings. A distinction could be made between this accident, and a vessel scudding with the wind on one quarter, being

A tactic advocated by William Hutchinson for dealing with a confident opponent lying to and expecting submission without a fight: disguising his attention as long as possible, his ship (1) begins its attack on the enemy's weather quarter (2), shooting up into the wind until the whole lee broadside can be fired with effect; the ship is then boxed around on her heel until the wind is far enough aft to allow her to make rapid headway (3), passing under the enemy's stern (4) for a very damaging raking volley as the guns bear. Note that both ships are fighting under topsails alone. From A Treatise on Naval Architecture *(London 1794; reprinted 1969).*

brought by the lee, that is, having the wind cross the stern, to the other quarter, throwing the canvas aback. The evil consequences were the same.

Lying to was the choice when there was little sea room, or if it was feared that scudding might be too dangerous. The tack that would best keep the ship clear of danger was chosen. Enough sail was set to keep the ship's head seven or eight points from the wind, with the helm well over to lee. In small vessels, the helm might be lashed a-lee, but in bigger ships it would be tended. If the rudder were carried away, the ship would fall off, rather than run up into the wind, and throw the square canvas aback. If no canvas would stand, the Elizabethans spoke of lying a-hull. They would have chosen to try under one of the lower sails, whereas in the 1800s the reefed main topsail was preferred. Acting at the end of a longer lever, it did a better job of ameliorating heavy rolling, and did not lose the wind, when the ship was in the trough of the sea. A lower storm staysail had the advantage that it could not fly aback.

Main sail aback, whether arising from bad steering or a sudden wind shift, was a serious matter, since the wind pushing on the backed sail, acted to hold the bow up to the wind, and keep the sail aback. If uncorrected, the ship would lose headway, and indeed start to sail backwards, perhaps losing her rudder. A fore sail thrown aback, on the other hand, tended to push the bow off the wind, and in this way itself helped to correct the problem.

In uncertain weather, and particularly at night, when it would be difficult to see a squall coming, getting sail off in a hurry might prove difficult, and it was best if the ship were snugged down in good time. The wind striking the lofty sails tended to knock the ship down, and the hazard was greatest if the wind came from abeam. When hit by a squall, royal and topgallant halliards were let go, and the mizzen and main sail brailed up as quickly as possible. In emergency, the lee sheets could be let go, to

get the pressure off the masts. The officer of the deck had two options in a squall: to bear away, or luff through it. Luffing would instantly spill some wind out of the sails, while bearing away dropped the relative wind speed, and by having the after sails shelter the forward ones, facilitating the task of the men taking them in.

In battle

In a fleet engagement shiphandling was necessarily kept to a minimum, since primitive systems of command and control made manoeuvres difficult and dangerous. Furthermore, the majority of the crew were required to man the guns, with a minimum assigned to sail trimming. The line of battle itself meant sailing at the speed of the slowest ship and in practice the approach speed was even slower to allow all ships to keep station. As a result, battle was usually joined with ships carrying topsails only, with courses brailed up; this allowed the deck officers a better view of developments and meant that in an emergency the courses could be dropped quickly to increase speed. A further advantage was that in a seaway, reduced canvas caused less of a heel, allowing weather-gage ships to run out their lee guns with less danger of taking in water through the lower deck gunports.

After breaking the opposing line became a commonly attempted manoeuvre an increase in readily available reserve sail may have been necessary, and paintings of the Napoleonic period often show ships with topgallants sheeted home but not hoisted; raising the topgallants would have given a quick increase in sail power.

There were exceptions to these practices, notably in 'general chase' engagements like

Cape Passaro and Quiberon Bay where the enemy was in flight and sail was piled on by the pursuing forces. In these situations, as individual ships came up with an opponent, the ensuing battle was often more akin to a series of individual single-ship actions, where manoeuvring for tactical advantage was more common. However, battleships were not as nimble as frigates and sloops, so once it was clear the enemy could not escape, engagements tended to become close-quarter slugging matches under reduced sail.

On the other hand, the smaller ships had a wide variety of options and many single-ship battles involved preliminary skirmishing for tactical advantage before closing for a gun duel and/or boarding. This very much depended on the skill of the opposing captains and the willingness of both parties to engage (if one was set on escape, then she had to be disabled before a decisive combat would result); in these sorts of actions, many manoeuvres were possible, and most were tried at some time; furthermore, some of these manoeuvres had to be carried out with damage aloft, so the shiphandling involved was often of the highest order.

Anchoring and getting under way

The ship approached the anchorage under easy sail. A sufficient length of cable was hauled up on deck, and flaked down, ready to run, with a turn taken on the bitts. The stoppers securing the anchor were removed, with the exception of the ring-stopper. Under shortened sail, the ship ran up into the wind, the anchor buoy streamed, the ring-stopper let go, and the cable allowed to run out as the ship dropped back. Additional cable was then veered, using the bitts as a veering cleat, and secured with deck-stoppers. If the ship was under the influence of

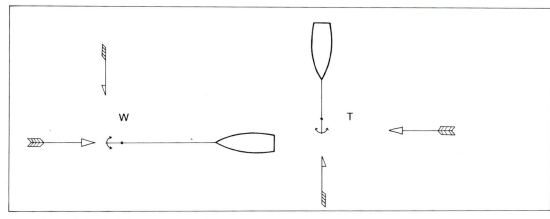

At anchor, wind-rode (W) and tide-rode (T).

nippered to the cable, and the capstan hove around. The stoppers were got off and the turn taken off the bitts. The cable was then hove in, until the anchor came in sight. The cat-tackle was hooked in the ring, and the anchor swung up to the cathead and secured with the ring-stopper. The fish-tackle was hooked to the crown of the anchor and the shank swung up into the horizontal position, and the shank and flukes secured. These operations were known as catting and fishing the anchor.

The diagram depicts the sequence of getting under way from single anchor. It assumes that

the wind (W in the diagram), she was said to be wind-rode, and if in the grip of the tide (T), she was tide-rode. If just sufficient cable were veered so that the cable was in line with the forestay, she was said to be at short stay.

By dropping two anchors, the ship rode to one cable with the ebb and the other with the flood tide. The circular space taken up as she swung was much less than with a single anchor down, and hence mooring was preferred in crowded anchorages. However, if close attention were not paid at change of tide, there was a danger that the cables would wrap themselves round each other, resulting in a foul hawse.

It might be assumed that, once at anchor, the sails were not touched, but this was not the case. In the first place, the canvas had to be loosed to dry at frequent intervals if it were not to rot; and in the second place, at change of tide, the ship's people needed to set appropriate sail, brace the yards, and make use of windlass (or capstan) and rudder. This was necessary if the ship were to be shifted in the correct direction, the hemp cable kept taut and so far as possible off the bottom, keeping the anchor turning in the ground and the cable clear of the protruding arm. The diagram shows the sequence as the ship is manoeuvred over to the west, at change of tide.

Before weighing anchor, the messenger was got up and the capstan rigged. The cable was

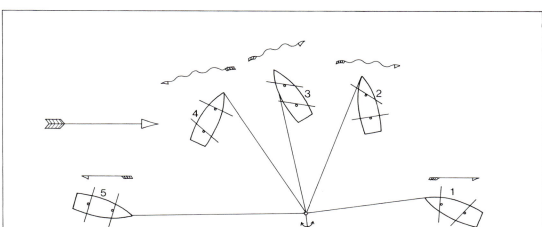

The sequence of shifting a ship at the change of tide.

The sequence of getting under way from a single anchor:
1. *Yards backed but after sail set for port tack*
2. *Making sternway; backed head sail pushing bow to starboard, rudder pushing stern to port*
3. *Wind abeam; fore sail braced round, all sail fills and*
4. *ship forges ahead.*

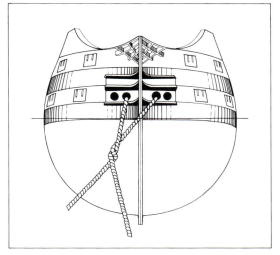

A foul hawse.

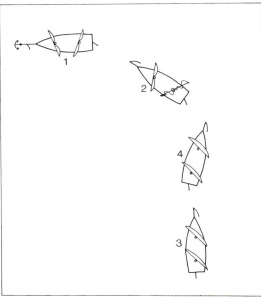

Riding to two anchors.

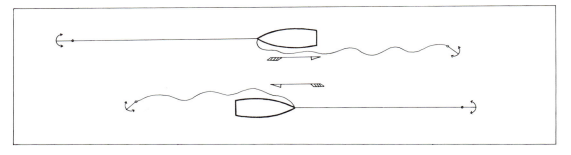

A lively eighteenth-century drawing of pinnaces coming alongside a ship; note the use of boathooks for fending off and hooking on. The drawing captures well the relative fragility of boats, ships on service frequently reporting their boats 'stove' (smashed) in the general course of their duties. (NMM)

the ship is riding to the port anchor, with the wind ahead and no tide. The cable was hove in to short stay (1), and sufficient canvas set to ensure control of the ship, once the anchor was a-weigh. The headyards were braced as for the starboard tack, with topsail aback, and the after yards laid the other way, with the helm a-starboard, so that the instant the anchor broke out of the ground, the backed headsails pushed the bow to starboard, while the rudder caused the stern to go to port, as the ship gathered sternway. As the wind came abeam (2) and (3), the canvas on the main and mizzen masts filled, and the ship began to forge ahead. The headsails were then braced around, and the ship brought under control, with appropriate rudder and trimming of yards, as the anchor was catted and fished.

Boat work

For the relatively unhandy warship of the age of sail its boats performed a multitude of functions unknown to their modern counterparts. Most manoeuvres under sail required space in which to conduct them safely, so big ships usually anchored rather than coming alongside a quay in the current manner. In these circumstances the boats became the link with the shore. They were used for personnel transport, for storing and watering the ship, and in emergencies they could be rigged to carry really heavy weights like guns (slung under the biggest workboat, the longboat or launch).

At sea the same restrictions on manoeuvrability meant that all but the most telegraphic communication between ships was done by boat, and for warships on blockade duty, for example, boats were needed to board neutral or suspected enemy merchant ships. More aggressive captains could also use their boats to extend the reach of their ships by mounting boat attacks on harbours and coastal installations – surprise 'cutting-out' raids aimed at capturing sheltering enemy merchantmen or warships were a particularly popular variation. Another possibility was to arm the better-sailing boats to act as miniature privateers, which was especially popular where the mother ship was a harbour-bound guardship.

Boats often functioned rather like an auxiliary engine, being capable of towing their ship when becalmed or manoeuvring her in confined waters, although it is unlikely that even the most powerful crews could move a ship against wind and tide. However, apart from directly towing, a boat might also carry out an anchor so that the ship could warp herself to the desired position by heaving in on the capstan; although it was slow and backbreaking work, progress could be made by repeating this process – known as kedging – and ships carried special kedge anchors for this purpose.

Important as they were, boats were always a problem to stow on the crowded deck of a warship. Boats slung from the familiar davits were a relatively late development (around 1800) and they were never employed for more than a minority of the ship's boats. There is plenty of evidence that boats were regularly towed at sea until the later eighteenth century, when the development of athwartship waist booms made them easier to stow without disabling the guns; before that they were stowed on deck or on a 'bridge' of spare spars between the forecastle and quarterdeck. Swinging them out, using tackles from the mastheads and yardarms was a tricky operation and in a seaway must have required considerable judgement – this must have lain behind the preference for towing boats and probably inspired the introduction of davits for the seaboats (those earmarked for instant use – for lifesaving or boarding duties).

Once in the water, boats required similar handling skills to the ship herself, although on a smaller scale. Most boats could be either rowed or sailed, even if some were better at one than the other: barges and pinnaces, for example, were principally pulling boats whereas cutters and yawls were better under sail. Since boats were effectively ambassadors for their ships, smart boatwork was much prized as a reflection of the efficiency and skill of the whole crew and their officers. In peacetime the rivalry between the boat crews of different ships was channelled and formalised into regular races and regattas, which were considered to be good for morale and team spirit.

John Harland

14

Naval Tactics

THE sail-propelled warship which began to appear in royal battlefleets at the end of the Middle Ages lacked the tactical mobility of the oared galleys which had hitherto dominated naval warfare, but at first naval tactics were not greatly affected by the change of warship type. Galley tactics were focussed on boarding the enemy, for which purpose they were equipped with a boarding spur, and by the fifteenth century with artillery to clear the enemy deck before the boarding party went over. Sailing vessels also sought to manoeuvre to board the enemy, and first acquired artillery to assist in boarding. The difficulty of sailing a heavy ship alongside the enemy, however, and the high sides of sailing ships, tended to give a greater advantage to the defence. By building fore and after castles on the ends of the sailing ship, and giving the hulls a pronounced tumblehome, this defensive strength was increased. As a result, sailing ships could defend themselves with smaller crews, and could be used profitably for trading purposes, as well as for war. Their capacity to carry victuals and water sufficient for their smaller crews gave them a strategic mobility which enabled them to conduct operations at a much greater distance from base, and over more extended periods of time, than galleys were ever able to undertake.

When in the sixteenth century warships began to make extended voyages in the open ocean, the high defensive castles became a structural weakness which could endanger the ship. One of the ships John Hawkins took with him on his West Indian voyages was the high-charged *Jesus of Lubeck*, and his experience with her was formative in his reconstruction of the English fleet in the 1580s. When the high castles were cut away, however, it became necessary to depend more upon the guns both for offence and defence. It had become possible to do so when the technique was learnt, in England in 1543, how to cast cannon from iron. Although inferior in quality to bronze guns, cast iron ordnance was so much less expensive (one-third to a quarter of the cost of bronze), that large numbers of them could be mounted on the sailing warships, transforming them into floating batteries which no galley could safely engage.[1] The *Mary Rose* in 1512 carried 250 soldiers for boarding, and only 120 sailors, who handled the great guns, but the *Triumph* of 1603 more than reversed those proportions, carrying 120 soldiers and 340 sailors.[2]

Before the line of battle

In the sixteenth and early seventeenth centuries warships sought to provide all-round defence with their guns, 'so as that,' as Captain Boteler wrote, 'upon the least yaw of the helm some one piece or other may be brought to bear'.[3] Tactics reflected this arrangement. Ships were manoeuvred in battle so that each gun could be brought to bear in succession. 'A principal thing in a gunner at sea is to be a good helmsman,' wrote Sir William Monson, 'and to call him at helm to loof, or bear up, to have his better level, and observe the heaving and setting of the sea to take his aim at the enemy'.[4] Nathaniel Butler wrote that the captain of a warship should edge up to his enemy, discharge small shot at anyone on deck, and then

Turning tactics as applied by the English against the Spanish Armada in 1588.

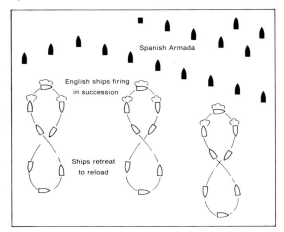

Spanish Armada

English ships firing in succession

Ships retreat to reload

'fire your bow pieces upon her, and then your full broadside; and letting your ship fall off with the wind, let fly with your chase pieces, all of them, and so your weather broadside. The which being done, bring your ship about, that your stern pieces may be given also'.[5] Compared to later practice, a larger number of seamen were required on deck to make radical sail changes in action.

Having discharged its pieces, the ship would then, if possible, withdraw out of range to reload, protected by other ships in the fleet. The small size of warships made it necessary to lash the guns in place so that they would not recoil during action, and the gunners were required to climb outside the ship for reloading. Mutual support, and especially support of the admiral's ship, was the most important tactical rule laid down in the admiral's fighting instructions.

In the battle against the Spanish Armada (1588) the English fleet had 1972 guns to the Spanish 1124 guns, the Spanish fleet having more of the larger types of cannon and cannon perrier.[6] Witnesses were greatly impressed by the discharge of these guns, and gunpowder was burnt at unprecedented rates. Nevertheless, the guns served more to harass than to injure. The smooth bore cannon was not engineered to a high standard in modern terms, and so was inaccurate. For a fleet armed with them to project a really damaging firepower, the fire from many guns had to be concentrated.

The first step was to redesign the ships themselves in the early seventeenth century, so

1. Carlo M Cipolla, *Guns and Sails* (London 1965), pp36–56, and *passim*.

2. Michael Lewis, *The Navy of Britain* (London 1949), p293.

3. W G Perrin (ed), *Boteler's Dialogues*, Navy Records Society, Vol LXV (London 1929), p259.

4. M Oppenheim (ed), *The Naval Tracts of Sir William Monson in Six Books*, Navy Records Society, Vol XLV (London 1902–14), p33.

5. Julian S Corbett (ed), *Fighting Instructions*, Navy Records Society, Vol XXIX (London 1905) p60.

6. Michael Lewis, *Armada Guns* (London 1961), p165.

that more guns could be brought to bear simultaneously, even though that meant that the guns were concentrated on the two sides of increasingly long and unmanoeuvrable ships. The construction of over-sized prestige ships which were incapable of turning easily to present their ordnance in succession, may have encouraged this development, and made possible, because of their larger size, the practice of allowing the guns to recoil inboard on firing so that they could be reloaded without turning away from the enemy. The fast frigates which were built during the English Civil War were relatively long for their beam and may also have had to depend on using their guns in broadside because of difficulty in turning. The size of ships continued to grow. A First Rate of 1677 was measured at 1540 tons, one of 1745 was measured at 1960 tons, and the *Royal George* launched in 1827 was measured at 2616 tons. This had less of an impact on the numbers of guns which could be carried than on the

The Battle of the Gabbard, 2 June 1653, probably the first occasion on which recognisable line of battle tactics were applied; if so, it provided the English with a significant advantage that translated into a clear victory. (NMM)

weight of shot which could be fired. The predominant English weapon at the time of the Armada battle in 1588, the culverin, fired a 17pdr ball. In 1755 a typical English First Rate line of battle ship was armed with 100 smooth bore cannon, ranging from 42pdrs on the lowest of its three gun decks, to 24pdrs and 12pdrs on its middle and upper decks, throwing a broadside weight of 2406lbs of solid iron shot.[7]

The line of battle

In order to employ this new broadside armament to maximum effect, new line of battle tactics were developed. Sometime during the Anglo-Dutch wars in the mid-seventeenth century, and certainly by the time of the Third Anglo-Dutch War, the line of battle was introduced into the English and Dutch fleets to bring annihilating fire against a decisive part of the enemy fleet, while the remainder was prevented from interfering. The vulnerable ends of each ship were protected by the ships next ahead and astern, and ships deployed in line ahead did not mask each other's fire. The French also adopted line tactics, not as a direct

result of tactical experience, but as part of Colbert's expansion of the French navy, under the influence of the mathematicians and scientists who were playing such an important part in French naval development as a whole.

The line of battle, however, created problems at the same time as it solved others. Line of battle tactics complicated the admiral's task of bringing his ships, with their broadside batteries, into action as rapidly as possible while exposing them to as little hostile fire as possible. In the 1780s Sir Charles Douglas successfully introduced gun-training tackles into the ships of the line he commanded so that their arc of fire was increased to 45 degrees each side of the beam, but up to that time battleships could only fire roughly at right angles to their line of advance, and even Douglas's innovations only served to reduce, not eliminate, the tactical problems. Consequently, tactical systems focused on the problem of the approach. Because the line of battle possessed both offensive and defensive value, its employment in action called for all the skills of the

7. *Ibid*, p31, and Brian Lavery, *The Ship of the Line* (London 1983), pp158–192.

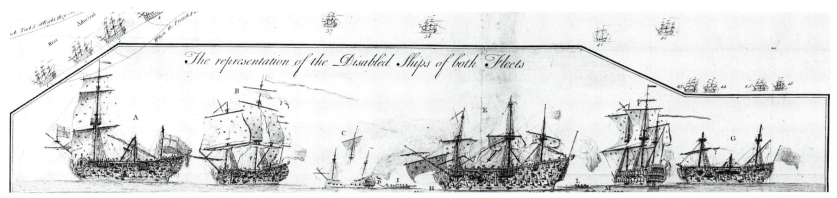

A detail from a contemporary print of the Battle of Toulon, 1744, showing the degree of damage sustained by ships of the line in a fleet engagement. (NMM)

A passing battle with fleets on opposite tacks rarely achieved decisive results.

admiral, and an ever increasing sophistication of technique.

The admiral could deploy his fleet end-on against the enemy's line, approaching each other like trains on parallel tracks so that the enemy was equally prevented from firing its batteries. This approach, however, ensured that the ships would pass each other at too great a speed for them to be able to disable or capture their enemy. Decisive results were the

Methods of approach to battle.

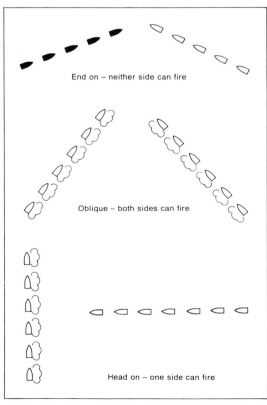

product of individual ships overwhelming their opposite so that its rate of fire slackened, and the damage inflicted became increasingly one-sided. This was unlikely to be effected in a passing action, or if the range was too long. Contemporary accounts speak of fighting at musket shot range, or even pistol shot, but these are elastic terms. Decisive action was probably possible at distances of up to 150yds, but in really close engagements ships might lie so close that they actually touched their enemies. Admirals' fighting instructions repeatedly cautioned captains not to open fire too soon, or until signalled to do so.

The English tended to favour an oblique approach on the same tack as the enemy so that ships could begin firing on part of the enemy line even if they had to shift targets as they advanced, but this approach was often ineffectual, especially if a ship or ships in the van (the head of the line) should be seriously disabled and so throw the whole approach into confusion. If a ship were damaged aloft it might well swing around broadside to the enemy, blocking the line of advance, and be forced to open fire at long range in self-defence. This could expose the lead ships, and prevent the rest of the attacking fleet getting nearer as they would mask each other's fire.

A bold head-on charge at the enemy line as at the battle of Trafalgar could be used to reduce the time exposed to long range enemy fire, but Vice-Admiral Nelson only attempted this very risky manoeuvre because he recognised that the French Revolution had undermined the technical ability of the French fleet.

Annihilating force

Having succeeded in his direct approach, Nelson's fleet prevailed at Trafalgar because the gunnery of the British ships was more efficient than that of their enemy. The British tended to favour three-decked ships, in part because of their heavier timbers which provided better protection in close action. It was

widely believed in the British fleet that the best way to obtain decisive results was to bring about a melée at close range where the advantage would rest with the fleet having the most effective gunnery and the best formed line from which to apply it. There is some truth in the belief that the British preferred to aim at the hulls of their enemy, while the French preferred to aim at the rigging. The hull was more difficult to hit but was the more decisive target. Alternative depressing and elevating of the guns, fired with reduced charges so as to cause the maximum amount of splintering in the enemy ship, could break up the hull and cause so many casualties that the enemy would soon lose the ability to resist. Battle damage and battle casualties were often disproportionate. In the Battle of the First of June (1794) the number of French killed in the six ships captured was more than three times that of the total killed in the whole British fleet.

If there was much of a sea running, however, it could be difficult to time the firing of the guns. It would be necessary to fire when the ship was on the right point of the roll, at which instant the enemy's hull might be obscured by a wave. The French generally fired on the upward roll of their own ship so as not to have shot fall into the sea, and this inevitably ensured that they would inflict a great deal of damage to the rigging. There were ways of reinforcing the rigging, but ultimately everything was vulnerable. Rigging and sails could be cut with bar or chain shot, and sometimes a mast could be cut through and felled, bringing down with it a mass of sails which might block some of the gunports. Damage to an enemy's rigging could facilitate a tactical withdrawal if the strategic situation called for that, or, if the enemy had the windward position, it could lead to individual ships drifting down to where they could be captured.

Based on the work of the French tactician Paul Hoste, this British work of 1762 by Christopher O'Bryan demonstrates the ease with which a superior fleet, when to windward, could detach ships to double the enemy's rear. (NMM)

Breaking the line, as attempted by Lord Howe during the Battle of the Glorious First of June, 1794.

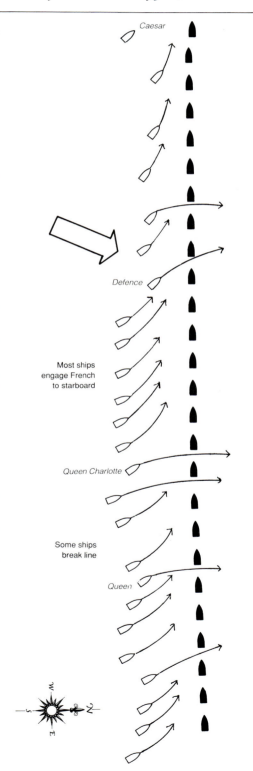

The self-confidence implicit in the British preference for close action and the melée was indeed an important element in battle, but generally admirals sought to retain greater tactical control so as to avoid the greatest risks, and to be able to take advantage of opportunities. Steadiness on the gundeck, and rapidity of fire, might ultimately be decisive in battle, but fleet tactics were necessary to ensure that the firepower was delivered with maximum effectiveness. In order to bring about a massive concentration of fire, without losing tactical control, admirals resorted to manoeuvring during the approach with the objective of using whatever ships they might be able to spare from the defensive requirements of the line to harass the van or rear of the weaker fleet. Ideally the extra ships could work around to the disengaged side of the enemy and put them between two fires, a manoeuvre known as doubling. The enemy would be forced to engage with both broadsides at once, which was a difficult task requiring high efficiency and morale (and ships did not have enough crew to man both broadsides completely at the same time). The doubling ships, on the other hand, had to be careful not to hit each other when firing at the enemy ships sandwiched between them.

A more sophisticated form of attack was to concentrate the bulk of the fleet against part of the enemy's line, leaving the remainder practically disengaged. The restricted arc of fire of broadside guns made this quite possible. As John Clerk of Eldin showed in *An Essay on*

Naval Tactics of 1782, ships in line ahead a cable apart could only fire on the same target if the enemy were over 720yds away, at which range the impact of broadsides was greatly reduced because of the spread of shot and dissipation of kinetic energy. Ships equipped with Douglas's gear for training guns were less restricted in their ability to support each other, but the principle was unaffected. Ships left unengaged could not swing themselves into position from which to open fire, because that risked upsetting the forward movement of their own line of battle. The best results seemed to be offered by massing ships against the enemy's rear. Much depended, however, on the extent to which the attackers could get into sufficiently close order to bring their superior weight of fire to bear and yet avoid obstructing each other. The defensive equivalent of this tactic was for the weaker fleet to space out their ships so as to leave some of the enemy ships without any target to fire at.

Still more sophisticated and ambitious was the manoeuvre of breaking the enemy's line. In theory this form of attack had many possible variations. It could be executed from windward or leeward, by all or part of the fleet, and at any point in the enemy's line. Lord Howe's special variation which he actually attempted at the battle of the Glorious First of June with some measure of success, was for his whole fleet to cut through the gaps between all the enemy ships. In doing so they could rake the bows and stern of the ships on either side of them as they passed through. The fleet which deployed its ships through the enemy line was, of course, also breaking up its own line of battle, so the success of this tactic depended on the morale and gunnery of the fleet undertaking it being equal to its boldness.

Forces

In order to carry out battle manoeuvres effectively it was necessary that the order of ships in the line of battle be such that units were not over-matched by the enemy opposite them. The division of fleets into squadrons was necessary to ensure effective control, and pre-dated the employment of line tactics. Admirals had to be provided with larger units, to accommodate them and their staffs, to support their authority, and because the oldest tactical idea was that admirals fought each other, supported by their subordinates. Heavy ships were stationed immediately fore and aft of each admiral to second him. Because it was necessary that the admirals place themselves in the line where they could be seen, usually at the centre, it was also necessary when drawing up a line of battle to provide large ships at the ends of each squadron, and especially at the ends of the fleet. These might have to take a heavy pounding without support, and leadership would be required of their commanders, who would inevitably be more senior officers. As the system was refined late in the eighteenth century, it was necessary to provide for the needs of the squadron deployed to cut or double the enemy. In the American War of Independence those British ships which had been coppered to retard marine growth were formed together into a fast squadron.

No battlefleet could be composed entirely of the largest class of ship, the cost of which was very much higher than that of smaller units. The masts and timbers of the largest ships were hard to obtain, and therefore expensive, and each one required larger crews, and more expensive dockyard arrangements. In 1764 a British First Rate ship cost £40,750 per year for service in the Channel, while a Third Rate 74-gun ship cost £30,688, and a 64 cost £24,396.[8] It was necessary to spread resources over a larger number of less capable ships so that the enemy would not have a numerical superiority which would enable them to overwhelm part of the line. Third and Fourth Rate ships which were easier to maintain were also required to provide ships for admirals on foreign stations. The French in particular made some use of the 74-gun ships because it was fast, and carried a good armament, although it was relatively expensive to build and maintain, in part because

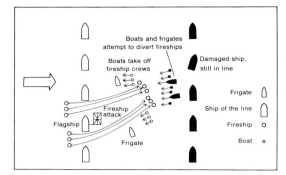

Typical tactics for the employemnt of, and defence against, fireships in the seventeenth century.

two-deckers of that length stressed badly in a seaway.

Fleets also needed small vessels, frigates and sloops, to extend their visual contact range, and to relay signals, as well as to carry out tasks like trade defence which did not require heavy units. In the sixteenth and seventeenth centuries fleets also made use of fireships, small vessels loaded with combustibles, which sheltered on the disengaged side of the line until the moment came for them to attempt to lay themselves alongside the enemy and set them on fire. The leeward fleet would need a flotilla of small craft to tow the fireships away before they made contact.

Manoeuvres

Tactics could not be based entirely on the capabilities of the smooth bore cannon, and its organisation into a broadside. The capacity of naval tactical systems to compensate for the limitations of naval armament was complicated by the limited tactical mobility of the ship of the line. At the beginning of the seventeenth century Sir Walter Raleigh had warned against the trend towards larger ships, writing that 'a ship of 600 tons will carry as good ordnance as a ship of 1200 tons, and where the greater hath double her ordnance, the less will turn her broadside twice where the great ship can wind once, and so no advantage in the overplus of guns'.[9] One of the reasons line tactics were adopted in the seventeenth century was that the new ships answered so badly to their helm that, in Boteler's words, 'being closed and shuffled up together, and being heavy and wieldly withal, [they] can never use save one, the same beaten side'.[10] Sailing performance was improved in the late seventeenth century by the addition of fore and aft sails on the stays, and braces on the yards, but it could never match the performance of the modern sailing yacht, let alone mechanically propelled ships.

At no time could an admiral make use of more than five-eighths of the sea around him because his fleet could not sail directly into the wind. Even when running before the wind it was generally best to go quartering to and fro, because when the wind was directly astern the aftermost sails blanketed the forward sails. These limitations, which of course applied equally to both sides, had to be used to gain an advantage. No admiral, however, could undertake new manoeuvres beyond the capability of his captains, who might not approve of innovations, and might not be skilled enough to carry them out, especially at the beginning of a war.

In 1690–91 Père Paul Hoste, a mathematician and protegé of Admiral Tourville, published *L'Art des Armées Navales* which described a series of tactical formations and the means of manoeuvring a fleet from one to another. French fleets were carefully drilled in such manoeuvres, which allowed French admirals to retain greater tactical control than was usually available to English admirals. Admiral Vernon complained in 1754 that English 'sea officers despise theory so much, and by trusting only to their genius at the instant they are to act, have neither time, nor foundation whereby to proceed on,' but believed that to be the lesser of evils. 'Where officers are determined to fight in great fleets,' he wrote, ''tis much of the least of the matter what order they fight in.'[11]

Sophistication in the 'order of sailing' of a fleet on patrol was as important as was the 'order of battle' because of the enormous difficulty that was experienced in bringing fleets into a line of battle, which might stretch beyond the horizon, ready to engage the enemy. Admiral Sir Charles Knowles the Elder remembered that before the Seven Years War, when a fleet left port in three squadrons, the second in command would always be given the place of honour on the commander-in-chief's starboard, and the captains in each squadron would be disposed alternately to starboard and port of their respective flagships in order of seniority 'without the least regard had to the station of each ship prescribed in the line of battle given out by the Commander-in-Chief'. Deployment into line of battle, with the vice-admiral leading the line when it was on the

8. Nicholas Tracy, *Navies, Deterrence and American Independence* (Vancouver 1988), p9.

9. Sir Walter Raleigh, *Works*, Vol 8, (London 1829), p627.

10. W G Perrin (ed), *op cit*, p256.

11. *An Enquiry into the Conduct of Captain Savage Mostyn* (1754).

A plate from Hoste's L'Art des Armées Navales, *showing what he called his third order of sailing, in which the flagship (A) was always at the apex of an oblique angle and to leewards whatever the point of sailing. (NMM)*

starboard tack, was incredibly confused.[12] The failure of the British fleet at the Battle of Toulon (1744) was largely the result of Admiral Mathews' failure to get his fleet into station on the previous evening. It took a long time for modern ideas of efficiency to prevail. The younger Sir Charles Henry Knowles published a set of *Fighting and Sailing Instructions* in 1780 in which he proposed a revolutionary order of sailing in parallel lines ahead with the admiral stationed two points on the weather bow of the leading ships. In 1790 Admiral Lord Howe employed a sailing order in three columns, and instructed his captains to keep their places in the column even when a change of tack transformed the place of honour into the rear of the line. All the same, the Battle of Trafalgar might have achieved even more spectacular results had Nelson been able to get the whole of his fleet into closer order without delaying his attack.

There were advantages to fighting from the windward position, especially for an admiral who was determined to seek tactical victory. The windward position tended to confer the choice of whether, when, and how to attack, and it had an effect on morale. Once they were engaged and taking damage aloft, individual

captains in the windward line would have difficulty hanging back. As a result, the manoeuvres preliminary to a battle were often concerned with keeping, gaining or disputing the windward position, or 'weather gage'. To maximise the difficulty of an enemy trying to work to the windward, the 'close-hauled' line ahead was adopted as the standard preliminary tactical formation. British fleets always steered seven points (78 degrees) from the wind when close-hauled, even though six points (67 degrees) was possible, so as to enable ships which had fallen to leeward to work up again to their station. Well-trained French fleets before the Revolution could manage six points off. Great responsibility rested on captains leading the fleet on either tack in line of battle ahead. Leading the line or lines and station keeping in general were especially important and especially difficult when the ships were in line of bearing, the so-called 'bow and quarter line', and en echelon from each other.

Not all the advantages lay with the windward position, as John Clerk of Eldin pointed out. It was easier for individual ships in the leeward line to withdraw should they be badly damaged, and

A diagram depicting the advantages and disadvantages of the weather gage.

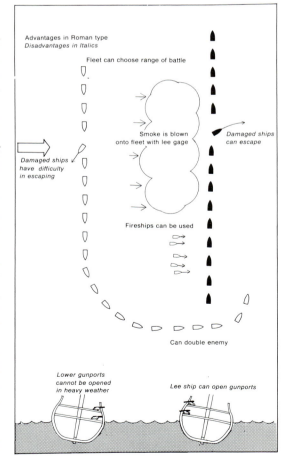

for the rest of the fleet to protect them, and possibly withdraw with them. For this reason the French, who subordinated the pursuit of tactical triumph to an overall strategy of survival, were less inclined to seek the weather position. In heavy weather, ships in the leeward line were more likely to be able to use their lower deck guns without risk, because the heel of the hull would bring them well clear of the sea. By the same measure, on the other hand, ships in the leeward position were rendered more vulnerable to being holed below the waterline.

When attacking a fleet already formed in line of battle, it was customary to make a slow and stately approach, with the lower courses furled. This enabled the attacking ships to maintain their alignment and not mask each other's fire by running too far ahead or accidentally steering across the line of approach of another ship. Even with a stiff breeze in their favour they might well be advancing at only about four knots. Hours and even days might be spent in trying to get into the desired order of battle before launching the attack.

Command and control

Limits were imposed on tactical innovation not only by the capabilities of guns, the sailing abilities of ships, and the skill of captains, but by the system of tactical control. Communication between ships at sea was so limited that admirals had to depend largely upon obtaining a common understanding with his captains before he met the enemy. This he did by drafting a collection of hypothetical instructions which he issued to his captains. Most articles of the instructions included a signal so that the admiral could indicate at sea when he wanted his captains to carry it out. This system of command depended upon the admiral having anticipated the particular circumstance. Inevitably the so-called 'fighting instructions', grew in length and complexity as successive admirals devised means of resolving the problems they encountered. In the British navy they constituted one chapter in what became the permanent *Sailing & Fighting Instructions for Her* [later *His*] *Majesty's Fleet.*

Standard methods of signalling had become established in the English, Dutch and French navies well before the end of the seventeenth century, and apart from developments in codes and techniques, they remained unchanged un-

12. Admiral Sir Charles Knowles, *Observations on Naval Tactics and on the claims of Mr Clerk* (London 1830), pp20–22.

A page from the Admiralty Day Signal Book for Ships of War, *1799, the first officially issued numerical code book.*

til after 1815. In port, in daytime, signals were made with guns and by moving sails. At sea flag signals were best for communicating with the fleet, guns being used to draw attention to the signal, but only in the eighteenth century was the system of employing frigates to relay signals developed. In the seventeenth century it was usually necessary in battle for orders to be sent through the fleet by boat. At night signals were made by fastening lanterns in the rigging, burning false fires, and firing sky rockets. Fog signalling was very limited in scope, and was made with guns, bells and muskets firing in distinct patterns, and always in the same direction.

Until the mid-eighteenth century, flag signals were encoded by the position in the rigging from which they were flown as well as by their colour and design. After the Seven Years War, which ended in 1762, the British navy developed under Lord Howe's leadership a numerical system employing two flags and a weft (a partially furled flag) which greatly increased the possible number of signals, and increased the speed of transmission. As early as 1776 when Howe commanded on the North American station he conceived the idea of separating signals and tactics, which greatly improved the speed of transmission and the accuracy with which signals could be read. In 1782 he applied his new system to the Channel Fleet, and in 1790 he gave the Royal Navy a true numerical system of signalling.

The final developments of British tactics and signalling in the age of sail, after the issue of the first official Admiralty Books of 1799, are gathered together in the Admiralty Signal Book of 1816. This incorporated Admiral Home Popham's *Telegraphic Signals or Marine Vocabulary* of 1803 which had finally made it possible, by means of three-flag hoists, to convey orders in the British navy which had not been thought of in time to be entered in the fighting instructions.

The French also continued to develop their tactical systems. In 1763 Admiral the Vicomte de Morogue produced in *Tactique Navale*, a work which sought to reduce tactics to formulae, and in 1776 Captain du Pavillon introduced a signalling system into d'Orvillier's fleet using grid tablature to allow two-flag hoists, flown where most easily seen, to convey hundreds of messages. The American War of Independence was the highest competitive point in French and British tactics. Beginning

Numeral Flags.	Figures represented	REMARKS.
	1	The flags are intended to represent the figures placed opposite to them in the annexed table. A flag hoisted alone, or under another flag, is to represent units; when two flags are hoisted, the upper flag is to represent tens; when three are hoisted, the uppermost is to represent hundreds, the next tens, and the lowest units.
	2	
	3	When the substitute flag is hoisted under other flags, it is to represent the same figure as the flag *immediately* above it: when the substitute pendant is hoisted under two flags, it is to represent the same figure as the upper flag of the two. For example, to represent the Nº 33, the substitute flag will be hoisted under the flag representing 3, and to represent the Nº 303 the cypher flag will be hoisted under the flag representing 3, and the substitute pendant under both.
	4	
	5	
	6	In blowing weather, or when much sail is set, as it may be inconvenient to hoist three flags at the same place, the two upper flags may be hoisted at one part of the ship, and the lowest flag, or the substitute pendant, at any other part.
	7	
	8	If the Admiral should have reason to believe that the enemy has got possession of these signals, he will make the signal for changing the figures of the flags, and when that has been answered by every ship, he will hoist the numeral flags, two or three at a time, the uppermost flag of those first hoisted is to represent 1; the next below it, 2; and so on till all the flags have been hoisted, the tenth flag representing the cypher, and the last being the substitute flag. To prevent mistakes, every ship is to hoist the same flags as the Admiral, and in the same order; the flag officers are to be particularly attentive to see this done, and to shew the distinguishing signal of any ship in which they observe a mistake. The figure which, by the new arrangement, each flag is to represent, is to be immediately entered in every ship's signal-book.
	9	
	0	
	Substitute	
	Substitute †	The flags are always to represent the figures placed opposite to them in the annexed table, in signals made in port, or to the signal posts on shore; or by ships meeting accidentally at sea. But an Admiral may make any other arrangement for the use of the fleet he commands, while at sea.

† Affirmative answer from private ships.

with the Vicomte de Grenier in 1777, the demand in the French navy for offensive tactics increased. As late as 1806, however, the French Navy rejected the proposed adoption of a numerical system of signalling, by a vote taken at each of the naval bases, and voted instead to continue using du Pavillon's tabular system, which they retained until after the end of the Napoleonic Wars.

Any tactical system is a product of all the technical and human limitations which affect both sides. Admirals were confronted by the limited abilities of their fleets, but were able to exploit the limited abilities of the enemy. Some

of the technical factors changed over time, as limitations in ship design, for instance, were reduced, or at any rate changed. Limitations in the human element, on the other hand, were more constant. Officers may have been trained to a higher degree of technical skill, which may have enabled the admiral to undertake more demanding manoeuvres, but this may have undermined the morale of simple men faced, as they saw it, with a straightforward task which had to be done. In the end, the employment tactics was more an art of the possible than a science.

Nicholas Tracy

Bibliography

Compiled by Robert Gardiner with the assistance of the contributors. The understanding of many aspects of the sailing warship has expanded enormously in this century, gaining particular momentum in the past twenty years. This has resulted primarily from work on documentary sources, but archaeology has also made a significant contribution. Nevertheless, there are still many dark areas: small craft in general have been studied in little depth, while major navies like those of the Netherlands and Portugal still lack a comprehensive technical history even in their own languages, let alone English. The list that follows aims to highlight the main gaps as well as directing readers to those works which will extend their knowledge beyond what can be gleaned from this book.

After a section of general works, the division of this bibliography follows the chapter order of the book. With a few specific exceptions, operational histories are confined to the Introduction.

GENERAL

Reliable fleet lists are surprisingly rare for the ships of this period and even where names and principal data are known there is rarely any sense of design history or rationale. For this reason many of the more general works discuss trends in development with little or no reference to specific ships. Studies of individual navies and the main ship-oriented journals are included in this section, although they are relevant to most other chapters as well.

ANON, *Der Geöffnette See-Hafen* (Hamburg 1705; reprinted 1989).
An early nautical dictionary covering a period for which there is little else available.

The American Neptune (Salem, MA 1941–).
The most prestigious US academic maritime journal, similar to the earlier *Mariner's Mirror* (*qv*). Quarterly.

R C ANDERSON, *Lists of Men of War 1650–1700: Part I English Ships*, Society for Nautical Research Occasional Publications No 5 (London 1935, revised edition 1966).
One of a series giving dimensions and basic data, arranged chronologically by launch date.

E H H ARCHIBALD, *The Wooden Fighting Ship in the Royal Navy* (London 1968).
Some useful material, though the text is superficial by present day standards; numerous, if rather crude, artist's impressions.

GERVASIO DE ARTIÑANO, *La Architectura Naval Española* (Madrid 1920).
A general history of Spanish shipbuilding; not comprehensive, but well produced for its time with numerous illustrations and some valuable data in the appendices.

HANS-CHRISTIAN BJERG and J ERICHSEN, *Danske Orlogskibbe 1690–1860*, 2 vols (Copenhagen 1980).
A large and well illustrated volume providing a general survey of Danish warship building; English language summary. Volume 2 is mainly devoted to ship decoration.

T R BLANCKLEY, *A Naval Expositor* (London 1750; reprinted Rotherfield 1988).
Contemporary dictionary, particularly useful by virtue of the fact that it was written earlier than its published date and so reflects a period on which little has been written; also valuable, if crudely drawn, illustrations.

H J BORJESON, P HOLCKE, H SZYMANSKI and W VOGEL, *Lists of Men of War 1650–1700: Part III Swedish/Danish-Norwegian/German Ships*, Society for Nautical Research Occasional Publications No 5 (London 1936, revised edition 1974).
One of a series giving dimensions and basic data, arranged chronologically by launch date.

D K BROWN, *Before the Ironclad: Development of Ship Design, Propulsion and Armament in the Royal Navy 1815–1860* (London 1990).
A major study by a naval architect, mainly concerned with the steam era but good on the technical improvements to the last sailing warships.

HOWARD I CHAPELLE, *The History of the American Sailing Navy* (New York 1949; numerous reprints).
The standard technical history of the ships illustrated with many plans; important work but devalued by lack of quoted sources and author's habit of reconstructing parts of the plans without careful attribution. Some additional material in his earlier *History of American Sailing Ships* (New York 1936) and later *Search for Speed under Sail* (New York 1967).

F H AF CHAPMAN, *Architectura Navalis Mercatoria* (Stockholm 1768; reprinted Rostock 1984).
Chapman's great work is much prized for its magnificent portfolio of ship drawings. Most of these are mercantile or of his own proposed designs but there are also a few draughts of actual warships (gleaned from years of foreign travel) up to frigate size. There have been a number of modern reprints but the edition quoted above is probably the most commonly available.

JOHN CHARNOCK, *History of Marine Architecture*, 3 vols (London 1800–2).
Rambling, opinionated and often wrong, Charnock is the source of many misconceptions about the sailing warship, but was much-quoted simply because his was the only general ship history available for so long. Does contain much based on original sources and contemporary prints.

PIERRE CLEMENT (ed), *Lettres, Instructions et Memoires de Colbert, Tome III/1: Marine et Galères* (Paris 1864).
A collection of documents relating to Colbert's administration of the French navy.

J J COLLEDGE, *Ships of the Royal Navy: An Historical Index*, 2 vols (Newton Abbot 1969; revised edition London 1989).
A dictionary-type listing of basic data; essential first stop but information per ship is very limited.

PIERRE LE CONTE, *Lists of Men of War 1650–1700: Part II French Ships*, Society for Nautical Research Occasional Publications No 5 (London 1935, reprinted 1975).
One of a series giving dimensions and basic data, arranged chronologically by launch date.

J DAVIS, *The Seaman's Speculum or Complete Schoolmaster* (London 1711; reprinted Bethesda, MA 1985).
A little known but useful early nautical dictionary.

CHARLES DERRICK, *Memoirs of the Rise and Progress of the Royal Navy* (London 1806).
Very useful statistics and ship lists; some of this material is reproduced as appendix matter in Archibald (*qv*).

WILLIAM FALCONER, *An Universal Dictionary of the Marine* (London, various editions 1769–1815).
Probably the most serviceable of contemporary encyclopaedias, Falconer covers a wide range of topics with more accuracy than many works of the period, which were prone to plagiarism. Both the earliest edition of 1769 and the much expanded 1815 edition (revised by William Burney) have been reprinted recently (Newton Abbot 1970 and London 1974, respectively).

JAN GLETE, 'Ship Lists as Source Materials (Locations)', *Warship* 45 (1988).
An invaluable article listing, navy by navy, sources for ship lists. with comments on their scope, reliability, etc.

GUSTAV HALLDIN (ed), *Svenskt Skeppsbyggeri* (Malmö 1963).
A general history of Swedish shipbuilding but covering sailing warships in some detail; well illustrated.

JOHN D HARBRON, *Trafalgar and the Spanish Navy* (London 1988).
A polemical work setting out to dispute the poor opinion of the Spanish navy underlying most English language histories; some technical detail and a valuable appendix (by C de Saint Hubert) listing Spanish ships of the line from 1714 to 1825.

D G HARRIS, *F H Chapman: The First Naval Architect and his Work* (London 1989).
A biography but with considerable attention paid to his innovative work on both large warships and Sweden's special inshore flotilla.

FRANK HOWARD, *Sailing Ships of War 1400–1860* (London 1979).

Concerned with general developments, the book concentrates on the kinds of details of interest to modelmakers; much useful data but poorly organised and lacking an index. Many good illustrations.

The International Journal of Nautical Archaeology (London 1972–   ).

A quarterly mostly given over to archaeology underwater but by no means confined to early periods; some relevant information published, particularly relating to the contents of warships rather than their structure.

BRIAN LAVERY, *Nelson's Navy: The Ships, Men and Organisation 1793–1815* (London 1989).

An encyclopaedic work containing sections, among others, on ship design and construction, armament and gunnery, seamanship and tactics; some analysis of other navies.

The Mariner's Mirror (London 1911–   ).

The quarterly journal of the Society for Nautical Research, the doyen of all publications devoted to the study of maritime antiquities. In recent years it has tended to concentrate on broader aspects of maritime history but many of its early volumes were much taken up with questions of ship development and many seminal papers were published.

Model Shipwright (London 1972–   ).

A quarterly devoted to top quality ship modelling but occasionally publishing articles of historical interest.

Nautical Research Journal (Washington, DC 1971–   ).

The quarterly journal of the Nautical Research Guild, who are mainly modelmakers; the journal reflects their interests but has published many research pieces.

Neptunia (Paris 1945–   ).

Published by the Friends of the French Maritime Museum, this is a well produced quarterly, which has published many fine pieces on ship history.

ADMIRAL E PARIS, *Souvenirs de Marine*, 6 vols (Paris 1882–1908; reprinted in 3 vols, Grenoble 1974–5).

A magnificent collection of plans and data relating to many ship types, nationalities and periods; naturally, strong on French material but with some Dutch, Spanish and Scandinavian naval interest. Based on contemporary plans and models for the most part and reasonably reliable back to the late seventeenth century. A number of modern reprints have been issued but that quoted above, with large format pages, is probably the most satisfactory.

ENRIQUE MANERA REGUEYRA, *et al, El Buque en la Armada Española* (Madrid 1981).

A general book on Spanish warships with some good illustrations and a fleet list (although the latter is far from complete or entirely reliable).

J H RÖDING, *Allgemeines Wörterbuch der Marine* (Hamburg 1793; reprinted Amsterdam 1969).

Comprehensive German language nautical dictionary.

JOHN SMITH, *The Seaman's Grammar* (London 1653 and later).

Although an expansion of a work originally written about 1620 this nautical dictionary represents practice around the beginning of the period under review. The earlier 1627 edition was reprinted London 1970).

ADMIRAL W H SMYTH, *The Sailor's Wordbook* (London 1867; reprinted 1991).

A late contribution to the genre of nautical dictionaries whose value lies in its comprehensiveness and the sly wit of the definitions.

G A SYMCOX, *The Crisis of French Sea Power 1688–97* (The Hague 1974).

Some material on the neglected topic of French shipbuilding during this period.

JACQUES VICHOT, *Repertoire des Navires de Guerre Français* (Paris 1967).

A French equivalent of Colledge (*qv*), but with little detail and an inability to differentiate between genuine warships, privateers and even East Indiamen.

PATRICK VILLIERS, *La Marine de Louis XVI, Vol I: Vaisseaux et Frégates de Choiseul à Sartine* (Grenoble 1983).

A boxed set of plans of French ships of the period with background notes on the naval administration and design; other volumes were planned but it seems that they were never published.

A VREUGDENHIL, *Lists of Men of War 1650–1700: Part IV Ships of the United Netherlands*, Society for Nautical Research Occasional Publications No 5 (London 1938, revised edition 1966).

One of a series giving dimensions and basic data, arranged chronologically by launch date.

INTRODUCTION

MARTINE ACERRA and JEAN MEYER, *Marines et Revolution* (Paris 1988).

A stimulating account of the effects of the Revolution on the French navy.

R C ANDERSON, *Naval Wars in the Baltic during the Sailing Ship Epoch, 1522–1850* (London 1910; reprinted 1969).

——, *Naval Wars in the Levant 1559–1853* (Liverpool 1952).

Both books give very detailed accounts of neglected areas of conflict, but without much political background.

SIR W LAIRD CLOWES, *et al, The Royal Navy. A History from the Earliest Times to the Present*, 7 vols (London 1897–1903; reprinted New York 1966).

This compilation work is still the standard history of the Royal Navy's principal activities, although it is thin on administrative and political background.

SIR JULIAN CORBETT, *Some Principles of Maritime Strategy* (London 1911; reprinted 1972).

Covers many aspects of the theory and practice of naval warfare.

——, *England in the Seven Years War*, 2 vols, (London 1907).

Deals with military as well as naval operations on the level of grand strategy.

WILLIAM JAMES, *The Naval History of Great Britain, 1793–1820*, 6 vols, (3rd edition London 1837; many later editions).

A very detailed and accurate chronicle, but short on historical and strategic perspective. Originally published in 5 vols in 1822–4, the expanded 3rd edition was the basis of most later editions.

P M KENNEDY, *The Rise and Fall of the Great Powers* (London 1988).

A modern account, giving an overall picture, and a counterbalance to the navalism of Mahan, below.

PIERS MACKESY, *The War for America* (London 1964).

Deals mainly with the overall strategy and diplomacy of the war, but naval strategy plays a big part in this.

A T MAHAN, *The Influence of Sea Power upon History, 1660–1783* (London 1890; reprinted 1965).

A classic work intended to argue the vital importance of sea power, but also giving a good 'blow-by-blow' account of Britain's naval conflicts.

——, *The Influence of Sea Power on the French Revolution and Empire, 1793–1812*, 2 vols (London 1892).

Essentially a continuation of the above, with slightly more detail.

HELMUT PEMSEL, *Atlas of Naval Warfare*, (London 1977).

A valuable concept, but not really detailed or reliable enough.

SIR HERBERT RICHMOND, *The Navy in the War of 1739–48*, 3 vols (Cambridge 1920).

Detailed and useful study of a war which set the pattern for much of the eighteenth century.

C G M B DE LA RONCIÈRE, *et al, Histoire de la Marine Français*, 6 vols (Paris 1899–1932).

The French navy lacks an objective modern study of its history and this is still the best available, although out of date in many respects.

THE LINE OF BATTLE SHIP

ANON, *American Ships of the Line* (Annapolis, MD 1970).

Includes a detailed listing, with the careers of each.

JEAN BOUDRIOT, *The Seventy-Four Gun Ship*, 4 vols (Paris 1986–8).

Both more and less than its title suggests, this phenomenally detailed work describes every aspect of the design, construction and service of a typical French 74 of about 1780; it includes much about administrative aspects of the French navy as well, but does not give any sort of design history of the 74 as such. Superbly illustrated by the author's own hand, it is as definitive a work of its type as will ever exist. Translated from an earlier French edition.

A BUGLER, *HMS Victory: Building, Restoration and Repair* (London 1967).

A detailed report on the work that restored the ship to her Trafalgar appearance. A revised edition is in prospect.

FRANK FOX, *Great Ships: The Battlefleet of Charles II* (London 1980).

A surprisingly detailed appraisal of the battleships of the period, with some reference to smaller craft and other navies; beautifully illustrated with contemporary drawings and paintings, especially the work of the incomparable van de Veldes.

C H HANCOCK, *La Couronne, A French Warship of the Seventeenth Century: A Survey of Ancient and Modern Accounts of this Ship* (Newport News, VA 1973).

A summary of the conflicting information about this influential early seventeenth-century ship.

ANDREW LAMBERT, *The Last Sailing Battlefleet: Maintaining Naval Mastery 1815–1850* (London 1991).

An integrated study of politics, economics and ship design that is mainly concerned with the rationale for the battlefleet, but throws much new light on many aspects of the Royal Navy's ship procurement after Waterloo.

BRIAN LAVERY, *The Ship of the Line*, 2 vols (London 1983).

The definitive work on British line of battle ships, the first volume is devoted to historical development 1650–1850 and includes a very detailed listing of all ships by class, with design notes; Vol 2 covers general technicalities like design, construction, rigging, armament etc.

——, *The 74-Gun Ship Bellona* (London 1985).
An 'Anatomy of the Ship' volume devoted to the archetypal line of battleship of the later eighteenth century analysed in depth with the aid of many drawings.

——, *The Royal Navy's First Invincible* (Portsmouth 1988).
Partly a report on the excavation work on the wreck, the book also covers the important period in which the 74-gun ship was developed in France and imported into Britain.

JOHN McKAY, *The 100-Gun Ship Victory* (London 1987).
Nelson's famous flagship given the 'Anatomy of the Ship' treatment utilising many drawings.

THE FRIGATE

Many of the titles already quoted in the general section of this bibliography are applicable to this chapter, but the following additional works are particularly relevant.

JEAN BOUDRIOT, 'Les Frégates la *Flore*', *Neptunia* 109 (1973), pp37–48.
Contains a brief history of French cruiser design by France's leading expert on the sailing warship.

——, 'Des Vaisseaux de 50 Canons aux Frégates de 1er Rang', *Neptunia* 167 (1987), pp37–44.
The replacement of the 50-gun ship by the big frigate in the French navy.

——, 'L'Egyptienne' *Neptunia* 175 (1989), pp10–16.
The 24pdr armed frigate and its history in the French navy.

——, 'La Frégate dans la Marine Royale, 1660–1750: La Frégate Légère', *Neptunia* 181 (1991).
A brief account, with fleet list, of the lightest frigates of the French navy.

JEAN BOUDRIOT and H BERTI, *La Belle-Poule – Le Coureur* (Paris 1985).
Primarily an elaborate monograph with modelmakers' plans, but the first part, on the *Belle Poule* of 1769, includes a good history of the 12pdr armed frigate in the French navy.

——, *La Venus 1782* (Paris nd, but c1988).
As above, but with history of the 18pdr frigate in considerable detail.

ROBERT GARDINER, 'The First English Frigates', *The Mariner's Mirror* 61 (1975), pp163–172.
Discusses the circumstances of the introduction of the 28-gun Sixth Rate into the Royal Navy.

——, 'The Frigate Designs of 1755–57', *The Mariner's Mirror* 63 (1977), pp51–70.
An analysis of the complex origins of the first 12pdr frigates in the Royal Navy.

——, 'Les Frégates français et la Royal Navy', *Le Petit Perroquet* 21 (1977), pp4–25; 24 (1978), pp4–28.
A comparison of English and French design and construction philosophies as reflections of differing tactical and strategic considerations.

——, 'Frigate Design in the 18th Century', *Warship* III (1979), pp2–12, pp80–92 and pp269–277.
A development of the ideas advanced in the above, but with less technical data and more considered conclusions.

JAN GLETE, 'Sails and oars: Warships and Navies in the Baltic during the 18th century (1700–1815)', in *Les Marines de Guerre Européennes XVII–XVIIIe siècles*, MARTINE ACERRA, JOSÉ MERINO AND JEAN MEYER (eds), (Paris 1985), pp369–401.
Useful summary of Danish, Swedish and Russian naval activity with tables of fleet strengths and ship types.

PETER GOODWIN, *The 20-Gun Ship Blandford* (London 1988).
In the 'Anatomy of the Ship' series, a detailed monograph based largely on drawings. This volume covers the British Sixth Rates of the 1719 Establishment.

JOHN McKAY, *The 24-Gun Frigate Pandora* (London 1991).
An 'Anatomy of the Ship' volume covering one of the small 'post ships' of the late eighteenth century; the smallest type to be regarded as a frigate.

PORTIA TAKAKJIAN, *The 32-Gun Frigate Essex* (London 1990).
The American frigate of 1799 given the usual detailed 'Anatomy of the Ship' approach.

DAVID WHITE, *The Frigate Diana* (London 1987).
An 'Anatomy of the Ship' volume detailing a British 38-gun *Artois* class vessel of 1794.

SLOOP OF WAR, CORVETTE AND BRIG

There are few works specifically devoted to sloops and brigs, and certainly no definitive history, so the interested reader must pick up snippets of information from many and varied sources. Howard Chapelle's *American Sailing Navy*, already listed, makes more than passing reference to small craft design in other navies as do his other books *American Sailing Ships* and *The Search for Speed Under Sail*, although many of his judgements are compromised by his failure to quote any sources. The titles listed below will be useful for particular aspects of the history of square rigged naval small craft.

R C ANDERSON, 'The Rig of the Pepysian Sloops', *The Mariner's Mirror* IX (1923), p214ff.
Many of the early issues of this journal of the Society for Nautical Research were concerned with establishing a clear chronology for sailing rigs and types; this article provided some incontrovertible evidence for the sloops of the 1660s. Other useful notes by Anderson can be found in Vols VIII (pp109–16) and XX (p371) on brigantines.

WILLIAM A BAKER, *Colonial Vessels: Some Seventeenth-Century Ship Designs* (Barre, MA 1962).
Mostly concerned with American colonial period small merchantmen, but useful on ketches and other contemporary rigs.

——, *Sloops and Shallops* (Barre, MA 1966).
Further thoughts on colonial types, but much of relevance to naval sloops.

——, *The Mayflower and Other Colonial Vessels* (London 1983).
A posthumous work updating ideas published in earlier books, so a valuable coda to the above.

JEAN BOUDRIOT, 'Les Barques Longues', *Neptunia* 117 (1975), pp12–16.
The origins of the corvette in the French navy, with visual evidence for their appearance.

JEAN BOUDRIOT and H BERTI, *Le Cygne* (Paris nd, but c1987).
A monograph on a 'brick de 24' of 1806, but including a brief history of the brig in French service, with fleet lists.

——, *La Creole* (Paris 1990).
Another monograph, devoted to a corvette of 1827, but including a history of the type from the earliest days.

JOHN FINCHAM, *A History of Naval Architecture* (London 1851, reprinted 1979).
Early sections are a rehash of published sources, but good detail on the sailing trials of 1820–45; his own designs were involved so he is not entirely objective.

L G CARR LAUGHTON, 'HM Brigantine *Dispatch*, 1692–1712', *The Mariner's Mirror* VII (1921), pp354–9.
Details of the Williamite brigantines gleaned from a reading of the log of one of the longest lived.

SIR ALAN MOORE, 'Rig in Northern Europe', *The Mariner's Mirror* 42 (1956), pp6–37.
A succinct summary of rig development, tackling some of the problems associated with small naval craft, particularly in the 1660–1720 period. His book *Last Days of Mast and Sail* (Oxford 1925, reprinted 1970) also has a small amount that is relevant.

E W PETREJUS, *Modelling the Brig-of-War 'Irene'* (Hengelo, Netherlands 1970).
Although ostensibly a modelmaking manual using a captured British *Cruizer* class brig as its subject, in fact the book covers much history as well as details of the ship itself.

W H SHOULDER, 'An English Ketch-Rigged Sloop', *Model Shipwright* 3–8 (1973–74).
A series devoted to a model of a *Speedwell* class sloop of 1752 but some background included.

FORE AND AFT RIGGED WARSHIPS

These vessels have received some attention in print but with a few American and French exceptions their specifically naval applications remain to be studied.

JEAN BOUDRIOT, 'Identification of Lateen-Rigged Craft: Barque, Polacre, Pinque', *Nautical Research Journal* 25 (1979).

——, 'The Chasse-Marée and the Lugger', *Nautical Research Journal* 26 (1980).
Two useful articles on neglected topics.

——, *The Cutter Le Cerf* (Paris (1982).
Details of this short-lived vessel (1779-80) combined with a history of the cutter in French naval service.

——, *Lougre Le Coureur* (Paris 1985).
The same detailed monograph approach as above applied to naval luggers; jointly bound with the monograph on the frigate *Belle Poule*.

——, *Schooner La Jacinthe* (Paris nd, but c1988).
A vessel of 1825 treated as the centrepiece of a study of French naval schooners.

——, *Xebec Le Requin* (Paris 1991).

Includes a broad survey of Mediterranean types as well as concentrating on this vessel from 1750.

W V Cannenburg, *Beschrijvende Catalogus der Scheepsmodellen en Scheepsbouwkundigen 1600–1900* (Amsterdam 1943).

The catalogue of ship models, plans and related material in the Dutch maritime museum; of general relevance but given the importance of the Dutch contribution to fore and aft development, probably more applicable to this section than any other.

Howard I Chapelle, *The Baltimore Clipper* (New York 1931; reprinted 1968).

One of Chapelle's earliest works, devoted to the development of sharp-lined schooners; also useful material in later works like *American Sailing Navy* and *Search for Speed under Sail* (see General section above).

G C E Crone, *De Jachten der Oranges* (Amsterdam 1937).

Information on the early history of the yacht in the Netherlands.

Harold M Hahn, *The Colonial Schooner 1763–1775* (London 1981).

Partly devoted to modelmaking but also covering the history of the first generation of Royal Navy schooners, employed in North America.

E Keble Chatterton, *Fore and Aft Craft: The Story of the Fore and Aft Rig* (London 1927).

A good general survey in its day but now superseded in many details.

I H King, *The Coast Guard under Sail: The US Revenue Cutter Service 1789–1865* (Annapolis 1989).

A general history of the present US Coast Guard's forebears but containing some material on the vessels they employed.

Karl Heinz Marquardt, *Schoner in Nord und Süd* (Rostock and Bielefeld 1989).

A well illustrated history of the schooner, with much technical detail aimed at modelmakers, and full plans of selected vessels, both naval and mercantile. An English edition is in prospect.

——, 'The Origin of Schooners', *The Great Circle* 10 (1/1988).

Some thoughts on the early history of the rig.

E P Morris, *The Fore and Aft Rig in America* (New Haven, CT 1927; reprinted London 1974).

Now outdated but for its day a good survey of American developments.

W F Ryan, 'Peter the Great's English Yacht', *The Mariner's Mirror* 69 (1983), pp65–87.

An influential article that first proposed the *Royal Transport* as the prototype naval schooner.

Graham Smith, *King's Cutters* (London 1983).

A general history of the British revenue services but with much incidental detail on the development of cutters.

The fireship and bomb vessel

A truly neglected area of ship development, neither fireships nor bomb vessels have attracted much interest among historians. Some insight into fireship tactics can be obtained from Brian Tunstall's *Naval Warfare in the Age of Sail* (full reference under Tactics below) but there is little on their technical characteristics (even the prolific Boudriot has not devoted a monograph to them). Bomb vessels are only marginally better understood; what there is in print is listed below.

Jean Boudriot, *Bomb Ketch La Salamandre* (Paris 1991).

An excellent survey of bomb vessels in the French service, with many drawings of the workings of the mortars and the mode of employing bombs.

——, 'L'Artillerie de Mer Français de 1674 à 1856', *Neptunia* 97–99 (1970).

Three articles in this series on naval guns devoted to mortars and bomb vessels; largely superseded by the above but still useful.

Peter Goodwin, *The Bomb Vessel Granado 1742* (London 1989).

An 'Anatomy of the Ship' volume devoted to one of the best documented British bomb ketches.

Bob Lightley, 'Granado', *Model Shipwright* 16–19 (1976–7).

A very detailed description of building the award-winning model in the National Maritime Museum at Greenwich, necessarily dealing with many aspects of bomb vessel practice.

John Winton, *Below the Belt* (London 1981).

A general survey of 'novelty, subterfuge and surprise' in naval warfare but containing descriptions of fireships and explosion vessels in action.

David Wray, 'Bomb Vessels: Their Development and Use', *Model Shipwright* 19, 25–27 (1977, 1978–9).

The most detailed account to date of English bomb vessels, their development and the techniques of employing them; some reference to other navies.

The oared fighting ship

The literature relating to oared warships in the period 1650–1840 is very uneven, with a strong emphasis on the French galley fleet in the age of Louis XIV and the Swedish archipelago fleet in the latter half of the eighteenth century. There is practically nothing about Spanish, Italian or Ottoman oared vessels and the huge Russian oared fleet is mainly known from a historical ship list (in itself admirable). There is an obvious need for more systematic and comparative studies on the subject.

This chapter is mainly based on the author's forthcoming study *Nations and Navies: Warships, Navies and State Building in Europe and America, 1500–1860*, a book which in no way provides the systematic study needed. Some results from that study were published in 'Sails and Oars: Warships and Navies in the Baltic during the 18th Century (1700–1815)', in Martine Acerra *et al*, *Les marines de guerre européennes XVII–XVIIIe siècles* (Paris 1985). In the absence of published studies about eighteenth-century Mediterranean galley fleets the author found the reports about them by contemporary Swedish officers and shipbuilders to be valuable. One of the most important of these reports is summarised by R C Anderson in 'Mediterranean Galley-Fleets in 1725', *The Mariner's Mirror* 42 (1956), pp179–187. Another, a report from 1749, with detailed information about dimensions is in Kungliga Biblioteket, Stockholm, Manuscript X 827.

Books and articles of value to this subject are as follows:

R C Anderson, *Oared Fighting Ships: From Classical Times to the Coming of Steam* (London 1962, 1976).

A broad and systematic survey of the available evidence, although by necessity very brief.

Paul W Bamford, *Fighting Ships and Prisons: The Mediterranean Galleys of France in the Age of Louis XIV* (Minneapolis 1973).

A scholarly study, mainly about why galleys were maintained and the condition for the oarsmen.

Lars Otto Berg, 'Svenska flottans fartyg 1808–1849, skärgårdsfartyg. En tabellarisk framställning', *Forum navale* 24 (1968), pp91–142.

A complete list of Swedish oared craft 1808–49, including auxiliaries.

René Burlet and André Zysberg, 'Le travail de la rame sur les galères de France vers la fin du XVIIe siècle', *Neptunia* 164 (1986), pp16–35 and 'La galère sous voile vers la fin du XVIIe siècle', *Chasse-marée* 29, pp32–51.

Two important articles about how French galleys were rowed and sailed.

Howard I Chapelle, *The American Sailing Navy* (full details in the General section above).

This book has a chapter about the early nineteenth-century American gunboat designs with drawings. Further information about the American gunboat navy can be found in two articles in *The American Neptune* 43 (1983): Spencer C Tucker, 'Mr Jefferson's gunboat navy' (pp135–141) and Frederick C Leiner, 'The "Whimsical Phylosophic President" and His Gunboats', (pp245–266).

Edouard Desbrière, *Projets et tentative de debarquement aux iles britanniques*, 4 vols (Paris 1900–02).

Primarily a source publication on the Boulogne flotilla and the plans for an invasion of England. A mine of information, although comparatively little about technical questions.

Jean Fennis, *Un manuel de construction des galères* (Amsterdam and Maarssen 1983).

A publication of important French documents about galley design.

Karl Gogg, *Österreichs Kriegsmarine, 1440–1848* (Salzburg 1972).

A list of Austrian oared craft, including the last Venetian galleys and gunboats transferred to Austria 1798.

Daniel G Harris, *F H Chapman* (full details in General section above).

Covers Chapman's designs of oared warships. Excellent illustrations, including several drawings never before published. The Appendix with warships built to Chapman's design is not complete, as several hundred unnamed gunboats and other light craft are excluded. Further information about Swedish oared craft by the same author in 'Admiral Frederic af Chapman's Auxiliary Vessels for the Swedish Inshore Fleet', *The Mariner's Mirror* 75 (1989), pp211–229.

Pierre Le Conte, *Lists of Men-of-War* (details in General section above).

Includes a list of French galleys although without details. The list must be regarded as preliminary as the source material poses several problems.

L Th Lehmann, *De galeien: Een bijdrage aan de kennis der zeegeschiedenis* (Amsterdam 1987).
A short study of galleys in general. Based on a broad survey of the literature and manuscript sources from several countries but not very systematic in its presentation.

Oscar Nikula, *Svenska skärgardsflottan, 1756–1791* (Helsingfors 1933).
A scholarly study of the Swedish archipelago fleet, including the development of technology and naval doctrine. Includes an appendix of its ships although incomplete (unnamed gunboats excluded) and not entirely correct.

F F Olesa Munido, *La galera en la navegación y el combate* (Madrid 1971).
A substantial work about Mediterranean galleys, although mainly about pre-1650 conditions.

Svenska flottans historia, Vols 2 and 3 (Malmö 1943–45).
The chapters about the technical development of oared craft (mainly by Gustaf Halldin) are valuable although far from definitive. Several drawings are reproduced.

Birger Thomsen, 'De Dansk-Norske Kanonbåde, 1780–1850', *Marinehistorisk Tidskrift* 3/1975, pp56–83 and 4/1977, pp98–115.
A concise technical history of the Danish gunboats with a complete list of such craft.

Feodor F Veselago, *Spisok russkich voennich sudov s 1668 po 1860* (St Petersburg 1872).
List of Russian warships 1668–1872. Still the best source available about Russian oared craft, although without illustrations.

Fleet support craft

There have been a number of fine studies of dockyard administration in recent years which add to the general understanding of naval infrastructure, but little on the ships involved. Howard Chapelle covers some US yard craft in *American Sailing Navy* (see General section above) but otherwise information is scattered through a number of works incidental to the subject.

F Abell, *Prisoners of War in Britain 1756–1815* (London 1914).
Deals mainly with social conditions afloat and ashore, but with some information on the hulks.

Daniel A Baugh, *British Naval Administration in the Age of Walpole* (Princeton, NJ 1965).
A pioneering study of naval administration with chapters on the dockyards and overseas bases.

A Currie, *Henley's of Wapping*, National Maritime Museum Monographs and Reports No 62 (London 1988).
A study of a typical company from which the Royal Navy hired vessels; comparatively little on the ships themselves, but concentrating on the organisation of the company and its trade.

G Doorman, 'Dredging', in *History of Technology*, C Singer (ed), 7 Vols, (London 1954–78), Vol 4, pp629–43.
Useful section on the history of dredging, a subject neglected elsewhere.

R J B Knight, *Portsmouth Dockyard Papers 1774–1783: The American War* (Portsmouth 1987).
A very useful collection of documents relating to most aspects of a large dockyard's work during one war.

B Lavery, *Nelson's Navy* (see General section above).
Contains sections on dockyards, prisoners of war, the transport service, etc.

C Lloyd and J L S Coulter, *Medicine and the Navy, Vol III: 1714–1815* (London 1961).
Includes a short section on hospital ships.

John McKay, *The Armed Transport Bounty* (London 1989).
An 'Anatomy of the Ship' volume devoted to Bligh's infamous command, a ship typical of hundreds of small merchant vessels taken up for naval employment.

Roger Morriss, *The Royal Dockyards during the Revolutionary and Napoleonic Wars* (Leicester 1983).
An excellent academic study of the workings of the dockyards during the period of their greatest trial.

J H Parry, *Trade and Dominion* (London 1971).
A general overview, but including a section on exploration.

D Syrett, *The Siege and Capture of Havana 1762*, Navy Records Society (London 1970).
Some documents on the transports used for the operation.

——, *Shipping in the American War: a Study of British Transport Organisation 1775–1783* (London 1970).
Important history of the operation of the Transport Service, including the surveying and hire of ships.

Design and construction

The level of understanding about these aspects of the sailing warship has improved significantly in recent years, largely driven by the ship modelmaking fraternity, which seeks to replicate in miniature every feature of the full size prototype with ever increasing accuracy and attention to detail. As a result of this market, all the most important contemporary naval architectural treatises have been reprinted and a number of modern studies have been devoted to the arcane details of draughting techniques and ship carpentry. As a general introduction to ship design, the early sections of Chapelle's *Search for Speed under Sail* (full reference under the General section above) are recommended, while for construction the relevant chapters of Jean Boudriot's *The Seventy-Four Gun Ship* (see The Line of Battle Ship section above) are among the best, but the latter deals only with French practice of a specific epoch. The following list is not exhaustive but is confined to the most accessible and those works on very specific topics not covered elsewhere.

W A Baker, 'Early Seventeenth-Century Ship Design', *The American Neptune* 14 (1954), pp262–77.
By the designer of the *Mayflower* replica who was America's leading expert on the ships of the colonial era; strictly speaking, too early for the period covered by this book but the article's description of the state of naval architecture might be stretched to about 1650.

J Dodds and J Moore, *Building the Wooden Fighting Ship* (London 1984).
Curiously old fashioned book, apparently unaware of the research of the last twenty years and so rather superficial by contemporary standards; partially redeemed by some good illustrations.

J Furttenbach, *Architectura Navalis* (Frankfurt 1629; reprinted Hamburg 1968).
One of the earliest printed treatises; contains much of value on seventeenth-century ships and shipbuilding.

Peter Goodwin, *The Construction and Fitting of the Sailing Man of War 1650–1850* (London 1987).
Very detailed in approach, with many technical sketches, but flawed by uneven handling of source material and a lack of proper historical perspective.

Brian Lavery (ed), *Deane's Doctrine of Naval Architecture 1670* (London 1981).
An edited version of the first full treatise in English on ship design, with supporting documentation from contemporary sources; more concerned with design than construction.

——, *Building the Wooden Walls: The Design and Construction of the 74-gun Ship Valiant* (London 1991).
A relatively general book following the life of a single ship from inception to service, it is a good starting point for those with little prior knowledge of the process.

C Nepean Longridge, *The Anatomy of Nelson's Ships* (London 1955).
Although it is essentially about making a model of the *Victory*, the first chapter is a good introduction to the full size shipbuilding techniques of the period.

Marmaduke Stalkartt, *Naval Architecture* (London 1781; second, 1787 edition, reprinted Rotherfield 1991).
One of the most spectacular treatises by virtue of its large and detailed plates (although not representing actual ships); the text is a practical disquisition on shipbuilding rather than a theoretical exposition of naval architecture, and Steel borrowed freely from it for his later work.

David Steel, *Elements and Practice of Naval Architecture* (London 1805; reprinted London 1977).
One of the best known, and most quoted, treatises, with a fine portfolio of drawings. Much of the material seems to have been pirated by Abraham Rees for the Marine volume of his *Cyclopaedia* of 1819–20 and this was reprinted as *Rees' Naval Architecture* (Newton Abbot 1970) in a far cheaper edition than the full facsimile of Steel's book itself.

William Sutherland, *The Ship-Builder's Assistant* (London 1711; reprinted Rotherfield 1989).
The only early eighteenth-century English writer on shipbuilding, Sutherland's works usefully fill a chronological gap.

David White, 'Understanding Ship's Draughts', *Model Shipwright* 46, 48, 50, 52, 54, 56 (1983–85).
A very detailed series on the nature and function of plans, the geometry of drawing them, and a short account of their historical development; principally confined to the Admiralty Collection and its conventions.

——, 'Traditional Wooden Shipbuilding', *Model Shipwright* 47, 49, 51, 53, 55, 57, 59, 61, 63 (1983–88).
Companion to the above, a series on shipbuilding at the detailed level of carpentry techniques and fastenings; essentially dealing with British, predominantly naval, practice.

Nicholaes Witsen, *Architectura Navalis et Regimen Nauticum* (Amsterdam 1671 and later; 1690 edition reprinted Netherlands c1970).
Allowing for the usual time lag between practice and publication at this time, the book probably represents Dutch shipbuilding in its golden age; the historical survey of ship development since Classical times is largely useless.

RIGS AND RIGGING

As for design and construction, most of the recent study of rigs and rigging has been for the benefit of modelmakers. Many original treatises have been reprinted, and for naval vessels at least, modern books have analysed the minutiae of rigging right down to cordage sizes and types of blocks. Some of the more important contemporary works are listed with the modern studies below, but as with all naval treatises of the time it is important to remember that they do not always represent official practice. Some of the naval architectural works quoted in the previous section, like Deane and Sutherland, also cover rigging.

R C ANDERSON, *The Rigging of Ships in the Days of the Spritsail Topmast 1600–1720* (Salem, MA 1927; reprinted London 1982).

One of the first modern analytical books on the subject and, unlike many later ones, international in outlook. Based on the author's unrivalled knowledge of contemporary models and manuscript sources. A reduced version, confined to English practice, was published as *Seventeenth-Century Rigging* in a paperback format (Hemel Hempstead 1955; reprinted frequently since).

JOHN FINCHAM, *Treatise on Masting Ships and Mastmaking* (London 1829 and later; final, 1854 edition reprinted London 1982).

A valuable work by a practising shipwright covering the masting of the enlarged ships of the post-1815 period; details on mastmaking and proportions of spars. Later editions also included reference to merchant ships and steamers.

R KIPPING, *Rudimentary Treatise on Masting, Mastmaking and Rigging of Ships* (Portsmouth 1853; many later editions).

Primarily relating to mercantile practice, but gives mast and spar dimensions for Royal Navy vessels towards the end of the era of pure sail.

JAMES LEES, *The Masting and Rigging of English Ships of War 1625–1860* (London 1979; second edition 1990).

A masterly survey by the man who conserved the incomparable collection of ship models at the National Maritime Museum at Greenwich; very detailed and well illustrated but confined to the three-masted ship rig. The second edition contains greatly expanded appendices of tabular data.

DANIEL LESCALLIER, *Traité Pratique du Gréement des Vaisseaux et Autres Bâtiments de Mer* (Paris 1791; reprinted Grenoble 1973).

The leading French work of the period, principally concerned with naval usage but with some reference to other craft; data not as detailed as Steel, but well illustrated.

KARL HEINZ MARQUARDT, *Eighteenth-Century Rigs and Rigging* (London 1992).

Combining the international scope of Anderson with the detail of Lees, this book is also valuable for covering smaller craft and a wide variety of rigs. Translated and expanded from the earlier German edition *Bemastung und Takelung von Schiffen des 18 Jahrhunderts* (Rostock and Bielefeld 1989).

C H ROMME, *Description de l'Art de la Mâture* (Paris 1778; reprinted Grenoble 1972).

French treatise on masting with dimensions for typical naval vessels and a few merchant ships; some fine engraved illustrations.

——, *L'Art de la Voilure* (Paris 1781; reprinted Grenoble 1972).

Companion to the above, dedicated to sails and sailing, including some rigging information and a glossary of terms.

DAVID STEEL, *The Elements of Rigging and Seamanship*, 2 vols (London 1794; reprinted London 1978).

The best known (probably because it is the most detailed) of contemporary works; covering both mercantile and naval practice, large ships and small, it ranged from mast making to seamanship, with very extensive tables of dimensions for virtually every item. It was eventually expanded to four separate volumes and an epitome of these, edited by Claude S Gill was published in London in 1932 as *Steel's Elements of Mastmaking, Sailmaking and Rigging* (itself reprinted in New York in c1970). A later edition of the rigging volume was reprinted in Brighton in 1974 as *Steel's Art of Rigging 1818* and there have been other reprints of parts of the opus.

C F STEINHAUS, *Die Schiffbaukunst in Ihrem ganzen Umfang & Die Construction und Bemastung der Segelschiffe* (Hamburg 1858, 1869; both editions reprinted together Kassel 1977).

A late German treatise on shipbuilding, of relevance to our period primarily in its masting and rigging aspects.

FITTINGS

Many of the more general books on ships cover fittings in some detail, particularly those of Jean Boudriot and the second volume of Brian Lavery's *Ship of the Line*. Numerous issues of *Model Shipwright* and the *Nautical Research Guild Journal* have published articles on particular fittings, but the few references listed below are the only works giving any kind of overview.

ROBERT GARDINER, 'Fittings for Wooden Warships', *Model Shipwright* 17, 19 (1976–77).

The first part is a general introduction dealing with some little known areas like ventilators; the second part is devoted to boats and adds some material to the work of W E May (*qv*).

BRIAN LAVERY, *The Arming and Fitting of English Ships of War 1600–1815* (London 1987).

The most comprehensive work available, covering steering gear, ground tackle, underwater protection, pumps, internal fittings, accommodation and boats. A coherent history of development rather than a compilation of statistics; its only drawback is its end-date of 1815, so that innovations of the last decades of naval sail are not addressed.

W E MAY, *The Boats of Men of War*, National Maritime Museum Monographs and reports No 15 (London 1974).

A short but fact-filled history of British naval boats down to the steam era. Includes data on numbers and types carried by various classes.

GUNS AND GUNNERY

Contemporary treatises, although often quoted, need to be used with care since they do not always represent official or even up-to-date practice, and rarely differentiate between land and naval service weapons. Although there are a number of modern books on particular aspects of naval artillery in the age of sail, there remains a need for a single volume combining specific details on guns with an historical account of the development of gunnery at sea; the interplay between technology, tactics and ship design would make a very enlightening study.

H L BLACKMORE, *The Armouries of the Tower of London*, Vol I: Ordnance (London 1976).

An inventory of the huge collection of guns, naval and land service, from many countries kept in Britain's oldest arsenal. It contains drawings of many of the weapons, a useful glossary and appendix listings of gun data.

JEAN BOUDRIOT, 'L'Artillerie de Mer de la Marine Française, 1674–1856', *Neptunia* 89–101, 103 (1968–71).

A series of important articles in the author's usual beautifully illustrated style encompassing every aspect of French naval guns and their equipment (including mortars). Many data tables. There was also a series on naval small arms in issues 83–85, 87 (1966–67).

SIR HOWARD DOUGLAS, *A Treatise on Naval Gunnery* (London, six editions 1820–61; 1855 edition reprinted London 1982).

Howard was the son of the famous gunnery innovator Charles Douglas and a prominent artillerist himself. Although a polemical work enshrining many of its author's prejudices, the much expanded later editions cover most aspects of the last generation of naval guns from the Napoleonic Wars onwards.

MERRITT EDSON (ed), *Ship Modeler's Shop Notes* (Washington 1979).

A compilation of many short pieces from the *Nautical Research Journal*, Chapter 9 being devoted to ordnance. Intended for modelmakers, the articles tend to concentrate on visual details and precise dimensions.

ROBERT GARDINER, 'Fittings for Wooden Warships: Part 3 Guns', *Model Shipwright* 20 (1977).

Some aspects of the historical survey have been superseded by later research but still valuable for its compilation of data, particularly the tables of all the British gun establishments.

MELVIN H JACKSON and CHARLES DE BEER, *Eighteenth-Century Gunfounding* (London and Washington 1974).

The complexities of gunfounding are better illustrated than described and this book reproduces fifty drawings by Jan Verbruggen, the great eighteenth-century gunfounder. A better quality facsimile of these drawings has recently been published in Britain.

BRIAN LAVERY, *The Arming and Fitting of English Ships of War 1600–1815* (London 1987).

A large scale encyclopaedic work, nearly a quarter of which is devoted to naval guns, their mountings and equipment, with much new and precise information. It deals with the relationship between guns and warships although not with gunnery itself, and as its title indicates it is confined to Royal Navy usage.

PETER PADFIELD, *Guns at Sea* (London 1973).

A very general history of the employment of artillery and its influence on fighting at sea. Superseded in many details, but for the 1650–1840 period useful for much telling quotation from contemporary sources on the gunnery aspects of naval warfare.

SPENCER TUCKER, *Arming the Fleet: US Navy Ordnance in the Muzzle-Loading Era* (Annapolis 1989).

A broad survey that briefly outlines the early history of guns at sea and gunfounding before dealing with specifically American developments. Stronger on the nineteenth century than earlier; very full bibliography, but missing a few of the latest works.

DECORATION

Despite its apparent attraction there has only been one major work in English on this topic, and foreign language works are no better represented. However, because both models and the more reliable marine artists are prime sources for the appearance of ships, a few of the more significant catalogues of such works have been listed here.

G S LAIRD CLOWES, *Sailing Ships: Their History and Development as illustrated by the Collection of Ship-Models in the Science Museum*, 2 parts (London 1932).

The historical notes which form Part I are now rather out of date, but the inventory in Part II is still the most complete list of the Science Museum's substantial holdings; the descriptive notes are extensive, but there are few illustrations.

L G CARR LAUGHTON *Old Ships Figureheads and Sterns* (London 1925; reprinted 1991).

Largely based on a study of models, it gives some idea of the overall development of decoration and attempts to deal with all the major navies. It is well illustrated for its day and despite its age it is still the only serious work on the subject.

JOHN FRANKLIN, *Navy Board Ship Models 1650–1750* (London 1989).

A study of the form and function of these exquisitely detailed official models, but with much to say about decoration; also information on fittings.

M S ROBINSON, *Van de Velde Drawings: A Catalogue of Drawings in the National Maritime Museum made by the Elder and the Younger Willem Van de Velde*, 2 vols (Cambridge 1958 and 1974).

This father and son team of Dutch artists who emigrated to England were the most accurate and prolific illustrators of the ships of their working lifetimes, which stretched from the late 1630s to just after 1700. The drawings include many detailed sketches of named ships and provide an unparalleled source of information on their appearance and decorative details. Robinson also catalogued the principal Dutch collection in the Boymans-van Beuningen Museum, Rotterdam.

——, *The Paintings of the Willem Van de Veldes: A Catalogue of the Paintings of the Elder and the Younger Van de Velde*, 2 vols (London 1990).

A companion to his previous work; many of the paintings also depict named ships and the detail of colouring and carved work is invaluable.

US NAVAL ACADEMY MUSEUM, *Henry Huddleston Rogers Collection of Ship Models* (Annapolis, MD).

One of the world's great collections of sailing warship models, its core was the Sergison Collection, originally put together by Pepys' successor at the Navy Board. Unfortunately the cataloguing leaves a lot to be desired, but this publication at least reproduces a photo of each model.

J VICHOT, *Musée de la Marine: Palais de Chaillot* (Paris 1943).

An inventory of the holdings of the French maritime museum but short on illustrations.

A H WAITE, *National Maritime Museum Catalogue of Ship Models: Part 1 Ships of the Western Tradition to 1815* (London nd, but c1980).

A spiral bound loose-leaf catalogue originally intended to be updated but no revisions were issued. This is undoubtedly the best collection of its kind in the world and with so little of it now on display it is very important to have a catalogue like this that includes at least one photo per model. However, the descriptions are inadequate, some of the dating dubious, and in most respects the text is a backward step from the simpler R C Anderson catalogue of the 1950s.

SEAMANSHIP

Many of the contemporary manuals have been reprinted in recent years; these are perhaps more valued for their illustrations of rigging detail than any exposition of seamanship or shiphandling, accounts of which are often difficult to follow. However, there has been one modern book which makes sense of much contemporary teaching and this and the principal manuals are listed below.

P M J DE BONNEFOUX, *Manoeuvrier Complet* (Paris 1852).

WILLIAM N BRADY, *The Kedge Anchor* (eighteenth edition New York 1876 reprinted 1970).

The most popular American manual on seamanship.

C BURNEY, *Young Seaman's Manual* (Jersey 1869).

ADOLPH EKELOF, *Lärobok i Skeppsmanöver* (Stockholm 1881).

JOHN H HARLAND and illustrated by MARK R MYERS, *Seamanship in the Age of Sail* (London 1984).

A remarkable collaboration between a leading marine artist and a writer with a command of many languages, the book is a superbly illustrated synthesis of earlier writings on the subject. Predominantly confined to naval shiphandling and the three-masted ship rig. Includes a very full bibliography of contemporary works on the subject.

DARCY LEVER, *The Young Sea Officer's Sheet Anchor* (second edition London 1819 reprinted New York 1963).

The best illustrated manual of the time.

G P J MOSSEL, *Manoeuvres met Zeil- en Stoomschepen* (Amsterdam 1865).

GEORGE S NARES, *Seamanship* (second edition Portsmouth 1862; reprinted Woking 1979).

Originally published in 1860 as *The Naval Cadet's Guide*.

FRANZ UFFERS, *Handbuch der Seemannschaft* (Berlin 1872; reprinted Kassel 1981).

NAVAL TACTICS

Naval historians tend to concentrate on strategy rather than tactics; as a result the number of studies is small but with the recent publication of an edited version of the late Brian Tunstall's life's work, there is at least one modern comparative study.

SIR JULIAN CORBETT, *Fighting Instructions 1530–1816* (London 1905; reprinted 1971).

Corbett was the first to make a systematic study of signal books and official fighting instructions as a key to the development of tactics. This volume is an edited compilation of such works from Tudor times to the end of the Napoleonic Wars.

——, *Signals and Instructions 1776–1794* (London 1909; reprinted 1971).

A follow-up to the above concentrating on a tactically important period and made possible by the discovery of much new material.

S S ROBINSON and MARY L ROBINSON, *A History of Naval Tactics* (Annapolis, MD 1942).

A series of excerpts from printed secondary sources and not an analytical history.

BRIAN TUNSTALL edited by NICHOLAS TRACY, *Naval Warfare in the Age of Sail: The Evolution of Fighting Tactics 1650–1815* (London 1990).

A monumental survey (even edited to half its manuscript length) based almost entirely on study of primary sources – fighting instructions, signal books and logs. Regarded by Tunstall as the completion of Corbett's work but an original and enlightening study in its own right.

Glossary of Terms and Abbreviations

Compiled by Robert Gardiner. This list assumes some knowledge of ships and does not include the most basic terminology. It also omits those words which are defined *in situ* on the only occasions in which they occur in this book.

Admiralty. The office responsible for the administration of the affairs of a navy, and in particular the Royal Navy. Originally headed by a Lord High Admiral, but for most of the period of this book his duties were discharged by a Board of Commissioners known as the Board of Admiralty, comprising civilian politicians, senior sea officers and a secretariat.

Admiralty pattern. Of anchors, the familiar type with iron shank and arms and a stock (usually wooden) set in a plane at right angles to the arms. When the arms were curved it was a round crown type; when they were straight and met at a point, it was called an angle crown pattern.

advice boat. Small craft intended to carry information (a seventeenth-century meaning of 'advice') either in the form of dispatches or as intelligence from reconnaissance. In both roles speed was the primary requirement. Related to the French *aviso*, which became the equivalent of the British rating sloop.

advis-jacht. A Dutch advice boat (*qv*).

angle crown. Type of anchor. *See* Admiralty pattern.

apostis. The outrigger structure of a galley; as it enabled the pivoting point for an oar to be outboard, it allowed the use of a longer and more efficient stroke.

armateur. French entrepreneurs who organised and funded privateering (*qv*).

bace, burr or **burrel.** Seventeenth-century term for case or canister shot (*qv*), although it might comprise irregular pieces of iron more akin to langrel (*qv*).

baghla or **bagala.** Lateen rigged dhow of the Persian Gulf region.

Baltimore clipper. An imprecise term applied to fine-lined American topsail schooners with an emphasis on extreme speed; not so much a specific type as a concept, their heyday was approximately 1870–1820.

bar (shot). Ammunition designed to damage spars and rigging; usually two hemispheres connected by a bar, but the term was also loosely applied to other forms.

barge. (1) A long, light pulling boat, usually carvel-built, often associated with pomp and ceremony, as with the City of London livery company boats; a warship's barge was normally the transport of a senior officer or admiral.

(2) A heavy riverine or coastal cargo carrier, usually sail propelled; there were many local variations.

bark or **barque.** As understood in the nineteenth century, a vessel with three or more masts, square rigged on all but the mizzen, which set only fore and aft canvas. In earlier times it carried more elusive meanings, but a particular naval application was to the lateen rigged corvette-like small craft used by the French navy in the Mediterranean up to the 1780s.

barque longue. A French term, also occurring in related languages as *barca longa*, originally meaning an undecked small craft that could be rowed as well as sailed. In the French navy the type was the ancestor of the corvette (*qv*) and therefore the late seventeenth-century equivalent of the English sloop. (*qv*)

barquentine. A nineteenth-century term applied to a vessel with a full square rigged foremast but fore and aft rigged main and mizzen. Not much used for warships, except auxiliary steamers; later vessels had four or more masts.

bâteau cannonier. A French gunboat, designed to be sailed as well as rowed; usually armed with one gun and a landing gun.

bâtiments interrompus. The category for miscellaneous small craft in the French seventeenth-century rating system, below the five *Rangs* or Rates of major warships and the light frigates.

batterie couverte. Nineteenth-century French corvette type with main battery covered by a spar deck, as opposed to the open flush-decked *batterie à barbette* type.

beakhead bulkhead. An athwartship bulkhead at the forward end of the forecastle at upper deck level; the small platform thus formed forward of it was known as the beakhead. With the introduction of the round bow (*qv*), in which the hull side planking was carried up to the top of the forecastle, both beakhead and bulkhead disappeared.

beam ends. The deck beams joined the frames at the sides of the ship, so a ship was said to be on her beam ends when heeled right over; this was a position of extreme helplessness and the phrase was metaphorically extended to any similarly dire situation.

Beaufort Scale. A method of describing wind strength, still in use, developed by Sir Francis Beaufort, the British Hydrographer of the Navy from 1829 to 1855. This replaced vague descriptions with a scale from Force 0 to Force 12 dependent on wind speed; each Force number has an accompanying designation (Force 6, for example, is Strong Breeze), an estimated wave height and a description of the appearance of the sea in deep water at each Force level.

becket. Any device used to secure loose items of rigging or equipment; could be applied to hooks or brackets but most common meaning was short rope with a knot in one end and an eye in the other.

bed. Of a gun carriage, the base, later the stool bed (*qv*); when specifically applied to mortars, the solid supporting timbers forming a swivelling mounting.

belfry. The ornate structure under which was hung the ship's bell; usually located at the break of the forecastle.

bergantino. Variant of *brigantin* (*qv*); from the 1770s used in the Spanish navy list for brigs.

Bermuda sloop. An extreme version of the sloop rig with raked aft mast, long bowsprit and relatively large main sail. In eighteenth-century Britain this was known as the **Bermudian** or **Bermudoes** rig after its supposed place of origin. Some craft carried triangular courses, from which the modern bermudian masthead rig derives.

bezan rig. Rig employed by some Dutch yachts bearing a close similarity to later sloops: single mast with bowsprit, jib headsails and fore and aft main set from short gaff and long boom.

bilander. A two-masted vessel with square rigged fore mast and square main topsail but a main sail set from a lateen; this latter was not triangular but had a vertically cut forward edge or luff. Not a regular naval rig and most common in North Sea and Baltic traders.

binnacle. The cabinet housing compasses, log glasses and watch glasses. Usually positioned directly before the wheel and divided into three compartments, with compasses in the outer ones (so that one was visible to the helmsman whichever side of the wheel he stood) and a light box between to illuminate them at night. Originally known as a bittacle.

bitts. A frame of strong upright timbers and a cross piece to which ropes and cables were made fast. The most important were the riding bitts (double in ships of any size) to which the cables were secured when at anchor but there were others associated with the rigging.

black stuff. Dockyard term for an antifouling composition made of tar and pitch. *See also* white stuff and brown stuff.

bobstay. Piece of standing rigging between the end of the bowsprit and the ship's stem, designed to counteract the upward pull of the jibs.

bojort. Baltic version of the Dutch boyer (*qv*); two-masted (main and mizzen), usually sprit rigged with square main topsail and lateen mizzen, but versions known with square main, resembling a seventeenth-century English ketch.

bolster. Any item designed as a reinforcement against chafing, such as the moulded wooden pieces under the hawse holes (*qv*) or the pads of tarred canvas protecting the collars of the stays from rubbing the woodwork of the masts.

boltrope. Strengthening rope sewn around the extremities of a sail; divided according to position on the sail as head-, leech- and foot-ropes (top, sides and bottom, respectively).

bomb vessel. A specialist bombardment craft designed to carry heavy mortars firing explosive shells. Earliest versions were ketch rigged and they were often, erroneously, called bomb ketches even when ship rigged from the 1760s onwards.

bombard. Some Mediterranean navies so described their bomb vessels (*qv*).

bomkin. *See* boomkin.

bonaventure mizzen. The fourth mast carried abaft the mizzen proper by some large late sixteenth- and early seventeenth-century ships; set a triangular lateen sail.

bonnet. An addition to the foot of lower sails for fair weather; after the late seventeenth century they were replaced on all but small craft with deeper sails that were reefed (*qv*) in heavy weather.

boom. (1) A relatively light spar, such as a studding sail boom; most commonly applied, without qualification, to the spar that extended the foot of a spanker (*qv*).
   (2) Ships' boats were originally stowed amidships with the spare spars or booms, so when more permanent transverse beams were fitted they continued to be called booms or boat booms.
   (3) A movable defence to the mouth of a harbour or anchorage, usually comprising a chain supported by baulks of timber.

boomkin, bomkin or **bumkin.** A small outrigger spar used to extend the corner of a sail; if used without qualification the term usually applied to those either side of the bow for the windward corner of the fore sail.

Borda-Sané system. The French scheme of standardisation introduced by the Chevalier de Borda, the Inspector of Naval Construction from 1784 and Jacques-Noel Sané, the most highly regarded French ship designer of his day. It fixed principal dimensions and for some classes even specified preferred designs.

bower anchor. The ship's main working anchor, so named because it was carried at the bow; ships usually had a best bower and a small bower although in late eighteenth-century British practice they were normally the same size (indeed rated ships carried four bowers). *See also* sheet anchor, kedge and stream.

bowline. Rope attached via three or four bridles to the leech (side) of the sail; led forward to hold the leech up into the wind when the ship was close-hauled (*qv*), from whence 'on a bowline' became synonymous with this point of sailing.

bowsprit. Heavy spar (in effect, a lower mast) angled forward over the bow which provided the support for the fore mast stays and allowed sail to be set far enough forward to have a significant effect on the balance of the rig.

boxhauling. A method of going about (*qv*) in which the ship sailed up into the wind; fore yards were then backed and the ship actually sailed backwards in an arc until stern to wind, when she would gather way forward, and was gradually brought up to the wind on the new tack. Often used to recover from a failed attempt to tack (*qv*).

boyer or **boeier.** Dutch coastal craft; in seventeenth century usually two-masted, with sprit rigged main and square main topsail, plus small mizzen lateen.

bp. Between perpendiculars, sometimes given as pp: modern, designer's measurement of length, omitting the overhang of stem and stern structures, as opposed to length overall; roughly equivalent to length on the lower deck as understood in the eighteenth century.

brace. (1) Rope used to pivot the yards; to brace up was to swing them to as sharp (*ie* smallest) an angle with the keel as feasible; bracing in was the opposite.
   (2) Also applied to the gudgeons (*qv*) of the rudder.

breast rail. The upper rail of the barricade at the fore end of the quarterdeck and the after end of the forecastle.

brick de guerre. French navy term for a brig of war.

brick-aviso. French navy nineteenth-century rating for small brigs designed as advice boats (*qv*).

brig. A two-masted square rigged vessel but with a fore and aft gaff-and-boom main sail; very similar to a snow (*qv*). Introduced to naval service from the 1770s but widely used in the merchant marine earlier.

brigantin. In seventeenth-century and earlier usage a small galley-like vessel as often rowed as sailed; originated in the Mediterranean.

brigantine. Originally more a hull form than a rig, presumably derived from *brigantin* (*qv*), the term was associated with oared craft. By the nineteenth century it came to denote a two-masted rig, square on the fore mast and fore and aft on the main; it was sometimes called a brig-schooner in some European countries.

broach to. To suddenly and uncontrollably fly up into the wind, when there was a danger of the canvas being thrown aback; this might mean the loss of the masts or the ship might be capsized.

brown stuff. Dockyard term for an antifouling composition made of brimstone mixed with tar and pitch. *See also* white stuff and black stuff.

bumpkin. *See* boomkin.

buntline. Rope from the foot of a square sail passing over the forward surface to the yard; used to spill the wind from a sail when necessary.

burr, burrel. *See* bace.

burthern. A measurement of capacity in tons calculated by formula from the dimensions of the ship. The formula varied over time and was different from country to country; it greatly underestimated the real displacement but may be regarded as a crude forerunner of gross tonnage (*ie* a measure of internal volume).

burton tackle. Consisting of a pair of blocks, one of which was fitted with a hook; useful for lifting weights and particularly used in setting up or tightening the shrouds (*qv*).

buss. A relatively small craft of about 50–70 tons associated with English and Dutch herring fisheries; two- or three-masted with simple square sails lowered for reefing.

calibre. The internal diameter of the bore of a gun, and consequently of the ammunition or shot fired from it.

camel. A very buoyant pontoon in two halves designed to assist deep-draught ships over sandbars or shoal water. Once securely strapped to either side of the ship, water was pumped out of the camels reducing the draught of the ensemble.

canister shot. Anti-personnel ammunition comprising a thin case filled with small shot, whence also termed case shot. *See also* bace.

cannon. Latterly loosely used of any muzzle-loading smooth bore ship's gun, but originally a distinct species of medium length, large calibre battering pieces.

cant frame. Timbers at the bow and stern which were angled, or canted, in relation to the keel, as opposed to the square frames which were perpendicular to it.

capsquare. Iron hinged strap over the trunnion of a gun to secure it to the carriage.

capstan. A machine for moving great weights, particularly the anchors, using the winding principle. It comprised a vertical barrel that could be turned by men pushing against a radial pattern of bars inserted in sockets in the head of the capstan, twisting a rope or cable around the body. *See also* crab, drumhead and trundlehead.

carronade. A design of short lightweight ship's gun developed by the Carron Ironworks in Scotland in the 1770s.

cartouche. Box used for the transportation of made-up cartridges of powder from the magazine to the guns; more usually called a cartridge box.

carvel. A form of ship or boat construction where the planks are laid edge to edge, not overlapped as for clinker (*qv*); this form of building requires a frame to be erected first.

cascable. The moulding at the breech end of a

muzzle-loading gun, including the button and latterly a breech ring.

case shot. *See* canister shot.

cat tackle. Used to haul the anchor up to the cathead (*qv*) after weighing.

catharpins. Lines used to constrict the lower shrouds (*qv*) in order to tighten them, and to allow the yards to be braced up as sharply as possible.

cathead. Projecting beam of timber from each side of the bow, used as a form of davit (*qv*) to keep the anchor clear of the hull before letting go or after weighing but prior to being secured with the fish tackle (*qv*).

catting the anchor. *See* weighing anchor.

chain shot. Ammunition comprising two round shot connected by a short length of chain, designed primarily to disable the rigging of an opponent.

chaloupe. A French term related to sloop and shallop; usually applied in the navy to the equivalent of a British barge or pinnace, as opposed to the longboat-like *canot*.

chaloupe-cannonière. French harbour defence gunboat designed for rowing or sailing; usually armed with three guns.

channel. (1) The navigable part of a river or stretch of water.
(2) The platforms projecting from the hull abreast each mast to spread the shrouds (*qv*) and prevent them chafing against the hull (term derived from 'chain-wales').

chase. That portion of the barrel of a gun between the trunnions and the muzzle.

chase guns. Those firing forward or aft, used when chasing or being chased, as opposed to the broadside guns.

chasse-marée. French lug rigged coastal craft.

clew or **clue.** Lower corner of square sail or after corner of a fore and aft sail; on square sails a tackle called a clewline (or clew garnets on the courses) hauled them up to the yards.

clinker. A form of construction in which planking is overlapped and fastened along the overlap (also called clench or lap construction). It allows a hull shell to be built without prior framing, although internal strengthening is usually added later; mostly confined to small craft and boats.

close-hauled. The point of sailing as near to the direction of the wind as possible (about 70 degrees for a square-rigger although fore and aft vessels could point somewhat closer).

compass timber. Curved, crooked or arched timber for shipbuilding.

constructeur. French equivalent of shipwright.

corsair. Originally applied to the piratical ships and men of the North African Barbary states, but in English usage often extended to encompass any enemy privateer (*qv*).

corsia. The centreline catwalk over the rowing benches of a galley.

corvette. French term for small unrated cruising

vessels derived from the *barque longue* (*qv*), equivalent to the British sloop. By the nineteenth century corvettes were sometimes regarded as intermediate vessels between frigates and sloops.

counter. The area of overhang at the stern, beneath the cabin windows; usually divided into upper and lower counters.

courses. The lowest, and hence principal, sail on each mast; a lateen mizzen or spanker was also considered a course.

crab. A primitive form of capstan where the bars went right through the head, limiting the number to about four, all of which were necessarily at different heights; portable versions were used for cargo handling. Replaced by the drumhead type (*qv*).

crank. Describes a ship that is unstable or liable to large angles of heel, so unable to carry much sail without danger. Opposite of stiff.

cringle. A small circle of rope or hole, usually in sails and sometimes lined with a metal ring or thimble, to which ropes can be secured without stress on the sail cloth.

cromster or **crompster.** A sixteenth-century sprit rigged coasting vessel with a couple of big guns, employed as makeshift warships by the Dutch and English.

crossjack. Pronounced 'crojack'; the lowermost mizzen square yard that extended the clews (*qv*) of the mizzen topsail. Unlike the fore and main yard it did not regularly set its own sail; the lateen mizzen, and later the spanker (*qv*), were considered the mizzen course.

crown. Of an anchor, the end of the shank where the arms joined.

culverin. A medium calibre gun of very long barrel length. The whole culverin fired a shot of about 17lbs and the demi-culverin of about 9lbs. The term died out after about 1700.

cutts. A short barrelled version of standard gun types: *eg* demi-culverin cutts, popular in the seventeenth century.

cutter. (1) Ship's boat, usually clinker-built (*qv*), seaworthy and handier under sail than oars.
(2) Sharp lined fast-sailing coastal craft, originally clinker-built in the English Channel ports; carried a single-masted fore and aft rig of large area, and popular as smuggling craft, revenue cruiser and small warship.

cutter-brig. A vessel with a cutter-style hull but rigged as a brig.

cutwater. The timber forming the foremost extension of the stem that in a ship under way actually divided the water.

dandy rig. A sloop or cutter setting a small mizzen lugsail, usually abaft the sternpost in the manner of a modern yawl.

davit. A beam of timber acting as a crane; originally applied to the fish davit that was used to hoist up the arms of the anchor, but from the late eighteenth century similar devices were used to sling boats from the quarters and stern of warships. The word has survived to the present in this latter boat-handling sense.

deadeye. Used in tensioning the shrouds (*qv*), these discs of wood were set up in pairs, one attached to the shroud itself and the other, via chains, to the hull. Tensioning was achieved by a lanyard rove through three holes in each deadeye and bowsed tight.

demi-batterie. A French term referring to an armament layout where one deck (usually the lowest) carried only a partial battery of guns.

demi-galère. French term for a half-galley or smaller version of the regular war galley.

dinghy. Originally an Indian local craft but the name was adopted for a warship's smallest boat.

dogger. A North Sea fishing vessel (whence Dogger Bank), usually setting square sails on a main and mizzen like a ketch or galiot (*qv*).

dolphin. Lifting handles of early guns, particularly those of bronze, which were usually modelled in the form of an arch-backed dolphin.

dolphin striker. Short spar beneath the bowsprit, perpendicular to its end, over which the martingale (*qv*) ran in order to guy the jibboom from below.

double shallop. In the seventeenth century a large undecked boat that could be rowed or sailed; ancestor of the sloop in the English service as the *double chaloupe* was of the *barque longue* in the French navy.

double-headed shot. Various forms of ammunition designed to dismantle the enemy's rigging; usually comprised two bars, roundshot or hemispheres, joined by a bar or chain.

downhauler. A line used to pull down a jib or staysail; a downhaul tackle was also used to strike the yards in bad weather.

drabbler. An addition to the bottom of sails for fair weather, usually added after the bonnet (*qv*); for large warships superseded by reefing (*qv*) but still employed in the early nineteenth century for the occasional square canvas of schooners and other fore and aft rigs.

drake. Species of seventeenth-century ordnance characterised by a short, lightweight barrel and, generally, a bore that tapered from muzzle to powder chamber.

driver. A sail set on the mizzen that was originally a fine weather addition (initially a square sail but later a fore and aft extension of the mizzen) and finally a temporary replacement for a smaller gaff mizzen. Finally replaced by the spanker (*qv*) with which it is often confused.

drumhead capstan. Improvement over the crab type (*qv*), introduced in the 1670s; a separate slotted disc, called the drumhead, allowed a far larger number of capstan bars to be inserted around its circumference.

dumb lighter. Unpowered cargo-carrying barge.

dumb truck. Baulk of timber replacing the two rear wheels, or trucks, on some nineteenth-century gun carriages.

earing. Small rope used to fasten the upper corner of a sail to its yardarm; there was also one at the level of each reef band to perform the same function for the reefed sail.

elliptical stern. Method of framing that replaced Seppings' round stern (*qv*) from the 1830s. There were a number of detail variations, but in general it was regarded as retaining most of the strength of the round stern design while returning to the elegance of the traditional square stern.

Establishment. A formalised set of standards pertaining to shipbuilding, rigging or armament that specified numbers, dimensions and characteristics of each item for each class or Rate of ship.

falcon. Small gun of the culverin type (*qv*) firing a shot of 2½-3lbs; the **falconet** was an even smaller version firing a ball of about half that.

faux pont. French term for the orlop, but by extension sometimes applied to the continuous lower deck of a frigate or corvette that was structurally very light.

felucca. Small lateen rigged galley-type vessel used in the Mediterranean.

fid. Bar of wood or iron locking the heel of a separate topmast or topgallant in place to the head of the mast below; from this, a mast made up of separate sections was described as a fidded mast.

fife rail. The uppermost rail of quarterdeck and poop barricades; also applied to the framework around the main mast carrying belaying pins for the running rigging.

Fifth Rate. In the British rating system originally a ship carrying no more than 24 guns (1651), but from the 1660s the Rate encompassed ships of up to 36 guns and for most of the eighteenth century it included those of 30–44 guns; after the Napoleonic Wars the re-rated 38-gun frigates (then officially 46 guns) were added.

fireship. A vessel either converted or purpose-built to be expended as a floating incendiary device; special fittings enabled the fireship to be ignited at the last moment, thus allowing the crew a chance of escaping by boat before collision with the target.

First Rate. Always the largest ships in the fleet, of 100 guns or more, but the lower end of the spectrum varied in British practice from 60 guns in 1651 to 80 guns in the 1660s and 100 guns after about 1700.

fish tackle. Used to catch the arms of the anchor and haul it up to its stowage position on the gunwale or fore channel, for which purpose a davit (*qv*) was employed.

fishing the anchor. *See* weighing anchor.

flagship. The ship from which an admiral or senior officer commanded, so called because it flew the admiral's distinguishing flag.

flaked. Coiled (of a cable); either as laid out on deck in preparation for anchoring or as stowed in the cable tier.

fleet in being. A strategic concept that argued for the preservation at all costs of a naval force as a bargaining counter, rather than risking it unnecessarily. The idea is often said to have been first crystallised by Lord Torrington after his defeat at Beachy Head in 1690.

flojt. *See* fluyt.

floor. The hull bottom; floor timbers are the lowest elements in a frame (*qv*).

flush deck. One without a break or step; later applied to ships with an open weather deck, lacking quarterdeck and forecastle structures above.

flûte. French term for a large naval storeship; sometimes warships were fitted for the role, with reduced main batteries, whence it derived the phrase 'armed *en flûte*'.

fluyt. Characteristically Dutch merchant ship of large carrying capacity, extreme tumblehome (*qv*) and narrow stern. Because they were such cost-effective carriers they were adopted by other nations, who spelt the name in a variety of ways, such as *flute* or *flojt*; the English referred to them as fly-boats.

forecastle. A structure over the forward part of the upper deck; in medieval times a castle-like addition, but by 1650 a relatively lightweight platform useful for handling the headsails. When forecastle and quarterdeck (*qv*) were combined into a spar deck, the forward portion was still known as the forecastle.

'forty thieves'. Derisive nickname for a large class of British 74-gun ships built from 1807 which were regarded as bad bargains and much criticised.

Fourth Rate. Smallest Rate to regularly justify a place in the line of battle, it comprised ships of 30–40 guns in 1651, 40–50 in the 1680s and 50–60 thereafter.

fowler. Small breech-loading anti-personnel weapon.

frame. The structural ribs of a wooden ship; strictly speaking a framed bend, comprising overlapping pairs of floor timbers, a number of tiers of futtocks, and toptimbers.

fregata. In many Romance languages denotes a small fast vessel but its exact characteristics are very vague; obviously the origin of the English term frigate (*qv*).

frégate d'avis. Small French cruising ship, precursor of the *frégate légère* (*qv*), and analogous to the English sloops of the late seventeenth century.

frégate légère. French light frigate, equivalent of British Sixth Rate, of about 20 guns; superseded by corvettes in the early eighteenth century.

frigate. As commonly understood, a fast and seaworthy cruising ship, too small for the line of battle, but large enough for independent action. However, it was originally applied to any nimble, lightly constructed vessel: for example, the frigates of the English Commonwealth were noted for these qualities – unlike the earlier great ships (*qv*) – even though they themselves eventually acquired enough guns to lie in the line of battle; by about 1700 the term was reserved for smaller craft.

futtock. *See* frame.

futtock staves. Iron or wooden bars fastened along the lower shrouds below the tops to which the catharpins (*qv*) were secured.

gabare. French naval transport, smaller than a *flûte* (*qv*).

gaff. A short spar to extend the head of a fore and aft sail; usually hoisted with the sail, for which purpose it was equipped with jaws that fitted around the mast. A larger permanent (standing) gaff was sometimes called a half-sprit (*qv*).

gaillards. French expression encompassing both forecastle and quarterdeck.

galejer. Danish rowing craft introduced around 1654 for defence of Norwegian coast.

galeota. Small galley, sometimes called a half-galley.

galère extraordinaire. Especially large galley usually employed as a flagship.

galiot or **galliot.** Dutch coaster type with standing gaff main and small lateen mizzen; also used for similar English vessels.

galiot à rames. Synonymous with *brigantin* (*qv*).

galiot à bombes. French term for bomb vessel, almost universally rigged as a ketch until the nineteenth century.

galleon. Sixteenth-century description of the large square rigged big-gun armed warship that was then a novelty; archaic after 1650 but retained for particular applications, such as Spanish treasure ships, which were always called galleons whatever the ship type involved.

galley-frigate. Cruising ship originating in the 1670s in which the lower deck was predominantly, if not exclusively, designed for rowing; some had proportions optimised for oared propulsion.

garland. Piece of timber between gunports or around hatch coamings with a row of hemispherical recesses to stow round shot as ready-use ammunition; so called because originally shot was stowed inside wreath-like rope grommets.

garnet tackle. Tackle fixed to the main stay for hoisting up heavy weights.

gig. A light, narrow ship's boat, better under oars than sail.

girdling. A process of improving the stability of a ship, increasing breadth by adding strakes of timber in the region of the waterline; a common seventeenth-century recourse but isolated examples are known as late as the 1840s.

going about. The manoueuvre of passing from one tack (*qv*) to the other, so the wind comes from the other side of the ship. This could be achieved by passing the bow through the wind (called tacking) or by wearing (*qv*), in which the stern passed through the wind. *See also* boxhauling.

gooseneck. A hook-shaped piece of iron usually on the end of a boom to allow it to be fitted and removed easily.

Gover gun. A British patent short 24pdr, of about 70 per cent the weight of a standard gun, designed by Captain Gover in 1805.

grand canot. The main boat of a French warship (equivalent to a British longboat or launch).

grape shot. Anti-personnel and dismantling shot comprising a bundle of small shot parcelled up to the rough appearance of a bunch of grapes. Individual grape shot was larger than case shot (*qv*), and nine was a typical number per round.

great ship. The large galleon-derived capital ship of the early seventeenth century; became Second Rates under the system of the 1650s and were superseded under the English Commonwealth by lower, faster and more manoeuvrable frigates (*qv*).

grommet. A ring of rope, used for a number of purposes including attaching staysails to their stays; a **grommet wad** was also used to secure shells in the bore of a gun before firing.

guardship. A stationary harbour defence vessel charged with the security of the port; also used for the ready reserve of those ships that could be fitted for sea at short notice.

gudgeon. The part of the rudder hinge that was attached to the ship, containing a ring into which the pintle (*qv*) of the rudder itself fitted. *See also* brace.

guerre de course. The strategy of war on the enemy's commerce, brought to a fine art by France but adopted by most other sea powers from time to time.

gunboat. Large boat equipped to carry a small number of guns (often one only); originally little more than ship's boats, they tended to become larger and more seaworthy in the late eighteenth and early nineteenth centuries.

gun-brig. A British term for small but seagoing craft, derived from gunboats, but brig rigged. Commanded by a Lieutenant rather than the Master and Commander of a brig sloop.

gun-vessel. A short-lived British term intended to denote something larger and more seaworthy than a gunboat but not quite a sloop.

gundeck. The main battery deck or decks, the number of which categorised a warship: even when quarterdeck, forecastle and possibly poop were heavily armed, it was the upper and lower gundecks that gave the two-decker its description.

gunnade. Nineteenth-century hybrid gun, somewhere in length and weight between a long gun and a carronade.

gunter. Fore and aft rig characterised by a hoisting sail headed by a long gunter pole that when set was almost an extension of the mast, so could be differentiated from the shorter gaff which took up a less acute angle to the mast.

half-galley. *See* galeota.

half-sprit. A long standing gaff (*qv*) that may have developed from the sprit (*qv*).

halyard. Rope or tackle used to hoist sail or yard; sometimes spelt **haliard** or **halliard**.

hances. The steps in the upperwork rails (properly called drifts) and in the rear profile of the rudder.

harpin. The specially cut, sharply curved sections of ribband that hold the fore and aft cant (*qv*) sections of the frame in place during construction.

hawse hole. The openings either side of the bow through which the anchor cable is paid out or hauled in.

head. The fore part of the ship; here were situated the crew's sanitary facilities, from whence to this day lavatories aboard ship are commonly called heads.

heart. A form of deadeye (*qv*) but with only one large aperture in its centre; used to set up the stays as deadeyes set up the shrouds.

heated shot. With great care solid shot could be brought to red heat in a furnace and fired before it cooled too far. In theory, highly combustible wooden ships were vulnerable to this form of attack but there are few examples of success, and those were from coast defences rather than other ships; there were experiments but it was usually thought too dangerous to take heated shot to sea.

hemmema. A special design of inshore frigate designed for the Swedish Archipelago Fleet by F H Chapman in the 1760s.

hog. Because of their fine lines fore and aft, a ship had more buoyancy amidships, which could cause the ship to arch upwards, distorting the structure and breaking the sheer, as it was described. This propensity to hog was enhanced in longer and more lightly constructed ships and was a major problem until the structural improvements inspired by Sir Robert Seppings from the end of the Napoleonic Wars gradually reduced hogging to manageable proportions.

hooker. Small hoy-like vessel usually employed for fishing.

horse. (1) Rope suspended below the yard as footing for men working on that yard.
(2) Vertical rope guide for controlling the hoisting of a sail or yard.
(3) A rod or beam across a deck on which the sheet block of a fore and aft sail slides when the ship goes about.

houario. Mediterranean two-masted small craft rigged with sliding gunter (*qv*) sails.

hound. The portion at the head of a mast, swelling out beyond the round section, that supports the structure of trestletrees (*qv*) and top (*qv*).

howitzer. Short barrelled gun designed to fire explosive shells at relatively high trajectories; more cannon-like than mortars (*qv*), with trunnions in the middle of the barrel instead of the end. Called *obusiers* in France, their limited naval employment was largely superseded by carronades (*qv*).

hoy. Small coasting craft, usually sloop rigged, for the transportation of passengers and/or cargo; often employed as a dockyard workboat.

hulk. A stationary ship, usually too decrepit for sea service, employed for various harbour duties, such as accommodation ships and hospitals; their masts were normally taken out.

Ingénieur-Constructeur-Général. The senior French technical officer, roughly the equivalent of the British Surveyor of the Navy.

jacht. Dutch fast sailing craft; although the origin of the English word yacht, in Dutch usage the term implied a hull form rather than a rig.

jack. Flag flown from the bows or end of bowsprit by means of a jackstaff; often the mark of a warship. In British warships the Union flag is flown as a jack (hence the common misnomer of Union Jack for the flag itself) but other navies have special flags for the purpose.

jackass frigate. Derisive nineteenth-century term employed in the Royal Navy for up-rated quarterdecked sloop. Sailors tended to use the term jackass for any faintly ridiculous novelty, unconventional rigs, for example, often being called **jackass barques**.

jackstay. A tautly set up rope, batten or, later, iron bar on a yard or spar to act as a traveller or to fasten the head of the sail to.

jakt. Danish small craft, probably derived from the Dutch *jacht* (*qv*), but possibly fore and aft rigged.

jeer. Heavy duty tackles used to hoist the lower yards.

jekt. Norwegian traditional inshore craft with single-masted square rig.

jewel block. Small block fitted at the end of upper yards to direct the halyard of the respective studding sail.

jibboom. An extension of the bowsprit (in effect its topmast); from the end of the eighteenth century, a further extension, called the **flying jibboom**, was added.

jollyboat. Often the smallest ship's boat, the all-purpose hack for light duties. The term was common until the end of the seventeenth century but thereafter died out in naval usage until a century later, when it was often applied to the smallest cutter.

kanonjolle. Swedish design of small gunboat with one gun firing aft; introduced in 1778.

kanonslup. Swedish gunboat design of the 1770s, with one heavy gun at each end. Danish and Russian imitations described as **kanonjoller** and **kanonerskia lodki** respectively.

katt or **cat.** Merchant ship much used in the coal and whaling trades; characterised by bulbous round stern with narrow transom above, and plain stem.

kedge. Small anchor used to manoeuvre the ship in confined water; could also be employed to move the ship forward, by carrying out the anchor some distance by boat and then heaving in on the capstan once the anchor was in the ground – a process known as kedging.

ketch. A two-masted rig characterised by a main and mizzen (often said to be a ship rig without a fore mast); originally square rigged, but fore and aft versions became common later.

knightheads. Bollard timbers supporting the bowsprit near the stem; so called because their tops were originally carved in the form of the head of an armed man.

koff. Dutch two-masted coasting type with sprit or gaff courses and square fore topsails.

kreiare, kray or **crayer.** Baltic trader with a rig like a nineteenth-century barque: square rigged fore and main with only a gaff-and-boom mizzen.

langrel. Anti-personnel ammunition made up of irregular pieces of iron, nails etc; also called **langrage** or **langridge**.

lanyard. Short piece of rope or line used to secure an item or act as a handle, such as the lanyard to a gunlock which allowed it to be triggered from a safe distance; lanyards between the deadeyes (*qv*) were used to tauten the shrouds (*qv*).

lateen. Triangular sail set from a long yard that was slung from its mast at a 45-degree angle; any vessel whose principal driving sails were of this kind was said to be lateen rigged. The rig is ancient in origin and was employed by galleys and most kinds of Mediterranean war vessels; the sail also formed the mizzen course of square riggers until the late eighteenth century.

launch. A large relatively flat-sheered boat, initially employed on dockyard duties, but taken to sea from the 1780s as a substitute for the more seaworthy but less capacious longboat (*qv*).

lazaretto. Quarantine accommodation, sometimes a building but often a hulk.

lee. The side or direction away from the wind or downwind (**leeward**). A ship which when sailing towards the direction of the wind (close-hauled – *qv*) lost ground downwind was said to be **leewardly**.

leeboard. A plate of timber attached to the side of shallow draught vessels to reduce their leeway (drift downwind) when sailing into the wind, on the same principle as the centreboard of a modern yacht. They were pivoted from the top so that the lee-side board could be let down below the level of the ships's bottom; the windward board was then hauled up out of the water. Leeboards are strongly associated with Dutch inshore craft, but the principle was widely applied wherever shallow waters restricted draught.

leech. Sides of a square sail; after edge of a fore and aft sail.

leechline. Rope from the leeches of the courses to haul the sides up to the yard.

lie to. In heavy weather, to carry just enough canvas to keep headway on (to allow the rudder to act and to make as little leeway as possible); the heading was usually seven or eight points (*qv*) off the wind. The alternative was to scud (*qv*).

lift. Rope from masthead to yardarm, used to square the yards (*ie* keep it perpendicular to the mast).

lighter. A capacious barge originally used to lighten seagoing ships in harbour, but later applied to working craft of similar form used for a variety of ancillary duties around dockyards and anchorages.

line of battle. Tactical formation with ships more or less in a single line ahead, designed to exploit in battle the broadside firepower of the sailing ships of this era; the overwhelming domination of this tactic led the vessels to be known as line-of-battle ships, from which the modern term battleship is derived.

lofting. The process in shipbuilding of transferring shapes from a scaled plan to the full size timbers; these were usually drawn out on the floor of a large attic space called a mould loft, whence lofting.

longboat. The largest ship's boat, used for heavy duty carrying; seaworthy and strongly built but often complained of as too difficult to stow. Replaced by the launch (*qv*) from the 1780s.

luff. The leading edge of a fore and aft sail and the weather leech (*qv*) of a square one; **to luff** meant to bring the ship's head nearer to the wind.

lug. A rig characterised by a four-sided sail with a head about two-thirds the length of the foot; hoisted on an angled yard with about a quarter of its length ahead of the mast.

lugger. A lug rigged coastal craft, two- and sometimes three-masted which could also set lug topsails; fast and weatherly, they were popular with smugglers and privateers but not much used by the Royal Navy. France and Spain employed the similar *chasse-marée* and *barca longa* for some naval and paramilitary duties.

martingale. The stay tensioning the jibboom from below, set up over the dolphin striker (*qv*).

messenger. The main cable was of too large a circumference to be wound around the capstan (*qv*), so a smaller rope, made up as an endless loop between the capstan and a block in the bows of the ship, was employed; this was known as the messenger. It was lashed, or nippered (*qv*), alongside the cable as it came through the hawsehole, and unlashed as the cable passed down to the cable tier.

minion. A small culverin-type gun firing a shot of about 4lbs.

mizzen. The aftermost mast of a ship or ketch, and the yards, sails and rigging pertaining to it.

monkey-tailed. Having a curved extension; applied to the handle of swivels and some early carronades.

moonraker or **moonsail.** Unofficial light weather sails set above skysail (*qv*); such occasional sails were generically termed flying kites.

mortar. Very short gun intended to fire explosive or incendiary ammunition at high trajectories; some had fixed base plates, but others were fitted with trunnions at the breech end.

morterchalup. Danish term for a gunboat (*qv*) whose main armament was a mortar rather than a long gun.

murderer. Small breech-loading anti-personnel weapon; by extension applied to all small calibre guns employed on the same service, particularly those on early seventeenth-century ships pointing into the waist from the forecastle (*qv*) and quarterdeck (*qv*) which were designed to clear the deck of boarders.

musketoon. Large musket supported by a swivel fitted along the rails and in the tops; superseded by swivel guns in the eighteenth century.

naveline. Light rope used to keep the parrel (*qv*) from jamming when hoisting or lowering a yard.

Navy Board. The Principal Officers and Commissioners of the Navy, the body charged with the technical and financial administration of the Royal Navy under the direction of the Admiralty. The Navy Board was responsible for ship design and construction, and the dockyards, and oversaw the work of subsidiary organisations like the Victualling Board and the Sick and Hurt Board. Comprised of long-term professional members, both civilian and sea service, it was often at odds with the more politically appointed Admiralty and was abolished in 1832 to end the potentially damaging division of interest.

Navy List. The official listing of ships, their rating, and commanding officers; for the Royal Navy this was originally issued by a commercial publisher but was formalised in the nineteenth century.

nipper. The temporary lashings used when weighing anchor to attach the cable to the messenger (*qv*), and by extension applied to those who carried out the task.

nominal rating. Round numbers of guns were often used to rate a ship, which might actually carry a few more; however, after the introduction of carronades (which were not counted as carriage guns), the nominal rating and the real gunpower diverged considerably, to the point where an 18-gun sloop might carry 28 guns. In 1817 the Royal Navy reformed the system, adopting nominal rates which were generally the same as actual numbers carried, although some ships of the line still had a few small poop carronades uncounted.

obusier. French term for howitzer (*qv*); the first French attempt to imitate the carronade was known as the *obusier de vaisseau*, and more closely resembled a howitzer than the British weapon.

oorlog-jacht. Naval version of the Dutch fast-sailing *jacht* (*qv*).

oorloge convoyerts. North Sea convoy escort; normally a converted sprit rigged coasting vessel.

(in) Ordinary. Usually applied to ships laid up. So called because the permanent establishment of the Royal Navy, including ships not in sea pay, was paid for out of the Ordinary estimate; the other estimates were Sea Service and Extraordinary (which included shipbuilding).

Ordnance Board. An institution in Britain independent of the Navy and charged with the design, manufacture and supply of weaponry for both land and sea services.

Ordres. In the French rating system, the main *Rangs* (*qv*) were sometimes further subdivided into *Ordres*.

orlop. A deck, or system of platforms in the hold, used mainly for storage, but often containing warrant officers' cabins. The term is thought to derive from the Dutch *overloop*.

packet or **pacquet.** Fast mail-carrying craft; usually government sponsored like British Post Office packets.

palm. The leaf-shaped spade at the end of the arm of an anchor.

parancelle or **paranzello.** Mediterranean single-masted lateen rig, used by the Neapolitan navy for gunboats.

parrel. An assemblage of beads called trucks and wooden dividers called ribs strung onto a series of horizontal ropes. Forming a collar between the upper yards and their masts, and designed to allow the yards to be hoisted or lowered easily, it vaguely resembled a flexible abacus, although the beads were intended to revolve and reduce friction while the ribs stopped them moving from side to side.

pawl. A pivoted pin that prevented the capstan springing back by engaging the whelps (*qv*) or, later, the stops on a pawl rim.

peak. The uppermost corner of a gaff-headed, sprit or lateen sail and the related end of the yard.

pendant. (1) Pronounced pennant; a long, narrow swallow-tailed flag flown from the masthead of a warship in commission; a broad pendant was a shorter swallow-tailed burgee, denoting the senior officer or commodore of a detached squadron.

(2) Short ropes, more or less permanently set up, to which a block or tackle could be attached by a thimble spliced into the end; the fore and main stay tackle pendants, for example, were used to hoist up the boats or other heavy objects.

periagua. Two-masted fore and aft rig with masts steeply raked fore and aft, away from one another, and gaff-headed sails; Mediterranean in origin but adopted for some US gunboats.

perrier. Originally stone-firing short-barrelled lightweight guns, the larger calibres were obsolete by 1650 but some smaller sizes survived as anti-personnel weapons; the French continued to call swivel guns *pierriers*.

petit canot. French version of the jollyboat (*qv*).

petrero or **pederero.** Small calibre breech-loading anti-personnel weapon; obsolete by 1700 but some still remained in use.

pink. A vessel characterised by a very narrow stern, all such craft being described as pink-sterned. Originally used by the English to describe the smaller Dutch *fluyts*, and ship rigged versions of naval ketches were so rated; in the Mediterranean the term (sometimes spelt pincque) was applied to xebec-like merchant ships.

pinnace. In the sixteenth century a small fast vessel, often used as a scout, that could usually be rowed as well as sailed but was decked like a ship. This usage survived into the mid-seventeenth century, in parallel with its application to a ship's boat; in the latter sense, a pinnace was a fairly seaworthy boat of up to 35ft proportioned like a longboat, but by the eighteenth century it had become a narrower, lighter craft and in many respects a smaller version of a barge (*qv*), for the use of junior officers.

pintle. The part of the rudder hinge fixed to the rudder itself, consisting of a downward-facing pin engaging the gudgeon (*qv*) on the sternpost, and a two-armed securing brace.

planksheer. The top timber or gunwale of the quarterdeck and forecastle bulwarks; when these bulwarks were later built up, the planksheer (sometimes given as plansheer) survived as a moulding representing the original sheer line.

points of the compass. The circumference was traditionally divided into thirty-two points, each of 11° 15′, and each given a name – clockwise from North, they ran North-by-East, North-North-East, North-East-by-North, North-East, North-East-by-East, East-North-East, East-by-North, East; the same principles then applied for the other quadrants.

polacre. Mediterranean trading vessel, originally lateen rigged; later examples acquired square topsails but these set on single-piece masts (*ie* no separate upper masts) and thereafter the term came to denote pole-masted.

polehead. The extension of the head of the uppermost mast, from which a flag could be flown or an additional sail set temporarily.

poop. Deck above the quarterdeck; often no more than the roof of the cabins below. A few very large ships had a deck above the poop called the **poop royal** or topgallant poop.

port-piece. Small breech-loading anti-personnel weapon, effectively obsolete by 1650.

portfire. Quickmatch; an inflammable composition used to ignite the priming powder of a gun. It was sufficiently resilient not to be extinguished by the resulting flash from the gun, obviating the need for a long train of powder to the vent and so speeding up ignition.

port tack. *See* tack.

Post Captain. In the Royal Navy any officer in command of a ship – even a lowly Lieutenant in a gunboat – was accorded the honorific 'captain', but only a Post Captain could command a ship of one of the six major Rates. His position differed from all lower ranks in that his future promotion was guaranteed by seniority, and if he lived long enough he must eventually become an admiral.

Post Ship. A Royal Navy term dating from the late eighteenth century for a small Sixth Rate of 20–24 guns, too small to be properly regarded a frigate but large enough to be commanded by a Post Captain (*qv*); the next Rate down was the sloop which was the province of a Master and Commander.

powder monkey. The member of a gun crew told off to bring powder cartridges up from the magazine.

pram, prahm or **prame.** Originally a lighter with a flat sloping bow used in Holland and the Baltic; the term was adopted for floating batteries with vaguely similar characteristics used in Baltic warfare.

premier rang extraordinaire. French late seventeenth-century rating for very large ships of over 100 guns.

pressing tender. A small craft, usually hired, employed on the business of impressing seamen.

preventer. Term applied to occasional reinforcements to the rigging (*eg* preventer stays), usually set up before battle or the onset of a storm to take over if the primary item was carried away.

privateer. A privately-funded warship licensed to attack enemy shipping; the privateer's sole purpose was warlike, but the otherwise similar Letter of Marque was issued to merchant ships which were thereby allowed to take prizes if the opportunity arose during the normal course of trading.

quarter piece. The timber – often carved and decorated – that formed the after extremity of the quarter gallery when seen from the broadside and the outer edges of the taffrail (*qv*) from aft.

quarter-galley. A small Mediterranean rowing and sailing craft, particularly associated with the Barbary powers. *See also* brigantin.

quarterdeck. A deck covering the after end of the uppermost complete deck; the area from which the officers controlled the ship, so by extension the term came to refer collectively to the officers themselves (in contradistinction to the 'forecastle' in merchant ships or the 'lower deck' in the navy, which from their place of berthing referred to the seamen).

quickmatch. *See* portfire.

quoin or **coin.** Wedge placed between the breech of a gun and the bed of the carriage to facilitate elevation and depression.

Rang. The French navy divided its order of battle into *Rangs* as the English did into Rates. There were usually six divisions, depending on the number of guns, but the details varied over time.

ratline. Light line across the shrouds which was a foothold for seamen going aloft.

razee. From French – a warship structurally cut down to a lower rate, usually by the equivalent of a single gundeck. Thus a two-decker might be made a frigate (*qv*), and by the loss of its forecastle (*qv*) and quarterdeck (*qv*) a frigate could be made into a sloop (*qv*). A useful modification for ships regarded late in their careers as too small for the current standard; retaining their more powerful main batteries, they then became formidable additions to their new rating.

receiving ship. Any vessel, usually a hulk (*qv*), serving as a collection point and temporary accommodation for seamen before they were sent on active service.

reef. The portion of a sail which could be shortened. A sail had one or more rows of reef points along a reef band which when hauled up and secured to the yard produced a fold in the reefed area of the sail, reducing the depth of canvas exposed to the wind. As the wind strengthened sail was progressively shortened to the first, second and third reef bands, when the ship was said to be single-, double- and triple-reefed, respectively.

reef points. Short lengths of cordage used to secure the sail when reefed.

reef tackle. A relieving tackle that helped to haul up the edges of the sail during reefing.

ribband. In shipbuilding, a thin lath connecting the exterior of the frames (*qv*) and holding them in place during construction. *See also* harpin.

roband. Corruption of rope-bands; short lengths of cordage used to secure a square sail to its yard.

robinet. Very small culverin-type (*qv*) gun firing a ball of less than 1lb.

round bow. Design in which the timbers of the bow were carried up to the top of the forecastle, eliminating the beakhead (*qv*) platform; common in small ships for most of the eighteenth century, for frigates from the 1750s and for line of battle ships from the early nineteenth century.

round crown. *See* anchor.

round stern. Design of stern attributed to Sir Robert Seppings in which a radiating pattern of substantial vertical frames replaced the flimsy transoms and windowed framework of the old square stern. Introduced just after the Napoleonic Wars, it claimed greater strength and all-round defensive fire as its advantages; but it did not please the seaman's eye and was replaced by the elliptical stern (*qv*) after a couple of decades.

rowle. The pivot of a whipstaff (*qv*).

royal. The regal implications of the word ensured

that it was applied to the ultimate in many aspects of the ship: eg the uppermost sail was called the top-gallant royal, which was soon shortened simply to royal; the rare structure built on the poop of very large ships was the poop royal; in the pre-1650 Royal Navy the few vessels rated larger than great ships (*qv*) were known as ships royal. In France and Spain the equivalent *Reale* or *Real* were used in a number of similar ways.

rudder. Hinged vertical timber at the after end of the keel used to steer the ship.

running backstay. An element of the standing rigging supporting upper masts; its lower end was set up with a block instead of the deadeyes (*qv*) and lanyards (*qv*) of standing backstays

running rigging. Those ropes and lines used to control the yards and the sails; in order to function they generally had to be capable of movement, unlike the standing rigging (*qv*), which was fixed.

sabot. Wooden base attached to the ammunition of early shell guns to ensure a snug fit in the chamber of the gun.

sacoleva. Single-masted sprit rigged coastal craft of the Levant.

saker. Small culverin-type (*qv*) gun firing a shot of about 5 ¼lbs.

sambuk. Type of Arab dhow with a two-masted lateen rig.

Sané system. *See* Borda-Sané system.

scantling. In shipbuilding, the dimensions of an individual piece of the structure; the principal measurements were the sided dimension (the width of timber, usually the same throughout its length) and the moulded (thickness, shaped from a mould, which might well vary).

schooner. Gaff rigged vessel with two or more masts, originating around 1700; later examples had square topsails. *See also* tern schooner and topsail schooner.

scud. In heavy weather, to run before the gale under reduced canvas; could only be employed if there was sea room to leeward, the alternative being to lie to (*qv*).

scupper. Drainage apertures, usually metal-lined, in the ship's side to carry water off the decks.

Second Rate. The Royal Navy's old great ships (*qv*), of 50–60 guns, were so rated in 1651, but by the 1680s this category included ships of more than 80 but less than 100 guns; there were no significant alterations thereafter.

settee. A form of lateen sail with what appears to be a rectangular lower extension, giving it a shape not unlike a lug (*qv*); also applied to Mediterranean small craft carrying this sail.

shallop. In the early seventeenth century, a large seaworthy boat, possibly the ancestor of the sloop (*qv*); the term continued to denote a boat type, although a rather lighter and more decorative craft, down to the nineteenth century.

shank. The main shaft of an anchor (*qv*).

sheathing. A protective layer added to the bottom of ships to protect them from the effects of marine borers and to act as antifouling. Originally thin wood, lead sheathing was tried without success in the seventeenth century but the ultimate answer was copper, which was adopted widely from the 1770s.

sheer hulk. Generally an old warship cut down and equipped with sheer-legs (a primitive form of crane) in order to hoist in the lower masts of ships moored alongside.

sheet. The rope confining the lower corners of square courses (and the after one of fore and aft sails), drawing them aft. *See also* tack.

sheet anchor. The strongest anchor, although in later years no larger or heavier than the other bowers (*qv*); proverbially, the seaman's last hope.

shell gun. A special design of gun to fire explosive shells introduced in the 1830s; by the 1850s most guns could fire either shell or solid shot and the term died out.

shifting backstay. An additional preventer support for the upper masts rigged whenever wind and weather required.

ship of the line. A major warship, usually with at least two full gundecks, arranged to fire on the broadside. The smallest ships so regarded carried at least 50 guns from the 1670s, 60 from the 1750s and 74 from about 1800, although ships as small as 30 guns had originally been admitted in the first decades of line of battle (*qv*) tactics.

ships royal. In the early Stuart navy a handful of the very largest ships; classified as First Rates from 1651.

shroud. Heavy rope supporting a mast from behind and transversely. *See also* backstay, stay and deadeye.

Sixth Rate. The smallest ship in the Royal Navy commanded by an officer of full Captain's rank; originally including ships of less than 16 guns (1651), by the eighteenth century it encompassed vessels of between 20 and 28 guns.

skaerbåde. Danish **skerry boat**, a rowing and sailing gunboat for the defence of inshore waters.

skampavej. A small Russian type of galley from the early years of the eighteenth century.

skiff. Small light boat, generally rowed rather than sailed.

skuta. Baltic merchant ship type; exact characteristics unknown; possibly related to the Dutch *schuyt*.

skysail or **skyscraper.** An occasional light weather sail set above the royals (*qv*).

slings. Rope supports for the yards in addition to the jeers; chain slings were introduced during the Napoleonic Wars for additional safety in action.

sloep. Dutch version of sloop (*qv*).

sloop. Originally a boat designation (*see* shallop), the term came to have two broad areas of meaning:
(1) In the Royal Navy it developed into a small cruiser, below the six Rates and commanded by a Master and Commander; it virtually became the seventh Rate, being applied to any vessel so commanded, such as the larger brigs and even fireships and bomb vessels when assigned cruising duties.
(2) As a rig it denoted a single-masted gaff rigged vessel with fixed bowsprit and jib headsails, and usually no square topsails.

slops. Ready-made clothing and bedding for seamen.

smack. Small inshore fishing craft, usually cutter (*qv*) rigged.

smak. Dutch coastal craft with a sprit (*qv*) or standing gaff main and lateen mizzen.

smasher. Nickname for the early large calibre carronades (*qv*).

snau. Danish small cruiser; possibly rigged as a snow (*qv*) in early days, but later it became an administrative term equivalent to the Royal Navy's sloop (*qv*).

snaw. Swedish small craft; the word if not the type is related to *snau* (*qv*) and snow (*qv*).

snotter. A form of becket at the foot of the mast supporting a sprit (*qv*).

snow. Two-masted square rigged vessel, with gaff-headed main course; in later eighteenth-century definitions, this gaff sail had to be hoisted on a rope horse (*qv*) or separate trysail mast (to distinguish the snow from the brig (*qv*), which hoisted its gaff course directly on the main mast).

spanker. Large gaff-and-boom sail; the main course of a brig and ultimately the replacement for the lateen mizzen on ships.

spar deck. Originally any light (often temporary) deck but later applied to the deck over the skid beams in the waist that effectively made the forecastle (*qv*) and quarterdeck (*qv*) into a single continuous deck; such vessels were termed spar-decked.

speel-jacht. A Dutch pleasure craft of the seventeenth century; examples are known with a primitive forerunner of the schooner rig (*qv*).

sprit topmast. The small mast carried by seventeenth-century warships at the end of the bowsprit from which a small square sail called the **sprit topsail** was set; it survived in large ships until about 1720.

spritsail. A fore and aft sail extended by a spar called a sprit running from the foot of the mast to the top outer corner of the sail.

squadron. A division of a fleet; actual numbers varied. In English usage the fleet was divided into Red, White and Blue squadrons, each flying an ensign of those colours (the White Ensign did not become the exclusive naval flag until 1864).

standing gaff. A spar that extended the head of a fore and aft sail and was more or less permanently in position. Possibly derived from the spritsail (*qv*) so sometimes called a half-sprit, it differed from the shorter hoisting gaff in that sail was taken in by brailing up the canvas to the mast and yard rather than by lowering the gaff.

standing rigging. The permanently set up support for the masts and tops – stays, shrouds etc.

star shot. Ammunition designed to dismantle the enemy's masts and rigging, formed of a series of bars hinged to a ring that opened out into a star-shaped pattern when fired.

starboard tack. *See* tack.

stay. The principal element of the standing rigging (*qv*) supporting a mast from forward. Fore and aft sails set from such rigging were known as **staysails**.

sternpost. The near-vertical extension of the keel aft on which the rudder was hung; the principal element in the construction of the stern.

stiff. Having a good reserve of stability and hence able to carry sufficient sail in all weathers; the opposite of crank (*qv*).

stock. (1) The wooden cross piece of an anchor, designed to make it easier for the arms to dig in to the ground.
(2) Wooden post to support a swivel gun (*qv*).
(3) Wooden blocks forming the base for the keel in shipbuilding; hence a ship under construction was said to be on the stocks.

stool bed. Flat plate of timber supporting the quoin (*qv*) of a gun carriage; replaced the solid base of the carriage in the mid-eighteenth century.

stoppers. Short lengths of rope used to grip the cable when riding at anchor; lashed to the cable and secured to an eyebolt in the deck. There were various forms, called deck-, dog- and ring-stoppers, the last being the final stopper to be cast off.

stream. Anchor smaller than the main bowers but larger than the kedge (*qv*); used for short-term mooring and occasionally kedging.

strike. To send down or haul down; used of upper masts and yards, and colours when surrendering.

studding sail. Additional fair weather square sails set on each side of the principal sails with removable yards and booms; pronounced **stuns'ls** and often written as **stunsails**.

Surveyor of the Navy. In the Royal Navy the senior official of the Navy Board charged with the design, construction and repair of the ships; originally a single post, there were two joint Surveyors from the mid-eighteenth century and three during the height of the Napoleonic Wars.

sweep. (1) Long oar used as auxiliary propulsion by some ships.
(2) Arc of timber used to support the end of the tiller on large ships; running the tiller ropes around the face of the sweep improved the geometry and made the helm more responsive.

swivel gun. A small anti-personnel weapon mounted along the rails and in the tops of ships; it was fitted into a swivelling crutch thrust into a wooden stock (*qv*).

tack. When sailing with the wind anywhere but aft, a rope used to extend to windward the lower corners of courses (*qv*) and staysails (*qv*) as sheets (*qv*) confined them to leeward; by extension it also applied to the parts of the sail to which it was attached. When so sailing, either the port or starboard tacks were said to be on board, from whence came the phrases port tack or starboard tack and the term **tacking** for the manoeuvre of changing course from one oblique angle to the wind to the other.

tackle. An arrangement of one or more ropes and blocks used to give mechanical advantage in the raising or securing of heavy weights about the ship, particularly as regards the rigging.

tafferal or **taffrail.** The decorated upper section of a ship's stern; from the Dutch word for a picture, seventeenth-century ships of the United Netherlands having a large pictorial or heraldic device above the stern windows.

tartana or **tartane.** A single-masted lateen rigged Mediterranean coasting vessel sometimes used as an auxiliary warship.

tender. (1) A small vessel assigned to attend on a larger one or on a port.
(2) Crank (*qv*), lacking in stability.

term. A supporting statue or bust borrowed from architectural practice by ship carvers.

tern schooner. A three-masted schooner; probably American in origin.

Third Rate. In the Royal Navy originally a two-decker of 40–50 guns (1651), it later encompassed ships of 64–80 guns and included some 80-gun three-deckers. The most numerous battleship Rate.

three-decker. Ship with three whole gundecks plus upperworks; the largest type of sailing warship, although the Spanish *Santisima Trinidad* and some late First Rates had a continuous spar deck that might be regarded as a fourth gundeck.

throat. The part of a gaff (*qv*) nearest the mast.

thwart. The transverse benches in a boat on which the rowers sat.

tide-rode. The situation of a ship at anchor in which the position at which she was riding was dictated by the tide. *See also* wind-rode.

tiller. An horizontal lever extending from the rudder head to facilitate steering; also by analogy an extension of a swivel gun used to point it.

top. A platform at the lower mastheads, principally needed to spread the shrouds (*qv*) of the topmasts but forming a convenient position for sharpshooters in action or to martial men working in the rigging.

top hamper. General term for masts, spars and rigging.

topgallant. The mast, yard, sail and rigging above the topmast (*qv*).

topgallant poop. A small deck above the regular poop (*qv*) in a few very large ships; also referred to as a **poop royal**.

topmast. The portion of a mast (and its rigging) above the top, usually separate from the lower section; its sail was called the **topsail**, which gave its name to the yard and running rigging (*qv*).

topsail schooner. A schooner (*qv*) with square canvas on at least one topmast.

toptimber. In shipbuilding, the uppermost element in a frame (*qv*).

trabaccolo. A lug rigged Adriatic coaster.

trabucco. A type of mortar (*qv*) with trunnions (*qv*) at its breech end.

trailboard. The timbers (usually decorated) between the cheeks and the knee of the head (*qv*), below the headrails.

traveller. A ring or hoop moving up or along a mast or spar to facilitate the hoisting or running out of a yard or sail.

trestletree. Fore and aft timbers supporting the top (*qv*), forming a framework with the transverse crosstrees (*qv*).

trucks. Round pieces of wood with various shipboard employments: as wheels to gun carriages; as the cap of the uppermost mast or flagstaff; as the rolling elements in a parrel (*qv*); and hollowed out as fairleads attached to the shrouds for the falls of particular ropes.

truck carriage. General term for the standard ship's gun carriage, with a truck, or small solid wheel, at each corner.

trundlehead. The lower head of a double capstan (*qv*) when arranged to work on a single spindle with the capstan on the deck above.

trunnions. Short cylindrical extensions at right angles to the barrel of a gun used to retain it to its carriage with a capsquare (*qv*); the trunnions formed the axis on which the gun was elevated and depressed.

trysail. A gaff-and-boom sail set from an auxiliary (trysail) mast or rope horse; the trysails that replaced staysails were called spencers in nineteenth-century navies. Trysail was also used of the reduced storm canvas employed by small craft in place of the regular main.

tumblehome. The curving-in of the ship's side above the waterline; this feature was abandoned in the nineteenth century, the resulting ships being described as wall-sided.

turuma. A class of inshore frigates designed for the Swedish archipelago fleet by F H Chapman in the 1760s; a smaller version of the hemmema (*qv*).

two-decker. A ship with two complete gundecks plus upperworks; always the most common arrangement for line of battle ships. When frigates acquired a complete upper (spar) deck, they were described as double-banked rather than two-decked since they had no additional upperworks.

tye. Tackle used to hoist upper yards.

udema. An unconventional design of inshore frigate by F H Chapman for the Swedish inshore fleet, characterised by pivoting guns on the centreline which could be fired on either broadside.

upperworks. The structures above the highest complete gundeck – forecastle, quarterdeck, poop and their bulwarks.

uytlegger. A Dutch inshore guardship. *See also* Wadden convoy ship.

vangs. Braces from the peak of a gaff or sprit to the rails.

veering. Letting out or paying out, particularly of rope. In earlier usage synonymous with wearing (*qv*).

vischhoeker. Dutch inshore fishing craft with square main sail and fore sail.

Wadden convoy ship. A small but quite powerfully armed guardship, usually a converted coaster, employed on convoy protection duties along the German North Sea coast (known as the Watt or Wadde) in the seventeenth century. Usually smak (*qv*) rigged, shoal draught and sometimes fitted with leeboards (*qv*).

wales. The broader and thicker strakes of planking around the hull at approximately the level of the decks; originally standing proud of the rest of the planking and painted in contrasting colours, the wales were eventually faired in and so became less evident.

wardroom. The mess area of the commissioned officers and often used collectively of the officers themselves.

watt-convoyer. *See* Wadden convoy ship.

wearing. The manoeuvre of going about (*qv*) by turning away from the wind, when the stern would pass through the direction of the wind. *See also* tack.

weather. As of side or direction, windward (*qv*).

weather gage. The windward station; in action this position gave the initiative to the ship or fleet holding it since it was easier to run downwind on the enemy than beat upwind towards them.

weighing anchor. The process of disengaging the anchor from the seabed, hauling in the cable and stowing the anchor. The anchor was heaved up by the action of a capstan (*qv*) or windlass, possibly acting through the medium of a messenger (*qv*). When the anchor was in sight, a cat-tackle was hooked to its ring and it was hauled up to the cathead (*qv*); then a fish-tackle from the davit (*qv*) was used to heave the crown of the anchor into the horizontal position where it was secured. This was known as catting and fishing the anchor.

whelps. The buttress-like extensions from the barrel of a capstan or windlass to allow the cable better grip.

wherry. A light fine-lined pulling boat mostly used on rivers for the transportation of small numbers of passengers.

whipstaff. A vertical lever at the end of the tiller which enabled the helmsman to be positioned at least one deck higher and possibly in sight of the sails. It was not mechanically efficient and was replaced in the early eighteenth century with a wheel; this was connected by ropes to the tiller so could be sited on any deck level.

white stuff. Dockyard term for an antifouling composition made up of oil, rosin and sulphur.

wind – true and relative. The true wind was the strength and direction experienced by a stationary observer, whereas relative wind was as experienced by a ship in motion. In general, when heading downwind, relative wind is less than true wind, and the converse is the case when heading towards the wind.

windage. In artillery, the small difference between the interior diameter of the bore of a gun and the size of the shot fired from it; in tables often quoted as a fraction of the bore diameter.

wind-rode. The situation of a ship at anchor in which the position at which she was riding was dictated by the wind. *See also* tide-rode.

windlass. A form of horizontal capstan (*qv*) favoured by merchant ships and small craft; it needed less space than a capstan but was far less powerful because fewer men could heave on it simultaneously.

windward. The side or direction from which the wind blows; in this context, weather is virtually synonymous with windward. The opposite of lee (*qv*) or leeward.

woolding. Rope windings around joints or scarphs in a mast to strengthen it; later replaced by iron bands.

xebec, chebec or **zebec.** Mediterranean fast-sailing craft, originally lateen rigged but later acquiring square canvas on polacre masts. Used by both navies and privateers.

yacht. From the Dutch *jacht* (a fast-sailing hull form), in English the term came to imply a craft whose main activity is sport or pleasure; early royal and naval yachts were frequently employed in war.

yaw. To wander from intended course.

yawl. A two-masted fore and aft rig in which the mizzen is very much smaller than that of a ketch (*qv*) and usually stepped abaft the sternpost.

zebec. *See* xebec.

Index